4

D0891819

'76

ONE WORLD

AND *THE CANTOS*

OF EZRA POUND

'76

One World
and *The Cantos*
of Ezra Pound
by Forrest Read

MIDDLEBURY COLLEGE LIBRARY

The University of North Carolina Press Chapel Hill

5/1982
Am. Lit.

PS
3531
.082
C296

© 1981 The University of North Carolina Press
All rights reserved
Manufactured in the United States of America

Library of Congress Cataloging in Publication Data

Read, Forrest.
  '76, one world and the Cantos of Ezra Pound

  Includes bibliographical references and index.
  1. Pound, Ezra Loomis, 1885–1972. Cantos.
I. Title.
PS3531.0820296   811'.52   80-15892
ISBN 0-8078-1455-5
ISBN 0-8078-4076-9 pbk.

Excerpts from unpublished writings by Ezra Pound © 1981
by the Trustees of the Ezra Pound Literary Property Trust

Excerpts from published writings of Ezra Pound and
writings by Ezra Pound in books published by other authors
and copyrighted by New Directions Publishing Corporation,
publishers and agents for the Ezra Pound Literary Property
Trust, are reprinted by permission of the publisher

To my wife, Heather

And my children—Nicholas and Daniel

Emily and Anthony

Forrest and Zachary

They endured

CONTENTS

FOREWORD

Though Ezra Pound (1885–1972) is acknowledged one of the inventors of twentieth-century poetry, his own poetry still raises controversies about its subject matter, its intelligibility, and its aesthetic values while the man remains notorious for having seemed to be a vituperative anti-Semite and a fascist. Both he and his poetry have been charged with ideological immorality or obtuseness. For broadcasting from fascist Italy to America during World War II he was indicted for treason. Declared mentally unfit to stand trial he spent thirteen years in an American government asylum. In 1958, without having stood trial, he was released as incurably insane.

Amid controversies he either responded to his accusers obliquely and evasively or seemed to confirm the charges with cocky self-assurance. In 1963 he reportedly asserted himself to have been wrong all his life and repudiated his works. After 1963 he lapsed into enigmatic silence. Yet he continued to publish additions to his long epic *The Cantos*, read parts of the poem in public, and recorded parts on tape. The work, the reputation, and the man have become virtually a myth. "The Pound myth" has clouded almost all efforts to understand and assess what he did and its value.

Whenever he was pressed or spoke directly to the point—and the whole drift and tenor of his life bear it out—Pound asked to be judged by his work. Refusal to answer various charges can be explained largely by a poet's desire to be read in his own time and to await judgment from succeeding generations. But reticence about his poetry did not begin with the political controversies or the treason charges. Although from the beginning of his career he allowed himself to be overheard in essays and prose books, he was always reserved about what he was doing and how he was doing it. Guardedness about both the large outline and its details fostered the assumption that he had no form of his own but was using forms derived from other poets in order to comprehend ideas and materials that came to hand. Publication begun in 1917 proceeded until, when he died in 1972, nearly 120 cantos had reached some 800 pages issued in a series of instalments, the last fragmentary. "Work in progress" always caused readers to await completion, assured by Pound that a form would then appear. The assumption of provisionality and the fragmentary ending are still precluding any accurate, convincing description of the intention, the subject, the form, and the end.

Problems of reading *The Cantos* have all involved the kinds of intelligibility needed for and expected from a long poem. What is the argument? Does an overall form relate or integrate the parts? How can we read a poem constituted of so much unfamiliar history and containing so many elliptical allusions, not only historical but also personal? In a narrative poem using varied data and often written as a texture of images, what is the principle by which one moves through a canto and from canto to canto? How does one correlate comprehensive definitions of the poem with details of varying magnitudes, from single words, images, and passages to single cantos, groups of cantos, instalments of cantos, and groups of instalments?

This book seeks to show that intention, subject, form, and end have inhered since *A Draft of XVI. Cantos for the beginning of a poem of some length* was published in 1925 and that from the beginning a mind in the process of making itself up over an era and a lifetime derives simultaneously, while turning them into narrative, forms of tradition, biography, government, and art. It would demonstrate that the first canto is an intricately designed epitome of the whole; that the first draft constitutes a prototype for a series of analogously formed instalments; that one instalment metamorphoses into another while sequence accrues toward a whole prophesied by historical materials and realized by the activity of what claims to be an archetypal revolutionary mind.

It should be self-evident, though the point has never been pressed, that *The Cantos* is an epic of revolution. The title of this book reflects an overall form and its concomitants inherent in American history and in American revolution prophesied by previous histories and projecting a world future. The varied subject matters may be local, but surely *The Cantos* is an historical narrative by an American mind informed at every point by its own native heritage.

Scrutiny both in the large and in meticulous detail has convinced this writer that a distinctive, discoverable form inheres in a subject matter chosen and arranged to be prophetic as well as literal, and that before he published his first definitive draft Pound had correlated and universalized the symbols and documents of '76 in a revolutionary Calendar for a new era dated from his birthday. The Calendar, as yet little known and never investigated, implies origins for world history. As I seek to show, both substantively and mathematically, it derives from the Seal of the United States a dynamic process of historical evolution caught at various points "in the course of human events," and correlates the Seal symbolism with a philosophy of revolution, an epic evocation, and a vision of justice found in the Declaration of Independence and the Constitution. Tradition, personality, and justice are to be consummated in a continuation of world revolutionary epic delineating a new world civilization.

Evidence for such early beginnings—from 1904 or 1905, Pound said in several places—appears here abbreviated (see pp. 64–65) from a subsequently written complementary book, *The Search for Oneself: Shaping Up Personae and The Cantos, 1907–1926*, parts of which elaborate further Pound's early American background (1885–1900) in his family and in college. The first chapters of *'76* itself describe an overall scope, subject, argument, and emerging form of *The Cantos*. Succeeding chapters present external evidence and a special kind of symbolic internal evidence ("arcana"). I should be content to omit some of this evidence here and also the record of composition from the so-called rejected or Ur cantos toward the first draft, and to leave such to its full elaboration in *The Search For Oneself*, did it not seem necessary to try to forestall objections to revolutionary interpretations which will doubtless boggle some minds. I hope that what is presented here and what is presented in *Search* will resolve at last the dispute between the disintegrators, who argue that *The Cantos* is but a ''rag-bag'' of ''notes'' for a poem (Pound's own terms), or a ''cento,'' or a ''loose series''; and on the other hand, the superimposers, who advance without sufficient evidence formal schemes of their own.

Subsequent chapters follow a transforming, constituting mind as it tries to work its inherited and personal materials toward conclusion, perfection, and focus. Since *The Cantos* is a poem of texture and structure investing each other, and since each metamorphoses into the other as the poem unfolds, in a sense each canto is an integral poem epitomizing the whole poem. But each canto, group, instalment, and group of instalments applies the paradigm differently according to changes of theme. Each unit must therefore be understood in itself as well as in relation to larger groupings. Each canto is thus considered both separately and within its contexts, in sufficient though not complete detail. Only so can one clarify both a canto's internal ordonnance and its place in a prototype; only so can one clarify instalments repeated with differences until a whole has revealed the structure of a mind clarifying its own texture as it experiences and promotes metamorphic growth.

The method is necessarily descriptive in order to have grist for interpretation. The aim is to clarify forms discoverable and intelligible to a reader who would follow a deliberately created impression of derivation and discovery aimed at defining a twentieth-century historical mind. It would be possible to reduce description to a mere table of cantos and divisions of cantos building toward a whole; but that would preclude integrity of subject, not to speak of the effects of poetry. To do any one thing justice requires four books in one: Pound's vision of history, his autobiography within it, his theory of history as revolution resulting in just government and viable order, and his transformation and consummation of world poetry—all this with sufficient consideration of his other poetry, his prose, his sources, and the like.

What follows makes little effort to expose Pound's sources. Self-evident matter of history is supposed to express developing themes being made gradually intelligible as world history evolves and as the mind grows. Exploration of sources, useful as a check against error, has been done sufficiently for that purpose. But the aim of *The Cantos*, which guides this book, is to relieve the reader of masses of historical data so that he may come to discern a fruitful direction toward a desirable pattern.

Again like *The Cantos*, this book must finally persuade by a growing sense of internal consistency, coherency, and proportion accentuated by myriad arcana. Accordingly no effort is made to build on previous studies of *The*

Cantos. Concordant with a purpose Pound stated variously (if obliquely) both within *The Cantos* and without, and concordant with arcana like the Calendar as loci for all such statements, this purports to be a "classic" reading of a poem deliberately intended to be the latest in a series of classics of world poetry.

One may read *The Cantos* in any way one wishes. But a classic reading must be rooted in the ground of the poem—the whole poem—and built upon its foundations. As Pound tried to make history speak for itself, so the serious reader or critic must, as a first step, try to make *The Cantos* speak for itself. Not only the Calendar but also designs, paradigms, and arcana planted within the poem were intended one day to be found, and, if the "new *forma mentis*" had generated enough interest, to be used to unlock the mind of history as a twentieth-century American had envisioned and lived it. One reads for oneself. But one can also read in the way Pound wrote, as a catechumen for posterity. When the thing itself has been grasped, felicities can be appreciated intelligibly and the reaches of pleasure and judgment may begin.

This book draws on the standard Pound works in their first editions if these have remained definitive, or on later definitive editions; distinctions are made in the text. Periodical pieces later collected in books are cited by first printing, for chronology; appearance in later collections can be found in Donald Gallup's *A Bibliography of Ezra Pound*, London 1963. Much of the supporting evidence comes, however, from periodical articles never reprinted (e.g., from Italian periodicals during World War II) and from unprinted materials. I think I can safely say that I have consulted almost all Pound's printed work, in several countries and languages, and all unpublished matter known to me (mostly in library collections). From all I have culled discussions and remarks which throw light on *Personae* and *The Cantos*. Much of the known material is used in a new way, while the new material is used for the first time. My interpretations find external support in the range, coherency, and relevancy of manifold materials refined to acuity.

For permission to quote from Pound's published works and unpublished writings I thank the Trustees of the Pound Estate. I thank the following libraries for permission to publish Pound holdings in their collections: The Collection of American Literature, Beinecke Rare Book and Manuscript Library, Yale University; The Humanities Research Center, The University of Texas at Austin; The University of Chicago Library for the *Poetry* Magazine Papers, 1912–36; the Cornell University Library; and the Houghton Library, Harvard University.

Forrest Read
Chapel Hill, N.C.

'76

ONE WORLD

AND *THE CANTOS*

OF EZRA POUND

CHAPTER ONE

ONE WORLD AND '76:

BIBLIOGRAPHY AND LIFE

"We are at the crisis point of the world."
  Tami Kume, 1924[1]

Ezra Pound was an American in love with a beautiful European tradition which had sought continually to extend its scope to the limits of the known world and beyond. While Greek, Roman, and medieval traditions were being revived during the Italian Renaissance, explorers had sought Cathay and found America; the result was to be Pound's own native tradition. By his own time the evolving tradition had come full circle. A single panorama of world history was in the process of evolving some kind of destiny both inherent in the past and at work in the present.

Such a view of history informs all Pound's life and work, from the first stirrings of a poetic vocation and from his earliest poetry. During the 1910s he published more than ten volumes of poems and translations aimed at perfecting his craft, at gathering world traditions, and at bringing them to bear on the conditions of his own time. These and many prose works were deliberate preparations for what he called "the tale of the tribe." Inheriting "the tale" from many sources, he continued it with the aim of unifying several traditions so that a single tradition projected through a single life might result in the first epic poem of a post-Renaissance One World. The ultimate aim was to promote both peaceful interaction and mutual enrichment among the world's peoples, whether by cultures or by persons.

The Cantos presents the reader, as history presents the twentieth-century mind, with a bewildering mosaic of fragments, mythic and historical, from many cultures. It follows the quite commonplace idea, however, that conceptions of One World originated in Europe and that their scope was finally defined during the Renaissance, which rediscovered and reinterpreted its own past while reaching beyond Europe toward China. The unexpected discovery

---

1. Tami Kume, an oriental painter friend, died in 1924. Placed at the end of Pound's translation of the Confucian *Ta Hsio* done at "D.T.C., Pisa: 5 October–5 November, 1945," the warning analogizes the ends of World Wars I and II, "the 'repeat in history.' "

of America resulted in the transplantation of European culture to the new continent and in the evolution there of a new civilization which in turn influenced its European source. During the Renaissance too, almost on the heels of Columbus's discovery, the world had been circumnavigated and so completed geographically, opening up China from all directions.

Culturally, however, Europe failed to realize the promise of the Renaissance on its own ground; instead it evolved competing nations and empires, therefore lost its ties with its American colonies, and finally brought the world together only under an irresponsible imperialist capitalism to fight a first world war. North America had evolved through revolution against Europe a new society under a form of government new to the world and had offered a model for political and cultural accord on foundations of liberty and justice for all. But it also succumbed to plutocracy and rejoined imperial Europe during World War I. The Orient too was forced into the world capitalist and militarist system.

Though European and American traditions had once offered promise they had sacrificed their best elements to pursue power and profit. Only the Orient offered traditions still to be explored. In the spirit of the original Renaissance, therefore, and in the original Spirit of '76, it might be possible to revive neglected or lost traditions, to explore new ones, and to redirect each culture singly and all together toward a better world of the future.

Traditions exist in the mind, both individual and collective. But they once originated in myth and religion, and however they may have changed they retain vestiges of their origins. Like myth and religion they direct choices and actions even if their original qualities have degenerated into ideas held by such a secularized popular mind as that of our own time. Pound's aim was to alter a popular mind which, having lost touch with its original creative values under a dominant plutocracy, had been easily incited to destructive war. To change that mind he undertook to make his own mind a medium through which creative values could manifest themselves and so effect change by education. He chose poetry because poetry originates in the myths and religions of the world's peoples, because poetry works its effects by dealing with what is already in people's minds whether latently or consciously, and because poetry appeals to all human interests, concerns, and faculties.

Moreover, poetry works by example, not only through manifestations of all kinds but also, in a personal poem, by the example of its author. By making his own mind the medium through which old traditions could be given new life and through which new ones could be formed from old, and by making his own life the embodiment of the history of his own times, he could give collective authenticity to his reconstructions and therefore to his projections of a better tradition, through a dismal present, toward a better future. A tradition derived from mythic and religious origins, and borne witness to in a twentieth-century life, could be an objective foundation at once impersonal and personal, individual and collective. The test of its value, given such foundations, would be less historical inclusiveness, or even perfect historical accuracy, than the appeal of all the resources of language characteristic of poetry. Such had been the effect of Homer's poetry, "the education of Hellas," and of other grandiose works from Roman Virgil and Ovid to medieval Dante and Chaucer; such had been the aim of certain Renaissance, Neoclassic, and Romantic poets and of Pound's immediate American ancestors Joel Barlow of *The Columbiad* and Walt Whitman of *Leaves of Grass*.

Pound claimed that conceiving *The Cantos* began as early as 1904. He was well into his subject before World War I all but crushed modern civilization. During the first seven years after 1917 he published fourteen cantos in periodicals; not until 1925 did he publish in book form—as a deluxe illustrated folio—*A Draft of XVI. Cantos for the beginning of a poem of some length*. These sixteen cantos altered the order of the cantos previously published in periodicals, removed some parts of cantos, and added new materials, so that the draft evolved from a Renaissance tradition, via the Renaissance itself as a modern tradition, to the decline of that tradition into twentieth century world capitalism, world war, and world revolution.

A second deluxe illustrated folio, *A Draft of The Cantos 17–27* (1928), continued and elaborated the same subjects in new perspectives. The two drafts of twenty-seven cantos were augmented in 1930 to constitute *A Draft of XXX Cantos*, a deluxe quarto, which made minor changes in a few of the earliest cantos but otherwise did no more than focus the Renaissance as a twentieth-century tradition foreshadowing world capitalism and world revolution via an as yet only hinted intermediary: the American Revolution of '76.

American revolution prophesied by the Renaissance emerged in a third draft. *Eleven New Cantos XXXI–XLI* (1934), later subtitled from its main subject "Jefferson-Nuevo Mundo," presents the American Revolution and its evolution to date as consequences of the Renaissance via Columbus's discovery and via transplantation in America of an original Mediterranean mythic spirit.

The Fifth Decad of Cantos XLII–LI (1937), later subtitled from financial and governmental reforms in seventeenth-century Siena and in eighteenth-century Tuscany "Siena-Leopoldine Reforms," presents an ideal form of European revolution free of the yoke of capitalism to which the American experiment had succumbed. In a hindsight prophesied by the beginning of the poem and worked out mythically in relation to the revolutionary histories, the four drafts of *Cantos I–LI* reveal the Mediterranean mythic spirit "ELEUSIS," which gives a unified *LI Cantos* its mythic-historical title as a "paideuma."[2]

2. "Fragments," "cantos," and "cantares," "drafts," "decads," "paideumas," and "phases" —all part of the meaning of the "opus" and all taken from the poem itself—will be differentiated in due course. Cantos are referred to by draft and number or simply by number. I take *The Cantos of Ezra Pound I–CXX* (New York: New Directions, 1972; hereafter cited as *The Cantos*) to be definitive but retain from first editions of the successive volumes the designation of some cantos "Canto" and the arabic numbering of *Los Cantares 85–109* and of *Canto 120*; these distinctive

Paideuma means for Pound in one sense a cultural tradition still nourished by its mythic roots, and in another—relevant to what he is doing in *The Cantos*—"our way of thinking in poetry."[3]

Coordinate with "ELEUSIS" *LI Cantos* as elements of world paideuma are the two drafts (or "decads") of *Cantos LII–LXXI* (1940), recurrent Confucian revolution over Chinese millennia entitled "KUNG" (*LII–LXI*), and the entire American Revolution of '76 in a world perspective rather than as an offshoot of "ELEUSIS," "JOHN ADAMS" (*LXII–LXXI*). *Cantos I–LXXI* in six drafts constitute three paideumas—"ELEUSIS," 'KUNG,'" and "JOHN ADAMS"—of a world revolutionary tradition (*LXXI Cantos*). The culminating and definitive form is the American; emerging from the discovery of 1492 and the colonization at Massachusetts Bay in 1628, it is carried by Adams's generation from the preparations of revolution, through the revolutionary process of 1760–91, to an ongoing revolutionary civilization. "Jefferson-Nuevo Mundo," though its title suggests the discovery of 1492 and revolution beginning with Jefferson's writing of the Declaration of Independence in 1776, in fact begins during the Constitutional Convention of 1787.

The world revolutionary tradition *LXXI Cantos* emerged from World War I as an effort to revise dominant traditions which had resulted in World War I and in Marxist world revolution. "Jefferson-Nuevo Mundo" takes Italian fascist revolution as a successor to '76 and as a revision of capitalist perversion and of the Marxist alternative; "Siena-Leopoldine Reforms" roots fascist revolution in a neglected part of its own tradition. Confucian revolution in "KUNG" and a revision of '76 in "JOHN ADAMS" were intended to modify and enrich the Italian model and its Eleusinian spirit so that the sequel would result in a synthetic One World paideuma carried from the past into the present by a contemporary revolutionary protagonist, Pound himself. The aim was to prevent a recurrence of World War I.

The aim failed, so that during World War II Pound carried out his opposition to capitalism and communism journalistically in Italy and by radio broadcast from Italy to England and America. The collapse of fascist Italy as the putative contemporary model for focusing a world revolutionary paideuma resulted in an effort to reconstitute the paideuma, if not its historical realization, *The Pisan Cantos LXXIV–LXXXIV* (1948). Written as the war was ending, in a U.S. army concentration camp at Pisa where Pound had been imprisoned under indictment for treason for his radio broadcasts to America, this seventh draft emerges in a mode of personal experience from the foregoing mode of tradition. Further, while bringing tradition to life in a personal

---

meanings were obscured when all canto headings were regularized to mere roman numerals in the London collection of *I–CIX* (1964) and after the New York collection of *I–CXVII et seq.* (1970). It has been reported that Pound wanted all designations synchronized eventually to roman numerals, but the record of the evolving poem better accentuates its form.

3. "Confucius to Cummings," Pound's preface to *Confucius to Cummings: An Anthology of Poetry* edited by Ezra Pound and Marcella Spann (New York: 1964), p. ix.

present, it is also turning tradition and personal struggle toward a mode of new justice for a new world future.

The eighth and ninth drafts were written in a U.S. government insane asylum near Washington, D.C., where Pound was confined from 1945–58 under adjudication of mental inability to stand trial on the treason charges. As their titles suggest, the two drafts extend tradition, personal struggle, and justice to the forming of governments as foundations for building a new civilization. The keynote for *Section: Rock-Drill 85–95 de los cantares* (1955) is "the basic principles of government": the texts show Chinese revolution forming a new dynasty from an old, defense of the American Constitution against the plutocratic forces of the Jackson era, and new perceptions of Eleusinian justice. *Thrones 96–109 de los cantares* (1959), presented as a consequence of the foregoing principles and ideas, includes an Eleusinian constitution, a Confucian constitution, and a form of the American Constitution imposed upon world materials, all culminating in the English Magna Charta and its elaborations into English constitutional law. The aim of the two drafts is to provide materials for founding a new world government.

The 109 cantos in nine drafts, completed in the spirit of an anticipated fulfillment of the revolutionary theme, remain virtually as originally written and published. There is no substantial evidence of provisionality or of an intention to make significant revisions.[4] The case is different, however, with what can be presumed to have been an intended eleven cantos of a tenth draft, which Pound wrote after the treason charges had been dropped in 1958 on grounds of incurable insanity so that he could return to Italy, where he lived the rest of his life. The deluxe folio *Drafts & Fragments of Cantos CX–CXVII* appeared in 1968 and *Canto 120* was added posthumously in 1972. "Drafts" refers to drafts of *Cantos CX–CXVI*, some completed and some not. "Fragments" refers to "Addendum for C," two fragments dated "Circa 1941" and intended then for a Canto 72 or 73, neither of which appears in the canon;[5] and to three "Notes for *CXVII* et seq.," presumably fragments for undrafted *CXVII*, *CXVIII*, and *CXIX*. *Canto 120*, though formally complete and completing a 120-canto form, is mournfully shorter than any of the fragments, or any of the cantos. *The Cantos* thus ends with *Drafts & Fragments* of cantos, which constitute formally but not substantively a tenth draft.

The accompanying table lists the ten drafts. It also lists cumulative collections correlated with four phases of Pound's life as a revolutionary gathering a tradition, emerging as its revolutionary protagonist or epic hero, enacting the role of a revolutionary statesman constituting the laws, and trying to complete

---

4. Though he did write once "Part of the job is *finally* to get all necessary notes into the text itself. Not only are the LI Cantos a part of the poem, but by labeling most of 'em draft, I retain right to include *necessary* explanations in LI–C or in revision." To John Lackay Brown, April 1937, D. D. Paige, ed., *The Letters of Ezra Pound 1907–1941* (New York: 1950). Hereafter cited as *Letters*.

5. On the missing Cantos 72 and 73, see pp. 295–96.

the latest versions of "an epic is a poem containing history" or "the tale of
the tribe." *Seventy Cantos I–LXXI*, the first phase, was not published until
1950, in England, probably because of the war. The phasal collections have
two functions, to accumulate drafts of revolution while building cantos symbolic of its aim, a new civilization. As will be seen, the preliminary collection
A Draft of XXX Cantos (1930) and the transitional collection *The Cantos
(1–95)* of 1964 have special ancillary meanings in relation to those of the four
phasal collections.

BIBLIOGRAPHY & LIFE

Drafts	Collections	Life
1. *A Draft of XVI. Cantos*, Paris 1925		
2. *A Draft of The Cantos 17–27*, London 1928		
	A Draft of XXX Cantos, Paris 1930	
3. *Eleven New Cantos XXXI–XLI*: "Jefferson-Nuevo Mundo," New York 1934		
4. *The Fifth Decad of Cantos XLII–LI*: "Siena-Leopoldine Reforms," London 1937		Pound wrote the six drafts of Cantos *I–LXXI* during and after World War I, up to World War II—from about 1915–39—while living in London, Paris, and Rapallo (Italy).
Cantos LII–LXXI, London 1940		
5. "KUNG" *LII–LXI*		
6. "JOHN ADAMS" *LXII–LXXI*		
	Seventy Cantos I–LXXI, London 1950	
7. *The Pisan Cantos LXXIV–LXXXIV*, New York 1948	*The Cantos I–LXXXIV*, New York 1948	Pound wrote the *Pisan Cantos* during 1945 while imprisoned in a U.S. army concentration camp for criminal soldiers at Pisa, under indictment for treason.
8. *Section: Rock-Drill 85–95 de los cantares*, Milan 1955	*The Cantos (1–95)*, New York 1964, copyright 1956	Pound wrote the 2 drafts of *Los Cantares 85–109* while confined under indictment for treason, but declared mentally unfit to stand trial, during about 1953–58 in a U.S. government hospital near Washington, D.C.
9. *Thrones 96–109 de los cantares*, Milan 1959		He was confined there from 1945–58 until he was

BIBLIOGRAPHY & LIFE (continued)

Drafts	Collections	Life
	The Cantos I–CIX, London 1964	released adjudged incurably insane.
10. *Drafts & Fragments of Cantos CX–CXVII*, New York 1968		Pound wrote the last draft from 1958, when he returned to Italy to live, until his death on 1 November 1972.
Canto 120 (1969)	*The Cantos 1–120*, New York 1972 (posthumous)	

These simple bibliographical facts have never been noticed. Nor has the fact of the life. Nor has the correlation between them. Without these simple facts and their correlation, all efforts to read *The Cantos* as it was written, and all efforts to interpret it comprehensively, have been, are, and will be doomed to myopia. Without them one is one of a pack of blind men clustered around a creature with legs like tree trunks, with a nose like a hose, with ears like sails, with a tail like a rope, with sides like walls, and with a skin wrinkled as a prune.

CHAPTER TWO

LIVING NEW WORLD

HISTORY AND '76

So there is no drop not American in me
Aye we have noticed that said the Ambassador
John Adams, "*JOHN ADAMS*" *LXVI*

From the beginning of *The Cantos* matter is being gathered from past history and from the present by voyages, and is being brought to life and incorporated into Pound's own mind and experience. All the matter is matter of revolution from many cultures; all is being worked toward a single world revolution against twentieth-century conditions and for a revolutionary ideal that evolves as the poem progresses. The voyages are of two kinds. The mythic voyage of Odysseus to consult the dead about how to return home runs through *The Cantos* from beginning to end; Pound takes the Homeric nostos as a pattern for his own effort to turn the world from war and destruction to new constructivity and peace. Odysseus's voyage to the dead (*I*) opens up the gathering of a world tradition (*LXXI Cantos*). His return from the dead to Circe's, his passage through Scylla and Charybdis, the loss of his crew, and the wreck of his raft off Phaeacia are touched as mythic models for the wreck of Pound's effort recorded in *Pisan*. In *Section: Rock-Drill* he receives aid from the sea nymph Leucothoe, an agent of divine justice against Odysseus's nemesis Poseidon, and in *Thrones* he reaches shore in Phaeacia, the classical paradise and utopia of ideal justice. In *Drafts & Fragments* Odysseus's return to Ithaca is a pattern for Pound's return to Rome and Venice.

At the same time that the mythic voyage is mythifying Pound's experience in history by the Odyssean thread and by changes of mode from traditional to personal to justicial to poetic, it is mythifying historical voyages by means of which One World was discovered and, in *The Cantos*, is being rediscovered and perfected. The historical voyages are one means of proceeding from draft to draft. After an oceanic voyage (Odysseus's) has introduced *XVI. Cantos*, a local Mediterranean voyage introduces *XVII–XXX*; together they introduce the Renaissance tradition as a twentieth-century tradition being incorporated by Pound (*XXX Cantos*). The Renaissance then follows the historical voyages of Columbus, first to "Nuevo Mundo" and then back to Europe for "Siena-

Leopoldine Reforms.'' From there drafting continues the eastward voyage until a circumnavigation perfects a revolutionary tradition emergent in ''Jefferson-Nuevo Mundo'' and passing via ''Siena-Leopoldine Reforms'' and ''KUNG'' to a culmination in ''JOHN ADAMS.'' Continuing, circumnavigation defines the three paideumas ''ELEUSIS,'' ''KUNG,'' and ''JOHN ADAMS'' consummated personally in *Pisan*. The same form appears when *Section: Rock-Drill* is added and in *Thrones*, though the mode of justice dominates. The Odyssean voyage carries *Section: Rock-Drill* to *Thrones* and *Thrones* to *Drafts & Fragments* for the culmination.

While Pound is following the pattern of the Odyssean mythic voyage and using it to mythify the Columbian voyage and his own extensions of it, he is prosecuting the voyages for the purpose of evoking the spirits of places on their own grounds so that he may enter into those spirits and give the matter of history new life through his own life for his own time. According to this theme he is bringing the world paideumas to life as a revolutionary tradition through his own life in the first half of the poem (*LXXI Cantos*); in the second half (*LXXIV–120*), having been made into a twentieth-century revolutionary protagonist by the tradition he has incorporated, he is using the now living tradition for his own ends. ''Odysseus the name of my family'' (*Pisan LXXIV*) defines the locus for his historical personae in *LXXI Cantos*; in *LXXIV–120*, having incorporated the spirits of the paideumas on their own grounds, Pound takes all grounds and spirits as his own and speaks with and for his personae on equal terms.

These two themes—voyage adapted to the discovery of historical matter and rites used to evoke the spirits of places so that matter may be brought to life—are the first two themes of New World history, the discovery of 1492 and the colonizations of the early 1600s;[1] Odysseus opens them up archetypally in *I* and both run concurrent from *I* to the end of the poem. After he had finished ''Jefferson-Nuevo Mundo'' and was working on ''Siena-Leopoldine Reforms'' Pound told an interviewer ''I am leaving Rome in the direction of China: along the way I shall become increasingly different from what I was when I left. At Peking I shall be presented with a vast and unforeseen horizon. I would not have been able to reach that point [achieve that scope] if I had not departed in the first place.''[2] ''If I had not departed in the first place'' refers to a latter-day Columbus's voyage from America in 1908 to settle in Europe, to an American's discoveries of Europe and China, and to his rediscoveries, in European and world contexts, of his own native America.

''I shall become increasingly different from what I was when I left'' refers to his expatriation conceived as an actual colonization of Europe and to figu-

---

1. '' 'America of the Instant' is newer than anyone thinks. The European dates it from 1492, or 1630, or 1776. One cannot consider it as older than 1870.'' ''Patria Mia'' I, *New Age*, London, 5 September 1912.

2. ''Conversazione con Pound,'' Gino Protto, *L'Ambrosiano*, Milan, 12 April 1934, my translation.

rative colonizations of the other cultures. "The American colonization," initiated by Henry James, concludes "FOUR PERIODS" of English literature since Chaucer in *ABC of Reading*.[3] In some unpublished notes sent to Carlo Linati just after he had published *XVI. Cantos* and while he was working on *Cantos 17–27*, Pound insisted that American interest in Europe had entered a "New situation, new phase: exiles." Americans no longer came to Europe to find models for building civilization in America, but "to stimulate a reawakening in Europe, to be part of the life of the intelligence of Europe, element like the Greeks who were also exiles from Constantinople [and who] stimulated the Renaissance." They were "no longer students" "not 'naive' Americans who came to be impressed," "no longer representatives of the capitalists." "They are not a colony, in the sense that a colony represents the organized government. They are exiles, they are a new species of European."[4]

The third phase of New World history is revolution, which discovery and colonization precipitated during the 1760s, 1770s, and 1780s, or, if the Declaration of Independence is a definitive beginning, in 1776. Revolution precipitated by Odysseus in *I* as the revolt of the dead runs concurrent with discovery and colonization in its own several phases (themselves also concurrent) from beginning to end. In *The Cantos* Pound drafts a history of the world by using the Odyssean mythic voyage as a line and historical voyages of circumnavigation to keep circling One World while world political and economic revolution is evolving. He drafts his own autobiography (again based on Odysseus's) as a medium for bringing the matter of One World to life. But neither of these forms accounts for a poem of revolution. A poem of revolution is drafted in ten drafts rigorously constructed and rigorously deployed according to a revolutionary argument, revolutionary motives, revolutionary forms of justice, and revolutionary poetry.

It is clear from the beginning, and it emerges in the drafts entitled *Section: Rock-Drill* and *Thrones*, that cantos are being drafted and constituted as documents while also being shaped as stone and being built toward the ultimate 120 cantos. But it is evident from simple bibliography that the means of achieving this end is the drafting of a single revolution in ten drafts each of which has a different major subject. The ten drafts, each begun with a keynote canto and each consisting of ten cantos with or without a coda of one or more cantos, carry a single revolutionary argument embodied in ten major subjects which evolve thematically.

The four drafts of "ELEUSIS" derive from Mediterranean myth and from Western millennial history a philosophy of history and a theory of revolution inspired by the paideuma "ELEUSIS" and revealing an inherent form. This

---

3. *ABC of Reading* (New Haven: 1934), p. 121.

4. To Carlo Linati, 6 June 1925, Collection of American Literature, Beinecke Rare Book and Manuscript Library, Yale University. Hereafter cited as Collection at Yale.

myth of revolution, embodied finally in ideal European revolution, is followed by and used to elicit ideal Chinese and American revolutions (''KUNG'' and ''JOHN ADAMS''), which are presented not as mixtures of myth and history but, in the light of the derived ideal, as straightforward histories, millennial and generational respectively. The philosophy of history and its resultant ideal revolutions prepare and justify the emergence from a world revolutionary tradition of an independent, contemporary revolutionary protagonist in *Pisan*. In *Section: Rock-Drill* and *Thrones* a protagonist prepared by tradition and personal experience turns to the task of forming new government for the future. He aimed to perfect a drafted epic of revolution and to perfect a monument of cantos in *Drafts & Fragments*.

The form of this argument is that of the American Declaration of Independence, which derives from millennial history a revolutionary philosophy in four evolving premises; applies them to two historical cases (against King George III and ''our British brethren''); makes a resultant declaration of independence; declares the independent status of a new nation and assumes the appropriate governmental powers; and concludes with a pledge to continue the revolution already in progress. The opening paragraph both states the historical motive to separate and assumes as a premise a political destiny of self-determination for all peoples under ''the laws of nature and of nature's God.'' The self-evident natural rights, government by consent to secure those rights, and, when governments violate those rights, recourse to revolution, complete a timeless philosophy nevertheless derived from a past rooted in myth. Timeless premises applied to cases against the immediate past make an argument for separation. Returning to the present occasion which necessitated the argument, formal declaration of the right to separate draws from the argument its inevitable conclusion. Declaration of a new nation and of its governmental powers projects past and present into the future. The pledge binds all time into an ideal of continuing revolution.[5]

In *The Cantos* the whole Declaration is derived, as we shall see, through its four premises, and both the four premises and the whole Declaration project subsequent phases of a revolution defined not only by its mythic sources (the premises and their antecedents), and not only by the projective Declaration, but also by revolutionary personae, revolutionary justice, and revolutionary poetry; the last is intended to manifest and realize through the completed monument of 120 cantos an a priori vision of a new civilization. Pound focused the intricate structure of *The Cantos* in various symbols and arcana, both textual and visual. One such arcanum, near the beginning of *Rock-Drill 92*—

5. The facing pages tabulate the documents of '76 as they are correlated in the ensuing text.

BILL OF RIGHTS

AMENDMENT I.

Congress shall make no law respecting an establishment of religion, or prohibiting the free exercise thereof; or abridging the freedom of speech, or of the press; or the right of the people peaceably to assemble, and to petition the Government for a redress of grievances.

AMENDMENT II.

A well regulated Militia, being necessary to the security of a free State, the right of the people to keep and bear Arms, shall not be infringed.

AMENDMENT III.

No Soldier shall, in time of peace be quartered in any house, without the consent of the Owner, nor in time of war, but in a manner to be prescribed by law.

AMENDMENT IV.

The right of the people to be secure in their persons, houses, papers, and effects, against unreasonable searches and seizures, shall not be violated, and no Warrants shall issue, but upon probable cause, supported by Oath or affirmation, and particularly describing the place to be searched, and the persons or things to be seized.

AMENDMENT V.

No person shall be held to answer for a capital, or otherwise infamous crime, unless on a presentment or indictment of a Grand Jury, except in cases arising in the land or naval forces, or in the Militia, when in actual service in time of War or public danger; nor shall any person be subject for the same offence to be twice put in jeopardy of life or limb; nor shall be compelled in any criminal case to be a witness against himself, nor be deprived of life, liberty, or property, without due process of law; nor shall private property be taken for public use, without just compensation.

AMENDMENT VI.

In all criminal prosecutions, the accused shall enjoy the right of a speedy and public trial, by an impartial jury of the State and district wherein the crime shall have been committed, which district shall have been previously ascertained by law, and to be informed of the nature and cause of the accusation; to be confronted with the witnesses against him; to have compulsory process for obtaining witnesses in his favor, and to have the Assistance of Counsel for his defense.

AMENDMENT VII.

In suits at common law, where the value in controversy shall exceed twenty dollars, the right of trial by jury shall be preserved, and no fact tried by a jury, shall be otherwise reexamined in any Court of the United States, than according to the rules of the common law.

AMENDMENT VIII.

Excessive bail shall not be required, nor excessive fines imposed, nor cruel and unusual punishment inflicted.

AMENDMENT IX.

The enumeration in the Constitution, of certain rights, shall not be construed to deny or disparage others retained by the people.

AMENDMENT X.

The powers not delegated to the United States by the Constitution, nor prohibited by it to the States, are reserved to the States respectively, or to the people.

THE DECLARATION OF INDEPENDENCE

4 JULY 1776

THE UNANIMOUS DECLARATION OF THE THIRTEEN UNITED STATES OF AMERICA

When in the course of human events, it becomes necessary for one people to dissolve the political bands which have connected them with another, and to assume among the powers of the earth the separate and equal station to which the Laws of Nature and of Nature's God entitle them, a decent respect to the opinions of mankind requires that they should declare the causes which impel them to the separation.

We hold these truths to be self-evident, that all men are created equal, that they are endowed by their Creator with certain unalienable rights, that among these are life, liberty, and the pursuit of happiness. That to secure these rights, governments are instituted among men, deriving their just powers from the consent of the governed. That whenever any form of government becomes destructive of these ends, it is the right of the people to alter or to abolish it, and to institute new government, laying its foundation on such principles and organizing its powers in such form, as to them shall seem most likely to effect their safety and happiness. Prudence, indeed, will dictate that governments long established should not be changed for light and transient causes; and accordingly all experience hath shown, that mankind are more disposed to suffer, while evils are sufferable, than to right themselves by abolishing the forms to which they are accustomed. But when a long train of abuses and usurpations, pursuing invariably the same object evinces a design to reduce them under absolute despotism, it is their right, it is their duty, to throw off such government, and to provide new guards for their future security. Such has been the patient sufferance of these Colonies; and such is now the necessity which constrains them to alter their former systems of government. The history of the present King of Great Britain is a history of repeated injuries and usurpations, all having in direct object the establishment of an absolute tyranny over these States. To prove this, let facts be submitted to a candid world.

He has refused his assent to laws, the most wholesome and necessary for the public good.

He has forbidden his Governors to pass laws of immediate and pressing importance, unless suspended in their operation till his assent should be obtained; and when so suspended, he has utterly neglected to attend to them.

He has refused to pass other laws for the accommodation of large districts of people, unless those people would relinquish the right of representation in the legislature, a right inestimable to them and formidable to tyrants only.

He has called together legislative bodies at places unusual, uncomfortable, and distant from the depository of their public records, for the sole purpose of fatiguing them into compliance with his measures.

He has dissolved representative houses repeatedly, for opposing with manly firmness his invasions on the rights of the people.

He has refused for a long time, after such dissolutions, to cause others to be elected; whereby the legislative powers, incapable of annihilation, have returned to the people at large for their exercise; the State remaining in the meantime exposed to all the dangers of invasion from without and convulsions within.

He has endeavoured to prevent the population of these States, for that purpose obstructing the laws for naturalization of foreigners; refusing to pass others to encourage their migration hither, and raising the conditions of new appropriations of lands.

He has obstructed the administration of justice, by refusing his assent to laws for establishing judiciary powers.

He has made judges dependent on his will alone, for the tenure of their offices, and the amount and payment of their salaries.

He has erected a multitude of new offices, and sent hither swarms of officers to harass our people, and eat out their substance.

He has kept among us, in times of peace, standing armies without the consent of our legislatures.

He has affected to render the military independent of and superior to the civil power.

He has combined with others to subject us to a jurisdiction foreign to our constitution, and unacknowledged by our laws; giving his assent to their acts of pretended legislation:

For quartering large bodies of armed troops among us:

For protecting them, by a mock trial, from punishment for any murders which they should commit on the inhabitants of these States:

For cutting off our trade with all parts of the world:

For imposing taxes on us without our consent:

For depriving us in many cases of the benefits of trial by jury:

For transporting us beyond seas to be tried for pretended offences:

For abolishing the free system of English laws in a neighbouring Province, establishing therein an arbitrary government, and enlarging its boundaries so as to render it at once an example and fit instrument for introducing the same absolute rule into these Colonies:

For taking away our Charters, abolishing our most valuable laws, and altering fundamentally the forms of our governments:

For suspending our own Legislatures, and declaring themselves invested with power to legislate for us in all cases whatsoever.

He has abdicated government here, by declaring us out of his protection and waging war against us.

He has plundered our seas, ravaged our coasts, burnt our towns, and destroyed the lives of our people.

He is at this time transporting large armies of foreign mercenaries to compleat the works of death, desolation, and tyranny, already begun with circumstances of cruelty and perfidy scarcely paralleled in the most barbarous ages, and totally unworthy the head of a civilized nation.

He has constrained our fellow citizens taken captive on the high seas to bear arms against their country, to become the executioners of their friends and brethren, or to fall themselves by their hands.

He has excited domestic insurrections amongst us, and has endeavoured to bring on the inhabitants of our frontiers the merciless Indian savages, whose known rule of warfare is an undistinguished destruction of all ages, sexes, and conditions.

In every stage of these oppressions we have petitioned for redress in the most humble terms: our repeated petitions have been answered only by repeated injury. A prince whose character is thus marked by every act which may define a tyrant, is unfit to be the ruler of a free people.

Nor have we been wanting in attention to our British brethren. We have warned them from time to time of attempts by their Legislature to extend an unwarrantable jurisdiction over us. We have reminded them of the circumstances of our emigration and settlement here. We have appealed to their native justice and magnanimity, and we have conjured them by the ties of our common kindred to disavow these usurpations, which would inevitably interrupt our connections and correspondence. They too have been deaf to the voice of justice and of consanguinity. We must, therefore, acquiesce in the necessity, which denounces our separation, and hold them, as we hold the rest of mankind, enemies in war, in peace friends.

We, therefore, the Representatives of the United States of America, in General Congress assembled, appealing to the Supreme Judge of the world for the rectitude of our intentions, do, in the name, and by authority of the good people of these Colonies, solemnly publish and declare, That these United Colonies are, and of right ought to be Free and Independent States; that they are absolved from all allegiance to the British Crown, and that all political connection between them and the State of Great Britain is and ought to be totally dissolved; and that as Free and Independent States they have full power to levy war, conclude peace, contract alliances, establish commerce, and to do all other acts and things which independent States may of right do. And for the support of this declaration, with a firm reliance on the protection of Divine Providence, we mutually pledge to each other our lives, our fortunes and our sacred honor.

and as engraven on gold, to be unity
but duality, brass
        and trine to mercurial
shall a tetrad be silver
        with the smoke of nutmeg and frankincense
and from this a sea-change?

—refers to the Declaration as "to be unity," (1–10), or a projection; as "duality," its argument against the past (1–6) supporting its projection of a new future (7–10); as "trine," its premises (1–4) modulating into its argument for independence (4–7) modulating into its projection of a new nation (7–10); and as "tetrad" its argument (1–6), its declaration (7), its projection of a new nation (8–9), and its pledge to continuing revolution (10). The metamorphosis of metals and the metamorphosis of divisions would undergo a final metamorphosis into the projected gold and unity.

The Declaration "to be unity" projects again, as it did in '76, a new revolutionary tradition, except that Pound has used a different method of effecting a "revolt of intelligence."[6] Taking for granted as a definitive form of revolution the conceptual and historical themes of the Declaration as formulated in 1776, he derives it from and imposes it upon the millennial revolutionary histories gathered by voyage and brought to life by colonization. The Declaration conceptualizes tradition; Pound particularizes the conceptualization. In that way he constitutes in *The Cantos*, over a whole revolutionary argument "to be unity," a new revolutionary tradition.

In the four drafts of "ELEUSIS" a world revolutionary destiny and natural rights emerge from the Renaissance, government by consent is instituted in America, and, when American government fails, ideal continuing revolution is found in Siena and Tuscany; each of these drafts contains mythic cantos which imbue the actual history with mythic value for the premises. The case against King George is applied to differentiating good and bad Chinese emperors. The case against "our British brethren" is applied both to American separation from Europe and to new relations based on mutual independence. The autobiographical *Pisan* declares independence from the old order in favor of a new. *Section: Rock-Drill* and *Thrones* look toward new world government. In *Drafts & Fragments* Pound makes his pledge to continuing revolution even though he cannot bring it to a successful conclusion.

This ten-draft argument is prophesied by epitome cantos in the prototype decad *I–X*, the subject of which is Renaissance revolution against an atavistic medievalism. *I–IV* derive the premises from a Renaissance tradition of Greek (*I*), Roman (*II*), and medieval (*III*) poetry consummated in Renaissance poetry derived from its antecedents "ply over ply" (*IV*). The rest of the decad

6. "The Revolt of Intelligence" I–X, *New Age*, London, November 1919–March 1920.

applies "the vision" to raw history viewed in "the arena" of history and so as yet untransformed into poetry. Canto *V* applies it to cases from millennial history which culminate in trying the case of a Renaissance political assassination; *VI* applies it to cases involving the medieval love codes and love courts. Historical argument shifts in *VII* to a twentieth-century protagonist's autobiographical declaration of independence from received traditions, for the derived Renaissance tradition. In *VIII* and *IX* Duke Sigismundo Malatesta of fifteenth-century Rimini tries to exercise independence and sovereign powers against the conditions of his time by reordering his duchy and by transforming Rimini's Christian cathedral into the neopagan Tempio Malatestiano. In *X*, though caught in the political intrigues of his times and excommunicated by the church, he receives an omen from an Eagle and pledges himself and his men to a new effort against the papal armies. The inspiration from the Eagle turns the decad into the new poetry of Renaissance revolution.

The theme of the Declaration as "duality" is revolution old and new carried from idea into action by former revolutionaries and then by their contemporary heir, who from the beginning is "formando di disio nuova persona" (*XXVII*), or "forming a new person from desire." In the first half of *The Cantos* the contemporary protagonist is subordinated to his historical personae, by drafts certain leaders of Italian Renaissance city-states, leaders who sought to unify Renaissance Italy, the collective men of '76, rulers of Siena and Tuscany, Chinese emperors (Confucian and otherwise), and finally, focusing all, John Adams. Pound emerges via his "protagonista civile"[7] Adams into his role as a twentieth-century "nuova persona"—as a struggler for independence, as a founder of governments, and as an epic poet—for the rest of the poem.

The document of '76 for new personae, projected by the dual Declaration, is the Preamble to the Constitution formulating the will ("disio") of "WE the People" out of the struggle for independence and then turning that will toward the writing of the Constitution. For his purposes Pound assumes a precedent and inherent "WE the people" and aligns with the Declaration's six-part argument for separation the six motives ("disii") of the Preamble—"to form a more perfect union, establish justice, insure domestic tranquility, provide for the common defense, promote the general welfare, and secure the blessings of liberty to ourselves and our posterity." The enacting motive—"do ordain and establish this Constitution for the United States of America"—is aligned with the Declaration's declaration of independence.

At the same time, to accomplish a double purpose—first to project a Constitution aimed by the Declaration's argument from a "more perfect union" toward "the blessings of liberty" for individual states and cultures, and then to project a Constitution aimed from achieved liberty to a new "more perfect union" on a world scale—Pound aligns a reversal of the Preamble, from

7. "Narrare," *Lettere d'Oggi*, Rome, June/July 1941.

liberty toward the new world union, with the Declaration's four-part projection of a new future. The enacting motive aligned with the seventh draft for the first Preamble serves the reversed Preamble as well. "WE the People" is assumed at the end as at the beginning. In fact Pound emphasizes the extremes union to liberty and then liberty to union more than the detailed motives, which in both the prototype decad and in the drafts are more generally diffused than discrete. Union to liberty was the achievement of past personae; liberty to union is the aim of their twentieth century successor. As we shall see Pound provided arcana both without *The Cantos* and within for this intricate ideal structure.

The theme of the Declaration as "trine" is "thinking out a sane state"[8] for the new One World reality and, from it, thinking out a new world order of such states. *The Cantos* begins with Renaissance city-state, elaborates it into the Renaissance and twentieth-century nation-state, shifts to the geographically organized American federation of states, and arrives in "ELEUSIS" at an anticipation of an economically organized corporate state (Siena) within the Duchy of Tuscany. "KUNG" offers the lesson of Confucianism as a means of sustaining or restoring order within an empire. "JOHN ADAMS" thinks out the American Constitutional system within a world context. *Pisan* seems to have been intended, before the debacle of fascism, to delineate the contemporary Italian corporate state modeled on Siena within Tuscany and modified by the Chinese and American lessons. Vestiges of "the effort" "to dream the republic" persist in *Pisan*, carrying along the original intent despite the debacle.

"Thinking out a sane state" takes place within the form of the Constitution interpreted for states' rights within a world order. For Pound a states' rights Constitution consists of four Branches, Congress, Presidency, Judiciary, and States (Articles I–IV) interacting with and modulating into four amending Powers (Articles IV–VII)—States initiating an amending process, Amendment defining it, the Constitution as the Supreme Law of the land testing it, and Ratification completing it. The Declaration's premises and argument culminating in a declaration of independence project, through the Preamble's union projecting liberty, seven draft-Articles for thinking out an independent state.

When the Declaration's premises become a single revolutionary philosophy (cf. the four drafts of the single paideuma "ELEUSIS"), the argument for independence (1–4 and 4–7 as the first and second thirds of "trine") projects through the Preambles (union to liberty turned from liberty toward new union) four paideumatic Branches (1–4, 5, 6, 7) for a world union of independent states. The Declaration's projection of a new future projects through the reversed Preamble the third third of "trine" (7–10), or world powers. It can

8. "The State Should Move like a Dance," *British Union Quarterly*, London, October/ December 1938.

be seen from the middle third that the two halves of the Constitution interact with each other so that the four Branches are amended by the four amending Powers and the four amending Powers are guided by the four Branches. The Constitution is thus, in Pound's handling, a dynamic, self-amending system of government.

For amending the geographically organized American state to an economically organized corporate state, Pound educes Congress from Renaissance cooperation toward order and constructivity (*XVI. Cantos*) and Presidency from Renaissance egoism and individualism (*XVII–XXX*).[9] American thinking about government and economics takes place as an expression of Judiciary, which the Renaissance neglected. Since America forsook states' rights, Sienese economic and political founding advances States as a fourth Branch while initiating an amending process aimed at extending a model for a corporate state toward the world. To this end "KUNG" contributes Confucian Amendment and "JOHN ADAMS" thinks out the Constitution as Supreme Law. Pound ratifies the corporate ideal if not the fact in *Pisan*.

Modulating out of this form, world Congress comes to focus in the West in Siena, China contributes the model of the Confucian emperor for Presidency, and America contributes through John Adams a model for a government of laws, not men, or Judiciary. Pound adds the corporate ideal for States as a world Branch initiating (as a Power) the amending process for perfecting the world form. New revolutionary founding, Constitutional defense, and new visions of Justice add Amendment in *Section: Rock-Drill*. The constitutions of *Thrones* add Supreme Law. *Drafts & Fragments* ratifies the world form if not its realization. As we shall see later the Constitutional themes and forms are also embodied prophetically in the prototype decad as independence passing to communal order.

Pound suggested his amendment of the Constitutional functions in "The State Should Move Like a Dance": "Any man trying to think out a sane state, must separate various kinds of human being, *e.g.*, those suited to the executive, those suited to the advisory, and (point not sufficiently developed in former sociology) those suited to *perceptive functions*. . . . The belief that THE STATE SHOULD MOVE LIKE A DANCE is not merely a poetic moonbeam projected into an unattainable future." The "kinds of human being" and their functions, the fourth being "poetic," go with the four Branches as Pound conceived them in the kind of corporate state he was "thinking out" in

---

9. In "Patria Mia" VI (*New Age*, London, 10 October 1912) Pound found the model of "our present constitutional government" in medieval free cities "now here, now there," which "contrived to hold out against the feudal system." He went on to analogize the feudal system based on arms and the industrial system based on money, which led him to guild socialism. Most of the analogy and other passages were excised when, in 1913, he rearranged "Patria Mia" I–XII (September–November 1912) and "America: Chances and Remedies" I–VI (*New Age*, May–June 1913) into the book *Patria Mia*, "lost" and then not published until 1950. I use the original essays.

The Cantos, a mixture of American states' rights theory, European guild socialism, Italian fascist practice, and Confucianism. In such a state varied economic and professional interests, the corporations, would act as States to initiate and exercise the Powers. With the guidance of a Congress or council of corporations, in which they would have representatives, the corporations would initiate, direct, and execute social and economic policy. Their efforts to effect change (Amendment) would be guided by a central government under a single Presidential Figure who would advise and arbitrate. Change would be subject to the Supreme Law interpreted by a Judiciary. The corporations and the people at large would be the measure of social well-being, the source of a communal will and of new ideas, the constituency for policies and practices, and the final authority for ratifying change.[10]

The Constitutional forms are rooted in the paideumas of the three cultures. "The European nature"—"to act, observe, and believe.—in this order of processes"[11] is embodied in the Greek, Roman, and medieval revolutionary poetry of *I*, *II*, and *III*; this spirit of "ELEUSIS" culminates in Amor in the fourth canto of the Renaissance poetic tradition (*IV*). The Chinese analogue is the Confucian "FOUR TUAN," Love, Duty, Propriety, and Wisdom, cited in *Rock-Drill 85* and *Thrones 99* but inherent in the beginning.[12] The American analogue is the revolutionary process defined by the Declaration, the Preamble, the Constitution, and the Bill of Rights, which (as we shall see) inheres in the Declaration's premises; hence the projection of the myth of revolution to the form of government to be achieved by it. All these forms can be universalized for One World into tradition, personality, justice, and poetry.

Drafting by constitutional "trine" is coordinated with and supported by the drafting and shaping of cantos being constituted and built into a monument. The three federal Branches consist of 71 clauses: Congress 1–53, Presidency 54–65, and Judiciary 66–71. The whole is completed by the Branch/Power States (72–78), Amendment (79), Supreme Law (80–82), Ratification (83), and, for Pound, a clause memorializing, signing, sealing, and delivering the Constitution (84). Drafting a states' rights Constitution in seven Articles thus

10. Between 1946 and 1951, in a letter to an unspecified correspondent, (The Humanities Research Center, University of Texas at Austin, hereafter cited as Humanities Center at Texas) Pound explained that to him the corporate state meant American Constitutional government modified simply by formal representation and responsible participation of the trade unions, and by a "division of powers, judicial, executive and rule-making" within the unions themselves. By "unions" he meant all trades and professions.

11. From a letter to Douglas Fox transmitting an unpublished essay "European Paideuma," 7 August 1939, Humanities Center at Texas.

12. Pound was familiar with the "Four TUAN" from Ernest Fenollosa's account of a Ban-Gumi or series of Noh plays (*'Noh' or Accomplishment*, by Ernest Fenollosa and Ezra Pound, London, 1917, p. 10). See the scheme sent to Santayana, pp. 73, 74. The process lies behind all Pound's efforts to correlate Western and Eastern philosophy (see further Chapter Fourteen and Appendix D).

converges with drafting, shaping, and building eighty-three cantos of Constitutional constituents plus the eighty-fourth. Clauses do not inform cantos one by one, but serve as a matrix upon which draft-Articles are composed.

At the same time drafting six drafts into three world paideumas—"ELEUSIS" *I–LI*, "KUNG" *LII–LXI*, and "JOHN ADAMS" *LXII–LXXI*—has converged with the clauses of the three federal Branches (Congress 1–53, Presidency 54–65, Judiciary 66–71); the overlapping of states' rights drafts and world paideumas signifies the modulation from states' rights to One World, and the overlapping of cantos and paideumas signifies separation and balance but also interrelatedness. Convergence of clauses 72–84 not only with Ratification of states' rights, but also with the Branch/Power States as a fourth paideuma containing clausally the amending Powers, initiates an amending process designed to be completed in the remaining three drafts of the poem.

Drafting and shaping cantos as Constitutional constituents continues within these last three drafts. The Constitution's eighty-three clauses plus an eighty-fourth are grouped into xxiv Sections plus Section xxv, the complement of *Los Cantares 85–109*. The eighty-four clauses and xxv Sections are grouped further into VII Articles plus Article VIII, the complement of *Drafts & Fragments CX–CXVII*. The anomalous *CXVII*, which is part both of the titular *Drafts & Fragments of Cantos CX–CXVII* and of the *Fragments of Cantos* "Notes for *CXVII* et seq.," serves both as Article VIII for drafts of cantos and as a first of four for what should have been *CXVII–120*. Thus the three fragments and the posthumous *120* can be seen within the form of four Branches interacting with four Powers, or the Branches/Powers dynamic employed by the Constitutional mind draft by draft throughout the poem.

The theme of the Declaration as "tetrad" is paideuma, or "our way of thinking in poetry"; so four drafts culminate in the Mediterranean paideuma "ELEUSIS," so four paideumas culminate in the world paideuma *Pisan*, and so four phases of the whole poem were intended to perfect new world epic poetry in *Drafts & Fragments*. If the mode of the Declaration "to be unity" is tradition, as "duality" personality old and new, and as "trine" justice old, new, and timeless—states' rights, a model world state, and a new union of such states—the mode of the Declaration as "tetrad" is a poetry of new tradition, a poetry of new revolutionary personality working within the tradition it has inherited and shaped, a poetry of new justice derived from tradition by personality, and a poetry of poetry made possible by the foregoing—i.e., a poetry free of time and place and therefore religious and divine. Such are the ten drafts accumulated by collections in four phases of a revolution, a life, a form of government, and a poem: *LXXI Cantos*, *Pisan*, *Los Cantares*, and the unperfected *Drafts & Fragments*.

The form for "thinking in poetry" is the Bill of Rights, the ten Amendments of which activate the ten-part Declaration until, through the Preambles and the Constitutions, idea and action converge. The Bill is interpreted freely as a warrant to exercise various specified rights protected from governmental injustice (First–Eighth), and various unspecified rights not explicitly granted to government by the Constitution (Ninth), through powers not specifically granted to government by the Constitution (Tenth). A span from freedom of religion, speech, and assembly (First), to powers reserved to the States, or to the people (Tenth), makes the mode of the Bill the justified, active, poetic imagination.

Pound takes straight as an epitome the freedoms of religion, of speech, and of assembly to seek a redress of grievances (First). The military arms of the Second are made sensibilities for apprehending natural phenomena epiphanically. Soldiers are prohibited entry into houses (Third) unless they are also lawmakers. Privacy is protected (Fourth) except under warrant of poetic invocation, which opens up secrets and rituals. Due process of law (Fifth) and fair trial with all legal rights (Sixth) govern cases against political tyranny. The common law by which civil cases must be tried (Seventh) is made the universal law of nature. Cruel punishments (Eighth) are suffered but overcome by the will and by accesses of vision, which are both cruel and beneficent. Retained rights (Ninth) open the rights further. Reserved powers (Tenth) provide a "poetic license"—the spirit of the Bill as a whole—for making such interpretations. As will be seen, these adaptations are especially prominent in the prototype *I–X*, whence they govern the ten drafts.

The Bill is not an argument like the Declaration, a means to an end (union to liberty, liberty to union) like the Preambles, or an organized governmental mechanism like the Constitution. It is a list, though it does have a logic from rights to powers. Pound thus groups the loosely listed amendments according to the tightly organized Declaration, with whose parts they often have a surprising affinity. The Declaration's premises are activated by Amendments First–Fourth, the private rights. The cases are activated by due process and fair trial, the criminal rights (Fifth–Sixth). The declaration is activated by Pound's adaptation of common law rights (Seventh). Less relevantly, but adaptatively, asserted independence and sovereignty are activated by what may be called political rights (Eighth–Ninth). The pledge is activated by the reserved powers (Tenth).

Drafting a ten-draft revolution in four concurrent phases converges with building a monument of 120 cantos in four discrete, sequential phases. The form is the heraldic symbol of '76, the Seal of the United States; taken as an a priori form for "REVOLUTION . . . in the minds of the people . . . during the fifteen years before Lexington" (so John Adams defines '76 in *XXXII*, *XXXIII*, and *L*), it is realized as a symbol for a new civilization through the documented revolutionary process.[13] The Eagle of war (arrows) and peace

---

13. The ensuing interpretation of the Seal and its symbolism is derived from Pound's apparent interpretation and use of it for *The Cantos*. For the official interpretation by the Continental Congress, which adopted it in 1782, see Appendix A.

(olive branch) on the dark obverse or front, inspired by Providence in the triangular space above the pyramid or Mount on the light reverse or back, envisions a form in four geometrical symbols one built upon the other from dark to light and each voiced by a revelatory motto or commemorative date. The Eagle, an antecedent locus for all personae (as is their poet), builds the received vision. Shield, constellation, Mount, and sun-vision constitute Pound's version of a Statue of Liberty embodying its own builder and inspiration in the revolutionary process that shaped and built it. The Eagle finds his materials in the form of a fragmented Statue of Constitutional fragments and reconstitutes them while making them new.

All symbols are different, but all repeat thirteen being unified, all take related forms, and the four geometrical shapes are all voiced by the inspired Eagle who drafts and builds up to his inspiring Providence. The a priori, all-encompassing, revolutionary Eagle unites in his head, or in his eye and mind, nine tail feathers for direction, two talons for grasping symbols of war and peace, and two wings for power; in this respect he symbolizes the ship for the voyage of discovery. The thirteen arrows symbolize Pound's handling "luminous detail" or "the limbs of Osiris"[14] being gathered by a voyage turned from war to peace; the matter is to be brought to life by the olive branch (of colonization) with its thirteen leaves and olives. These symbols are subsumed in "REVOLUTION . . . in the minds of the people" to be realized by voices.

Thirteen stripes unified by the blue field on the shield voiced E PLURIBUS UNUM (Out of Many, One), project the Declaration. Thirteen stars unified as a constellation on a blue field voiced NOVUS ORDO SECLORUM (A New Order of Centuries), project the old and new Preambles. Thirteen tiers of stone built on a foundation inscribed MDCCLXXVI project the overlapping Constitutions. Thirteen sun-rays encircling a triangular space and the eye of Providence, celebrated ANNUIT COEPTIS (He Favored Our Beginnings), project the Bill of Rights while completing the Seal edifice. (Pound's means of translating thirteen to ten must await the next chapter.)

The shield E PLURIBUS UNUM both *is* unity and is "to be [new] unity" by metamorphoses of its stripes and by additions and constitutings of "duality," "trine," "tetrad," and a "sea-change." By its downward point it symbolizes the inspiration of Providence descending to the Eagle to be planted and founded in the dark of the past, symbolically the underworld; its downward point makes the shield at once a foundation for and (reversed) a pattern for the upward-pointing triangular Mount; both foundation and pattern will be figured in the mediating constellation.

The pentagram stars (a shape of the Eagle without its directing tail) transform the stripes into twelve personae surrounding a central persona; the re-

14. "I gather the Limbs of Osiris" I–XII, *New Age*, London, November 1911–February 1912.

sulting hexagram constellation figures the Eagle flying downward with his inspiration while building upward to realize it. As "duality"—as interpenetrating ten-star triangles or tetraktyses pointing respectively downward and upward—the constellation transforms the shield into stars while projecting from the stars the erected Mount; in this respect it is a plan derived from the past by personae who project it toward the future. Its duality symbolizes the Preambles projecting the overlapping Constitutions. Duality subsumes unity (the shield) in a transitional unity (duality itself) while constituting duality with the shield; by its shape it foreshadows "trine," "tetrad," and a "sea-change."

The tiers of the Mount transform the shield stripes while the stones transform the stars of the constellation. The triangular Mount built on the shield according to the stellar plan subsumes unity and duality in a transitional unity (trine); it *is* "trine" by its triangular shape and it *constitutes* trine with the shield and the constellation; by pointing toward its own culmination in the light it foreshadows "tetrad" and a "sea-change." Constituted trine symbolizes the modulating halves of the states' rights Constitution while projecting the world Constitution to be perfected beyond the material Mount in the idealizing light.

The rays of the sun transform stripes, stars, and tiers of stones. The circular sun-vision perfects the preceding shapes while containing the shape of all previous symbols as a shrine for the eye of Providence. The sun-vision transforms each prior symbol in itself as "tetrad" while constituting "tetrad" out of the four symbols. A "sea-change"—not only the metamorphoses of symbols but also a modulation from dark to light—realizes the whole as the new unity inspired by Providence and evolving according to Her inspiring vision.

Each symbol is a whole, each symbol is a phase of an evolving four-phase whole, and each symbol metamorphoses its predecessors into new constituents and a new form. Taken together these several aspects account for drafting by concurrent voices while drafting and building by sequential voices. Another characteristic of this simultaneity is the unfolding of accruing four-phase subjects draft by draft as the overall revolution is being drafted and built toward the culminating four phases. Pound called this characteristic changing "mass relations."[15] It is symbolized by an open-ended Mount ending in ideal light rather than in stone, and it is announced by a concluding voice that keeps celebrating the same divinely favored beginnings from the vantage point of new endings. "Mass relations" are changed by adding a new subject to the previous four-phase subject so as to form a new four-phase subject. In the first draft, which contains evolving epitomes and prototypes for the whole poem, "mass relations" change by the addition of cantos. From that basis, "mass relations" change by the addition of drafts. Detailed exposition of this unusual form, especially in the first draft, will have to await closer examination; here it can only be sketched.

First, however, it must be pointed out that as "REVOLUTION . . . in the minds of the people" the Seal symbolizes the myth and millennial history behind the Declaration's premises, or "ELEUSIS" and Western millennia from Homeric Greece via the Renaissance and '76 to the twentieth-century present. With the Renaissance date of the first canto, 1538, instead of MDCCLXXVI, the Seal symbolizes a Renaissance tradition making Greece, Rome, and the Middle Ages new as a revolutionary tradition prophesying what it precipi-

---

15. Pound wrote to "G/S" (16 May 1935, Collection at Yale) while he was working on *The Fifth Decad* "what I haven't yet done . . . will modify the mass relations of what is already printed"; that the "weight" of the mass relations "shd crush the 'documentation' to succulence" suggests that the evolving form would gradually reveal itself by major subjects.

tated, New World or American history in four analogous thematic phases: Columbus's discovery of 1492, the colonizations begun in North America during the early 1600s, the Revolution of 1776, and the civilization embodying continuing revolution inaugurated when the Bill of Rights was ratified in 1791. The Seal also symbolizes four analogous phases that emerged in the middle of New World history, declaration, struggle, founding, and continuing revolution, which modulates back into the consummation of New World history. The overlapping of New World history and '76 is explained by the fact that the revolution was dated during its middle phase when the Constitution of 1787 commemorated an American era beginning with the Declaration in "MDCCLXXVI." In the actual unfolding of *The Cantos* the themes are laid "ply over ply" while the millennial, epochal, and generational histories they inform evolve according to a general chronology.

All the forms and themes so far described are nonetheless completely prophesied by being overlaid upon the Odyssean voyage to consult the dead (*I*) translated out of Homer, via Renaissance Latin, in an adaptation of medieval "seafarer metre," by Pound's own "modern metre."[16] The linguistic overlay carries concurrency. Sequentially, a crew makes a voyage of discovery, performs rites of colonization evoking the spirits of place (the dead), and undergoes the revolt of the dead (which is thereby made their own) before Pound interrupts and takes over the narration for continuing revolution. At the same time the revolt of the dead is made the revolt of the living by the myriad dead declaring, by an individualized dead seeking recompense for the common struggle, by a seer delivering the destiny of the living as a new divine justice, and by Pound recognizing his poetic predecessors in the continuing revolution and delivering the invocation to the Muse or Providence of his new epic poem, Aphrodite atop her Mount. Pound has made old history and old revolution new by taking over Odysseus's narration and by replacing Odysseus's Providence, Circe, with his own. His entry at the end has made *I* both an epitome of all that follows and a first canto joining all that follows in "mass relations." He has drafted and built a canto in the form of all cantos, the "triangular space" containing the eye of Providence, which culminates the three material symbols in an ideal (a divine or mythic or poetic) fourth.

"These triangular spaces" (*CXIV*) are the Constitutional spaces of a Constitutional mind to be filled with appropriate materials and built into the same triangular form (the Mount). Pound apparently imagined such a Mount built of tiers of triangles placed alternately upon base and apex. He apparently planned a Mount of "100 or 120 cantos."[17] If history answered to his concep-

16. On 3 December 1914 (letter at Houghton Library, Harvard University, hereafter cited as Houghton Library) Pound sent Thomas Bird Mosher eight Cathay poems and "The Seafarer," mentioning also "some of the eleventh book of the Odyssey, in 'modern metre.' " He told Iris Barry "I have tried an adaptation in the 'Seafarer metre,' or something like it, but I don't expect anyone to recognize the source very quickly" (20 July 1916, *Letters*).

17. To Felix E. Schelling, 9 July 1922, *Letters*.

tion during his lifetime, a neo-Dantean 100-canto Mount would be suspended from a tier of one triangle via tiers of three, five, seven, etc., down to a tenth tier and foundation of nineteen. If history did not answer to his conception during his lifetime, a 120-Mount would be built in the form of the Renaissance Mount, a twenty-one-triangle foundation rising via nineteen, seventeen, fifteen, etc., to a tenth tier of three, beyond which would lie the ideal model for further extension into the next era. The Renaissance Mount would build an earthy foundation under the ideal medieval Mount.[18] Either Mount would end in the light and in celebration if completed; uncompleted, as *The Cantos* is, it would end like its principal model, the Renaissance and the Tempio Malatestiano, "In the gloom, the gold gathers the light against it." Such too is *I*, a module and an epitome for which Pound invokes the new light of Aphrodite to replace the light of Circe and the dark of history—invokes, but cannot guarantee. All he can guarantee is "the effort" of "the life vouchsafed."[19]

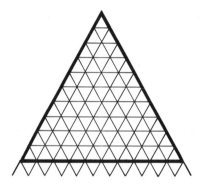 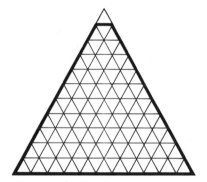

From standing by itself epitomizing all subjects, themes, and forms as an old Statue of Liberty being remade new, *I* evolves from European millennia a mythifying Seal-vision. The Seal-vision mythifies the European era by being derived from a Renaissance tradition of Greek (*I*), Roman (*II*), and medieval (*III*) poetry consummated in Renaissance poetry derived from its antecedents "ply over ply" (*IV*). The four cantos project "renaissance" as a universal mythic and historical principle. The mythifying poetic selections and the

18. Cf. "In architecture, medieval work means line; line, composition, and design: Renaissance work means mass. The medieval architect envied the spider his cobweb. The Renaissance architect sought to rival the mountain. They raised successively the temple of the spirit and the temple of the body. The analogy in literature is naturally inexact; Dante, however, sought to hang his song from the absolute, the centre and source of light; art since Dante has for the most part built solidly from the ground." "Montcorbier *Alias* Villon," *The Spirit of Romance*, 1910.

19. "An Interview with Ezra Pound," *Paris Review* 28, Summer–Fall 1962. Hereafter cited as *Paris Review* 28.

unmythified historical passages are all instances of revolution against a status quo, so that a myth of "renaissance" contains a myth of revolution.

As we shall see the epitome *I* evolves through its four speakers "to be unity" by duality, trine, and tetrad until the fourth (Pound) provides the "sea-change" to a gold-clad Aphrodite. The Seal-vision evolves similarly. Homeric "to be unity" (*I*) evolves Homeric-Ovidian duality (*II*), these transformed and augmented with the medieval *Poema del Cid* to form Dantean trine (*III*), and all consummated in Renaissance tetrad (*IV*). Canto *IV* turns historical dark (*I*), natural dark and light (a "half-light," *II*), and justicial light (*III*) into full religious light while effecting within itself a "sea-change" from silver to new gold.

As "REVOLUTION . . . in the minds of the people" this vision projects through the Declaration's premises the whole Declaration and thus the whole revolution. The occasion for declaring separation and the destiny of free peoples projects the Declaration "to be unity" *I–X*. The destiny and natural rights project the Preambles *I–VI* and *VII–X*. The destiny, natural rights, and government by consent project the Constitutional trine *I–IV*, *IV–VII*, and *VII–X* (a form for independence modulating into a form for communal order). The destiny, natural rights, government by consent, and continuing revolution project the Declaration as tetrad activated by the Bill and sealed by the discrete phases of the Seal-vision, *I–VI*, *VII*, *VIII–IX*, and *X*. This complex form is possible because each Seal symbol is a differently formed whole and because a new formal whole is constituted by "mass relations" as each symbol is added. At the same time, by the Seal's simple discrete sequence, *I* projects *I–VI*, *II* projects *VII*, *III* projects *VIII–IX*, and *IV* projects *X*.

The four-canto Seal-vision constitutes a prototype for all four-phase subjects. It evolves first to Renaissance revolution *I–X*, a prophetic prototype for the revolutionary process of '76. Each canto of the prototype decad projects thematically, through the first and keynote canto of each draft, the major subject of that draft in the revolutionary process. At the same time the decad and its coda, *XI–XVI*, project according to the prototypic paradigm "ONE, ten, eleven, *chi con me* 目 tan?" (*Thrones 97*)—English, Italian, Chinese, and transliteration—an extension of Renaissance revolution to twentieth century world revolution (*XVI. Cantos*). The decad and its coda provide a prototype for each of ten decads informing ten drafts: the decad drafts revolution while the draft both drafts revolution and builds a tier of the Mount. Uniquely, as we shall see, *XVI. Cantos* not only consists of a decad extended by a coda but is also a four-phase epitome draft projected by *I*, *I–IV*, and *I–X* toward the convergence of ten drafts and four phases in a single poetic Mount to be constituted and built of 120 cantos.

Expanding by "mass relations" has resulted in a Renaissance projection of twentieth-century world revolution. Twentieth-century revolution continues, but the main subject of the second draft, *Cantos 17–27*, is the continuation of the Renaissance seen from new perspectives until it declines as a phenomenon confined to Europe. A four-phase subject was not completed, however, until cantos were added to constitute *XXX Cantos*, which formalizes the "death" of the local Renaissance with the death of the Borgia Pope in 1503. A four-phase form for the completion of the historical Renaissance before the discovery of "Nuevo Mundo" appears as arcanum in a plan for Malatesta's Tempio at Rimini, itself a type of the Renaissance dream of a new civilization. Although the historical Renaissance "dies," the Malatestan plan is extendable beyond the historical limits. It takes new root via Columbus in "Nuevo Mundo."

Extension of the apparently "dead" Renaissance to revolution continuing in "Nuevo Mundo" (*XLI Cantos*) is constituted of four decades; when '76 succumbs to plutocracy a coda introduces Italian fascist revolution as a revision of the Renaissance and American failures. Taking a cue from the return to fascist Italy, four decades evolve four drafts. Out of Renaissance and American forms continuing revolution more economic than civil emerges in seventeenth-, eighteenth-, and nineteenth-century Siena and Tuscany (and in the world) in the fourth draft of "ELEUSIS" (*LI Cantos*).

Completion of the four drafts of "ELEUSIS" within the ten-draft poem realizes the Seal-vision as "REVOLUTION . . . in the minds of the people" projecting the prototype decad. The result of the mythic Seal-vision derived from and applied to millennial Western history is ideal European revolution (in Siena and Tuscany) coming out of a Renaissance tradition modified by its consequences in "Nuevo Mundo." "Jefferson-Nuevo Mundo" has made explicit the themes of New World history and of '76 implicit in the Renaissance tradition. For New World history, the Renaissance has instigated discovery and colonization, "MDCCLXXVI" has emerged in the middle, and continuing revolution has been found in Siena and Tuscany. For '76, Renaissance declaration and struggle have precipitated American revolution during the writing of the Constitution of 1787, when "Jefferson-Nuevo Mundo" begins. Declaration and struggle have been derived from and imposed upon the Renaissance; again continuing revolution has been found in Siena and Tuscany.

As indicated in the table of his Bibliography & Life (see p. 8), Pound published *The Cantos* not only as ten drafts reflecting the revolutionary process, but also as five collections (plus a transitional sixth) reflecting the historical forms and the building by drafts and phases of cantos. The first collection, *XXX Cantos*, reflects not only the pre-"Nuevo Mundo" Renaissance but also discovery and colonization, which within "ELEUSIS" were subsumed in declaration and struggle but which, when "new" revolution breaks out in "Jefferson-Nuevo Mundo," stand out as discovery and colonization. The *XXX Cantos* is then subsumed in *XLI Cantos*, a declaration of a world revolutionary tradition defined by its culminating draft.

Pound suggested that *XLI Cantos* constitutes a first "episode," presumably of four.[20] In the perspective of emergent '76 being amended and augmented for world revolution, "Jefferson-Nuevo Mundo" declares against plutocracy, "Siena-Leopoldine Reforms" extends declaration to a personal struggle against the identified villains Geryon and Usura, "KUNG" extends declaration and struggle to revolutionary founding based on Confucian principles, and "JOHN ADAMS" consummates New World history and revolution in an at last completed pattern of revolution emerging from a world tradition and projecting its perfection. As an indication of the drafting and building of "the first phase of this opus" (*XLVI*) Pound collected *Seventy Cantos* in 1950.[21] *LXXI Cantos* focuses a four-phase revolutionary tradition. "JOHN ADAMS," as we shall see, is also written so that the concurrent phase of the Declaration "to be unity" is condensed for or by the Seal-vision into a first phase: *XXX Cantos* having revealed the voyaging, colonizing Eagle inspired by Providence, *LXXI Cantos* focuses the shield and E PLURIBUS UNUM projecting the rest of revolutionary drafting and building.

The three paideumas "ELEUSIS," "KUNG," and "JOHN ADAMS" are consummated in the world paideuma *Pisan LXXXIV Cantos*, collected in 1948, which not only completes a four-phase world paideuma consummated by a change of phase from traditional to personal and contemporary, but also completes a seven-draft, eighty-four-canto Constitutional form for states' rights within a twentieth century world reality (principally economic). As a second phase *Pisan* continues the phases of drafting and building. It also uses the ten cantos of the typical draft to condense the concurrent Preambles—the "duality" union to liberty and liberty to new union—into the subsuming, projecting constellation and its voice NOVUS ORDO SECLORUM.

Publication of *Section: Rock-Drill* in 1955 and of *Thrones* in 1959, both in Italy, was followed in 1964 by the transitional *Cantos (1–95)* published in America and copyrighted 1956, and by *Cantos I–CIX* published in England. Functionally *Cantos (1–95)* takes a place between *LXXXIV Cantos* and *CIX Cantos*; as its parenthesized title and its text indicate, it has an ad hoc meaning which is superseded when *Thrones* is added to complete a third phase; the ad hoc meaning may be left until later. As a third phase *Los Cantares 85–109*, composed upon a matrix of Constitutional sections, condenses the overlapping Constitutions into ten subjects in "trine," which realize the material Mount in the voice MDCCLXXVI. The ten subjects transform the previous, current, and coming drafts. The tenth, foreshadowing the fourth phase, makes *CIX*

20. "The founding of the Monte dei Paschi" in "Siena-Leopoldine Reforms" is a "second episode" following "the Malatesta cantos" and their "effect"—that of the "factive personality" (Chap. 31, "Canti," *Guide To Kulchur*, 1938). A first episode presumably extends through "Jefferson-Nuevo Mundo"—Jefferson and Mussolini as heirs of Malatesta, as the text supports.

21. "This case, and with it / the first part, draws to a conclusion, / of the first phase of this opus" refers to "ELEUSIS." "The first part" may also refer to the first third of "trine" for the whole "opus."

Cantos a four-phase subject revealing building by phases: building a tradition (*LXXI Cantos*) and building by personal struggle (*Pisan*) break into the justicial light of the architecturally entitled *Section: Rock-Drill*, a justicial means, and *Thrones*, a justicial end. In this perspective all the cantos are revealed to have been and to be at once drafted "Sections" of the law (Constitutional constituents), and shaped stones of the law cut to the proportions of the Golden Section.

Finally, all previous four-phase subjects come to a focus in the uncompleted *Drafts & Fragments* and in the posthumously collected *Cantos 1–120*. The forecast form of *Drafts & Fragments*, though unrealized, is the ten cantos of the typical draft used to condense the ten drafts according to the consummating, illuminating sun-vision and its voice ANNUIT COEPTIS. Pound is trying, as an emerging poet, to perfect the Declaration as "tetrad" with the activating Bill of Rights and the perfecting phasal Seal. In *Canto 120* he looks back upon his whole work from within a final "triangular space" with the eye of an Eagle who has tried to realize the inspiration of his Providence. He has tried to rebuild what the Renaissance achieved, and to build new what it dreamed, by making new the fruits of its principal prophecy, the revolutionary form achieved by his own native American tradition.

Looking back with the Eagle and Providence to the whole poem's epitome, we see what the epitome prophesied both sequentially and concurrently. The voyage has discovered One World prostrate in darkness and rites of colonization have been performed to evoke the spirits of place, here the dead; these two archetypes project the drafts *XVI. Cantos* and *XVII–XXX* united into *XXX Cantos*. Revolt by the myriad dead against their condition projects the drafts of a world revolutionary tradition, *LXXI Cantos*. The revolt of an individualized dead projects the draft of personal struggle, *Pisan*. The prophecy of the seer projects the drafts of new justice, *Los Cantares*. The revolt of the Renaissance translator of Homer, who first spoke for the narrator Odysseus, projects the draft of consummating revolutionary poetry, *Drafts & Fragments*.

Throughout *I* the narrator has been the old Eagle Odysseus inspired by his old Providence Circe to make the voyage of discovery and to perform the rites of colonization. When he becomes responsive to the revolt of the dead, who have spoken through him, they become his personae and he becomes their spokesman. All along, however, all have spoken through the encompassing new Eagle Pound, who invokes his new Providence Aphrodite at the end. In this perspective the symbols and voices of New World history and of '76 have been prophesied and have spoken in their temporal sequence. In effect the static Seal and all it symbolizes has been transformed into dynamic voices that have made history and that will be able to make new history. They will make new history through several thematic voices emerging from one voice and carried by one voice while being translated or transformed into another voice.

So the epitome reads as "ONE," or as if in linear, horizontal time. When it joins with its sequels, however, linear, horizontal time combines with simultaneous, vertical time, as though the epitome sent its themes, symbols, and voices through every one of its coordinate forms. Hence the concurrency of the Seal voices as the voices of the documents. In effect Pound discovers the materials of One World as prerevolutionary data portending revolution and performs the rites of poetry to evoke the spirits of places on their own grounds, to bring them to life, and to incorporate them into a prerevolutionary self. By doing so he precipitates the voices of revolution, which subsume and transform the voices of discovery and colonization. The voice of discovery is subsumed in the voice of a revolutionary tradition, the Declaration. The voice of colonization is subsumed in the voice of revolutionary struggle, the Preamble. The voice of justice is the voice of the Constitution. The voice of revolutionary poetry is the voice of the Bill of Rights.

The accompanying table shows the concurrent documents precipitating the discrete phases over the whole poem.

	Shield E PLURIBUS UNUM (Declaration)	Constellation NOVUS ORDO SECLORUM (Preambles)	Mount MDCCLXXVI (Constitutions)	Sun-vision ANNUIT COEPTIS (Bill of Rights)
Declaration (shield E PLURIBUS UNUM)	*Cantos I–LXXI* (1–6)	*Pisan LXXIV–LXXXIV* (7)	*Los Cantares 85–109* (8–9)	*Drafts & Fragments CX–CXVII* (et seq.) (10)
Preambles (constellation NOVUS ORDO SECLORUM)	*Cantos I–LXXI* (1–6)	*Pisan LXXIV–LXXXIV* (7)	*Los Cantares 85–109* (8–9)	*Drafts & Fragments CX–CXVII* (et seq.) (10)
Constitutions (Mount MDCCLXXVI)	*Cantos I–LXXI* (1–6)	*Pisan LXXIV–LXXXIV* (7)	*Los Cantares 85–109* (8–9)	*Drafts & Fragments CX–CXVII* (et seq.) (10)
Bill of Rights (sun-vision ANNUIT COEPTIS)	*Cantos I–LXXI* (1–6)	*Pisan LXXIV–LXXXIV* (7)	*Los Cantares 85–109* (8–9)	*Drafts & Fragments CX–CXVII* (et seq.) (10)

The Seal is arranged in horizontal headings for linear time. The documents are arranged in vertical headings for simultaneous time. The parentheses in the headings mean that the Seal symbolizes and inspires the documents while the documents are realizing the Seal. The vertically arranged documents (reading across) run through the whole poem; the horizontally arranged Seal (reading down) is precipitated out by phases. A Seal-phase applies to only one phase. Each of the documents, "moving concurrent . . . ply over ply," applies to all phases.

More generally the voices are conducting a "revolt of intelligence" against an existing tradition, formulating a new ethic through the motives of a collective "nuova persona," "thinking out a sane state," and "thinking in poetry." The voices of tradition, personality, justice, and poetry can be formulated as other tetrads. Some are history, nature, government, and art; ideas, motives, forms, and acts; past, present, future, and timelessness (or all time); dead facts, live facts, symbols, and gods; intelligence, ethics, politics, and religion. One derives such formulations from the subjects of *The Cantos*, from its symbolic arcana, and from statements and paradigms found elsewhere in Pound's writings. No one such set of categories suffices, as none sufficed for Pound. All must be entertained as approaches to an unstatable statement, i.e., to a symbol. That symbol is the Seal, which is rooted in the earth but rises to the heavens.

Theoretically we may follow through every canto, draft, and phase in the evolving order of the epitome, the voices of six themes being gathered into the voices of four themes while the voices of four themes are being focused by and in one voice. Practically, however, we read by drafts. Drafts offer sufficient amplitude for including the variety of matter being brought to life and directed by the four revolutionary voices. Only the first draft, which evolves an epitome, a four-phase prototype, a prototype decad, and a four-phase draft, deploys the voices canto by canto. Thereafter, except for the keynote canto of a draft and sometimes an initiating Seal-vision, the voices may appear in any order within a canto or within the draft itself; the only requirement is that they accord finally with the general evolution of the draft's major subject toward its climax or focus. After the prototype draft, therefore, we read by four-phase subjects as concurrent voices precipitate themselves out to dominate a subject's respective phases. Like the concurrent voices the voices of all subjects project the final four-phase whole. With *Canto 120* concurrency returns the single-drafted, builded poem to the epitome from which it has sprung.

CHAPTER THREE

THE INTEGRITY OF A

VISION: EXTERNAL EVIDENCE

The Revolutionary Calendar

"Toutes mes choses datent de quinze ans."
    Constantin Brancusi

Before he published *XVI. Cantos* in 1925, Pound devised and published a
form for translating the static, visual Seal with its symbolisms of thirteen into
the dynamic, documentary form of '76 with its complements of ten, so that
the documentary form would rebuild the broken edifice from whose still vital
spirit and form it had been derived. The form was a neopagan or Renaissance
Calendar for a new era dated from Pound's thirty-sixth birthday, 30 October
1921. It appeared anonymously in *The Little Review*, New York, in Spring
1922. The Seal does not appear in its own form in the Calendar, and neither
the Seal nor the Calendar appear in their own forms in *The Cantos*. But versions of the Seal symbols appear in the Calendar and a version of the Calendar
derived from the Seal and realizing the Seal-vision, having been embodied in
other verbal and visual forms since the epitome *I*, appears in this form at the
end of *Rock-Drill 88*:

And

fifty

2

weeks

in

4

seasons

The heart symbolizes the sun-vision, the diamond symbolizes the Mount built on the shield in light of the sun according to the stellar plan, the club symbolizes the constellation, and the spade symbolizes the shield on the Eagle's breast. Providence inspires while the Eagle builds. From heart to spade the four suits symbolize a descent of inspiration; from spade to heart they symbolize realizing the inspiration by phasal building.

The Calendar phrase reverses the four suits in the order of reading temporally. The black suits underlie "And fifty 2 weeks," the year measured by the moon; the red suits underlie "in 4 seasons," the year measured by the sun. The Calendar phrase realizes the four symbols "in 4 seasons" of voices both concurrent and sequential while the four voices are being unified in the voice that focuses days (unstated), weeks, months (unstated), and seasons into one year. While the four suits refer to all four-phase subjects, the Calendar phrase refers in general to each draft and to ten drafts; in particular, by disposing words and numbers symbolically, it refers to the drafted Seal-vision "ELEUSIS" *LI Cantos*, which is constituted of fifty-one Cantos ("And fifty") in halves old and new ("2 weeks") in four drafts ("in 4 seasons").

What this Seal/Calendar arcanum symbolizes is opened up on pages 38–39. The key (see p. 40) is the translation of the Seal symbols into the timeless, hand-drawn, revolutionary cycle suspended within an architectural tabulation which it builds. The year "turns upon" HORUS, the Eagle, at the center. From there it expands to the cycle through ISIS, PAN, POSEIDON, and BACCHUS, who preside over the four discrete geometrical symbols.

On the cycle ZAGREUS and PAN, both "of no era," translate the arrows and the olive branch; each projects an undivided cycle; together they project hemicycles. Thirteen radial segments (twelve months and the eccentric arm "of no era") translate the stripes of the shield into a divided cycle. Circumferentially named gods and goddesses translate the stars of the constellation into divided hemicycles with HORUS at the center. Emerging beyond the divided cycle (shield formation) and hemicycles (stellar plan) while continuing them, the Mount is outlined by the names of the female months and by the phases POSEIDON and BACCHUS extrapolated outside the cycle and culminating in a Providential PAN; divided cycle and hemicycles are shield foundation and stellar plan. The eccentric arm containing "INCIPIT" and the arrow translates the rays of the sun-vision into radii while representing on the cycle the "triangular space" of Providence ("of no era"); the radii carry discrete phasal forms and all the concurrent, overlaid forms into the tabulation arranged around the revolutionary cycle, which builds the whole while illuminating it from within with the whole cyclic form.

The emerging Mount defines a vertical axis that rises (though moving downward to the eye) from the hemicycle of six gods under ISIS, through HORUS, to the hemicycle defined by PAN, POSEIDON, and BACCHUS, to the same hemicycle named by the six goddesses outside the cycle in the shape of the Mount, to the Mount culminating axially in POSEIDON, BACCHUS, and Providential PAN. Inwardly the second hemicycle is dominated by PAN while projecting POSEIDON and BACCHUS. The axially defined Mount, subsuming ISIS and PAN while projecting BACCHUS, is dominated by POSEIDON. While male phasal divinities group "the warm months" (female) "two by two," the vertical axis redivides POSEIDON into halves. The result is ten radial segments, six for the first hemicycle under ISIS, two grouped as one under PAN, two under POSEIDON, and two grouped as one under BACCHUS. In this way phases, cycle, hemicycles and the axial Mount work together to symbolize the phasal form of the Declaration (radial segments) realized via the Preambles (six gods and six goddesses), and via the Constitution (cyclic foundation, hemicyclic plan, and emerging Mount), in the illuminating, "sealed" Bill of Rights (all symbols transformed into radii).

The feasts work out the detail on the cycle. ZAGREUS projects cyclic discovery and PAN projects cyclic colonization; in sequence ZAGREUS projects the circumnavigation completed by the first half of the poem (*LXXI Cantos*), which subordinates Pound to personae of the past, and PAN projects the colonization of the second half (*LXXIV–120*), in which the emergent Pound subordinates the past to new revolutionary life. ZAGREUS is a god of rebirth and liberty, while PAN is a god of living nature and liberty. ZAGREUS is individual (hence Pound's birthday) and PAN is collective (his feast transforms All Soul's Eve). Together they also symbolize two aspects of "WE, the People" for the Preambles carried by the gods and goddesses of the months.

The "Feast of Figures" (14 HERMES) celebrates "REVOLUTION . . . in the minds of the people" taking the form of the Seal-vision and marks the Declaration's ideal premises and the first third of "trine" for the Constitutions. The "Feast of Political Buncomb, ancient feast of fools or feast of the ass, Mort de Caesar, Jules" (15 MARS) marks ironically the Declaration's shift from revolutionary ideality to revolutionary fact. The feast of PRIAPUS (1 KUPRIS) marks individual passion and inaugurates the culmination of a states' rights Constitution under the phase PAN (KUPRIS and JUNO). The feast of "EPITHALAMIUM, ancient Corpus Domini" (15 JUNO) ritualizes passion and marks a transition from a Constitution for states' rights to a comprehensive world Constitution. The feasts of FAUNUS or Roman Pan (6 ARTEMIS), and of Apeliota or East wind and Auster or South wind (14 ARTEMIS), are less easy to specify;[1] perhaps they herald the coming consummation under BACCHUS and focus in ZAGREUS and PAN, who end one cycle while beginning another in the continuing revolution for which the Calendar represents only "YEAR 1."

The Calendar works from HORUS outward via the four phases and the cycle to the tabulation and its titles as the epitome (*I*) works out via the Seal-vision (*I–IV*) and the revolutionary decad (*I–X*) to the revolutionary draft

---

1. In *The Cantos*, perhaps because Pound mistook his winds, AUSTER becomes (correctly) Zephyrus.

THE SEAL OF THE UNITED STATES
as a
STATUE OF LIBERTY

YEAR 1 p. s. U.

1921 O. S.
ZEUS

S		4 11 18 25
M		5 12 19 26
T		6 13 20 27
W		7 14 21 28
Th	1	8 15 22 29
F	2	9 16 23 30
S	3	10 17 24 31

Jan. 1922 O. S.
SATURN

S	1	8 15 22 29
M	2	9 16 23 30
T	3	10 17 24 31
W	4	11 18 25
Th	5	12 19 26
F	6	13 20 27
S	7	14 21 28

HERMES

S		5 12 19 26
M		6 13 20 27
T		7 14 21 28
W	1	8 15 22
T	2	9 16 23
F	3	10 17 24
S	4	11 18 25

1921-1922
Old Style

And

fifty

2

weeks

in

4

seasons

1921 O. S.
HEPHAISTOS

S		6 13 20 27
M		7 14 21 28
T	1	8 15 22 29
W	2	9 16 23 30
Th	3	10 17 24
F	4	11 18 25
S	5	12 19 26

MARS

S		5 12 19 26
M		6 13 20 27
T		7 14 21 28
W	1	8 15 22 29
Th	2	9 16 23 30
F	3	10 17 24 31
S	4	11 18 25

PHOEBUS

S	2	9 16 23 30
M	3	10 17 24
T	4	11 18 25
W	5	12 19 26
Th	6	13 20 27
F	7	14 21 28
S	1	8 15 22 29

DEMETER

S	1	8 15 22 29
M	2	9 16 23 30
T	3	10 17 24 31
W	4	11 18 25
Th	5	12 19 26
F	6	13 20 27
S	7	14 21 28

KUPRIS

S	7	14 21 28
M	1	8 15 22 29
T	2	9 16 23 30
W	3	10 17 24 31
Th	4	11 18 25
F	5	12 19 26
S	6	13 20 27

HESTIA

S		6 13 20 27
M		7 14 21 28
T	1	8 15 22 29
W	2	9 16 23 30
Th	3	10 17 24 31
F	4	11 18 25
S	5	12 19 26

ATHENE

S	2	9 16 23 30
M	3	10 17 24 31
T	4	11 18 25
W	5	12 19 26
Th	6	13 20 27
F	7	14 21 28
S	1	8 15 22 29

ARTEMIS

S		3 10 17 24
M		4 11 18 25
T		5 12 19 26
W		6 13 20 27
Th		7 14 21 28
F	1	8 15 22 29
S	2	9 16 23 30

THE LITTLE REVIEW
CALENDAR

JUNO

S		4 11 18 25
M		5 12 19 26
T		6 13 20 27
W		7 14 21 28
Th	1	8 15 22 29
F	2	9 16 23 30
S	3	10 17 24

Note to Calendar

The Christian era came definitely to an END at midnight of the 29-30 of October (1921) old style.

There followed the Feast of ZAGREUS, and a Feast of PAN counted as of no era: the new year thus beginning as on 1st November (old style), now HEPHAISTOS.

The new months, replacing the old months: of cold months HEPHAISTOS (for November), and then in the following order ZEUS, SATURN, HERMES, MARS, PHOEBUS APOLLO; and the warm months; KUPRIS, JUNO, ATHENE, HESTIA, ARTEMIS and DEMETER, the male months being also under ISIS, and the female months, two by two, under PAN, POSEIDON and BACCHUS.

The following feasts are instituted, to ZAGREUS on the 30th Demeter; to PAN on the 31st Demeter; Feast of Figures on the 14th Hermes; Feast of Political Buncomb, ancient feast of fools or feast of the ass, Mort de Caesar, Jules, 15th Mars; PRIAPUS, 1st Kupris; EPITHAL-AMIUM, ancient Corpus Domini, 15th Juno; FAUNUS 6th Artemis; AUSTER and APELIOTA 14th Artemis.

The year turns upon HORUS.

Forms & Symbols Evolving Concurrently

Cycle
&
Hemicycles

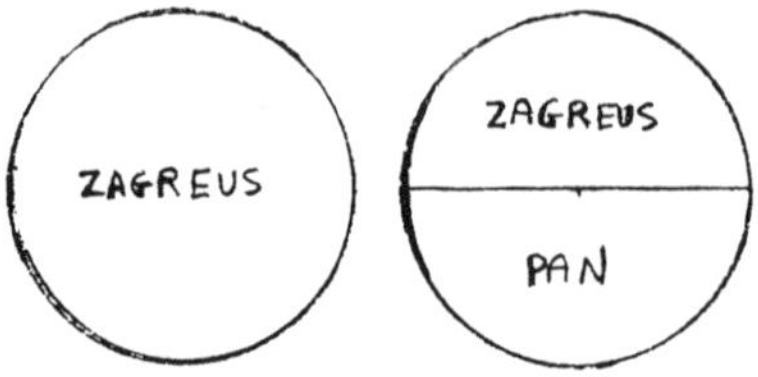

Radial segments
(shield)

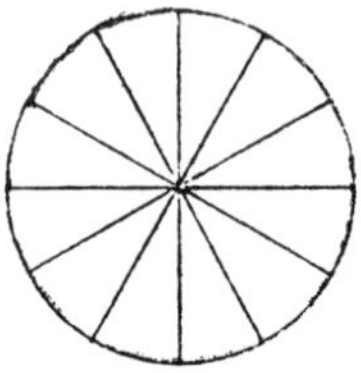

Circumferential names
(constellation)

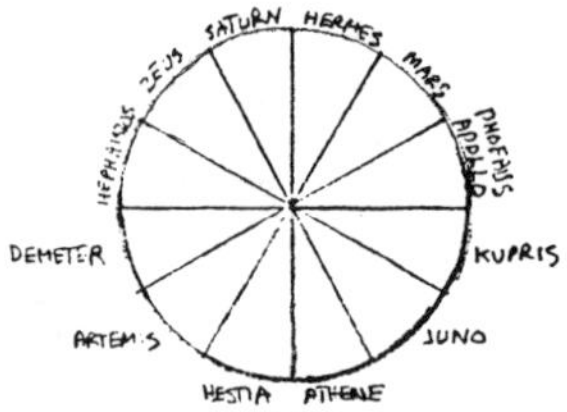

Emerging form
(Mount)

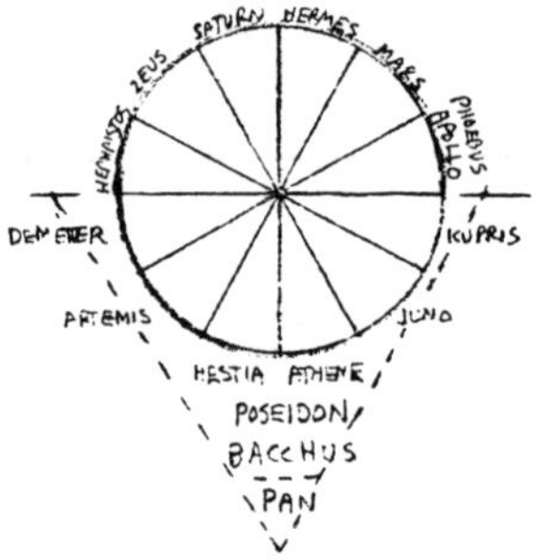

Irradiated building
(sun-temple)

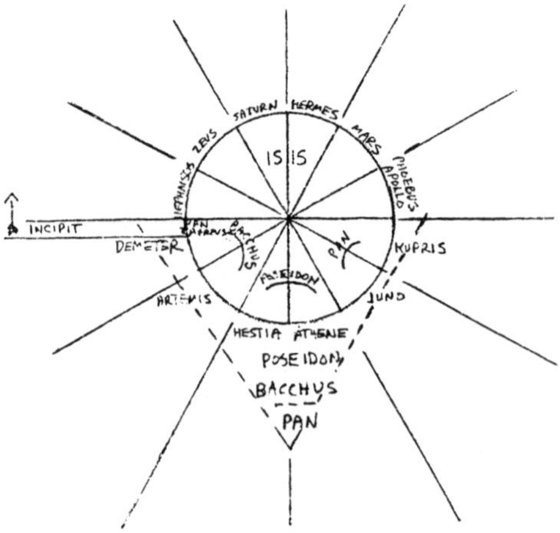

(*XVI. Cantos*); or, as the first draft works out via "ELEUSIS" and the ten decads of the ten drafts to ten drafts building 120 cantos in four phases. "INCIPIT" and the titles of the Calendar are related to the Seal's mottoes for the beginning, for the new era, for the dating of new style from old, and for the consummation that would extend beginnings in continuing revolution. "YEAR 1 p.s.U." seems to focus all the mottoes in "YEAR 1 post scriptum Ulysses," which would commemorate the fact that Joyce's *Ulysses* was finished on Pound's birthday in 1921 and that it was "an epoch-making report on the state of the human mind in the twentieth century (first of the new era)"; out of Joyce's "retrospect" on the European mind that had caused and tolerated World War I was coming the "pro-spect" opened by the Odyssean beginning of *The Cantos*.[2] That would be reading and looking rightward with Providence. Looking leftward with the Eagle would read "United States [of] Pound 1 RA[E]Y," a version of E PLURIBUS UNUM within Providence's ANNUIT COEPTIS.

Pound wrote H. L. Mencken in 1922 "the Christian Era ended at midnight on Oct. 29–30 of last year. You are now in the year 1 p.s.U";[3] in 1928 he wrote "the State of Pound did very largely sever 20 years ago. It is the only state in which I have any preponderant authority or even influence. . . . I try what I can to keep the Bill of Rights waving above the Paris office at the Chicago Trib. . . . States Rights surtunly, sah. But if not them, at least our own."[4]

"X-Ray" and "Ray" were this Yankee Doodle's earliest boyhood nicknames; the "rays" ideogram, used on the cover of *Cathay* (1915), became the frontispiece to *Cantos LII–LXXI*, "KUNG," and "JOHN ADAMS." "Beat, beat, whirr, thud," the Calendar cycle sounded by the dancesteps of a circle of nymphs and satrys (*IV*), turns a line from Whitman's "Drum-Taps" ("beat, beat, whirr, pound") into a mythic signature of Ez Ra Loomis Pound (cf. "X-Ray" and "Ez-Ray"); puns like Ies-Ra abounded within Pound's circle while he was confined during 1945–48. Such is Yankee Doodle's polyglot, macaronic, neo-Whitmanian "natural language."

Constituting the Seal's myriad elements into thirteens, thirteens into four geometrical symbols, geometrical symbols into halves governed by the male Eagle and female Providence, and halves into a single edifice, corresponds with constituting days into weeks, weeks into months, months into seasons, seasons into cold and warm, and all into a single year. On the Calendar the principle is male-female dichotomy throughout, whether across the center HORUS month by month or, sexually reversed, across the horizontal diameter that divides the phase ISIS from the phases PAN, POSEIDON, and BACCHUS. Not named but present in all the male divinities is the sun-

2. "Ulysses," *Dial*, New York, June 1922, and Chap. 13, "Monumental," *Guide To Kulchur* (1938).
3. 22 March 1922, *Letters*.
4. 3 September 1928, *Letters*.

god OSIRIS, husband of the moon-and-earth goddess ISIS (who focuses all female divinities) and father of HORUS. Figured is the effort of HORUS to "gather the Limbs of Osiris" (Pound's title for a 1911–12 manifesto, see below pp. 53–56) so that the universal god may be reassembled. Prefigured are reconstitution of OSIRIS's Holy Family on their Mount and a holy re-marriage in their temple. The limbs of Osiris, fragments traditional, personal, justicial, and poetic, all contribute to the Constitutional fragments out of which a new Statue of Liberty is to be built.

Arranged around the revolutionary cycle and its extensions, the tabulation is irradiated by all the forms. The whole Calendar thus symbolizes simul-taneously, "ply over ply" like the cycle, the Eagle with a cyclic shield on its breast; the constellation arranged around a central star; the Mount containing the cycle as a plan and a means for building it; and the sun-vision surrounding the temple of Providence. The "triangular space" of Providence is defined by the names of the phases surrounding HORUS. HORUS receives the divine in-spiration and performs all the activities of drafting and building while singing the revolutionary epic in the four voices.

The tabulated months are also arranged around the cycle by phases (the six gods under ISIS, KUPRIS and JUNO under PAN, ATHENA and HESTIA under POSEIDON, ARTEMIS and DEMETER under BACCHUS). This di-rect projection of the cycle to the tabulation results too in a simple visual reversal of the downward pointing cycle for building upward in the direction of the "INCIPIT"-arrow. With reference to the Seal edifice juxtaposed to the Calendar on the above facing pages, the tabulated female months show the shape of the Eagle and shield (wings DEMETER and KUPRIS, legs ARTEMIS and JUNO, shield HESTIA and ATHENA). The cycle takes the place of the constellation. The tabulation of male months (ZEUS excepted) shows the shape of the Mount. ZEUS, who "favored (ANNUIT) our begin-nings," and a beginning (COEPTIS) during "1921–1922 Old Style," flank "YEAR 1 p.s.U." just as ANNUIT COEPTIS flanks the sun-circle and the "triangular space" of Providence. The symbolic foundation and Mount are reversed from male and female to female and male. The double direction of the tabulation—downward for inspiration and upward for building—reflects the double direction of the Seal/Calendar arcanum's four suits. The cycle, on the other hand, reflects the single direction of the Calendar phrase—drafting and building.

The geometry of the Seal includes all the simpler forms used for symbolism and for building, triangle, square, pentagram, hexagram, and octagram (for vertical, horizontal, and diagonal axes, defined by an eight-appendaged Eagle: tail, legs, wings, halves of the E PLURIBUS UNUM banner, and head; this will be verified in Chapter Five from illustrations to the deluxe editions). These figures culminate in or define circles while all are being included within the circular forms of front and back. Within the cycle the phase-names delineate the "triangular space" of Providence while the arcs with PAN, POSEIDON, and BACCHUS delineate the pentagram star or Eagle. The Calendar cycle divided by twelve defines three, four, and six for triangle, square, and hexagram. On the circumferences the feasts mark diagonals for adding axes. Outside the cycle the hand-drawn names and dispositions mediate between the cycle and the tabulation: the names of the goddesses delineate with POSEIDON, BACCHUS, and Providential PAN the Mount, and the eccentric arm projects the radii and defines the "triangular space." The interior of the cycle, the circumference, the projections beyond the cycle, and the tabulations, all working together, define a containing Golden Section within which the Calendar is constructed. While the "triangular space" symbolizes each canto and a Mount built of such cantos, the Golden Section defines drafting and building by "mass relations" or what is called "gnomonic growth."[5]

A Golden Section is a rectangle of such proportion that a square taking its dimension from the longer side, when added to the original Golden Section, results in a new and larger Golden Section. The square is the Golden Section's "gnomon." Another square may be projected from the longer side of the new, larger Golden Section, etc. The result is "gnomonic growth" by "whirling squares," which transcribe an expanding spiral.[6] Such a spiral evolves as the cycle turns while expanding from HORUS through the four phasal divinities to the radial segments, to the monthly gods and goddesses, to the Mount delineated outside the cycle, to the eccentric arm, to the tabulated months. At the same time the "INCIPIT"-arrow is a module defined by the cycle and expanding by Golden Section "whirling squares" to the including Golden Section which contains and defines the tabulated months.

The accompanying diagram shows a four-phase expansion by "whirling squares" from a module or epitome defined by the arrow.

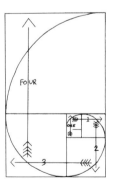

5. The details of Golden Section construction are described in some detail in my "The Mathematical Symbolism of Ezra Pound's Revolutionary Mind," *Paideuma*, Orono, Maine, Spring & Fall 1978. The method and its history are described by Matila Ghyka, *The Geometry of Art and Life* (New York: 1946).

6. Ghyka relates how an American autodidact, Jay Hambidge, a virtual antecedent of Pound

The module arrow is expanded by phases from itself ("ONE") via 1, 2, 3, and 4 to "FOUR." A cycle of added squares transcribes a spiral expanding by additions while building upward. Expansion by phases results in a replica of the originating epitome "ONE." A series of wholes all show the same proportion on a larger scale, so that "what I haven't yet done . . . will modify the mass relations" of a periodically augmented whole accruing by cantos within the first Seal-vision, decad, and draft, and by decads and drafts within the whole poem. Four is the form at once of what is added to, of what is added, and of the result (cf. "and the whole creation concerned with 'FOUR,'" *Rock-Drill 91*).

Each added square is a function of what preceded, or is shaped and prophesied by what preceded. So units of *The Cantos* are projected by the a priori fourfold Seal ("REVOLUTION . . . in the minds of the people") and by the fourfold revolutionary process, which takes its form from the Seal through the Declaration. Expanding "to be unity" by duality, trine, and tetrad reflects the Golden Section form. The Declaration's argument expands by wholes as one part is added to what preceded, except for the complementary cases (5–6) and the complementary separation and assumption of sovereignty (8–9), as reflected in *Cantos LII–LXXI* ("KUNG" and "JOHN ADAMS"), in *Los Cantares 85–109*, and in their counterparts in the prototype draft. One can imagine the first canto establishing a preliminary Golden Section form with archetypal discovery and colonization and then adding the fourfold revolt of the dead, each phase of which is also (as we shall see) a whole projecting the whole canto. The same form occurs when *XXX Cantos* is expanded draft by draft in four drafts to the first phase (*LXXI Cantos*) and thence phase by phase in four phases to the whole poem.

The mathematics of the Seal and the Calendar reflect Pythagoreanism, which originated in Egypt with the building of the pyramids, evolved through the mysteries of Eleusis, and was transmitted via Platonism, Roman stonemasons, neo-Platonism, and medieval guilds of masons and builders to the speculative Freemasonry of the Enlightenment in Europe and America.[7] The ultimate result was architectural forms for buildings, music, painting, and sculpture, for revolutions and forms of government, even for the forms of the natural order, which Pythagoreanism and the Golden Section presume to relate to the constructions of the human mind. Pound found the same phenomenon in the Chinese *Li Ki* or *Book of Rites*, a Calendar of the months and seasons which ritualizes the government of all human occupations, from the Son of Heaven to the whole people of the empire; the *Li Ki* lies behind and

---

and Buckminster Fuller, rediscovered Golden Section construction and what he called "Dynamic Symmetry" and "whirling squares" just after the turn of the century. Hambidge gave lessons in European museums during 1919–20.

7. Ghyka, *Geometry of Art*, "The Transmission of Geometrical Symbols and Plans," Chap. 7, is the source for the next few pages.

within the Chinese millennia inspirited by "KUNG" as "ELEUSIS" lies behind and within European millennia including New World history and as "JOHN ADAMS" lies behind and within the American era and the generation of '76. The Tempio Malatestiano, a "Confucian universe . . . of interacting strains and tensions,"[8] a "system of government" of separated, distributed, balanced powers founded on principles as infallible to Adams "AS . . . a demonstration of Euclid" (*LXII*), and the Seal and the Calendar all proceed from the same kind of mind.

In the Pythagorean system expansion of the "Great Ordering One" by "fluxion," the constant change of infinitesimal calculus, was guided by the dyad, the triad, the tetrad, the pentad, and the decad, a "Society of Numbers." Out of the monad came the dyad, the first even, female, number, and the triad, the first odd, male, number. United the two formed the pentad, the number of love. The pentad became a symbol for Microcosmos, or Man (cf. Pound's Eagle) and the decad became a symbol of Macrocosmos, the World; the link or "proportional mean" between them was sometimes the Temple. Nicomachus of Gerasa, the most explicit exponent of Pythagorean number mysticism, described the properties of the decad in relation to infinity and unity:

> But as the whole was illimited multitude . . . an Order was neces-
> sary . . . and it was in the Decad that a natural balance between the
> Whole and its elements was found to pre-exist. . . . That is why the All-
> Ordering God (literally: the God arranging with art) acting in accordance
> with his Reason, made use of the Decad as a canon for the Whole . . .
> and this is why the things from Earth to Heaven have for the whole
> as well as for their parts their ratios or concord based upon the Decad
> and are ordered accordingly. . . . [The Decad] was used as a measure
> for the Whole, as a set-square and a rule in the hand of the One who
> regulates all things.

The decad was related to the monad, the dyad, the triad, and the tetrad by the tetraktys, numerologically the sum of the first four integers $(1+2+3+4)$ and geometrically a four-tiered triangle:

$$
\begin{array}{ccccccc}
 & & & \cdot & & & \\
 & & \cdot & & \cdot & & \\
 & \cdot & & \cdot & & \cdot & \\
\cdot & & \cdot & & \cdot & & \cdot \\
\end{array}
$$

Members of the Pythagorean Brotherhood took their oath not to betray their mathematical and other secrets in the name of the Tetraktys, in which was found the source and root of eternal Nature.

The interpenetrating tetraktyses found in the constellation inhere in Pound's

8. *Paris Review* 28.

symbol for the ultimate social and architectural achievement of "ELEUSIS," the Monte dei Paschi Bank of Siena rooted in and founded upon nature, and in the four suits of the Seal/Calendar arcanum:

	And
	fifty
	2
	weeks
	in
	4
	seasons

The Mount shows unity, duality, and trine down to a tetradic foundation. Heart = monad, diamond = dyad, club = triad, and spade = tetrad. The reverse tetraktys (which transforms the shield foundation) is implied. The perfection of the tetraktys, via the Mount, is the sun-circle containing the "triangular space" of Providence.

The Seal symbols and voices have analogues in all cultures. The Calendar transforms the Seal-vision into a universal poetic process. As an arcanum it universalizes all religious mysteries and all mystic traditions. In terms of a gnostic tradition originating in Egypt, throughout universal history sacred mysteries had been preserved and perpetuated, despite antagonistic dogmas, among certain visionary religionists, philosophers, and artists who had sought, so inspired, to manifest their apprehensions in works of the human mind. The mind was to be perfected through knowledge, self-discipline, a reverence for the mysteries, and guardianship of the holy. The aim of the mind was to achieve freedom from man-made tyrannies and to celebrate the vision of perfection by realizing it on earth.

Pound discovered a Pythagorean continuity in the theistic psychology of Ovid's *Metamorphoses*, which passed that psychology to Christianity and to the poetry of the Middle Ages. In Pound's view troubador lyric poetry, the Italian *dolce stil nuovo*, and even Dante's *Divine Comedy* constituted a subversive or even revolutionary tradition within ecclesiastical Christianity. This tradition came through the Renaissance into the Enlightenment. The exploratory Renaissance and the cosmopolitan Enlightenment reached simultaneous acmes in Tuscany ("ELEUSIS" *XLII–XLIV*), in Manchu China ("KUNG" *LVIII–LXI*), and in America ("JOHN ADAMS") before the old ecclesiasticism, joined with an emerging plutocracy and a manipulated democracy, subjected it to a new and even more oppressive tyranny.

During the Middle Ages the tradition was in the keeping of the guilds of builders and masons and of Gothic master builders, keepers of a fundamental Gothic master diagram; such a plan lies behind the medieval phenomenon "All rushed out and built the duomo, / Went as one man without leaders / And the perfect measure took form" (*XXVII*), which shows up the failure of French and Russian revolutionary leaders to provide a constructive plan for the Jacquerie and the Tovarisches. During the Renaissance the tradition produced architects like Leon Battista Alberti, who was employed by Malatesta for the Tempio. It gave rise to Freemasonry, in Europe speculative or philosophical as well as practical, and, therefore, revolutionary. Among artists Mozart, whose letter to the Archbishop of Salzburg in 1777 is read "*inter lineas*" by a fellow conspirator (*XXVI*) to conclude a rise and decline of the Renaissance constructive vision, was a Freemason. So were many American founders, among them Franklin and Washington. Pound takes the versatile Jefferson, the land surveyor Washington, the legal architect Adams, and the visionary libertarian and world revolutionary Tom Paine to be exemplars of the same spirit.

Many arcana in *The Cantos* are like the mason's marks or seals used as signs or passwords by members of the brotherhood to identify each other and to decorate keystones, effigies of the Master Architect, shields, and funeral plaques; all are partial manifestations of a "ground-lattice," a geometrical background that allows an infinite number of combinations. In this same spirit the form of *The Cantos* sometimes seems Homeric, sometimes Ovidian, sometimes Dantean, sometimes Confucian, sometimes Whitmanian—but always Poundian. Accordingly too Pound not only explores and seeks to incorporate aboriginal mysteries and rites, but also writes in the spirit of such styles as the Provençal *trobar clus* (secret song) and medieval allegory. Extending these (as they were indeed extended by the speculative Freemasonry of the Enlightenment) he conceives himself to be a revolutionary conspirator among revolutionaries of a timeless tradition. Arcana, multiple meanings, and analogies take a cue from revolutionary polemics, half-hiding and half-disclosing a revolutionary motive, as in Lenin's "Aesopian language (under censorship) / where I wrote 'Japan' you may read 'Russia' " (*Thrones 100*). The revolutionary mind, certain that "the Divine Mind is abundant / unceasing / *improvisatore* / Omniformis / unstill" (*Rock-Drill 92*), views itself in the role of a protagonist who is "Waiving no jot of the arcanum / (having his own mind to stand by him)" (*Rock-Drill 91*). At the end of the poem he would "enter arcanum" ("Notes for *CXVII* et seq."). The sun-temple of Providence is OSIRIS's temple of Amor, Wisdom, and Liberty to be built and entered by an initiate.

The Calendar and its mathematics are not ends in *The Cantos*, but means. They are referred to indirectly in the text, they appear in many visual arcana, and they organize the text into its proportions and sequences. But as Pound was wont to insist, "The *what* is so much more important than how."[9] He meant that all arcana refer to the forms of '76 according to which he is trying to conduct a "revolt of intelligence," to evolve a revolutionary "nuova persona," and to "think out a sane state," all by "thinking in poetry." The documents of '76 have mathematical aspects and the Seal is a mathematical form. The one is dynamic and the other static. He had to find a way to translate the static into the dynamic and to make the dynamic the means of creating or recreating the originating static form—to recreate it so that the static form would include the dynamism in order to be continually alterable for whatever a new future might bring. We therefore do not look for the Calendar in the work, but rather for the forms the Calendar symbolizes, the forms of '76, and for what matter realizes the forms.

It seems fair at this point, preparatory to presenting further external and internal evidences and before entering in detail the texts themselves, to anticipate skepticism about the foregoing analyses of and applications to *The Cantos*. To allay such skepticism, particularly as it might argue numerical complements and divisions to be coincidences, it seems timely to bunch here, as will not be possible elsewhere, certain coincidences, arcana, and focuses. All will be explored in due course, but otherwise perhaps too distantly from each other to make a concerted effect.

The Epitome *I*-as-ONE

To begin, four old voices (Odysseus, Elpenor, Tiresias, and Divus) under an old Providence (Circe) will become four renewed voices (Odysseus, Elpenor, Tiresias, and Pound) under a new Providence (Aphrodite). The transformation will be brought about by ten narrated events in the fourfold form ONE: 4 + 2, + (2-as-) 1, + 2,+ (2-as-) 1 becoming a renewed ONE (ONE: ten/ ONE).

The canto will be constituted of seventy-one lines of narration extended by invocation to seventy-six lines. Odysseus will speak for tradition in lines 1–53 (Congress 1–53). For personae, Elpenor addressing Odysseus "But thou, O King" (54) and Tiresias naming him "Odysseus" (65) will frame Elpenor's request for burial and Tiresias's challenge and command, lines 54–65 (Presidency 54–65). For justice Tiresias's prophecy, Pound's acknowledgment of Divus, and Pound's completing of the narration by sending Odysseus back to Circe's (lines 66–71) will complete judgments and destinies (Judiciary 66–71).

Pound's retroactively recognized translation, acknowledgment, and completion will have been anticipated (in fact preceded) by an everywhere implicit lines 72–76, which deliver an expected, missing, formal epic invocation consummating tradition, personae, and justice in inspired, continuing, renewed poetry. Lines 72–76 will precipitate what in fact begins at the beginning, *The Cantos* as a states' rights amending process emerging with States (72) and culminating in an epitome of seventy-six lines symbolic of '76. Structure and themes thus become emblem. Thence the title of this book, " '76."

The ten events unfold from ONE (an inspiration) constituted into a basic ten (the narration) and coda (the invocation); the pattern is "ONE, ten, eleven, *chi con me* 目 tan?" (*Thrones 97*). The "ONE, ten" of *I*-as-ONE projects a prototype de̅cad *I–X*, which for *XVI. Cantos* is completed by the coda *XI–XVI*. The *XVI. Cantos* also constitutes a four-phase prototype draft. The prototype decad and the prototype draft project in turn each of ten drafts of ten cantos with or without coda, and ten drafts of a whole poem with or without coda.

Seal ONE: FOUR/ONE

The Seal will be explicitly elaborated draft by draft in the four drafts of "ELEUSIS" by the pattern ONE: FOUR/ONE. The Eagle appears to Malatesta and his men at the end of the prototype (*I–X*) and at the beginning of its coda (*XI*); Pound exits from Hell as an Eagle with a shield tied to his breast (*XV*). The imagery of the second draft comes to a visual focus as a plan for a new, nonmilitarist Gibraltar (a Mount) at the very center of *XXII*, the middle canto of the original *Cantos 17–27*. A materialized, monolithic Mount perverts '76 in "Jefferson-Nuevo Mundo" *XXXIV*. "Siena-Leopoldine Reforms" *XLII* repluralizes the American monolith to its ideal form; the Sienese polylith projects completion of ONE: 4 as "ELEUSIS" focused by light and by ideogram (*LI*), ideogram as "right name" lexically and by "E P" macaronically.[10]

Continuing Revolution: ONE: ten/ONE

The ten drafts will have for tradition (the Declaration) the form ONE (the prototype *I–X*): 4 (the four drafts of "ELEUSIS") + 2 ("KUNG" and "JOHN ADAMS" completing a first phase) + (2-as-) 1 (*Pisan* a second phase) + 2 (*Rock-Drill* and *Thrones* constituting a third phase) + (2-as-) 1 (*Drafts & Fragments* trying to complete a fourth phase and a whole poem).

For personae old and new (the Preambles) the ten drafts will have the form 1–6 + drafts 7–10.

For new states' rights and New World union the ten drafts will have the

10. *Paris Review* 28.

form drafts 1 through 7 (Articles I–VII) generating and overlapping drafts (1–4-as) new-1 through draft (10-as) new-7 (new Articles I–VII).

For continuing revolution (the Bill of Rights) the ten drafts will have accrued in FOUR phases to a newly perfected Seal (ONE: FOUR/ONE).

Continuing Revolution Draft by Draft

After the Seal projected through "ELEUSIS," the Chinese *Books of Rites* (*LII*) provides for "KUNG" a natural twelve months for a revolutionary ten cantos. The lexical ideogram for revolution (*LVII*) is by visual macaronics a dead ringer for the American Seal's Eagle.

The plantations settled by the Adamses (*LXII*) embody for "JOHN ADAMS" the Seal in the form of the Seal/Calendar arcanum. Issuing from this symbol, "ten head 40 acres @ 3/ (shillings) per acre" builds from a prototype ten a Mount of 120 shillings (cantos).

In *Pisan*, "Canto 77 Explication" rearranges ideograms into a mystical 13 becoming natural 12 becoming revolutionary "1–10." The form is also phasal (ONE: FOUR/ONE) for *Pisan LXXVII* as a pattern for the whole poem, and dual for the phase of personae traditional ("1–6") and renewed ("7–10").

The "rock-drill" of thirteen oversized ideograms (*85*), a new form of the antecedent arcana, will be adjusted by the text via 12 to 10; from 10, for a third phase, it will subsume ONE: FOUR/ONE and duality in trine. The Seal/Calendar arcanum is an all but explicit form for ONE: FOUR/ONE as a Branches/Powers dynamic. The alchemical paradigm (*92*) unites fourfold concurrency, sequence, and "mass relations." "The trigger happy mind" "going six ways a Sunday" and then returning "Six ways to once / of a Sunday" (*93*) cloaks personal duality.

"ONE, ten, eleven, *chi con me* 旦 tan?" (*97*) makes "ONE" new prototypically.

"Thru the 12 Houses of Heaven / seeing the just and the unjust, / tasting the sweet and the sorry, / Pater Helios turning" (*CXIII*) could hardly be more explicit.

The formal consistency of the foregoing is supported and enforced by the revolutionary subject. Among the several revolutions presented only historical '76 gives the revolutionary subject its detailed revolutionary form.

Constitutional Constituents in "Triangular Spaces"

Finally, either by itself, or, more inevadably, in conjunction and convergence with the foregoing consistencies and concurrencies of drafting, can the Constitutional complement for building be coincidence? Must it not be design?

Cantos I–LIII extend pluralistic "ELEUSIS" to Kung himself (*LIII*), Kung passes via his dynastic aftercomers (*LIV–LXI*) into John Adams's tradition and struggle (*LXII–LXXV*), and Adams adds Constitutional founding and continuing revolution (*LXVI–LXXI*). The clauses of three Branches (Congress 1–53, Presidency 54–65, Judiciary 66–71) converge with three paideumas the themes of which are plurality (Congress), unity (Presidency), and balance (Judiciary).

If this should still be regarded as coincidence, consider the complements of *Pisan*, which synthesizes and focuses a world paideuma (collective) through a single persona (individual): *Cantos (72–) LXXIV–LXXXIV* reflect the amending clauses 72–84. Consider too seven drafts focusing world paideuma and Articles I–VII of a states' rights Constitution.

If all that can be taken as coincidence, what about *Cantos I–LXXXIV* made new in *Cantares 85–109* according to a theme of revolutionary founding and amending, coincident with Constitutional clauses 1–84 condensed to Sections i–xxv?

Add to that *Cantos I–LXXXIV* and *Cantares 85–109* intended to be perfected in what became *Drafts CX–CXVI/CXVII*, and clauses 1–84 condensed to Sections i–xxv condensed to Articles I–VII/VIII. Add further *Cantos*, *Cantares*, and *Drafts* condensed to *Fragments*, and clauses, Sections, and Articles condensed to Branches/Powers in fragmentary *CXVII–120*.

Add finally a ten-draft, 120-canto Calendar Mount drafted and built by a cyclic revolutionary mind in "triangular spaces" out of Constitutional constituents with the major divisions and junctures during a lifetime. Clauses 1–51 modulate into 1–53 + 54–65 + 66–71 during the first phase of Pound's life, 72–84 during his second phase, 85–109 during his third phase, and 110–17 modulating into 117–20 during his fourth phase.

Is it plausive to reason that all this—*all* this—could be mere chance, or unconscious? Is it plausive that it could be arbitrary numerology, and not '76? Could other verbal and pictorial forms correlate in such meticulous detail as do the documents of '76 and the symbolic Seal?

Can *The Cantos* plausibly be random? If not, can any comprehensive hypothesis but '76 account for it all? Occam's razor tells us "No."

"Se non è vero è ben trovato?" No, "Fuori di ben trovato è anche vero." That is the meaning of Pound's troubador and Whitman's poet as "maker and finder of songs"; '76 is found in history, and history is made into a song (Pound's "fugue") of '76. "An epic is a poem containing history." *The Cantos* makes all history into epic poetry of revolution by orchestrating '76 into song. "This is not a work of fiction, nor yet of one man" (*Thrones 99*). "Only a musical form would take the material, and the Confucian universe as I see it is a universe of interacting strains and tensions." Pound's mythology is not *devised* from history by eclectic personal selection, like Yeats's system, but claims to be *found* in history in both matter and form.

CHAPTER FOUR

THE INTEGRITY OF A

VISION: EXTERNAL EVIDENCE

Early Prose and the "Personae" Volumes

"It is all part of a prologue . . . the great line of a life work counts."
   To Harriet Monroe, 1915

If one looks for explicit external evidence to verify that the Calendar is Pound's, and that he applied it to twentieth century history (and therefore without question to *The Cantos*), one will look long and hard and will be astonished at its paucity (though one might be alerted by its anonymous publication). A 1933 letter, however, dispels any doubts: "I enc photo indicating that I did not wait for the march on Rome or for Mr. Douglas [the Social Credit economist] to announce a NEW ERA. The calendar was pubd a year before the Eyetalyans started dating their calendars from actuality. The calendar WAS because something Damn well had to bust & new start had to BE. . . . The date of new year [i.e., his birthday] was not due to Evangeline Adams or any astrologic computation. That is when the NEW YEAR begins. When the HELL will people learn to perceive things."[1] That the fascist era began one year after Pound's meant more for himself and *The Cantos* than could easily be stated here. Four years later he dated an essay "Jan. 8 anno XV of our Era—anno XVI of my personal and particular era as I can show by demonstrable evidence which also shows the discrepancy between my sense of reality and Benito Mussolini's. His time sense is better than mine and I would be a pig-headed fool not to admit it."[2] Both remarks are as serious as playful, as factual as imaginative. One year is not much amid millennia.

As to explicit internal evidence in *The Cantos*, the Seal and the Calendar inhere in the subjects, themes, and forms of the texts and in the visual symbols; all are arcana in that they refer to something beyond themselves, but all

1. To H. R. Hays, 20 November 1933, Collection at Yale.
2. "Intellectual Money," *British Union Quarterly*, London, April/June 1937.

are also integral matter of the poem. The only explicit reference to the detail of the Calendar appears in Pound's dating of John Adams's birthday "Born 1735; 19th Oct. old style; 30th new style John Adams" (*LXII*). The HORUS born on the feast of ZAGREUS for '76 has been succeeded by the HORUS born in 1885 to renew the destiny.

Beyond casual remarks and inherency, however, a few bits of evidence point directly at the Seal and the Calendar as models for literary form. Some of these come from earlier in his career than 1921–22, which suggests a greater integrity for his poetic vision and for the principal forms it took, the "personae" volumes of 1908–21 collected and rearranged in *Personae* (1926) and *The Cantos*. This early evidence suggests that Pound was working on the Seal/Calendar form for *The Cantos* all along, and that his "personae" poems were indeed deliberately designed as a single "prologue" to a "life work."[3]

Parts of a Prologue

Though the Calendar was not published until 1922, the Calendar (and thus the Seal) are obviously related to Pound's first elaborate prose manifesto, "I gather the Limbs of Osiris," which speaks of gathering elements of world poetry in a circle around an individual center (Pound, the Eagle, or HORUS) and thence "erecting" one's "microcosmos" by arranging four "distinct phases of consciousness . . . about one's own."[4] Pound's model was Dante, who defined his center in his *Vita Nuova* and erected his microcosmos in the *Divina Commedia*. Pound had already, in *The Spirit of Romance* (1910) defined the four senses of the *Divina Commedia* by a mathematical analogy that

3. "One thing I want insisted on is 'the work as a whole.' . . . It is all part of a prologue . . . the great line of a life work counts. Not the single isolated point, valuable as it may be in the whole. I decline to be judged save as a whole, each part of the work in relation to the rest. . . . The verse at least the collected poems [*Personae* 1909, *Exultations* 1910, *Canzoni* 1911, *Ripostes* 1912, republished together as a "collected edition" in 1913] with Cathay [1915] and some selection of the other translation works into a single volume . . . I might say that there is very little repetition in the books as they stand, though I shall make some excisions before I regard the work as finished." To Harriet Monroe, Spring 1915, the University of Chicago Library for the *Poetry* Magazine Papers, 1912–36, hereafter cited as *Poetry* Papers.

4. "I gather the Limbs of Osiris" I–XII, *New Age*, London, 1911–12. Pound tipped the Calendar in a concurrent letter to the *New Age*, "On the 'Decline of Faith' " (21 December 1911): "Sir,—It is true that we no longer believe that the supreme and controlling power of this universe is a bigoted old fool or a Hebrew monopoly; this much the Rationalist has done for us. Our creed may run riot somewhat as follows:—I believe in the Divine, the ruler of heaven and earth, and in his most splendid protagonist, Christ Jesus our Lord, born of the Virgin Diana, succoured of Pallas Athene, Lord of Horus, Lord of Raa, Prince of the House of Angels; but to say that we are faithless in an age without faith is an absurdity. E. P." He tipped the Calendar too in "Patria Mia" IX by using Ceres (Demeter), Juno, Aphrodite (Kupris), Pallas Athena, and Artemis to define female social types.

applies exactly to the mathematics of the Seal and the Calendar. In "Vorticism" (1914)[5] he applied the same mathematical analogy not to the rising dimensions of a narrative poem but to the increasing intensities of the new imagist or vorticist poetry he himself was trying to write.

In "I gather the Limbs of Osiris" Pound posited "a 'new Method of Scholarship,'" "the method of Luminous Detail," for assembling instances of "donative" writers who had added something new to world poetry; his exhibits were his well-known translation of "The Seafarer," the keynote of the series, and poems by Guido Cavalcanti and Arnaut Daniel. In "On Virtue" (VI), however, he revealed his own poetic aims. As a metaphor for expressing "certain relations," he posited that "the soul of each man is compounded of all the elements of the cosmos of souls, but in each soul there is some one element which predominates, which is in some peculiar and intense way the quality or *virtù* of the individual; in no two souls is this the same." "It is the artist's business to find his own *virtù*"—to find it in relation to the virtues of others, so that he may become like the angel in Dante's *Vita Nuova* "the centre of a circle which possesseth all parts of its circumference equally." In "Vorticism" Pound called this effort "the 'search for oneself,'" for "'sincere self-expression,'" for "the real."

By the time of writing "I gather the Limbs of Osiris" he had defined a Renaissance poetic tradition in *The Spirit of Romance* (1910), *Personae* (1909), *Exultations* (1909), *Canzoni* (1911), and the about-to-be published *Riposes* (1912), the keynote of which is his translation of "The Seafarer." *Riposes* would complete a first four-phase definition of his own "*virtù*" through different kinds of poems deployed for different purposes in each of the four volumes. The "dramatic lyrics" of *A Lume Spento* (1908), which was incorporated mostly into *Personae* (1909) but also into *Exultations*, *Canzoni*, and *Riposes*, were spoken by personae.[6] "Exultations" were proportionally arranged passionate expressions of "life 玊 ," a monogram for "E. P."[7] "Canzoni" were not the emotional moments of "personae" and "exultations," but the formal "high mass" of poetry.[8] "Riposes" were "my compositions."[9] All the poems of 1908–20 come finally under the title *Personae* (1926).

Having discovered and expressed his *virtù*, "the artist may proceed to the erection of his microcosmos." Having discovered his own he will "be more likely to discern and allow for a peculiar *virtù* in others. The erection of the

---

5. "Vorticism," *Fortnightly Review*, London, 1 September 1914.

6. To William Carlos Williams, 21 October 1908, *Letters*.

7. To Viola Baxter Jordan, ?–1910, Collection at Yale. '玊' seems to be a stylization of the initials E[zra] L[oomis] P[ound], superimposed, and probably also of the Christian cross with an earthly ground under it and a heavenly roof over it. Thus "life" defined as the scope of personal action within an intelligible cosmos.

8. A note to *Canzoni*, cancelled in proof, Humanities Center at Texas.

9. To Harriet Monroe, 18 August 1912, *Letters*.

microcosmos consists in discriminating these powers and in holding them in orderly arrangement about one's own.'' Dante performed it ''in the most symmetrical and barefaced manner,'' yet Pound would ''stretch the fabric of my critique'' on ''four great positions,'' or ''four men in especial virtuous, or, since virtues are so hard to define,'' on ''four phases of consciousness.'' These are Homer of the *Odyssey*, ''man conscious of the world outside him''; Dante in the *Divina Commedia*, ''man conscious of the world within him''; Chaucer, ''man conscious of the variety of persons about him, not so much of their acts and the outlines of their acts as of their character, their personalities''; and Shakespeare, ''man conscious of himself in the world about him—as Dante had been conscious of the spaces of the mind, its reach and its perspective.'' This formulation looks toward a poem like *The Cantos*, but the subject is ''man conscious'' and the spirit is that of renaissance, not revolution. Still, the form for the Seal/Calendar tabulation built from and by the Seal/Calendar cycle is evident in the *virtù* and the microcosmos and in their mutual relations.

In ''Vorticism'' he shifted from defining himself in relation to the poetry of others to defining himself by four kinds of his own poems, in rising intensity toward perfection of the ''Image.'' His definition was ''psychological or philosophical,'' '' 'from the inside' . . . autobiographically,'' ''based on one's own experience.'' He subsumed the search for ''Osiris'' in the new categorization:[10]

> In the ''search for oneself,'' in the search for ''sincere self-expression,'' one gropes, one finds some seeming verity. One says ''I am'' this, that, or the other, and with the words scarcely uttered one ceases to be that thing.
>
> I began this search for the real in a book called *Personae*, casting off, as it were, complete masks of the self in each poem. I continued in long series of translations, which were but more elaborate masks.
>
> Secondly, I made poems like ''The Return,'' which is an objective reality and has a complicated sort of significance, like Mr. Epstein's ''Sun God,'' or Mr. Brzeska's ''Boy with a Coney.'' Thirdly, I have written ''Heather,'' which represents a state of consciousness, or ''implies,'' or ''implicates'' it.
>
> A Russian correspondent, after having called it a symbolist poem, and having been convinced that it was not symbolism, said slowly: ''I see, you wish to give people new eyes, not to make them see some new particular thing.''

The personae are obviously impersonal, at least by convention. Pound also called the second and third impersonal, and ''Imagisme.'' For a fourth illus-

---

10. Cf. the previous categories ''personae,'' ''exultations,'' ''canzoni,'' and ''my compositions.''

tration he described elaborately how he had come to write "In a Station of the Metro," perhaps the prototype Imagist poem. This perfect "Image" tries to "record the precise instant when a thing outward and objective transforms itself, or darts into a thing inward and subjective." This obviously personal "image" perfects in the scope delimited here the search for oneself, for sincere self-expression, for the real.

The relation of "I gather the Limbs of Osiris" to the Calendar is obvious; its relation to the Seal is more general. The Seal, the source of the Calendar's mathematics, is more evident in the mathematical analogy. It is applied to discrete kinds of poems in "Vorticism," but as has been said it had already been applied to Dantean cosmic narrative. I quote at length from Pound's explanation of how the four poems are Vorticist:

> Vorticism is an intensive art. I mean by this, that one is concerned with the relative intensity, or relative significance of different sorts of expression. One desires the most intense, for certain forms of expression *are* "more intense" than others. They are more dynamic. I do not mean they are more emphatic, or that they are yelled louder. I can explain my meaning best by mathematics.
>
> There are four different intensities of mathematical expression known to the ordinarily intelligent undergraduate, namely: the arithmetical, the algebraic, the geometrical, and that of analytical geometry.
>
> For instance, you can write
>
> $$3 \times 3 + 4 \times 4 = 5 \times 5$$
>
> or, differently, $3^2 + 4^2 = 5^2$.
>
> That is merely conversation or "ordinary common sense." It is a simple statement of one fact and does not implicate any other.
>
> *Secondly*, it is true that
>
> $$3^2 + 4^2 = 5^2, 6^2 + 8^2 = 10^2, 9^2 + 12^2 = 15^2, 39^2 + 52^2 = 65^2.$$
>
> These are all separate facts, one may wish to mention their underlying similarity; it is a bore to speak about each one in turn. One expresses their "algebraic relation" as
>
> $$a^2 + b^2 = c^2.$$
>
> That is the language of philosophy. It MAKES NO PICTURE. This kind of statement applies to a lot of facts, but it does not grip hold of Heaven.
>
> *Thirdly*, when one studies Euclid one finds that the relation of $a^2 + b^2 = c^2$ applies to the ratio between the squares on the two sides of a right-angled triangle and the square on the hypotenuse. One still writes it $a^2 + b^2 = c^2$, but one has begun to talk about form. Another property or quality of life has crept into one's matter. Until then one had dealt only with numbers. But even this statement does not *create* form. The picture is given you in the proposition about the square on the hypotenuse of the right-angled triangle being equal to the sum of the

squares on the two other sides. Statements in plane and descriptive
geometry are like talk about art. They are a criticism of the form. The
form is not created by them.

Fourthly, we come to Descartian or "analytical geometry." Space
is conceived as separated by two or by three axes (depending on whether
one is treating form in one or more planes). One refers points to these
axes by a series of co-ordinates. Given the idiom, one is able *actually*
to *create*.

Thus, we learn that the equation $(x - a)^2 + (y - b)^2 = r^2$ governs
the circle. It is the circle. It is not a particular circle, it is any circle and
all circles. It is nothing that is not a circle. It is the circle free of space
and time limits. It is the universal, existing in perfection, in freedom
from space and time. Mathematics is dull ditchwater until one reaches
analytics. But in analytics we come upon a new way of dealing with
form. It is in this way that art handles life. The difference between art
and analytical geometry is the difference of subject-matter only. Art is
more interesting in proportion as life and the human consciousness are
more complex and more interesting than forms and numbers.

This statement does not interfere in the least with "spontaneity"
and "intuition," or with their function in art. I passed my last *exam*, in
mathematics on sheer intuition. I saw where the line *had* to go, as clearly
as I ever saw an image, or felt *caelestem intus vigorem*.

The statements of "analytics" are "lords" over fact. They are the
thrones and dominations that rule over form and recurrence. And in like
manner are great works of art lords over fact, over race-long recurrent
moods, and over to-morrow.

Great works of art contain this fourth sort of equation. They cause
form to come into being. By the "image" I mean such an equation; not
an equation of mathematics, not something about *a*, *b*, and *c*, having
something to do with form, but about *sea*, *cliffs*, *night*, having something to do with mood.

The image is not an idea. It is radiant node or cluster; it is what I can,
and must perforce, call a VORTEX, from which, and through which,
and into which, ideas are constantly rushing.

A "Note," presumably related to erecting his microcosmos according to
the mathematical analogy, saw "nothing against a long vorticist poem." The
Japanese, who had evolved the hokku (cf. "In a Station of the Metro"), had
also evolved the Noh plays. Each play consisted of or was gathered about one
image enforced by movement and music, and several were united in a series
(the Ban-Gumi).

Arithmetic refers to the Seal's arbitrary heraldic symbols, which are not
repeated. Algebra refers to the Seal's numerology of thirteen, which relates
all the symbols. Geometry refers to the Seal's four geometrical symbols.

Analytics refers to the voices of the symbols uttered by the Eagle who receives the inspiration and creates the "image." In discrete sequence arithmetic refers to the unitary shield voiced E PLURIBUS UNUM, algebra to the dualistic constellation voiced NOVUS ORDO SECLORUM, geometry to the triadic Mount built on its foundation MDCCLXXVI, and analytics to the tetradic, circular sun-vision that has inspired the whole, that completes it, and that is voiced ANNUIT COEPTIS.

The mathematical analogy, not the four poems, is related to the Seal. The substance of the Seal requires a poem like *The Cantos*, which was in conception and probably also by now in composition. But the mathematical analogy, the four poems, and the Seal all relate together to the famous definition "an 'Image' is that which presents an intellectual and emotional complex in an instant of time. . . . It is the presentation of such a 'complex' instantaneously which gives that sense of sudden liberation; that sense of freedom from time limits and space limits; that sense of sudden growth, which we experience in the presence of the greatest works of art."[11] The creative aesthetic worked out from the Seal's mathematics makes the "Image" a dynamic "radiant node or cluster," "a VORTEX, from which, and through which, and into which, ideas are constantly rushing." The Calendar cycle is a dynamic "Image," properly a "VORTEX," while the finished Calendar is a fixed "Image" containing the dynamic mental process by which it has been constituted and built. The Calendar is a comprehensive paradigm for "Image" containing a "VORTEX" that creates a new "Image."

As the scopes of both "Osiris" and "Vorticism" imply, the "personae" volumes of 1908–21 and the culminating *Personae* (1926) constitute "the 'search for oneself,' " for "sincere self-expression," for "the real" by bringing the world past to life through one's own life and times and by making one's own life and times an extension of the world past. The "personae" poems constitute a new tradition or a "better tradition" by ranging through many cultures; the result is a world tradition in the lyric and satiric mode corresponding to the world tradition defined narratively and epically in *The Cantos*.

As to form, the "personae" poems show generally a development from volumes of single poems, to volumes of poems grouped to define cultures, to formal series poems that define eras through more broadly conceived "personae." The first four volumes, reprinted together in 1913 as "Collected Poems," constituted a first four-phase definition of oneself dominated by European culture, especially by "The Spirit of Romance" (in *The Cantos* "ELEUSIS"). In 1915 Pound added his own "discovered" *Cathay* (1915), a volume defining China at a certain stage of her civilization and analogizing it to European culture by including "The Seafarer." In 1916 he added *Lustra*, which concentrated on an American view of all cultures through Roman eyes

---

11. "A Few Don'ts by an Imagiste," *Poetry*, Chicago, March 1913.

while also extending, deepening, and making more personal kinds of poems of the first four volumes; as *Cathay* had included "The Seafarer" to analogize Europe and China, *Lustra* contained *Cathay* to comprehend the several cultures of a world tradition. With *Lustra*, his sixth volume, Pound had defined himself in relation to an assembled tradition of world poetry made new in his own evolving poetic forms and poetic languages. He had also defined himself stylistically by subsuming his work to date in the four poems of "Vorticism" and had ventured to apply this projective mathematical analogy to his own work both achieved and to come.

The rest of the "personae" poems are formal series. "Langue D'Oc" I–IV (originally "Homage à la Langue D'Oc" I–V) and "Moeurs Contemporaines" I–VIII (originally I–IX) constitute a complementary dual series juxtaposing translations and adaptations of Provençal songs with modernist satires; one can see how they evolve from and focus the principal tones, lyric and satiric, and the principal European subjects, Provence and modernity, of the first six volumes. "Langue D'Oc" and "Moeurs Contemporaines" were published along with "Homage to Sextus Propertius" I–XII in *Quia Pauper Amavi* (1919). Pound makes Propertius's ability to write poetry of lyric passion and satiric exposure within the hostile Augustan empire (and get away with it) a mirror (or "persona") of his own achievement within the twentieth-century British Empire.[12] The final "persona" poem is the dual series *Hugh Selwyn Mauberley* (Life and Contacts) (1920) consisting of I–XII plus the coda "Envoi" (1919) and of I–IV plus the coda "Medallion."[13] In *Mauberley* the titular persona dies or is killed by his times while a recording persona survives to tell Mauberley's story, to learn the lesson, and so to move on to the work already in progress, *The Cantos*. In *Poems 1918–21* Pound ordered the three series poems as "Three Portraits" in the historical order Rome, Provence, and modernity.[14] In *Personae* (1926) he returned to "Langue D'Oc"/"Moeurs Contemporaines" as the first, and followed it with "Mauberley" and "Proper-

12. Pound insisted over and over on the analogy between the Roman and British (or even American) Empires and between Propertius's plight and his own. For instance, "Augustus living spit of Wilson. Ovid and Propertius really up against thing very much as one is now; and similarity does not apply to any other known period of history" (to his father, 25 March 1919, Collection at Yale); "If possible I shd. even have wished to render a composite character, including something of Ovid, and making the portrayed figure not only Propertius but inclusive of the spirit of the young man of the Augustan Age, hating rhetoric and undeceived by imperial hogwash."(To A. R. Orage, April 1919, *Letters*).

13. The presence of twelve-part series poems in the "personae" volumes is not accidental. The prototype, "Und Drang" (*Canzoni* 1911), was Pound's first formal, published, poetic statement of his personal situation, motives, methods, and ends. "Und Drang" shows clearly the Seal/Calendar form. It served as a model for "Propertius" and *Mauberley*. It was broken up after *Mauberley* had appeared in 1920, but its second half, grouped two by two, was restored as six separate poems, "The House of Splendour" through "Au Jardin," which conclude the first section of *Personae* (1926), "Personae (1908, 1909, 1910)."

14. To John Quinn, 9 October 1920, in Daniel Pearlman, *The Barb of Time* (New York: 1969), Appendix A.

tius." As a result the poet who cannot deal with imperial tyranny is survived by the poet who can.

This reversal of composition and historicity points up the evolving theme of the volume, renaissance to revolution. Behind the first volumes is the theme of renaissance or "make it new" laid out from late Rome via the Middle Ages to the Renaissance in *The Spirit of Romance* (1910). The spirit is lyric and positive. With the encroachment of modernity, however, the spirit begins to range from irony to satire to diatribe. It begins lightly in *Ripostes*. By chance or by design, the poems of *Cathay* reflect elegiacally a declining culture falling into mismanagement and destructive war as the world was doing when the volume was published. The spirit of *Lustra* is mainly ironic and satiric. The spirit of "Moeurs Contemporaines," especially by contrast with "Langue D'Oc," is corrosive. "Propertius" achieves the urbane irony of a revolutionary poet who is able to survive. *Mauberley* returns to irony and satire fortified by diatribes against the destructiveness of World War I. The personal voice of "Propertius" and the recording voice of *Mauberley* are definite revolutionary voices, the one from within tyranny and the other on the way out of it. To such an end had Pound's hope for a new Renaissance come. Whatever *The Cantos* may have been originally planned to be, it now had to be the Renaissance generating revolution as a means of fulfilling the original Renaissance dream.

On the way toward the final *Personae* (1926) Pound devised further four-phase categories to deal with new "mass relations" as the volumes accrued. To *Umbra* (1920), which reconstituted the four volumes of "Complete Poems" while adding some other poems and translations from 1912, Pound appended the tabulation below.

PERSONAE AND PORTRAITS

Main outline of E.P.'s work to date

Personae—	*Sketches (in "Lustra")*—	
La Fraisne	Millwins	
Cino	Bellaires	
Audiart	etc.	
Marvoil	*(Later)*	*Etudes*—
Altaforte	I Vecchii	Guido
Vidal	Nodier Raconte	Arnaut
	etc.	Langue d'Oc

Sketches (in "Ripostes")—	*Major Personae*—
Portrait d'une Femme	Seafarer
Phasellus Ille	Exile's Letter (and
Girl	Cathay in general)
An Object	Homage to Sextus Propertius
Quies	

As a ''main outline,'' and being Pound's, the arrangement doubtless has symbolic value. One may think ''Personae and Portraits'' to be relevant to two columns, and can note that the second column inverts the first while elaborating it with larger forms and bringing a fourfold whole to a focus. One may think of the inverted, focused form of the Seal/Calendar arcanum. One may also find in ''Personae and Portraits'' individuals and social types, or ''halves of a seal.''

Such speculations yield fruit, but they require too much analysis. Here it is enough to note that the earlier ''fours''—the volumes of ''dramatic lyrics'' evolving to ''my compositions,'' and the autobiographical and stylistic ''four'' of ''Vorticism''—have yielded to four kinds of poems evolving social history: simple ''Personae'' evolve simple ''Sketches,'' simple ''Sketches'' evolve more complex ''Sketches'' deepened by ''Etudes'' (the ''Later'' Sketches are from ''Moeurs Contemporaines''), and all evolve ''Major Personae.''[15] If ''Personae'' include ''Major Personae'' as well as being culminated by them, then each of the four categories spans all of ''E. P.'s work to date.'' The three ''Major Personae'' epitomize the Anglo-Saxon spirit (and its later emergence in America), the Chinese spirit, and the Mediterranean spirit. A fourth ''Major Persona,'' not included but published simultaneously with *Umbra*, was Hugh Selwyn Mauberley, a twentieth-century parody of what the three paideumatic spirits (they are also revolutionary) had become.

It may be noted that there are no ''Portraits,'' only ''Sketches'' for ''Portraits.'' The designation ''Portraits'' appeared when ''Homage to S. P.,'' the dual series ''Langue D'Oc''/''Moeurs Contemporaines,'' and the dual series *Hugh Selwyn Mauberley* were grouped as ''Portraits'' of three eras in *Poems 1918–21*.

By 1921, whether by chance or by design (I suspect design), Pound had published nine volumes of ''personae,'' the ninth reordering the three series of the seventh and eighth. For 1926, in the perspective of what he had done in *The Cantos*, he completed the ''personae'' by reorganizing the nine volumes into a tenth volume constituted of ten sections in four phases. *Personae* (1926) is designed in much more intricate detail than can be described here; indeed, one has to follow the volumes from the beginning to be aware of all that Pound was doing both along the way and in the final revision.[16] Here it is

15. ''Study'' and ''Etude'' were first experiments with the Provençal and Italian canzone, which first appeared as ''Canzoniere: Studies in Form'' in the third section of *Provença* (1910). They constituted the first half of *Canzoni* (1911), the second half of which consisted of a lyric history beginning with a translation from Propertius and culminating in Pound's first personal study in form, ''Und Drang'' I–XII. After many intervening experiments, *Mauberley* became in one of its dimensions a culminating ''study in form'' (To Felix E. Schelling, 9 July 1922, *Letters*). ''Study in form,'' an expression of the emerging Mount, is characteristic of third phases: *Canzoni* is the third volume of ''collected poems'' (1913), ''Etudes'' inform the third phase of ''Personae and Portraits,'' and *Mauberley* becomes the third phase of *Personae* (1926).

16. Pound applied to the ''personae'' volumes, for *Personae* (1926), the kind of revision he did not need to apply to *The Cantos*.

hoped that, in the light of what has been said so far, a brief description will persuade that Pound "had a design."[17] The description passes over exclusions and new inclusions of individual poems within sections, which are important but do not affect the overall form.

The divisions of *Personae* (1926) can be followed by the large-type title page for each section, with the exception that the two parts of "Mauberley" are the eighth and ninth sections. Pound greatly abbreviated *Personae, Exultations,* and *Canzoni* as "Personae of Ezra Pound (1908, 1909, 1910)." "Ripostes (1912)" appears as was, by itself. The title "Lustra," without its date 1916, comprehends the next four sections. The first third of *Lustra* (1916) appears as was, as "Lustra" (undated). It is followed by "Cathay" dated 1915, or as *Cathay* was included in the middle of *Lustra* (1916). "Cathay" is followed by a brief new section, "POEMS FROM BLAST (1914)" in the boldface type of that magazine; these poems had never appeared previously in book form. Finally comes "Poems from *Lustra* (1915)," the poems that followed *Cathay* in *Lustra* (1916). By condensing the first three volumes into one section, and by letting *Lustra* (1916) appear as its three sections while adding "POEMS FROM BLAST," Pound reflected the chronology of composition of the six volumes that constituted (and still constitute) a world tradition. But the effect is different. Now irony and satire begin earlier and assume greater proportion. Further, the note of decline and encroaching war in *Cathay* is not only earlier but is enforced by "POEMS FROM BLAST (1914)," which has more effect by title, typography, and date than by the poems included. The need to extend renaissance to revolution is made peremptory.

"Langue D'Oc"/"Moeurs Contemporaines" returns to its place as the first of the series to point up the dual theme, tone, and perspective and to accentuate the need for change. "Hugh Selwyn Mauberley," in its two parts as "Life and Contacts" (Pound later said the two parts reflect instead "Contacts and Life"),[18] takes a new place as a third phase; art and the poet die out

---

17. Pound often complained that "designs" of his prose books had been missed. He claimed that *Prolegomena*, an intended "Collected Prose Work (Folio)" prepared in 1929 and intended to run from *The Spirit of Romance* (1910) as a "work in progress" accompanying *The Cantos* would show "some proof" that he had "started with a definite intention," and that what had appeared to be "an aimless picking up of tidbits" had been "governed by a plan which became clearer and more definite as I proceeded" ("Postscript [1929]" to "Praefatio Ad Lectorem Electum" to *The Spirit of Romance* when that work was printed as *Prolegomena 2*, 1932). He fulminated to the editors of *Hound & Horn*, Cambridge, Mass.: "The folio mind has died out and the world is no better for its absence. I am the last bhloody rortin rhinocerous. My one vol of prose is no more a series of four little vols. than my cantos are a series of lyrics. My books were crippled, incomplete from the 1909 Personae to the Liveright 'Collected Poems, Personae.' Same thing with the prose. It is NOT a series it is a single chunk, and the components need the other components in one place with them. There is a difference between Ulysses and a series of Hen. Jas. novels" (30 August 1930, Collection at Yale).

18. *Paris Review* 28.

in the contemporary world, but the spirit of art and the poet's work live on as always to instigate necessary change. "Homage to Sextus Propertius" takes a new place as a fourth phase to affirm through style and tone that the poet can survive and has survived for a larger mission. Dating the two parts of "Mauberley" respectively 1919 and 1920, and "Propertius" 1917, accentuates the fact that spirit and art can rise above the death or at least moribundity of a culture.

Tradition, personality, and justice perfected in poetry appear to be as much the evolving themes of *Personae* as of *The Cantos*, and the Seal/Calendar form appears to be equally applicable, though the subject matters, scopes, and modes are vastly different. Too, although he may have had a general design for *Personae* as a "prologue" to *The Cantos*, he evolved it by revision along the way and on into the final form; for *The Cantos* the form had become fixed so that virtually no revision was necessary after *XVI. Cantos* had been published. The reason is the detailed application of the forms of '76 in *The Cantos* but not in *Personae*. *Personae* follows the Seal/Calendar form as a simple archetypal form of ten and four evolving by a looser version of "mass relations" than employed in *The Cantos*. Pound probably did not have the documents of '76 in mind for *Personae*; when he applied them to a Seal/Calendar form that must have preceded that application cannot be known from present evidence, most of which is in the works themselves, in their evolutions, and in their relations to each other.

We can, however, follow Pound's thinking about the relation between the Renaissance and America and about renaissance and revolution, especially in A. R. Orage's guild socialist weekly *The New Age*, London, after "I gather the Limbs of Osiris." Previously, while working on *The Spirit of Romance*, Pound had formulated in "What I Feel About Walt Whitman" (dated 1 February 1909, but not published until 1955), a personal manifesto for applying the Renaissance and American visions to his own career.[19] "Patria Mia" I–XI envisions an American renaissance symbolized by a new version of the Statue of Liberty (I), adduces the phases of New World history (I), uses five of the six goddesses of the female hemicycle to define female social types (IX), and begins to view millennial political and economic history in the perspective of constitutional government and of guild socialism (VI).[20] "America: Chances and Remedies" elaborates an analogy between conditions that made the Renaissance and similar contemporary conditions.[21] With the outbreak of

19. Herbert Bergman, "What I Feel About Walt Whitman," *American Literature*, Concord, N.H., March 1955.

20. On the constitutional heritage, see Chapter Two, n. 9. On the goddesses, see above, n. 4. "I believe . . . in the imminence of an American Risorgimento. Of 'Liberty' beautifully proportioned, of 'Liberty' without that hideous nightgown wherein Bartoldi has arrayed her" (I). At the end of the epitome Canto *I* Pound redresses Liberty as Aphrodite and makes her his Providence.

21. *New Age*, May–June 1913. This series became with "Patria Mia" the book *Patria Mia*.

World War I he begins to argue against America's neutrality as a symptom of the "Provincialism" of the American mind,[22] and, from there, to study more rigorously the same character in the British imperial mind.[23] As a result his thinking moves from hoped-for renaissance to necessary revolution, not the violent revolution of Marx and Lenin but "a conspiracy of intelligent men" aimed at remedying social, political, and economic flaws in present systems.[24] These series of essays culminate after the Treaty of Versailles and the establishment of the League of Nations in "The Revolt of Intelligence" I–X, a declaration of a revolutionary vocation already millennially, autobiographically, formally, and poetically prepared.[25]

Preparations for Epic Narrative

In *Pisan LXXVII*, where he rederives a Seal/Calendar form ideogramically (see pp. 322–23), Pound dates the beginning of *The Cantos* from "A.D. 1904, somewhat previous but effective / for immediate scope," which was apparently to find some middle way between the unjust "privileges" of "le beau monde" and "Sochy-lism." He corroborated this early date in a 1962 interview. Asked when he began *The Cantos* he replied:

> I began the Cantos about 1904, I suppose. I had various schemes, starting in 1904 or 1905. The problem was to get a form—something elastic enough to take the necessary materials. . . . Obviously you haven't got a nice little road map such as the Middle Ages possessed of Heaven. Only a musical form would take the material . . . the first thing was this: you had six centuries that hadn't been packaged. It was a question of dealing with material that wasn't in the Divina Commedia. . . . The problem was to build up [cf. the Calendar tabulation?] a circle of reference [cf.the Calendar cycle?]—taking the modern mind to be the medieval mind with wash after wash of classical culture poured over it since the renaissance. That was the psyche, if you like. One had to deal with one's own subject.[26]

The "subject" and the "psyche" evolved from "1904 or 1905" until they were fully sketched in the prototype *XVI. Cantos*. Pound had an a priori form: much work was "thrown away" because it didn't "function within my form," didn't "embody a value needed." Not only the matter but also, necessarily,

22. "American Chaos" I–II, September 1915; "This Super-Neutrality," October 1915; "Provincialism the Enemy" I–IV, July–August 1917.

23. "Studies In Contemporary Mentality" I–XIX, August 1917–January 1918.

24. "What America Has to Live Down" I–VI, August–September 1918; "The Regional" I–XVIII, June–November 1919.

25. I–X, November–March 1919–1920.

26. *Paris Review* 28.

the form itself was "historic . . . but not fiction." His myth could not be personal, like Yeats's, but had to be an historic myth like the Renaissance tradition evolving New World history and '76.

The well-known first hint of *The Cantos* is the Browningesque dramatic monologue "Scriptor Ignotus," written in 1906 and published in 1908 in Pound's first book, *A Lume Spento*, with a dedication to his "2nd friend,"[27] the American pianist Katherine Ruth Heyman, who became the dedicatee (and Providence) of his second book, *A Quinzaine For This Yule*. In "Scriptor Ignotus" Pound's speaker, a fictional eighteenth-century poet and Dante scholar, promises his lady (an organist of Ferrara) that he will follow the example of Dante and write for her, after a work like Dante's *Vita Nuova*, a "great forty-year epic" modeled on the *Divina Commedia*.

Even more explicit is another Browningesque poem written at about the same time, in any case no later than 1907, "To R. B.," which has never been published.[28] In it the speaker, a fellow poet though of lesser stature, argues with Browning about the common aim of their respective poetries, the speaker's "Cavalcanti" and Browning's "Sordello"; the argument prefigures the 1917 Ur *I–III*, where Pound begins by arguing with Browning about Browning's poem *Sordello*, about Browning's persona Sordello, and about the historical Sordello, before hitting on the Homeric voyage to the dead as his own definitive beginning (relics of the argument open the present *II* and *III*).

Pound's persona posits (to Browning) in prose: "Begin with a different or a new idea And as we grow, following that idea in all its byways and branches, so we grow to comprehend it but a part of some greater thought tree, seen before in some other part and not known of us to be the same. So my Cavalcanti growing, joins Sordello. Sordello whom my faint understanding failed to comprehend till Guido stood ready for the acting." From prose he breaks into verse by extending the metaphor of the "greater thought tree":

> Then looking on the fruits of both these men
> For fruit is the tree's token,
> Lo thou one branch, and I
> A smaller stem have broken,
> Both of one tree and in quality the same,
> Though show'st th'incomprehensions self
> Being greater and poet.
> I being, or striving to be what [I?] would be,
> Show the outward act of this same lack of grasp.
> Thy script stands sealed
> To them who may not read,
> Mine plainer writ is yet unto the blind a secret,

27. To Iris Barry, 29 August 1916, *Letters*.
28. The text is in the Collection at Yale. See Appendix E.

> May hap we work to one same end
> Thou greater and I less.

The "thought tree" is one of Pound's symbols for the Seal/Calendar arcanum. An explicit example will be a Seal/Calendar arcanum using the successive names ("ply over ply") of the settlements at Massachusetts Bay leading up to the Adams's Braintree (*LXII*):

> Merry Mount become Braintree, a plantation near Weston's
> Capn Wollanston's became Merrymount.

or:

> Sun Mount become Constellation, Shield planted near Weston's
> Eagle 'n' shield 'n' stars became Sunmount.

Weston's was the plantation of Pound's ancestors. The lines read backwards and forwards (like the up-and-down Seal, Calendar, and Seal/Calendar arcanum); other meanings will be explained later.

The speaker then goes on to discuss "thought's circle" as a means of showing "not all truth" but "just so much of truth we see, / As best may help our stumbler on the road to All ends." After a parable and further discussion, he catches himself up with a figure that strongly suggests the Calendar cycle as a symbol for the previously described "thought tree" and "thought's circle":

> But I ramble as ever
> Thought half-cut from next thought
> Two radii ill seen are blurred to one.
> And in o'er great confusion
> The priest and levite passing,
> See no radii, as such, at all;
> Nor even guess the circle and its laws
> Or know a centre and that lives lead thither.
> Or living mid mixed lines,
> Have no chance to hear
> The harmonies of thought God-leading.

We may take "thought tree" to be an organic term for the Seal edifice, with Cavalcanti and Sordello as Eagles. We may take "thought's circle" to be the Calendar cycle for assembling and discriminating thoughts, whether in "personae" being written or in cantos to come. There is no hint as yet of the Calendar tabulation.

Another hint of the mathematical scheme occurs in "Guillaume De Lorris Belated: A Vision of Italy" (*Personae* 1909), an imitation of the pre-Dantean allegory *Romance of the Rose* applied to Pound's own vision of the cities of northern Italy in the form of beautiful women both ideal and real. The key to the poem is a dream encounter with Verona, Dante's refuge in his exile, in which Pound's soul becomes "enfranchised" from earth so that he receives a vision of "all time" and an "*in*formation" (a form of inner inspiration) of all that occurred within the dream state. When "the transfusion / Of all my self through her and she through me" had passed, he perceived that she (his Providence) "enthroned" two things, "Verona, and a maid I knew on earth." Thus "dulled some while from dream, and then become / That lower thing, deductive intellect,"

> I saw
> How all things are but symbols of all things,
> And each of many, do we know
> But the equation governing.

In "my rapture at this vision's scope" he "saw no end or bourne to what things mean" and so praised Pythagoras. Raised once more by his rapture to "the house of Dream" he envisioned other cities, including Venice, "Princess of the Opiates," and "Ligurian Genoa," "Cornelia of Colombo of far sight, / That, man and seer in one, had well been twain, / And each a glory to his hills and sea." Pound recalls this vision while discovering "my Holy city" Siena among the cities of Tuscany ("so that the echo turned back in my mind: Pavia, / Saw cities move in one figure, Vicenza, as depicted / San Zeno by Adige," *XLII*).

A footnote to "I saw / How all things are but symbols of all things" refers to the mystical philosophy of the twelfth-century philosopher Richard of St. Victor, which Pound placed behind *The Romance of the Rose*, Dante's *Divina Commedia*, and his own post-medieval adaptation. Pound's footnote reads:

> Ref. Richard of St. Victor. "On the preparation of the soul for contemplation," where he distinguishes between cogitation, meditation, and contemplation.
> In cogitation the thought or attraction flits aimlessly about the subject.
> In meditation it circles round it, that is, it views it systematically, from all sides, gaining perspective.
> In contemplation it radiates from a centre, that is, as light from the sun it reaches out in an infinite number of ways to things that are related to or dependent on it.
> The words above are my own, as I have not the Benjamin Minor by me.
> Following St. Victor's figure of radiation: Poetry in its acme is expression from contemplation.

Richard's "gradation of processes," derived from the philosophies of the ancient world, arcane and rational, and from the early medieval Neo-Platonism of Scotus Erigena (died 877), leads to a fourth dimension, the actual creation of poetry. Pound cites Richard frequently throughout his works as a definitive model and uses it as a measure of other "gradations of process," European, Chinese, and American.[29] Richard's philosophy is embodied formally and definitvely in the visionary *Rock-Drill 90*.

The early external clues to *The Cantos* itself culminate in the application of the mathematical analogy to Dante's *Divina Commedia*. In one sense the *Commedia* is a sequence of discrete cantos and discrete realms (*Inferno*, *Purgatorio*, and *Paradiso*) like the lyrics, volumes, and phases of *Personae* and like *The Cantos* as discrete cantos, drafts, and phases; in another sense it is a single, sustained, polysemous narrative like *The Cantos* alone. After he had his mathematical Seal/Calendar form in *XVI. Cantos*, Pound tried to explain what he had done in a simpler archetypal form in a well-known letter to his father of 11 April 1927. He tried to make an even more elaborate explanation to Yeats in March and October 1928, which Yeats recorded in "A Packet For Ezra Pound" (1929) and included as an introduction to his revised *A Vision* (1936). The explanation to Yeats confuses more than clarifies. But it does elaborate the letter to Pound's father by describing a Renaissance model for all the forms, the frescoes of the Room of the Months in the Estean Palazzo Schifanoia at Ferrara; the frescoes, each in vertical compartments or tiers, turn the room into a calendar of the year analogous to Pound's own. In a 1958 interview Pound corrected a crucial error in Yeats's account of the frescoes and hinted that the frescoes might be a "clue" to "something similar" he had done (the Seal/Calendar form) and to his own poetry.

In "Il Maestro," *The Spirit of Romance* (1910), Pound introduced his discussion of the *Divina Commedia* with his mathematical analogy. Reordering the "four senses" in which the *Commedia* is written from literal, allegorical, moral, and anagogical to literal, allegorical, anagogical, and ethical he explained:

> For this form of arcana we find the best parallel in the expressions of mathematics. Thus, when our mathematical understanding is able to see that one general law governs such a series of equations as $3 \times 3 + 4 \times 4 = 5 \times 5$, or written more simply, $3^2 + 4^2 = 5^2, 6^2 + 8^2 = 10^2$, $12^2 + 16^2 = 20^2$, etc., one expresses the common relation algebraically thus, $a^2 + b^2 = c^2$. When one has learned common and analytical geometry, one understands that this relation, $a^2 + b^2 = c^2$, exists between two sides of the right angle triangle and its hypotenuse, and that likewise in analytics it gives the equation for the points forming the circumference of any circle. Thus to the trained mathematician the cryptic $a^2 + b^2 = c^2$ expresses:
>
> *1st*. A series of abstract numbers in a certain relation to each other.
> *2nd*. A relation between certain abstract numbers.
> *3rd*. The relative dimensions of a figure; in this case a triangle.
> *4th*. The idea or ideal of the circle.

29. See Appendix D.

Literal and heraldic correspond with arithmetical, or discrete instances all embodying thirteen. Allegorical and numerological correspond with algebraic, or a principle that governs repeated units of thirteen. Anagogical and geometric precipitate from these relations visual forms. Ethical and mathematical correspond with the method of analytics by which a perfected maker may perfect his work.

He then explained how the four levels of meaning govern Dante's narrative. In a literal sense the *Commedia* is "a description of Dante's vision and a journey through the realms inhabited by the spirits of men after death." Allegorically it is "Dante's own mental and spiritual development." Anagogically "Dante or Dante's intelligence may come to mean 'Everyman' or 'Mankind,' whereas his journey becomes a symbol of mankind's struggle upward out of ignorance into the clear light of philosophy." Ethically the *Commedia* is "an expression of the laws of eternal justice" envisioned by, embodied by, and manifested through one man (cf. the Eagle) who has undergone a universal process while "imaging" it in a work of art. Pound went on to define Dante's Hell, Purgatory, and Paradise as "states" (of mind), not places, and to suggest their relation to Richard of St. Victor's gradation.

The four senses are mutually copresent or concurrent at any point in Dante's poem. Shifting the order of moral and anagogical to anagogical and ethical, along with later formulations, suggests that Pound saw the four senses precipitating the discrete, sequential *Inferno*, *Purgatorio*, and *Paradiso* plus a fourth unrealized by Dante, the divine vision to be realized on earth after Dante's return, which the very telling of the *Commedia* implies (cf. also Richard's gradation extended to the creation of poetry). Pound's anagogical turns Dante's mystical sense into the perfection of human rationality, which Pound will make into the mode of political justice. Ethical throws "the laws of eternal justice," which Pound will make into the laws of the poetic imagination, back upon human action, or, historically, upon the Renaissance effort to build the Dantean vision on earth and upon Pound's effort to achieve an historical (not a Dantean) "paradiso terrestre."

This modification appears in a much later formulation, "for 40 years I have disciplined myself . . . to write . . . an epic poem that begins in the Dark Forest and, passing through the Purgatory of human error, finishes in the light, and among 'the masters of those who know.'"[30] Here Pound's fourth turns Dante's Limbo into a neopagan Elysium. In the prototype Seal *I–IV* Dantean trine (*III*) transforms Homeric Erebus into *Inferno*, Ovid's anthropomorphic nature into a neo-Dantean *Purgatorio* and "paradiso terrestre," and My Cid's quest for justice into a Dantean Paradiso; the tetradic *IV* tries to perfect the whole Renaissance tradition received through the Dantean form. In the prototype draft, where three phases of Renaissance tradition are being

---

30. From the opening sentence of *Introduzione alla Natura Economica degli S.U.A.* [Introduction to the Economic Nature of the United States of America] (Venice: 1944), my translation.

applied by the twentieth century (*I–VII*, *VIII–XI* and *XII–XIII*), "the modern mind" is emerging as "the medieval mind with wash after wash of classical culture poured over it since the renaissance," a culminating neo-Dantean vision (*XIV–XVI*) turns Dante's Limbo into a Renaissance and post-Renaissance Elysium of "founders, gazing at the mounts of their cities" (*XVI*).

The letter to his father translates Dantean triadic narrative into fugal form:

> Afraid the whole damn poem is rather obscure, especially in frag-
> ments. Have I ever given you outline of main scheme ::: or whatever
> it is?
> 1. Rather like, or unlike subject and response and counter subject
> in fugue.
> A. A. Live man goes down into world of Dead
> C. B. The "repeat in history"
> B. C. The "magic moment" or moment of metamorphosis, bust thru
> from quotidien into "divine or permanent world." Gods, etc.

The fugal analogy suggests the combination of concurrency and succession, whether Dante's senses and realms or the documents and Seal of '76. But the musical form demands a resolution or finale and the letters on the left demand a concluding "A. A." for the suggested process of cyclic metamorphosis. In fact, a fourth theme, "Gods, etc.," is appended to the end of the third, so that a fourth line would read "A. A. Gods, etc." (this will be corroborated in the frescoes). The letters would then suggest the four suits and the Calendar tabulation read down for inspiration, and up for building, while the themes would state the Calendar phase and the cycle unfolding toward realization. The distinction between a third and a fourth is that between a process of meta-morphosis from "quotidien" to " 'divine or permanent world,' " and elabora-tion of the permanent world as "Gods, etc." For Pound "Gods" are perfected states of mind. The new "A. A. Gods, etc." signifies how a live man has metamorphosed the historical "states of mind" of the dead via natural and justicial "states of mind" into imaginative "states of mind" symbolized by "Gods, etc." Though the terms are religious like Dante's, the modes are all human.

In fact, Pound went on to illustrate the main outline by adducing from *XX* a recapitulation of all European myth and history in the whirling Renaissance mind of Duke Niccolò d'Este of Ferrara, whose successor Duke Borso com-pleted the Palazzo Schifanoia and its Room of the Months. Este's mind con-summates Dantean trine in Renaissance tetrad, revealing a cycle building an historical mind. Este's mind is a model for Pound's as the Schifanoia frescoes are a discovery of what Pound had already done in his own Seal/Calendar form.

If we apply the fugal form to '76, the letters represent the Seal abstracted and the themes represent the revolutionary phases made archetypal. Themati-cally "A. A. Live man goes down into world of Dead" represents discovery and the Declaration "to be unity"; the mode is historical events, which happen only once. "C. B. The 'repeat in history' " represents colonization and struggle toward the dual Preambles; the mode is nature, the mode of living men, through whom history may repeat itself in similar form but in different substance (i.e., by metamorphosis). "B. C. The 'magic moment' or moment of metamorphosis, bust thru from quotidien into 'divine or permanent world' " represents revolution aimed at founding (the Constitutions in trine), which metamorphose the previous phases into the transcendant mode of permanently instituted justice. "A. A. Gods, etc." represents continuing revolution or one tetradic process activated by the Bill of Rights and perfected by the Bill and the tetradic Seal; the mode is religion, a religion of the creative poetic imagination.

In his account, before coming to the frescoes, Yeats corroborates many formal aspects of *The Cantos* as so far described. Many of his separate descriptions, however, are incomplete, and together they do not add up to any coherent whole. He seems to corroborate the metaphor of dealing out card suits, which appear in the illustrations to *I–IV* and in at least one verbal arcanum before emerging in the Seal/Calendar arcanum. He cites 100 cantos, though Pound had previously cited "100 or 120," his alternatives.[31] When the hundredth canto was finished, the poem would "display a structure like a Bach Fugue," though clearly that form is revealed at the beginning in the concurrent and successive voices. The poem would have "no plot, no chronicle of events, no logic of discourse"—obviously Pound did not confide to Yeats his historical "curves of time" and the logics of '76. Instead of these conventional forms it would have "two themes, the Descent into Hades from Homer, a Metamorphosis from Ovid, and, mixed with these, medieval or modern historical characters." Homer and Ovid indeed provide "halves of a seal" in *I* and *II*, but medieval and Renaissance poetry in *III* and *IV* complete Seal-vision *I–IV*. Yeats does not pick up the fourfold form of Mediterranean mythic history taking Renaissance form while being inherited as a modern tradition.

Yeats reports thus Pound's effort to explain how these characteristics and themes were being deployed dynamically:

> He has scribbled on the back of an envelope certain sets of letters that represent emotions or archetypal events—I cannot find any adequate definition—A B C D and then J K L M, and then each set of letters repeated, and then A B C D inverted and this repeated, and then a new element X Y Z, then certain letters that never recur, and then all sorts of combinations of X Y Z and J K L M and A B C D and D C B A, and all set whirling together.

The four groups of letters suggest beginning, middle, end, and everything in between. Presentation in sequence, with repetitions and inversions, may sug-

---

31. To Felix E. Schelling, 9 July 1922, *Letters*.

gest fugal concurrency and sequence. Inversion may suggest descent and ascent. Whirling suggests all being drawn into the cyclic revolutionary mind. Knowing the Seal/Calendar form and the forms it takes gives the description a certain chaotic intelligibility, but without these it creates only confusion.

Pound must have known his dynamic description was confusing, for he turned from it to the Schifanoia analogy, the kind of architectural end toward which the dynamic mind works:

> He has shown me upon the wall a photograph of a Cosimo Tura deco-
> ration in three compartments, in the upper the Triumph of Love and the
> Triumph of Chastity, in the middle Zodiacal signs, and in the lower cer-
> tain events in Cosimo Tura's day. The Descent and the Metamorphosis—
> A B C D and J K L M—his fixed elements, took the place of the Zodiac,
> the archetypal persons—X Y Z—that of the Triumphs, and certain
> modern events—his letters that do not recur—that of those events
> in Cosimo Tura's day.

The frescoes show descent and ascent, with ascent a metamorphosis from "quotidien" to "Gods, etc." as in the 1927 fugal letter. But why the Descent should appear in the middle with the Metamorphosis instead of at the bottom or beginning (as it does in *The Cantos*) is unclear. In fact, everything is viti-ated by the fact that while Yeats saw (at least describes) three compartments, the bottom compartment consists of two parts, giving the complement of four and so according the frescoes properly with Pound's form. (The illustration below gives March, presided over by Minerva; Yeats was looking at March and April, the latter presided over by Venus.)

In a 1958 interview, asked about Yeats's citation of a fugue and of the frescoes as structural patterns for *The Cantos*, Pound described the frescoes (see below, pp. 68, 74) and explained:

> his idea of fugue was very vague so he can't have known what the hell
> I was talking about. And the Schifanoia Frescoes I discovered after I
> had done something similar. The Schifanoia does give—there is an
> analogy there. That is to say, you've got the contemporary life, you've
> got the seasons, you've got the Zodiac and you have the *Triumphs*
> of Petrarch in different belts—I mean, that's the only sort of map or
> suggestion of a map. No, the Schifanoia, that might give a clue, but I
> don't think Yeats knew what a fugue was . . . the analogy there would
> create more confusion than light.[32]

History, nature, cosmic order (the source of justice), and the gods presiding over human arts square with the four themes of all Pound's arcana, both in *The Cantos* and out. The four belts moving around the Room of the Months,

---

32. "An Interview with Ezra Pound" by D. G. Bridson, edited from a BBC broadcast of 1959, in *New Directions in Prose & Poetry 17* (New York: 1961).

analogous to the Seal symbols and voices articulated by the concurrent documents, in effect build the four-tiered frescoes and thence, figuratively, the new building. The "something similar" Pound had done is the Calendar derived from the tiered Seal.

Finally, Yeats mentioned "the mathematical structure" and speculated that "when taken up into imagination" (which Pound's poem works toward) it might appear "more than mathematical, that seemingly irrelevant details" might "fit together into a single theme." They never did. But while Yeats's descriptions cannot be put together in themselves, the Seal/Calendar form clarifies each one and their relations like a circle emerging from tangents, or like "the rose in the steel dust," or like '76 informing *The Cantos*.

This Renaissance "clue" rises in Pound's eyes according to the European nature evolving by act, observe, and believe to Amor or "ELEUSIS." Its Chinese counterpart is a graphic "clue" sent to George Santayana about 1951.[33] Below (p. 74), a process descends from the single ideogram *tuan*[1], to Pound's eye a virtual picture of halves of the Seal (left and right) and also of the Eagle (left) building a rising Mount upon a rooted shield (right). Descending from the ideogram yields (*Rock-Drill 85*):

THE FOUR TUAN[1]

Or foundations.

Ascending builds the ideogram. As noted earlier, the "Confucian Four TUAN" were familiar to Pound by 1915 in Ernest Fenollosa's account of a Ban-Gumi or series of Noh plays.

The European process is that of a voluntarist intelligence and the Chinese process is ethical. The American process is the political process of '76 and its corresponding "clue" is the Seal. The three processes are universalized in the poetic process of the Calendar for a new era. To complete a universal four we may juxtapose the four-tiered fresco, the tiered "Four TUAN," the Seal, and the Calendar. We see, in the sequence of *The Cantos*, Eleusinian historical revolution, Confucian ethical revolution, and American political revolution, all universalized in world religious revolution.

The three cultures also provide three epic traditions consummated in the world tradition of *The Cantos*. In Homer's *Odyssey* intelligence opens up past history "to be unity." Ovid's *Metamorphoses* explore psychological types or types of personality defined by transformation from human nature into general nature, or from an old state of being to a new; both changes of external forms

33. To George Santayana, 1951, Humanities Center at Texas.

EUROPE: Schifanoia frescoes (March)

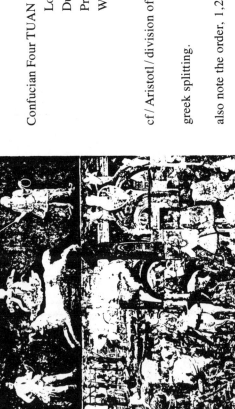

CHINA: Confucian Four TUAN

端

Places you start to build from
principles, or if analyzing
clues.

1

2

3

4

Confucian Four TUAN

Love

Duty

Propriety

Wisdom.

cf / Aristotl / division of faculties (teXne   in Nicomac/
omitted in Mag/Moralia.

greek splitting.

also note the order, 1,2,3,4

AMERICA: Seal of the United States

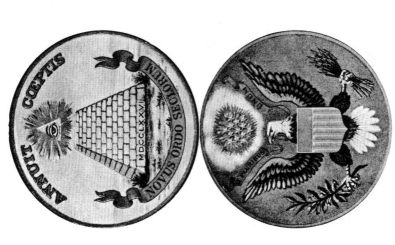

WORLD: Calendar

YEAR 1 p. s. U.

1921-1922
Old Style

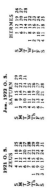

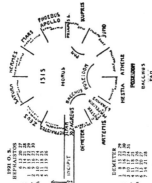

THE LITTLE REVIEW CALENDAR

(inner states remain constant), and cultural change from the Greek mind to the Roman, result in "duality." Dante's *Divina Commedia* subsumes history and spiritual change in triadic justice, and the Greek and the Roman minds in the medieval. The Renaissance produced consummating works like Malatesta's Tempio or the Schifanoia frescoes, which subsume the modes of tradition, personality, and justice in art. The principle of change in each work and mind and the changes from one to the other manifest the all-suffusing, all-embracing revolutionary theme.

For China, Pound altered the traditional Confucian "four books" and their order by translating from 1928 to 1954 his own Confucian canon. Though all the works deal with social and political ethics, the *Ta Hsio* or *Great Learning* stresses tradition, the *Lun Yu* or *Analects* stresses Confucius's personality as a teacher among his disciples, the *Chung Yung* or *Unwobbling Pivot* stresses government, and the *Shih Ching* or *Odes* is Confucius's anthology of Chinese poetry. All themes run through all the books, but the *Odes* appear in and provide explicit authority for all before taking their own form as the culminating book.

Behind Pound's choice of his European epic tradition lies what it anticipated, an American unfinished tradition consisting of Joel Barlow's *Columbiad*, Walt Whitman's *Leaves of Grass*, and Pound's *Cantos* as a third American epic and as a first world epic (also American). The *Columbiad* surveys American history and its myth in the context of world history of the past and future. It is an epic of the intelligence applied to the arts and sciences. It emphasizes discovery and the Declaration. Barlow's mind and his achievements in his political and poetic writing caused him to be named President Madison's official ambassador to Russia and former President Jefferson's unofficial courier to Paris, a mission referred to in the keynote Canto *XXXI*; Pound thought such a mission ought to have been entrusted to him by the American presidents of his time. That is Pound's only mention of Barlow, but the major themes of his poem permeate *The Cantos* everywhere, especially in the first phase.

Leaves of Grass is the epic of the New World personality emerging from Old World personality. Its mode is nature newly apprehended on the new continent. In Pound's view it is the epic of colonization—the Manifest Destiny of the continent—and of personal struggle—the Civil War, in which Whitman participated as chronicler, nurse, and poet. Pound focuses the same modes and roles, especially in *Pisan*, where he chronicles a phase of twentieth-century history from among his fellow prisoners and turns chronicle and autobiography into poetry. Whitman of course paid his tributes to the Old World, to the "organic compacts" of '76, and to the arts and sciences; he looked ahead to justice and poetry perfected in America for the whole world. But the essence of his theme is personality in nature and the will of "WE the people"—of the people of Democracy beyond the listed motives of the

Preamble. That is why Pound mentions him and concentrates his spirit in *Pisan*.[34]

There can be no doubt that Pound is the explicit poet of the Revolution of '76 and of world revolution, that *The Cantos* stress and adopt in detail the documents and symbol of '76, and that the main document is the body of the Constitution. It is Pound who is at work on revolutionary founding and who emerges in the third or Constitutional phase free to use the tradition because he is shaping it and being shaped by it, and free to act as the revolutionary personality because he has become its medium. The same would be even truer of the consummation of world tradition, world personality, and world justice in a world epic of continuing revolution if Pound and his poem had not encountered the intractabilities found and faced in *Drafts & Fragments*. Still, ''it''—the dream—''coheres all right / even if my notes''—the last draft and phase or the whole *Cantos*?—''do not cohere'' (Canto *CXVI*).

34. A subsequently written book—''. . . *what I was pleased to do'' : Walt Whitman's Making of Leaves of Grass 1855–1881*—deals in Chapter 10, ''American Epic,'' with some relations among Barlow's, Whitman's, and Pound's uses of the American myth.

CHAPTER FIVE

THE INTEGRITY OF A

VISION: INTERNAL ARCANA

The "Seal" Illustrations 1925 and 1928

"[The] 'algebraic relation'. . . is the language of philosophy. IT MAKES NO PICTURE. This kind of statement applies to a lot of facts, but it does not grip hold of Heaven."
   "Vorticism" 1914

Insofar as single cantos refer to Constitutional constituents, as four-phase subjects refer to the Seal, as ten-canto drafts and ten drafts refer to the process and documents of '76, and as all refer to the Seal/Calendar form, everything in *The Cantos* is arcanum. But there are many special arcana, both textual and visual. The first three of these were the illustrations to the deluxe folios of 1925 and 1928. All but one were dropped for *XXX CANTOS* of 1930, and subsequent drafts had one or two visual symbols until Chinese ideograms entered more profusely with "KUNG" and "JOHN ADAMS." Still, these seemed only to highlight the texts and to carry no special form or meaning. In *Pisan*, however, ideograms take on a special symbolic function from a profusion in *Pisan LXXVII* and from their gathering into the specially formed and extended coda "Canto 77 Explication." In *Rock-Drill 85* thirteen oversized ideograms form a central vertical axis within a text itself filled with smaller ideograms; *Section: Rock-Drill* also contains the Seal/Calendar arcanum. The "rock-drill" of *85* and the Seal/Calendar arcanum apply in particular to a third phase, *Los Cantares*, subsuming the first and second while projecting a fourth. *Drafts & Fragments* has few ideograms, but those too take a significant form.

   In general the deluxe illustrations reflected the Seal, which was and is expressed textually in the Seal-vision *I–IV* as the first elaborated four-phase subject. Removal threw the emphasis onto decads and drafts, the major constituents of the poem. The shield stripes symbolizing the Declaration simply took the form of drafts; hence the relative scarcity of visual symbols in the first phase *LXXI Cantos*. But the drafts are also drafts emphasizing personae for the Preambles; these take the visual form of the stars of the constellation, so that each draft is symbolized by one or more stars. This symbolic form is touched by a placard in *XXII* and by ideograms in subsequent drafts of the first phase until drafts symbolized by the stars take the form of the ideograms of *Pisan* and of the coda "Canto 77 Explication."

Each draft is also a tier of the Mount, a form also touched by visual symbols in the first phase and by visual arrangements in *Pisan*; tiers are symbolized by the vertical ideogram-axis of *Rock-Drill 85*, which is in turn refined for phasal drafting and building by the Seal/Calendar arcanum. The drafts as rays of the sun-vision were to be consummated in the fourth phase, which would transform principally the stripes of the shield. The loci for these visual arcana are the first four cantos of each phase, each a Seal-vision in a different mode. This economy, replacing the excessive elaboration of the deluxe illustrations, allows for modulation and metamorphosis over a ten-draft, 120-canto poem. Still, before describing the phasal arcana, it is worthwhile to pay some attention to the cancelled illustrations for their relation to the Calendar.

Illustrations 1925–1930

As might be expected from their relations with the Seal and the Calendar, at least some of the illustrations reflect not only the substance of the text, which as it were realizes the simple heraldic symbol in "verbal manifestation," but also the numerological, geometric, and analytic dimensions, which cannot be reflected in the text and are not. Instead the mathematical dimensions symbolize thematic phases of tradition, personality, justice, and poetry. So they do for the Seal-vision *First*, *Second*, *Third*, and *Fourth*. A tailpiece to *Seventh*, the first predominantly autobiographical and modern canto, makes the mathematical dimensions (and indeed the relation to the Calendar) most evident to the curious eye and mind. *Eighth*, *Ninth*, and *Tenth* illustrate building the Seal edifice and its Calendar equivalent. The remaining illustrations expand the prototypic symbols of a Renaissance tradition toward their analogues in America and China and toward a culminating neo-Dantean heraldry of '76 projecting world revolution.

The illustrated capital to the epitome *First* canto pictures all that the text will imply but only partially narrate, the whole Odyssean voyage from Troy to Ithaca. The ship is shown voyaging from Circe, the daughter of the sun, past a Siren and past benighted Kimmeria, down to Erebus; but it will then return upward and pass between Scylla and Charybdis back to Circe's, after which Odysseus alone will find refuge in Phaeacia and finally return to Ithaca. The order of the *Odyssey* is somewhat violated by the compression, which is deliberate and necessary. The compression accentuates the Seal symbolism. The ship is the Eagle and Erebus is the shield. The ship's crew are persons

ᴛᕼᴇ ᴀɪʀsᴛ ᴄᴀɴᴛᴏ

ND then went down to the ship,
Set keel to breakers, forth on the godly sea, and
We set up mast and sail on that swart ship,
Bore sheep aboard her, and our bodies also
Heavy with weeping, and winds from sternward
Bore us out onward with bellying canvas,   Νέκυομαντεία
Circe's this craft, the trim-coifed goddess.
Then sat we amidships, wind-jamming the tiller,
Thus with stretched sail, we went over sea till **day's end.**
Sun to his slumber, shadows o'er all the ocean,
Came we then to the bounds of deepest water,
To the Kimmerian lands, and peopled cities
Covered with close-webbed mist, unpierced ever
With glitter of sun-rays;
Nor with stars stretched, nor looking back from heaven,
Swartest night stretched over wretched men there.

symbolized by the constellation; the figure praying to the sun is the Eagle and central star. The ship must "bust thru" the lower half of the "A" and strike a balance between Scylla and Charybdis, symbols of retributive justice. The sun shining above the Charybdis-Mount symbolizes both Circe's and Ithaca. The personae in the ship project *Second*, the Scylla and Charybdis Mount projects *Third*, and the sun projects *Fourth*. The capital is entirely heraldic and traditional, only symbolizing the other dimensions and modes.

In the *Second* capital, moving cyclically, the ship subsumes *First*, the accentuated troubador keynotes *Second*, seawaves taking the form of a Mount project *Third*, and a metamorphosis of the ship by a god projects *Fourth*. The troubador juggling six symbols represents the Eagle with the constellation above his head and the central star. The six symbols represent six parts of *First* transformed for the Preamble (see pp. 18–19). The troubador's arms and head represent the Preamble reversed in the three phases of the second hemi-cycle. Diamonds and clubs on the troubador's coat (above and below his waist) suggest a medial vertical axis topped by the juggling-circle (heart) and founded on the legs (spade). The mast uniting the ship with metamorphosis of it (also the first and fourth of the cyclic symbols) suggests the same axis on the

THE
SECOND
CANTO

ANG it all, Robert Browning,
  there can be but the one "Sordello";
  So-shu churned in the sea,
  Seal sports in the spray-whited circles of cliff-wash,
  Sleek head, daughter of Lir,
    eyes of Picasso,
  Under black fur-hood, lithe daughter of Ocean;
  And the wave runs in the beach-groove:
"Eleanor, ἑλέναυς and ἑλέπτολις!"

left. Overall the illustration has the shape of the second realized phase, the club. The six symbols extend heraldry to numerology. The troubador stresses personality. Interpretations could be extended, but the text is there for that.

Gods ruling an orderly mythic nature—sky, land, and waters—symbolize in the *Third* capital ideal justice. The illustration framed by the "I," the caption, and the text has the geometrical proportion of a Golden Section, the symbol for drafting and building the tiered Mount. Ideal justice turns to bad weather in a tailpiece, but the enclosing triangle is the form for building Pound's actual, material Mount as a triangle of triangles.

The *Fourth* capital begins with Diana and her nymphs bathing in their grove and runs down both sides of the page. On the left Cabestan's lady tries to fly from a window (the "triangular space" of Providence) but is falling; the tail of the "P," having begun with the goddess and the lady, descends to a

THE THIRD CANTO

SAT on the Dogana's steps
For the gondolas cost too much, that year,
And there were not "those girls," there was one face,
And the Bucintoro twenty yards off, howling "Stretti,"
And the lit cross-beams, that year, in the Morosini,
And peacocks in Koré's house, or there may have been.
Float:
       Gods float in the azure air,
Bright gods and Tuscan, back before dew was shed.
Light: and the first light, before ever dew was fallen.
Panisks, and from the oak, dryas,
And from the apple, maelid,
Through all the wood, and the leaves were full of voices,
A-whisper, and the clouds bowe over the lake,
And there are gods upon them,
And in the water, the almond-white swimmers,
The silvery water glazes the upturned nipple.
    Scarabs, green veins in the turquoise,
Or gray steps, lead up under the cedars.

Palazzo
dei Leoni

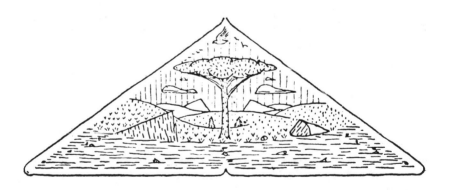

spade. On the right Diana sends the dogs after Actaeon changed to a stag.
Below a spade runs through a circle (the cycle) to a heart. This is all heraldic.
But in a tailpiece, fishtails focusing toward a center from which others are
expanding define circles or spirals expanding or contracting within a square.

THE FOURTH CANTO

ALACE in smoky light,
Troy but a heap of smouldering boundary stones,
ANAXIFORMINGES! Aurunculeia!
Hear me. Cadmus of Golden Prows!
The silver mirrors catch the bright stones and flare,
Dawn, to our waking, drifts in the green cool light;
Dew-haze blurs, in the grass, pale ankles moving.
Beat, beat, whirr, thud, in the soft turf
           under the apple trees,
Choros nympharum, goat-foot, with the pale foot alternate;
Crescent of blue-shot waters, green-gold in the shallows,
A black cock crows in the sea-foam;

And by the curved, carved foot of the couch,
      claw-foot and lion head, an old man seated,
Speaking in the low drone . . . .
             Ityn!
Et ter flebiliter, Ityn, Ityn!
And she went toward the window and cast her down,
     "All the while, the while, swallows crying:
Ityn!
     "It is Cabestan's heart in the dish."
     "It is Cabestan's heart in the dish?
     "No other taste shall change this."
And she went toward the window,
               the slim white stone bar
Making a double arch;
Firm even fingers held to the firm pale stone;
Swung for a moment,
            and the wind out of Rhodez
Caught in the full of her sleeve.
         . . . the swallows crying :
    B*i*

Geometric is being varied by analytic for multiplicit creation. The tailpiece "seals" a vision completed by the "whirling squares" of Golden Section expansion. It also happens to have the shape of Egyptian *shen*, symbol of eternity.

The capitals of *Fifth*, *Sixth*, and *Seventh* are more simply heraldic and confined to their texts, though *Seventh* contains much suggestive symbolism. In phasal projection of the Seal-vision *First* projects *First–Sixth* and *Second* projects the *Seventh* tailpiece, a complete medieval-Renaissance symbol of the revolutionary mind as a fortune wheel. Its importance as a locus for techniques used partially in other capitals and tailpieces is emphasized not only by its place at the end of the first contemporary and personal canto but also by its having been embossed on a copy of the deluxe folio which Pound had bound for himself in 1932.[1] By this placing it introduced an image of what Pound was seeking, a book suggesting a medieval illuminated manuscript given the form of a Renaissance printed folio. It reflected his theory that "the modern mind is the medieval mind with wash after wash of classical culture poured over it since the Renaissance." It also unites heraldic, numerological, geometric, and analytic.

The relation to the troubador's cycle of *Second* is self-evident. Heraldically the spokes symbolize the stripes of the shield while reflecting an eight-appendaged Eagle (tail, legs, wings, halves of the banner E PLURIBUS UNUM, and head—a skeptic may refer to the design on the helmet of the

---

1. At Trinity College, Hartford, Conn.

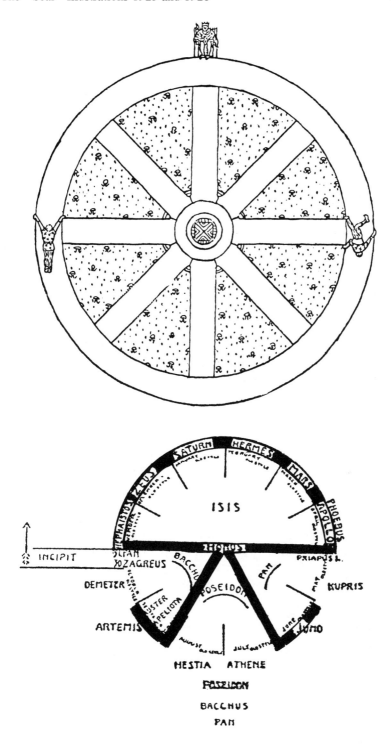

horseman in the *XXVII* tailpiece, below p. 97. The field between or showing through the spokes reveals dotted phenomena being precipitated into mushroomlike stars the pattern of which is the Calendar cycle demarcated into four phases; the figure implies the pentagram Eagle while foreshadowing the hexagram constellation and the Mount built on the shield foundation. Taken together spokes and stars symbolize a dynamic prophecy of Old Glory from the older glory of the Renaissance tradition. On the wheel rim troubadors descend and climb; above the wheel rim the king presides in seeming permanence, but he must achieve a justice that incorporates change in order to keep his place.

Numerologically the phenomena and the four-phase stars work with the eight spokes. Geometry is self-evident. Analytics and building inhere in the proportions of the mathematically patterned axle extended by concentric circles to a hub, to a ring just beyond the intersection of the spokes with the hub, to the wheel rim.[2] These are also proportioned to the widths of the spokes and the wheel rim, which in turn is a function of the eccentric arm of the Calendar and of the ''INCIPIT''-arrow, a module both for creating the fortune wheel and for building the Calendar. All the heraldry, numerology, geometry, and analytics are carefully worked out to make the fortune wheel and the Calendar (both cycle and tabulation) functions of each other working from the same center. The technique and the proof are mathematical, but can be easily done by anyone who is familiar with such mathematical construction. It would be too detailed to be rehearsed here.[3]

The ensuing four Malatesta cantos, the first sustained subject of *The Cantos*, historicize the mythic Seal-vision with a Renaissance effort. *Eighth*, *Ninth*, and *Tenth*, however, complete the decad of Renaissance revolution architecturally. *Eighth* and *Ninth* have been projected by the geometry of the *Third* and (from its text) by its Mounts being sat on, climbed, and descended.

The *Eighth* is the nearest to the Schifanoia frescoes. A painter stands on the floor of the Tempio Malatestiano. Having painted Malatesta paying tribute to the holy Roman emperor, he is working on a painting of Malatestan architecture. The third tier, a completed battle scene, depicts ironically Renaissance politics and order. The fourth tier is a pair of mullioned windows. Each glass is dual and four-tiered and each is crowned with a glass that joins each into a whole (cf. the Providential window of *Fourth*). The designs (cf. ''Gods float in the azure air,'' *III*) direct attention respectively down from God (the left) and up to God (the right). The windows both deliver and consummate a

2. Of this new *''forma mentis''* he wrote later ''We no longer think or need to think in terms of monolinear logic, the sentence structure, subject, predicate, object, etc. We are capable or almost as capable as the biologist of thinking thoughts that join like the spokes in a wheel-hub and that fuse in hyper-geometric amalgams'' (''Epstein, Belgion and Meaning,'' *Criterion*, London, April 1930).

3. The mathematics is described somewhat more fully in ''The Mathematical Symbolism of Ezra Pound's Revolutionary Mind,'' *Paideuma*, Spring & Fall 1978.

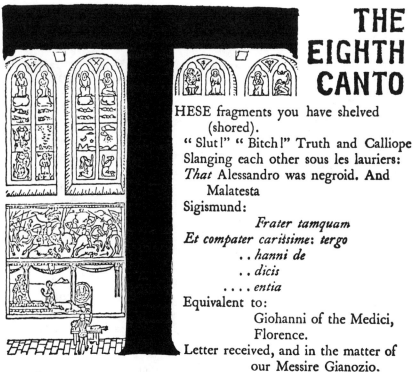

THE EIGHTH CANTO

HESE fragments you have shelved
        (shored).
" Slut!" " Bitch!" Truth and Calliope
Slanging each other sous les lauriers:
That Alessandro was negroid. And
        Malatesta
Sigismund:
                    Frater tamquam
        Et compater carissime: tergo
                    . . hanni de
                    . . dicis
                    . . . . entia
Equivalent to:
                    Giohanni of the Medici,
                    Florence.
Letter received, and in the matter of
                    our Messire Gianozio,
One from him also, sent on in form and with all due dispatch,
Having added your wishes and memoranda.

fourfold inspiration. The top of the next chapel begins to realize a text of Seal-inspired poetry; Malatesta's letter to Medici is indeed "sealed" by the salutation (front) and by a fragmented rear ("*tergo*").

The *Ninth* illustrates transporting stone for the Tempio dominated by Malatesta's sculptured tomb (in one of the chapels).

The *Tenth* capital, encompassing the whole first page (cf. the *Fourth* and this fourth phase of the decad), is a triumphant architectural commemoration. The architrave (symbolizing the stripes) entitles "The Tenth Canto." The frieze shows Malatesta's life in thirteen images (the constellation) centered by the burning of his effigy by the Roman Catholic Church, which convicted him as a pagan, a heretic, even an anti-Christ. The facade images Renaissance political history as a siege of a fortress-Mount, again an irony. The fortress's tower is open to the heavens, but the triangular roof closes it in. The whole reads up or down while heading a Malatestan text "between the two columns," an image to be sustained through *XXX Cantos* for Renaissance treachery and luxury (especially Venetian).

ᏦᏂᎬ ᏁᏆᏁᏖᏂ ᏟᎯᏁᏖᎾ

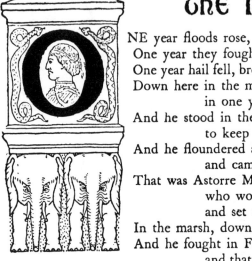

NE year floods rose,
One year they fought in the snows,
One year hail fell, breaking the trees and walls.
Down here in the marsh they trapped him
        in one year,
And he stood in the water up to his neck
        to keep the hounds off him,
And he floundered about in the marsh
        and came in after three days,
That was Astorre Manfredi of Faenza
        who worked the ambush
        and set the dogs off to find him,
In the marsh, down here under Mantua,
And he fought in Fano, in a street fight,
        and that was nearly the end of him;

The *Tenth* is sealed in the middle by a Poundian concoction from several Malatestan seals. A version of the eagle and shield introduces a Papal account of the burning of Malatesta's effigy, a self-condemning banner issuing from its mouth, on the steps of St. Peter's. The shield commemorates the union of Sigismundo and his inspiring mistress (later third wife) Isotta, for whom he built the Tempio, or symbolizes Malatesta's Renaissance versus Christendom's, which extends medievalism beyond its flowering to political violence and religious tyranny. The elephant (which also supported Malatesta's tomb in the *Ninth*) is the dominant animal symbol in the Tempio; as Malatesta's Eagle it holds in its trunk at Isotta's tomb a banner inscribed with Isotta's motto "Tempus loquendi, tempus tacendi," which will carry the Renaissance spirit via Columbus to "Nuevo Mundo" and to the revolution of '76 (cf. the opening lines of "Jefferson-Nuevo Mundo"). A decad of Renaissance revolution ends when the providential Eagle validates the Malatestan tradition against the Pope's and warring Christendom's.

As an historical Seal-vision the Malatesta cantos turn *First–Seventh* into a twentieth-century inheritance of a Renaissance tradition by "mass relations" while themselves defining revolutionary personality on the Renaissance model. In this perspective Malatestan tradition (*Eighth*), Malatestan contemporary chronicle (*Ninth*), and Malatestan justice (*Tenth*) are set against their ortho-

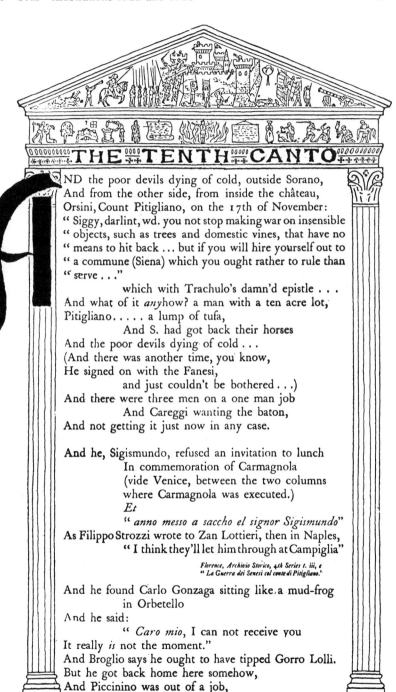

THE ✠ TENTH ✠ CANTO

AND the poor devils dying of cold, outside Sorano,
And from the other side, from inside the château,
Orsini, Count Pitigliano, on the 17th of November:
" Siggy, darlint, wd. you not stop making war on insensible
" objects, such as trees and domestic vines, that have no
" means to hit back ... but if you will hire yourself out to
" a commune (Siena) which you ought rather to rule than
" serve . . ."
              which with Trachulo's damn'd epistle . . .
And what of it *anyhow?* a man with a ten acre lot,
Pitigliano. . . . . a lump of tufa,
              And S. had got back their horses
And the poor devils dying of cold . . .
(And there was another time, you know,
He signed on with the Fanesi,
              and just couldn't be bothered . . .)
And there were three men on a one man job
              And Careggi wanting the baton,
And not getting it just now in any case.

And he, Sigismundo, refused an invitation to lunch
              In commemoration of Carmagnola
              (vide Venice, between the two columns
              where Carmagnola was executed.)
              Et
       " *anno messo a saccho el signor Sigismundo*"
As Filippo Strozzi wrote to Zan Lottieri, then in Naples,
       " I think they'll let him through at Campiglia"

              Florence, Archivio Storico, 4th Series t. iii, e
              " *La Guerra dei Senesi col conte di Pitigliano.*'

And he found Carlo Gonzaga sitting like a mud-frog
              in Orbetello
And he said:
       " *Caro mio*, I can not receive you
It really *is* not the moment."
And Broglio says he ought to have tipped Gorro Lolli.
But he got back home here somehow,
And Piccinino was out of a job,

NTEREA PRO GRADIBUS BASILICÆ S. PIETRI
EX ARIDA MATERIA INGENS PYRA EXTRÚITUR IN
CUJUS SUMMITATE IMAGO SIGISMUNDI COLLOCATUR
HOMINIS LINEAMENTA, ET VESTIMENTI MODUM ADEO
PROPRIE REDDENS, UT VERA MAGIS PERSONA, QUAM
IMAGO VIDERETUR; NE QUEM TAMEN IMAGO
FALLERET, ET SCRIPTURA EX ORE PRODIIT, QUÆ
DICERET: SIGISMUNDUS HIC EGO SUM
MALATESTA, FILIUS PANDULPHI, REX PRODITORUM,
DEO ATQUE HOMINIBUS INFESTUS, SACRI CENSURA
SENATUS IGNI DAMNATUS;

                                              SCRIPTURUM

MULTI LEGERUNT. DEINDE ASTANTE POPULO, IGNI
IMMISSO, ET PYRA SIMULACRUM REPENTE FLAGRAVIT.
                          COM. PIO II. LIV. VII, P. 85
                          YRIARTE, P. 288

dox counterparts; the Malatestan testament perfected as poetry is set against orthodoxy in *Eleventh*.

The *Eleventh* capital expands diagonally in circles to a ring commemorating Malatesta (cf. the Calendar cycle) and to a rectangular frame (cf. the Calendar tabulation). The circles evolve four scenes: a petitioner approaches a ruler beneath windows like those of *Fourth* and *Eighth*; a mounted army approaches a city; a galley rows from one coastal city toward another; sea-

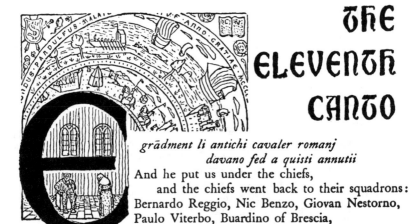

THE
ELEVENTH
CANTO

grādment li antichi cavaler romanj
davano fed a quisti annutii
And he put us under the chiefs,
        and the chiefs went back to their squadrons:
Bernardo Reggio, Nic Benzo, Giovan Nestorno,
Paulo Viterbo, Buardino of Brescia,
        Cetho Brandolino,

going ships break an oceanic horizon. The ships imply the coming voyages of discovery though the ring and frame hold the scope here to Renaissance Italy. The first lines of the text (repeating the last of *Tenth*) refer to the providential Eagle—cf. "quisti annutii" and ANNUIT COEPTIS—or Malatesta's Rome versus Christendom's.

The *Twelfth* and *Thirteenth* look beyond Renaissance Italy and the horizon to America in the West and to China in the East (or, by circumnavigation, further west). A perverted American paradise and a genuine Chinese paradise constitute a third phase (halves of a seal) which extends the Renaissance spirit to the other major civilizations of the world. The *Twelfth* capital (not shown here) shows American commerce moving out from the New York skyline and the Statue of Liberty, to Constantinople and further east. It also shows a beached ship whose cargo of corn is salvaged to fatten pigs for the market. The consequence of the vignettes is a rain of money down the whole left side of the page, a symbol of plutocratic America's God Mammon as its contribution to the rest of the world (displacing the heritage of '76). The *Thirteenth* capital illustrates a Confucian paradise beneath a tentlike canopy of flowers; within it a sage practices instruction and music. As a third phase the two cantos symbolize the Branches of the Constitution perverted but amendable by new Powers not yet operative in the western mind.

Capitals *XIV*, *XV*, and the *Sixteenth* try to perfect a Dantean form of the first three phases in a neo-Dantean or Renaissance cosmos opening up toward a world historical "paradiso terrestre." A tetradic form tries to turn the mythic Seal-vision (*I–IV*) historicized by the Malatestan Seal-vision (*VIII–XI*) into a Seal-vision fusing myth and history. The *XIV*, *XV*, and *Sixteenth* capitals consummate the Seal / Calendar heraldry, numerology, and geometry, if not in analytics, in symbols that include the revolutionary process carried out through the documents of '76.

The "XIV" surmounts the hell mouth of the *XIV* capital, which transforms *First*, as a unity (a Statue of Liberty). It divides into triangular eye-bumps containing the eyes of a perverted Eagle (later to be defined as Geryon, or Fraud) and of a perverted Providence (later to be defined as Usura). These halves of a seal expand with the tusks to four. The tusks also flank on a hemicyclic upper lip eight teeth, forming with them a perverted symbol of the ten-part Declaration; the lower jaw holds ten teeth representing on the horizontal diameter the rest of the cycle and symbolizing a perverted activating Bill of Rights. Interaction of the inaugurating Declaration and the consummating Bill makes the Seal symbolism dynamic through the Calendar cycle. The sea monsters in a striped sea pervert the gods and goddesses (motives of the Preambles). The seven-tentacled figure between the two upper front teeth symbolizes a perverted Constitution.

The wheel of the *XV* capital transforms the troubador's circle of *Second* and the fortune wheel of the second phase of the decad (*Seventh*). The "XV" governs the center like HORUS or like the central star of the constellation.

O vieni in luogo d'ogni luce muto;
The stench of wet coal, politicians
. . . . .e and . . . . . .n, their wrists bound to
            their ankles,
Standing bare bum,
Faces smeared on their rumps,
            wide eye on flat buttock,
Bush hanging for beard,
            Addressing crowds through their arse-holes,
Addressing the multitudes in the ooze,
            newts, water-slugs, water-maggots,
And with them . . . . . . r,
            a scrupulously clean table-napkin
Tucked under his penis,
            and . . . . m
Who disliked colloquial language,
Stiff-starched, but soiled, collars
            circumscribing his legs,
The pimply and hairy skin
            pushing over the collar's edge,
Profiteers drinking blood sweetened with shit,
And behind them . . . . f and the financiers
            lashing them with steel wires.

For the Preambles the second hemicycle is opened up and the sea monsters recur, but now whirling in concentric circles.

HE saccharescent, lying in glucose,
the pompous in cotton wool
                    with a stench like the fats at Grasse,
the great scabrous arse-hole, shitting flies,
                    rumbling with imperialism,
ultimate urinal, middan, pisswallow without a cloaca,
. . . . . .r less rowdy, ... Episcopus
            . . . . .sis,
        head down, screwed into the swill,
his legs waving and pustular,
        a clerical jock-strap hanging back over the navel,
his condom full of black beetles,
        tattoo marks round the anus,
and a circle of lady golfers about him.

For Dantean "trine" the *Sixteenth* transforms three cantos into a composition of a neo-Dantean Hell, Purgatory, and Paradise looking toward a "paradiso terrestre." Hell is hidden behind the doors but is viewed from both Mounts. From the left or west Mount (according to the text) Dante sees Hell in his mirror and Sordello looks on it in his shield (as Pound did in *XV*); St. Augustine gazes toward "the invisible." On the right or east Mount Blake gestures wildly against "the evil" while running from it. The plain between the Mounts depicts pools of purgatorial cleansing and an Elysium of constructive "founders, gazing at the mounts of their cities"; at least one of the founders rises from his pool and heads off upward toward the horizon, presumably to build his city.

THE
SIXTEENTH
CANTO

ND before hell mouth; dry plain
            and two mountains;
On the one mountain, a running form,
            and another
    In the turn of the hill; in hard steel
The road like a slow screw's thread,
The angle almost imperceptible,
            so that the circuit seemed hardly to rise;

The west Mount, a focusing spiral of ten left-handed threads, symbolizes the Declaration rising in the dark of the containing "A" as an expression of revolution inaugurated by the contemplative life of philosophy. The east Mount, a focusing spiral of ten right-handed threads interacting with the west Mount, symbolizes the activating, consummating Bill of Rights rising in the light under the free heavens where birds fly. The figures represent the motives of the Preambles. The form of the Mounts is that of the "bust thru" of the third phase. The two Mounts thus manifest the dichotomies of the interacting, self-amending Constitution spread over the ten-part evolution. The various cycles of the foregoing cantos have taken this form for building.

The mediating scene combines the climb of Dante's Purgatory toward a Christian "paradiso terrestre" with a climb toward an historical "paradiso terrestre" beyond contemplative Paradiso. With his Mounts and his climb Pound is trying to restore the vitality of the medieval mind by mixing it with '76 and Confucianism.[4] Within the text, however, historical "paradiso terrestre" devolves into World War I and the necessary but equivocal Russian revolution.

Though "paradiso terrestre" cannot be pictured within the concluding nightmare of the first draft, the first capital of the second draft images a mythic antecedent. In the XVII capital Diana directs her hounds not after Actaeon but after a rabbit, which leads toward an ideal city (Venice). Otherwise the hunt

---

4. See the interpretation in Chapter Ten, pp. 171–72.

THE
XVII
CANTO

O THAT THE
vines burst from my
fingers
And the bees weighted
with pollen
Move heavily in the
vine-shoots:
chirr—chirr—chir-rikk—
a purring sound,
And the birds sleepily in the branches.
ZAGREUS! IO ZAGREUS!

and the rapes of the lower vignette carry the epitome *Second* into the keynotes for the second draft of four in "ELEUSIS" and of ten in the whole poem.

The illustrations for the deluxe *XVI. Cantos* were executed by a young American artist then in Paris, Henry L. Strater, in cooperation with William Bird, the American publisher of the Three Mountains Press; both obviously worked under some considerable direction from Pound himself. The illustrations for the deluxe *Cantos 17–27* were executed by Gladys Hynes. They follow the same heraldic conventions derived from the Seal and the same numerological conventions derived from the Seal via the Calendar. But so far as I have been able to determine their geometrical symbols remain merely heraldic and numerological; no mathematical proportions like those of the fortune wheel link these capitals and tailpieces to the construction of the Seal and Calendar. As a prototype *XVI. Cantos* embodies all dimensions in the heraldic. The second draft precipitates numerology from heraldry while only adumbrating constructive geometry and mathematics.

The capitals and tailpieces of *Cantos 17–27* symbolize the three major dimensions of the draft: myth, its consequence Renaissance history, and their joint consequence twentieth-century history; as a result of the derivation from myth the histories are themselves mythified, either as positive symbol or as symbol perverted. Thus the mythic *XVII* capital is ambiguous, as the histories will be. Significant illustrations can be most advantageously cited along with interpretations of the texts. For now the culmination, a myth of the reborn "nuova persona" and a numerological heraldry of the Renaissance projecting '76 from its wars and its personae, will suffice.

The *XXVII* capital consummates the unifying theme of the first two drafts, a nightmare of history relieved only by "in the gloom, the gold gathers the light against it" (*XI, XVII, XXI*). But the Renaissance dream and the effort are reborn through a twentieth-century "colonist" and revolutionary protagonist who has awakened the dead and has himself awakened from the nightmare. While subsuming symbols from many previous headpieces and tailpieces, a mythic capital and a Renaissance tailpiece transform the neo-Dantean '76 of the *XIV, XV,* and *Sixteenth* with emphasis on personae rather than tradition. In the capital an archetypal revolutionary sleeps on a ten-part half-shell symbol-

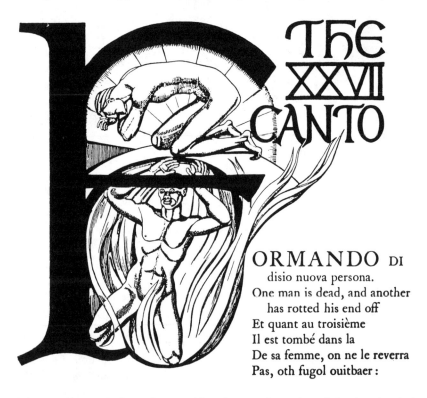

ORMANDO DI
disio nuova persona.
One man is dead, and another
has rotted his end off
Et quant au troisième
Il est tombé dans la
De sa femme, on ne le reverra
Pas, oth fugol ouitbaer :

izing mythic revolution (cf. *XIV*). The sleeper of a cycle and first hemicycle is reborn in the fire of his own passion in a second hemicycle (cf. *XV*). The reborn mind and "nuova persona" signs himself at the end of *The XXVII Canto*, of *XXVII Cantos*, and of two drafts "Explicit Canto XXVII/E.P./*Sep-*

tember 1927," which reads both "Canto XXVII ends" and "Canto XXVII explicates" (cf. the similar colophons of *XXX* and *XXXI* and "Canto 77 Explication").

The achievement is "sealed" by an historical tailpiece that sums up '76 in Renaissance heraldry and numerology, both of which project the impending emergence of '76 and its consequences. The form personalizes that of the *Sixteenth*, two mounts between which a protagonist climbs. It subsumes the sleeper and the "nuova persona" as the *Sixteenth* subsumed *XIV* and *XV*. The foundation, decorated with nine symbols directed from each end toward a

unifying circle, symbolizes the Declaration interacting with the Bill. The flowers on the horse's caparison symbolize the eight-part Preamble projecting the seven-Article Constitution; an analogous symbol of the eight-appendaged Eagle appears on the helmet (in the mind) of the horseman. The flower on the horseman's shield symbolizes a Constitution for new union in three drafts preceding a definitive seven. The flowers on the foot soldiers' shields symbolize a states' rights Constitution in seven definitive drafts followed by three. While the horseman facing west symbolizes the Eagle and his mind, the foot soldiers looking east with Providence symbolize the Constitutional dynamic building from shield to Mount. Both the foundation and the foot soldiers symbolize the hemicyclic and stellar dichotomy that mark the second of four phases.

When the two drafts were collected in *XXX Cantos* (1930) all the illustrations except one in the middle of *XXII* were dropped and the capitals were supplanted by avant-garde Vorticist designs executed by Pound's wife and suggesting ideograms. Each capital is accompanied by a Roman numeral except the capital for *XIII*, whose stylized "K" is followed by ideograms for

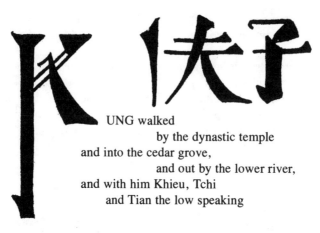

UNG walked
    by the dynastic temple
and into the cedar grove,
    and out by the lower river,
and with him Khieu, Tchi
    and Tian the low speaking

Kun (not K'ung) Fu Tzu drawn to look like ''XIII.'' But Kun, downstroke, drawn erroneously either deliberately or involuntarily, divides the first word of the canto, ''KUNG,'' from Fu Tzu, sage, which looks like ''E P.'' ''KUNG'' and ''E P'' thus constitute halves of a seal within a Chinese-Roman Vorticist palimpsest. After *XXX Cantos* all capitals (past and to come) became simple Roman capitals, as all are now.

CHAPTER SIX

THE INTEGRITY OF A

VISION: INTERNAL EVIDENCE

Phasal Arcana

"And the whole creation concerned with 'FOUR' "
Rock-Drill 91

The detail and consistency of the illustrations, and the symbolisms that often go far beyond the text they presume to illustrate, should lay to rest any doubts that Pound had in mind a form which the text refers to as "arcanum." Nor should there be any doubt that the visual arcana are the Seal and the Calendar. But Pound wisely removed the illustrations and allowed the texts to unfold their themes gradually through subject matter, relations, and proportions. Had he not, the illustrations could easily have drawn the kind of attention they have drawn here and thus distracted attention from matter to form. As it is he let numerologies and proportions be carried by the complements of cantos and drafts and by ordinary textual symbolism and arcana, resorting to visual reminders and indications only after the texts had established themselves. Thus we can draw assurance for interpretation from scholarship by recognizing and analyzing the illustrations (and the Seal, the Calendar, his remarks, and *Personae*) as evidence from the early constructive stages of the poem. Still, however, we must face the poem itself in its own terms and in its definitive form. In that perspective neither Chapter Two nor Chapter Five has added anything to the overall reading proposed in One; it has only supported it.

The Seal-vision *I–IV*, the decad *I–X*, and the draft *XVI*. *Cantos* provide sufficient arcana, all of it textual, for "ELEUSIS," for a poem of four-phase subjects, for a poem of decads informing ten drafts, and for a first phase of drafts in which visual arcana seem only conventional (though, as we shall see, they reflect the Seal). But each phase has its own arcanum subsuming all others while distinctive to its theme. Each appears in the first four cantos of the phase except the arcanum for the first, which has a more explicit form than Seal *I–IV*. The arcanum for the first is for a narrative of events informed by revolutionary argument, the Declaration. The arcanum for the second is for the personae of "WE the People," of the Preambles. The arcanum for the third is "the basic principles of government" and form of the Constitution. The arcanum for the fourth is for the activating, irradiating Bill of Rights in the form of the Calendar.

The arcanum for a narrative carrying a revolutionary argument and pro-jecting all other modes is the fugal paradigm Pound sent to his father:[1]

A. A. Live man goes down into world of Dead
C. B. The "repeat of history"
B. C. The "magic moment," or moment of metamorphosis, bust
thru from quotidien into "divine or permanent world." Gods, etc.

The fourth event (A. A. transformed) is the whole consummated in Niccolò d'Este's whirling mind and being built into a temple (*XX*). The four phases apply to Seal *I–IV*, the paradigm for all four-phase subjects. The theme applies to a poem of ten drafts symbolized by the shield and by the Calendar cycle's radial segments.

As noted earlier the seventh draft and second phase focuses within a poem by drafts a poem by personae, who are focused first by Pound's emergence in *Pisan LXXIV* as "Odysseus / the name of my family" (of personae), then by the musical score of the bird canzone "not of one bird but of many" (*LXXV*), then by ideograms formed in progress into "Canto 77 Explication," and finally into the transformation of all these into evolving surges of lyric poetry which voices less Pound himself than all men and their common world. Here we shall only explicate "Canto 77 Explication" as a form of the Seal, the Calendar, and '76 appropriate to the second phase.

Though "Canto 77 Explication" has other specific meanings in its context, *Pisan*, it is a paradigm for the single canto (*LXXVII*) out of which its ideo-grams have been drawn to be rearranged; for a prototype decad (the first trans-formed phasally in *Pisan*); and for a poem of ten drafts informed by personae. The ideograms numbered in the "Explication" appear in the text unnumbered in four groups, 1–6 scattered within the text, 7 in a column on the right of the text, 9 and 8 (in that order) in a different column to the right of the text, and 10 doubled to form two columns at the end of the text. The ideogramic sen-tence on the upper right is not translated in the text; nor does the text include the upper right made into an English sentence to join the two columns hori-zontally. Too, 8, 9, and 10 are disposed differently in the "Explication."

The dominant theme is the upper right translated ideogram by ideogram and then Englished in the personal "to sacrifice to a spirit not one's own is flattery (sycophancy)." The ideogram "seals" are bird-stars drawn in a per-sonal orthography with the head of each looking left (like the Eagle). The substantive Seal-symbol for the whole is thus the constellation of symbolized personae.

1. 11 April 1927, *Letters.*

CANTO 77 Explication

1 - middle

2 - precede

3 - follow

4 - how (is it)

    far

5 - dawn

6 - mouth

7 - not

one's own

spirit

and

sacrifice

is

flattery

bi gosh

To sacrifice to a spirit not one's own is flattery (sycophancy).

8 - halves of a
tally stick

9 - direction
of one's will

10 - perfect or
focus

With reference to the Calendar, the columns represent the cycle's dichotomy of gods interacting with goddesses. The horizontal sentence divides two hemicycles. In both Seal-symbols and Calendar form the "Explication" represents two Preambles.

But the symbols and form of the second phase also contain the four phases of '76 sequentially by the Seal and concurrently by the documents. In sequence the ideograms on the left above the horizontal come to a focus in the declarative E PLURIBUS UNUM. The horizontal states NOVUS ORDO SECLORUM personally. Below the horizontal the justicial MDCCLXXVI comes to a focus in the poetic ANNUIT COEPTIS.

For concurrency we can follow the construction of the "Explication" from heraldry to numerology. Ideograms alone form two vertical columns of ten each (the eighth on the left is a sentence made from the upper right). The columns are joined first by the horizontal sentence and then by the enumerations 1–10, which combine vertical and horizontal. The left column is impersonal for the ten-part Declaration. The right column is personal for the Preambles and religious for the Bill of Rights. The two columns joined by the sentence and by numbers 1–7 constitute a states' rights Constitution; joined by numbers 1–10 they constitute a Constitution for new union.

All forms begin simultaneously at the top of the two columns. When the numbers are added, all forms begin simultaneously at the top of the two columns and end simultaneously at the bottom right. All are subsumed in the now enumerated ten-part Declaration (left to right) coming to focus with the ten-Amendment Bill (right).

The Declaration's philosophy of revolution (1–4) is a mental "process" (so called in the text, where it culminates " 'How is it far if you think of it?' "). The result of applying the ideal process to the facts of a revolutionary case (see the text) is a sunrise both natural and mental (5–6); out of "the sun that is god's mouth" (see text) comes a voice declaring personal independence (7). The personal voice becomes a formal voice for projecting a government (8), which governs a merging of formal with personal (9) and religious (10).

Simultaneous with the Declaration, but within it, begin the personal Preambles (upper right). Motives from union to liberty inhere in the Declaration's argument against the past (1–6); motives from liberty to union emerge with the personal declaration of independence (7) and proceed toward "10-perfect or focus."

The states' rights Constitution (1–7), inherent in the Declaration's argument leading to independence and in the Preamble's motives toward liberty, is ratified by the emergent personal declaration (7). The world Constitution, coming out of the Declaration's premises and the states' rights Branches (1–4), turns from Branches to Powers through the personal declaration and ratification of states' rights (7); it moves through the symbol for the Constitutional third phase (8) and through the formalization of retained rights (9) to its own ratification (10).

The right column reflects the Bill both thematically and by divisions. The personal theme of the Preamble is religious for the Bill. The eight ideograms in the negative reflect Amendments First–Eighth, which specify what government *may not* do to infringe the rights of the people. The positive rights retained for what the people *may do* are reflected by "9-direction of one's will." The positive powers reserved to the States or to the people to effect their rights are reflected by "10-perfect or focus."

Yankee Doodle's calligraphy also shows as through a glass darkly initials and names of the revolutionary personae of '76, who are brought together in the order of their responsibility for the respective phases and documents on the first page of *Canto XXXI*, where '76 is first elaborated: Jefferson of the Declaration; Washington for the struggle that resulted in de facto independence, in the Constitutional Convention (of which he was president), and in the Preamble; Adams of the Constitution; and Tom Paine of the Bill of Rights. The lower half of the bottom left ideogram, which Pound adapted as a personal monogram for the cover of *Lustra* (1916), shows "E P," their poet;

taking this cue reveals "E π" and "E P" in the bottom right ideograms. Further scrutiny shows in the lower half of the first ideogram of "8-halves of a tally stick" "T J," and in the lower left quarter of its other ideogram (the "E" of "E P") "J A"; "T P" appears in the right-hand elements of these two ideograms taken together. On second look the bottom right ideograms unite "T P" and "E P." Pressing still further one can find "TOM PAINE" spelled out down the upper right and, cloaked in the whole left column, "WASHINGTON."

Such macaronics, which are characteristic of the Yankee Doodle style, continues the revision of Jefferson to Adams for world declaration (in the first phase) by revising Washington's domination in American mythology of the struggle and of the Constitutional Convention. Washington and Paine vie during a first phase until Paine instead of Washington speaks through Pound in the second. In the third phase "E P" unites all the men of '76 to amend the Constitution drafted under Washington. In the fourth "E P" makes himself a successor to "T P" for the Bill of Rights.

The "Explication," like other such arcana and brief reference (only the citation in *Canto XXXI*), shows that Pound became a successor to the men of '76 through the Johnny-come-lately colonist, catalyst, penman, and world revolutionary Paine; that he made Paine an American OSIRIS (Paine's body disappeared) to his own HORUS under ISIS as their mutual Providence and universal Liberty; and that he made Paine's lifetime effort the principal model for his own. Paine's struggle during "the times that try men's souls" and then during the French Revolution, which led to substantial participation but then to imprisonment in the Bastille and nearly to the guillotine, has special relevance to Pound's struggle for and against twentieth-century heads of state, to his struggle in Italy before and during World War II, and to his imprisonment at Pisa and then in Washington.

In *Los Cantares* the ideograms resume the classic form of those of the first phase.[2] The first of two arcana for the third phase takes the form of a "rock-drill" of thirteen oversized ideograms headed by a doubly oversized ideogram translated "Our dynasty came in because of a great sensibility" and penetrating the keynote *Rock-Drill 85*, a Confucian summation of "the basic principles of government." The "rock-drill" is an instrument containing the pattern MDCCLXXVI to be inscribed on the foundation of the Mount, and an instrument for cutting and shaping stone for building the Mount. The doubly oversized ideogram symbolizes the foundation of the Mount, the inscription MDCCLXXVI, and a first of thirteen tiers completed by the rest. For the Calendar the "rock-drill" symbolizes the vertical axis of the "bust thru" from the cycle, which subsumes cycle and hemicycles into the downward-pointing Mount or into Constitutional trine and the Constitutional phase while projecting tetrad and a fourth phase. The Calendar adjusts thirteen by phases to ten for drafts of the Constitutional Articles in the form of stones of the law. Ten projects the ten Constitutional subjects (subsuming and projective) of *Los Cantares*.

The second arcanam for the third phase is the Seal/Calendar arcanum at the end of the fourth canto of the phase (*Rock-Drill 88*). Though general for the whole poem it has special relevances to the third phase. It symbolizes the Constitutional dynamic, Branches interacting with Powers. It also symbolizes that the thirteen-ideogram "rock-drill" is constituted by the Calendar into ten parts in four phases, so that through its ten subjects in four phases the third phase subsumes all previous drafts and phases while projecting itself and the consummation of all drafts and phases.

The keynote four cantos of the first phase were simply cantos symbolizing stripes and the Calendar cycle; the four keynote cantos of the second phase contained visual symbols culminating in "Canto 77 Explication" symbolizing stars and the hemicycles; the keynote four cantos of the third phase began with visual symbols symbolizing tiers of the Mount and the Mount "busting thru" the cycle and hemicycles, and ended with the Seal/Calendar arcanum. We would expect the keynote four cantos of the fourth phase to symbolize

---

2. Tailpiece ideograms are added to six cantos of "KUNG" in a still different rough calligraphy in *Seventy Cantos* (1950), but were never added to American editions (see "KUNG," Chapter Fourteen). Two occurrences of *chung*[1] were altered to a different style in later printings of *Pisan*.

the rays of the sun-vision containing the "triangular space" and the eye of Providence, and the Calendar Mount and Calendar cycle completed together in irradiating light. We would also expect a return to an emphasis on cantos without ideograms for the transformation of stripes in the dark to sun-rays; this is almost the case.

Canto *CX* is divided formally into tetrad by a first hemicycle and phase without ideograms followed by a second hemicycle in three phases, each marked by two ideograms. This form reflects the Calendar's first phase of six cold, male months under ISIS followed by the second, third, and fourth phases of warm, female months two by two under (respectively) PAN, POSEIDON, and BACCHUS. The light shines directly through ISIS and shines through the darkening rest of the canto in ideograms. "From CXII" ends, as we shall see, with a version of the fortune wheel of *Seventh* and of the Seal/Calendar arcanum. Canto *CXIII* reveals in action the irradiating revolutionary mind which has been moving throughout the poem,

> Thru the 12 Houses of Heaven
> > seeing the just and the unjust,
> > tasting the sweet and the sorry,
> Pater Helios turning.

After "God's eye art 'ou, do not surrender perception" a mournful coda ends

> > Out of dark, thou, Father Helios, leadest,
> but the mind as Ixion, unstill, ever turning.

Canto *CXIV* refers to the female dichotomies of the cycle "present in heaven and hell" and to its "moving . . . from the inward . . . in these triangular spaces." But since a broken cycle cannot complete a Mount, Pound's effort to perfect a Malatestan Tempio and '76 ends like Malatesta's Renaissance, "In the gloom, the gold gathers the light against it."

In detail and in gradual evolution *The Cantos* is intended to satisfy the mind that is making it and the minds of those who would follow the writer's in the same intellectual and aesthetic spirit. But it is also intended to have the immediate impact of "reading matter, singing matter, shouting matter, the tale of the tribe."[3] It sets the American Revolution to music to try to realize the vision of the Seal, the back of which has never been engraved—a sign that, despite erection in New York harbor of a Statue of Liberty (conceived and constructed in Europe), '76 and American civilization have yet to be realized. And what other poem has tried to deal with the salient facts of the twentieth century, capitalism, imperialism, economic justice, and revolution?

In a 1962 interview Pound went back to an anecdote first used in 1918 (whence he had dated "began investigation of causes of war, to oppose

---

3. To John Lackay Brown, April 1937, *Letters*.

same''),[4] but probably applicable to the claim made in the words of the Roumanian sculptor Constantin Brancusi, ''toutes mes choses datent de quinze ans,''[5] and to an adage applied to the Russian composer Igor Stravinsky, ''dream of youth accomplished by the ripe man.''[6] (Both Brancusi and Stravinsky were ''colonists''—from Eastern Europe rather than from America—who tried to transform from within, with fresh blood and imagination, Western European art and culture.) Asked after *Los Cantares* had been published and he was working on a final draft, ''Are you more or less stuck?'' he acknowledged, ''Okay, I am stuck'' and then summarized:

> An epic is a poem containing history. The modern mind contains heteroclite elements. The past epos has succeeded when all or a great many of the answers were assumed, at least between author and audience, or a great mass of audience. The attempt in an experimental age is therefore rash. Do you know the story: ''What are you drawing, Johnny?''
> ''God!''
> ''But nobody knows what He looks like.''
> ''They will when I get through!''[7]

The anecdote simplifies things as intricate as the Seal, the Calendar, the illustrations, and *The Cantos* itself. As the Ur-Imagist T. E. Hulme said, ''All a man ever thought would go onto a half-sheet of notepaper. The rest is application and elaboration.''[8] Pound's ''half-sheet'' is the Calendar symbolizing visually New World history and its revolutionary process of '76; ''application and elaboration'' is his works.

As to the ethical and moral dimensions of Johnny's effort, which kept Pound true to his vocation and to his vision even in the face of two world wars, of a personal debacle during the second, and of many personal errors, he phrased it simply in the ''Savoir Faire'' Chapter (22) of *Guide to Kulchur* (1938): ''To act on one's definition? What concretely do I myself mean to do? I mean to say that one measure of a civilization, either of an age or of a single individual, is what that age or person really wishes to do. A man's hope measures his civilization. The attainability of the hope measures, or may measure, the civilization of his nation and time.''

4. ''Autobiography,'' *Selected Poems* (New York: 1949).

5. The epigraph to ''Postscript (1929)'' to ''Praefatio Ad Lectorem Electum'' to the *Spirit of Romance* in *Prolegomena 2*, 1932.

6. ''Igor Stravinsky, by Boris De Schloezer; Translated from the French by Ezra Pound'' appeared in seven instalments in *Dial*, New York, October 1928–July 1929.

7. *Paris Review* 28. Pound first used the anecdote to mock H. G. Wells's *The Soul of a Bishop, A Novel (With Just a Little Love in It) About Conscience and Religion and the Real Troubles of Life*, 1918, in which Wells presented a clergyman's discovery of The New God (''Joyce,'' *Future*, London, May 1918).

8. ''Condensare,'' *Townsman*, London, January 1938; reprinted as the last of ''Addenda: 1952'' to *Guide To Kulchur*, 1938.

CHAPTER SEVEN

LIBERTY "ONE":

NEKUOMANTEIA

A Roman lawyer came and sat on my chest other evening, with "Language of the law and of the state" as I think Johnnie Milton calls it. Long after midnight and just about as he was convincing or convictin me that some of my earlier Cantos cd. do with a bit of explainin, the hotel keeper came round and allowed some of the other inhabitants of the buildin cd. do with a bit of sleep.

Rome Radio, Ezra Pound Speaking 1941?
from *If This Be Treason......*[1]

The first draft is deployed by concurrency and by sequence so that a single, all-inclusive archetype of revolution (*I*) evolves four-phase "REVOLUTION ... In the minds of the people" (*I–IV*), so that these evolve the ten-part argument of the Declaration in concurrency with the documents it projects (*I–X*), and so that all project not only a prototype decad with a six-canto coda but also the first drafted subject *XVI. Cantos.* This opening of *The Cantos* is intended thus to be read. *I* is set off from its sequels by beginning anonymously and by being narrated by Odysseus before Pound interrupts, takes over the narration, and delivers a conventional epic invocation. From standing alone *I* becomes the first of Seal *I–IV*, which is set off from its sequels by constituting a Renaissance poetic tradition. Seal *I–IV* is subsumed in Renaissance revolution *I–X*, which is focused as destiny, prophecy, and history by the Malatestan subject and the validating revolutionary Eagle. Finally *XVI. Cantos* is derived from mythic archetype, from millennial vision, and from Renaissance revolution for the culminating subject (inherent all along) of the four-phase draft, twentieth-century continuing revolution. Since each grouping projects the whole draft and the whole poem, this exposition follows that evolution.

This pattern reflects not only the unfolding of New World history and '76 from a Renaissance destiny and prophecy, but also their symbols, the Seal and the Calendar. The archetype *I* (as "ONE") embodies the Eagle's vision of the

1. Five broadcasts edited under Patrick Henry's rubric by Olga Rudge (Siena: 1948).

Seal edifice as a Statue of Liberty inspired by Providence and focused in Providence's "triangular space," the epitome of a canto as a Constitutional constituent for building. The canto passes from Old Style to New Style via the narration of Odysseus, who is guided by Circe, to the narration inherited and extended by Pound, who invokes Aphrodite. By the Calendar *I* is HORUS's vision of a whole cycle (Odysseus's narration inherited and completed by Pound) within a whole tabulation (Pound's narration extended by his invocation to a perfected "triangular space" containing Aphrodite). The epitomized unitary Seal and the epitomized unifying Calendar are contained within the archetypal subject of *I*, Eleusinian myth coming through the Homeric Nekuomanteia—the voyage to consult the dead to learn an historical destiny through prophecy of the future, in this case whether and how to get home. The Nekuomanteia contains as prophetic archetype the form of New World history evolving '76.

But for Pound's interruption and invocation, *I* is a single narration evolving the comprehensive archetype in its definitive sequence. *II*, *III*, and *IV* each contains a major narration for the evolution of a Renaissance poetic tradition, but these narrations appear amid varied fragments and images, past and present. Unlike *I*, each of these cantos also begins with Pound speaking. Together *I–IV* constitute four symbols in four voices of an edifice to be built by the Eagle under and toward Providence. According to the Calendar the Eagle (and Providence) HORUS moves from the center to the four phasal divinities ISIS, PAN, POSEIDON, and BACCHUS, who project a cycle to be completed as a means of building the tabulation. The Seal and Calendar forms symbolize "REVOLUTION . . . in the minds of the people" derived from the Renaissance poetic tradition and to be realized by the revolutionary process.

Renaissance revolution *I–X* is informed by the ten-part Declaration containing concurrently its projected sequels. On the Seal the form is symbolized by the repeated thirteens of the four geometrical symbols adjusted to ten and metamorphosing one into the other while evolving sequentially. On the Calendar HORUS moves through the four phases to the cycle, whose concurrent and sequential cycle, hemicycles, emerging Mount, and irradiating sun-rays activate the static Seal.

For twentieth-century revolution the four sequential phases of *I*, having emerged in *I–IV* and been projected to *I–X*, culminate in four sequential phases of *XVI. Cantos*; using "triangular spaces" fulfilled as Constitutional constituents, *XVI. Cantos* perfects the Seal edifice and the Calendar tabulation built by the ten-part cycle. *XVI. Cantos* is a prototype and first draft of a ten-draft whole built of cantos—i.e., of tiers of stone—in four phases.

With these principles in mind, we turn to more detailed consideration first of *I*, then of *I–IV*, then of *I–X*, and finally of *XVI. Cantos*. Since all are prototypes composed with special care, they demand the most detailed consideration of any cantos in the poem. *I* demands most, then *I–IV*, and so on.

Before proceeding, however, and to introduce the perspective of *I* as a prehistoric, archetypal "ONE," we may note the special application of the formula "ONE, ten, eleven, *chi con me* 旦 *tan*?" to *XVI*. *Cantos* and therefore also to the epitome for the whole poem. "ONE" refers to *I* as an archetype. *I–IV* is not referred to in the formula. "Ten" refers to *I–X*, in which *I* has become a first. For a coda "eleven" extends "ten" in its own terms (the fourth of four Malatesta cantos, *XI*). "*Chi con me*" (who's with me?) shifts to the personal for the American *XII*. The ideogram for *dawn* refers to the hopeful Chinese *XIII*. The transliteration of *dawn*, also Cretan for god or Zeus,[2] refers to the neo-Dantean *XIV–XVI*, not with "paradiso terrestre" but with world war and the equivocal Russian Revolution ("?"). This form is prepared in *I*-as-"ONE" by Pound's invocation of an irradiating amelioration of the gloomy Nekuomanteia. Both the epitome/keynote and its projection are also integral subjects divided into four phases.

The Archetypal Epitome: *I*-as-"ONE"

For Pound the *Odyssey* marked the passage in European values from the brute force and war of the *Iliad* to intelligence and peace. The Nekuomanteia, which Pound considered the oldest part of the *Odyssey*, not only caught that shift at its earliest but also represented the European mind's passage from myth to historical consciousness as a guide to intelligence. Other values are Odysseus's responsibility for his crew, his obedience to the gods, the destiny of intelligence because it is intelligence, a shift from the vindictive gods of the *Iliad* and from the "spiteful Neptune" of the *Odyssey* to gods who dispensed an equitable justice, and Odysseus's desire to return home—which would bring peace and a new order where the disorder of the old order had supervened. Various kinds of revolution are implied, not the least of which is political revolution aimed at changing former social and political relations in the light of a new justice replacing the old. This archetypal change of values reflects all such changes, the latest of which is a need to turn away from One World dominated by world war and in mortal need of revolutionary reversal.

The Greek Nekuomanteia is translated from Renaissance Latin into medieval "Seafarer metre" taken to be a proper "modern metre" for Pound's own epic poem. Such translation—translation is itself revolution—reflects a tradition of continuing revolution laid "ply over ply" and "moving concurrent." Concurrency is also reflected by Odysseus being the narrative spokesman for all the dead, who thereby become his personae, and by Pound's making Odysseus his persona. It is further reflected by the construction "to be unity"

2. "Igon Tan," a pseudonym used during his confinement 1945–58, abbreviates [EP] Igon Tan, epigon of the dawn or of Zeus.

via duality, trine, and tetrad. As to sequence, Pound follows the order of the Homeric Nekuomanteia exactly, but he foreshortens some speeches, makes certain slight variations, and cuts off the Homeric narration (which continues much further) at a point that will fit his discovery in the Nekuomanteia of the proportions, themes, and forms of New World history and '76. He also adjusts the diction at certain points to hint at (i.e., to prophesy) his own American future. Selection and adjustments are designed to make the Nekuomanteia his own inheritance of an archetypal revolutionary tradition and epic vocation.

The Nekuomanteia is narrated by a single narrator in a casual rhetoric ("and then") of "human events," but studied casualness is designed to give an impression of gradually revealed predestination and prophetic forms. A Seal-vision permeates the canto while finding sequential loci of symbols and voices.[3] The ship with its "swart" hull, its mast, its tiller, its oars, and its sails manifests the Eagle erect from tail to head and borne by legs and wings. The narrating captain speaks its mind and eyes through a mouth bearing the banner E PLURIBUS UNUM; he unites the voyagers, will unite the dead, and will unite all voices while also emerging as one of many and singling out Elpenor. The locus for the arrows is his sword, which becomes a spade to dig "the ell-square pitkin" and then is used to beat off the dead; it becomes Elpenor's oar, Tiresias's golden wand, Divus's pen, and Aphrodite's "golden bough of Argicida." The locus for the olive branch is the place "aforesaid by Circe" where rites (of colonization) are performed, in part by the sword adapted from war to peace. Odysseus pacifies the nameless myriad dead, his former comrade Elpenor, and Tiresias; Pound pacifies Divus. The Eagle HORUS discovers by cyclic voyage and brings to life by colonization under ZAGREUS and PAN "of no era."

The "ell-square pitkin," dug as a shield-foundation for a Mount, brings from Erebus the unified dead clamoring for blood—for a new tradition, for new life, and for new justice; around the fosse the dead and living recognize their common human fate. Personae grouped around a central persona like the stars of the constellation begin with the voyagers, the benighted Kimmerians, the voyagers as ritualists, and the myriad dead; they find their locus, however, in the individualized Elpenor, who presents a stellar plan for a personal tomb that will give him a new life; the ghosts of Odysseus's mother Anticleia, of Tiresias, and of Divus carry the personae to the end.

Within the narrator's overall E PLURIBUS UNUM (under ISIS), Elpenor utters NOVUS ORDO SECLORUM (under PAN). From Circe's house Mounts pass through the Kimmerian cities deprived of sun and stars, to the pyre, to Erebus, and again to Circe's house, from the roof of which Elpenor fell to his death; the locus is the new Ithaca prophesied by Tiresias in the voice of new

---

3. The explications of Seal I–IV can be compared to the illustrations of the deluxe XVI. Cantos in Chapter Five.

justice MDCCLXXVI (again within Odysseus's voice, now under POSEI-
DON); sequels are Divus's publishing house, again Circe's, and Aphrodite's
"munimenta."

After descending from Circe the daughter of the sun and the sun itself,
the voyagers entered the dark; the sun returns figuratively when Pound takes
over Odysseus's narration in a consummating ANNUIT COEPTIS (under
BACCHUS) and recognizes his source Divus; it returns actually when he
sends Odysseus back to the old Providence Circe and invokes a new Providence atop her Mount, in the sun, within her shrine. An old Eagle has descended under an old Providence while a new Eagle has been drafting and
building toward a new Providence.

The Seal-vision symbolizes the destinies of living and dead, past, present,
and future. An overall destiny of revolutions against status quos prophesies
revolution in the four-phase form of New World history. The living discover
Kimmeria and Erebus and perform rites of colonization which elicit the revolt
of the dead, a counterpart of revolt against conditions of their own world; four
major events culminate in Pound's inheritance of continuing revolution. After
discovery and colonization, revolution (the third phase) opens up in four
phasal events, all through Odysseus and Pound: the myriad dead make a
declaration, Elpenor voices struggle toward a new life, Tiresias delivers a
new justice, and Pound again consummates continuing revolution. Revolution
as a single event has taken four-phase forms as the four major events of New
World history and as six major events of New World history opening up the
form of '76.

Simultaneously, however, just as the Seal symbols permeate Odysseus's
narration while precipitating the sequential voices, the four events and the six
events are overlaid by a ten-part "course of human events," the background
out of which comes the Declaration's argument. Predestined men descend
from Providential Circe's to their fates, which carry them from the light into
the dark; there they discover their own destiny and causes for revolution in the
wretched "Kimmerian lands and peopled cities" cut off from the sun and
stars ("the laws of nature and of nature's god"). Having come to "the place /
Aforesaid by Circe," the crew observes rites of colonization under natural
rights while the leader digs with his sword the "ell-square pitkin"; they
propitiate the spirits of place and acknowledge natural rights by pouring
libations "unto each the dead." For government by consent the leader prays
to "the sickly death's heads" and performs the blood sacrifice "as set in
Ithaca" to evoke the prophet of new justice Tiresias. The rites draw "Souls
out of Erebus," who deny consent to the living and their rites and revolt
against their general condition by falling upon the sacrifices intended for
Tiresias alone. History as general premises passes into historical evidence in
a first turn for trine.

As the dead crowd around "with shouting" they are first described with sympathy by one who knows the condition of the world all have come from (many were killed in war). And when they cry for more beasts the terrified leader at first "slaughters" (not very ritually) and cries to the gods, especially the tyrants over the dead, Pluto and Proserpine. But then he draws his sword to keep "the impetuous impotent dead" from the blood till he should hear Tiresias. The revolt of the dead has resulted in a case against executive tyranny, not only the gods' but the speaker's. But pity and responsibility fuse in the leader's recognition of one of "our . . . brethren," who comes as evidence not only against a leader but also against a friend:

> But first Elpenor came, our friend Elpenor,
> Unburied, cast on the wide earth,
> Limbs that we left in the house of Circe,
> Unwept, unwrapped in sepulchre, since toils urged other.

He laments "pitiful spirit" and cries in hurried speech (breaking into his own narration)

> "Elpenor, how art thou come to this dark coast?
> Cam'st thou afoot, outstripping seamen?"

The pity and the question complete an identification of the plights of living and dead. They complete an argument against the past with a turn from the single speaker with whom the narration began "to be unity" to a second speaker for "duality." The single speaker of E PLURIBUS UNUM has opened up a tradition which also carries and projects new life, new justice, and a new order sought by both living and dead. He will continue until his own unity passes into Pound's new unity, but exponents of duality, trine, and tetrad will speak for themselves.

The leader has opened up "A. A. Live man goes down into world of Dead"; Elpenor opens up "The 'repeat in history.' " By relenting and letting Elpenor speak the leader allows him to draw from premises and cases a projection of freedom from the dismal past. Elpenor sums up the Declaration's argument against the past in a present declaration of independence for the future. Looking back, he laments his death at Circe's and repeats the voyage of the living and its consequences:

> And he in heavy speech:
> "Ill fate and abundant wine. I slept in Circe's ingle.
> "Going down the long ladder unguarded,
> "I fell against the buttress,
> "Shattered the nape-nerve, the soul sought Avernus."

Turning toward his own future, a destiny all men hope for, he expresses the deads' version of the home to which the living are seeking to return and projects the return voyage to Circe's:

> "But thou, O King, I bid remember me, unwept, unburied,
> "Heap up mine arms, be tomb by sea-bord, and inscribed:
> "*A man of no fortune, and with a name to come.*
> "And set my oar up, that I swung mid fellows.'"[4]

Elpenor's appearance at Erebus and his speech have been predestined since the departure from Circe's. His speech subsumes the leader's account of the descent of the living to the dead while projecting the rest of the canto. It constitutes with the leader's account duality, and it is duality. It modifies the leader's singlemindedness by asking for recognition of individual cases under the laws of comitatus and ritual burial, which are prescribed to men by the gods and cannot be ignored with impunity. Both the leader's narration and Elpenor's narration and request carry all themes, but while the leader's emphasized tradition Elpenor's emphasizes personality. The dual voice of a second phase is NOVUS ORDO SECLORUM.

Having yielded to Elpenor and now supported also by the rites and by his own purposes, Odysseus lets Tiresias assert his own independence by challenge and command and assert sovereign powers by prophesying Odysseus's. Tiresias recognizes the narrator and challenges the acts and motives of the living in descending to the dead:

> "A second time? why? man of ill star,
> "Facing the sunless dead and this joyless region?"

He translates the motives of the dead and Elpenor's personal lament and request into a command for personal gratification:

> "Stand from the fosse, leave me my bloody bever
> "For soothsay."

Having identified the "man of ill star" with the dead and with Elpenor and caused him to step back, he drinks, and, "strong with the blood," names the narrator and prophesies:

> "Odysseus
> "Shalt return through spiteful Neptune, over dark seas,
> "Lose all companions."

The challenge subsumes the leader's account of the voyage to the dead. The command subsumes the desires of the dead and Elpenor's request, which expresses their own form of "soothsay." Tiresias's soothsay, however, is the

---

4. Elpenor recounts his death from excess (KUPRIS's passion) and requests burial, tomb, and epitaph under JUNO's ritual restraint. The goddesses will preside two by two in this fashion: passionate KUPRIS and regal JUNO; martial ATHENA (Tiresias's challenge and command) and domestic HESTIA (Tiresias's prophecy of return home and Anticleia); severely just ARTEMIS (Pound's restraint of Divus) and maternal, all-accepting DEMETER (Pound's commemoration of Divus and completion of Divus's Latin).

will of the gods or "B. C. The magic moment or moment of metamorphosis, bust thru from quotidien into divine or permanent world. Gods, etc." It reveals a new destiny and a new, equitable justice different from the vindictiveness of "spiteful Neptune"; accordingly, unlike the dead, who are not allowed to speak at all, and unlike Elpenor, who is queried, Tiresias speaks out of his presumed authority without being spoken to.

If Elpenor's speech is a turn from "to be unity" to duality, a second turn for trine, and a second turn (and therefore a second phase) for tetrad, Tiresias's speech, after Anticleia the dead mother has been beaten off in a return to the claims of public duty, is a third turn and a third phase for tetrad. In its two parts—before drinking the blood and after—it asserts independence and sovereignty. In its three parts it subsumes tradition and personality in justice while prophesying through Odysseus's turn to Anticleia new civilization and the rest of the canto.

Odysseus's last words, "And then Anticleia came," portend a reevocation of Ithacan beginnings in anticipation of prophesied Ithacan ends and new beginnings. But Pound, who since the beginning has taken words out of Odysseus's mouth by taking them out of the mouth of his Renaissance translator, interrupts to reveal that he has been transforming the concurrent themes of tradition, personality, and justice into new poetry. While focusing the concurrency in the Declaration's pledge he also consummates Odyssean "to be unity," Odyssean/Elpenorean duality, and Odyssean/Elpenorean/Tiresian trine in Odyssean/Elpenorean/Tiresian/Poundian tetrad, or into a tenth event and fourth phase.

Pound's interruption inherits Odysseus's narration of ten events containing the forms of New World history and '76 while emphasizing four encounters with the dead; Pound has given the past new blood by translating, or formed a new tradition.

Also in Seal-form, Pound's address to his translator—

> Lie quiet Divus. I mean, that is Andreas Divus,
> In officina Wecheli, 1538, out of Homer

—recognizes a tradition given new life, individualizes the translator, cites Divus's book by publishing house and date, and names the original poetic source. Echoing the quelling of the clamorous dead by the naming of Elpenor, it fulfills Elpenor's request that he be remembered by historical memorial as *"A man of no fortune, and with a name to come"*; it does so by making the book Tiresian prophecy of Pound's work and by letting Pound get his own oar into Homeric beginnings for his own.

Completing Odysseus's narration—

> And he sailed, by Sirens and thence outward and away
> And unto Circe

—inherits Tiresias's transformation of tradition and personality into prophecy and sets prophecy into motion. "And he sailed" begins realizing a cyclic destiny. Sailing "by Sirens" (an alteration of the sequence in the *Odyssey*) glances at an evasion of Elpenor's fate. Sailing "outward and away" from threats of the dark and of the Sirens realizes a first stage of the destiny prophesied by Tiresias. Returning to Circe clinches a cyclic destiny augured since the beginning.

Inheritance of a tradition, of personalities, and of new justice precipitates Pound's invocation for his own new poetry:

> Venerandam,
> In the Cretan's phrase, with the golden crown, Aphrodite,
> Cypri munimenta sortita est, mirthful, orichalchi, with golden
> Girdles and breast bands, thou with dark eyelids
> Bearing the golden bough of Argicida. So that:

"Venerandam," which mediates between Circe and the invocation of a new style Providence, introduces the Latin of tradition in the phrase of "the Cretan," another Renaissance personality and poet. His phrase and Pound's translation invoke atop her Mount, in the light, the goddess looking from her dark eyelids and bearing the golden bough of Hermes, the slayer of the hundred-eyed guard Argus; her magic (like poetry) will guide the new poet on his own venture into the underworld. Aphrodite has inspired the initial beginning; beyond the causal "So that" she will inspire a continuation and a new beginning. Pound pledges "our lives, our fortunes, and our sacred honor" of all his personae and poets to a better destiny than that achieved by and since Homer, through ages and epochs of "the course of human events," to the moment of writing. His four-phase consummation memorializes, signs, seals, and delivers an epitome of the cyclic Declaration.

The cyclic Declaration's argument against the past (1–6) and projection of the future (7–10) contain and project halves of the Seal generating hemicyclic Preambles marked by the motives of the living yielding to the motives of the dead. "WE the People," the living, bring from Circe's the motive "to form a more perfect union" by returning to Ithaca, but the impact of the dead and the coming of Elpenor force Odysseus to yield to the demands of liberty, which he does by querying Elpenor and letting him speak (1–6). Circean liberty— too much wine and climbing too high—caused Elpenor's death, but his request that his limbs be composed and his plan for a tomb (7) project both his own interests and the livings' toward a new union. The motive toward new union is carried on through Tiresias (8–9) until Divus stirs and Pound placates him, uniting the voices of living and dead with his own (10). Pound then confirms the will of "WE the People" both living and dead with his celebratory invocation.

The Declaration's premises (1–4) and revolutionary argument declaring independence (4–7), and its revolutionary argument (1–7) projecting a new union (7–10), contain and project the overlapping Constitutions. For the dynamic Branches/Powers, forms brought by the living arouse the dead, the dead demand new forms from the living, and the dead project new union both for themselves and for the living. The living act within inherited Branches to effect normal change (1–4) but the dead seek states' rights by applying the Powers (4–7), which culminate in Elpenor's response and request. The integrity of the rites has been protected, however, so that through Elpenor's assertion of states' rights the Powers applied by the dead become Branches for new union (4–7). Thus Tiresias's challenge and demand for blood propose Amendment (8) and his blood-inspired prophecy utters Supreme Law (9). Elpenor's Ratification and prospective memorializing, signing, sealing, and delivering of states' rights (7)—"be tomb by sea-bord, and inscribed: / "*A man of no fortune, and with a name to come.* / "And set my oar up, that I swung mid fellows"—thus becomes Pound's commemoration of Divus and his completion of the Odyssean narration (10), which he makes new in an invocation ratifying new union.

The Declaration's argument against the past (1–6), declaration (7), assertions (8–9), and pledge (10) contain and project the activating Bill and the sealing Seal. After Odysseus has run "Thru the ten voices of the tradition" (*Thrones 99*) uttered by living and dead and expressing old law, new law, and divine law, Pound reveals that the whole has been carried "By the ten mouths of the tradition" speaking through his own. Voyages inspired by Circean religion assemble for free expression demanding a redress of grievances (First) like those they find in Kimmeria. They perform the general rites with the sword turned to an instrument of peace (Second). The leader becomes a soldier-lawmaker (Third) building a symbol of government to intrude into the house of the dead; he prays for religious warrant and spills the blood that will open up Tiresias's secrets. Warrant has opened up the deads' secrets (Fourth). But the dead demand the due process of one law while the leader is trying to enforce that of another (Fifth). When Elpenor comes, however, the leader breaks his silence by granting Elpenor the right to plead his own case as his own witness and counsel (Sixth). Granted the right, Elpenor presents his case under an archetypal version of the common law (Seventh), the right to burial. After the leader has recurred to his sword to beat off Anticleia, a cruel punishment, Tiresias laments the cruelties inflicted both on the dead and on the "man of ill star" (Eighth) before demanding the blood, which will bring an access of painful vision; Tiresias prophesies under the retained rights (Ninth) while extending them to the crew, who will use them to violate prescribed rituals, and to Odysseus, who will adhere to prescribed rituals as he does now by turning to Anticleia. Finally Pound appropriates reserved powers (Tenth) employed since the beginning to complete, memorialize, sign, seal, and deliver a prophetic epitome of continuing revolution. The cyclic narration has drafted and built a Seal/Calendar epitome perfected by Aphrodite's new Mount. The canto is also an epitome of a "triangular space" or Constitutional constituent.

The Calendar cycle and hemicycles under ZAGREUS and PAN "of no era" discover and colonize, the radial segments declare, the circumferential gods and goddesses motivate, the emerging axial Mount founds, and the irradiating radii illuminate a drafted, edificial canto—all "moving concurrent." It is evident too that each concurrency is condensed or "sealed" into a sequential phase. Deference to Elpenor before Tiresias comes causes Odysseus's narration to condense into a first phase the Declaration symbolized by the shield and voiced E PLURIBUS UNUM (under ISIS). Elpenor's lament and request condense into a second phase the Preambles symbolized by the interpenetrating constellation and voiced NOVUS ORDO SECLORUM (under PAN). Tiresias's challenge, command, and prophecy condense into a third phase the overlapping Constitutions symbolized by the Mount voiced MDCCLXXVI (under POSEIDON). Pound's narration, recognition of Divus, implementation of the prophecy, and invocation condense into a fourth phase the whole activated by the Bill, which is symbolized by the sun-vision and voiced ANNUIT COEPTIS (under BACCHUS).

Yankee Doodle's "macaroni" also makes the translation of Homer a feather in a country boy's cap. Odysseus's discovery of "the Kimmerian lands" foreshadows in anagram Columbus's discovery of America. Digging "the ellsquare pitkin" relates "E L P" via "Odysseus / the name of my family" to Pound's colonial ancestors who settled in New England before the Adamses (cf. Adams's "Braintree, a plantation near Weston's," *LXII*), and thus to all the colonial revolutionaries of '76. The "square" pit anticipates graves "bien carré, exact" ordered dug by French burying squads under fire during World War I (*XVI*) and Jefferson's model for a capitol, "the Maison Quarrée of Nismes" (*XXXI*). Jefferson, who formalized "REVOLUTION . . . in the minds of the people" in the Declaration, will become the Odysseus of '76 in *Canto XXXI*, where the men of '76 will be named in their phasal order Jefferson, Washington, Adams, and Paine.

Odysseus's terrified praise of "Pluto the strong" and "Proserpine," rulers over the dead, probably alludes to American plutocracy (see "Jefferson-Nuevo Mundo") and, through "pro-serpent" in the queen's name, to Usura. His naming of "Elpenor" links "E L P" and "Paine," whose scattered limbs have never been found and properly buried (cf. OSIRIS and his stand-in PAN); at the time of writing Paine was considered a drunk and, thanks to President Teddy Roosevelt, a "dirty little atheist." Odysseus's query whether Elpenor came to Erebus on foot anticipates President Jefferson offering Paine return passage to America (*XXXI*):

> "in hopes you will find us returned to sentiments
> worthy of former time.....in these you have laboured as
> much as any man living. That you may long live to
> continue your labours and to reap their fitting reward....
> Assurances of my high esteem and attachment."

In recognizing Elpenor, Odysseus shifts from Jefferson's role to Washington's, who as General Washington worked with the "pen-man" of the struggle (cf. "Elp-," "-pen-," and "-or," the last "gold" or "oar") but who as President Washington neglected him almost mortally while Paine was seeking to continue the revolution in England and France. Elpenor's "the soul sought Avernus" plays on Washington's comfortable resting place at Mount Vernon, a repose Paine will not find until his lost limbs have been reassembled and he has been memorialized on earth. Elpenor's *"a name to come"* not only calls attention to his own name (which means "man of hope") but also looks toward Divus's and therefore Pound's.

Given such style Anticleia becomes a figure for the motherland neglected when Odysseus was called to war and Tiresias becomes a figure for "Patria Mia" (see Pound's 1912 essays under this title). Anticleia's name, "anti-history," becomes relevant to a revolutionary tradition that needs recognition and revival. Pound had only Washington available as "the Father of His Country" at the time of writing, and so left the figure for the Constitutional phase open. Canto *XXXI* proposes either Franklin or Adams. In *LXII* Adams succeeds Jefferson and Washington as "pater patriae." Tiresias's recognition that the "man of ill star" has come "A second time,"[5] either a translator's error or a deliberate alteration of Homer, applies to a twentieth-century traveler who is named "Odysseus" only after having deferred to "Patria Mia" as the prophet of his destiny. Odysseus (HORUS) then receives "Matria Mia" (ISIS), through whom the final *"name to come"* is Andreas Divus, an antecedent of Paine and a figure, through his resurrected *Odyssey*, of OSIRIS.

Andreas Divus is "Andreas Divus Justinopolitanus," where Justinopolis was Capodistria, east across the Gulf of Venice.[6] Pound speculated that Divus's name might mean "Signore Dio, Signore Divino, or even Mijnheer von Gott." "Capo d'Istria" was a marginal gloss to Divus both in "Three Cantos" *I–III* (*Quia Pauper Amavi*, 1919) and in "The First Canto" (*XVI. Cantos* 1925). A macaronic reading might find the "God" of *I*-as-"ONE" to have come from a "Just City" or "Head of History," making him the "chief histrion" of a prophesied world vision as Columbus was of Whitman's (cf. "Passage To India" and Whitman's "last poem," "A Thought of Columbus"). The cyclic narration has rounded back to its initial figure.

"I mean, that is" reflects Yankee Doodle's sensitivity to his own borrowing of a non-native tradition and to his countrymen's distance from a shared tradition, even their own. The locution is akin to what Pound described when asked if he thought free verse is a particularly American form: "I'll tell you a

<hr>

5. Divus's "Cur iterum" should be "Cur autem," "Why," indeed. Continuation of Divus's error is a lucky destiny—se non è vero è ben trovato. Such "errors" are part of history. Pound accepts many—indeed deliberately creates some of his own.

6. "In the year of grace 1906, 1908, or 1910 I picked from the Paris quais a Latin version of the *Odyssey* by Andreas Divus Justinopolis (Parisiis, In officina Christiani Wecheli, MDXXXVIII)" ("Early Translators of Homer" II, *Egoist*, London, September 1918).

thing that I think *is* an American form, and that is the Jamesian parenthesis. You realize that the person you are talking to hasn't got the different steps, and you go back over them. In fact the Jamesian Parenthesis has immensely increased now. That I think is something that is definitely American. The struggle that one has when one meets another man who has a lot of experience to find the point where the two experiences touch, so that he really knows what you are talking about.''[7]

Yankee Doodle builds his macaroni toward ''Venerandam,'' with which a New Eagle announces a New Providence and Statue of Liberty emerging from their ''Old'' counterparts. ''Venerandam,'' grammatically ''She must be worshipped'' but macaronically ''Venus and I'' and ''I venerate [Venus] and [therefore] I am,'' asserts Yankee Doodle's revolutionary vocation.[8]

In the form ''ONE, ten, eleven, *chi con me* 曰 tan?'' *I*-as-''ONE'' stands alone. Four-part New World history, six-part New World history opening up '76, and four-part '76 subsuming New World history, enable it to combine with its sequels in ''mass relations'' to form an evolving Seal *I–IV*. The four phases perfected by Odysseus's narration of the revolt of the nameless myriad dead, of Elpenor, and of Tiresias, and by Pound's succession, have varied meanings. Events and their argument precipitate archetypal personae. Odysseus is the type of directive, active intelligence, Pound's ''factive personality'' or ''executive'' type for declaration. Elpenor is the type of the sensitive ordinary man, ''advisory'' for ''WE the People'' of the Preambles. Tiresias is the type of the prophet and lawgiver, ''perceptive'' for the Constitution. Divus is Pound's ''poetic'' type for the Bill and Seal. Odysseus changes to meet the four waves of dead until he himself changes into Pound.

Odysseus and Pound interacting with the four waves of dead voice the revolutionary documents, which the structures of the speeches make all inherent in Odysseus's from the beginning. Constitutionally the ''executive'' Odysseus interacts as Congress with the myriad dead, who bring new ideas of change through the Power States (their ''states of mind''). ''Advisory'' Odysseus assumes Presidency when advised by Elpenor through Amendment. ''Perceptive'' Odysseus assumes Judiciary when he defers to Tiresias, whom the blood drink has inspired to envision new justice through Supreme Law. Odysseus is about to become ''poetic'' for the Branch States, but Pound takes that role to acknowledge the poet Divus for Ratification. Forms of events, personae, and justice culminate in forms of art, the Seal as ''ONE,'' a Statue of Liberty.

7. *Paris Review* 28.

8. ''Amo ergo sum, and in just that proportion,'' *Pisan LXXX*; one of Pound's letterheads from St. Elizabeths was ''J'ayme donc je suis.'' Cf. also ''UBI AMOR IBI OCULUS,'' macaronically ''You be Amor, I be the eye,'' *Rock-Drill 90*.

CHAPTER EIGHT

SEAL *I–IV*: RENAISSANCE

POETIC TRADITION

"Poetry is a centaur. . . . The poetic fact pre-exists."
   "The Serious Artist" 1913

Ur to Echt

I-as-"ONE" projects from its fourfold form becoming a sixfold form (New World history becoming revolution) four cantos. Each canto is informed by four themes while each emphasizes one, viz., tradition (*I*), personality (*II*), justice (*III*), and poetry (*IV*). The four cantos also have the form "to be unity," duality, trine, and tetrad. But *I–IV* were not always thus. In the Ur *Cantos*—fourteen cantos published in periodicals from 1917–24—the present *I* was the second half of Ur *III*. The present *II* was Ur "Eighth" with an Homeric opening; for *II* the Homeric opening was replaced by the keynote of Ur *I*, the first line of an argument with Browning about his poem *Sordello*. The present *III* was made for 1925 by greatly condensing Ur *I* and *II*. However, *IV* remains virtually the same. In Ur *I–III*, therefore, Ur *I* and *II* led up to discovery of the Homeric Nekuomanteia as an archetypal Seal/Calendar form; Ur *IV*, the Seal/Calendar form in a new poetic mode, then confirmed it as it does now via *II* and *III*, Seal/Calendar forms in mediating modes. Ur "Eighth," the "Seal sports" canto, revealed the Seal/Calendar form mythically preparatory to historicizing that form in the Malatesta cantos (then Ur *IX–XII*), which do the same thing in the definitive version. There is thus less change than at first appears.

Each of Ur *I–III* is a fourfold or "square" canto like *I–III*. Ur *I* argues with Browning about his poem *Sordello* as a possible "art form" to develop and extend. In conducting the argument Pound draws upon "Ghosts . . . patched with histories" for a "background" or tradition. Through his own presence there he elicits spirits of place as sources for personae. He casts about among originators of millennial law and justice—the gods of the Golden Age (cf. the present *III*), Hotep-Hotep, Atlas, Prometheus, Moses, and Confucius—for a beginning of a millennial "progress." Finally, after wondering whether his "visions" are valid, he confirms the possibility of "new form" from Renaissance and modern (Vorticist and Cubist) inspirations. The argument proceeds projectively and cumulatively, as though the four themes were both evolving concurrently and building in a mode of argument dominated by the theme of tradition. While Browning wrote "pre-Dante" looking toward Dante's vision of Rome, Pound wants to write post-Dante for the Renaissance.

Ur *II* draws from Ur *I* several literary kinds: lyric, novelistic, epic and dramatic, and personal anecdote. Within these, each rooted in a place where Pound sets himself and each expressing the spirit of its place, Pound casts about for a Sordello. Moving from Sordello's Mantua through a Browning lyric to Provence, Pound seeks his persona among "ancient peoples" (not "ghosts" or "phantoms"). Starting with a Provençal songbook he translates Provençal, Chinese, Greek, and Roman lyrics so that "the murk opens." From "When I was there" in Provence he finds that "ancient people" still "wrap the earth here" with "Ply over ply of life"; "Catch[ing] at Dordoigne" he retells an affair of courtly love as a "novel." Moving from Provence he elicits (again through "When I was there") "A flood of people storming about Spain" and opens up epic and drama in a political mode. The medieval Cid seeks justice (cf. the present *III*); injustice is illustrated from the Renaissance drama of Lope de Vega and from the Renaissance epic of Camoens (in Portugal). Modulation of literary genre through the Dutch Renaissance results in a Renaissance tradition which "brings you to modern times." Not having found a Sordello in the past, however—though My Cid will be retrieved for *III*—Pound has to settle through the Whitmanian "I knew a man" for an American painter educated in Europe who has returned to paint in middle Indiana and has thus been reduced to "talking Italian cities, . . . dreaming his renaissance." "Take my Sordello!" is Pound's last word.

Ur *III* subsumes poetic form and tradition, the spirit of place and personality, in voices of general philosophy, of human law, of divine law, and, consequently, of formal poetic invocation. Renaissance Neo-Platonism and its conventions deliver voices that describe "pure form" and the "omniform intellect." The "Roman speech" of the Renaissance Latinist Lorenzo Valla, who becomes a genuine Sordello by having his Latin compared to the political poetry of the historical (not Browning's) Sordello, is elevated above "the Roman city" and "the eagles" as "the law's voice." Divus's Renaissance Latin Nekuomanteia opens up the voices of tradition, personality, and divine justice, as in the present *I*. Assured at last of a coherent tradition whose personae are seeking justice, and the theme of renaissance having turned to the theme of revolt, Pound adapts "the Cretan's phrase" to a formal invocation for his own epic poem.

Divus's Nekuomanteia, the first sustained narrative in Ur *I–III*, turns "catching at" "many fragments" in Ur *I*, Ur *II*, and the first half of Ur *III* into an assured form with the comprehensive persona Odysseus and other distinctive personae, and with a definitive beginning at once archetypal and historical. Through Odysseus the discovery of Kimmeria subsumes the search for a form and a tradition, Ur *I*; the rites to evoke the dead subsume the search for personae, Ur *II*. Through Odysseus too the myriad dead subsume the "ghosts" of Ur *I*, Elpenor subsumes the "people" and personae of Ur *II*, and Tiresias subsumes the philosophical and justicial voices of Ur *III*. Pound's invocation turns Ur *I–III* and the Seal/Calendar form of the Nekuomanteia toward *IV*, which transforms all that has preceded into an illuminated Renaissance poetic tradition "ply over ply." The modes of argument, personal discourse, and philosophical and justicial discourse, always culminating in poetic discourse, anticipate the detailed forms of '76 symbolized by the Seal and deployed through the Calendar but not formally realized until the prophetic Nekuomanteia.

Pound published "Three Cantos" *I–III* in *Poetry* (Chicago, in June, July, and August 1917) and almost immediately condensed them somewhat for the American *Lustra* (1917). He published them in England in 1919 in *Quia Pauper Amavi* between the dual series "Langue D'Oc" and "Moeurs Contemporaines," and the series "Homage to Sextus Propertius"; simultaneously he "*Privately* printed, for author's convenience, NOT published" *The Fourth Canto*.[1] "The Fourth Canto" was published in *The Dial* (New York), in June 1920 coincident with the retrospective reorganization of the four volumes of "collected poems" (1909–11), *Umbra*, and with the retrospective view of the poet of those volumes and his subsequent fate, *Hugh Selwyn Mauberley*. The "Fifth," "Sixth," and "Seventh" cantos, in versions that like the "Fourth" go into *XVI*. *Cantos* of 1925 without significant change, appeared in *The Dial* in August 1921; the "Fourth" through "Seventh" were grouped in *Poems 1918–21* as "Four Cantos" following "Three Portraits"—of the Roman Empire ("Propertius"), of medieval Provence and its modern counterpart ("Langue D'Oc"/"Moeurs Contemporaines"), and of definitive modernity ("Mauberley"). The simultaneous publications and the rearrangements suggest that "personae" and "cantos" were influencing each other, that Pound was experimenting with ways of relating periods of millennial history to each other and to modernity, that he was extending and deepening the evolution of renaissance to revolution as an historical principle, and that he was preparing his own life and his own vision as means of organizing historical poetry. The possibilities are too detailed to be explored here. We only note that they extend the methods described in pages 60–64 for the "personae" volumes evolving from 1908 to 1926.

The next simultaneous publication was even more important: when the Calendar appeared anonymously in the Spring 1922 *Little Review*, the "Eighth" or "Seal sports" canto appeared in May 1922 in the *Dial*. Before "Seal sports" can be explained as *II* in Seal *I–IV*, its place has to be explained as "Eighth" in relation to the "Malatesta Cantos (Cantos IX to XII of a Long

---

1. See Donald Gallup, ed., *A Bibliography of Ezra Pound* (London: 1963), entries A 16 and A 17.

Poem),"[2] the first of which became the new *VIII* when Ur *I–III* became *I* and *III* so that an altered "Eighth" could be moved forward.[3]

Pound's unpublished letters tell the story of Malatesta originally intended to be a ninth canto but then expanding from one canto to four. The letters and unnumbered periodical versions of the Confucian canto (now *XIII*) and of half the American canto (now *XII*), in that reverse order, refer to the cantos after Malatesta. But there are so many contradictions in Pound's letters about what he was doing after the Malatesta that conjecture about his intentions from such evidence are less credible than the evidence of the poem itself.[4] The letters also refer to revision of the beginning sometime before July 1923, the month when the Malatesta cantos were published as "IX to XII." But as we shall see the Malatesta cantos are so written that even as "IX to XII" they were prepared to take their place as the last two phases of the prototype decad projecting the prototype draft. They were also prepared, as a unit, to become the second phase of the four-phase prototype draft.

On 9 July 1922, Pound tried to justify his work in the face of harsh criticism by Felix E. Schelling, an eminent scholar from his own university, Pennsylvania:

> Perhaps as the poem goes on I shall be able to make things clearer. Having the crust to attempt a poem in 100 or 120 cantos long after all mankind has been commanded never again to attempt a poem of any length, I have to stagger as I can.
>
> The first eleven cantos are preparation of the palette. I *have* to get down all the colours or elements I want for the poem. Some perhaps too enigmatically and abbreviatedly. I hope, heaven help me, to bring them into some sort of design and architecture.[5]

The evidence presented so far, both outside and inside *The Cantos*, makes it evident that Pound did not lack a design; his misgiving here is that he has not yet been able to make it "clearer." "The first eleven cantos" does not refer to design and to the final *I–XI*, but probably to the Renaissance materials and their extensions to China and America: if the Malatesta were only one canto and Ur *I–III* were not condensed to *I* and *III* to allow for moving "Eighth" to *II*, "the first eleven cantos" would comprise the Ur cantos published before *XVI*. *Cantos*—Ur *I* to "Eighth," a Malatesta canto (a ninth), a Chinese canto (a tenth), and an American canto (an eleventh). Pound would thus be

---

2. *Criterion*, London, July 1923.

3. In January 1924, in the *Transatlantic Review*, Paris, appeared "Two Cantos," "One Canto" the Confucian canto (now *XIII*), and "Another Canto" (now *XIII*). No more cantos were published in periodicals; next was the definitive *XVI. Cantos* of 1925.

4. Myles Slatin, in "A History of Pound's *Cantos I–XVI*, 1915–1925," *American Literature*, Durham, N.C., May 1963, follows *Letters* and most of the Yale letters. His hypotheses about how Pound arrived at his form, however, reflect the narrow ground on which they are built.

5. *Letters*.

referring to the "palette" in the Ur cantos as he had written and was writing them, but not to the "design and architecture."

The "design and architecture" are in the subject and form of the Malatesta cantos, a Seal-vision historicized according to the Calendar cycle ("design") and to the Calendar tabulation and Seal-edifice ("architecture"). "Design and architecture" had already inhered in Ur *I* and *II*, emerged in the Nekuomanteia of Ur *III*, and been manifested in *IV*. The middle of the prototype decad, *IV–VII*, remains substantially as first published in periodicals (though *VI* was refined for the 1930 *XXX Cantos*, as we shall see). If the Nekuomanteia is an inherited Seal/Calendar form for the beginning of a Seal-vision (under ISIS), and if *IV* is a constructed Seal/Calendar form for the end of a Seal-vision (under BACCHUS), then "Eighth" was (and *II* is) a constructed Seal/Calendar form for the middle of a Seal-vision projected to the decad. As such it subsumed the Seal/Calendar form in a dominant subject appropriate to the third phase (under POSEIDON); POSEIDON's symbols in turn contain and project the light of a new religion under BACCHUS. But already such an all-encompassing Seal/Calendar form, "Eighth" could be moved to Seal *I–IV* when it and a new *III* (written from Ur *I* and *II*) were placed between the Nekuomanteia (from Ur *III*) and *IV*, a Seal/Calendar climax in both Ur and Echt. When "Eighth" was moved forward two Malatestan POSEIDON cantos on building the Tempio (*VIII* and *IX*) and one Malatestan BACCHUS canto on alternate forms of religion were ready for their new places as third and fourth phases of the decad.

What counts is reading "Seal sports" as a sequel to the Nekuomanteia in the context of *I–IV*; its place as Ur "Eighth" following Ur *I–VII* and projecting the Malatesta cantos may be touched after it has been interpreted in its definitive location as *II* and can be seen in both lights.

Seal *I–IV*

Seal *I*: Prophecies

Seal *I* projects or prophesies Seal *I–IV* in two ways. First, Odysseus's voice projects Seal *I*, the prophecies; Elpenor's voice projects Seal *II*, personal epiphanies; Tiresias's voice projects Seal *III*, justices; and Pound's voice projects Seal *IV*, inspirations for poetry. Second, each canto has the same four-phase form under its dominant theme. Thus Odysseus's voice projects the first phase of each of Seal *I–IV*, Elpenor's projects the second, Tiresias's projects the third, and Pound's the fourth. This form supports the unfolding "to be unity" via duality, trine, and tetrad. Seal *I* having been sufficiently detailed as "ONE," we may now turn to Seal *II–IV*.

Seal *II*: Epiphanies

While the dominant element of *I* is tradition projecting the other dimensions, the dominant element of *II* is tradition being subsumed in POSEIDON's element, out of which natural "Seal sports" are generating the Seal-forms of revolution. But nature does as well for PAN when the originally written POSEIDON canto becomes a second phase; although the Mount is emerging or "busting thru" in each part of *II*, it will emerge definitively under POSEIDON the builder (of Troy) source of Venice in the newly constructed *III*. Again, while the unifying theme of *I* is the prophecies of the gods being received through the ritually evoked dead, the unifying theme of *II* is gods entering human affairs through the elements (which they govern) and being perceived through personal epiphanies.

"Eighth" and *II* differ only in their opening lines, which reflect their respective placings in the prototype decad; the recurring, all-inclusive "square" canto allows the shift in place. The overall theme is a metamorphic tradition being made new by Pound. For duality and personality Homeric poetry leads up to the middle of an Homeric metamorphosis, which modulates into an Ovidian metamorphosis; completion of the Ovidian metamorphosis, as it were inside the Homeric, modulates into completion of the Homeric metamorphosis and of the canto. The Homeric beginning, Ovidian middle, and Homeric end result in a triadic birth of justice out of the sea, out of rape, out of war, and out of godnapping. Dividing the Ovidian middle (like the Homeric metamorphosis) into halves (of a seal) yields a tetradic theme of poetry. Each and all are symbolized by the Seal and each metamorphoses what preceded it (including *I*-as-"ONE"). Hence "Seal sports."

"Eighth" began (after a transition from *VII*) with the Muse weeping for the passing of the Homeric epic of adventurous voyage. It then keynoted the main subject of the canto as the rape of Tyro by Neptunus in an image of a natural Mount enclosing personae:

> Tyro to shoreward lies lithe with Neptunus
> And the glass-clear wave arches over them;

the Roman name of the god linked the Homeric telling of the story with the Ovidian analogue to be generated out of it. This opening was succeeded by "Seal sports in the spray-whited circles of cliff-wash," out of which the rest of the canto evolved as in *II*.

For *II* in *XVI. Cantos* the Muse's lament was replaced by the opening line of Ur *I* (with Browning's name added) about Browning's poem:

> Hang it all, Robert Browning,
> there can be but the one "Sordello."

For the 1930 *XXX Cantos*, when the historical Sordello's story was added to the end of a condensed *VI*, the question of the poem was augmented by the question of a persona and his native place:

> But Sordello, and my Sordello?
> Lo Sordels si fo di Mantovana.

For the Tyro-Neptunus keynote was substituted

> So-shu churned in the sea,

part of an image that opens the last part of the canto. The "Seal sports" line then opened up the rest of the canto as in "Eighth."

The abbreviated argument with Browning sums up the whole lesson of Ur *I–III*, that Browning's poem is unique, that there is a difference between a fictionalized persona and an historical persona, and that the historical persona is the only objective one. Here the argument is preceded by the Nekuomanteia, whose lesson it draws. It also makes the question of personae, not the passing of heroic epic, the keynote.

Therefore So-shu, a Chinese demiurge churning in the natural element (under PAN) as if he were the central star of a whirling cyclic constellation (a vortex), but not yet showing form, replaces the image of Tyro and Neptune shown within a form of the Mount. "Seal sports" then projects all dimensions of the canto by symbolizing the Seal emerging from nature. Natural "Seal sports" foreshadow the activities of the Eagle. Picking up So-shu's churning, "Spray-whited circles" suggest the clouds surrounding the constellation and perhaps too the Calendar cycle. The cliff suggests the Mount. That the seal is a sea-nymph—

> Sleek head, daughter of Lir,
>   eyes of Picasso,
> Under black fur-hood, lithe daughter of Ocean

—suggests Providence. "Eyes of Picasso" suggests the eyes of Eagle and Providence looking respectively left and right. "Under black fur-hood" recalls Aphrodite looking from beneath her dark eyelids (*I*). Indeed, through "And the wave runs in the beach-groove," the sea-nymph prophesies " 'Eleanor, ἐλέναυς and ἐλέπτολις!' "

The fragments of argument and straight historical narrative modulate through the mythic "Seal sports" into blind Homer's ear picking up from the "sea-surge" the droning plea of the elders on the wall at Troy that Helen, despite her divine beauty, be sent back to the Greeks lest she bring evil upon the city. Aural hypnosis passes to an hypnotic image of Tyro and "the sea-god" (not named) "tented" within a wave in bright sunlight. The wave leads into a "Naviform rock overgrown" with algae, giving off "a wine-red glow in the shallows," and showing "a tin flash in the sun-dazzle." As an illusion to POSEIDON's vengeful transformation of the Phaeacian ship that carried Odysseus to Ithaca, this image suggests the whole Seal edifice founded on the shield, which is presumably responsible for the "tin flash."

This first part shows the Calendar phases as truncated, prophetic images. ISIS lies behind the intimation of Sordello's history. Nature prophesies, through Helen, minion of KUPRIS, under PAN. The rape of Tyro by POSEIDON seems at first destructive like the rape of Helen, but it will yield a new conception of justice (the Ovidian story), out of which it will bring a new birth. The "Naviform rock" looks from retribution against Odysseus to the Ovidian story of BACCHUS, who punishes sacrilege but rewards worship with new liberty.

The truncated images prophesy through the "Naviform rock," and the "sun-dazzle" precipitates from the "Naviform rock," a complete, single narration divided into halves (and phases) and inherited by Pound (like the Nekuomanteia, *1*). The story of Bacchus carrying his new religion from Asia to Europe is pre-Homeric in origin but enters European poetry through Ovid.

A brief first phase of the Ovidian narration tells how a ship's crew offered passage to "a young boy loggy with vine-must" (cf. Elpenor) but then, "mad for a little slave money" (the economic theme), mutinied against the captain and took the ship off its course. A long second phase (longest of the account) identifies the boy as Dionysus by "god-sleight," the narrator as the captain Acoetes, his convert, and the listener as King Pentheus of Thebes, who is being warned not to deny the new god and the new religion lest he (like the crew) suffer divine retribution. "God-sleight" consists in stopping the ship "stock-fast in sea-swirl" (cf. "So-shu churned in the sea") and in metamorphosing it to a jungle of the god's vines and beasts. The narration is even more hypnotic than that of Tyro and the sea-god. The ship is presented as though it were a petrified ship of state suspended in dry dock while new life encases it. Lyaeus (Dionysus as the carefree) announces his new religion, makes Acoetes a priest of his new religion, and prescribes rites. Acoetes is a "nuova persona" and the rites and altars constitute a stellar plan metamorphosing Elpenor's burial and tomb.

For a second half of the Ovidian narration and third phase of tetrad, "The back-swell now smooth in rudder-chains" hints at the back of the Seal and the ship turned to a "Naviform rock." The god's justice metamorphoses the crew to fish while Acoetes retells his own change to a priest by personal epiphany ("I have seen what I have seen" and "I said: / 'He has a god in him, / though I do not know which god' "). Pentheus had better listen to Tiresias, the persona for justice, and Cadmus (in *IV* a persona for new civilization), lest he suffer the crew's fate (as he will). Pound ends Acoetes's story and inherits the Homeric and Ovidian traditions in "a later year" by inviting the reader to lean with him over "the rock," where they will see the coral face of

> Ileuthyeria, fair Dafne of sea-bords,
> The swimmer's arms turned to branches,
> Who will say in what year,
>> fleeing what band of tritons,
> The smooth brows, seen, and half seen,
>> now ivory stillness.

This underwater statue of Liberty (the nymph's name means Liberty) symbolizes the ship of state as a petrified Constitution, its living arms turned to
unalterable Branches. Avoidance of rape, unlike Browning's rape of history,
the rape of Helen, the rape of Tyro, and the godnapping, has resulted not in
productive metamorphosis or change but in sterility.

As a single four-phase narration in a triadic canto the Ovidian story is
constituted of the godnapping, the metamorphosis that leads to the announce-
ment of a new religion, the justice meted out to the crew and threatened
against Pentheus, and Pound's inheritance.

The third part and fourth phase begins by revealing that the keynote image
contained a Chinese metamorphic tradition analogous to the Homeric and
Ovidian: "So-shu churned in the sea, So-shu also, / using the long moon for
a churn-stick." The tradition and the persona modulate through the ellipsis
into the suspended rape of Tyro, but now Poseidon is named and the truncated
rape evolves narratively to its climax. Consequent Dionysian imagery color-
ing the water suggests that the Ovidian story interposed in the midst of the
rape was Poseidon's conception and that the now engendered conception has
precipitated a new birth. The new birth is a Seal-scene. A "rock-slide" (the
Seal in fragments) and wings of a portentous fish-hawk casting "grey shadows in water" suggest the front; for the back, the edifice and bird unite by
simile in "The tower like a one-eyed great goose / cranes up out of the olive
grove." This fourth and culminating Seal-form is extended by the coda

> And we have heard the fauns chiding Proteus
> > in the smell of hay under the olive-trees,
> And the frogs singing against the fauns
> > in the half-light.
> And...

A Seal/Calendar form has been set finally in a "paradiso terrestre." Proteus,
focusing all the metamorphoses and their agents in a figure for continuing
change, would be a Providence cloaking OSIRIS; the rebellious fauns cloak
PAN and the rebellious frogs cloak ZAGREUS. The "half-light" indicates
something less than "the sun-dazzle" but more than the dark of *I*. "And..."
(not in "Eighth") points through the eccentric arm and the "INCIPIT"-arrow
to a new beginning (*III*) in continuing revolution.

The violence of *II* reflects violence in history because of inevadable characteristics of nature, of human nature, and of the gods, who rule over all.
Violence is necessary to change or revolution. Revolutionary change is linked
to sexuality and beauty through the rapes. Beauty is a power for destruction or
constructivity; the result of either can be a new beauty that civilizes. Browning
violated history and caused argument, but wrote *Sordello*. The abduction of
Helen destroyed Troy but produced the Homeric poems, "the education of
Hellas." The rape of Tyro results in new birth the conception for which is
the attempted godnapping of Bacchus. The godnapping results in a new priest

of a new justice and a new religion of liberty. The violence in the canto moves toward greater constructivity and order, but just as *II* was necessary to bring *I* to life, so *III* will be necessary to formalize natural powers with justice and *IV* will be necessary to beautify justice with the poetry that can create civilizations.

As *I* tried to reflect the shield-form by successive events directed downward toward the dead while prophesying upward, *II* tries to reflect the constellation as a mind whirling about its center while precipitating from disparate images (the stars) interpenetrating tetraktyses pointing downward and upward. Hence the keynote "So-shu churned in the sea." Hence variegated "Seal sports." One result is concentricities or "Chinese boxes," which reflect an inner hexagon of six stars and an outer hexagram of six stars all whirling about the central star. Arguing with Browning and chiding Proteus circumscribe "Seal sports" begun and completed. "Seal sports" circumscribe the prophesied doom of Troy and the "rock-slide," which is set beside another proud tower. Troy and the tower circumscribe the circumscribing rape of Tyro. The rape circumscribes Acoetes's story and Pound's inheritance. At the center, just as Odysseus/Pound emerged as HORUS the Eagle presiding over a unifying shield, Acoetes/Pound becomes HORUS the central star. Concentricities and the interpenetrating duality of the metamorphic narratives reflect the interpenetrating stellar tetraktyses transforming the shield while projecting the Mount.

The ten events and Homeric unity of *I* having projected a whole form of revolutionary tradition, the multiple personae and the Homeric-Ovidian duality of *II* project a whole form of personae (the Preambles). The rape of Tyro forming "a more perfect union" culminates in Lyaeus's proclamation of new liberty; proffering the new liberty to Pentheus culminates in consummated rape as a more perfect union. At the same time *II* joins with *I* to constitute front and back of the Seal and the Calendar hemicycles. In this form emphasis shifts from tradition to personae. As symbolized by the troubador juggling six symbols in the headpiece to *The Second Canto* (p. 81), the horseshoe symbolizes the luck of "Circe's craft" for the voyage "to form a more perfect union," Odysseus uses his sword to dig the "ell-square pitkin" to "establish justice," the top symbolizes keeping off the dead to "insure domestic tranquility," the shield represents Elpenor's arms to "provide for the common defence," the goblet symbolizes Tiresias drinking the blood to "promote the general welfare," and the whip (Osiris's whip of justice and immortality) symbolizes Pound's restraint but liberation of Divus to "insure the blessings of liberty." Odysseus and Pound carry "WE the People" and unite the disparate motives in the enacting motive, which Pound sums up in the invocation. The personae of the four phases of *II*, again with Pound carrying the enacting motive, turn the motives from the liberty offered by Lyaeus to the new union perfected by Tyro and Poseidon; "WE the People" come to a focus overhearing the fauns and frogs.

Seal *III*: Justices

Seal *III* is divided like *I* and *II* into duality, trine, and tetrad, but its structure is simple, open, and discrete. Its unifying element is the stones of the law symbolizing a single quest for justice. Stones appear first as steps of the Mount to sit on and climb, then direct climbing and descending the Mount before ending in ruins. In a first discrete image, Pound recalls an earlier effort to discover a tradition in Venice; in a second he enters into the aboriginal spirit of Tuscany. These images of Pound's quest for justice, a first half for duality, modulate into a complete narrative of the medieval revolutionary My Cid Campeador's. A final image of ruins continues the narrative for trine while constituting a separate image for tetrad. The four parts transform Constitutional "stones" into a Mount and into the four Branches/Powers before breaking back into fragments.

Seal *III* is brief. It was constituted for *XVI. Cantos* from parts of Ur *I* and *II* by the "bust thru" of the third phase. In the justicial light of *III* the four-phase forms of *I* and *II* show like *III* the Constitutional dynamic. It also transforms Homer and Ovid into the first two thirds of a medieval (Dantean) trine, so that both *III* as trine and *I–III* as trine will project a triadic justicial whole. As trine, *I*, *II*, and *III* will constitute the shield, the constellation, and the Mount rising toward the irradiating sun-vision but not achieving it. The sun-vision waits the consummation of a Renaissance poetic tetrad in *IV*.

The first image elaborates a passage from Ur *I* in which Pound compared himself to Browning sitting on "Your 'palace step' " in Venice possessed of "a background" but seeking from " 'those girls' " (of Venice) inspiration for a form and a persona. Pound's alteration of the passage for *III* reads

> I sat on the Dogana's steps
> For the gondolas cost too much, that year,
> And there were not "those girls," there was one face,
> And the Buccentoro twenty yards off, howling "Stretti",
> And the lit cross-beams, that year, in the Morosini,
> And peacocks in Koré's house, or there may have been.

Only the first and third lines have counterparts in Ur *I*. The rest is elaboration in the light of the revolutionary theme and Seal-vision as evolved in the new *I* and *II*. Since "that year" was "1908, 1909, 1910" (*XXVII*), Pound is pushing the conception for a revolutionary epic back to the date of his first formal effort to "discover" Europe. The overt autobiographical opening makes his own search for justice subsume the preceding *I* and *II* while preparing to envelop the rest of *III*.

If "And then went down to the ship" keynotes prophetic tradition, and if "Hang it all, Robert Browning" keynotes personal epiphany, "I sat on the Dogana's steps" subsumes these in a quest for new justice. By chance or by destiny Pound "sat" (like a legislator or judge) on the steps of the customs-house by which the Venetian government had controlled its trade for centuries. That he lacked money to continue his voyage from America into the storied city reflected economic injustice. Like Browning he had a background and had found a possible Providence (cf. " 'one face,' " Aphrodite, *I*, and Ileuthyeria, *II*). Part of both was the Buccentoro, the symbolic ship of state from which the doges wed the Adriatic with rings (to promote their trade). But the Buccentoro had become a boat club, in the same building as the Dogana, from whose rooms came a modern lovesong: a tradition had declined, but its traces still remained (as paideuma). Lights in a palace suggest a live tradition still persisting across the Grand Canal; the repeated "that year" touches the dating of the Seal. "Koré's house" refers to Venice as Hell, which may or may not have retained symbols of its ancient pride. By this brief passage the discovery and declaration of *I* have been metamorphosed into Pound's own. The voice, however, has settled from anxious and fearful into matter-of-fact and legal.

"Gods float in the azure air" opens an epiphany of prehistoric gods ruling air, woodlands, and waters during a Golden Age "back before dew was shed," in "the first light." The gods are spirits of Tuscany. They transform the violent gods of *II* into gods of a Dantean "paradiso terrestre" atop Purgatory. The epiphany is not hypnotic like the epiphanies of *II*, but again takes the measured legal tone. The epiphany comes with little change from the phase of justicial beginning of Ur *I*. But in 1930 Pound both objectified it and emphasized again the Renaissance perspective by attributing it to the Renaissance humanist Poggio. Out of the epiphany come two lines which recall the possible Egyptian and Chinese beginnings of Ur *I*,

> Green veins in the turquoise,
> Or, the grey steps lead up under the cedars.

These lines turn discovery and declaration "on the Dogana's steps," and colonization and struggle of the epiphany, into a preamble to the narration about My Cid.

Whereas Odysseus and Acoetes spoke for themselves before Pound made them his personae, "My Cid" belongs from the start to a mind already "the medieval mind with wash after wash of classical culture poured over it since the Renaissance." For *XVI. Cantos* Pound turned the discovery of My Cid as a justicial persona of Ur *II* into a Seal-form for the third phase of the third canto of Seal *I–IV*: the narration takes a four-part revolutionary form, adds lines for the Seal and the Constitution, adds the economic theme, and takes the form of the Mount "busting thru" the Calendar cycle.

Modulating out of "the grey steps lead up," "My Cid rode up to Burgos" and beat with his lance-butt on "the studded gate between two towers" (cf. the Declaration and the dichotomies). His challenge brings "una niña de nueve años" to a gallery over the gate, between the towers, where she reads in a Providential voice ("voce tinnula") the king's writ proscribing My Cid

from the city of his residence and eventual burial (cf. struggle and the Preambles). She concludes for halves of the Seal, for the Seal edifice, and for the
Constitution:

> "And here, Myo Cid, are the seals,
> The big seal and the writing."

My Cid's quest for justice has subsumed Dantean Hell and Purgatory into an
ironic reversal of Paradise with the niña as My Cid's Beatrice. My Cid
accepts the irony and the form of the law with a wink at the niña, then goes off
to try to achieve his own "paradiso terrestre."

"My Cid rode up to Burgos" turns backward and downward in "And he
came down from Bivar, Myo Cid" (cf. the Calendar "bust thru"). His
destitution reflects economic injustice, but he has outwitted the usurers by
pawning to them a trunk full of sand "To get pay for his menie" so that he can
break his way to Valencia and new justice. So Pound is imagining his own
plight and a way out of it. But Myo Cid's effort modulates into the murder of
Ignez da Castro and into medieval and Renaissance ruins relieved only by silk
tatters bearing the motto "Nec Spe Nec Metu" (Neither by Hope nor by
Fear—will one achieve one's ends).[6]

The king's writ condemns instituted medieval justice (cf. the Malatesta
cantos). That My Cid accepts it with a wink at the sympathetic niña illustrates
respect for constituted forms. That he turns from medieval justice toward
what became Renaissance justice represents a continuing effort. That the
Renaissance ended in ruins shows a failure to realize the medieval dream of
justice on earth. But to a twentieth-century Yankee who has entered a tradition
of revolutionary justice and has found a revolutionary protagonist, the Renaissance ruins reveal that justice will be achieved "Neither by Hope nor by
Fear" but by continuing revolution along the lines so far laid down. We can
read Pound's whole attitude toward what America of '76 had become through
My Cid's relation to medieval Spain.

Hell, Purgatory, Paradise, and an unachieved "paradiso terrestre" are also
correlated with the literal (Pound in Venice), the allegorical (the gods), the
anagogical (the upward-leading steps modulating into My Cid riding up), and
the ethical (Myo Cid riding down to the ruins with their challenging motto). A
letter from Pound to his mother virtually applies to this canto: "The word
'anagogical' is explained somewhere or other. The greek word originally
means 'leading up to'; I shd. think you might take it as meaning: leading up to
a sense of things in general. But as I haven't looked at that passage in Dante's
prose for some time; wont swear that he uses it in this exact sense. However it

---

6. Ignez da Castro's story, cited in Ur *II*, was added in 1930 when her story was used at the end
of the third decad (*XXX*) to travesty rebirth (renaissance); here allusion to her story replaced an
allusion to "Dante's music." In two lines of Ur "Eighth," cancelled when it became Seal *II*,
Acoetes relied on the god against implicit threats by Pentheus "I was frightened, / but I am not
afraid any longer."

is in the Commedia, a third strata of meaning. The literal, i.e. Dante 'havin vision,' or going through hell etc; the allegory, states of mind depicted, the anagogy: the general significance.'"[7] Since Dantean form prophesies the Constitutional form of '76, the three operative parts of *III* each symbolizes a Branches/Powers dynamic consummating the Constitutional myth of *I–III*: Pound in Venice projects an American entering "ELEUSIS," the gods symbolize his entry into the paideumas, and My Cid symbolizes his active search for justice. By *III* as tetrad, however, Pound brings a Congressional mind to the State of Venice, a Presidential mind to the amending gods, a Judicial mind to My Cid's quest for Supreme Law, and a mind of the Branch States to Ratification of a Renaissance justicial tradition.

The structure of *III* clearly follows the structure of the Seal, the Calendar, and '76. The Eagle in Venice finds data for the stripes of the shield, the segmented cycle, and the Declaration. The gods represent the constellation, the hemicycles of circumferential gods and goddesses, and the Preambles. My Cid riding up and down traces the shape of the Mount, the shape of the Mount "busting thru" the cycle and hemicycles, and the Constitutions overlapping in the gods as amending Powers and as amended Branches. The ruins find the form of the completed sun-vision, temple of Providence, and Providence, the form of the irradiating cycle, and the spirit of the Bill of Rights, but only the motto filters through. The whole canto builds constitutional "steps" and "stones" toward a tetradic, triadic, dual edifice, but at the end unity recurs to fragments. Nor is there light or a "sea-change."

Adding *III* to *I* and *II* brings out myths for overlapping Constitutional forms, states' rights evolving a larger order. Odysseus interacting with his crew and with the myriad dead becomes Congress/States. Odysseus/Elpenor becomes Presidency/Amendment, Odysseus/Tiresias becomes Judiciary/Supreme Law, and Odysseus/Anticleia passing to Pound/Divus becomes States/Ratification.

Odysseus interacting with all the living and dead having culminated in Pound/Divus for States/Ratification, Pound/Divus as Congress/States modulates into the evolving constitutions. In *II* Pound embodying Congress interacts with States (of mind) embodied in Browning, Sordello, So-shu, the Trojan elders, "the sea-god," and the "Naviform rock overgrown" (states' rights in desuetude). Dionysus and Acoetes work through Amendment to a new Presidency. The Supreme Law of Dionysus's new justice and new religion is being expounded to Pentheus by Acoetes through the form of a new Judiciary. A myth of states' rights is ratified through the consummation of the rape of Tyro by Poseidon, which in turn precipitates new States.

Through Congress Pound modulates states' rights into the larger order of States inherent in Venice. Poggio remarks through the eyes of Presidency the gods of nature for Amendment. Pound (Judiciary) presents My Cid's quest for

7. 13 March 1926, Collection at Yale.

Supreme Law. Through a form of States the medieval and Renaissance ruins ratify a myth of Constitution extended from the mode of tradition and personality to the mode of justice, or from the mode of history to evolving modes of nature and civilization.

Seal *IV*: Inspirations

The key to the transformation of Ur *I–III* into *I–III* is *IV*, which emerged from Ur *I–III* to clinch Ur *I–IV*, determined the reordering into new *I–IV*, projects *IV–VII* (Ur and Echt), and through itself and through all these projects the form of all tetrads in the poem. And why should it not, since it is a simple, straightforward, explicit Seal/Calendar canto? As such it brings to a focus through Ur *I–III* culminating in the Nekuomanteia, and from the Nekuomanteia via the new *II* and *III*, a Renaissance poetic tradition. From either form it projects from itself *IV–VII*, which have retained their main subjects and themes since they were first published in 1921, and (via "Seal sports" or not), the Malatestan tetrad. In *XVI. Cantos* it opens up and illuminates "ONE" and *I–IV*, projects the prototype decad *I–X* in both ten cantos and four phases, and projects a four-phase *XVI. Cantos*.

The unifying element of *IV* is rays of the sun-vision, which illuminated the historical dark of the Nekuomanteia of Ur *III* directly and which illuminate the Nekuomanteia of *I* via the natural chiaroscuro or "half-light" of *II* and the justicial "first light" of *III*. Whereas the tone of *I* was dismal, of *II* hypnotic, and of *III* legalistic, the poetic *IV* includes all these tones while raising them to the ecstatic. Seal *IV* begins with an explicit, formal, fourfold Renaissance poetic invocation, which projects the canto as a phasal tetrad; in that respect it opens up the fourfold structure of each preceding canto, Ur and Echt. But the four phases, which consist of images, narratives, and anecdotes, are also deployed (or the canto is divided) into ten irradiating paragraph-images inspired by the Calendar deities and realized through the ten Amendments of the Bill of Rights. These ten images—all vivid and many clinched formally— open up and illuminate the ten events of *I* and give every canto potentially such a ten-part form, though for all but a few key cantos the standard remains four. As to the form "to be unity" via duality, trine, and tetrad, *IV* incorporates concurrency "ply over ply" in its first phase and lets the others unfold in simple sequence while a Seal-vision and Renaissance poetic tradition perfects itself and undergoes a "sea-change."

As argued in pages 65–66, Pound's Seal/Calendar form and beginning a "great forty year epic" modeled on *Sordello* are hinted in 1907. The Renaissance perspective, New World history, the Calendar, and many of the materials of Ur *I–III* are already moving through his early writings. He had translated the Nekuomanteia into "modern metre" by December 1914. The conception, form, and matter of Ur *I–III* can be ascribed to 1907–14, while completion apparently extended to just before publication in 1917. Nothing sure about *The Fourth Canto* appears in his letters until 1919 itself; it can therefore be inferred that from 1917–19 Pound was working the detailed Seal/Calendar form, already "found" in the Nekuomanteia by working from Ur *I* to Ur *III*, into his own Seal/Calendar *IV*, which is definitive in subject matter as well as in theme and form. Since he had finished *V–VIII* by December 1919, it must have taken a long time to consummate Ur *I–III* in *IV*, whereas *IV* enabled him to write the next "four" rather quickly. If it took him more than two more years to publish "Seal sports," it was due more to other activities than to a creative impasse. It took him less than a year to write the Malatesta and, after that, no more than a year and a half to write the rest of the sixteen cantos and to shape up the first draft.

This perspective means that he composed *IV* with Ur *I–III* behind him and a sure knowledge of *V–VIII* ahead; he must have known the themes and forms of cantos after Ur *I–VIII*, but probably did not know the exact subjects. Thus the four phases of *IV* could consummate Ur *I–IV* and project all other four-phase subjects, while the ten paragraphs of *IV* could project the prototype decad *I–X*. To do so the first four paragraphs would be written from Ur *I–IV* and the next three would be written toward a known Ur *V–VII*. The last three paragraphs, however, had to be written toward known themes but toward unknown subjects. Such is indeed the case. Though we cannot validate and explicate this intricate "ply over ply" in complete detail, it can guide the explication that follows. We can rely on the method of "ply over ply," on the necessary looseness which Pound had to allow himself, and on the nature of the dominating Seal/Calendar form. As usual we shall follow the final text, citing earlier variants or later emendations if and when they aid interpretation.

The opening lines look from the Renaissance behind the Nekuomanteia to prehistory:

> Palace in smoky light,
> Troy but a heap of smouldering boundary stones.

The fragments of an old era (cf. Liberty as a broken Calendar tabulation and Constitutional constituents) glare through the smoke ready to be gathered and rebuilt by a drafting mind.

Against this background HORUS the Eagle invokes the four phases of the Calendar cycle in the four voices of the Seal,

> ANAXIFORMINGES! Aurunculeia!
> Hear me. Cadmus of Golden Prows!

Greek Pindar celebrated Apollo as "lord of the lyre." Roman Catullus celebrated Aurunculeia in an epithalamium.[8] Pound commands justice as a

---

8. The stylistic conventions of *The Cantos* make Aurun-culeia a play on *Golden Ass*, Apuleius's book of post-Ovidian metamorphoses. Among other second-phase archetypes Elpenor's relation to Odysseus hints at Greek love, Acoetes means "bed-mate" and his relation to the young boy

self-motivated protagonist with a "medieval mind" being made new by
Renaissance classicism. He celebrates the mythic founder of Europe, a voyager, colonizer, lawgiver, and inventor of an alphabet. Inherently the six gods
under ISIS will culminate in Apollo, KUPRIS's love will be ritualized by
JUNO's feast of EPITHALAMIUM under PAN, revolutionary founding and
building will "bust thru" under Pound's special tutelary POSEIDON, and a
vision of a new era of continuing revolution will culminate under BACCHUS,
Cadmus's grandson.

"Silver mirrors" of a faceted Renaissance mind (cf. "shall a tetrad be
silver") catch light from the smouldering stones and recreate a mythic dawn
("of no era") and a ritual dance. "Beat, beat, whirr, thud," a take-off on
"Beat, beat, whirr, pound" from Whitman's "Drum-Taps," cloaks Ies Ra
*Loom*is Pound (italics mine) as ZAGREUS; Whitman, one of Pound's "spiritual fathers," is an OSIRIS, and *Leaves of Grass* are his limbs.[9] "Goat-foot"
PAN is included in a circle-dance of satyrs and nymphs (the male-female
cycle). From the mythic landscape and from the "sea-foam" a black cock
crows phallic generation. Inspiration for the smoky vision, the invocations,
the circle-dance, and the annunciation has been received from HEPHAISTOS,
artisan of the silver mirrors (cf. Achilles's shield in the *Iliad*), and activated
by the freedoms of religion, speech, and assembly.

The invocation and the first paragraph introduce two stories in five paragraphs. In each story a Greco-Roman myth being relived in medieval Provence is being told in a Renaissance voice until, for a moment, the narrator
seems to be the second Provençal participant. But he returns to himself and
modulates into Pound, who tries to participate in the story before summing up
the whole Renaissance poetic tradition in a first phase.

The first story and second paragraph are introduced by the mythic dance
turned into Renaissance furniture from which an old man speaks in "the low
drone" of historical narrative. But he tells the story of a Provençal lady who,
when her troubador lover's heart was served to her to eat, tried to imitate
Philomela by flying like the swallows, who called her in the voice of the child
Itys served to his father Terreus. Inspired by ZEUS she exercized her right to
bear the arms of imagination. Her passion and her act were so real that even
the swallows changed from the accusative "Ityn" to the nominative and
macaronic " 'Tis. 'Tis. Ytis!" (it is).

This story of myth recreated by passion triggers the story of Actaeon,
which is prepared by an hypnotic paragraph describing the golden sunlight
beating on the trees of Diana's sacred grove as if they formed a fish-scaled

Dionysus carries similar overtones, and the nature spirits of *III* display Ur-sexuality. Cf., more
broadly, Whitman's cameradoes.

9. Pound accepted Whitman as "my spiritual father" in "What I Feel About Walt Whitman,"
written in 1909; another native spiritual father, Henry James, is introduced by pun later in *IV* and
as a Sordello in *VII*. His European "spiritual father" is Browning (to René Taupin, May 1928,
Letters). Confucius is of course a Chinese "spiritual father."

cathedral roof; beneath it Diana and her nymphs bathe naked in silver water in an almost perfect dark. Into this SATURN-inspired scene breaks the interloping soldier-huntsman Actaeon. But suddenly the old man who retold the Cabestan story and created Diana's hypnotic setting has become the Provençal troubador Piere Vidal speaking, a new Actaeon "stumbling along in the wood." That revelation appears to a bona fide Renaissance narrator and to Pound himself.

When the dogs leap on Actaeon-Vidal as in the myth, the new narrator tries to save the doomed stag by calling him to a safe place as the goddess's hair, previously pale in the dark, now blazes like gold in a blazing sunlight. The narrator is inspired by HERMES, protector of spirits, who provides a warrant for probing into the secrets of the dead and of rites.

As a result of the affinity between them, the narrator hears Vidal "muttering Ovid." Inspired by MARS, Vidal has justified his intrusion into the past and into sanctities by discovering how to revive the past—to relive its forms. The narrator clinches the inspiration and due process of law applied to historical cases with the image "The empty armour shakes as the cygnet moves," which gathers the black cock and the swallows into the old shield being given new life by a reborn Eagle (cf. Achilles's shield and armor).

A causal "Thus" carries the revived Renaissance tradition into a vision of sunlight pouring as water from the gods "Ply over ply." Figures like Cabestan's lady and Vidal are vindicated by fair trial along with oriental counterparts. Inspired by APOLLO, the brilliant, fluid light of a Renaissance revolutionary mind has realized the invocation "ANAXIFORMINGES."

A first phase has validated the exploration of Browning's *Sordello* in Ur *I* with Pound's own troubador tradition, which dominated Ur *I–VI* before the tradition of *IV* was read back into the new *I–III*.

It should not be forgotten that in Pound's conception sexual impulse drives the mythic power and enlightenment that make revolutionary history; that has been amply illustrated so far and will become clear in mythic interpenetration of political revolution in the four drafts of "ELEUSIS." But, as in *I–III* and in the Philomela and Actaeon stories, sexual passion is violent as well as creative. Therefore personal history—Pound "At Gourdon that time," in Provence—recalls marriage rites in the old Greco-Roman form of Aurunculeia's—the same torches, the same sky, the same dress, the same cries of "Hymen, Io Hymenae!" Sexuality instigating rapes under KUPRIS but ritualized in marriage under JUNO asserts common law. A second phase (under PAN) is clinched by the image "One scarlet flower is cast on the blanch-white stone." From the Seal a new life symbolized by the constellation is augured by the son of the Muse of Astronomy and by the historical rite taking new natural form against the stone background (the Mount).[10]

---

10. Before being cancelled for *XVI. Cantos* (1925), a final "Amaracus, hill of Urania's son" accentuated the constellation.

A whole tradition validating personal experience not only transforms Ur *II* (and *II*) but also points ahead to the same theme developed autobiographically in *VII* as a search through personal passion for a "New Eros."

Revolutionary justice is validated by one Chinese courtier arguing with another that the wind belongs not to the king but to the whole people, and by camel drivers (the people) challenging "Danae! Danae! / What wind is the king's?" The liberal courtier, "opening his collar," is inspired by ATHENA against cruel punishments;[11] later removal of quotation marks from his "No wind is the king's wind. / Let every cow keep her calf," and from "No wind is the king's" (making both Pound's), fulfills more explicitly the invocation "Hear me." The camel drivers are inspired by HESTIA to assert retained rights. They allude to the imprisonment of Danae in a tower by her king father to prevent her having a son predestined to kill him. Zeus, however, in a shower of gold, fathered Perseus, slayer of the Gorgon, of tyrants, and (accidentally) of his mortal grandfather. The Chinese palace and the stairs looking down on "Ecbatan of plotted streets" symbolize the Mount under POSEIDON.

The ninth paragraph ends enigmatically:

> Smoke hangs on the stream,
> The peach-trees shed bright leaves in the water,
> Sound drifts in the evening haze,
> > The bark scrapes at the ford,
> Gilt rafters above black water,
> > Three steps in an open field,
> Gray stone posts leading...

Pound wrote the justicial theme from Ur *III* dominated by "the law's voice," toward what would become "Seal sports" and Malatesta in Ur and the Tempio cantos (under POSEIDON) in Echt. Phasally he was also writing toward what would become the new *III*. The text sounds like arrival at an oriental or Venetian palace followed by climbing steps of a Mount as in new *III*. The camel drivers sitting on stairs recall Pound "on the Dogana's steps." "Leading" recalls the anagogue and My Cid's quest for new justice. The ellipsis, which in 1925 read "nowhither," probably to cut off "Hear me" before fulfilling "Cadmus of Golden Prows!," suggests an opening toward new poetry and civilization. New *III* in Seal *I–IV* projects this third phase in *IV*, and both project "Seal sports" as "Eighth" and the Malatestan Tempio cantos.

A consummation of metamorphic powers, the reserved powers inspired by ARTEMIS and DEMETER under BACCHUS, realizes "Cadmus of Golden Prows!" in a consummating sun-vision and eye of Providence. A Père Henri

---

11. "Mentally I am a Walt Whitman who has learned to wear a colar and a dress shirt (although at times inimical to both." "What I Feel About Walt Whitman."

Jacques (Anglice: Father Henry James) would speak with Chinese spirits atop a sacred Chinese Mount. The foregoing metamorphoses (with others) are catalogued. Aurunculeia lies behind Danae elaborated in "upon the gilded tower in Ecbatan / Lay the god's bride, lay ever, waiting the golden rain." Two visions of goddesses are contrasted: Pound saw "By Garonne," which was "thick like paint," a statue of the Madonna moving "like a worm in the crowd";[12] Cavalcanti had seen her in a Veronese garden amid a "thin film of images." The contrast foreshadows the conflict between medieval Roman Catholic orthodoxy and Malatesta's Renaissance vision; "The Centaur's heel plants in the earth loam" anticipates the Eagle at the end of X. Here "the poetic fact," which "pre-exists," is taking root in "the rich loam in which a new literature may germinate."[13] Seal $I–IV$ and a Renaissance poetic tradition have been completed, validated, and brought to life. A concluding transition—"And we sit here . . . / there in the arena" (added for 1925)—turns the Seal-vision toward and upon the "Great bulk, huge mass, thesaurus" of raw history (V et seq.).[14]

Seal I precipitates each of the variably divided cantos of Seal $I–IV$ into an integral canto according to this scheme:

	I	II	III	IV
I "to be unity"	10			
$I–II$ duality	6	4		
$I–III$ trine	4 / 4 / 4			
$I–IV$ tetrad	(6) + (1) + (2) + (1) 1 + 1 + 1 + 1			

12. "The worm of the procession had three large antennae, and I hope to develop the motive later, text clearly states that this vermiform object circulated in the crowd at the church of St. Nicholas in Toulouse. Not merely medieval but black central African superstition (*sic*) and voodoo squalling infant, general mark and epileptic religious hog wash with chief totem being magnificently swung over whole." To his father [October] 1919, Collection at Yale.

13. "Poetry is a centaur. The thinking, word-arranging clarifying faculty must move and leap with the energizing, sentient, musical faculties. . . . In the verse something has come upon the intelligence. In the prose the intelligence has found a subject for its observations. The poetic fact pre-exists." ("The Serious Artist" *New Freewoman* IV, London, 15 November 1913). "If Benda is not the rich loam in which a new literature may germinate he is at any rate a fine disinfectant" ("The Island of Paris: A Letter," *Dial*, New York, October 1920).

14. "The Centaur's heel plants in the earth loam" presumably symbolizes too a concluding, rebeginning ZAGREUS and PAN. For *XVI. Cantos* (1925) Pound made the Centaur line into an eleventh paragraph-image for ZAGREUS and added the arena line for PAN (cf. "Zagreus/Zagreus" focused at the end of *Pisan LXXVII* and opening onto "Canto 77 Explication").

Seal *IV* builds and completes building while undergoing and precipitating the "sea-change" to new unity. Each integral canto now manifests the appropriate Seal symbol: the shield in the historical dark, the constellation in a natural light, the Mount in justicial light, and the sun-vision revealing divinity. Each symbolizes a revolutionary phase and its document latent in "REVOLUTION . . . in the minds of the people." Each is thus prepared to undergo a "sea-change" into a premise of the Declaration, through which each projects its respective concurrent and sequential phase of prototypic Renaissance revolution *I–X*: *I* projects the Declaration and *I–VI*, *II* projects the Preambles and *VII*, and *III* projects the Constitutions and *VIII–IX*; *IV* projects the Bill of Rights and *X*, which completes another Seal-form as the Calendar cycle.

CHAPTER NINE

RENAISSANCE REVOLUTION *I–X*

E gradment li antichi cavaler romanj
  davano fed a quisti annutii,
    X and *XI*

Seal *I*, a myth of declaration, projects a Renaissance Declaration culminating in Malatesta, apparently negated by the Papacy but validated by the Eagle (*I–X*). Seal *I–II*, a myth of struggle generating as halves of a seal the motives of the Preamble, projects the struggles of personae of a Renaissance tradition first from union to liberty (*I–VI*) and then from liberty to union (*VII–X*). Seal *I–III*, a myth of founding, projects by trine a Constitutional form for Renaissance states' (and individual) rights (*I–IV, IV–VII*) modulating into a Constitutional form for a new Renaissance union (*I–VII, VII–X*). Seal *I–IV*, a myth of continuing revolution sustaining justice and liberty, projects a perfection of the Renaissance Declaration by the activating Bill of Rights: a Renaissance argument consisting of premises and facts has been activated by private and legal rights (*I–VI*), a declaration of independence has been activated by common law rights (*VII*), a projected new order has been activated by political rights (*VIII–IX*), and a pledge has been activated by reserved powers (*X*). For all these forms the Renaissance poetic tradition comes through the Provence of the troubadors to the efforts of Malatesta, which are apparently thwarted by medieval atavism but which are validated and projected by the Eagle toward the future. As perfection of Seal *I–IV* precipitates the decad *I–X*, so the appearance of the Eagle precipitates a new future through the coda *XI–XVI* and through the four-phase *XVI. Cantos*, which in the new perspective has been perfected from the mythic Seal *I–IV* through the historical Malatesta *VIII–XI*.

So we are intended to read, noting dominant modes, grouped subjects, and focusing images. Seal *I–IV*, Ur or Echt, is a Renaissance poetic tradition culminating in "The Centaur's heel plants in the earth loam." Seal *V* and *VI* make the poetic tradition an historical tradition by adding a "Great bulk, huge mass, thesaurus" of millennial facts and by culminating in Pound's history of Provence and the troubadors (this culmination is clearer in Ur *I–VI*, where this history evolves from the argument with Browning through every canto). Seal *VII*, precipitating the twentieth-century presence evident since the start but keeping it within a Renaissance frame, sums up the Renaissance

141

tradition autobiographically and seizes upon Renaissance personality. The subject of *VIII–XI* (confining ourselves to Echt) is Renaissance revolutionary constructivity (its version of justice and founding) applied to the Tempio Malatestiano. Seal *X* shifts to Renaissance justice for the papal excommunication of Malatesta, which contains more poetry (of its sort) than truth, and for Malatesta's countering vision of the Eagle. We shall see after we have followed it how the four-phase, ten-canto prototype modulates into the four-phase *XVI. Cantos*.

Renaissance Revolution *I–X*

As unitary Liberty (*I*-as-"ONE") precipitated Seal *I–IV*, so the "sea-change" of Seal *IV* precipitates Seal *I–IV* as "REVOLUTION . . . in the minds of the people" in the prototype decad. "REVOLUTION . . . in the minds of the people" projects the Declaration's premises concurrent with appropriate personae, with the first Constitutional dynamic, and with the poetry of the Bill's private rights.

Seal *I*: Revolutionary Destiny

It is tempting to see each four-phase canto in the form of Seal *I*, where tradition, personality, justice, and poetry evolved in discrete sequence. If that pattern prevailed in every canto (if that were possible), then themes could be read from canto to canto in the same tiered order or in belts like those of the Schifanoia frescoes. Odysseus and the dead would proclaim the Declaration's revolutionary destiny, Odysseus and Elpenor would be moved "to form a more perfect union," Odysseus and Tiresias would confront each other in the form Congress/States, and Divus and Pound would have activated the whole according to the freedoms of religion, speech, and assembly. But in the decad concurrent events, personae, justicial relations, and symbols spread these themes over the whole canto. The living and the dead proclaim through Odysseus/Pound the revolutionary destiny. The living and the dead unite "to form a more perfect union" (HEPHAISTOS). Odysseus/Pound interacting with both living and dead manifest the form Congress/States. All have taken advantage of the freedoms to seek a redress of grievances against the laws that govern the rendered world.

Seal *II*: Natural Rights

The natural mode of Seal *II* expresses equality of creation and the self-evident rights to life, liberty, and the pursuit of happiness, to the extremes of rape and godnapping. Natural rights are modified by the motive to "establish justice"

(ZEUS) expressed through the Trojan elders but principally through Dionysus and Acoetes; the motive is accentuated by the symbolic wall, wave, rock, coral, and tower, all of which touch on the equivocal relation between rights and justice. Pentheus and Acoetes focus the conflict while confronting each other in the forms of Presidency and Amendment. Pound focuses all themes and forms in Ileuthyeria, who denied natural rights to the tritons in preference to her own conception of justice and whose arms turned to petrified branches, a symbol of a Constitution unamendable by the right to bear varied kinds of arms: So-shu's churn-stick, Poseidon's arms holding Tyro, Ileuthyeria's arms, and the voices of the fauns and frogs are generalized in epiphanic perception and imagination; all are symbolized by metamorphosis as the Power Amendment itself.

Seal *III*: Government by Consent

The justicial mode of Seal *III* expresses the self-evident truth that governments are instituted among men, deriving their just powers from the consent of the governed. Pound witholds consent from the government of Venice but accords it to the gods of the Golden Age; My Cid consents to the king's writ but seeks new justice. The gods are a locus for "insuring domestic tranquility" (SATURN), which is uncertain in Venice but is observed at Burgos. Judiciary is the form for the laws of Venice and Spain, but the gods manifest a Supreme Law sought by both Pound and My Cid. Pound and My Cid are both intruders and My Cid is literally a soldier denied quarters in Burgos. But since both are would-be lawmakers their entries are justified despite discouraging conditions and proscription. The dangers of admitting militarists are illustrated by the murder and the Renaissance ruins.

Seal *IV*: Continuing Revolution

The inspirational mode of Seal *IV* reveals the self-evident truth that revolution is necessary and defines its scope through Cabestan's lady, Vidal, and the debaters against authority; the methods—reliving the past and debate—are ritualized both in themselves and by marriage ("Prudence indeed") imposed upon natural impulse. To "provide for the common defense" (HERMES) moves the effort to save Vidal. Inspirations come through States (of mind) invoked and realized (Ratification) by the emergent Renaissance/twentieth-century narrator. At the same time the world scope and the varied "states of mind" open up an expanded form of Congress which looks toward new union. The initiating invocations warrant opening up the secrets of the dead and sacred mysteries.

Executive Tyranny *V*

The mythic premises of Seal *I–IV* modulate through "And we sit here... / there in the arena" into the "Great bulk, huge mass, thesaurus" of millennial history from Ecbatan to Egypt through Greece, Rome, and Provence to the Renaissance. But first "the clock ticks and fades out" so that "the vision" of Seal *I–IV* (much of it in echoes and imagery more recognizably from Ur *I–IV*) is imposed upon it. Still, however, though the vision is always there, "flitting and fading at will," it is "on the barb of time," or guided (like the Declaration's premises) by millennial history; "the vision" and millennial history interanimate each other, the one bringing the ideal (here Neo-Platonic) and the other giving it substance.

Busy commercial Ecbatan and flourishing agricultural Egypt generate the Neo-Platonic vision, which itself opens up Greek and Roman poetry as though they were fresh. But a decadence begins to enter because social order and natural fertility are subordinated to personal passion. Separation of collective well-being and personal desire expands in stories of troubador wanderings and adulteries, which bring back the Trojan War. This decline, which has evolved in a mode of poetry, has nevertheless regressed from pure vision back toward raw history. It breaks into raw history with the Renaissance as "Clock-tick pierces the vision" opens up Renaissance political murders.

The murder of John Borgia in Rome and other such murders are presented as mere slander or ironically. But the Florentine historian and jurist Benedetto Varchi sets a Medici murder in millennial perspective, gathers all the facts, and explores the motives of victim and assailant to try whether it was just or unjust. Pondering Brutus and the slayers of Agamemnon, Varchi tries to decide whether Lorenzaccio murdered his cousin Duke Alessandro for love of Florence or from personal malice. He interviewed Lorenzaccio to probe his motives, which, if Varchi were Dante, would justify condemnation to Hell. He found that Alessandro's assassination had been forecast in his horoscope, so that the Duke had resigned himself to a destiny. Was it patriotism, malice, or destiny? Was Alessandro a tyrant or a weakling? Was Lorenzaccio a patriot or a murderer? Varchi cannot decide. He ends impressed most by Lorenzaccio's resolute and terrible deliberation about how to kill Alessandro so that the Duke would know his assassin.

Varchi focuses a millennial theme of executive tyranny by trying a case involving it. Was Alessandro a tyrant? Was Lorenzaccio a mere egoist? Were either moved to promote the general welfare (MARS)? They are related to each other as Presidency (for a Renaissance union) and Amendment (for states' rights). Varchi has amended Dantean moral judgment by applying due process of law historiographically to seek an historical judgment. Of his having left the case open Pound wrote: "Christianity lends itself to fanaticism. Barbarian ethics proceed by general taboos. The relation of two individuals is so complex that no third person can pass judgment upon it. Civilization is individual. The truth is the individual. The light of the Renaissance shines in Varchi when he declines to pass judgment on Lorenzaccio."[1] The Renaissance and the so-called Renaissance man, particularly the case against mere egoism, remain open. Malatesta will open up the question further. But the case will not be decided on a world scale until the fifth draft reveals the Confucian means of dealing with political tyranny and violence.

Justicial Tyranny *VI*

Ur *VI* followed Ur *I–V* compositionally and then in the same form followed the new *I–VI* in the 1925 volume. For 1930, however, "But Sordello and my Sordello? / Il Sordels si fo di Mantovana" was added after the first two lines of Seal *II*, and Seal *VI* was drastically overhauled in form and materials if not in general subject. For the new *VI* the beginning was radically expanded, the earlier version was severely condensed to make up a new middle, and the line introducing the historical Sordello was repeated from *II* to open up the newly added story of Sordello and his inamorata Cunizza da Romano. Other alterations gave the canto a Greek frame and analogue for the first phase. The new *VI* thus became a more explicit transitional canto subsuming *I–V* in the end of a phase of Renaissance tradition while projecting Renaissance personality, justice, and poetry.

    Ur *VI* completed a Renaissance tradition coming through the troubadors since Ur *I* argued with Browning about his *Sordello*. The personae of the lyrics and the "novel" of Ur *II*, Sordello the historical poet of Ur *III*, and Cabestan's lady and Vidal of *IV* had lived their poetry and poeticized their lives. The troubadors of *V*, seen in the light of "the vision," simply lived their passions as raw history and so became negative evidence in an historical case. Ur *VI* applied "the vision" to the complete case of Provençal civilization in its medieval setting, illustrating negative and positive values. Ur *VI* was written as the case of a whole civilization motivated to "secure the blessings of liberty to ourselves and our posterity" (APOLLO). Medieval law and the new law of the love courts and the love code manifest the dynamic Judiciary / Supreme Law, the latter for states' rights and the former for a new Renaissance union. The case is prosecuted by a fair trial of the historical evidence and its personae. In the new *VI* of 1930 the case is pointed more sharply, the motive toward liberty is elaborated, forms of justice are more clearly marked, and fair trial is accentuated with witnesses and counsel for the defense.

    The opening of Ur *VI* puts Odysseus on trial before a bar of universal justice with " 'The tale of thy deeds, Odysseus' "; accuses Guillaume, ninth duke of Aquitaine, for having sold out his ground rents; and evolves this millennial history "Till Louis is wed with Eleanor," which makes it also dynastic history from Guillaume to his grand-daughter Eleanor of Aquitaine.

---

1. "De Gourmont: A Distinction," *Little Review*, New York, January–February 1919.

It puts the whole sweep on "the wheel" of fortune, which a refrain from Bertran De Born "('Conrad, the wheel turns and in the end turns ill')" gives a dismal cast. The whole aim of the canto is to develop the bleakness of medieval fortunes, personal, familial, and political, but to show shining through them a revolt against prevailing conventions stemming from Provence and promising better forms of civilization. The end of the canto shows that the revolt has been centered in Eleanor, the head of the love court and administratrix of the love codes, and carried out by genuine lovers and troubadors against conventional political leaders and political marriages.

Eleanor's marriage to Louis, an arranged dynastic marriage and therefore loveless, does not survive his jealousy and suspicions of adultery. He does not punish her, however, nor does war result—the customs of V would have suggested either or both—but legally divorces her and casts her down the wind to fortune, even though that means losing her patrimony, Aquitaine and Poitiers. The wheel delivers her to Henry Plantagenet, about to become king of England, who marries her for her political value as Louis had. Louis becomes angry, but again, instead of war, the matter between the French and English dynasties is settled by ceding to Henry and Eleanor's firstborn certain cities; if there is no issue, the cities shall revert to France. The young prince dies (and is mourned by Bertran De Born's "Planh"), but Henry keeps the cities anyway. Consequently wars break out between Henry on the one side and, on the other, Eleanor and her son Richard Coeur-de-Lion. Born's wheel refrain again laments ill fortune, but Henry holds the cities against Louis's successor even though one of them is the dowry of Louis's daughter.

The background for these complex dynastic dealings is the Crusades, the first of which drew Guillaume, the second of which drew Louis and Eleanor, the third of which Richard concluded with a treaty, and the fifth of which Frederick II, emperor of Germany, concluded with a treaty. The emphasis is on the Third Crusade for its drawing Richard to Messina in Sicily on the way to Jerusalem. There chivalric jousting was more "to the era" than peace treaties, but nevertheless quarrels among the leaders of the Crusade were resolved by the Convention of Messina, in which the French King Phillipe Auguste agreed to cancel the marriage contract between his sister Alix and "our noble brother" Richard and reaffirmed that the cities of Aquitaine remain with the English crown.

Still Bertran De Born's wheel refrain recurs. But the canto ends "before all this" with an inherent element so far not touched. Eleanor, in her role as head of a love court, receives from the troubador Bernart of Ventadour a plea that she send word to Eblis, who to keep his wife away from Bernart has deprived her of her freedom and her joys, that " 'you have seen that maker / And finder of songs,[2] so far afield as this / That he may free her, / who sheds such

2. "Poems and the materials of poems shall come from their lives, they shall be makers and finders," from "Mediums," is quoted along with "Camerado, this is no book; / who touches this

light in the air.' '' This spirit lies behind the legal rather than violent methods of handling dynastic and cultural disputes. It is a new civilizing form. It could make men and women brethren and sistren. Love has humanized politics. Bertran's resigned and elegiac poetry, which has come through the language of chronicle, personal passion, and legal documents, takes on a new and more hopeful tone in Bernart's poetic speech, which draws on the best of the troubador spirit and expression.

Still, however, though a new set of values is coming through the old, a new equivocation comes with it: the ethic of the love courts and the troubadors carries the argument of separation but does not bring with it a new sense of social responsibility and public order. Both this insufficiency and a new myth are accentuated in the new *VI*, which is modeled on the sequential four-phase forms of Seal *I*, *III*, and *IV*, and remodeled as a transition between *I–V* and *VII–X*.

The new *VI* opens with four elliptical fragments which transform Seal *I–IV* while accentuating the cases against Odysseus and Guillaume:

> What you have done, Odysseus,
> We know what you have done...
> And that Guillaume sold out his ground rents
> (Seventh of Poitiers, Ninth of Aquitain).
> "Tant las fotei com auzirets
> "Cen e quatre vingt et veit vetz..."
> The stone is alive in my hand, the crops
> will be thick in my death-year...

The case against Odysseus places in dispute the destinies of both plaintiffs and defendant while implying a need to turn from the wandering life toward home (cf. *I*). Guillaume ''sold out'' so that he could pursue life, liberty, and happiness as a troubador (cf. *II*). He sang how he governed the ladies by fucking them 188 times (cf. ''those girls,'' ''one face,'' and ''Stretti,'' *III*; also the Spanish My Cid, *III*, and ''Poictiers, you know, Guillaume Poictiers, / had brought the song up out of Spain / With the singers and viels,'' *VIII*). He handed on a continuing revolution of natural fertility through his sexual prowess and artistry even if he did not hand on means for achieving sufficient communal order (cf. *IV*).

''The vision'' having been condensed as the Declaration's premises, Louis and Eleanor are put into the raw chronicle history of *V* generationally:

> Till Louis is wed with Eleanor
> And had (He, Guillaume) a son that had to wife
> The Duchess of Normandia whose daughter
> Was wife to King Henry e maire del rei jove...

---

touches a man,'' from ''So Long!'' in affirmation of the American spirit and of Pound's own vocation, ''Patria Mia'' XI (1912).

They are taken off the wheel of fortune, which means complete removal of Bertran De Born from the canto and thus a greater emphasis on human responsibility and opportunity for achieving justice. The main subject then recurs to *I* and the opening of *VI* by applying ''Went over sea till day's end'' to Louis and Eleanor's voyage to the Second Crusade. Eleanor's discovery that her uncle, who had ''known her in girlhood,'' commanded at Acre, elicits a new tag from a poem by Arnaut Daniel and an analogy to Theseus's abduction of Helen of Troy when she was a girl. The innuendo and alleged meeting with the Mohammedan leader Saladin caused the jealous Louis to divorce her, ''divorcing thus Aquitaine.'' In that year Odyssean Henry ''dodged past 17 suitors'' and married her, angering Louis. But the treaty ceding cities to an English heir and the later treaty freeing ''Richard our brother'' from the contracted marriage with Alix settled disputes of two generations. Removal of all family, dynastic, and religious conflicts emphasizes further the supersession of military solutions by legal solutions.

The case against the Odysseuses of this first phase, each motivated by his own kind of liberty against prevailing conventions, has been given fair trial within the dynamic Judiciary/Supreme Law. The argument for separation has been made but the case (like that against Lorenzaccio in *V*) has also opened up means of liberalizing and humanizing political and erotic relations justicially without resort to tyranny and violence. These themes continue in three more phases, which also project the rest of the Declaration for the rest of the decad.

Ventadour's plea to Eleanor in her love court shifts from dynastic history and legal documents to semidramatic, quasi-poetic personal appeal (cf. Elpenor's appeal to Odysseus, *I*). It projects a declaration of independence to *VII*.

The addition to new *VI* consists of a third phase, the stories of Sordello the poet and lover and of his inamorata Cunizza, and a fourth, a snatch of Sordello's poetry about Cunizza. Sordello's story tells how his prowess in poetry made him accepted at the court of Richard Saint Boniface. But he turned a conventional court into a love court by falling in love with Richard's wife Cunizza and freeing her from a loveless marriage in the spirit of the new code. Sordello's assertion of independence projects Malatesta's in *VIII*.

Cunizza's will, quoting legal Latin and validated by witnesses, tells how she freed her slaves and so was worthy of a troubador's love. The same Latin tells how Sordello ''subtracted'' her from her husband and lay with her, so that she became a source of inspiration for his poetry. This version of proclaiming sovereign powers projects Malatesta's inspiration, Isotta degli Atti, for whom he built the Tempio (*IX*).

The culmination of the new *VI* and of Sordello's inspiration is a quatrain of Sordello's own poetry:

> ''Winter and Summer I sing of her grace,
> As the rose is fair, so fair is her face,

> Both Summer and Winter I sing of her,
> And snow makyth me to remember her.''

Such was the kind of thing for which Malatesta was excommunicated but which qualified him to receive the Eagle (*X*). Sordello's pledge to Cunizza foreshadows Malatesta's pledge under the Eagle to his men.

After part of a line beginning another troubador story, an anecdote about the saving of Theseus gives *VI* and *I–VI* (cf. also drafts first–sixth) a Greek frame. The coda sums up all the Odysseuses of the canto in a case against Theseus newly arrived incognito in his father's court and about to be poisoned at the behest of his father's wife. Recognition of a family heirloom, the shape of his sword-hilt, saved him. Like the whole canto this is a separation from the past and a new dispensation, but the application is almost entirely to the individual case and the scope is more liberation from than construction of. Though a code for a communal order is in the making within the argument for independence and for states' rights, the forms for a larger communal order will be perceivable only when a declaration of independence and a form of states' rights have been completed (*VII*) and have precipitated the broader scope of Malatestan constructivity.

Canto *VI* is noteworthy for its female inspiration, from Odysseus's and Guillaume's women to Eleanor, to the lady of Eblis, to Sordello's Cunizza. Looking back we can be struck by the inspirational roles of Circe and Aphrodite (*I*), of Cabestan's lady and Actaeon-Vidal's Diana (*IV*), and of love poetry modulating into Lorenzaccio's possible "love of Florence" (*V*). These inspirations reflect the gods under ISIS of the first hemicycle. It is evident that subject, theme, form, and the emergence of a tradition dominated by Odysseus/Sordello E PLURIBUS UNUM make *VI* a frame with Seal *I*. Passage from the dark of tradition to the light of a new personality, justice, and poetry will be accompanied by greater initiative from males associated with PAN, POSEIDON, and BACCHUS.

Another noteworthy aspect of *VI*, more emphatic in Ur *I–VI*, is the sustained use of Provence and the troubadors in every canto until *VI* presents a whole history. Provence was "my background" cited in Ur *I* and already developed as the dominant period in the "personae"; it continues to have an important place in *VII* and is linked with Malatesta for *VIII–XI*. There is reason to think that Pound analogized Provençal "background" with his American "background"—that Provence was to medieval orthodoxy what America had been to the atavistic medievalism of Europe since 1492 and what America could be again to the atavistic medievalism of the twentieth century. A paragraph in the chapter about Arnaut Daniel in *The Spirit of Romance* ("Il Miglior Fabbro," II) suggests the first stirrings of the Renaissance and Pound's revolutionary Calendar for a new era: "While the highest minds of the age were passing systematic legislation for the most orderly angels, and reconstructing the laws of God with a fascinating preciseness, the architects, illumined, one supposes, by some glimmer of the esoteric doctrine, were applying the Greek laws of proportion to buildings meet for the new religion, and the Troubadours were melting the common tongue and fashioning it into new harmonies depending not upon the alternation of quantities but upon rhyme and accent. Some temperamental sympathy may prejudice me in favour of this age." Again, in "Provença" (III), Provençal civilization is idealized America, its poets were the kinds of poets Pound looked for in America and tried to be, and its poetry is the kind of poetry Pound always tried to write: "The poetry, as a whole, is the poetry of a democratic aristocracy, which swept into itself, or drew into it, every man with a wit and a voice." "My spiritual father" Whitman was a "maker and finder of songs" whose poetry came from life lived, and such he predicted. "My Sordello . . . dreaming his renaissance" at the end of Ur *II* is a Whitman/Pound.

From such points Pound extends his whole handling, in essays, in "personae," and in *The Cantos*, of Provençal history, life, justice, civilization and poetry. Cantos *I–VI* (Ur and Echt) culminate in a whole rendering of its values and of prophesied values of '76. That rendering is sharpened by the new *VI* of 1930, a condensation of the Declaration itself, to account for diminished emphasis on Provence in the new *I–VI* and for the coming Jefferson-Adams *Cantos XXXI–XXXIII*, which were published in 1931 before *Eleven New Cantos* or "Jefferson-Nuevo Mundo" was published in 1934.

If such an analogy between Provence and America, between a troubador and Pound, seems fanciful, one need but note the draft epitomized by *VI*, paideumatic America presented in the sixth canto "JOHN ADAMS," where the protagonist is in one aspect an heir to "ELEUSIS" through Guido Cavalcanti's love canzone (*XXXVI*). Too, as we shall see, "JOHN ADAMS" has the same form as *VI*: five drafts summed up by fragments in a sixth and a sixth projecting seventh through tenth, or again a condensation of the Declaration of Independence into the culmination of the first phase.

Declaration of Independence *VII*

Canto *VII* consummates the Renaissance tradition in poetic autobiography while incorporating the tradition into the autobiography; it epitomizes *Pisan*. In 1919 Ur *VII* came out of Ur *I–VI* in the model of *IV*, which then first suggested the epochal sequence embodied in Seal *I–IV* for 1925. It now, without significant change, continues from *VI* while summing up the Renaissance poetic tradition (*I–IV*) and historical tradition (*I–VI*) on its first page. It then modulates into its main subject, Pound's poetic autobiography from 1909 to 1919, before a concluding frame affirms and selects the Renaissance historical tradition identified in *V* as a locus for revolutionary personae.

The rubric—"Eleanor (she spoiled in a British climate)"—refers both to the historical Eleanor who married Henry II and to a visionary beauty Pound brought with him when he came to London in 1908 and began to settle there in 1909. Homer, Ovid, and medieval poetry (summarized in that order) were still viable, but a gap existed between that poetry and the next viable literary medium, nineteenth-century realist prose, which (in the hands of Flaubert and Henry James) had to deal with a reality dominated by material furnishings and by psychological enervation. For this summary of *I–VI* (Ur or Echt) James, in the role of a Sordellan guide, introduced Pound to London (if not to the Renaissance tradition):

> And the great domed head, *con gli occhi onesti e tardi*
> Moves before me, phantom with weighted motion,
> *Grave incessu*, drinking the tone of things,
> And the old voice lifts itself
> > weaving an endless sentence.

The Italian describes Dante's moralist Sordello. The Latin describes the slow, heavy tone enforced by the subjects James had to deal with.[3]

Guided by James "We" made "ghostly visits . . . seeking for buried beauty." Pound recalls his first entries into London and Paris in the perspective of a return to Paris after World War I, in 1919. All he found was empty rooms and a strange concierge in place of "the gouty-footed" (cf. PAN). Skeptical of apparent cultural exhaustion and stubbornly refusing to accept it, he seeks the living. Even the "personae" of 1909–12—"The wilted flowers / Brushed out a seven year since, of no effect"—were at least passionate. But the "personae" respected a separation between past and present. Here his passion damns the partition and breaks it by linking Greek and Chinese personae with his own surroundings so that "Time [is] blacked out with the rubber." The Champs-Élysées continues a name and a bus gives him "a date for a peg" (cf. the "clock-tick" and the "barb of time," *V*). Only the furnishings are "in 'time.'" "The passion endures."

The objective account of the tradition and the passionate rejection of mere modernity pass into hypnotic recollection. Is his imagined Eleanor or Helen as dead as Tyro in the seven years since he turned from impassioned lyric to irony and satire? (Tyro, who would come alive in Ur "Eighth," has already come to life in *II*). She comes to life again through Ovidian and Provençal imagery in a "Nicea" envisioned in Provence before the war and carried with

3. The single recurring tribute to James, from "Patria Mia" (1912) through "Provincialism the Enemy" (1917) to "Henry James" (1918), is "his propaganda, his continuing labour for individual freedom" ("Patria Mia" VIII). All James, however, is brought to bear: his guidance on "the remaining great adventure, the approach to the Metropolis"; his effort to stave off war by promoting international understanding; and his novelist's treatment of a major force in world affairs, "race." "Henry James" is a mine for understanding *VII*, as, for "the passion endures," is "[Rémy] De Gourmont: A Distinction" (1919). In *Make It New* (1934) Pound grouped as "General summary of state of human consciousness in decades immediately before my own, the H. James and De Gourmont compendium." Their successors were Joyce and Eliot, whose *Ulysses* and *The Waste Land* constitute one of the backgrounds for *I–VI* culminating in *VII*. Cf. the first line of *VIII*, p. 153.

him ever since. Only she and he have "being" among locust-like men droning in locust-like voices. Between sham classical decorations and beneath the jazz persists "Shell of the older house," but it is "expulsed" by "this house."[4] Amid the same old talk a contrast between Nicea and a dancer reminds him that his original inspiration is "ten years gone" (since 1909). The old talk preserves her in a "petrifaction of air" and the old room stifles the young. Passion to take off into a Dantean paradise ("O voi che siete in piccioletta barca") is weighted down by a sentimentalized Dido weeping for her dead Sichaeus and drowning with her tears a "New Eros" instead of founding Carthage. Still "the life" goes on in nature and "Flame leaps from the hand" in "Passion to breed a form in shimmer of rain-blur." But still Eros remains drowned in Dido's tears.

Life mocks husks that move, words that rattle, and "shells given out by shells" until "The live man, out of lands and prisons," shaking "the dry pods" and probing for "old wills and friendships," revives the figures of the Medici assassination. A new light affirms Varchi's Renaissance historiography and suspension of judgment. From objective and passionate, then hypnotic, then elegiac and yearning, the tone becomes excited. Lorenzaccio, voluntarist and factive personality (cf. Odysseus), is more alive than the dead living because "more full of flames and voices." With him "the tall indifference" Alessandro, visionary and victim (cf. Elpenor), moves "a more living shell." United they "Drift in an air of fate, dry phantom, but intact." The phase of the epiphanic personality ends apostrophizing Alessandro as a visionary Henry James, doomed but still an "Eternal watcher of things, / Of things, of men, of passions." A concluding image—

> Eyes floating in dry, dark air,
> E biondo, with glass-grey iris, with an even side-fall of hair
> The stiff, still features.

—suggests the stars of the constellation or the Eagle inspired by Providence. In 1925 Pound's fortune wheel (see p. 85) immediately followed.

In the large *VII* defines an inheritable or usable tradition objectively and then affirms it autobiographically. The summary from Homer to a medievalized James, though "spoiled," is distinct. The autobiographical affirmation is homogeneous, but it is marked by reaffirmation that "the passion endures" (validated by Nicea), by "Passion to breed a form," and by the live man's self-liberation before he focuses both tradition and autobiography in Renaissance personality. The canto thus has its own form of four phases—a more organic one appropriate to personality—but the major form is the stellar form of Seal *II*, metamorphosis of old life to new framed between expectancy and new birth (here rebirth). As a unity—as *VI* made a first phase emphasize the

4. Until 1930 the shell was less forcibly "expulsed" but "not extinguished."

Homeric quest for a new tradition—an Ovidian quest for new life is set in a context of men turned to locusts.

The quest for new life is a declaration of independence. The protagonist reachieves the liberty of *VI* and redirects it under KUPRIS and JUNO toward a new Renaissance union. The "states of mind" of the tradition are ratified by his own "states of mind," which ratify a states' rights form (*I–VII*) while modulating through the Branch/Power States toward new union. The protagonist is activated by a common law of timeless passion rooted in nature and in human nature presided over by PAN.

As a second phase of the decad *VII* precipitates under PAN a twentieth-century protagonist's struggle against twentieth-century medievalism contained within and so defined by Renaissance protagonists' struggles against medievalism itself. After a tradition of dead personae inspired by Eleanor and seeking liberty—Homer, Ovid, Dante, Flaubert, "the old men," and James—has summed up *I–VI*, the living Pound turns the motivation from liberty toward union of living and dead.

The second phase not only manifests the Preambles (as *VI* summarized the Declaration) but also (again like *VI*) projects the rest of the Declaration. The new and main subject of *VII* is the reaffirmation through Nicea that "the passion endures," a declaration of independence from the locust-world. The quest for a "new Eros" by "Passion to breed a form" resulted first in "Seal sports" as Ur "Eighth" and then in Malatesta, but the present Malatesta *VIII* and *IX* were written so that conceiving and building the Tempio would manifest the assuming of independence and of sovereign powers. The live man's union with Lorenzaccio and Alessandro resulted in Malatesta's pledge with his men under the Eagle (*X*).

Independence *VIII*

When Pound removed "Seal sports" as a transition between *VII* and Malatesta he added to the opening of *VIII* a summation of the modes of tradition and personality:

> These fragments you have shelved (shored).
> "Slut!" "Bitch!" Truth and Calliope
> Slanging each other sous les lauriers:
> *That* Alessandro was negroid. And Malatesta
> Sigismund:

The first lines refers to the question of usable history as in the argument with Browning. Here, however, the alternatives are probably Joyce's *Ulysses*, in which Leopold Bloom's history resides in the books on his shelves, and Eliot's *The Waste Land*, in which the Fisher King's fragments of history have either been gathered from shored wreckage of the sea or used to shore up a

falling structure. In neither case does the past reveal a viable, usable form for
the present, as *The Cantos* has claimed, is claiming, and will claim. The argument between Truth and Calliope, Muses of fact and fiction, applies the same
argument to personae. Was Alessandro "biondo," as at the end of *VII*, or
"negroid"? In fact, Alessandro dei Medici was the latter. But Pound "busts
thru" the argument by substituting a new and more satisfactory persona for
both the factive Lorenzaccio and his contemplative victim. Again we might
sense Joyce's Homeric Ulysses and Eliot's Ovidian Tiresias giving way to a
persona who can put many-mindedness and sensitivity to use constructively in
the service of an historical destiny.

These new lines were added to the opening of Ur *IX*, Malatestan halves of
a seal unified by Pound as an introduction to a phase of constructive effort
toward a new order:

> *Frater tamquam*
> *Et compater carissime*: *tergo*
>   *...hanni de*
>   *..dicis*
>   *...entia*
> Equivalent to:
>   Giohanni of the Medici,
>   Florence.

"Brother, as it were, and dearest comrade"[5] subsumes the first two modes as
the front of the Seal shared, one Eagle to another. "*Tergo*," back, seems to
reveal "*hanni de*" (years of) for NOVUS ORDO SECLORUM, "*dicis*"
(you say) for MDCCLXXVI, and "*entia*" (things) for stone reaching toward
a summit. Pound's irradiating interpretation resolves the enigma by constituting the new fragments in the voice ANNUIT COEPTIS so that the new subject
can begin with a letter from Sigismundo to Giovanni. The subject is European, the "fraternal deference" (*XIII*) is Chinese, and the form is American.
Halves of a seal project Malatesta conceiving a new order crowned by the
Tempio (*VIII*) and working to crown that new order with the Tempio (*IX*).

Malatesta is presented at once as an expression of his times, as a victim of
his times, and as a revolutionary innovator. Over the four cantos he appears as
one of his times' foremost condottieri, one of those military leaders whose
skill and prowess made him much in demand among the warring city-states of
quattrocento Italy. He was also therefore involved in the many intrigues and
treacheries that followed necessarily from such a system; he tried more than
others to be honest and aboveboard, but his temperament and his other interests made him less than a match for more skilled players at power politics.
His main interests were the current discoveries of the classical past, the re-

5. Ur "Malatesta" began simply "Frater," etc., with no link to antecedents—i.e., provisional
as to substantive integration.

sultant new humanism, the creation of a thriving, enlightened, independent community for his Duchy of Rimini, and, as a crowning achievement, transformation of Rimini's Duomo into the neopagan Tempio Malatestiano. To finance these interests he undertook his many military jobs. But he was no saint in his private life. Among other things he was suspected of and charged with killing two wives (like Browning's Duke in "My Last Duchess") and of raping a woman after having killed her. Still he was devoted to his mistress and then third wife Isotta degli Atti, to whom he dedicated the Tempio, and to their family. He was the Renaissance man in broader terms than either Lorenzaccio or Alessandro dei Medici.

Malatesta thus becomes the first fully explored cultural revolutionary in *The Cantos*, second in magnitude and importance only to the "protagonista civile" John Adams. It is no accident that the frontispiece of *Guide To Kulchur* is a Malatesta seal given "to indicate the thoroughness of Rimini's civilization in 1460." Also: "If ever Browning had ready an emphasis for the 'reach and grasp' line it was waiting for him in Rimini. And the Malatesta had his high sense of justice, for I think Gemisto [Plethon, the Byzantine Platonist from whom Malatesta got ideas for the Tempio and about government] wd. be even more forgotten without Sigismundo's piety."

> In a Europe not YET rotted by usury, but outside the then system,
> and pretty much against the power that was, and in any case without
> great material resources, Sigismundo cut his notch. He registered a state
> of mind, of sensibility, of all-roundedness and awareness. . . . All
> that a single man could, Malatesta managed *against* the current of
> power. . . . The Tempio is both an apex and in a verbal sense a failure.
> It is perhaps the apex of what one man has embodied in the last 1000
> years of the occident. A cultural "high" is marked.[6]

For himself:

> To act on one's definition? What concretely do I myself mean to do?
> I mean to say that one measure of a civilization, either of an age or of a
> single individual, is what that age or person really wishes to *do*. A man's
> hope measures his civilization. The attainability of the hope measures,
> or may measure, the civilization of his nation and time.[7]

As Pound wrote also in *Guide To Kulchur* "There is no mystery about the Cantos, they are the tale of the tribe. . . . No one has claimed that the Malatesta cantos are obscure. They are openly volitionist, establishing, I think, the effect of the factive personality, Sigismundo, an entire man."[8] But the four cantos as well as *VIII* and *IX* are constructed to constitute a second

---

6. Chap. 24, "Examples of Civilization," *Guide To Kulchur*, 1938.
7. Chap. 22, "Savoir Faire," *Guide To Kulchur*, ibid.
8. Chap. 31, "Canti," ibid.

phase of the draft. They also contain a very important textual arcanum. Consequently it is necessary to explore the form in which Pound has deployed his materials.

Canto *VIII* introduces a revolt against medievalism with primary historical documents, the mode of the tradition and the Declaration. It then shifts to contemporary chronicle, the mode of struggle generating the motives of the Preambles; to judgment of Malatesta from the foregoing evidence, the mode of founding and the Constitution; and to judgment of Malatesta in the light of timeless poetry, the mode of continuing revolution and the Bill. Canto *VIII* establishes the modes for *IX–XI*. At the end of *VIII* Malatesta comes to life for contemporary chronicle, the mode of *IX*, which also contains (within the chronicle) the fresh documentary evidence of Malatesta's captured postbag. Documents and contemporary chronicle continue into *X*, but the main mode of *X* is the historical judgment delivered against Malatesta by papal excommunication. At the end of *X* a contrary judgment from beyond historical justice, the appearance of the Eagle, clinches Malatesta *VIII–X* and the whole decad as revolutionary poetry and thus introduces a final poetic judgment of Malatesta in *XI*.

Four-phase *VIII* enables it to embody Constitutional Branches as a first half (with *IX*) of a third phase of the decad; but it is also written as a ten-part Declaration to become first of Malatesta *VIII–XI*. Canto *IX* is written both as Constitutional Powers and as two Preambles. Canto *X* is written as a Bill in Seal form for the tenth canto and fourth phase of the decad, and as a Constitutional dynamic for a third of four. These forms enabled the three cantos to move forward in the decad when "Seal sports" was removed and, with *XI* as a ten-part form of the Declaration perfected by the Bill, to become a second phase of the draft.

The letter to Giovanni dei Medici introduces the premises and extends to the cases. In the midst of war against Cremona, contracted to Venice, Sigismundo nevertheless welcomes as a destiny the suggestion that he arrange peace between Florence and Naples (1). Further, he asks Giohanni to advance his negotiations with Piero della Francesca about helping decorate the Tempio and about endowing Piero for life as a resident artist in Rimini (2). A condottiere's contract with Florence is negotiated with the consent of the Duke of Milan (3). It is honored when Malatesta marches his contracted forces into Tuscany through the lands of the Malatestan founders, on which Malatesta meditates (4). As an enlightened executive he invokes the spirits of the land in a lyric praise of Isotta (5), but interruption of song by war rounds him back to his opening letter to "Frater" Giohanni (6).

Chronicle records in the midst of continuing wars a celebration in Rimini of the wedding of the Duke of Milan, conversation with the Byzantine Platonist Gemisto Plethon in Florence, and an incident in which Sigismundo is trapped in a besieged city while trying to patch up a treaty. For a declaration (7), the conversations with Plethon concern war over the temple at Delphos; Plethon's

Platonism, in which "POSEIDON" was *"concret Allgemeine,"* concrete universal; and Plato's ideas of government in the *Republic.* Plethon's revival of the pagan gods and his emphasis on Poseidon went into Sigismundo's conception of the Tempio. Plato's observation that tyrants were the most efficient rulers, but inability to persuade his model, Dionysius of Syracuse, to any "amelioration," doubtless went into Sigismundo's policy of efficient but enlightened rule at Rimini.

Historical judgment derived from document and chronicle lead into a catalogue of the opposition to Sigismundo's independence (8), which judges them, and into a simple statement of what his sovereignty (9) accomplished against them—*"templum aedificavit,"* built a temple—which judges him.

Poetic judgment (10) is made not in the sanguine terms of the troubador song brought by Guillaume Poitiers out of Spain (cf. *VI*)—the mud flats of Romagna did not provide a setting like Provence—but in the terms of Greek tragedy. The Malatestan founder ("Mastin") had been condemned to Hell by Dante along with his son Paolo (of Paolo and Francesca fame), Parisina Malatesta was executed by her husband Niccolò d'Este for adultery and incest (cf. *XX, XXIV*), and Sigismundo's destiny also appears dark. Yet Pound has sensed a kindred vision and force of continuing revolution. Accordingly, in the spirit of the pledge (10), he sees the stormy dark of history abate so that Sigismundo's life of struggle and constructivity reopens in the new mode of contemporary chronicle, which carries his exploits at twelve years old "by night over Foglia" (a river), through an elliptical "and...," into *IX*.

Within the third phase of the decad (see *IX*) four phases of *VIII* embody the Branches. Within the decad unified *VIII* formalizes independence from medievalism and seeks to provide against it a common defense (ATHENA). Malatesta (in a Presidential role) proposes Amendment of medievalism and *VIII* proposes an Amendment of Malatesta's historical reputation, imposed mainly by the church, as a moral monster. The materials claim a right to new historical life against the confinement and cruel punishment of anarchic quattrocento Italy; Pound gives it. Out of Malatesta's struggle has come to his poet a new access of vision, the "bust thru" that reveals the emerging Mount as the Tempio built under POSEIDON. The dominant themes of founding and building epitomize *Section: Rock-Drill.*

Sovereign Powers *IX*

Contemporary chronicle is enforced by the "And"-rhetoric and by insistence on "that year," so that *IX* opens in "One year" and carries Malatesta's biography to a second conclusion. Caught in continuing wars and intrigues, Sigismundo's life of constructivity appears only in interludes. First he is knighted by the Holy Roman Emperor, promotes a debate between Greek and Latin humanists, has a male heir (who died along with its mother), and builds Rimini's fortress-castle, "the great Rocca," to his plan. In the midst of further struggle he "began building the TEMPIO" and his second wife died. Building the Tempio requires stone, which he is accused of stealing from Classe. In a third phase the chronicler is able under *"Casus est talis"* to exculpate him of that charge but cannot clear him of rape and has to admit that in his "messianic year" (of dedicating the Tempio, 1450) he was "Poliorcetes," taker of cities, and was being a bit too "POLUMETIS" or many-minded (Odysseus's epithet). Further intrigues and more wars ensue until a postbag from Rimini to the front is intercepted and appropriated by Sigismundo's employers, this time Siena. The letters in the postbag evidence continuing work on the Tempio and continuing family affairs in a spirit of civic harmony and constructivity even while the moving spirit is away earning money for his ambitious hometown plans. On that evidence Pound focuses and "seals" the postbag, the canto, and the third phase poetically by memorializing the Tempio, inspired by Isotta, as Sigismundo's crowning lifework.

Within the decad Sigismundo uses his sovereign powers in war and peace and seeks domestic tranquility (HESTIA) despite war. He is exculpated from stealing stone but not from rape and other excesses in the mode of Judiciary/ Supreme Law; the harmony and constructivity in Rimini evidence governance of Supreme Law, not simply Malatesta's will but the best spirit of his time. The works at Rimini have been promoted and illustrate rights retained by the people, not only by Sigismundo in the face of his times but also by his subjects. The achieved civic order epitomizes the constitutional orders of *Thrones*.

As halves of a seal, the third phase of the decad, *VIII* and *IX* manifest in their four-phase forms the Branches, Sigismundo's idea, and the Powers, the efforts to realize it. The documents of *VIII* define his place among the leaders of his time (Congress); his mastering idea (Presidency) is guided by Plethon's Platonism; historical judgment is made in the mode of Judiciary; poetic judgment is made in the mode of the Branch States and new life begins turning the Branch to a Power. The Power States evolves in *IX* in the activities of the revived life; Amendment governs the turn from political struggle to building the Tempio; the cases against Malatesta are argued under Supreme Law, the postbag ratifies his lifework. Together *VIII* and *IX* epitomize *Los Cantares*.

The postbag is the equivalent of a whole canto, Sigismundo's Renaissance in full swing but about to be suffocated under papal supremacy (*X*). It contains a major arcanum for the prototype decad, for the particular subject of *XXX Cantos*, and thence for the whole poem. It is introduced by a Seal-arcanum consisting of the size of Sigismundo's adversary's land ("a ten-acre lot"), of his possession of "two lumps of tufa" (halves of a Seal), of his comfort within his plentifully provisioned besieged castle, and, outside, of Malatesta's "poor devils dying of cold" (the people of the Bill of Rights, as in the rubric to *X*). The contents of the postbag then consist of nine letters or parts of letters interspersed with snippets carrying on the works at Rimini, all focused and sealed (tenth) by Pound. The form and spirit are a revolution being perfected by the Bill.

It should come as no surprise that Pound was reading '76 back into Malatesta as he had read it back into the prior history and cantos; he will read Malatesta forward to '76 in the third draft, "Jefferson-Nuevo Mundo."[9] Thus Malatesta has in *VIII* the role of Jefferson of the Declaration. That he "crossed by night over Foglia" suggests a change of role from Jefferson writing the Declaration to Washington crossing the Delaware.[10] The December situation before Sorano foreshadows Washington's before Trenton in 1776 or perhaps at Valley Forge. Parts of three letters (1–3) from men at work on the Tempio about the plans and about the architect, Leon Battista Alberti, hint by subjects, by diction, and by puns at '76. In the first—

> "I advise yr. Lordship how
> "I have been with master Alwidge who
> "has shown me the design of the nave that goes in the middle,
> "of the church and the design of the roof and..."

—"master Alwidge" hints at the designer of '76 Jefferson; "JHesus" opening the second suggests "John Hancock." The second, from a workman—

> "Sence to-day I am recommanded that I have to tel you my
> "father's opinium that he has shode to Mr. Genare about the
> "valts of the cherch...etc...

—hints at Tom Paine's *Common Sense* ("Sence . . . recommanded"), at "WE the People," at Paine's relations with the father of his country, at the relations of both to an overseeing mind ("Mr. Genare"), and at the barbaric yawp of "valt" Whitman. The third—

> "Giovane of Master alwise P. S. I think it advisabl that
> "I shud go to rome to talk to mister Albert so as I can no
> "what he thinks about it rite

—hints at "WE the People" recurring to a higher wisdom and to a supreme authority for designing the Constitution and adding a Bill of Rights. The Bill then inheres in a bill of lading for stone for the Tempio, which contains a

9. What Pound is doing may be intimated in a remark to Kate Buss in a letter of 14 July 1922 (Collection at Yale): "Have blocked in five more Am Cantos," "Am" presumably abbreviating "American" and "five" referring to what was at that time—before Malatesta expanded from one canto to four—a complement for a first draft.

10. So Columbus crossed the Atlantic (cf. the *Columbiad*). The end of *IX*, "old sarcophagi, / such as lie, smothered in grass, by San Vitale," jokes about *Leaves of Grass* while acknowledging its irrepressible vitality. The ends of *X*, the Eagle, and of *XI*, Sigismundo's last will and testament, hint at Pound's succession. (See also the American *XII*, pp. 123, 205).

Seal/Calendar arcanum for continuing revolution for the Renaissance and for the whole poem. We shall analyze this design in a moment.

The four planning extracts obviously transform Seal *I–IV*. Two letters from scribes about domestic matters—about Isotta and the young heir Salustio (5–6)—transform the dynastic *V* and *VI* from conflict to harmony. A letter from Salustio himself (7) transfers the domestic theme to a new generation, bettering *VII*. Interspersion among the domestic letters of snippets about the works in progress carries the works from planning through building to a two-part letter—about acquiring stone (8) and about the status of various works (9)—from Sigismundo's general secretary "PETRUS GENARIIS" (cf. the planning letters), whose name hints at "stone-generator," a St. Peter to "Magnifice ac potens domine," "JHesus," and other such recurring salutations. This letter condenses Malatesta *VIII* and *IX*.

Finally Pound (10), entering in his own voice, sums up the postbag as evidence of civic harmony and constructivity, "seals" Malatesta's inspiration and effort with words from a medal struck to Isotta, signs " 'and built a temple so full of pagan works' " with "i.e. Sigismund," and judges the Tempio in the light of universal art: the style is " 'Past ruin'd Latium' " like Walter Savage Landor's Neoclassicism, the filigree hides the Gothic, and there is "a touch of rhetoric in the whole." Pound's judgment anticipates the Papacy's in *X*. Malatesta is the Eagle persona and Pound the Eagle poet. The concluding "And the old sarcophagi / such as lie, smothered in grass, by San Vitale" seals Sigismundo's lifework with a hint of revivable spirit. "Filigree hiding the gothic" hints at the veiled arcanum not only of the Tempio but also of the postbag and of Pound's poem, for which Sigismundo's effort and the Tempio are becoming Renaissance models.

The bill of lading, deliberately redesigned from Pound's source,[11] derives from stones of the Renaissance a Seal/Calendar form:

"First: Ten slabs best red, seven by 15, by one third,
"Eight ditto, good red, 15 by three by one,
"Six of same, 15 by one by one.
"Eight columns 15 by three and one third
        etc...with carriage, danars 151

The quantities of stone refer to quantities of cantos as "triangular spaces" evolving from epitome, "First," and to be filled by Constitutional constituents.[12] For any four-phase subject, however, four lines are completed by a

11. Charles Yriarte, *Un Condottiere au XVE Siècle/RIMINI/Études sur les Lettres et les Arts à la Cour des Malatesta D'Après Les Papiers d'État des Archives d'Italie/Avec 200 Dessins D'Après les Monuments du Temps* (Paris: 1882), pp. 398–99. The bill of lading was not even in the postbag; Pound extracted his materials from a much longer document, altered even what he took, and imposed his own design. See Appendix B.
12. For what follows one may keep in mind the technique and comparison of "Picabia is the

coda which ends with a macaronic numerical pun, "151" = CLI = "Seal
Eye"; the "15" repeated in every line is thus "Seal." The four lines read by
shapes of stone, slabs as a foundation for columns; by red and black (= no
color), the four Seal-suits; by "15," "Seal" defined as one symbol metamorphosing into another; and by changing measures, which reverse the four
Seal-suits by shape. "One third," the spade as the Eagle's head above the
shield, unifies three. Three by one, the club as the constellation above the
Eagle's head, inverts and pluralizes. "One by one," the diamond, balances
the Eagle's dually directed head and joins the transformed, illuminated spade
and club into the founded Mount. "Three and one third," the heart, consummates the three symbols in the sun-vision containing the "triangular space"
and the eye of Providence. The "Seal Eye" focuses four lines in an infinitely
extendable coda which sums up the cost and transportation of stone in kinds
and quantity of coins.

The four lines and coda symbolize the Calendar's hand-drawn cycle transmitted by the eccentric arm to the tabulation. The cycle emerges from the
quantities of stone, a broken tabulation, and builds a new tabulation. The first
line is written so that "ten slabs best red" can be a cyclic form referrable to
all lines, while spelled-out "seven" joins with "First" to constitute "Eight"
cantos, or ONE: *I–VIII.* "Eight ditto" then completes *XVI. Cantos*, "Six of
same" refers to the first half of the second draft (*XVII–XXII*), and "Eight
columns" refers to the second half (*XXIII–XXX*). The bill of lading thus
emerges from the Renaissance and projects a four-phase plan for Renaissance
XXX Cantos. In such a reading the coda is included in *XXX*.

In another reading of the first line "seven" is a measure and "First: ten" is
eleven cantos, which with "Eight ditto" and "Six of same" constitute xxv
"slabs" of Constitutional Sections. "Eight columns" then becomes Constitutional Articles modulating into the coda, Branches/Powers. In this way
Pound prepared for a new Renaissance in either 30 cantos or 36. In a 100-
canto poem, 70 cantos would have been followed by a transformed *XXX
Cantos* for a world Renaissance. In the 120-canto poem Constitutional clauses
are allowed to run to 84, after which *Los Cantares* adds Sections (*85–109*)
and *Drafts & Fragments of CX–CXVII* adds Articles, which for Branches/
Powers modulate into "Notes for *CXVII* et seq." plus *Canto 120.* In a 100-
canto poem Sections would have had to overlap clauses and the coda would
have been included in *Canto 100.* As it was Pound opened up the middle of
the poem with *Pisan* and then tried to build upon *LXXXIV Cantos* the new
Renaissance projected by the bill of lading expanded fully to its complement
of 36.

---

only man I have ever met who has a genius for handling abstract concepts with the ease and
surety a chartered accountant would have with a bill (ordinary) of lading." "D'Artagnan Twenty
Years After," *Criterion*, London, July 1937.

Pledge X

The postbag anticipates what should have been the perfection of Renaissance revolution (under BACCHUS) in a pledge involving a whole society, in efforts to establish justice and form a more perfect union (ARTEMIS and DEMETER), and in Ratification of a governmental form, all activated by reserved powers. But the first line of X, "And the poor devils dying of cold, outside Sorano," and a partial repetition of the arcanum that introduced the postbag, make X supersede the postbag as an overlay upon—as a suppression and perversion of—the Malatestan Renaissance and the thriving community seeking to achieve it. For a fourth phase "And the poor devils dying of cold" keys an ironic Bill of Rights, a positive version of which thus inhered in the postbag. Contemporary chronicle carries a series of judgments that increasingly impugn Sigismundo while extending the system of unmitigated power politics. Only at the end is the predatory Renaissance momentarily reversed by the Eagle's confirmation of a revolutionary mind in the reviving libertarian spirit of BACCHUS.

A familiar but trenchant letter from Pitigliano inside his besieged castle mocks Malatesta for making war on trees and vines while serving a commune (Siena) he ought to rule rather than serve; the pledge and Malatesta's life, fortune, and sacred honor are twitted. Increasingly unsavory instances of pledges betrayed result in murder.

Into these breaks a block-letter Latin description of a pyre before the steps of St. Peter on which the effigy of Sigismundo was burned; protruding from its mouth (cf. the Eagle) is the inscription "I am Sigismundo Malatesta, son of Pandolph, king of criminals, dangerous to men and God, condemned to the fire by decree of the Holy Senate."

The pyre opens up indictment and conviction in absentia by the papal court acting under orders of the Pope himself. This travesty of the pledge ratifies by excommunication the negative forces against which Sigismundo has been struggling; all Italy and all Christendom are arrayed against his singlehanded effort to achieve an alternative to the monolith that made orthodox history.

The result is further travesties of pledges during a quattrocento version of world war until finally, beset by papal forces, Sigismundo makes a positive pledge while reaffirming his motives to establish justice and form a more perfect union in an alternative Ratification: when an Eagle alights on his tent pole as papal troops are advancing, he cites the Roman precedent for such auguries ("*quisti annutii*") and exhorts his troops

> All I want you to do is to follow the orders,
> They've got a bigger army,
>> but there are more men in this camp.

The Eagle inspired reserved powers for reversing "The poor devils dying of cold" and the foregoing travesties, if not in achievement then at least in spirit.

The Eagle precipitates and Malatesta confirms (note "*annutii*") a cyclic revolutionary mind that has been working within the prototype decad against varying forms of orthodoxy and tyranny. The mind is Pound's and the Eagle clinches his epic form. The Bill of Rights has been travestied, but Sigismundo and Pound have held to it until the Eagle vindicates both. Canto *X* epitomizes what *The Cantos* could achieve, either a transformation of history or another historical failure but affirmation of spirit. The result: *Drafts & Fragments*.

CHAPTER TEN

WORLD REVOLUTION

XVI. CANTOS

In the gloom, the gold gathers the light against it.
    Malatesta *XI*

The Eagle precipitates a new subject, the mythic Seal-vision realized as a revolution against medievalism on its way from the Renaissance to the twentieth century. Canto *VIII*, an argument for Malatesta constituted of ten fragments in four phases, has opened up the Odyssean consultation with the dead. Canto *IX*, by bringing Sigismundo to life, has opened up the secrets of "Seal sports" *II*: sounds of the seawaves yield narratives of war and peace portending the Tempio, the rapes become Malatesta's rape, the "Naviform rock" reappears as gathering stone for the Tempio, and Poseidon's and Tyro's conception becomes the plans and activities found in the postbag. For *III* and *X* Pound in Venice becomes Sigismundo involved in Renaissance intrigues, the gods and the steps leading to a temple become Sigismundo's effigy atop the pyre, the proscription of My Cid becomes the excommunication, and the medieval effort culminating in ruins but the motto "Nec Spe Nec Metu" becomes the expanded wars but the affirming Eagle. Canto *XI*, like *IV*, consummates the evolving subject by irradiating it with light of ten paragraph-images. The invocations are unified in the Eagle and the paragraph-images remanifest the Calendar cycle. The substantive culminating form is the Bill of Rights.

In hints at the Seal and at the Calendar's cycle and edifice, the Eagle-inspired Sigismundo assembles his men under twelve chiefs (First) and wins a victory, but then, military arms and his own exemplary morale notwithstanding (Second), he suffers a series of defeats that cost him thirteen of his cities. Returning to Rimini as a soldier he sits in the Tempio observing the work and meditating justice for his family and his subjects (Third). But the writs of the Papacy and the papal seal ("*annulo piscatoris*") strip him of his domains until the millennial perspective of "the arena," opened by poetic warrant (Fourth), reveals only unrealized hopes. The spirit of "his young youth" remains, however—"Vogliamo, *che le donne*, we will that they, *le donne*, go ornate / As be their pleasure, for the city's glory thereby."

This irrepressible spirit sends him to Rome to try to assassinate the Pope but he is jailed along with the Roman Academy for alleged conspiracy. His friend Platina, asked about their singing to Zeus in the catacombs, claims justice under due process of law (Fifth) by describing a version of the Committees of Correspondence of '76 and of revolutionary planning conducted by conversations in restaurants and coffeehouses:

And they want to know what we talked about?
"de litteris et de armis, praestantibusque ingeniis,
Both of ancient times and our own; books, arms
And men of unusual genius,
Both of ancient times and our own, in short the usual subjects
Of conversation between intelligent men."

But the Papacy forces Sigismundo to return home like a convicted criminal bound by contract (Sixth) to limit his forces and to confine them in Rimini to watch the Venetians. Accordingly the narrator regrets his failure to effect the common law (Seventh) of revenge upon a "Little fat squab" whom the conclave declined to entitle "Formosus."

But the Malatesta tried again to avenge the cruel punishment (Eighth), so that the Pope had to surround himself with protective cardinals; nor do the papal punishments reduce Sigismundo's popular support, which re-emerges in a report that on his return from Sparta the people lit fires and turned out yelling "PANDOLFO!" In such light the retained rights (Ninth) both of Sigismundo and of the historian-poet presenting his case are affirmed "In the gloom, the gold gathers the light against it." In illustration, under reserved powers for the continuing revolution (Tenth), Sigismundo jokes with his officers in a mock last will and testament. He grants a green cloak with silver brocade to a friend on condition that for four months he will stand any reasonable joke Sigismundo might play, "And you can joke back / provided you don't get too ornry." After it had all been put down in writing the writing was memorialized, signed, sealed, and delivered *"Actum in Castro Sigismundo, presente Roberto de Valturibus / ..sponte et ex certa scientia...to Enricho de Aquabello."*

Sigismundo does not end tragically as in *VIII*, to be reborn in *IX*; nor is his life definitively memorialized, as at the end of *IX*, before being continued (*X*) from before the revealed plan; nor is "the judgment of history" (*X*) merely reversed under the Eagle for continuing revolution on his own ground (*XI*). Instead his spirit passes living into continuing revolution carried to the rest of the world and to the twentieth century. In the gloom Pound receives a mantle of hope (cf. Elpenor and "Nec Spe Nec Metu") decorated with Renaissance silver (cf. the "silver mirrors," *IV*). He hopes to make it pure gold by turning Old Style to New Style for a New Era.

By being expanded to a Seal-vision through "Seal sports" as Ur "Eighth,"

the Ur Malatesta realized Ur *I–IV.*[1] Accordingly, when Malatesta took the
place of "Seal sports," it became a second phase of the draft, which, as Seal
II, "Seal sports" still projects. Seal *I–IV,* the prototype for all four-phase
subjects, has projected first the prototype decad and then, evolving from it,
Malatesta *VIII–XI.* The first coda of the prototype decad (*XI*) having completed Malatesta *VIII–XI* as a second phase, Seal *I–IV* now projects a four-
phase draft.

The Homeric prophecies (*I*) projected a Renaissance tradition of continuing
revolution (*I–VI*); through it they now project a usable Renaissance tradition
continuing into the twentieth century (*I–VII*). The epiphanies of "Seal sports"
projected Renaissance protagonists awakening a twentieth-century protagonist
(*VII*); such protagonists now project a usable Renaissance protagonist and his
plan for a Renaissance (*VIII–XI*). The quest for new justice (*III*) projected
prototypic new founding (*VIII–IX*); thence it now projects new world founding, American *XII* and Chinese *XIII.* The inspirations of *IV* projected prototypic continuing revolution apparently thwarted in its own time and place but
vindicated by the Eagle (*X*); they now project through the Eagle a world
revolution continuing in the twentieth century (*XIV–XVI*).

By extending Malatestan spirit via Columbian discovery, the twentieth-
century protagonist finds the consequence of the Renaissance quest for justice,
American law in the hands of self-serving business entrepreneurs. By continuing Columbus's westward voyage he finds an as yet unincorporated alternative to both the Renaissance and America, Confucian Cathay. Like Venice
(*III*) both America and China are viewed in a perspective at once Renaissance
and Columbian. Through a rubric symbolizing the Mount—

> And we sit here
> > under the wall,
> Arena romana, Diocletian's, les gradins
> > quarante-trois rangées en calcaire

—America reveals its gods, money. Confucian China is opened up as if by
inspiration from other gods after a climb upward followed by a descent (cf.
Pound's and My Cid's):

> Kung walked
> > by the dynastic temple
> and into the cedar grove,
> > and then out by the lower river, . . .

America (and its influence on Europe), presented in four discrete anecdotes
(the third evolving into a fourth), takes the form of Constitutional Branches
usurped extra-governmentally and turned against the public interest. Confucius's integrating philosophy promises amending Powers. The two cantos also

---

1. Cf. the illustrations, pp. 78–98, for the Seal pictured.

incorporate themes from American and Chinese counterparts of the European epic tradition.[2]

Since the promises of the Renaissance and '76, both America and Europe taught by America have degenerated into financial opportunism, usury, and dirty jokes. Baldy Bacon, a latter-day Odysseus and Columbus, practices monetary chicanery in Cuba; later, as an insurance agent in Manhattan, he knows how to take care of "his people." Baldy's name hints that the spirit of Franklin ("Baldy") and Hamilton ("Bacon") has superseded "the Geo. Washington tradition," of which "Dirtiness and meanness are NOT a part."[3] "Habitat cum Quade, damn good fellow, / Mons Quade who wore a monocle on a wide sable ribbon" hints at a homosexual affair while suggesting a Providence to Baldy's Eagle.

Baldy is a perversion of the new man and Congressman perfected by the arts and sciences as envisioned by Columbus in the *Columbiad* of Joel Barlow, through whom Jefferson sends revolutionary correspondence to France (*XXXI*). His relation with Mons Quade modulates him into a European who has got the message, José Maria Dos Santos, a "Portugese lunatic" who bought corn apparently spoiled by seawater, mortgaged his patrimony to buy suckling pigs, and so made a fortune on "water-soaked corn." Dos Santos, a male Circe travestying Presidency, continues the parody of Whitman.[4] Parodied are Whitman's relations with his "Camerados" (cf. Odysseus's with his crew and Elpenor), his style ("Did it on water-soaked corn"), and his excessive bets that "poems and the materials of poems shall come from their lives, they shall be makers and finders" (cf. "Mortgaged all his patrimony, / e tot lo sieu aver" and the troubador "makers and finders of songs"). The end of the Baldy and Dos Santos anecdotes, "Go to hell Apovitch, Chicago ain't the whole punkin," expresses Pound's attitude toward the Whitman motto of *Poetry*, Chicago, of which he was the first foreign editor, "In order to have great poetry, it is necessary to have great audiences"; this symptom of provincialism caused him to cut his editorial ties. It also directs to Europe, where Pound already was, the poet of the American tradition: in the polyglot of the

2. In "Two Cantos" (*Transatlantic Review*, Paris, January 1924) the Confucian canto appeared as "One Canto" beginning "Kung walked / by the dynastic temple" but without "and into the cedar grove, / and then out by the lower river," which links it to "the gray steps lead up under the cedars," *III*. The American canto, only through "Go to hell Apovitch, Chicago ain't the whole punkin"—i.e., without the bankers and the story of the Honest Sailor—followed as "Another Canto."

3. To Viola Baxter Jordan, 3 November 1941. "Frank Bacon also turned up last week. Was damn glad to see him, after twelve years. Had just used part of his biography in my cantos. (Canto X.) Have now a rough draft of 9, 10, 11, 12, 13. IX may swell into two." To his father, August 1922, Collection at Yale, written before the Malatesta materials had expanded.

4. Pound probably derived "Dos Santos" from a remark in his obituary of the Belgian poet Emile Verhaeren (*Poetry*, Chicago, February 1917). Verhaeren's poems "of the Flammand country, of the dull sorrow of peasants, of the oppression of labor," and his "great sincerity, his great pity, and his simplicity of heart," made him and Whitman "the saints of one temple."

melting pot "Apovitch" reads in Welsh, Irish, and Russian "[Pound]son of [Whitman] son of [Barlow] son of [a bitch]," whether Circe or Anticleia. Pound's relation to Whitman is spoofed elsewhere in *The Cantos*, but the true relation to his "spiritual father" emerges in *Pisan.*

The *Columbiad* and *Leaves of Grass* are foundations but must be extended and altered. Pound receives his special epic matter, the struggle against usury, from the American lawyer and patron of the arts John Quinn, who at a sitting of American de facto government, a bankers' meeting travestying Judiciary, tells the story of the Honest Sailor. When drink had landed him in a hospital, he was tricked by the doctors into thinking that a child born to a poor whore in the woman's ward had been taken out of him. Sobered and reformed, he built up a steamship line and educated his son. On his deathbed, as the father was handing over "re-sponsa-bilities," the son demurred "But, father, / Don't talk about me, I'm all right, / It's you, father." The Honest Sailor replied

> "That's it boy, you said it.
> "You called me your father, and I ain't.
> "I ain't your dad, no,
> "I am not your fader but your moder," quod he,
> "Your fader was a rich merchant in Stambouli."

So America has a non-native, equivocal heritage. The Chaucerian diction glances at inheritance of an American tradition of *The Canterbury Tales*, *Tales of a Wayside Inn* by Pound's ancestor Henry Wadsworth Longfellow.

This latter-day Columbus-cum-Whitman-turned financier, a product of a capitalist system governed not by justice but by license, is at least constructive and concerned about his posterity. His methods and character subsumes those of Baldy and Quade, Dos Santos and his pigs, Quinn and the bankers, who have made the capitalist plutocratic system; but his reformation symptomizes the spirit of constructive states' rights. While his story parodies the American epic tradition, past and future, "Patria Mia" and "Matria Mia" unite in his confession as he hands his son his patrimony / matrimony. The undenominated heir prefigures Pound himself and his successors.

In the other half of the third phase Confucius appears among his disciples like an Eagle who has descended from a temple of Providence and passed through a grove of a "paradiso terrestre." Kung sums up, according to "THE FOUR TUAN," the wisdom of the *Ta Hio*, the ethics of the *Lun Yu*, the governmental principles of the *Chung Yung*, and the poetry of the *Shih*. "THE FOUR TUAN" descending from Love to Wisdom, analogies to the Branches, guide the Powers, "THE FOUR TUAN" reversed. For the Branch/Powers States Confucius queries his disciples and elicits from each a different answer, one in the lingo of James Whitcomb Riley or of days along the Wabash (where Pound had taught in 1907); Kung judges more Americanly than Confucianly "They have all answered correctly, / That is to say, each in his nature." Kung incited Amendment by raising his cane against Yuan Jang, his elder, for sitting by the roadside pretending to be receiving wisdom. The philosophy of beginning with oneself and spreading order outward because one can stand firm in the middle draws on Supreme Law. Confucius's philosophy is consummated or ratified in an anecdote, an admonition, and a confession. A king ruled with moderation and kept order because his historiography left blanks for what the historians didn't know. Character enables one to play music fit for the *Odes*, which in turn build character. Something like an *Ode* concludes with an eye to world civilization: "The blossoms of the apricot / blow from the east to the west, / And I have tried to keep them from falling." The theme of circumnavigation precipitated through Sigismundo is thus pointed explicitly toward the consummating phase of the draft, where Confucianism is known to the twentieth-century historian, chronicler, statesman, and poet who has discovered it, but not, as yet, to the West.

The Homeric Nekuomanteia having opened up a Renaissance tradition inherited by the twentieth century (*I–VII*) and Ovidian metamorphosis having revealed a model twentieth-century protagonist (*VIII–XI*), *XII–XIII* transform the first into Dantean Hell and the second into Dantean Purgatory while adding Dantean Paradise. Accordingly, completing a westward circumnavigation, the twentieth-century poet views the twentieth century in a timeless perspective through Renaissance eyes, or through Dantean form consummated in an historical "paradiso terrestre" (*XIV–XVI*). He enters a neo-Dantean Hell of twentieth-century intelligence (*XIV*) and continues through it (*XV*) until he recoils against it and exits into a version of ethical Purgatory. Having exited he looks back (*XVI*) from universal justicial viewpoints (including Dante's) upon Hell, undergoes a new Purgatory, and enters a new Paradise (*XVI*). Formally this process should perfect a twentieth-century "paradiso terrestre." Instead it falls into the nightmare of history that was World War I.

Four phases in three cantos constitute a culminating revolutionary cosmos in the form of a twentieth-century Seal-vision. The phases embody the form of '76, "to be unity" (*XIV*), duality (*XV*), trine (the first half of *XVI*), and tetrad (the second half of *XVI*); there is, however, no "sea-change." The phasal epitome is *IV*, which via Malatesta *XI* has projected the Calendar-Mount of a New Era irradiated with the light of the Bill of Rights perfecting the Declaration. But the formal neo-Dantean cantos remain Old Style to the twentieth century. Within them, seeking to break out into New Style, the protagonist-poet applies the revolutionary mind evolved in the prototype decad by carrying the Bill from confrontation to confrontation in the form unity + duality + trine + tetrad. But private and legal rights have been perverted or are observed only out of this world, the common law and political rights have been perverted to universal war mitigated only by a prospect of world revolution, and the reserved powers have been implemented to positive advantage only in Russia. With "comes the revolution" a New Era is in the offing. But since it does not conform to the New Era evolving in the poet's mind, darkness cannot be pierced and the vision remains as it has come—

through infernal images, through dream and unconsciousness, through other-worldly vision, and through nightmare.

The keynote to *XIV–XVI*, "Io venni in luogo d'ogni luce muto," gives a Dantean perspective for carrying an irradiating vision into a lightless temple of Providence.[5] It opens up a scatalogical vision of politicians addressing crowds "through their arse-holes," of betrayers and perverters (particularly of language, through the press), of the organized "pusillanimous" howling and raging, of agents provocateurs and religious bigots, of "the great arse-hole" inspiring vice crusaders to wave the Christian symbols, and of "the mouthing of orators" and "the arse-belching preachers" motivated by "Invidia"; all culminate in ". . . . .m Episcopus, waving a condom full of black beetles." The general condemnation "without dignity, without tragedy" and the inclusive characterization of monopolists as obstructors of knowledge and distribution focus a Hell of Intelligence presided over by capitalism. Despite motion and noise, everything is static under "the great arse-hole," a perversion of the Eagle. Its unity is proclaimed by the placard "ΕΙΚΩΝ ΓΕΣ," image of the world, which for modernity is Englished on an accompanying placard "THE PERSONNEL CHANGES." The single vision symbolizes the Declaration activated by the Bill and projecting its sequels (cf. the illustrated capital, p. 92). In the narrator's perspective the whole perverts the freedoms of religion, speech, and press and the right to assemble for a redress of grievances.

In *XV* capitalism takes the form of imperialism while stasis evolves in circles and moves in cycles (again, cf. the capital, p. 93). "The saccharescent" are exemplified by Episcopus "head down, screwed into the swill" with a circle of lady golfers about him. Imperialists, violent and nonviolent, are gathered around "the beast with a hundred legs, USURA" or spread in a great circle. When the narrator, now revealed to have a guide, asks "How is it done?" The guide explains "This sort breeds by scission," a perversion of polytheism. In this perspective a world united by "USURA" rotates so that the center ('the great arse-hole") passes over all parts in succession, "a continual bum-belch / distributing its productions." This half of the canto perverts the right to bear arms.

Against such perversion either the narrator or his guide ejaculates "Andiamo!" and they begin to move toward the exit over the "welsh of mud" and "the bog-suck like a whirlpool." The guides bids "Close the pores of your feet!" and the narrator turns to the horizon. The guide, now revealed to be Plotinus, directs him toward the door, bidding him keep his eyes on a mirror, a symbol for the constellation, lest he be turned to stone by Medusa. The mirror becomes a shield used by Plotinus to harden the morass into a track (a foundation) while Medusan heads (perversions of the stars) rise from it. "The unsinkable shield" becomes a means of transport as the narrator

5. For the neo-Dantean symbolism applied to '76, cf. the illustrations to *XIV*, *XV*, and *XVI*, pp. 91–93.

passes into oblivion, in which a snatch of the *Rubaiyat* is heard in a dream (of rebirth). The narrator awakes with Plotinus gone and the shield tied under him (he is a renewed Eagle, the shield a foundation). "Panting like a sick dog" he exits and bathes himself in purging alkali and acid, which opens his eyes to the sun. Blind with sunlight and swollen-eyed he rests, his lids sinking as he loses consciousness.

In *XV* a Hell and Purgatory of Ethics is constituted of the cyclic, mobile Hell and of substantiating metamorphoses used to pass from it to natural purgation and natural sun; these halves of a seal—duality for the Preambles—manifest the static shield taking new forms within the transforming, projective constellation. The right to bear arms and the guarantee against soldiers in the house have been violated in Hell but the entry of the narrator has been justified by his motives, by his having Plotinus as his guide, and by manifold use of the shield, defensive and constructive, until the Eagle-narrator carries it with him beyond the total dark and beyond the constellation on the horizon, above which the sun-break anticipates the next phase.

The first half of *XVI* transforms neo-Dantean Hell (Declaration) and neo-Dantean Purgatory (Preambles) for Constitutional trine while adding neo-Dantean Paradise (Constitutions). Intelligence and ethics, or panoramic history and personal experience, are subsumed in justice. Before Hell mouth, from a dry plain, rise two mountains, each a vorticial form in hard steel. The road rises on each like a screw's thread, almost imperceptibly. On the east mountain the type of the active revolutionary, Blake, is howling against "the evil," his eyes whirling like flaming cartwheels as he runs from it. On the west mountain appear types of the contemplative visionary; Dante looks at Hell in his mirror and Sordello looks at it in his shield while St. Augustine gazes toward the invisible. The two mountains and the figures on them allegorize a revival of the medieval mind via '76: "Modern Europe has merely dumped the medieval thought about *la vita contemplativa*. That doesn't mean that there are no Western mystics, but again the European schizophrenia has split their being. Instead of the *vita contemplativa* being conceived as the dynamo of the active life, it is merely sidetracked, and commonly regarded as useless."[6] The narrator's armature is whirling between two vorticial poles (Branches and Powers). Looking with the poetic imagination (e.g., the mirror and the shield) warrants opening up the secrets of the past. Past visionaries warrant their successor.

Visions of Hell pass to awareness of a new Purgatory beyond the two mountains. Passing those convicted of the crime of having acted ("'crimen est actio'"), who are lying in "blue lakes of acid," the narrator follows the road upward between the two hills. A later formulation explains the allegory: "Both Confucianism and Christianity propose a state of sincerity which is

6. "On the Degrees of Honesty in Various Occidental Religions," *Aryan Path*, Bombay, October 1939.

almost unattainable, but the Christian proposals are mixed with all sorts of disorder, whereas a Confucian progress offers a chance of a steady rise, and defects either in conduct or in theory are in plain violation of its simple and central doctrine."[7] "The criminal" have presumably overacted but the protagonist's action is Confucian, of the mean. Thus he bathes to free himself of the last vestiges of Hell and continues on to a lake containing bodies and limbs mingled "like fish heaped in a bin," from which extends an arm clutching a fragment of marble and which is receiving a new influx of embryos. Many known and unknown appear for an instant and then submerge. Regeneration of those who did not act sufficiently takes form only in fragments and glimpses before they pass back into generation. Between overacting and underacting, Purgatory allegorizes due process of law.

Having struggled upward and passed through such an ethical Purgatory, the narrator enters a benign natural landscape "under aether" (as if drugged). "Passing the tree of the bough" (cf. the golden bough, *I*) he finds grey stone posts leading to a passage "clean-squared in granite." Descending into the earth he enters another air, and new sky, with light as after sunset, where by their fountains, "the heroes, / Sigismundo, and Malatesta Novello, / and founders" are "gazing at the mounts of their cities." Discovering this Paradise or Elysium of calm, ritual, cut stone, and founders allegorizes justice. Discovery, identification, and vindication of "founders" by a narrator who has come through the Purgatory of "crimen est actio" allegorizes fair trial, especially eye-witness account. The first half of *XVI* in trine symbolizes the Constitution.

The Paradise of founders opens up in the distance a new plain where nymphs are weaving garlands in their fount-pools. Adumbrated "paradiso terrestre" draws one man from his fountain into the plain, to realize the vision of history. But his progress is broken into by the narrator's "Prone in that grass, in sleep; / et j'entendis des voix." In a tetradic second half of *XVI*, instead of dreaming his renaissance or making it, he hears in a nightmare voices from World War I.

One or more voices, perhaps even his own, recount a succession of wars from the Franco-Prussian (or even earlier) up to World War I. World War I at worst killed the individual intellectuals and artists who might have made a better world; at best it forced them to fight in the interest of capitalism and usury. The plain of a "paradiso terrestre" has been replaced by the western front. The common law has been perverted into destroying individual rights instead of preserving them.

Voices turn collective in conversation, in French, among poilus on the western front. They describe mental breakdowns, stupid officers, criminals, starving German troops who attacked like beasts simply to eat, deterioration of equipment, gentlemen shirkers, and, in culmination, soldiers forced to

7. Ibid.

bury dead comrades under enemy fire in perfectly dug graves, "bien carré, exact." These cruel and unusual punishments, mitigated by nothing more constructive than the art of digging graves, are summed up "Liste officiele des mortes 5,000,000," though perhaps deterioration of morale is even more devastating for the future.

A third voice tells an anecdote about German troops on the eastern front who teased a bolshevik "Looka vat youah Trotzsk is done, e iss / madeh deh zhameful beace!!" The bolshevik taunts back

> "He iss madeh deh zhamefull beace, iss he?
> "He is madeh de zhamevul beace?
> "A Brest-Litovsk, yess? Aint yuh herd?
> "He vinneh de vore."

The bolshevik explains

> "De droobs iss released vrom de eastern vront, yess?
> "Un venn dey getts to deh vestern vront, iss it
> "How many getts dere?
> "And dose doat getts dere iss so full off revolutions
> "Venn deh vrench is come dhru, yess,
> "Dey say, "Vot?" Un de posch say:
> "Aint yeh heard? Say, ve got a rheffolution."

This universaling account of consequences of World War I draws on the rights retained by the people.

Finally a fourth voice offers an authoritative explanation for revolution— "That's the trick with a crowd, / Get 'em into the street and get 'em moving" —derived from witnessing the Bolshevik Revolution. The instance, heard in Paris from Lincoln Steffens, is Lenin, who gave a short speech to a thousand, moved them on, and then gave it again to another thousand. His gist was that the mensheviks could do everything except act. Go hear them, but when they are through, come to the Bolsheviks. Lenin prepared the crowds so that "it broke" when the crowd heard a cossack say "Please." That got around in the crowd, so that when a lieutenant of infantry ordered the cossacks to fire into the crowd and the cossacks wouldn't, a student laughed. The lieutenant killed the student, a cossack cut down the lieutenant, "And that was the revolution... / as soon as they named it." The lesson, the eye-witness concludes, is that "you can't make 'em [revolutions], / Nobody knew it was coming." Lenin played on the reserved powers of the crowd and the crowd and the soldiers used them, though it is unclear whether planning or simply converging circumstances made the Russian revolution. If circumstances, then it is merely part of the nightmare. If planning then it may or may not be, depending on what went into the planning.

In fact the groundwork has already been laid for a revision of Marxist revolution by showing how Sigismundo's revolution, the Renaissance, and One

World came out of a millennial European tradition. The same will be true of American revolution emerging from the European tradition and prepared "in the minds of the people . . . in the course of fifteen years before Lexington"; of the fascist revolution; of the founding of the Monte dei Paschi "FIXED in the soul" of the Sienese Bailey, planned for ten years, and then extended by the Leopoldine Reforms 150 years later; and of millennial Chinese revolution informed if not instigated by Confucianism. All met emergencies, all evolved in accordance with conditions of their times and places, and all projected models rooted in their respective cultural heritages. By contrast Marxist ideology posited violent class struggle, rejected the cultural heritage, offered little more than a utopian withering away of the state, and was imposed from without on the least likely of all world powers because war had destroyed all order and morale.

The tetrad of world war and world revolution symbolizes the Bill of Rights. But the Western beau monde's attitude toward the whole tradition so far evolved and toward what was happening in the East is summed up "So we used to hear it at the opera." In fact they were paying attention to neither, but to hearsay from the western front:

> So we used to hear it at the opera,
> That they wouldn't be under Haig;
>   and that the advance was beginning;
> That it was going to begin in a week.

The irony of this coda is highly providential. A new Era is essential. There is good reason to declare the causes for a separation from the kind of One World that has evolved since the Renaissance.

The first decad has established that each decad and its coda will begin with an epitome "ONE," which will evolve a four-canto Seal-form, which will evolve a ten-canto decad, which will itself either be a draft or become a draft by addition of a coda. Each decad and draft will discover historical materials by voyage, either within itself or succeeding its predecessor, and each will bring the materials to life through the protagonist Pound. Each decad and its coda will evolve in four concurrent voices, "to be unity" for the Declaration, duality for the Preambles, trine for the Constitutions, and tetrad for the Bill and Seal perfecting the process. Completion of the decad will precipitate four successive phases manifesting the Seal and symbolizing the four documents, which will be condensed into their respective phases. Other forms may cause overlays upon this form in particular drafts, but such is Pound's basic means for ordering his poem.

Each of the first ten cantos is an epitome or "ONE" for a draft; it transmits itself by metamorphosis to the "ONE" of the draft itself, its first canto, and so is the epitome for the main subject of the whole draft. The basic form of each canto is a four-phase Seal-form symbolized by the culminating "triangular space'' of Providence, which inspires the form to be perfected in symbols by voices. Some cantos manifest the ten-part form, like the ten-part, four-phase unity perfectly integrated in the epitome *I*-as-''ONE.'' Irradiated into ten paragraphs, this ten-part form marks crucial cantos like Seal *IV*, which perfects Seal *I–IV*, and the first and last of Malatesta *VIII–XI*, in each case for the Declaration perfected by the Bill of Rights. It appears too in the postbag, a special arcanum by both subject and form. It will appear in some later cantos for the Declaration or the Bill (e.g., the first American canto, Jefferson canto *XXXI*) or in comprehensive arcana like ''Canto 77 Explication'' and the ''rock-drill'' of *85*. The four-part form will also, of course, govern Seal-subjects accruing by ''mass relations'' within the ten drafts of the poem.

As each canto of the prototype decad and draft has a main subject, or is grouped with other cantos from ''halves of a seal'' to a whole draft, so each decad or draft has a main subject. For the prototype decad it has been Renaissance revolution precipitated from an Eagle (Zeus) by an Eagle (Malatesta) to an Eagle (Pound), and twentieth century world revolution precipitated by Pound coming through Hell with a shield tied to his breast. The main subject of a draft defines the Seal-phase within its subject and the concurrent themes of '76 within the whole poem. Cantos may vary as to subject or era within a draft, but the main subject prevails and apparent disparateness is resolved by the theme appropriate to a canto's place in the draft. Main subjects must be induced deductively, but Pound has aided by subtitles like ''Jefferson-Nuevo Mundo,'' ''Siena-Leopoldine Reforms,'' ''ELEUSIS,'' ''KUNG,'' and ''JOHN ADAMS,'' or by symbolic indications like place for *Pisan* and justicial building for *Section: Rock-Drill* and *Thrones*.

With Renaissance revolution (*I–X*) and world revolution (*XVI. Cantos*) as initiating subjects and prototype forms, and with these generalizations about form in mind, we may turn to the unfolding of the poem.

CHAPTER ELEVEN

A DRAFT OF THE

CANTOS 17–27 & A

DRAFT OF XXX CANTOS

Formando di disio nuova persona.
  XXVII

. . .but he hath excogitated / a new form. . .
  XXX

The main historical subject of *XVI. Cantos* having been the rise of the Renaissance out of its own mythified history and its becoming a twentieth-century tradition, the main subject of *Cantos 17–27* (and its extension to *XXX*) is the rise of the Renaissance out of nature through personality while that too is becoming a twentieth-century tradition. In both cases the Renaissance declines into twentieth-century perversions and destructions, but now (*XXVI* and *XXX*) it definitively dies as an historical era. Against this historical background, however, and within rebirth of the mythic paideuma "ELEUSIS," old personality becomes new both for the Renaissance, and, through the protagonist, who seeks Renaissance models for "Formando di disio nuova persona," for the twentieth century. The dominant symbol is the symbol of the whirling revolutionary mind, the constellation evolved from the shield, projecting the Mount, and voiced NOVUS ORDO SECLORUM.

For the process of '76 in the whole poem the main historical theme is derivation from the Renaissance of the natural rights to life, liberty, and the pursuit of happiness, which is then perverted during the Renaissance until it becomes license in the twentieth century. For the personal theme Renaissance and twentieth-century constructivists seek to establish justice. Personality makes Presidency/Amendment the form for amending the Renaissance city-state and the modern nation. The mythic or poetic theme is the right to bear arms, whether the constructive imagination or imagination perverted by greed until the production and sale of munitions are pursued without regard to the obvious consequences.

The second draft is not only the second of the four-phase paideuma "ELEU-SIS" and the second draft of the process of '76 in the same form as the first, an epitome (*XVII*), a Seal-vision (*XVII–XX*), and a decad (*XVII–XXVI*) augmented with a coda (*XXVII* and then *XXVII–XXX*). It also, with the extension to *XXX*, completes the four-phase subject *XXX Cantos*, Renaissance civilization projected by the Malatesta bill of lading. Further, extension to *XXX Cantos* results in three decads of Renaissance revolution uncompleted in Italy but continued by projection to "Nuevo Mundo." This overlapping of subjects makes *XVII–XXX* the most heterogeneous draft of the poem, with many groupings arranged "ply over ply." Since these subjects are only precipitated by *XXX* (though previously prepared formally by the bill of lading and by the decad, and substantively by textually shifts), they have the effect of back-views from the vantage point of Providence, from whose inspiration all begin. We therefore read forward with the second draft of four and ten, then take up the matter of accruing phasal subjects.

As for the concurrent voices, the voices of discovery and colonization precede but also are subsumed in the voices of tradition for the Declaration "to be unity," of personality for the Preambles working between the dualities union and liberty, liberty and union, of justice for Constitutional trine, and of myth or poetry for the tetrad of the Bill and Seal. These thematic voices are spread through the draft as the stellar mind whirls or "churns." But they are introduced in their order in the epitome *XVII*, a Seal/Calendar canto in the natural mode.

A Draft of The Cantos 17–27

Canto *XVII*-as-"ONE" overlays the natural mode of *II* upon the traditional mode of *I* in a hypnotic monologue of personal epiphany. Through the conjunction that sent *I* into *II*, Acoetes speaks as a "nuova persona" awakening into a new life through the rites of his new god, Dionysus:

> So that the vines burst from my fingers
> And the bees weighted with pollen
> Move heavily in the vine-shoots:
>   chirr—chirr—chir-rikk—a purring sound,
> And the birds sleepily in the branches.
>   ZAGREUS! IO ZAGREUS!

In a morning light of mythic origins he descends from hill cities through a god-inhabited landscape to a sea-bord city, recognizably Venice, and in the evening embarks on a magic voyage in a light "not of the sun." The ship carries him "Between . . . the great cliffs of amber" to the Cave of Nerea, a transformation of Erebus and of the "Naviform rock." Through it the living seek the dead and the dead seek the living, an allegory for renaissance. He enters the cave into Renaissance myth and history. Nerea, "like a great shell curved / In the suavity of the rock," symbolizes the shield and the segmented cycle.

The Cave opens up to the Acoetean sensibility a field of the gods, an allegory for personae symbolized by the constellation. Zagreus feeding his panthers and other gods and goddesses of the circumferential hemicycles provide models for a "nuova persona." The gods and goddesses appear under almond trees with a circle-dance of nymphs on the right and a grove of fauns and nymphs on the left. "Between them," and between Hermes and Athena, the speaker trembled (he is now speaking retrospectively) "As shaft of compass" (cf. HORUS on the diameter). Between "the great alley of Memnons" and "the alley of cypress" he descends once again to the sea, which is "churning shingle," an echo of So-shu's metamorphic mind. So end two hemicycles.

Into the revolutionary churning, mirroring the magic voyage to the Cave of Nerea and the revolutionary godscape, one man churns a real gondola with his oar. Like Tiresias prophesying to Odysseus or Acoetes warning Pentheus, the gondolier transforms the Cave and the godscape from a plan into an eye-witness account of Venice rising from the sea, the "bust thru" of an emerging Mount. The narrator recognizes the mythic Venice already traversed to have been the thriving Renaissance model of civic order and justice which inspired Renaissance craftsmen and founders as it will now inspire a latter-day tourist. Nocturnal glamor both rears up from the water and is reflected in the element that gave it birth, a version of the Mount built on the shield. But as if in response to his romantic vision, the gondolier recalls from the history of the first draft the fate of Sigismundo and the Renaissance, "In the gloom the gold / Gathers the light about it." Mixed triumph and elegy need no more elaboration.

Seeking to renew the vision, as if waiting to be reborn, the narrator couched in a burrow squinting at the sea in Athena's grey light. Through a "peek-hole" (cf. the irradiating eccentric arm) he spied on the shore inspiring female figures. One, Kore, identified him as "brother of Circe" and so a son of the sun. As such he absorbed for three days an irradiating "splendour of Hermes"; so inspired he shipped back to "the stone place" over known water, completing an overall cycle. There he entered time (cf. the Calendar tabulation) in the definitive historical Venice that inspired and paid Renaissance lawmakers, condottieri, and builders like Sigismundo, but that treacherously betrayed or murdered them. His own passage between the cliffs to the Cave of Nerea, between the places, trees, field, figures, and thoroughfares of the field of the gods, and between mythic and historical Venice, has ended up "between the two columns" where Venice executed her public judgments. The ends of a day, of a life, of an era, and of justice are portended in a Chinese echo of the fertile (though soporific) bees of the opening, "Sunset like the grasshopper flying."

We recognize transformations of Odysseus and his personae. We recognize

"So-shu churned in the sea," the threat to Troy of Helen's beauty, Tyro and Poseidon, the "Naviform rock" rising from the waves, the new persona Acoetes, and the ambiguous conception of Tyro and Poseidon. The conception behind the Renaissance will evolve in the protagonist's mind from waveforms to a symbolic stellar plan. The protagonist's place "between" will appear in the dichotomy of old and new, the Renaissance and the twentieth century, which is being unified by the myth of one "nuova persona" (the central star) emerging from amid many. Against a background of Renaissance union evolving to twentieth-century liberty, and of Renaissance liberty trying to evolve a new Renaissance union, the "nuova persona" will emerge. At one extreme is the myth of the Renaissance man personified in Acoetes (*XVII*); at the other is the myth of the twentieth-century man personified in the Russian revolutionary Tovarisch (*XXVII*). The two, with their historical exemplars, provide extremes "between" which the evolving "nuova persona" may choose.

Myth and millennial history are complementary sources for the Declaration's premises, here emphatically natural rights. For this form and for the dichotomy of old and new Seal *XVII–XX* consists of mythic-and-Renaissance cantos framing two twentieth-century cantos. The Renaissance passes into the twentieth century through Marco Polo's account of Kublai Khan's invention of paper money (*XVIII*) as the official currency of his empire. To Polo it seems to be alchemy (metamorphosis). Kublai's "Seal sports" consist in using his imperial seal on his bills and in "sealing" the backs of his messengers' coats. To Polo, Kublai's policies have resulted in Xanadu. He appears to be less interested in central control of a stable currency than in how Venice might apply such policies to attain commercial dominance and wealth. We have already seen the Venetian result. As consequence, twentieth-century relations between nations are defined on the model of a vengeful Napoleon by a totally unpublicized munitions magnate, Sir Zenos Metevsky, a representative of unbridled capitalism, imperialism, and colonialism. Universal peace is impossible as long as such a clandestine private person can control " 'tew billions ov money . . . invested in the man-u-facture / 'Of war machinery.' " Metevsky's career is generalized "War, one war after another, / Men start 'em who couldn't put up a good hen-roost." Such uses of the inventive mind overwhelm the ingenuity of a Dave, who put a buzz-saw (a churning mind) to ebony logs and did two days' work in three minutes.[1]

The counterpart of privately motivated war (*XVIII*) is publicly acknowledged sabotage (*XIX*). In America industrial sabotage suppresses invention,

1. In the *XVIII* headpiece skeletal Death holding money bags dripped blood on workers laboring in a munitions workshop; to the right emerged a peaceful looking factory. The tailpiece mythified the canto with Geryon (Pound entitled *XVIII–XIX* "Geryon" to William Bird, 24 August 1926, *Letters*). In the *XIX* headpiece financiers manipulated puppet-rulers (at Versailles) from behind the scenes; a tailpiece mythified the canto with a sleeper's head in a (Venetian) lion's mouth.

Marx is a joke and business a "romance," problems of credit are ignored. Irish, Russian, and Czech revolutions are sabotaged, though the Czech results in "Short story, entitled, the Birth of a Nation." Still, despite revolutions, war industries and trade continue across national boundaries. Sitting around in armchairs making deals typifies real as opposed to apparent government. Mexico was governed successfully during its revolution from a train, which kept ahead of the lobbies, and inventive ingenuity found a way to drill for oil on government land without confiscating foreign interests. But life under capitalist imperialism is "sealed" by a Kiplingesque colonial:

> "Ten years gone, ten years of my life,
> Never get those ten years back again:
> Ten years of my life, ten years in the Indian army;
> But anyhow, there was that time in Yash (Jassy):
> That was something, 14 girls in a fortnight."
> "Healthy but verminous?" "That's it, healthy but verminous.
>   And one time in Kashmir,
> In the houseboats, with the turquoise,
> A pile three feet high on the boat floor,
> And they'd be there all day at a bargain
> For ten bobs' worth of turquoise."

In another version of the Seal/Calendar arcanum, three "times" culminate in an economic argument. "Ten years wasted," repeated five times (heart vs. "And fifty"), were compensated only by "14 girls in a fortnight" (diamond vs. "2 weeks") and by a time "in" Kashmir, "In" the houseboats, before a pile "three feet high" (club vs. "in") amid haggling natives (spade vs. "4 seasons"). A single narration and a conversation between two personae lead to an image of a Mount being haggled over in the spirit of the Bill. "Ten years" becoming "ten bobs'" (120 pence) "worth of torquoise" culminate an image of the Seal edifice. Mythically the speaker is in the lion's mouth of the original tailpiece.

Seal *XX* transforms the mythic-historical Seal *XVII* from history back into myth.[2] In an opening rubric poets of a Renaissance tradition transform the natural music and the mythic descent of *XVII* by playing Circean music in a lovers' paradise. Pound then opens up the Cave of Nerea by resolving a crux of Provençal poetry. The crux has resisted philological solution, but Pound resolves it by recreating imaginatively, in the spirits of Provençal song and Renaissance painting and sculpture, a mythic landscape in which the crux is interpreted to express the spirit of place.

The churning mind symbolized by the gods and goddesses is opened up through Duke Niccolò d'Este of Ferrara tormented by having had to execute

2. The capital to *XX* transformed the *XVII* into a lovers' "paradiso terrestre" above Odysseus wreathed in Circe's arms while his ships and crew were being "churned" in Charybdis.

for adultery his wife and his son by a previous marriage. Este's delirium churns up a vision of Estean founding and European history going back to the fall of Troy. Pound takes the apparently chaotic states of mind to be "jungle" and "wilderness" but also "Basis of renewals." "Lozenge of the pavement" and "clear shapes" suggest the stars of the constellation. "Broken, disrupted, body eternal" suggests the gods. Este's whirling mind opens up "HO BIOS," life, in sunlight and in "the faceted air," with, below, "sea churning shingle." Personae float in the air on rafts accompanied by the incense of Dionysus's rites, either falling over a cataract or bursting into vorticial flames.

Apart from the flow, the flame, and the onomatopoeic churning of the sea, "Shelf of the lotophagoi" opens up Venice rising from the sea. Protected in luxury, supercilious lotus-eaters "of the suave nails, quiet, scornful" prefer beauty to struggle and complain against the fate Odysseus brought on his crew, all of whom but Elpenor "died in the whirlpool" and remain but anonymous "clear bones, far down," so that he might have great fame and pleasure. What were they given? "Poison and ear-wax." The lotus-eaters' sardonic " 'Canned beef of Apollo, ten cans for a boat load' " brings back the Circean music with which the canto opened, "Ligur' aoide."

The inspiration received in the burrow and from the sunlight is opened up by a Malatestan vision of Renaissance glory. A Dionysian procession carries Isotta, Salustio, and "the form wrapped," presumably Sigismundo and his vision, over a plain "as of Somnus," through colors suggesting American Old Glory. A figure emerging from a cloud seems to materialize Sigismundo's spirit. The spirit modulates into (or irradiates) a perfected palace, a form of Sigismundo's Holy City or Renaissance, cut into a cliff. At last, however, a Circean Vanoka appears half-naked between gilded baroque columns, a "waste hall" behind her. The columns bring back the summation of dichotomies in the Venetian columns at the end of *XVII*; Vanoka would be a sinister Venetian Providence. Against this background, focusing the theme of war and peace evolved since the beginning of the poem (and stressed as a dichotomy in this draft), Sigismundo or Niccolò as it were deliver a testament to Niccolò's second successor as Duke of Ferrara, "Peace! / Borso..., Borso! "[3]

The two cantos of the historical cases, dynastic like *V* and *VI*, alternate old and new while interpenetrating each with the other and mythifying both. Canto *XXI* follows the Medici dynasty from its founding by Giovanni through its flowering under his son Cosimo, the father of his country, and under Cosimo's successor and grandson, Lorenzo Il Magnifico.[4] Giovanni founded the dynasty on hoards of "sealed" florins ("di sugello") almost to spite his snobbish fellow citizens. Cosimo used his wealth to control the state, to foster culture and the arts, to force peace on other states of Italy, and to control

3. A tailpiece found all the Seal symbols on a sarcophagus to be found in St. Apollinare in Classe, where Malatesta got stone for the Tempio (*IX*).

4. In the headpiece Cosimo and Lorenzo (who looks like Jefferson) flanked a decorative urn surmounting the Medici shield.

business and finance all over Europe. Cosimo's successors, however, reaped the resentment of his highhandedness. Lorenzo realizes that "honest" Nic Uzano (cf. *XLI*) saw the Medici coming and warned the Florentines, so that they would have murdered Cosimo if he hadn't bribed them. They did murder Lorenzo's brother Giuliano (cf. the Medici murder, *V*). It is difficult, Lorenzo has to admit, to live rich in Florence without "having the state."

Across the Medici example cut two "modern" American instances, Pound's grandfather who "sweated blood to put through that railway" (to be developed in *XXII*)[5] and Jefferson's search for European gardeners who could also play musical instruments and thus earn their way as colonists into the frugal economy of the emerging new nation. Jefferson's letter, to a Burgundian, was written from Monticello in 1778 while Jefferson was governor of Virginia and while the struggle for liberty was in progress. His idea is cross-referenced to Malatesta's desire to support Piero della Francesca at Rimini (*VIII*). It comprehends urbanely, without a passion for power or fear of reprisal, nature, human nature ("Sobriety and good / Nature"), a reasonable economy, and the arts. It mediates between Malatesta's letter and the opening up of '76 through Jefferson's letters in "Jefferson-Nuevo Mundo."

Lorenzo returns after the interpolation with an anecdote illustrating Renaissance dynastic greed, which elicits from Pound an echo of the modern war and sabotage cantos, "Another war without glory, and another peace without quiet." Pound then remarks dynastic gifts received (an assassin and a lion), a family fathered (including a pope), a university founded, near bankruptcy, and finally peace made "by his own talk" in Naples. The last four align Lorenzo with Jefferson.

Pound continues into Renaissance decline with a spate of images which extend "the vision" of Seal *XVII–XX* as *V* extended "the vision" of Seal *I–IV*, from which many of the images come. Key images and phrases are "grass on the floor of the temple," "Gold fades in the gloom" (under the starred roof of Galla Placidia's tomb), "we sit here / By the arena" watching a palace hang baseless in the dawn, and "Fools making new shambles." Still a lurid beauty is born in the dark, though an old man sweeping leaves complains " 'Damned to you Midas, Midas lacking a Pan!' " The clash of destruction and new creation brings back "the discontinuous gods" of *XVII* and "Confusion, source of renewals" from Niccolò d'Este's churning mind (*XX*). The resulting ritualized vision and envisioned myth link the dynastic old and new. The old man still "beating his mule with an asphodel" restates decline but sustains the motive toward renewal.

As *XXI* turned Seal *XVII* and *XX* dynastic, *XXII* turns Seal *XVIII–XIX*

---

5. Pound's grandfather stands in for Washington, man of '76 for the phase of struggle. This seems to have replaced: "There is a line in the Cantos, but haven't yet found where 'Gawd, mah gawd boy, you dun cut Massa Washington.' As thus died George, of an hemorage. I have always heard it occurred in the dark and was of course due to mistaken identity." To Richard Aldington, 18 August 1928, Collection at Yale.

dynastic. Like Lorenzo, Pound succeeds his grandfather, who sweat blood to put through a railway in Wisconsin and proposed educating the Indians instead of killing them off, until irresponsible, selfish economic interests beat him and broke up his business.[6] (He was also a lieutenant governor of Wisconsin and a member of Congress.) Pound continues his exposés of war and sabotage, extending them now to exposures of war production during World War I, of orthodox economic theory, and of orthodox publishing (books on economics and anthologies of poetry). Such is "Price of life in the occident." An Italian folktale about the creation of Eve from a foxtail suggests a common Providence for saboteurs both Renaissance and modern. Then, to culminate the Renaissance search for liberty, he goes back to the beginning of his own search by having voyaged from America in 1908. At the crossroads of the world, Gibraltar, on his way from Venice, he was introduced to world revolutionary "confusion." There the mythic "nuova persona" of *XVII* began to take twentieth-century form.

A voice behind him in the street accosted him portentously "Meestair Freer!" It was Yusuf, whom he had known from an earlier visit.[7] Yusuf introduced him to all sorts and conditions in his cafe, which churned up the placard

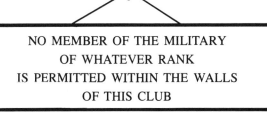

NO MEMBER OF THE MILITARY
OF WHATEVER RANK
IS PERMITTED WITHIN THE WALLS
OF THIS CLUB

—"That fer the governor of Gibel Tara." All Yusaf's friends were "For secession" from the British crown. To show up a fat tourist from Rhode Island who complained of being cheated in Gibraltar, Yusaf asked if the rich didn't rob the poor in his own country. Gibraltar was full of quarrels and lawsuits, a sink of cheating and license, but at Yusaf's synagogue Pound was received hospitably and found the ritual and the law observed reverently and cheerfully. Pound's final comment "Yusuf's a damn good feller" singled out an imitable modern persona even though a friend of Yusuf's of another race replied " 'Yais, he ees a goot fello, / 'But after all a chew / ees a chew.' "

6. Recalling *XVIII*, the headpiece to *XXII* shows a modernistic monster throned and operating some kind of controlling mechanism (or ship of state); it governs exhausted workers sitting about a transmission belt mechanism; on the right jumbled machinery is plowing up trees.

7. "1908 landed in Gibraltar with 80 dollar and lived on the interest for some time. Life saved by Yusuf Benamore. (tourists please note and use the Benamore family if couriers required.)" "Ezra Pound: An Autobiographical Outline," dated "Rapallo. 1932" but prepared in 1930, *Paris Review* 28.

The lawsuits in Gibraltar modulate into a failure of justice in the face of excessive liberty both Renaissance and modern. Execution between Venetian columns (*XVII*), twentieth-century war and sabotage (*XVIII–XIX*), Vanoka the Providence of "new shambles" (*XX–XXI*), and Eve made from a foxtail converge in a Siren or Circe on trial in an Italian Renaissance court for violating sumptuary laws. She evades a judge's condemnation of her veil with " 'at's a scarf,' " of her buttons " 'them's bobbles,' " and of her ermine " 'At's a lattittzo.' " To the judge's bewildered "And just what is a lattittzo?" she responds " 'It'z a animal.' " The protagonist old or new comments "Signori, *you* go and enforce it!" The "nuova persona" has emerged motivated by Renaissance liberty but now in need of being motivated toward whatever new union the Renaissance achieved as balance.[8]

The canto declaring independence, *XXIII*, is eclectic and transitional as the libertarian turns toward new union.[9] Its opening celebrates the free, polytheistic mind

"Et omniformis," Psellos, "omnis
"Intellectus est." God's fire.

—to which Malatesta's philosopher, referring to anarchic Christianity as a bar to new union, rejoins

Gemisto:
"Never with this religion
"Will you make men of the greeks.
"But build wall across Pelopenesus
"And organize, and...
            damn these Eyetalian barbarians."

The failure of new union is presaged

And Novvy's ship went down in the tempest
Or at least they chucked the books overboard.

The rest of the canto follows most closely Seal *I–IV*. The modern scientific mind investigates phenomena freely; correspondingly scientific philology coaxes out of a Greek lyric about sundown a meaning of Odysseus's descent to the dead; both sciences probe "Precisely, the selv' oscura" à la Dante. "And the rose grown while I slept" shifts for nature and personality to PANic music and dance on a peaceful hill above the sea where "a man might carry his oar up" (cf. Elpenor and Acoetes). The growth of the rose symbolizes,

8. A tailpiece adopts the colophon of the famous Renaissance Venetian printer Aldus, dolphins bound by ribbons flanking an anchor. Cf. the printers, *XXX*.

9. The headpiece to *XXIII* transforms and combines the heraldry and architecture of the *XX* tailpiece, the headpiece to *XXI* and the tailpiece to *XXII*.

despite the nightmare of history opened by modern voices in *XVI*, the growth of the "nuova persona" since the floral outburst of *XVII*.

The first two phases are positive, the second two ambiguous. Medieval justice is parodied in the Maensac brothers (cf. *V*) tossing a coin to see which would keep the family castle and which would go on the road as a jongleur. The result was not only the war caused by Piere for stealing a woman à la Helen of Troy but finally the destruction of Provençal civilization by the Albigensian crusade (cf. the justice and ruins of *III*). "And that was when Troy was down, all right" picks up Seal *IV* and Seal *XX* with the ambiguity of the latter. Anchises, on the way from Troy toward the founding of Rome, hears howling because Adonis died virgin; he replies "well, they've made a bloody mess of that city." The destruction of Troy and the death of Adonis are both "source of renewals," if ritualized. Anchises forgets both the ritual and his own liaison with Aphrodite, which resulted in the destruction of Troy but also in the founder-in-progress Aeneas. But Pound's recollection of the goddess's disguise when she accosted Anchises precipitates from the churning sea and mind of the previous canto

> and saw then, as of waves taking form,
> As the sea, hard, a glitter of crystal,
> And the waves rising but formed, holding their form.
> No light reaching through them.

The constellation has evolved from fluid to form, though the stars do not yet shine from it.

The two cantos for declaring new government are introduced by lawbooks and deal with Renaissance justice and building. The Este of Ferrara come like Malatesta *VIII* through documents, chronicle, judgment culminating in a symbol, and testament, forms for the Branches. Extracts from the "book of the mandates" reveal the justice and openhandedness of the Este and their intermarriages with the Malatesta, though the precedent of Paolo and Francesca shines through (cf. *VIII*).

Niccolò's personal life is recapitulated from his youthful travels in the eastern Mediterranean "in the wake of Odysseus" until he condemns his wife Parisina (a Malatesta) and his son Ugo for adultery; out of his grief he severely punishes other Ferrarese adulteries. "Affable, bull-necked, that brought seduction instead of / Rape into government, ter pacis Italiae auctor," he was honored by all Italy and received a coat of arms (a Seal) from Charles of France.

When he died he was buried nude as ordered in testament, with no decoration except the memorial "Ter pacis Italiae." His statue and Borso's lasted as monuments to peace until Napoleon's time, when they were melted down for cannon. But after his day had come dilettantes who made Ferrara "paradiso dei sarti." The Room of the Months, which had celebrated feats of the Este, the seasons, the zodiac, and the triumphs of the gods, then spoke only through the infant Hermes tricking the herder Apollo. The Palazzo Schifanoia itself lamented "Albert made me, Tura painted my wall, / And Julia the Countess sold to a tannery...".[10]

In *XXV* the Venetian "BOOK OF THE COUNCIL MAJOR" introduces the Powers of the amending process. Various prohibitory enactments culminate in a notarized birth certificate for new lions of St. Mark born in the cellars of the Ducal palace. Stone is assembled and artistic contracts are let so that the palace and its environs be "new built" (cf. the Tempio, *IX*). New building opens up to the evolving "nuova persona" a mythic Supreme Law for inspiring, envisioning, and realizing new form by architectural extension of the creative process evolved since "So that the vines burst from my fingers."

The "nuova persona's" interpretation of the new building breaks through the mist of history, which has obscured the palace's foundation (cf. *XXI*) to the conception behind the realization. He envisions a beloved (Sulpicia) amid growing vegetation (cf. the rose, *XXIII*) " 'as the sculptor sees the form in the air / before he sets hand to mallet, / 'and as he sees the in, and the through, / the four sides / 'not the one face to the painter.' " PANic flute music plays a lovesong against heavy voices of those who quarry stone without living concepts and so make nothing and set nothing in order. The amorous flute continues against "Noble forms" and dead words lacking life but keeping form. The cry "Civis Romanus" focuses a cluster of concepts dead because civic only and lacking "the solid, the blood rite, / The vanity of Ferrara," which can bring (has brought) the dead to life. The flute harmonizes passion until "thought," defined as "the deathless, / Form, forms and renewal, gods held in the air, / Forms seen," casts its "gods" back into "the νοῦς" (pure mind), leaving "Bright void, without image." In this conception the dark waves of *XXIII* take form as crystal, the flute music becomes "facets of air" (the stars of the constellation), and the mind moves before the notes "so that notes needed not move." The palaces of Venice and the Renaissance in general are rising new built to an architectural music churned from the sea by the "nuova persona's" mind. The source of civic order and building is passion-refining Amor.

After this focus of previous mythic passages the Venetian senate ratifies *XXIV–XXV* by revoking an artist's living. In 1513 Titian entered into a contract for painting the walls of the Ducal palace but failed to complete the work within the time contracted. In 1522 the Senate moved that he either finish or return moneys from a lien on customs-house duties. In 1537 it moved that he return all moneys received during the time he had not worked on the painting, "as is reasonable." Reasonable, yes, to the senatorial mind. But the artistic mind works by different laws. In any case, the end is ambiguous.

While the Renaissance has been evolving Pound has been moving into the

10. A gryphon tailpiece continues myth.

role of the mythic speaker who in *XVII* awakened to the Renaissance vision.[11] At the beginning of the pledge canto, *XXVI*, comprehending *XVII* from before the awakening to the end "between the two columns," he recalls his arrival in the wake of Malatesta, Este, and others for whom Venice was both an inspiration and a fatality.

> And
> > I came here in my young youth
> > > and lay there under the crocodile
> > By the column, looking East on the Friday,
> And I said: Tomorrow I will lie on the South side
> And the day after, south west.
> And at night they sang in the gondolas
> And in the barche with the lanthorns;
> And prows rose silver on silver
> > taking light in the darkness.

Renaissance Venice encourages a unity of Italy and of the world, but more for its own political and commercial interests than for justice and culture. In secret diplomatic documents her council, having held Malatesta's maker-of-seals Pasti, frees him on condition that he stay out of Constantinople and sequesters *Re Militari*, the book of Malatesta's military strategist Valturio. It intrigues to restore peace between Malatesta and the Pope (cf. *X*) and then uses duplicity and bribery in dealing for Malatesta's military services. Its main interest is trade.

Historical narrative reveals that "the vice luxuria" has infected the guilds and all Venetian life. Venice's only notable contribution here to Italian culture, her role as a commercial center, brings intellectuals (including Malatesta's Gemisto) from Constantinople; but even they draw the attention less of Venice than of the Este, the Medici, and the Malatesta. The constructive Renaissance and the effort to unify Italy end with the protagonist's laconic "And they are dead and have left a few pictures." The end is clinched historically by Venetian satisfaction that "Albizi have sacked the Medici bank," a unifying force and a force for peace, and by a Turkish treaty favoring Venetian commerce. Renaissance and twentieth century merge in a more odorous version of "Sunset like a grasshopper flying," "Wind on the lagoon, the south wind breaking roses."

The Renaissance decline is definitive. But four Renaissance letters, a form of revolution, keep alive at least the ambiguity of the Renaissance mind. Pisanello serves his patron as a horse buyer, but impatiently. Covering the head of St. George with silver and installing it as a relic is atavistic superstition. The conspiratory assassination of the revolutionary assassin Lorenzaccio

---

11. The headpiece to *XXVI* frames the page like the triumphal Malatestan capital (*X*); the large frame outlines a Golden Section and a small frame a square.

dei Medici cuts both ways. The painter Victor Carpaccio complains to a patron that one of his agents has swindled Carpaccio by carrying off a part of Carpaccio's painting of a Jerusalem. Artistry, though beset by stupidity, superstition, and greed, continues within its protective irony.

Looking beyond, the Renaissance revolutionary spirit lives on in a 1777 letter from Mozart to his patron, the archbishop of Salzburg (cf. Malatesta and the Pope, *X*), who will neither give him a decent income nor let him seek elsewhere. This one, read *"inter lineas"* by a later fellow artistic conspirator (cf. the Eagle, *X*), reveals a revolutionary diatribe; so revolution and '76 have lurked *"inter lineas"* since the beginning of *The Cantos*. Mozart's concluding "As is the sonata, so is little Miss Cannabich" clinches the decad of the second draft with an ironic musical version of the equivocal liberty and new union introduced by the hypnotic bird-and-bee music opening *XVII*. Indeed, one of the dualities between which the "nuova persona" has been moving is seductive music and inspiring music. Mozart's letter and the epigram clinch the decline of the Renaissance but sustain the spirit that has already taken new root in "Nuevo Mundo."[12]

As a coda *XXVII* transforms the historical *XI–XVI* in the mode of personality. The deluxe headpiece of 1928 accentuated the theme of waking from the nightmare of history to a "nuova persona" born of the flames of struggle.[13] "Formando di disio nuova persona" from a Cavalcanti love poem, celebrates "the American colonization" and the culmination of a revolutionary struggle. Leaving behind those who have died along the way the "nuova persona" catches glimpses of intelligence in modern Europe but sees them fade out in a general descent of darkness and folly. His own autobiography is marked by his having heard "Stretti" sung by the Bucentoro in "1908, 1909, 1910" (cf. *III*), by an old woman in 1920, and now ("this year '27") by seductive females in a drummers' hotel in Milan. Such Siren music, which defines the unchanging era, is peddled around the world as "Floradora in sheets." Set against his own change from old personality to new is a shrunk Indian head brought back from South America.

Cavalcantian love poetry and "Stretti," having defined historical perspective and opposing kinds of personality, open up a millennial political contrast. During the Middle Ages a universal assembly of the people ("Sed et universus quoque ecclesie populus") "All rushed out and built the duomo, / Went as one man without leaders" until "the perfect measure took form," its stones signed by their carvers. Thereafter theoretical masons, architects, and revolutionaries "wrote for year after year / Refining the criterion," perhaps excessively, or "rose as the tops [constructive leaders] subsided," bringing in the European eras from "Brumaire, Fructidor" (months of the French revolu-

---

12. A tailpiece links a checkered shield and a "Sigismundo-Isotta" shield with ribbons and festoons of flowers.

13. Cf. pp. 91–97 for the *XXVII* headpiece and tailpiece as transformations of neo-Dantean '76, *XIV*, *XV*, and *XVI*.

tionary calendar) to "Petrograd." A mythic "bust thru" reveals the cause of the decline by identifying the culminating "nuova persona" of these eras, not a constructive "factive personality" but Russian Tovarisch. Tovarisch materializes in the wind, under the sun, surrounded by three forms which he recognizes "This machinery is very ancient, / surely we have heard this before." His inspirations, the Xarites or three Graces "born of Venus and wine," stir dreams of building, but Tovarisch only rose up, wrecked the house of the tyrants, talked folly on folly, cursed and blessed without aim, and finally lay in the earth again. Having in *XI–XVI* followed the evolution of Renaissance revolution to the Russian, the narrator is rejecting post-'76 revolutions while differentiating a "nuova persona" in search of a new form.

He is also placing the betrayal of Renaissance artists (*XXVI*) in a mythic perspective. Tovarisch finally laments and complains as if from a sun-temple, in the voice of one of Cadmus's dragon's teeth who neither sailed with Cadmus nor survived to build Thebes. Three responses, precipitated by his complaint, define the distance the "nuova persona" has come since the mythic voice "So that the vines burst from my fingers." Tovarisch is first answered in the Mozartian spirit (*XXVI*) by Yankee Doodle:

> "Baked and eaten tovarisch!
> "Baked and eaten, tovarisch, my boy,
> "That is your story. And up again,
> "Up and at 'em. Laid never stone upon stone."

A visionary voice speaks from the midst of new birth:

> "The air burst into leaf."

A final voice alludes to a completed edifice and "paradiso terrestre":

> "Hung there flowered acanthus,
> "Can you tell the down from the up?"

In the mode of nature, personality, and epiphany Tovarisch defines millennial, the "nuova persona" replaces him, the pregnant air releases new forms, and the new forms touch on a descending providential inspiration revealing the interpenetrating triangles of the stellar plan, "down" for the shield and "up" for the Mount and sun-temple. As described in Chapter Five (see p. 97), the 1928 tailpiece arranged in Renaissance prophetic heraldry a transformation of headpiece *XVI* for the coming whole form of '76.

A Draft of XXX Cantos

The Cantos 17–27 ended with a mythic judgment of the end of *XVI. Cantos.* The Russian Revolution, in *XVI* presented as history without judgment, is adjudged in *XXVII* through personality indulging natural rights without being able to institute order or build. Tovarisch, who can only destroy and enjoy himself, stands at the other end from the Renaissance mythic persona of *XVII*, who, rooted in the mythic tradition incorporated by Pound as the draft evolved, is set against Tovarisch at its close.

This judgment concludes the second draft. But Pound still had to fill out the form of the Renaissance projected by the bill of lading and three decads of Renaissance revolution. He did so by carrying the coda of the second draft to *XXX*, which thus ends Renaissance civilization unextended to "Nuevo Mundo," and (again and still) a second draft. The key canto is *XXX*. Cantos *XXVIII* and *XXIX* are more or less filler cantos,[14] though Pound has taken advantage of them to elaborate the "nuova persona" in a principally modern, worldwide context (*XXVIII*) and to explore the dualities of the draft more philosophically (*XXIX*).

As to form, *XXVII* illustrates explicitly, in the mode of personality, the formulation Pound sent his father about this time. The "nuova persona" emerging from the dead and envisioning a mentally dead Europe becomes "A.A. Live man goes down into world of Dead." His hearings of "Stretti" mark "C. B. The 'repeat in history.'" Passage from historical building to the myth of Tovarisch expresses "B. C. The 'magic moment' or moment of metamorphosis, bust thru from quotidien into 'divine or permanent world.' Gods, etc." Tovarisch's complaint and the answering voices consummate the four phases as a new "A. A. Gods, etc." This Seal-form is extrapolated to Seal *XXVII–XXX*, which consummates the preceding Seal-clusters with appropriate themes, symbols, and voices.

If *XXVII* elaborates the "nuova persona's" descent to the dead (the shield), *XXVIII* elaborates the autobiography marked by "Stretti" by cataloguing mental types repeated from all eras in the twentieth century. An Italian folk-tale catches God having finished His creation and reflecting that something was lacking. He thought still more and decided it was the Romagnolo, so he stamped his foot in the mud and "Up comes the Romagnolo" declaring "Gard, yeh bloudy 'angman! It's me." Against Tovarisch the Romagnolo sets Malatesta, already known, and Mussolini to come (*XXXVIII, XLI*). Defiant individuality is augmented by "the force of his intellect" and by the "art and assiduous care" of a doctor who in 1925, in Siena, saved both mother and son by Caesarian section. These traits are augmented by a Renaissance ex-

14. When *XXVIII–XXX* first appeared (*Hound & Horn*, Cambridge, Mass., March 1930) Pound appended the note: "It is increasingly difficult to make the fragments of this long poem complete each in itself, and were they entirely so they would be wrong for their purpose as parts. I have no desire either for needless mystery or for writing equally needless explanations. In the case of the present three cantos, I believe the thoughtful reader, if he will take the risk of guessing their probable function in the poem as a whole, will probably guess right. If he is unwilling to hazard such guess he may as well go back and read Tennyson. 'The two lines of Provençal in Canto XXIX are from a poem of Sordello's.'"

plorer who advises that ships can be protected from cannibals in the New World by careful "watch and ward" and by resolute resistance.

Against these mental qualities of the "factive personality"—mythic, modern, and Renaissance—are set those of an artist who followed Emerson, " 'Too broad to ever make up his mind,' " and of a lady from Kansas whose "mind was made up" with the "ligneous solidness" of a cigar-store Indian. These two extremes, male and female, define devolutions into mental enervation, petrifaction, obsession, triviality, subversion, illusion (under drugs), and vacuity, all observed by a new kind of American colonist in all sorts and conditions of men and women who are passing between two worlds. Most of the anecdotes are about American expatriates and tourists in Europe, but some recall anecdotes about teachers and missionaries in Asia and some illustrate the decay of the European cosmopolitan mind. Only an extension of the anecdote about the man who "sweat blood to put through that railway" stands against a general mental disintegration. The canto ends by commemorating epically, "lest it pass with the day's news / Thrown out with the daily paper," anecdotes about the efforts of the 1920s to fly the Atlantic. Luck alone prevented disaster and Circean seduction dominated the male mind; but vestiges still remain of a Renaissance mind that looked and is still looking toward "Nuevo Mundo."

In separate parts, sustaining the Renaissance, modern, and mythic themes, *XXIX* contrasts destructive and creative female principles, and religious attitudes oriented toward death and toward life. The Seal, especially the back under Providence, and the Calendar cycle, especially the gods and goddesses of the months, are strongly suggested in jeu d'esprit.

The rubric,

> Pearl, great sphere, and hollow,
> Mist over lake, full of sunlight,

extends the "bust thru" that opened the myth of Tovarisch with a similarly ironic sun-vision. Accordingly it introduces a female Tovarisch, Pernella, a Renaissance concubine who poisoned her paramour's younger son, and from that instigated a war in which she expected the elder son to be killed so that her own son could inherit. An accomplice repented and told the elder son, who won back "that rock" (a Mount) from his father, who à la Tovarisch still doted on his concubine. The anecdote of this figure for lethal liberty, injustice, and destructive change is clinched imagistically by

> The sand that night like a seal's back
> Glossy beneath the lanthorns.

A "Seal sport" imposes the dark side of Pernella on the positive symbol. Pernella and her imagery are countered by

> From the Via Sacra
> > (fleeing what band of Tritons)
> Up to the open air
> Over that mound of the hippodrome,

which suggests passage from the dark front to the light back parenthesized with a recollection of Ileuthyeria (*II*), a Liberty who symbolized the Constitution's active arms turned to coral Branches. This image introduces an elaboration of Cunizza freeing her slaves, of her lineage, and of her varied love life. Her love life under Venus ("'The light of this star o'ercame me'") differentiates her from the murderous Helen Pernella and Ileuthyeria the petrifaction. Freedom in love leading to political freedom for her slaves symbolically gives justice (the Constitution) new constructive life.

The "bust thru" next takes the form of a contrast between visionary Platonism and quotidian materialism. Lusty Juventus (Yeats), looking from his theater to heaven, gives immortality and millennial history the form of his gyres (and Pound's vortex or churning mind): "Passing into the point of the cone / You begin by making the replica." Himself somewhat comical, he theorizes "Before the residence of the funeral director / Whose daughters' conduct caused comment." Yeats is seconded by "the old man" (the Platonist G. R. S. Mead), who did not know how he felt nor could remember what prompted his utterance, but rejoined testily "'What I know, I have known, / 'How can the knowing cease knowing?'" By the lawn of the senior elder he continued his "ambulation" with hints at Pound's idealized cycle of gods and goddesses proceeding from a single revolutionary vision (the eye of HORUS):

> "Matter is the lightest of all things,
> "Chaff, rolled into balls, tossed, whirled in the aether
> "Undoubtedly crushed by the weight,
> "Light also proceeds from the eye;
> "In the globe over my head
> "Twenty feet in diameter, thirty feet in diameter
> "Glassy, the glaring surface—
> "There are many reflections
> "So that one may watch them turning and moving
> "With heads down now, and now up.

He continued past the houses of the amateur student of minerals who later went bankrupt, of the local funnyman who had a camera and whose bow-legged daughter married the assemblyman's son, and of three retired clergymen too cultured to keep their jobs.

Pound has allowed himself to become playful. He generalizes the quotidian parodies of the ideal "Houses of Heaven" as "the osmosis of persons" expressed by languor crying out to languor, by the wail of the phonograph (or "pornograph") which has penetrated the marrow, and by the uninterrupted sound of cicadas (cf. *VII*). "With a vain emptiness the virgins return to their homes" parodies the goddesses; "With a vain exasperation / The ephèbe has gone back to his dwelling" parodies HORUS, with perhaps a play too on the gods culminating in PHOEBUS. "The djassban" has "hammered' them out of the material world, leading a gentleman of fifty to reflect "it is perhaps just as well, / Let things remain as they are"—without a transforming idealism.

The third "bust thru" dichotomizes male and female archetypally as intellectual and biological while defining degradation of the male mind. The mythological exterior on the moss in the forest stimulates the male's "burning fire of phantasy" and elicits a Dantean praise of woman so that she (perhaps a Circe to his Odysseus) would regret his departure. In a general drift she seeks a guide, a "mentor"; but his passion cools down to the ideal of an honorable career modeled on his elders'. Is there incomprehension between female and male, between young and old? If so it is ironically not so great as that between young and young, or so-called idealists. The young seek comprehension; the middle-aged seek to fulfill their desire. Who then seeks passionate creativity? In a prevailing atmosphere of wine, women, and song the mind of "slow youth" drifts like a weed or like Tovarisch's; the chief allure, woman, is an element, a chaos, an octopus, a biological process to the male's intellectual— if he exercizes it instead of subjecting it to his desire. One male knows the relation:

> "Nel ventre tuo, o nella mente mia,
> "Yes, Milady, precisely, if you wd.
> have anything properly made."

But he too says let's do it (to fulfill his desire?). Not in the palm-room, she balks—it's too cold there. Considerations, he expostulates, always considerations. Archetypal relations and fiery phantasy have devolved to mere seduction and manners.

The fourth "bust thru" extends "the osmosis of persons" to Arnaut (= T. S. Eliot) on a Provençal parapet confessing to Pound " 'I'm afraid of the life after death' " and, after a pause, " 'Now, at last, I have shocked him.' " On another day toward sundown by the arena a frayed aristocrat elicits from Pound an answer to both incidents, " 'But this beats me, / Beats me, I mean that I do not understand it; / 'This love of death that is in them.' " In response to such religious attitudes he recurs to the earliest known Provençal lyric— "nondum orto jubare," dawn has not yet risen, a translation of which was one of his earliest publications.[15] It brings back from the affirming mythic visions of the second draft his own religion ("A. A. Gods, etc."), here Phoebus or Helios as "Lord of the light's edge" with "April blown round the feet of the God," and "Beauty on an ass-cart / Sitting on five sacks of laundry" near

---

15. "Belengal Alba," *Hamilton Literary Magazine*, Clinton, N.Y., May 1905.

Perugia. To god-inspired eyes rises once again Venice terrestrial, aquatic, and ethereal.

Tovarisch's lament and the divine end of *XXIX* becomes explicitly "A. A. Gods, etc." in Artemis's "Compleynt" against Pity, which opens *XXX*. Canto *XXX* consists of complementary divine complaints, of two travestied marriages (medieval and Renaissance), of a letter about Renaissance printing in styles old and new, and of two interpretations of the Renaissance, one the "nuova persona's" and the other orthodox. This very brief, intensely formal canto—*XXVIII* and *XXIX* are long and rambling—condenses the dualities of the documents of '76 (and therefore also of the Seal and the Calendar) in entirely mythic and Renaissance terms.

Artemis's "Compleynt" against Pity, neo-Chaucerian in kind, diction, and cadence, complains that nature (her forests) has been corrupted because Pity spares evil, so that none may seek purity. The historical reference is to moribund or negative elements of the past allowed to encroach upon and befoul the present. That old clogs and tyrannies should be killed or let die expresses the Declaration's argument against the past. The complementary complaint, that Venus remains domesticated to the "doddering fool" Vulcan instead of going with young Mars "to playe," expresses the Declaration's projection of a new future. The mode of nature puts the whole Declaration into the claim of natural rights.

Artemis's "Nothing is now clean slayne / But rotteth away" and the aging of Vulcan are generalized "Time is the evil. Evil." Time the decayer but preserver introduces two historical marital travesties. When crown-prince Pedro of Portugal's secret wife Ignez da Castro was murdered by courtiers at the behest of his father, he walked baffled meditating vengeance. When he became king he had her body exhumed and forced the courtiers to do her homage as if she were queen, a corpse with the king still young beside her. In complement "Madame ῨΛΗ" (Lucrezia Borgia as Lady Matter), sponsored by her Pope father and richly dowered, arrived in Venice to meet her new fiancé Alfonso d'Este. Faced with the cynical challenge " 'Honour? Balls for yr. honour! / Take two million and swallow it" Alfonso simply picked up his bride without saying " 'O.' " The anecdotes express the Preambles: Pedro's union with Ignez results in a dead Liberty; the perverted Liberty "Lady Matter" is entering into a corrupt new union with Alfonso. The relevancy to already illustrated Renaissance love and politics is obvious.

The letter about printing is addressed from a Venetian publisher to "the Prince Caesare Borgia," the would-be unifier of Italy on whom Machiavelli modeled *The Prince*. Caesare is addressed also as Duke of Valencia (in Spain) and of Aemelia; but that the publisher has brought his men "in Fano Caesaris" indicates that he is also Duke of Romagna, having displaced the Malatesta. "We" printers (the people) have as it were carved the letter in permanent metal, "Here working in Caesar's fane." The publisher has brought cutters of letters, printers, compositors, and a notable die-cutter for Greek fonts and

Hebrew. This last has also "excogitated / a new form called cursive or chan-
cellry letters," i.e., *italics*; it was he who cut all the letters of Aldous, the
famed Venetian publisher, "with such grace and charm as is known." The
theme of Renaissance political union concludes ironically, but the arts go on
as at the end of *XXVI*. A new "Caesar" for Italy will fail, though perhaps he
anticipates Mussolini. The letter form is modulating from *XXX Cantos* toward
"Jefferson-Nuevo Mundo"; the "excogitated . . . new form" suggests the
activity of the revolutionary mind. Altogether the theme and form of the letter
is Constitutional, conventional printing for the Branches and new printing for
the amending Powers.

Pound picks up the printers in what amounts to an historical footnote to all
that he has printed.

> and as for text we have taken it
> from that of Messire Laurentius
> and from a codex once of the Lords Malatesta...

His source for the Renaissance in Lorenzo dei Medici would be well known
or old materials, his source in the Malatesta is new. His poet's right to his
materials has been guaranteed by the Bill of Rights. He has made the Renaissance new—as a prophecy of '76—in the twentieth-century mind. The values
of the text and codex (a collection of family papers, poems, constitutions, or
religious texts) are greater than the value of notorious events and persons,
here the Borgia family in the place Pound has allotted to the Malatesta, the
Este, and the Medici. Pound's new view of the Renaissance stands even
though in the old view it "died" with the death of the Borgia Pope, which
ends the canto and *XXX Cantos*

> And in August that year died Pope Alessandro Borgia
> Il Papa mori.

A colophon,

> Explicit canto
> XXX

means not only "Canto XXX ends" but also (like *"Hic Explicit Cantus"* to
canto *XXXI* or "Canto 77 Explication" to *Pisan LXXVII*) "Canto XXX
explicates"—explicates in the mode of personality what Pound has been
doing since the beginning of the poem and will continue to be doing *ad finem*.

Cantos *XXVIII–XXX* simply elaborate the dominant theme of the main
subject of a second draft of four, "Formando di disio nuova persona," and the
dominant themes of the main subject of the second draft of ten, natural rights,
to establish justice, Presidency/Amendment, and the right to bear arms. But
the poetic dimension of *XXX*, notably the complaints of "Gods, etc.," precipitates and clinches a four-phase Renaissance projected by the Malatesta bill
of lading, while the justicial dimension, notably the adjudged marriages and

the printers' form, precipitates and clinches Renaissance justice, a third decad of four.[16] The personal dimension of a second draft of four (the thus of ten) is simply reclinched by projecting the end of the Renaissance but the continuing revolutionary letters from *XXVI* to the same form in *XXX*. All endings come to a focus in the contrast between Pound's new continuing Renaissance and the dead Renaissance or an orthodox historical tradition.

In Providential backview a four-phase uncontinuing Renaissance—i.e., before its continuation by transmission to "Nuevo Mundo"—is dominated by Malatesta and measured by his bill of lading. The epitome *I*-as-"ONE" opens up a new tradition (*II–VIII*) focused in Malatesta. Malatesta is brought to new life as a new persona in *IX*, dominates his own cantos (*X–XI*), projects American and Chinese personae (*XII* and *XIII*), projects a world persona (Pound in *XIV–XVI*), and reappears with "founders, gazing at the mounts of their cities" as the "one man" who goes off into the plain (cf. also the single revolutionary Lenin). Renaissance justice imposed on Malatesta is introduced through Venice in the mythic *XVII*, is carried by the Este, Malatesta, and Medici (*XX–XXI*), and culminates in the girl being tried for violating sumptuary laws (*XXII*); this equivocal justice becomes blatant economic injustice in its continuation to the twentieth century (*XVIII–XIX*, *XXII*). Renaissance art (and religion), introduced by the omniform intellect as "God's fire" and by the Malatestan philosopher Gemisto's desire for a new civilization (*XXIII*), is carried by Ferrarese civilization (*XXIV*) and by Venetian civilization and mythified new building (*XXV*) before the decline (*XXVI*); it is continued equivocally by letters (*XXVI*) and by vestiges of its mythology and its imagination (*XXVII–XXIX*) to the Malatestan codex and the still equivocal focus of *XXX* itself.

A continuity of Malatestan achievement to Malatestan heritage accentuates four decads. The prototype clinched by the Malatesta Eagle at the end of *X* serves as a Declaration of new Renaissance tradition to be extended beyond Italy. It opens up Malatestan personality as a medium for "WE the People" seeking liberty in a world context (Malatesta to the "founders," *XVI*); *XVII–XX* turns mythic liberty revealed through Malatesta in Venice toward a new vision of Renaissance union evolved out of Este's whirling mind and focused by the Malatestan "form wrapped." Renaissance Constitutional founding is introduced formally in *XXI* by the Medici using their ledgers; Jefferson's letter (analogized to Malatesta's) accentuates the theme at the beginning of the third decad, anticipating the fourth.

Books carry the Constitutional theme of the third decad. After the Medici ledgers, modern books on new economics and new poetry are sabotaged, but scrolls of the law are respected (*XXII*). Malatestan books are lost overboard (*XXIII*). The Estean "book of the mandates" and the Venetian "BOOK

---

16. Ignez da Castro murdered (Seal *III*) and ironically brought to life (*XXX*) were added in 1930.

OF THE COUNCIL MAJOR'' dominate *XXIV* and *XXV*. Venice sequesters Valturio's *Re Militari* (*XXVI*). The twentieth century is ruled by "Floradora" sheet music like "Stretti" (*XXVII*). Pa Stadtvolk, a millionaire inventor of gutter-hangers, doesn't have a book in his house and a Baronet doesn't know what to make of Pound's four-volume Bayle (*XXVIII*). Cunizza frees her slaves by testament (*XXIX*). The printers are printing and Pound has printed from the Medici text and the Malatestan codex (*XXX*).

Constitutionally Florence has introduced states' rights (*XXI*) and Ferrara has continued them while looking toward all Italy (*XXIV*); Venice rules herself (*XXV*) and tries to extend her sway to all Italy and the Mediterranean (*XXVI*), but devolves into the chaos of modern nations (*XXVII*). States' rights evolving new union appears mostly in modern and mythic materials in *XXVII–XXIX*, but the return to the Renaissance in *XX* clinches the theme. It clinches it ironically, as it developed, because although the Renaissance evolved a transatlantic tradition and personae, it did not evolve a viable justice or governmental order. The justice unachieved by the Renaissance will come in a fourth decad of "New Cantos," introduced by the Malatestan heritage, which will transform a fourth decad to a third draft.

CHAPTER TWELVE

ELEVEN NEW CANTOS

XXXI–XLI: "JEFFERSON-NUEVO

MUNDO" & XLI CANTOS

"Thou shalt not," said Martin Van Buren, "jail 'em for debt."
   XXXVII

The main historical subject of *Eleven New Cantos* is the emergence from the Renaissance and from New World history of the revolution of '76. Pound's discovery of a Renaissance tradition and his bringing it to life on its own ground by colonization have fulfilled the first two phases of New World history. Simultaneously he has evolved a Renaissance declaration and a struggle yielding the motives of the dual Preambles. By voyaging to "Nuevo Mundo" in the wake of Columbus he brings the tradition of '76 to life through his own life; but since he carries with him the phase of declaration and struggle the tradition of '76 begins emerging explicitly with the Constitutional Convention of 1787, the third phase, and evolves under the Constitution (and the Bill of Rights) up to the twentieth-century present. The fourth decad of *The Cantos* (*XXXI–XL*) thus becomes revolution continuing from the Renaissance in the form of the Bill of Rights while informing the Constitutional draft of the paideuma "ELEUSIS." It becomes too, with the two drafts of *XXX Cantos* becoming discovery and colonization in a revision of '76 for world revolution, a draft of declaration in the four "episodes" of *LXXI Cantos*.

As the rise and decline of Renaissance civilization dominated the first two drafts, the rise and decline of American civilization dominates the third. The overall theme is thinking about government and trying to "think out a sane state" for a reality beyond the political reality dealt with during '76 itself, a new economic reality requiring continuing revolution. In Seal *XXXI–XXXIV* Jefferson and Adams deal with it in their letters and John Quincy Adams carries it into the next generation in his diary. Martin Van Buren (*XXXVII*) deals with it in his memoirs of the struggle against the national bank during the Jackson era. The struggle culminates during the Civil War and on into the twentieth century in a triumph of plutocracy over Constitutional government

198

(*XL*). The theme of trying to make Constitutional government meet the new economic reality is accentuated by an American triadic structure of the decad. The states' rights instituted in 1787 were saved during the Jackson era but the rise of the financial power already apparent during John Quincy Adams's career resulted in a new union under monolithic plutocracy.

At the same time Jefferson and Adams are thinking not only about American government and revolution but also about the emerging French revolution and the Napoleonic era. This preoccupation leads to a continuation of European revolution from the Renaissance into the nineteenth and twentieth centuries, and to a reconsideration of the minds behind revolutions in the West. The Renaissance mind inspirited by the paideuma "ELEUSIS" and the mind of '76 inspirited by both give way in the nineteenth and twentieth centuries to Marxist political sociology and Freudian psychology, both of which ignore the rich mythic tradition of positive, fruitful Amor. The decline of '76 and the rise of Marxism and Freudianism precipitate out the revolutionary sociology and psychology of Amor rooted in mythic nature and refined in the enlightened intellect, until a twentieth-century inheritance of the whole tradition of Amor, from the Renaissance tradition through '76, is discovered in Mussolini and the ongoing fascist revolution. The chief cantos for the reconsideration of the European tradition, intersticial to the American Constitutional trine, are the Amendment and Supreme Law cantos, for states' rights persons and states (*XXXV*) and an individualized poem (*XXXVI*), for new union the whole world (*XXXVIII*) and collective myth (*XXXIX*).

Beginning '76 at the time of writing the Constitution makes a new form of government the original American contribution to revolution, as the Renaissance originated declaration and struggle. The Renaissance also declared a revolutionary destiny and natural rights; as the third draft of ten "Jefferson-Nuevo Mundo" derives the justicial premise, new to history, of government by consent under a Constitution aimed at institutionalizing the revolutionary destiny and at securing natural rights. The American invention is taken to be both mythic and historical, but the mythic is enforced (as in the previous drafts) by cantos revealing the Eleusinian myth. In the face of an encroaching plutocracy, however, consent is being withdrawn and a need for new forms is becoming evident. (This is the way four decads are included in three drafts, or tetrad is anticipated in trine.) The purpose of government by consent, to insure domestic tranquility, motivates the American justicial mind and its antecedent, a ritualizing Eleusinian mind. Thinking out a government of laws, not men, takes place within the Branch Judiciary interpreting Supreme Law, which guides interpretation and validates the amending process. Lawmakers, statesmen, visionaries and other upholders of peace, justice, liberty, and civilization are working within various kinds of houses, but they are being displaced by militarists, munitions makers, plutocrats, and other destroyers and perverters.

Canto *XXXI*

American thinking about government, drawn from the justicial epitome Seal
III is elaborated in the draft epitome canto *XXXI*[1] by letters of '76 which are
applying the mind behind its achieved forms to a new situation. But first the
dual rubrics carry the first two drafts into the third. A Malatestan motto—

> Tempus loquendi,
> Tempus tacendi

—"A time for speaking, / A time for being silent," sums up drafts of Renaissance idea and act carried to "Nuevo Mundo" by Columbus. But it also, as
discovered tradition and as the essence of the uttering persona, turns *XXX
Cantos* into discovery and colonization ("Nuevo Mundo") preceding revolution ("Jefferson"). Jeffersonian transformation of the Malatestan rubric into
new idea and act—

> Said Mr Jefferson: it wd. have given us
>   time
> "modern dress for your statue.....

—translates the first two drafts retrospectively into their inherent American
terms as declaration and struggle. Had '76 seen the past as *The Cantos* has
revealed it, the Declaration would have given the mind of '76 a better understanding of the new tradition as all "time." "Modern dress for your statue"
would commemorate the man of action Washington as a new persona for his
role during the struggle, which at the time of writing has become his presidency over the Constitutional Convention. Jefferson's first letter is written to
Washington during that presidency. So, out of New World history and '76, the
Constitutional theme is prepared and opened.

   After the transitional openings, gists and fragments of letters are arranged
into a ten-letter epitome of '76 being made new even as it is being perfected.
The letters not only project the cantos of the decad/draft, but also transform
the comprehensive epitome *I*-as-"ONE," a prophecy of '76, to explicit '76.
They do so through such ten-part cantos as Seal *IV* and Malatesta *VIII* and *XI*,
through the postbag, through the ten-part *XIV–XVI*, and through the prior
decads. Canto *XXXI* makes the two "old" drafts "new" while projecting a
"new" prototype to the ten drafts, which thus themselves become "new."
Canto *XXXI*-as-"ONE" is thus projected back upon *I*-as-"ONE" while at the
same time serving as a kind of focusing lens between old and new, whether
between Circe's house and Erebus or between a Circean *XXX Cantos* and
XXX Cantos as the beginning of world revolutionary history.

   In prototypic arrangement, a first letter by Jefferson evolves from '76, even
as it is being instituted, a theme of economic revolution for the whole canto

1. Pound wrote A. B. Drew of the Production Department of his British publisher Faber &

("to be unity"). The first four letters evolve from a new destiny, from the personae of '76, from the conduct of government, and from continuing revolution a Seal-form containing the Declaration's premises and their projections—i.e., ONE/1, 1–2, 1–3, 1–4; the fourth modulates from American states' rights Branches to Powers and world Branches while French revolution is emerging as if from '76. The fifth and sixth add cases against European royalty and against brother European revolutionaries in the light of '76. The first six are unified by the emergence from political '76 of a new economic tradition, by the public lives of '76 directed toward new liberty, and by Jefferson and Adams, the ambassadors to France and England respectively, writing from or about France during the American Constitutional effort of 1787–88. The impression is that Jefferson is a medium for introducing cosmopolitan ideas and experiences into the minds of those like Washington and Madison who were writing the Constitution and trying to get it ratified.

The last four letters, written by Jefferson and Adams after their retirements from public life, give the impression that they are continuing and universalizing revolutionary ideas for the republic and for the world. The seventh reaffirms American states' rights and modulates from world Branches to world Powers while Jefferson enters a personal phase. The eighth and ninth turn from the personal seventh to a psychology and a political science for a founding phase of continuing revolution. The tenth (and a fourth phase) focuses a new prototype of continuing revolution by directing the older political and newer economic revolutions against the Roman Catholic Church and against the economic systems of Napoleonic Europe and imperialist England. The Amendments of the Bill have activated the whole, which is perfected phasally as a Seal-form and sealed "*Hic Explicit Cantus.*"

A comprehensive destiny ("ONE") evolving a Seal-form (1–4), two cases (5–6), a declaration (7), a theory and practice of government (8–9), and a pledge (10) carry a Declaration "to be unity." A public hemicycle (1–6) seeks new liberty and a private hemicycle (7–10) seeks new union. States' rights inheres in the American theme (1–4/4–7) while the French and European theme (4–7/7–10) is emerging for new world union. The private and legal rights (1–6) seal a tradition, the common law rights (7) seal personae, the political rights (8–9) seal a theory and practice of government, and reserved powers (10) seal continuing revolution in a religious mode. The gists and fragments are of such magnitude as to concentrate the themes. The following "explication" of that which "*Explicit Cantus*" (explicates *The Cantos*) refers directly or indirectly to the argument, to the Constitutional forms, and to the rights, but leaves the motives to the turn from liberty (public life) toward new union (private life). To avoid excessive congestion it draws the prototype into canto *XXXI*, leaving the projections of canto *XXXI* to be

---

Faber about Canto *LX* "Canto appears in heading where it is intended to be read aloud (if one is reading aloud)," 7 November 1939, *Letters*.

noted during explication of Seal *XXXI–XXXIV* and of Revolution *XXXI–XL* and its coda *XLI*.

Like Odysseus and Pound (*I*), Jefferson opens up a new tradition in the middle of an old. Washington had surveyed the western lands (discovery) for the purpose of opening them up to settlement (colonization); Jefferson had written the Declaration and Washington had led the struggle. The new, a prophecy, is economic revolution continuing out of still evolving political revolution. Anticipating Manifest Destiny, Jefferson enquires about Washington's idea of opening up "water communication between ours and the western country." He remembers having first enquired while he was sitting in Congress and Washington had retired with his idea or "states of mind" to his native Virginia. Now Ambassador Jefferson writes from France to General Washington presiding over the Constitutional Convention, which is in the process of uniting a nation politically while Jefferson is thinking ahead to unite it economically. Jefferson begins reassembling the men of '76 by and for the freedoms of the First Amendment.

The second letter is framed by fragments evincing the versatile Jefferson's stellar mind (cf. *II*). Restated as epiphanic perceptions are Dionysian natural rights ("....no slaves north of Maryland district...."), Dionysian nature ("....flower found in Connecticut that vegetates when suspended in air..."), the churning mind ("...screw more effectual if placed below surface of water," on invention of the screw propeller), and Acoetean "nuove persone" ("Excellency Mr Adams. Excellency Dr. Franklin," ministers from the new nation to England and France). From the central star of such a mind ("And thus") Jefferson writes Tom Paine after Paine's participation in two revolutions offering the former latest-arrived colonist and penman of the struggle passage back to America in a public vessel. Hoping that America has returned to sentiments "worthy of former time," praising Paine for his earlier labors while hoping he may continue them and reap fit reward, "Mr Jefferson (president)" amends the prevailing view of the natural rights philosopher, known imbiber of Bacchus, and "dirty little atheist." Jefferson's and Paine's minds are arms of the imagination. Citing the lies of English newspapers and recurring to "in a few years...no slaves northward of Maryland" complete the stellar frame. The first two letters have assembled the "nuove persone" of '76 in their order, Jefferson, Washington, Adams, and Paine. Even though the second letter is from Jefferson's public life under the Constitution, not dating it keeps the focus on 1787 while having Paine in France keeps the American-French connection.[2]

The third letter, from Paris in 1787, draws on Pound outside the Dogana of Venice, where "the gondolas cost too much that year," and My Cid outside

2. Jefferson wrote Paine in 1801. Presumably Pound suppressed the date to sustain the perspective of 1787 but introduced the letter from "(president)" Jefferson to the instigating, culminating man of '76 to fit the unfolding of his prototype form.

Burgos, both seeking economic justice (*III*).[3] Probing into the French policy on tobacco, Jefferson heaps up (the form of the Mount) the cost of imported raw material, manufacture, royal taxation, and the cost of tax collection, all borne by the consumer. From this practice of government he withdraws consent by declaring that collection costs too much. A Judicial mind has applied a Supreme Law of economic justice. The intrusion, because in the interest of lawmaking (again at the time of writing the Constitution), is warranted. The first three letters now constitute a triad of economic justice. Withdrawal of consent looks from within trine toward tetrad. Recurrence of this letter (*XLI*) to introduce a Jeffersonian summation of the American economic theme of this third draft accentuates that the letters are projecting not only "Jefferson-Nuevo Mundo" but, through its cantos, the ten drafts of the poem.

The mediating fragment "......for our model, the Maison Quarrée of Nismes.....," linking Mount and sun-vision, America and France, draws on the model of Troy, on the irradiating psychological states, and on the continuing and extended revolution of *IV*. Madison, a leading delegate at the Constitutional Convention, cannot divine any natural motives (states of mind) of a certain politician's acts without going deeper into human nature than he is willing to go.[4] Jefferson replies that the critical state of England ought to enable Adams to borrow there and that France is on the eve of a "XTZBK49HT," on which Pound comments "(*parts of this letter in cypher*)." Both the politician's motives and Madison's provincial unwillingness to explore (to irradiate) his states of mind more deeply contain seeds of an American decline. Jefferson's cosmopolitan state of mind irradiates the present states or conditions of the States of the world. Economic cooperation adumbrates world Congress. Cypher introduces French "revolution" modulating out of '76 to continuing revolution on a world scale. Madison respects privacy to the detriment of the nation being founded. Jefferson's and Pound's revolution by cypher is both prudent and warranted. Pound's interpolated comment marks four-phase culmination of an inherent Seal-vision for "REVOLUTION . . . in the minds of the people" taking the form of the Declaration's premises and its projections—motives from union toward liberty and a Branches/Powers dynamic being activated by the private rights of the Bill.

The fifth and sixth letters turn the eyes of '76 (in 1788) upon two cases from revolution emerging in France. The fifth, to General Washington after

3. Here the letter is dated "(from Paris, 1787)"; in *XLI* it is addressed "To the Count Vergennes, Paris, August, 1785." The 1970 edition "corrected" the first citation to "(from Paris, 1785)," whether with Pound's sanction I do not know. Thus, "1787" without an addressee sustains the impression of advice from abroad to the Constitutional Convention.

4. Madison is writing neither in 1787 nor to Jefferson; instead he is writing a "Memorandum as to Robert Smith," his secretary of the navy, dated April 1811 (Gaillard C. Hunt, ed., *The Writings of James Madison*, vol. III, p. 141). Again suppression of circumstances and date allow a thematic effect just as valid as chronicle history.

the Constitution has been written but before it has been ratified and implemented, draws on Varchi's weighing of Medicean government and political assassination. Jefferson reports that a French revolutionary (Beaumarchais) is determined "to make himself heard," presumably against the monarchy (cf. Lorenzaccio vs. Alessandro); he also recurs ("again the vision") to Washington's plan for opening up the West. These evidences join to the advantage of Washington in Jefferson's judgment that no crowned head in Europe has the talents or merits to be elected vestryman in any American parish. Washington, president of the Convention, is about to be elected first President under the American Amendment of former governments and their ways of selecting heads of State. The offered evidence and argument observe due process of law.

The sixth, drawing on the Provençal love code's revolt for personal liberty but unconcern for new forms of order (*VI*), measures the ignorance of Lafayette and other revolutionary "brethren" (including Franklin) by a Supreme Law of "government and history." Adams, in a Judicial role, recalls to Jefferson how Lafayette convicted himself by "harangue" (which was fair trial). While Jefferson heard silently Adams was astonished. If not Jefferson, then at least Adams is concerned with a deeper view of human nature than Provence's or Madison's. Not dating the letter (written in 1813) allows it to fit the time of writing the Constitution (in which Franklin participated) and of preparing the French Revolution.

In the first six letters a Seal-form has precipitated from American states' rights French revolution aimed at a newer and larger union. The Declaration's argument and the motivation from union toward liberty have been applied to new conditions. To conclude the new union projected by all documents and perfected by the Bill, the remaining letters jump over the presidencies of Washington, Adams, and Jefferson, and over the French Revolution, to Jefferson's and Adams's private lives (Washington and Paine have died) during the Napoleonic era. The division also precipitates the phasal Seal-form so that new tradition (shield) will be succeeded by new mind (constellation), new justice (Mount), and new religion (sun-vision). The documents continue while this phasal form is coming to a focus.

For a seventh letter four brief gists accent the continuation of Jefferson's stellar mind and revolutionary activity even though he moves from the duties of public life to the independence of private life. As Pound summed up and inherited a Renaissance tradition through his personal life in *VII*, so Jefferson sums up and continues '76 personally—while passing it on to Pound as the seeds of an epic tradition. Jefferson remains involved in European continuing revolution by dispatching from Monticello in 1811, via Joel Barlow (author of the *Columbiad*) then departing for Paris as ambassador to France, letters "not proper for the eye of the police." The other three gists refer to American states' rights retrospectively and finally currently. Recalling the "cordial aid" of his Secretary of the Treasury Gallatin during the financial struggles of his presidency echoes Paine's contribution during the Revolution. A characteristic "kink" in the American mind—believing the Indians of America to be descended from the Jews—reillustrates Madison's provincial view of human nature while seconding Jefferson's judgment of royalty and Adams's judgment of revolutionaries. A culminating argument against the alleged benefits of a public debt declares independence in the continuing economic struggle while ratifying states' rights:

> "But observe that the public were at the same time paying
> on it an interest of exactly the same amount
> (four million dollars). Where then is the gain to either
> party which makes it a public blessing?"
>   to Mr Eppes, 1813

Self-evident demonstration and the concept "public blessing" apply the activating common law to a declaration of independence, to states' rights, and to the phase of "WE the People."

The personal phase also sends "Mr Eppes" ("E P" backwards and forwards) to Europe with his epic tradition. Jefferson sends Pound on a world revolutionary mission via Barlow and the *Columbiad*. Pound takes with him via Gallatin the "cordial aid" of Whitman and his camaradoes. The American "kink" warns how Pound may be affected by his own destined subject, the integration of America with a world dominated by economic injustice. Jefferson's rejection of a national bank as a "public blessing" clinches the vocation of continuing revolution and challenges "Mr Eppes's" epic imagination. Canto *XII* has already burlesqued the American epic tradition. In *XXXIII* Adams's learning from Plato "that sneezing is a cure for the hickups" will refer to curing Barlow's couplets with Whitman's orotundities; Pound's verse is curing sneezing. In *Thrones 99* (see p. 396) Chinese-American macaronics urge "Yank" Barlow to nourish, and "Ma" Whitman to set out practical hemp instead of leaves of grass, so that "the middle," "me," and "cotton tongue" will all be in this thing together.

The eighth and ninth shift to complementary aspects of political philosophy, Adams's psychology and Jefferson's political science. Adams's draws on the delineation of the "factive personality" Malatesta (*VIII*) and Jefferson's on Malatesta's creation and the means of achieving it (*IX*). Adams cites a favorite subject of the French ideologues, "Man, a rational creature!," as described in an amusing anecdote by the Francophile Franklin. Franklin supposed a rational man stripped of his appetites, in his chamber, engaged in making experiments. When a servant announced dinner he expostulated "And must I break the chain of my thoughts to / go down and gnaw a morsel of damned hog's arse? / Put aside your ham; I will dine tomorrow." Whatever Franklin's tone, Adams makes a serious application to political philosophy: "Take away appetite, and the present generation would not / Live a month, and no future generation would exist; / and thus the exalted dignity of human nature etc...." Adams's psychology applies to the factive personality Malatesta while contradicting Madison's, the French revolutionaries', and Franklin's. Franklin's Amendment is countered by Adams's Amendment. While Franklin's rational man is claiming independence from the cruel punishments of appetite, Adams is turning the same principle back upon him. Adams is showing up the self-styled universalists with a broader, more human universality. Refuting rationalist theory with a theory which restores appetite suggests an interpenetration of theory and practice (cf. the Branches/Powers of the third phase).

The theoretical Adams's " '..wish that I cd. subjoin Gosindi's Syntagma / of the doctrines of Epicurus' "[5] (a philosophy directed by virtue toward repose), and the practical Jefferson's " '..this was the state of things in 1785...'," link halves of a seal (the Mount symbolizing the Constitution). Jefferson's fragment recalls the Constitutional crisis which arose when the two Constitutionalists were ministers abroad. It re-evokes, for '76, for the crisis, and for continuing revolution, the Committees of Correspondence initiated in " '73" to unite the colonies in a single purpose. The method echoes Malatesta and his people uniting to rebuild Rimini and the Tempio, as evidenced especially by the postbag. It applies now to amending the Constitution and to uniting the world (cf. the sending of Barlow). The rights retained by the people activate the assumption of sovereignty within a universal Supreme Law for political revolution. Theory and practice here interpenetrate in the practical method for exchanging ideas.

Tenth and last, gists draw on Malatesta's struggle against the Papacy's effort to extend its religious power to political and economic power (*X*). Returning from philosophy to the present situation, the two collaborators on the Declaration, fellow officials at home and ministers abroad during the struggle, contributors of ideas to the Constitution (though not present at the Convention), but opponents during the presidencies largely omitted from the canto, join finally (cf. the Malatestan Eagle) in continuing revolution under the pledge and under the reserved powers of the Bill of Rights. The adversaries are the old universal orthodoxy, "church of St. Peter," and the new, French and English imperialist economics. To Adams the church's exploitation of superstition overpowers "human reason, human conscience," in which he

5. This fragment, though assigned to "Mr Adams," is from a Jefferson letter to Charles Thompson, 9 January 1816, about the so-called Jefferson Bible made by cutting up the four Gospels and "arranging them on the pages of a blank book, in a certain order of time or subject" to extract "the Philosophy of Jesus" from excrescences imposed upon it. Jefferson wished he could "subjoin a translation of Gosindi's Syntagma of the doctrines of Epicurus, which, notwithstanding the calumnies of the Stoics and caricatures of Cicero, is the most rational system remaining of the philosophy of the ancients, as frugal of vicious indulgence, and fruitful of virtue as the hyperbolical extravagances of his rival sects." Jefferson intended his "Bible" to be used for educating the Indians to the new society, a subject elaborated in *XXXII*. Whether Pound erred in attributing the quotation to Adams, or meant something by it, I do not know. In any case the similarity of the Jefferson Bible to *The Cantos* is noteworthy.

believes. To Jefferson it corrupts the laws by translating "ancien scripture" as "*Holy Scripture,*" an error which the Christian revolt against classicism continues. Going back to the economic topic of the first letter, Adams and Jefferson together reject the new secular order, the French Revolution resulting in Napoleon's Continental System ("Bonaparte...knowing nothing of commerce...") and the system of Protestant imperial England ("...or paupers, who are about one fifth of the whole...").

Lest the paupers be taken for French or continental, the Eagle Pound adds the concluding parenthesis "(on the state of England in 1814)," then the colophon "*Hic Explicit Cantus.*" His coda and the colophon focus cosmopolitan economic revolution already in the mind of '76 and being inherited by a twentieth-century mind. The Latin rubric and colophon frame the mind of '76 within its source, the spirit "ELEUSIS." An archetypal revolutionary mind is still alive in the stones of the Renaissance and in the Seal and documents of '76 if not in the Statue of Liberty and in a petrified Constitution, its "arms turned to branches, / Who will say in what year."

Both the church and the new empires travesty the motive toward a new union and the revolutionary order sought. America has been a source of potential economic revolution (1–7) but the ideas have failed to enter the extension of revolution to the world via France (4–10). Jefferson, stressing liberty, practicality, and political economy, and Adams, stressing union, theory, and human nature, have nevertheless evolved a promising new revolutionary tradition modifying even that of orthodox '76. That it has failed in Europe and will fail in America is not their fault. It will emerge again in fascist Italy after having evolved since the colonization of America in Siena and Tuscany.

Yet even so-called "*Holy Scripture*" is a source of revolution. The opening Malatestan rubric is from the Bible. The Malatestan Renaissance and its successor '76 therefore embody a religion of continuing revolution evolved from old and new epitomes (the Nekuomanteia, Malatesta's postbag, and this canto). Canto *XXXI*, introduced through the Eagle who opposed the Pope in *X*, is overseen by the Eagle Pound through the Eagles of '76 until Pound (as he did in *I* and *IX*) clinches the whole with his parenthetical coda; so his "*parts of this letter in cypher*" clinched a Seal-form, which has projected the first four letters to the whole canto. In the Malatestan perspective, "paupers, who are about one fifth of the whole" recalls to a reader aware of arcana the concluding "151" of the bill of lading, or Pound here as "Seal Eye." "*Hic Explicit Cantus*" thus surveys and judges the whole canto from the vantage of the eye of Providence, in the voice ANNUIT COEPTIS, for new beginnings of '76 always in progress and now being prosecuted in the twentieth century. The whole canto and Pound's handling considered, it is no wonder that "*Hic Explicit Cantus*" should read (like the colophons of *XXX* and *Pisan LXXVII*) both "*Here ends the canto*" and "*This explicates The Cantos.*"

As a new epitome for the whole poem Liberty *XXXI* opens up and transforms Liberty *I* explicitly into traditional political '76 and into "new" economic '76. But it is also the first of "new" Seal *XXXI–XXXIV* within "new" Revolution *XXXI–XL*. To these we now turn.

Seal *XXXI–XXXIV* & Revolution *XXXI–XL*

Canto *XXXI*-as-"ONE" first epitomizes a "new" American Seal *XXXI–XXXIV* transforming a Renaissance poetic tradition into an American revolutionary tradition. New revolutionary traditions emerging first in America and then in France (1–6) project a traditional Seal *XXXI*, Jefferson after his retirement (7) projects a personal Seal *XXXII*, Adams's and Jefferson's governmental theory and practice (8–9) project a justicial Seal *XXXIII*, and their convergence against persisting and new orthodoxies projects as an American version of a poetic tradition a tradition of continuing revolution, Seal *XXXIV*. Seal *XXXI–XXXIV* reproject and project the four drafts of "ELEUSIS."

Through Seal *XXXI–XXXIV* as "REVOLUTION . . . in the minds of the people," the ten letters project from antecedents the eleven "new" cantos of a new prototype, explicit American revolutionary form and its historical consequences. Through Revolution *XXXI–XL* the "old" and "new" epitomes and prototypes reproject the ten drafts. Rather than separate explication of Seal *XXXI–XXXIV* and Revolution *XXXI–XL*, as was done for the first decad, it is convenient to view both evolving together from canto *XXXI* and the one in the process of evolving from the other.

Subsuming Odysseus opening the prophecies of the dead (*I*) and Renaissance (*I–X*) and world (*XVI. Cantos*) revolution, Jefferson's recollection of the Washington plan for developing the West (letter 1) projects at once a traditional Seal *XXXI* and a new revolutionary destiny (*XXXI*), later Manifest Destiny in America and revolution in the world. The men of '76 seek more perfect American and world union. Jefferson reassembles their states of mind in the form of Congress to assess universal human nature and the States of the world. Reassembly for new perspectives and purposes draws on the activating religious and political freedoms.

Subsuming the epiphanic "nuove persone" of Seal *II* and *XVII–XXX*, the stellar mind (letter 2) projects revolutionary personality through Jefferson in retirement (letter 7). In the rubric—

"The revolution," said Mr Adams,
"Took place in the minds of the people"

—Adams's central mind forms a collective mind of "WE the People" into a stellar plan. Adams and Jefferson take the Presidential role (for Amendment). Adams's definition amends to mental arms the better known French provision of military arms, which was motivated not to establish justice but to advance the old power politics. In the middle of the canto the retired Jefferson continues his myriad interests, seeks to improve the natural rights of "man oppressed," and maintains revolutionary communication with Europe. The Indians, some of whom are "instituting a government," should be civilized by education rather than by conversion. A luxury which banishes thought has made "their privileged orders . . . as mere animals." The middle is framed by "revolution . . . in the minds of the people" and by "Cannibals of Europe are eating one another again," which frames diatribes against the animalism of the privileged orders, against European royalty, and against the European policy of war. Adams opposes the animalistic mind by suggesting scientific animal breeding as an analogue for bettering an existing popular mind. Out of the refrain "The cannibals of Europe are eating one another again" Jefferson ends the canto as a Dantean Sordello ("a guisa de leon . . . quando si posa"). For the Seal, liberty and new union have interpenetrated each other à la constellation.

Subsuming the justices and Mounts of Seal *III* and catching "Jefferson-Nuevo Mundo" in progress, American theory and practice of government (letters 3 and 8–9) project the civil and economic revolution of '76 to the industrial revolution of the nineteenth and twentieth centuries. For the first half of Seal *XXXIII* Adams introduces the theory of a balance of governmental powers. Four passages of Adams theorizing about government toward the end of the Napoleonic era (1815) alternate with four Jeffersonian passages of practice, economic rather than civil, from the American struggle (1777–81). The themes and form manifest the Constitutional dynamic. In the second half of the canto Marx's critique of industrial conditions in *Das Kapital* introduces ten pieces of evidence which record nineteenth-century efforts to institute humane labor laws, but then decline into ideological, violent communist revolution and into capitalist means of sustaining its domination in the face of such threats. The theme and form is that of the Bill of Rights implemented but gradually perverted. The appended Bill reflects tetrad foreshadowed at the end of trine, like the Renaissance ruins at the end of Seal *III* or Malatesta's postbag at the end of the third phase of the prototype decad (*IX*).

The Seal theme is Constitutional. For the decad Adams and Jefferson are instituting government by consent but under new conditions consent is being withdrawn. The motive to secure domestic tranquility also fails. The Judicial Adams is interpreting a political Supreme Law, but under industrialism an economic Supreme Law implicit in Jefferson's economic concern supersedes it. Protection against quartering soldiers unless they be lawmakers like Adams, Jefferson, and objective critics of industrial capitalism is sustained until bloody revolutionaries and capitalists begin to take over the "houses" of government.

The irradiated Renaissance mind and universal extension of continuing revolution (Seal *IV*) are projected through letter four (Madison's opaque view of human nature and political motives, and Jefferson's illumination of States and continuing revolution), and through letter ten (Adams's and Jefferson's convergence against the Church and European economic systems), to the irradiating mind of John Quincy Adams continuing revolution into the next generation. Seal *XXXIV* opens with ten irradiating fragments of conversation about nature, international politics, commerce, and literature, which culminate in Adams's idea of a treaty of commerce with Russia. Transforming prior exercises of the Bill of Rights (especially that at the end of Seal *XXXIII*), Adams's continuing mind of '76 irradiates his posts as ambassador in Europe, as Secretary of State, as President, and finally as Congressman. For the decadal themes Adams applies the premise of continuing revolution to his declining times to provide for the common defense against encroaching plutocracy. States/(Ratification) modulates via Adams's career into new Congress/States. Privacy is respected but modified by Pound's proper revolutionary warrant to open up Adams's diary: a fourfold invocation having opened up ten paragraph images in Seal *IV*, in Seal *XXXIV* ten fragments move through four phases to a symbolic focus.

In his diary Adams records relations between America and Europe, the decline of the American mind and political morality, and the emergence of the financial power. The diary form and the elegiac tone accent his devotion to the ideals of '76 as the nation is growing away from them. From United States ambassador abroad to congressman marks the emergence from states' rights of the coming plutocratic union. Seal *XXXI–XXXIV* is sealed by a monolithic, materialized travesty of the pluralistic, idealized Mount of '76:

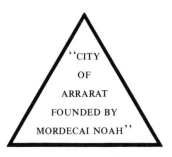

This symbol projects an "AGALMA" (monument) of plutocratic new union in *XL*. It projects the repluralized Monte dei Paschi of Siena as Adams's mind projects continuing revolution in "Siena-Leopoldine Reforms." Pound concludes by exalting Adams with Malatestan and Horatian mottoes enforced in later printings by ideogram, with which "Siena-Leopoldine Reforms" will also end:

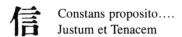

        Constans proposito....
        Justum et Tenacem

The Latin (constant in will, just and form) echoes the Malatestan motto with which the draft began. *Hsin*[4], faith, "The man standing by his word" (the words his mouth speaks) culminates and affirms the Four Tuan in the Wu Chang or Five Constants. The universal revolutionary protagonist's arrangement makes the end of the American Seal *XXXI–XXXIV* also Eleusinian and Confucian.[6]

The American Seal *XXXI–XXXIV* has emerged out of the spirit "ELEUSIS" through the Renaissance. Having done so it not only evolves itself but also provides a new perspective for viewing the European revolutionary tradition as it continues from the Renaissance. To the eyes of '76 the French Revolution emerges but subsides into the Napoleonic era. European revolution then emerges from Marxist sociological criticism and takes the form of the communist-capitalist struggle. Beginning with John Quincy Adams, America struggles against but finally declines into plutocracy, just as the Renaissance declined before. But the American expression of "ELEUSIS" continues to expose nineteenth- and twentieth-century decline of the European mind, both sociological (into the Marxist view) and psychological (into the Freudian view). The eyes of '76 have opened up the Renaissance tradition for reconsideration, which reveals alternatives to Marxism and Freudianism. Indeed, while America is evolving forward in time, reconsideration goes backward via the Renaissance and the Middle Ages to origins in the *Odyssey* and in its mythic background. Convergence of this perspective with the ultimate decline of '76 precipitates a new view of twentieth-century revolution as heir to a continuing and still viable Eleusinian spirit.

The case of millennial leadership culminating in Varchi's view of the Medici assassination (*V*) is projected through Jefferson's comparison of European and American leaders (letter five) to leadership measured by Marxist sociology and Freudian psychology (*XXXV*). "So this is (may we take it) Mitteleuropa" itemizes post-World War I Vienna in a series of Freudian case histories of the so-called social elite; both the cases and the Freudian perspective are treated as evidence of a breakdown of social cohesion, leadership,

---

6. Canto *XXXIV* reflects what Brooks Adams called in *Degradation of the Democratic Dogma* his grandfather's tragedy, his inability to realize the Washington plan for America adumbrated in Jefferson's opening letter to Washington. Part of the purpose was to turn Virginia away from negro slavery toward commerce and industry. Pound's reading of *Degradation* lies behind remarks in "Newspaper, History, Etc." (*Hound & Horn*, Cambridge, Mass., April/June 1930). A first phase of "THE SANE METHOD OF STUDYING HISTORY," "learning what certain great protagonists intended, and to what degree they failed in forcing their program on the mass," is illustrated by "Washington's limited objective re/ the Potomac waterway," by Jefferson's "continual struggle to import civilization from Europe (getting measurements of la Maison Carée, etc,)" and by "J. Q. Adams' intention of conserving national wealth for purpose of national education and civilization." "The second phase of the method is, obviously, the study of why the intentions failed or succeeded to the degrees recorded." Brooks Adams explored these two phases but did not "erect it into a principle," i.e., derive from his evidence and method "a science of history." "In his search for a science of history Henry Adams, I think, erred in that he started gunning about for an analogy outside history: i.e., in astronomy, before he had exhausted the study of relations inside the subject (history) itself."

and direction. The canto ends with a corroboration of the Marxist critique applied to the Renaissance, Venice seeking to monopolize commerce at the expense of her competitors. But inbetween the psychological and economic critiques Renaissance Mantua presents a plan to make the Mantuan cloth industry self-sufficient so that it will benefit the whole commune. Implied is a critique of the Marxist plan for achieving economic justice and prosperity. Foreshadowed are the coming innovations in Siena and Tuscany, which will not stand isolated as mere plan but will actually be established and will last on to the time of Pound's writing. For the decadal theme cases against Freudian, Marxist, and Venetian minds are modified by the Mantuan. Mantua would promote the general welfare. "We" are applying Amendment in a search for Presidential leadership and new ideas. The method observes due process of law. The subjects and theme will be treated more largely through the cases of dynasties and emperors in "KUNG."

The enlightened revolutionary love code of Provence (*VI*), "a cult of the emotions," is projected through Adams's criticism of the revolutionaries of his time (letter six) to the Tuscan refinement of the cult of Amor into "a cult of the harmonies of the mind."[7] Most of *XXXVI* consists of a probing, loving translation of Guido Cavalcanti's difficult, arcane love canzone "Donna mi prega," which provides an alternative to the Freudian emphasis on pathology in a psychology oriented toward inspired creativity.[8] The canzone turns Eleusinian psychology into a philosophy that has informed the mind of '76, as "JOHN ADAMS" will clearly show. That philosophy, rooted in concrete experience and translating inspirations and affections into will, intention, and reason, is generalized through symbols of justice ("thrones, balascio or topaze") and through the early medieval philosopher Scotus Erigena's dictum

7. "The cult of Provence had been a cult of the emotions; and with it there had been some, hardly conscious, study of emotional psychology. In Tuscany the cult is a cult of the harmonies of the mind," Chapter 5, "La Dolce Lingua Toscana," *The Spirit of Romance*, 1910. Both were expressions of "The Mediterranean sanity," first "the classic aesthetic, plastic to coitus" and then "the medieval clean line" based on the "dogma," "the central theme of the troubadours," "that there is some proportion between the fine thing held in the mind, and the inferior thing ready for instant comsumption." It is "the section d'or, if that is what it meant, that gave churches like St Hilaire, San Zeno, the Duomo di Modena, the clear lines and proportions. Not the pagan worship of strength, nor the Greek perception of visual non-animate plastic, or plastic in which the being animate was not the main principal quality, but this 'harmony in the sentience' or harmony *of* the sentient, where thought has its demarcation, the substance its *virtù*, where stupid men have not reduced all 'energy' to unbounded undistinguished abstraction." "Mediaevalism and Mediaevalism," *Dial*, New York, March 1928.

8. The bibliography on Cavalcanti begins with the "Etude" *Sonnets and Ballate of Guido Cavalcanti* (1912) containing an important theoretical "Introduction" dated 15 November 1910. Cavalcanti illustrates "I gather the Limbs of Osiris," 1911–12. The essays "Mediaevalism and Mediaevalism (Guido Cavalcanti)," "Donna Mi Prega," and "Guido's Relations" appeared in *Dial*, New York, March and July 1928, July 1929. An elaborate scholarly edition, *Guido Cavalcanti Rime* (Genoa: 1932), comprehended all the foregoing. "Cavalcanti" dated "1910/ 31," the essays of 1928–29, culminated *Make It New* (1934).

"Authority comes from right reason, / never the other way on,'" which Pound sets against "Aquinas head down in a vacuum, / Aristotle which way in a vacuum?"[9] In this perspective Sordello returns through "Sacrum, sacrum, inluminatio coitu," his slogan for poetic inspiration. Now, however, Sordello is also treated politically. When Charles of Anjou rewarded him for fighting in his army with lands, castles, and a dye-works, Sordello rejoined "what the hell do I know about dye-works?!" and "sold the damn lot six weeks later," preferring (in the pun Goito/Godio and in a concluding tag from his verse) his own rich thought and the life of a wandering minstrel. A dye-works had been integral to the Mantuan plan in *XXXV*. Sordello's Amor makes him a precursor of Cavalcantian philosophy, but indifference to social and economic well-being leaves him politically akin to the case studies of Mitteleuropa. The case of Charles's "brother soldier" ("Dilectis miles familiaris") shows that the Provençal love code liberates but does not lead to a new social order.

That Cavalcanti's canzone expresses a medieval revolutionary mind derived from "ELEUSIS" is the argument of "Mediaevalism and Mediaevalism," which opened attributing to the canzone "a tone of thought, no longer considered dangerous, but that may have appeared about as soothing to the Florentine of A.D. 1290 as a conversation about Tom Paine, Marx, Lenin and Bucharin would to-day in a Methodist bankers' board meeting in Memphis, Tenn." Cavalcanti leans not only toward proof by reason but also toward proof by experiment. He is thus "much more 'modern' than his young friend Dante Alighieri, *qui etait diablement dans les idées reçues.*" In "Partial Explanation,"[10] part of a further essay on the canzone, Pound noted that Cavalcanti was called "natural philosopher," "atheist," and "Epicurean"; hence the link with Scotus, who was labeled Manichean when the Albigensian crusade destroyed Provençal civilization. It is not so much what Cavalcanti says in his poem as the familiarity he shows with "dangerous thinking." He is in "'that tenuous line who from Albertus Magnus to the renaissance' meant the freedom of thought, the contempt, or at least a moderated respect, for stupid authority," for "the tyranny of the syllogism, blinding and obscurantist." The canzone conveys this effect "with the suavity of a song, with the neatness of a scalpel-cut."

Pound's translation also illustrates a complementary relation between government and art explained and emphasized marginally in *Jefferson and/or Mussolini*, a particular gloss to *Eleven New Cantos* and a general gloss to the operation of the revolutionary mind (Chapter 25):

> My next analogy is very technical. The real life in regular verse is an irregular movement underlying. Jefferson thought the formal features of the American system would work, and they did work till the time of

9. The British *Seventy Cantos* (1950) eased the scorn by adding "not quite in a vacuum."
10. *Dial*, New York, July 1928.

General Grant but the condition of their working was that inside them
there should be a *de facto* government composed of sincere men willing
the national good. When men of understanding are too lazy to impart the
results of their understanding, and when the nucleus of that national
mind hasn't the moral force to translate knowledge into action I don't
believe it matters a damn what legal forms or what administrative forms
there are in government. The nation will get the staggers.

The whole argument of *Jefferson and/or Mussolini* is based on the relation between de jure and de facto, Constitutional Branches and Powers. In "Jefferson-
Nuevo Mundo" the mind of '76 derived from "ELEUSIS" and established
de jure declines de facto into plutocracy while "ELEUSIS" itself is resurging
from formality, debility, and perversion with new de facto force. Cavalcanti's
whole poem is an "accident," in medieval philosophy an actual property or
manifestation (de facto) of an ideal form or object (de jure). A twentieth-
century mind informed by '76 is inheriting an embodiment of Eleusinian
form by translation; mythic roots will be revived at Circe's (*XXXIX*) and
"ELEUSIS" itself will be fully revealed in *XLVII*, the sixth canto of "Siena-
Leopoldine Reforms."

Canto *XXXVI* and the neo-Odyssean *XXXIX* are mythic cantos for deriving
the premise of the draft, the institution of government by consent; Cavalcanti
reflects it by consenting to a lady's request for definition and by accepting the
governance of a philosophy of love, while Sordello rejects it as too restrictive
to his liberty. Perhaps both are right, but Cavalcanti's philosophy is new, is
more refined, and transcends the individual case; his whole canzone is set
against Sordello's quatrain praising Cunizza's beauty (*VI*). For the decadal
theme Cavalcantian refinement tests the case of brother Sordello and Scotian
philosophy tests the cases of his brother philosophers. Philosophizing Amor
would secure (the emphasis is on "secure") the blessings of liberty. The
Judicial mind opens up the Supreme Law of Amor. The standards of Cavalcanti and Scotus give fair trial to Aquinas, Aristotle, and Sordello. As noted
above the Cavalcantian philosophy of Amor and the decadal themes will be
elaborated in "JOHN ADAMS" according to Adams's motto "not less of
order than liberty" and through his effort to reintegrate America into a world
order after the case against "our British brethren" has been won.

Canto *XXXVI* also completes the philosophy of '76 (the Declaration's premises) evolving through cases its antecedent, inherent philosophy of Amor. The
Eagle speaker of the love canzone affirms E PLURIBUS UNUM a unified
philosophic tradition. The tradition mends a schism between Aristotle's and
Aquinas's abstract impersonal philosophies and Sordello's asocial Amor. The
framing cantos *XXXI* and *XXXVI* reflect a unity of politics and psychology
which is splitting apart as the draft evolves but which the draft is seeking to
reintegrate.

Canto *XXXVI* also completes the philosophy of '76 The
The case against the past and the states' rights motives union to liberty have

carried states' rights to the verge of Ratification and evolved Congress, Presidency, and Judiciary for a new union. After Amendment/Presidency and Supreme Law/Judiciary derived from and applied to the European cases, a return to America in *XXXVII* declares independence against growing financial power and liberates the public treasury for an effort (doomed) toward "a more perfect union." The return to American Constitutional trine for Ratification of states' rights and for the Branch/Power States formalizes the effort. The common law is applied to the civic and economic rights of the whole people.

Pound's summary and choice of a Renaissance tradition (*VII*) is projected through the retired Jefferson's continuation of '76, his recollections of his public life, and his rejection of public debt and a national bank, which cloaked Pound's inheritance of a tradition and an epic vocation (letter seven). Pound inherits his vocation even more directly through Martin Van Buren's continuation of '76 culminating in the struggle against the national bank during the Jackson administration and his own, which Van Buren tells "in the mirrour of memory," from Italy, in his *Autobiography.* Canto *XXXVII* is also made contemporary (like *VII*) by the fact (not mentioned until *XLVIII*) that Van Buren's *Autobiography* remained unpublished until 1920, for Pound an evidence of the suppression of history by economic interests, and by publication in 1932 of the autobiography of Peggy Eaton, whose virtue the antibank forces rallied to protect when it was impugned as a means of embarrassing the Jackson administration. She also carries the psychological theme, which may either inspire Amor or reduce the achievements of the creative mind back into elemental nature. Van Buren's suave political opacity and his characterization of politicians of his time also carry the psychological theme. The evolution of Jacksonian Democracy, of which Van Buren is presented as an initiator, coadjutant, and heir, belies Marx's dogma of class struggle; Van Buren's understanding of the uses and abuses of finance evidence Marx's neglect of that mechanism for promoting or perverting social justice.

The neo-Biblical rubric " 'Thou shalt not,' said Martin Van Buren, 'jail 'em for / debt' " (cf. the Malatestan Biblical rubric "Tempus loquendi / Tempus tacendi") focuses economic declaration, liberty, states' rights, and common law (the last of which had in part this aim). Van Buren earns his spurs in his native New York State by supporting local autonomy and the rights of the people, both civic and economic. When he goes to Washington his character is attacked, from his first years as senator to the 1840 election, as servile, devious, luxurious, profligate, and unprincipled—in short, that of a mere "politician." But his place in history is assured by his role during the bank war and by his later clear account of its event and their meaning, that is, control of the government and of the economy either by the bank forces in their selfish interests or by the people for the well-being of the country at large. He closes by characterizing politicians of his time insofar as they promoted the principles of '76 or undermined them. He recognizes his own opaque political character but claims staunch adherence to '76 and to political

principles aimed at advancing the public good. Pound confirms the judgment
by commemorating Van Buren's establishment of an independent treasury.

HIC

JACET

FISCI LIBERATOR

This tomb of *"A man of no fortune, and with a name to come"* supersedes the
pyramid "CITY OF ARARAT" and extends the eulogy of John Quincy
Adams. Both '76 and Adams's heritage continued to Van Buren. But here the
good, like his *Autobiography*, is interred with Van Buren's bones. Van
Buren completing his testament "In the mirrour of memory" anticipates the
formula for Adams's testament (*LXX–LXXI*). His doing so in Italy projects
Pound's reconstitution of his own tradition and revolutionary self "In the
mirrour of memory" in *Pisan*.

Canto *XXXVII* has been not only a turn from liberty toward new union
and a second turn in trine but also a phase of struggle dominated by the
motives, which are shown through Van Buren's struggle to liberate the country from the bank and to unite the country behind an independent treasury.
Like Acoetes/Pound amid epiphanies in *II* and Jefferson writing to Paine,
like Pound at the center of a Renaissance tradition in *VII* and Jefferson at
the center of activities and memories upon entering his retirement, and like
Adams and Jefferson in *XXXII*—Van Buren's "mirrour of memory" is the
central star of a stellar "WE the People" struggling against the bank and
proclaiming with its defeat a NOVUS ORDO SECLORUM.

Cantos *XXXVIII* and *XXXIX* are projected from the factive personality
Malatesta (*VIII* and *IX*) through Adams's assertion of a psychology that
includes appetite (letter eight) and through Jefferson's recollection of the
means of uniting the colonies for '76 (letter nine). As halves of a seal and a
phase of founding (Branches interacting with Powers), both cantos draw from
both letters their theory and practice and their complementary themes. So the
same Malatesta materials are first tested theoretically (*VIII*) and then brought
to life (*IX*). So the political *XXXVIII* is interpenetrated with psychology, and
the psychological *XXXIX* is interpenetrated with politics.

A perspective for judging *XXXVIII* is provided by a Dantean epigraph,

il duol che sopra Senna
Induce, falseggiando la moneta.
Paradiso XIX, 118

As the Eagle in the Heaven of Justice, referred to often in *The Cantos*,
excoriates the policies of a medieval monarch, so the twentieth century will
be judged. For the decad a world financial tyranny and public opposition to it
assert independence of each other. Public opposition seeks to provide for the
common defense. Individual minds (Presidential) adduce Amendment to try

to free the world from cruel and unusual punishments. Canto *XXXVIII* projects principles of government and the Branches to *Section: Rock-Drill.*

Projected from Malatesta's efforts against his times, means for uniting the world constructively and peaceably beat futilely against irresponsible capitalist imperialism's promotion of wars. Peddling munitions continent to continent to both sides and manipulating international finance reflect wheelings and dealings in Congress: the result was World War I and will be another.

Varied new ideas from all over the world, some good some not, reflect lively minds (Presidency) bent on solving world problems. None, however, gets to the heart of the matter or comes up with a comprehensive solution.

That is left for a third part, the Social Credit theories of Major C. H. Douglas, an alternative both to capitalist imperialism and to Marxist revolution. Douglas's economic democracy depends on keeping a country's wealth in circulation as purchasing power and in keeping purchasing power up with the creation of total prices (the ABC Theorem). Neglect of Douglas's nonmaterialist ideas in a world of gross and dialectical materialism elicits from Pound the exasperated judgment (Judiciary) "and the light became so bright and so blindin' / in this layer of paradise / that the mind of man was bewildered."

Because new ideas are disregarded and Douglas's theories are ignored, the world remains in the hands of the munitions industry. Evidence since 1842 shows how the French and German munitions industries infiltrated all institutions of society and spread their influence and products to all the states of the world. After a century such de facto government is able to use parliaments, philanthropies, banks, chambers of commerce, and newspapers to increase war-profiteering at the expense of "the affairs of the nation."

Behind and within all social and political systems, and revolutions old and new, are the sexual sources of psychic and intellectual power. In *XXXIX* the evolving return to Eleusinian origins resolves the conflict between politics and psychology mythically and sexually. Canto *XXXIX* answers charges against Odysseus—by Tiresias (*I*) that he would "Lose all companions" and by the Lotophagoi (*XX*) that he used his crew to further his own curiosities and pleasures. It does so by starting with the *Odyssey* but by going behind it to certain implications which are universalized over the whole history of visionary Amor. The canto develops a scale of Amor from self-indulgent sexual fantasy to sexual abstention, both of which result in personal and collective death. Between these extremes control of sexual license and rejection of abstention ritualize sexuality in the interests both of personality and of the collective. Ritual stabilizes sexuality in marriage so that the bride realizes "Sacrum, sacrum, inluminatio coitu" as a conception of new life. The silent procreating male will not speak his realization until educated by the woman in the culmination of mythic "ELEUSIS," *XLVII.*

An opening phase relives Elpenor's sexual fantasies when he lay in Circe's ingle and atop her roof, which after his death is desolate. His luxurious

hypnotic language recalls the approach to Circe's house, her song, her animals, and the transformation of himself and his fellows into swine. Greek and
Latin from Homeric and Ovidian sources abounds; as the canto proceeds
Dantean Italian and Middle English will lend their tones to an English which
is seeking to translate myth and tradition into modern relevancy.

To Elpenor, Circe is a seductive sorceress. With five lines of Greek from
Circe's speech directing Odysseus to Hades to consult Tiresias about how to
return home to Ithaca, however, the tone changes. In *The Cantos* Odysseus
has already made the voyage (*I*), but he has not yet fully realized its relation
to sexuality; hence the opaque Greek will be translated when he celebrates a
new knowledge in *XLVII*. Here the Greek opens up an Egyptian ritual voyage,
the arrival at Aeaea and Circe's, Circe's recognition of Odysseus, and her
knowledge that he will have to go "to hell in a boat" to fulfill his destiny.
Before she knows Odysseus, Circe tries to lure him to her bed. But he refuses
as had crewman Eurylochus, the type of sexual abstention ("Macer," thin,
sterile), who later led the crew mutinously to destruction and who would have
been better off in the swine-sty than in his ultimate watery grave. On the other
hand Odysseus dominates Circe, thus causing her to recognize him as one
"Always with your mind on the past" and to ask "Been to hell in a boat
yet?" The voyage is a discipline refused by Elpenor; hearing Circe's instructions in her bed is an opportunity refused by Eurylochus. Controlled sexuality
preserves directive intelligence from animalism and asceticism so that it can
receive life-enhancing inspiration.

The result of this balance in both male and female psychologies and in
relations between them is then celebrated collectively in a ritual nuptial dance.
The cry "Fac deum!" is answered "Est factus." The result is "Ver novum! /
Thus made the spring." Male and female have been "Beaten from flesh into
light." She "Hath swallowed the fire-ball." Thus she first says ("Sic loquitur
nupta"), then sings ("Cantat sic nupta"), "His rod hath made god in my
belly . . . I have eaten the flame."

In the evolution of drafts *XXXIX* reveals even beyond Cavalcanti's love
canzone the mythic source for the premise of government by consent, in this
case the consent both of the male who accepts female direction and of the
female who accepts male sexual dominance. Ritual orders the otherwise chaos
of natural rights. Interacting with the Branches of *XXXVIII* Elpenor and
Eurylochus express the Power States, Odysseus amends both, the ritual dance
evokes sexuality as the Supreme Law Amor, and the bride's celebration of
new conception and new birth ratifies. For the decad order comes out of
sexual confusion ("source of renewals") as the Tempio came out of Malatesta's struggles and as '76 came out of Adams's appetent human nature and
Jefferson's Committees of Correspondence. The Supreme Law of Amor mandates order through a Judicial mind. The rights retained by the people are used
for ends broadly social as well as narrowly personal. Canto *XXXIX* projects
these themes to *Thrones*. As with the love canzone the many other felicities

and implications of this important, rich, dramatic canto must be left to a reader's pleasure.

The Constitutional theme, the Dantean paradisal perspective, Douglas's ideal social definition of a factory versus the antisocial uses of factories by militaristic plutocracy, the hollow monuments erected by capitalism and Circe's house as either a sty for animals or a birthplace of gods—such concepts, perspectives, and symbols join *XXXVIII* and *XXXIX* as a Mount of MDCCLXXVI caught between perversion and rectification.

Papal excommunication of Malatesta but the countering Eagle (*X*) are projected through Adams's and Jefferson's judgments of the Church and of European economics (letter ten) to the triumph of plutocracy but an Eagle's voyage out of it to new possibilities (*XL*). The triumph of plutocracy culminates American Constitutional trine in the decad of the third (and American) draft; the flight out of it results from the return to Eleusinian origins, which has carried a fourth decad of Renaissance revolution informed by the Bill of Rights and about to be "sealed." Decadally plutocracy usurps the pledge, the motives to establish justice and to form a more perfect union, Ratification, and the reserved powers while perverting (phasally) the Bill; the Eagle counters with their original spirit.

The men of '76 who pledged themselves to the Declaration are replaced in a contemporaneous rubric (from *The Wealth of Nations*, 1776) by the cabals of plutocracy:

> Esprit de corps in permanent bodies
> "Of the same trade," Smith, Adam, "men
> "never gather together
> "without a conspiracy against the general public."

A new economic declaration (from Jefferson) rejoins

> Independent use of money (our OWN)
> Toward holding OUR bank, own bank
> and in it the deposits, received, where received.

The principle had already applied in "Venice 1361" before being "shelved for a couple of centuries." Jefferson accentuates

> "whether by privates or public...
>   currency OF (O, F, of) the nation.

But such warnings and policies have been overwhelmed by the pursuit of palatial estates and extravagant sport.

The success of plutocracy is typified by J. P. Morgan, whose financial manipulations have been beyond the reach of Congressional committees investigating colossal wealth. Such manipulations overwhelm the plea "*If a nation will master its money.*" So great have become the powers of insidious intelligence and lucrous inspiration—Geryon and Usura—that by 1907 we find ouselves "With our eyes on the new gothic residence, with our / eyes on Palladio, with a desire for seignieurial splendours" of a Circean civilization. The cornerstone for "THE CITY OF ARARAT" seen by John Quincy Adams has become

> (ÀGALMA, haberdashery, clocks, ormoulu, brocatelli,
> tapestries, unreadable volumes bound in tree-calf,
> half-morocco, morocco, tooled edges, green ribbons,
> flaps, farthingales, fichus, cuties, shorties, pinkies
> et cetera

And so, "Out of which things seeking an exit," it is "PLEASING TO CARTHEGENIANS" (and ought to have been pleasing to Americans of 1908) that the Eagle "HANNO" (or Pound) voyage to explore new lands to colonize them by laying out new cities, and to report his (or his) findings and efforts in a straightforward style true to motives, facts, and achievements, whether physical or intellectual.

So Hanno sailed in the wake of Odysseus along the northwest coast of Africa in the third century B.C., so Columbus sailed westward across the Atlantic, and so Pound has returned eastward. The results are the *Odyssey*, Hanno's *Periplous* (here translated), America and '76, and *The Cantos* so far, which includes all its antecedents. Hanno's account carries the voyager beyond the material ÀGALMA to the ideal sun-vision, Providence, and ANNUIT COEPTIS:

> Out of which things seeking an exit
> To the high air, to the stratosphere, to the imperial
> calm, to the empyrean, to the baily of the four towers
> the NOUS, the ineffable crystal

The "NOUS," the top of the mind, seals the foregoing. It is signed by Hanno "Karxèdonīon Basileos." A final "hung this" (the narration) "with his map" (a geographical plan) "in their temple" (atop the Mount) pre- and post-figures Malatesta's design, Columbus's globe, the documents and Seal of '76, and Pound's Calendar. So the new prototype decad subsumes all that has prophesied and projected it and projects all that is to come.

The main subject of the third draft of ten institutes American government by consent, but that consent is gradually withdrawn until Pound exits with Hanno. Hanno's voyage not only frames with Odysseus's four decads of Renaissance revolution and perfects the decad of the new American prototype, but also perfects a first "episode" to be revised by eastward circumnavigation until Renaissance revolution and '76 have been revised and perfected for world revolution in "JOHN ADAMS." In this perspective the first two drafts become discovery and colonization behind the new prototype as a new Declaration, i.e., "Jefferson" to be extended to a new "Nuevo Mundo" which must accommodate itself to the new economic revolution and to a world scope. Hanno's voyage thus precipitates anew the scope of '76 evolved since canto *XXXI*; that scope will be made explicit by ongoing modern revolution in the coda *XLI*, just as the codas to the first two drafts (*XI–XVI* and *XXVII*) culminated in Marxist revolution.

Coda *XLI*

Having made explicit the informing revolution of '76 and its economic dimension, but having shown its decline, Pound needed a contemporary descendant of economic '76 different from rejected Marxism. He also needed a contemporary revolutionary politician with whom he could ally himself as revolutionary "penman," at once historian, polemicist, lawmaker, and poet.

Toward the end of 1932, having brought America through Van Buren's new view of the Jackson era, having brought capitalist Europe up to date, and having set Douglas's Social Credit principles against militaristic finance, Pound felt the need to set down for himself "my state of curiosity, that is my *personal* curiosity," about a possible and desirable economic system. In January 1933 he expounded his ideas "in the form more or less of a manifesto, more or less interrogative, which asked for an affirmative response."[11] Direction and tone were given by the first question, "Is an economic system that which yields greater fruits to those who make cannon to kill people rather than to those who cultivate grain and make useful machines?" Supersession of Marxism by Social Credit was assumed, the fascist revolution met Social Credit public policy, fascism differed from bolshevism in "the cultural level," and finally "the de facto government of Jefferson is more like the fascism of today than it is like the current American actuality. Isn't that so?" His notes to himself commented "any ameliorating mechanism (that is, economic-monetary) would be absorbed and set in motion faster by Fascism than by any other existent system."

The 18 questions are the basis for *ABC of Economics*, "a brief formal treatise" begun at the same time to "get the subject off my chest" and to protect himself against "charges of unsystematized, uncorrelated thought, dilettantism, idle eclecticism, etc." The questions may also, however, have been deliberately formulated to be presented to and to draw an affirmative from—as Pound put it in an opening note to *Oro e Lavoro* (1944)—"a personage in the Italian government" interviewed on "Monday, 30 January 1933 (anno XI) at 5:30 P.M." At that meeting the list apparently caused Mussolini to ask "Perché vuol mettere le sue idee in ordine?" Why do you want to put your ideas in order? (*Rock-Drill 87, 93*). Pound replied "Pel mio poema," for my poem (*Rock-Drill 93*).

11. Pound recalled this in "Di un sistema economico," *Meridiano di Roma*, Rome, 1 December 1940. I translate his Italian.

Mussolini also made the comment on *A Draft of XXX Cantos* with which *XLI* opens, " 'MA QVESTO,' said the Boss, 'è divertente.' " Noel Stock speculates that Mussolini had received *XXX Cantos* earlier, or glanced at a passage here and there, or perhaps was directed by Pound to certain lines. "Appropriately, as a famous statesman having his first meeting with a distinguished American poet, Mussolini remarked that he found the work, or the passage, 'divertente,' meaning entertaining. Pound seems to have taken this as a serious comment indicating that in a flash the statesman had seen through to the heart of the matter—the liveliness and strong flavour of the work—which was at once a proof of Mussolini's brillance and of the fact that the cantos were meat for strong men of affairs."[12] In *Guide To Kulchur* Pound labeled Mussolini "a great man, demonstrably in his effects of events, unadvertisedly so in the swiftness of mind, in the speed with which his real emotion is shown on his face, so that only a crooked man cd. misinterpret his meaning and his basic intention."[13] Mussolini had shown his response to *The Cantos* and had instantly "carr[ied] his thought to the root" in his question. For better or worse the interview answered the questions, made Mussolini the contemporary "factive personality" of the poem, and clinched *Eleven New Cantos*.

First, however, on 8 or 9 February Pound began *Jefferson and/or Mussolini*, which comes out of the composition of *Eleven New Cantos* and glosses its purport. He signed his "Conclusions or a Postscript in the Spring" to *ABC of Economics* (London 1933) "E. P. *Feb. 12, anno XI dell' era Fascista*," his first public use of the fascist calendar; it was also Lincoln's birthday. On 22 February (Washington's birthday) he finished *Jefferson and/or Mussolini* subtitled "L'Idea Statale: Fascism as I Have Seen It" and signed "Ezra Pound *Volitionist Economics*"; after having been refused by "40 publishers" it was published in 1935, in London, with a 1935 foreword and a "September (1933) Preface." A New York edition (1936) added another preface, dated autumn 1934. The dust jacket read "A parallel between two forms of government with reference to a third," i.e., a new form for One World and for Pound's New Era. Having entered "the course of human events" through *The Cantos* Pound had become a chronicler and matter for chronicle according to the principle formulated in the "September Preface": "Journalism as I see it is history of to-day, and literature is journalism that *stays* news. A.D. 1933." Chronicle is confirmed as matter of literature with *XLI*, *Eleven New Cantos*, and *XLI Cantos*, which carry "the tale of the tribe" "ad interim 1933."

Pound also derived economic thought from a millennial "course of human events" in a series of ten lectures, "An Historic Background for Economics," delivered at the Università Commerciale Luigi Bocconi in Milan, March

---

12. *The Life of Ezra Pound* (New York: 1970), pp. 306–7.
13. Chapter 15, "Values," p. 105.

21–31. He contrasted "forms of thought in two different systems," presumably the "old" scarcity economics and the "new" volitionist economics for the distribution of abundance, and explained "Why or how a poet came to be drawn into economic discussion." Insofar as the titles have reference to his other works, "Problems that have been there" recurs to age-old conditions. "Economics for Mohamed, Kublai Khan, the middle ages" are carried through "the transition," presumably the Renaissance (*XXX Cantos*). The lectures then follow *Eleven New Cantos*. "Economic ideas of the early and constructive American presidents: Jefferson, John Quincy Adams, Martin Van Buren," lead to "the 'new' economics in England" and to "Conclusions," which presumably come up to the 18 questions, *ABC of Economics*, and *Jefferson and/or Mussolini*. "What literature has to do with it—The function of good writing in the State" implies incorporation of "L'Idea Statale" and "Volitionist Economics" into "the tale of the tribe."[14]

Coming out of Hanno's voyage and colonization, which give those themes to the first two drafts in relation to a coming four episodes of revolution, the coda to a fourth decad, a third draft, and a first episode transforms the Malatestan and Marxist-Leninist revolutions of the coda *XI–XVI*, and the revolution of Tovarisch of the coda *XXVII*, while becoming a transforming coda to '76. It transforms the previous codas by reversing the Jefferson-Adams judgment "Bonaparte...knowing nothing of commerce...." with Mussolini, and "...or paupers, who are about one fifth of the whole... / (on the state of England in 1814)" with Italian prosperity in 1933. A Malatestan Eagle's (*XI*)

"MA QVESTO,"
　　　said the Boss, "è divertente."
　　　catching the point before the aesthetes had got
　　　there

aligns Mussolini's view of history with the view presented poetically in *XL Cantos*. Both he and Pound see it from the "NOUS," as though they were reading Hanno's account and interpreting correctly "his map in their temple." Mussolini's mind and his public works correlate "XI of our era," fascist 1933, with the new era projected by Pound's Calendar. His policies muster industrial capital for a cooperative planned economy and he deals summarily with capitalist profiteers for whom investment and profit are a "personal matter." Both he and Pound understand, or Pound explained it to him in the 1933 meeting, the Renaissance monetary policy of Nic Uzano, who saw

14. An invitation listing the principal topics of the lectures was supplied by Donald Gallup. According to Stock (*The Life of Ezra Pound*, p. 309) Pound "traced the history of banking from the Temple of Delphi," "claimed to discover principles of economics in the sayings of Confucius," and found many problems illustrated by "capitalist behaviour in the Roman Empire." "In order to show that it was possible for poetry to have an active part in economics and the study of history he read from his cantos."

through the Medici (cf. *XXI*): that there always be enough money in circulation to keep commerce and industry moving for the public good. Catching
new revolution already in progress goes beyond the Russian Revolution of
1917 in the constructive spirit of '76. The fascist revolution is a source of new
declaration.

A second phase goes back to show how Mussolini became a revolutionary
different from Tovarisch (*XXVII*). He was exploited and insulted as a worker
and then stupidly deployed as a soldier during World War I. As a politician he
found Italian national policy reflected in military affairs ("'ordine, contrordine
e disordine''); while the socialists, his own party, wanted any kind of peace
("'una pace qualunque''), he saw a "social content to the war.'' As a poet-
soldier on the Alpine front he remarked the contrast between the beauty of the
Alpine landscape and the slaughter. Finally he became so important a figure
that his opposition identified a hospital where he was recuperating so that the
enemy would bomb it. Italian stupidity, hypocrisy, and treachery are interlineated with a case from the other side: the empress of Germany gave a
young Uhlan officer a book on "Renewal of higher life / in the struggle for
German freedom,'' but he was never out of uniform from his eighth year until
Germany lost the war. So the alleged ideals of World War I betrayed all who
espoused them. Interlineating the making of revolutionaries on both sides
reflects a need for liberty and new union shown already being achieved by
Mussolini's policies after he had gained power.

A third phase sets Mussolini against the European governing mind exposed
in Mitteleuropa (*XXXV*) and in the munitions trade (*XXXVIII*). Here it leads
Europe into World War I and then out of it toward World War II. Cultureless
militarism exemplified by Hindenburg, the socialist "Una pace qualunque,''
mindless bureaucracy exemplified by a "seventh under cat's dogkeeper'' who
filed away the German ultimatum of 1914 while his superiors were on va-
cation, and anti-intellectual opportunism exemplified by Churchill—all are
shown up by Mussolini's Malatestan observation and interpretation of a revolutionary Eagle seen over Udine. Lust for another war, "That llovely unconscious world / slop over slop,'' and government of a nation's mind by a
so-called 'free' press, elicit Mussolini's mild " 'where there is no censorship
by the state / there is a great deal of manipulation...,' '' which Pound echoes
ironically "and news sense?''

This résumé of the third draft from a Mussolinian point of view precipitates
projection of a fourth, which rounds back to Mussolini and his public policies.
True "news sense'' is that Duke Cosimo of Tuscany anticipated Mussolini by
securing loans with the duchy's resources and credit, and that the Sienese
Monte dei Paschi lent at low interest and applied all profits to relief works.
And are Douglas's Social Credit proposals news? Is "Woergl in our time?''
The last refers to Silvio Gesell's theory of depreciating stamp-scrip designed
to promote his Natural Economic Order. It was tried in a town in the Austrian
Tyrol (see *Pisan LXXIV*) until the bankers of Vienna got wind of it and

suppressed it. Gesell complements Douglas's industrial perspective with a perspective rooted in agriculture.

The foregoing four phases of *XLI* bring the European dimension to "XI of our era" while transforming the first three drafts and projecting "Siena-Leopoldine Reforms." A coda to the coda-canto recapitulates the American dimension as a projection of its epitome letter in canto *XXXI*, Jefferson's critique of French tax collection now formally addressed, dated, and laid out tabularly to symbolize even more distinctly the Mount. For France the framing letter implies nineteen of twenty million Frenchmen "accursed . . . in every material circumstance." Extended to America it implies the seeds of the whole American decline observable by Jefferson during his lifetime. Predicting "THE CITY OF ARARAT" and the "ÀGALMA," fragments from Jefferson's letters build from all the American cantos a Mount of economic evidence for the decline, here nakedly and without mitigation.

The remedy would have been, had it been applied, Jefferson's points restated from *XL*, "Independent use of our money...toward holding our bank." But neither Jefferson's critique nor Mussolini's new policies have yet been able to disturb this international militaristic version of the plutocratic "ÀGALMA,"

> 120 million german fuses used by the allies to kill Germans
> British gunsights from Jena
> Schneider Creusot armed Turkey
> Copper from England thru Sweden...Mr Hatfield
> Patented his new shell in eight countries.

An unjust tax system has expanded step by step to world rule by war profiteers. Evidence from World War I illuminates "new" evidence pointing toward a new war. So the state of things is imaged as universal history and an epic poem now definitively "of our era" carry Pound "ad interim 1933."

Precipitation by *Eleven New Cantos* of a circumnavigation inherent since the beginning is indicated by Pound's remark in 1934: "I am leaving Rome in the direction of China: along the way I shall become increasingly different than I was when I left. At Peking I shall be presented with a vast and unforeseen horizon. I would not have been able to reach that point [that scope] if I had not departed in the first place." That it also precipitates a new Declaration is indicated by the adjuration "Ban 'fascism' and start talking about the corporate state. Mussolini has rewritten the Declaration of Independence and put in the punctuation. 'All men equal in respect to labour and the state, differ only in the grade and extent of their responsibilities.' THAT ought to be the phrase JUSTE." His dissociation of "Systems 'devised' from 'systems in act, or going into act' " differentiated the American system, which was not being used, from fascism's inheritance of the best of both (*Eleven New Cantos*).[15]

---

15. To T. C. Wilson, 3 November 1934, Collection at Yale.

His own "Declaration" appeared in *New Democracy*:

> We do not want a weakening but a strengthening of the DECLARATION
> OF INDEPENDENCE, it may have been all right in 17 hundred and
> whatever, but the term 'pursuit' is too ironical. EVERY MAN HAS THE
> RIGHT TO LIFE, LIBERTY AND TO A REASONABLE AMOUNT
> OF THE AMENITIES. *A reasonable amount in 1934 consists in any of
> the comforts and amenities not needed by someone else.* That assertion
> and definition can be used to emend the brass on the Aurillac monument
> (which displays the original text of the 'Droits de l'Homme').[16]

16. *New Democracy*, New York, 30 March/15 April 1934.

CHAPTER THIRTEEN

THE FIFTH DECAD XLII–LI:

"SIENA-LEOPOLDINE REFORMS"

& "ELEUSIS" *LI CANTOS*

"...my 'Holy City'..."
  To Wyndham Lewis

That hath the light of the doer; as it were
a form cleaving to it.
  "Siena-Leopoldine Reforms" *LI*

The main historical subject of *The Fifth Decad of Cantos* and fourth draft of "ELEUSIS," seen through eyes opened by the Renaissance and by redis-covered '76, is the founding of the Monte dei Paschi Bank in Siena during the 1620s and extension of its lesson from Tuscany, Italy, and Europe to the world and to modern times. Unlike Renaissance and American revolution, which succumbed to plutocracy, Sienese revolution has continued on its own ground until Pound observes it with his own eyes. Culminating and consum-mating Renaissance assertions of revolutionary destiny and natural rights and American assertion of government by consent, Siena precipitates the premise and fact of continuing revolution while its lesson is exposing the mythic archvillains of *The Cantos*, the perverted Eagle Geryon and the perverted Providence Usura. The motive is to "provide for the common defense." Constitutionally the Renaissance city-state, attempted Renaissance union, and American federation culminate in a Sienese corporate state and a Tuscan federation of such states; the originating local states define an ancestral model for the corporate state evolving in contemporary fascist Italy; a federation of such states projects a world Congress. The negative mysteries of Geryon and Usura are exposed by the warrant of poetry; so are their positive counterparts, the mysteries and rites of "ELEUSIS," which make Pound their catechumen and poet.

Italy is "rediscovered" in the wake of 1492, Sienese founding (*XLII–XLIV*) coincides with the beginning of the colonization of North America, the Leopoldine Reforms of 1766–91 (*XLIV* and *L*) coincide with '76 itself, and the forms of both New World history and '76 continue on to the time of Pound's writing. In this respect "Siena-Leopoldine Reforms" is not only a fourth draft of "ELEUSIS" and in itself a new form of Constitution. After the emphasis on the tradition of '76, its new popular emphasis makes it also a second episode expressing the will of "WE the People": a "volitionist" first episode having established "the effect of the factive personality, Sigismundo, an entire man," from the Renaissance through '76 to Mussolini; "The found-ing of the Monte dei Paschi," a "second episode," shows "the discovery, or at any rate the establishment, of the true bases of credit, to wit the abundance of nature and the responsibility of the whole people."[1] Finally, "Siena-Leopoldine Reforms" also turns the first paideuma "ELEUSIS" into a world paideumatic declaration.

Pound accounted for the overlapping of phases in "A Social Creditor Serves Notice," a manifesto and first contribution to the organ of the British Union of Fascists.[2] With millennia of revolutionary history in mind he declared "A vast and inane conflict results from failure to recognize different phases of the SAME great revolutionary PROCESS occurring SIMULTANEOUSLY in dif-ferent parts of the world at different levels of civilization." That "England and continental Europe are grossly ignorant of Jefferson and Van Buren" looked back to the beginning of the poem in the light of "Jefferson-Nuevo Mundo." "But," looking ahead, "America (and England) are blackly, blankly, and utterly ignorant of Italian traditions. Cobden went to Siena in 1847 to render homage at the shrine of Salustio Bandini. No Englishman or American today, or not one in a million, has ever heard of the Leopoldine Reforms. That British liberalism sprouted under the aegis of a Prince of the House of Lor-raine, would cause flesh-creeping in Manchester." From the Renaissance per-spective of the beginning to the perspective of Italy today opened in *XLI* and ready to emerge in "Siena-Leopoldine Reforms," "Italy has lived through any amount of political and economic culture. (Just as she lived through humanism, and any amount of aesthetic culture, before it got to the ultimate Briton)." From its political and economic culture, through its aesthetic cul-ture, Italy evolved a revolutionary tradition which has not got to the "ulti-mate Briton" and to his American offshoot—the "Englishman or American today"—any more rapidly than did the Renaissance aesthetic tradition.

"The different phases of the SAME great revolutionary PROCESS" are the phases of New World history evolving the phases of '76, which are about to be completed thematically by drafts as "ELEUSIS." Explicitly, however, they emerged with the subtitles "Nuevo Mundo" (1492) and "Jefferson" (1776) and with the beginning of *Eleven New Cantos* in 1787. The founding of the Monte dei Paschi during the 1620s is carried through the American

---

1. Chapter 31, "Canti," *Guide To Kulchur*, 1938.
2. *Fascist Quarterly*, London, October 1936.

colonial period to the Leopoldine Reforms of 1766–91. Chinese millennial history will culminate in the Manchu revolution begun in "1625/35" and running to 1776. "John Adams," running from the discovery through the colonizations of the early 1600s to '76, will consummate "the SAME great revolutionary PROCESS occurring SIMULTANEOUSLY in different parts of the world at different levels of civilization." In revising '76 for world revolution eastward circumnavigation carries discovery from one episode to another while Pound's life carries colonization. In this world revolutionary perspective, since "Jefferson-Nuevo Mundo," "Siena-Leopoldine Reforms," and "KUNG" all end with continuing revolution, "JOHN ADAMS" perfects definitive continuing revolution for the world. In a world paideumatic perspective, with "ELEUSIS" discovered in the wake of 1492, continued eastward circumnavigation will define three world paideumas consummated in a turn from independent paideumas toward a world paideumatic union.

Like its predecessors the decad is divided to accommodate all forms. Founding the Monte dei Paschi is an epitome (*XLII*-as-"ONE"). Founding (*XLII*), carrying the founding to the people (*XLIII*), the Leopoldine Reforms (*XLIV*), and a mythic diatribe exposing Usura (*XLV*) constitute a Tuscan Seal *XLII–XLV*. The cases are applied to Pound's prosecution of continuing revolution against revealed Geryon and Usura since 1918 (*XLVI*) and to a culmination of the case against Odysseus (*XLVII*), which reveals the sexual mysteries and rites behind "ELEUSIS" and continuing revolution. Declaring independence against Geryon and Usura (*XLVIII*) also celebrates the evolving fascist corporate state while turning toward world union. A voice of the Chinese folk asserts local independence (*XLIX*). Sovereign powers are asserted by explicitly analogizing '76 with the contemporary Leopoldine Reforms (*L*), which are now placed in the context of the European restoration arranged by the Congress of Vienna. All the foregoing, "ELEUSIS" as well as the decad, are summarized and focused in a version of the pledge (*LI*) on the way toward revolution continuing in millennial China, in John Adams's America, and in the contemporary One World.

The documents projected by the Declaration and "moving concurrent" by duality, trine, and tetrad can be followed as in former drafts. Liberty *XLII*, Seal *XLII–XLV*, and the decadal Declaration inform continuing revolution against Geryon and Usura. Cantos *XLII–XLVII* motivate liberty from Geryon and Usura and *XLVIII–LI* motivate from achieved liberty a new world union. States' rights form culminating in a corporate state free of Geryon and Usura (*XLII–XLV*, *XLV–XLVIII*) modulates into a projection of such a state to the world (*XLII–XLVIII*, *XLVIII–LI*). The Amendments of the Bill of Rights activate the Declaration's argument and its concomitants while precipitating the tetrad of the Seal.

But in this fourth draft, which is more homogeneous than its predecessors, the themes of cantos are subordinated to major subjects of the transitional draft. Seal *XLII–XLV* emphasizes states' rights and the financially free corporate state as achievements of "ELEUSIS." Thematically Pound's summary of continuing revolution (*XLVI*) and the revelation of "ELEUSIS" itself (*XLVII*) would project fifth and sixth drafts. They do. But here, as subjects, they historicize and mythify Eleusinian achievement, in effect focusing "ELEUSIS" as a separate paideuma. Accordingly *XLVIII–LI*, which in all documents project thematically the new union of drafts seven through ten, here transform the local Seal *XLII–XLV* into a projection from "ELEUSIS" to its world scope, foreshadowed since the beginning and about to emerge in "KUNG," "JOHN ADAMS," and *Pisan*. These major subjects overlay the decadal themes, which are allowed to speak as they will.

Liberty *XLII*

The opening of the epitome, the next after Canto *XXXI* to be labeled "Canto," sums up the foregoing drafts anecdotally while projecting the fourth:

> We ought, I think, to say in civil terms: You be
>   damned'
>   (Palmerston, to Russell *re* / Chas. H. Adams)
>   'And how this people CAN in this the fifth
> et cetera year of the war, leave that old etcetera up
> there on that monument!' H.G. to E.P. 1918
>   Lex salica! lex Germanica, Antoninus
> said law rules at sea
>
> FIXED in the soul, nell' anima, of the Illustrious College
> They had been ten years proposing such a Monte,
> That is a species of bank—damn good bank, in Siena

Circean direction, discovery, and the tone and terms of declaration are summed up in a British prime minister's will, thought, and speech that an American ambassador, John Adams's grandson, go to hell. H. G. Wells intimates to an American colonist during a new struggle what the people ought to do with a statue of Queen Victoria. Laws concerning male and female succession could be resolved by heeding a Roman emperor's assertion of a single universal law beyond the whims of nations and men. The three catch-phrases pass into a providential vision which has been looking toward a new kind of state and a new kind of economic system, one that would harmonize varied states, a collective will, and several communes of a single state. For the first time the emerging catechumen, now about to discover "my 'Holy City,' "[3] introduces the historical materials of a draft with his own comments.

   In the form of the four invocations that projected the epitome of continuing

---

3. In a letter to Wyndam Lewis Pound called *The Fifth Decad* "my 'Holy City,' " probably

revolution, Seal *IV*, and through the presence of the emerging catechumen, the four assertions modulate into four irradiating voices of "ELEUSIS." The fourth assertion and first voice introduces the documents of the "Istrumento di Fondazione del Monte dei Paschi," 1624, rearranged from the original like the Malatesta materials and the Jefferson-Adams letters. For the first time in the poem the catechumen is explicitly turning over the documents before him while taking them into a mind prepared to find contemporary relevance, to compose them into an order common to past and present, and to receive from the matter, from his activity, and from the result a manifestation of ideal form corroborated by universal myth. "FIXED in the soul" introduces notice that Siena's Bailey, its executive body, consulted with the Senate and with the Medici rulers of the Grand Duchy of Tuscany. Inspiration, motive, and method open up instances from among ten items of the Bailey's proposal, dated July 1623, for a new bank designed to extend credit to anyone in the commune who can "USE IT" to expand the communal economy. The bank will accept deposits from all citizens, will pay a modest interest, will charge only a minimum for administrative expenses, and at certain periods will distribute surpluses to the workers of the city's various wards and guilds. In the first of four such validations of the several acts of the governing authorities, the proposal is formally dated, sealed

>   Loco Signi
> ✠   [a cross in the margin]

and notarized.

Memorializing, signing, sealing, and delivering the proposal precipitates a voice warning that all human works, especially a limited liability corporation, must be ritually renewed (cf. Jefferson's "The earth belongs to the living," *Pisan LXXVII* and elsewhere in Pound's works):

>   wave falls and the hand falls
> Thou shalt not always walk in the sun
>   or see weed sprout over cornice
> Thy work in set space of years, not over an hundred.

In the light of the general human condition the Duchy's financial advisers, having examined the proposal, approve its financial soundness, its accessibility to all citizens, and its accessibility to other "towns" in the state. Accordingly a letter from the Duchy to the Bailey accepts the proposal and agrees to provide an initial capital secured by income from the Sienese grazing lands. The Duchy's letter, signed by the female and male regents of the young Duke, is sealed, delivered, and memorialized in the Sienese Calendar (cf. Pound's Calendar and those of the paideumas).

---

with reference to unrealized America and to Yeats's "holy city of Byzantium" (4 November 1937, Collection at Yale).

Accordingly "ACTUM SENIS" introduces enactment of the proposal by "Senatus Populusque Senensis / OB PECUNIAE SCARCITATEM" (because of a scarcity of money). This time the catechumen joins in with the notaries by intervening in a third irradiating voice,

> so that the echo turned back in my mind: Pavia:
> Saw cities move in one figure, Vicenza, as depicted
> San Zeno by Adige...

Siena and other cities of Tuscany thus realize the catechumen's "Guillaume De Lorris Belated: A Vision of Italy" (*Personae* 1909), which has remained "FIXED in *his* soul" since he dreamed of Italian cities and of their extension to America via Columbus. As "ACTUM SENIS" continues he also applies to himself the voice of nature, "(to be young is to suffer. / Be old, and be past that)."

The proposal "FIXED in the soul" of the Bailey, the stabilizing advice and consent from the Duchy, and enactment by "Senatus Populusque Senensis" are all recapitulated until public documentation "for public and private utility," providentially "foreseeing erection / legitimate and just" of "such a MOUNTAIN," precipitates a sealing vision of the Monte, of Siena, and of associated cities and states now actually seen "in one figure,"

Pound's three-tiered, six-lobed Mount on a foundation extends the Monte's two-tiered, three-lobed Mount on a foundation. The foundation implies four lobes, giving ten.[4] This polytheistic Mount transforms the sign of Gibraltar (*XXII*) and the monolithic "CITY OF ARARAT" (*XXXIV*) into a Sienese symbol extending to Tuscany, Italy, Europe, and the world.

Canto *XLII* epitomizes economic continuing revolution undertaken by a corporate state taking shape within a larger federation of states. Branches and Powers of the Commune of Siena and the Duchy of Tuscany have cooperated for a common good. Overall a new Constitutional Convention is affirming governmental sovereignties while extending continuing revolution to economic justice and well-being. The Renaissance city-state and the American

---

4. The Monte dei Paschi seal is a vertical oval ringed by "Montis Pascvorum," the upper half consisting of two levels (three lobes) in a white field and the lower half a black foundation. The bank's seal is in turn taken from the Chigi-Saracini seal, three levels (six lobes) surmounted by an eight-pointed star and the motto "Micat In Vertice" (It Shines on the Summit). As explained in pp. 45–46 Pound's version implies a shield foundation and the interacting ten-star triangles of the constellation. It is also a tetraktys, the Pythagorean name for the sum of the first four numbers (1 + 2 + 3 + 4) regarded as the source of all things.

geographical state are being amended by a model for the twentieth-century corporate state needed to cope with the new "economic reality." Inherent are Jefferson's principle "The earth belongs to the living" and the corollary "Definitions" of "Volitionist Economics," C. H. Douglas's "Increment of association: Advantage men get from working together instead of each on his own" and "Cultural heritage: Increment of association with all past inventiveness."[5] The "Definitions" revise Marx's "surplus value," a value siphoned away from economic cooperation. Sienese revolution combines the best of Renaissance revolution, of '76, and of Marxist revolution, revising all for the new reality. A final revision of psychological revolution, inherent in the four voices, will come in the voice of "ELEUSIS."

Canto *XLII* also focuses "a man trying to think out a sane state" by "thinking in poetry," the culminating mode of "ELEUSIS." His "thinking" has corroborated the premise that particular forms of government grow out of the millennial traditions or paideumas of respective cultures, the basis of states' rights. His few essays on government, all written about this time, insist on such paideumatic origins.[6] His ideal, however, "The State Should Move like a Dance," was based upon the American model for the separation, distribution, and balance of powers, which in his somewhat amended view called for distinct "kinds of persons" for its functions, "executive," "advisory," "perceptive," and "poetic" (see pp. 20–21). Such functions are loosely present in Siena and Tuscany, but rigorously applied in Pound's four-phase form.

The four voices project as usual the Seal and decadal forms. But here they project especially the political *XLVI* interacting with the psychological *XLVII* as halves of a seal (Branches and Powers), *XLVIII* as a summary of the first four drafts, the world-projecting *XLVIII–LI*, and a culminating Seal/Calendar form for all the subjects of the four drafts, *LI*.

Seal *XLII–XLV*

For "REVOLUTION . . . in the minds of the people" Seal *XLII* turns the vision "FIXED in the soul" into a declaration symbolized by the shield and voiced E PLURIBUS UNUM. Shifting through the stabilizing voice of nature to the cooperating Duchy and to "WE the People" itself, Seal *XLIII* becomes a struggle symbolized by the constellation and voiced NOVUS ORDO SECLORUM. Support by the Duchy frames the canto and recurs throughout.

5. The motto and key "Definitions" of *Social Credit: An Impact* (London: 1935).

6. Chief instances are "Race," *New English Weekly*, London, 18 October 1936; "'Our Own Form of Government," dated 1936 but not published until *Impact* (1960); "The Jefferson-Adams Correspondence" (written in 1936), *North American Review*, New York, Winter 1937/1938; and "National Culture: A Manifesto" (1938), presumably written in conjunction with Pound's joining the National Institute of Arts and Letters to rouse it to his "endeavour to stave off war," but also not published until *Impact*.

Similarly the process of founding is continued and repeated (churned up) over and over, but now with the purpose of informing the people and forming a popular mind. At last the instituted Mount moves forward in time and out from Siena to Tuscany, though the emphasis remains on the people of Siena. Within the churning, two key passages focus the dichotomy liberty and new union.

For liberty a "general / council of the People of the City of Siena" is assembled for "Symbolic good of the Commune" so that citizens might be satisfied, contented, and persuaded that the Monte has been proposed for the common good and "for gt. future benefit to the city"; Pound comments "Worthy will to the chosen end." The reasons have been shortage of coin, taxes, exchanges, and usuries, which have impeded legitimate business. The end itself is evidenced by the catechumen's own observation, "under my window" in Siena, of preparations for communal religious rituals. That Siena has sustained her rites up to the time of writing affirms the continuing revolution which failed during the Renaissance and in America. In Siena, and perhaps in all Tuscany and all Italy, the Monte has preserved economic liberty.

Personal experience corroborates that the Monte involved the "REE- / sponsibility" of all, so that (Pound comments) "there first was the fruit of nature / there was the whole will of the people" (cf. the second irradiating voice). For new union these judgments open up an adaptation from the source which foreshadows the building of a 120-canto Mount of Constitutional clauses, Sections, and Articles, all culminating in a Branches/Powers dynamic. Under the Glorious Virgin, Siena's patroness, was

> convoked and gathered together 1622
> general council there were 117 councillors
> in the hall of World Map, with bells and with
> voice of the Cryer (Il Banditore)
> shares of Mount to yield five scudi on each hundred
> per annum, and to be separate from the PITY
> with its own magistrates, its own ministers
> Ill^{us} Balia eseguisca in tutto
> Rescript of TTheir HHighnesses

A general council constitutes 117 clauses, Sections, and Articles in a Columbian One World context; all culminate in a Congress affirming a renewed State and States. The Presidential "voice of the Cryer" proclaims Amendment. Judiciary interprets Supreme Law for interest on the shares. That the Monte dei Paschi should be separate from the Monte di Pietà or public hock shop, that it should have its own magistrates and ministers, and that the Baily should execute the whole scheme, ratifies the new institution of the renewed State by returning to the proposal's origin. The whole is signed by "TTheir HHighnesses." The resultant "ACTUM SENIS" is open-ended: "blank leaves at end up to the index.'' Sealing echoes the mythic natural voice: "Grass nowhere out of place. / Pine cuts the sky into three" (four Branches?). "Thus BANK of the grassland was raised into Seignory"—a new union.

In Seal *XLIV* the Leopoldine Reforms are promulgated in Tuscany beginning in 1766 (all cities thus "move in one figure"), and both Tuscan reforms and the Monte outlast the French Revolution and the Napoleonic interregnum. Leopold's

> And thou shalt not, Firenze 1766, and thou shalt not
> sequestrate for debt any farm implement
> nor any yoke ox nor
> any peasant while he works with the same

results in a heavy grain crop. Leopold decrees free trade inside the Duchy and shuts down grain imports. The Monte has kept cash in circulation, has always paid its creditors, and has kept interest rates low until 1783 and 1785. The grain policy of Leopold's successor Ferdinand, who "declared against exportation / thought grain was to eat," elicits from the Sienese a protracted Fourth-of-July-like celebration for "this so provident law."

Such popular feeling is swept up, however, and Ferdinand is swept away, during the French Revolution and its consequences in Tuscany. French occupation brings violence, treachery, and then annexation to the Kingdom of Etruria "without constitution" and with taxes so heavy that they are thought to be more than paid by subjects of Britain. This analogy to British "taxation without representation" is contrasted with the low cost of operating the Monte.

To restore at least peace and order, Napoleon is partly rehabilitated for his Italian policy from the judgments of Jefferson and the Adamses. An urbane letter to the Bourbon queen of Etruria, about to be removed from the defunct kingdom, and his remark " 'Artists high rank, in fact sole social summits / which the tempest of politics can not reach,' " place him with Malatesta. That his law code remains a monument of civil wisdom places him with the founders of '76. That swamps were drained, cotton grown, merino sheep brought in, and the mortgage system improved places him with Mussolini. The balanced judgment " 'Thank god such men be but few' / though they build up human courage" acknowledges the lawmaker within the soldier.

Before him, however, and more the lawmaker, had been Pietro Leopoldo, whose reforms (and Ferdinand's) are now catalogued like a Bill of Rights. These have outlasted and perhaps been a foundation for Napoleon's. The Monte, Siena in Tuscany, and all in their relation to Europe come to a focus in a concluding " 'The foundation, Siena, has been to keep bridle on usury' " asserted by "Nicolò Piccolomini, Provveditore," the Chairman of the Monte under whom its history was begun in the 1890s and brought to a conclusion in 1925. Seal *XLIV* focused four-phase continuing revolution in a Constitutional

form symbolized by the Mount voiced MDCCLXXVI. The catalogued reforms and the "Provveditore's" (Providence's) judgment open up mythic
revelation.

As expected, the fourth canto of the fourth draft is a climax. The diatribe
"WITH *Usura*" (Seal *XLV*), describing life under Usura while delivering
against it (cf. the Anglo-Saxon "with-" of withstand or withold) the eco-
nomic lesson emergent from the whole poem, voices the symbolic Mount of
Seal *XLII* millennially and universally—as if divinely, or as if by an Old
Testament prophet. Archaism suggests the Renaissance English of the King
James Bible. Desecration of the lifegiving, fructifying spirit "ELEUSIS" is
summed up in perverted marriage:

> Usura slayeth the child in the womb
> It stayeth the young man's courting
> It hath brought palsey to bed, lyeth
> between the young bride and her bridegroom
>   CONTRA NATURAM
> They have brought whores for Eleusis
> Corpses are set to banquet
> at behest of usura.

Clarified in Siena and Tuscany, "REVOLUTION . . . in the minds of the
people" culminates in a Bill of Rights symbolized by the sun-vision and
voiced ANNUIT COEPTIS "with Providence" (Usura perverts Providence
as Geryon perverts the Eagle).

In a 1958 BBC interview Pound said "There is a turning point in the poem
toward the middle. Up to that point it is a sort of detective story, one is looking
for the crime."[7] "Usura" *XLV* precipitates "The *Usura* cantos" *XLVI–LI*,
each of which continues the evidence and argument against Geryon or Usura
or both. Taken together they muster against the mythic villains the paideuma
"ELEUSIS" and foreshadowings of the other paideumas, until the mythic
diatribe recurs (*LI*) not in archaic mythic language but in a contemporary
restatement.

Decad *XLII–LI*

"REVOLUTION . . . in the minds of the people" comes through Seal *XLII–
XLV* into the decad as the Declaration's premises, the concomitant motives,
and a Constitutional dynamic, all activated by the Bill's private rights. The
premises are applied to a summation of Pound's continuing revolution since

---

7. D. G. Bridson, "An Interview with Ezra Pound," *New Directions 17* (New York: 1961),
p. 172.

"1918 Began investigation of causes of war, to oppose same" (*XLVI*) and to a culmination of the case against Odysseus, which has evolved through the four drafts (*I, XX*, and *XXXIX* to *XLVII*). As Usura *XLV* is a negative mythic source, political and collective, for deriving the premise of continuing revolution, "ELEUSIS" *XLVII* is a positive mythic source, psychological and individual.

Two rubrics of *XLVI* introduce *XLVI* and *XLVII* as halves of a seal, the same form as the Amendment-Supreme Law cantos *XXXV–XXXVI* and *XXXVIII–XXXIX* in "Jefferson-Nuevo Mundo." The first opposes to Eliot's priestly view of a "waste land" a naturalist view of the ordeal being undergone by the revolutionary poet of "the tale of the tribe" for his contemporaries:

> And if you will say that this tale teaches...
>   a lesson, or that the Reverend Eliot
>   has found a more natural language...you who think
>   you will
>   get   through   hell   in   a   hurry...

The second derives from discrimination of bad weather and good a mythic perception applicable to ignorance and intelligence:

>   That day there was cloud over Zoagli
> And for three days snow cloud over the sea
> Banked like a line of mountains.
> Snow fell. Or rain fell stolid, a wall of lines
> So that you could see where the air stopped open
> and where the rain fell beside it
> Or the snow fell beside it.

In such terms Odysseus will apprehend "ELEUSIS," which will in turn project its paideumatic sequels. The rubrics introduce a summary of the first four drafts as Branches (*XLVI*) and as Powers (*XLVII*).

The refrain "Seventeen / Years on this case, nineteen years" turns the mythic diatribe into Pound's "CASE for the prosecution" since "1918 Began investigation of causes of war, to oppose same." His economic enlightenment began with the Douglas Social Credit theories, successors to Sienese policy, learned in the office of the Guild Socialist weekly *The New Age* in London. Here the office is analogized to the office of the socialist *Il Popolo d'Italia*, of which Mussolini was editor, and which Pound has just seen at the Decennio exposition of the evolving fascist state. A journalistic perspective in a Congressional mode charges a "CRIME / Ov two CENturies" up through World War I, a crime exposed in *The New Age*, *Il Popolo*, and now *The Cantos* despite the camouflage of snappy journalism. Other camouflage were suburban conversations among intellectuals and founders of new religions (Presidency) about ancient history, religious evangelism, and misunderstandings between representatives of empire and colonial peoples.[8] The "CRIME / Ov two CENturies" and the "first case" is defined by its founder's statement that the Bank of England

<u>Hath benefit of interest on all</u>
<u>the moneys which it, the bank, creates out of nothing.</u>

A Judicial Pound heaps up a "monumentum" of evidence from "ages of usury" as well as from immediate surroundings and cites as confession not only the founder but also some Rothschild's remark that few will understand the method, that those who do will be occupied with getting profits, and that the general public will probably not see that it is against their interest. Can we take it to court? Will any jury convict? The only court appears to be "the tale of the tribe."

In making his case Pound alludes to this "first case," which has evolved in four drafts, in the context of a "series" of cases which will constitute a "whole . . . CASE for the prosecution." Of this "first case" he says "This case, and with it / the first part, draws to a conclusion, / of the first phase of this opus." Further, he asks a "REVISION" and "enlightenment" in a case "moving concurrent." These terms refer to the Declaration, to "ELEUSIS," and to the revision of '76 for One World.

For "the first case" the causes coming through the premises have "evinced a design" to subject the world to Geryon and Usura. The "first part," "ELEUSIS," contains both "part of / The Evidence" and the positive ideal premises themselves; it is "the first part" of a two-part (premises and cases) or three-part (three paideumas) "first phase of this opus." "The first phase" will be an argument for separation from the world of Geryon and Usura.

The "REVISION . . . moving concurrent" will be the revision of '76 through the paideumas for a new world union built on more positive foundations. "This opus" will consist of a ten-draft "whole case" in four phases containing all "The Evidence" as "monumentum." The canto ends with Pound's own mythic identification of Geryon and Usura and with the cases of the states America (under Roosevelt), England, and France.

Discovery of the case of Siena and the mythic diatribe have made Pound an historical medium for opposition to Geryon and Usura; *XLVI* presents in a new perspective what has been seen and heard since the beginning of the poem. But Pound is also asking for a "REVISION" from negative to positive

---

8. Pound studied the British imperial mind most assiduously in his *New Age* series, from "Through Alien Eyes" (1913), a companion to "Patria Mia," to "The Revolt of Intelligence" (1919–20). The series most pertinent to *XLVI* was "Studies In Contemporary Mentality" (1917–18), a survey of the British mind through its newspapers and magazines, from popular to intellectual to religious; he wanted to add it to *Make It New* (1934) as a "sottisier," "customs which the visiting anthropologist or student of Kulturmorphologie would have noticed as 'customs of the tribus Britannicus,' the materials which the average man would have found easy to hand as printed matter in the city of London about 1918–1919." "Date Line," *Make It New*, 1934.

foreshadowed by the image of foul weather sharply demarcated from fair. Accordingly *XLVII* presents in a double perspective—from Circe's bed before going to Hades and from Circe's bed upon his return—what Odysseus has seen and heard. While millennial history and autobiography have been carrying Pound forward in time the Odyssean archetype has been moving both backward in time to disclose its original inspiration and forward in time to reveal a total inspiration in Pound's mind. Through an Odyssean canto in each of four drafts (*I*, *XX*, *XXXIX*, and *XLVII*) comes the mythic dimension for deriving the Declaration's premises. These cantos chasten or ritualize the revolutionary factive personality by turning him to a catechumen and poet of the paideuma "ELEUSIS" and thus presumptively of the other world paideumas.

In Seal *I* Odysseus narrated the arduous revolutionary destiny, the Nekuomanteia directed by Circe, in behalf of the collective desire to return to Ithaca; but the cost to comradeship opened up accusations against himself (*VI*) and against the "too POLUMETIS" factive personality Malatesta summarized "crimen est actio" (*XVI*). In the midst of "confusion, source of renewals" opened up through another mind committed to rigorous justice and duty (Niccolò d'Este's), the Lotophagoi—who claimed natural rights by "shelving" themselves from the nostos before arrival at Circe's—surveyed the cost both prior to and after the Nekuomanteia, implying that the factive personality was more absorbed in his own curiosity and pleasure than in his crew (*XX*). In *XXXIX* differing responses toward a goddess (government by consent in sexual terms) typed the several crewmen and Odysseus himself, but the factive personality's response proved the only means of securing protection against Circe's seductive powers while taking advantage of her powers of inspiration and prophecy; the resultant ritualized sexuality celebrated a bride's receipt of male seed and consequent conception. While the bride celebrated her consent in voice and song, the male was silent. Canto *XLVII* consummates the ritual with dual participation and male celebration. A larger dimension of natural fertility illuminates philosophically and religiously a creative balance between general nature and human nature. Revolution becomes ritual and the revolutionary becomes an initiate to natural mysteries.

The form and symbolism of *XLVII* is that of the four-phase Seal consummated in the sun-vision by the Eagle and Providence, here Odysseus and Circe as positive answers to Geryon and Usura. The narrator Odysseus's celebration of the human mind in the figure of Tiresias, "Who even dead, yet hath his mind entire!," introduces a fourfold ritualization of his own mind in relation to his sexuality. The rest of the canto, introduced "This sound came in the dark," consists mostly of a Circean providential definition and delimitation of the male mind in its human condition.

A first phase (the Power States) opens by translating the opaque Greek of *XXXIX* into Circe's revelation of Odysseus's destiny, that before he comes to his road's end he must voyage to Hell "Knowing less than drugged beasts" (the crew in the swine-sty) to consult all-knowing Tiresias. The voyage and the blood rite are turned into sexual ritual through the rites of Adonis, who is worshipped by floating lights (the mind) out into the night sea until the waters become as if streaked with blood.[9] "By this gate art thou measured" binds the mind to its sexuality. The life-and-death ritual is, however, a rebirth and fertility ritual, ritualizing equally the descent into Hell and the sexual act. The result is new growth.

Secondly, Circe describes female sexuality as an undirected life force which draws even Odysseus into a blind impulse à la Elpenor. There is no escape. But Amendment ritualizes such blind sexuality into plowing the fields in proper season, as prescribed (for instance) in Hesiod's *Works and Days*. While to the woman the stars are uncounted and but "wandering holes," to the man they measure out his seasonal occupations. Again the plowing ritualizes sexuality ("By this gate art thou measured"), but again the result is growth and (now too) gathering building stone. While female sexuality is defined by unrestrained liberty (or license), male sexuality is ritualized toward new union.

A mediating "Thus was it in time," whether spoken by him or by her, prepares a "bust thru" from tradition and nature into transcendance. Though "now" the small stars fall from the olive branch, though a bird's shadow falling on the terrace cares nothing for the man's presence, and though that presence is no more lasting than the bird's wing-print on the roof tiles (note the building), "Yet hast thou gnawed through the mountain" (for teeth read also phallic mind, or inspired phallus). Firm in the Supreme Law of mutual sexuality, the consenting woman teases

> Hast thou found a nest softer than cunnus
> Or hast thou found better rest
> Hast'ou a deeper planting, doth thy death year
> Bring swifter shoot?
> Hast thou entered more deeply the mountain?

Her teasing elicits from the silent male of *XXXIX* a celebration of his entry by light (by mind) and "by prong" into the cave, these hills, the hill. Subsuming the other phases of a ritualized process of mental and sexual revelation ("Sacrum, sacrum, inluminatio coitu," *XXXVI*), he celebrates with his Providence, as it were within the sun-vision atop the Mount at their altar, a new relation to his condition and a reborn self. Either he, she, or both together (the last seems aptest) bring all previous phases into the Adonis ritual as the almond tree "puts forth its flame" and as new shoots are brought to the altar in sacri-

---

9. Tags from Bion's *Adonis* ring changes on "DIONA" and "ADONIN" here and on "ADONIN" and "DIONA" at the end. Pound called this play of sound—also anagram, as in Kimmerian-American (*I*)—"Syrian syncopation" ("The French Poets," *Little Review*, New York, February 1918). He sought it in the meter of *Mauberley*, his "Major Persona" of the dead poet as renouncer of Aphrodite. Syncopation and anagram also play with interpenetrating, reversible male-female dichotomies.

fice. The sexual ritualizing of continuing revolution ratifies an "ELEUSIS" "that hath the gift of healing, / that hath the power over wild beasts," be they Adonis's boar or Geryon and Usura.

This substantive (though not formal) climax of "ELEUSIS" opens up a transformation of the local Seal *XLII–XLV* (States) into a Seal *XLVIII–LI* (a Congress of States) projecting world paideumas-and-paideuma as continuing revolution against Geryon and Usura. Through the four voices of Liberty *XLII* and their consequence Seal *XLII–XLV*, *XLVIII* condenses the four drafts of "ELEUSIS" and reorients them toward the One World projected by Seal *XLVIII–LI*. Behind the political summations and projections and therefore inspiriting them, lies the four-phase ritualized sexuality and psychology of "ELEUSIS" *XLVII*.

XLVIII restates world declaration in the light of the Sienese Bailey's proposal of the Monte dei Paschi:

> And if the money be rented
>> Who shd pay rent on that money?
>> Some fellow who has it on rent day,
>>> or some bloke who has not?

The principle elicits the kind of evidence which since the beginning of the poem has been cause for world revolution and which, in earlier and different circumstances, caused the founding of the Monte. The evidence is framed by a Rothschild's remark that nations are fools to pay rent for their credit.

Drawing on the defining of a "nuova persona" through the natural voice of Liberty *XLII*, a Dionysian rubric—

Δίγονος
DIGONOS; lost in the forest; but are then known as leopards
after three years in the forest; they are known as 'twice-born'.

—introduces folk customs, first local and then worldwide. Siena consulting the Duchy of Tuscany through its advisers, and Pound personally observing Sienese rites "under my window" (*XLIII*), are transformed into an agent advising a king about the pedigree, background, and characteristics of a dog the king has bought; the agent's careful investigation of facts on their own ground is interlineated by a President plying senatorial advisers with whiskey in order to assure appointment of a secretary of state. In place of the signature of the agent's letter to the king a voice "under my window" (Pound's) opens up exploratory world voyages interlineated with world economic manipulations. World voyages as qualifications for honor and responsibility extend the assembly of the Sienese general council "in the hall of World Map" to exorcize "REE- / sponsibility" (*XLIII*). Choosing a "nuova persona" links the two interlineated passages. As in Seal *XLIII* the forms and themes are old passing to new in popular terms, or liberty passing toward new union.

The revolutionary founding of "Jefferson-Nuevo Mundo" comes through

Pound's recollection of his youthful dream of united cities of Italy and through the Leopoldine Reforms (Seal *XLIV*). It is illustrated by a letter from Pound's daughter describing her pleasure in being present at a mountain town's celebration of a new priest's saying of a new mass (his first), in the new Italy, in "(dodicesimo anno E.F.)." The Fourth-of-July-like celebration makes new Siena's celebration of Ferdinand's "so provident law" (*XLIV*). It may also have been the twelfth anniversary of the March on Rome, 30 October 1933. The spirit, the theme, and the date recall Pound's Calendar and the Mount MDCCLXXVI. The child's pleasure and an obvious abundance in the town are intended to make the new Italian era hard to resist. So the young Pound must have felt on the Fourth of July in America, a feeling reflected in his early "Guillaume De Lorris Belated." The letter also celebrates the founding of a corporate state being projected as a world model.

"Siena-Leopoldine Reforms" itself is condensed via the symbolized Mount and via the mythic diatribe against Usura in a natural observation turned into a symbol of vengeance against Geryon and Usura. A caterpillar observed in Provence is taken as a symbol of the forces that destroyed Provençal civilization, which persists vestigially in ruins, in castles and villages, in archaeological layers ("ply over ply"), and in the paradisal setting; the civilization stood for states' rights; hence its destruction by the Albigensian crusade. In symbolic vengeance "Falling Mars in the air" takes the form of three ants who kill "a great worm" (the caterpillar), swallow its limbs, and haul its carcass up a tree trunk. This reversal focuses evidence for revolution, local customs, and a new state into recollection of a time when an old man could find employment at Venice's Lido by placing stones on beach costumes when the wind threatened to blow them away. The image mitigates the old man's " 'Damned to you Midas, Midas lacking a Pan' " (*XXI*). His basket of stones and his placing a stone contrast with Geryon's "eel fisher's basket" and destructivity, which will end *LI*.

In *XLIX* an anonymous voice of the Chinese folk ("by no man these verses") elaborates folk customs, local and worldwide, from Seal *XLIII* and the popular phase of *XLVIII*. The voice of "WE the People" builds up a powerful impression of local life bound to natural conditions. But it then turns to the larger imperial context by asking "State by creating riches shd. thereby get into debt?" and answering "This is infamy; this is Geryon." Work is ritualized in a Japanese transliteration of a sixteen-ideogram, four-square song reputed to be the first Chinese poem; Pound translates it:

> Sun up; work
> sundown; to rest
> dig well and drink of the water
> dig field; eat of the grain

In such light "Imperial power is? and to us what is it?" The answer:

The fourth; the dimension of stillness.
And the power over wild beasts.

Chinese paideumatic power alters the Eleusinian "gift of healing" (*XLVII*) to
the preservation of peace, but both are set against Geryon and Usura. *XLIX*
seeks to balance local liberty with imperial union. If foreshadows "KUNG."
     The American paideumatic locus opens *L*:

'REVOLUTION' said Mr Adams 'took place in the
          minds of the people
          in the fifteen years before Lexington'

It brings out through Pound's daughter's letter of *XLVIII* the analogy between
'76 and the Leopoldine Reforms which opened and closed Seal *XLIV*. Whereas
Seal *XLIV* drew Napoleonic Europe into a Sienese-Tuscan perspective, *L*
draws Tuscany through the Leopoldine Reforms into a transatlantic and European perspective. The Leopoldine Reforms are recapitulated concurrent with
'76 until a Tuscan historian (Zobi) makes America "our daughter," lauds
its admirable "popoli transatlantici," and places Washington with Leopold.
Tuscany then navigates through the French Revolution, the Napoleonic reac-
tion and invasion of Italy, Napoleonic Europe, Napoleon's defeat by the
concert of European powers, the Hundred Days, and Europe restored by the
Congress of Vienna, up until just before the revolution of 1848. Through a
usurist "Filth" that "stank as in our day," the viable state established by
Leopold retained its economic viability and its devotion to independence.
"As in our day" implies the fascist corporate state in the context of a world
organized by the Treaty of Versailles and the League of Nations.
     While "Siena-Leopoldine Reforms" was being written the League of Na-
tions imposed sanctions against Italy for its invasion of Ethiopia. Hence
Pound's scatalogical diatribes against earlier Vienna (read Geneva) and against
the European mind assembled there with usura in its soul, darkness in its
mind, and bloody repression in its hand, not to "reset . . . republics" but to
restore prerevolutionary Europe. Napoleon attributes his own failure to organize Europe not to "that league of lice" but to his similar thwarting of continuing revolution. Leagues and congresses of states limited to economic
cooperation take a better form in a Tariff League instituted among Italian
states during the 1840s under Leopold II, successor to the restored Ferdinand.
The people's "EVVIVA / Evviva the Tariff League / . . . Evviva Leopoldo /
Evviv' INDIPENDENZA" celebrates independence both from restricted trade
and from international economic control.
     So the Branch/Power States is passing to world Congress. The equivo-
cality of such a Congress, which though being foreshadowed paideumatically
has yet to be realized historically, is presumably symbolized in an image of a
new Renaissance and a new era trying to come to life, seemingly blotted by a
femme fatale, but freeing itself in a light natural and mental:

Lalage's shadow moves in the fresco's knees
She is blotted with Dirce's shadow
dawn stands there fixed and unmoving
   only we two have moved.

Recalled are Italian cities in the form of women moving "as one figure," behind which lay the warning "Thou shalt not always walk in the sun" and the proposal "FIXED in the soul" of the Sienese Bailey. Though the shadow of a cruel beauty (nature as femme fatale? Usura?) blots the poet's Lalage, she has moved in his vision, his vision itself has matured, and both have moved from night to a new day (a new dawn of the Bailey's idea?). However interpreted, the opaque image does seem to expand both canto and draft beyond locality. The new light also presumably augurs dispersal of all shadow when "we two" (also poet and reader) will have moved from *L* to *LI*.

Canto *LI* culminates all four-phase subjects—canto, cantos, and drafts—in an illuminated Seal/Calendar form. Four irradiating voices transform the framing prophetic epitome *I* in the light of Seal *IV*, whose four invocations in Calendar form projected ten paragraph-images for rebuilding the scattered stones of Troy. *LI* begins like *I* in the light and carries light into the dark of history, but it illuminates history with the declaratory voice "to be unity," the dual voice of "WE the People," and the triadic voice of founding, all projecting and accumulating toward an explicit Calendar tetrad. At the same time each voice expands its predecessor or predecessors by transforming addition.

The Eagle HORUS looks outside of time to

SHINES
in the mind of heaven God
who made it
more than the sun
in our eye.

Inspiration reveals "the mind of heaven" to be the revolutionary cycle made by the "God" OSIRIS. Divine light enters the dark mind of history through "Fifth element; mud," Napoleon's military remark applied symbolically. The resultant sublunary, idiomatic restatement of the diatribe "With *Usura*" (*XLV*) translates the cries of the dead into a declaration against the identified tyranny and toward a renewal of what it has thwarted, "Nature's increase" and human creativity. The diatribe projects "to be unity" toward a culminating Calendar exposure of Geryon and Usura.

An addition to the diatribe of Seal *XLV*, "Peasant has no gain from his sheep herd," modulates declaration of continuing revolution into a folk voice's meticulous instructions about how to make two kinds of fish fly and when to use them. An anonymous craftsman's rapport with nature for a productive end is given the form of the stellar plan. The first fly is named, the conditions for using it are specified, and the materials for making it are described. For the second, after the time of year for using both flies has mediated between them, the form is reversed: materials for making the second fly are described, the conditions for using it are specified, and it is named. Such folklore has been in the minds of the people since time immemorial. Through the popular theme it transforms the general human destiny expressed through Elpenor, descent to death at Circe's but a plan for the new life of a memorial tomb. Fishing symbolizes the prior declaration against Usura while projecting the culminating Calendar vision of "the eel-fisher" Geryon.

A "bust thru" to "the mind of heaven" being realized historically takes the form of Tiresias's Constitutional challenge, command, and prophecy. The antecedent to

> That hath the light of the doer, as it were
> a form cleaving to it

is the creation advanced by the foregoing two voices. This transformation of "With usury" begins with the objective historical creation ("That") and subordinates the revolutionary mind while projecting an end ("it"). Transformation of the popular voice begins with the doer's "adept intellect," which is "like God in some way," and culminates in natural creation and local order:

> Deo similis quodam modo
> hic intellectus adeptus
> Grass; nowhere out of place.

Out of these transformations evolve explicit terms for founding extended universally:

> Thus speaking in Königsberg
> Zwischen die Volkern erzielt wird
> a modus vivendi.

"Among the people is being achieved / a modus vivendi," quoted from Rudolph Hess, envisions a united Europe.[10] Each sentence of the "bust thru," one historical, one natural, and one justicial, looks toward a unity while the three constitute a unity. In Pound's terms a unifying "modus vivendi" would mean a Congress of corporate states extendable to the world.

Pound consummated *I* by revealing himself as an inheriting translator, by recognizing Divus, by sending Odysseus back to Circe's, and by invoking his new Providence. Here the timeless Seal/Calendar form of "SHINES / in the

---

10. "I haven't got to the Fuhrer, but some lines on Rudolph Hess in a draft/ not yet settled on where it can go . . ." (to J. D. Ibbotson, 20 April 1936, Collection at Yale). Then: "Some years ago Rudolph Hess said it should not be beyond European intelligence to work out a system of living together, meaning between European peoples" ("United States of Europe?" *Globe*, Milwaukee, Wis., November/December 1938).

mind of heaven" becomes historical recognition by the New Style cyclic mind of the perverted cycle of "ages of usury." The prophesied "modus vivendi" modulates into an exposure of the Old Style government declared against by the first voice:

> circling in eddying air; in a hurry;
> the 12: close eyed in the oily wind
> these were the regents;

The "God" of this "mind of heaven" perverts nature with a "sour song" from the folds of his belly:

> I am the help of the aged;
> I pay men to talk peace;
> Mistress of many tongues; merchant of chalcedony
> I am Geryon twin with usura,
> You who have lived in a stage set.

The New Style mind reveals the harvest of the grim drama,

> A thousand were dead in his folds;
> in the eel-fishers basket

Freed by exposure, however, the initiate looks back to the Renaissance and forward in ongoing circumnavigation:

> Time was of the League of Cambrai:

A Congress of States against Geryon and Usura was "the right word" of the Renaissance. "SHINES" and the ideograms frame the canto with ANNUIT COEPTIS. The ideograms also show an upright "E P" who has been the mouth for myth and history since the beginning.[11]

"Time was of the League of Cambrai," formed in 1508 against a chief villain of the first three drafts, commercial and militant Venice, looks back to the emergence of a Renaissance tradition of revolutionary poetry with Divus's Homer (1538) and to perfection of that tradition in the epitome for the four drafts of "ELEUSIS," Seal *I–IV*. It completes "ELEUSIS" *LI Cantos* as the drafted Seal-form of *The Cantos*, "REVOLUTION . . . in the minds of the people" evolving the whole revolutionary form. Beginning and ending at

---

11. "Anyhow the Ching Ming shd. enlighten the title page and close the MUZIK of 51. Make a classy finish for the wollumk." To F. V. Morley of Faber & Faber, February 1937, Collection at Yale.

about the same time centers *LI Cantos* in a Renaissance perspective which looks back to the origins of a tradition (*I–IV*) while looking forward to its consequences (the four drafts). The four drafts show that despite the apparent "death" of the Renaissance in 1503 (*XXX*) and in 1527 (*XLVI*), not only a poetic tradition (for the ideal premises) but also a governmental and economic tradition (evidence for the premises) inhered in a renewed Renaissance tradition as *The Cantos* defines it: in the creative efforts of Malatesta, in the efforts of Malatesta and other Renaissance leaders against the forces that destroyed the Renaissance, in the transplantation of the Renaissance spirit to America, and, by these lights, in revelations of a neglected Siena and Tuscany. If "Time was" turns back to the paideuma "ELEUSIS" as a single subject, the ideograms point "ELEUSIS" via the renewed Renaissance voyages toward a new world future in four episodes and four paideumas to be perfected in four phases of an evolving ten-draft poem.

Pound wanted to constitute the four drafts of "ELEUSIS"—states' rights Branches—as the integral paideuma "ELEUSIS" *LI Cantos*—world Congress. Having finished *The Fifth Decad* he wrote T. S. Eliot at Faber & Faber "What about a 50 deLOOKZ, at ten guineas? Whoo is in that line of bizniz/ or say it shd be 53//? By the time the press gits oil in its jintz//."[12] The "50" refers to "ELEUSIS" as a single paideuma while "53" cites its expression of a world Congress overlapping by clauses 1–53 into "KUNG," where Kung himself will focus the ultimate Congressman.

12. March 1937, Collection at Yale.

CHAPTER FOURTEEN

"KUNG" *LII–(LXI)* &

LXXI CANTOS

"MAKE IT NEW"
    "KUNG" *LIII*

Came KIEN, 40 years before 'our revolution' . . .
and as to the rise of the Adamses—
    "KUNG" (*LXI*)

"KUNG" *LII–LXI* and "JOHN ADAMS" *LXII–LXXI*, published together in 1940 as *Cantos LII–LXXI*, are coordinate paideumas with "ELEUSIS" *LI Cantos*.[1] Like "ELEUSIS" each goes back to mythic origins and evolves through its era to a perfection of its own special form of revolution, which enters the twentieth-century mind as a constituent of its world tradition. "ELEUSIS" and "KUNG" both prophesy the culmination of that tradition in "JOHN ADAMS," where definitive revolutionary form converges with its now fully emergent substance.

As European paideuma went back to Homeric beginnings and evolved a revolutionary tradition from venturesome Eleusinian intellect and Eleusinian sexuality, Chinese paideuma goes back to the *Li Ki* or *Book of Rites*, a ritual calendar designed to harmonize divinity and nature with the whole people through observances performed month by month and season by season by the Emperor, the central officer of the empire. This mythic-historical form of natural revolution becomes formalized in Confucian revolution, the pattern of which is to be found not only in the *Li Ki* but also in the Confucian books. The books become patterns for Confucian revolution over millennia until, like European revolution, Confucian revolution is perfected beyond the Chinese context, in a world context, by the MANCHU. Like Sienese and Tuscan revolution, MANCHU revolution evolves during the American colonial period

---

1. For the title page to *Cantos LII–LXXI* Pound wanted "the single ideogram criterion," *ch'eng*[2], literally words brought to a focus (see the ideograms of *Pisan LXXVI* and *LXXVII*, discussed in Chapter 17, pp. 320–27). "Might make a prettier title page than the Ching Ming though mebbe that will din it into the reader's head (if he has one)." To T. S. Eliot, 24 October 1939, Collection at Yale.

248

from "1625/35" to 1776. Over several reigns the MANCHU evolve a distinct pattern explicitly close to the phases of '76. This pattern then modulates into the complete form and substance of '76 prophesied by the European and Chinese paideumas.

The mythic source for "JOHN ADAMS" is New World history evolving '76 itself. The spirit of New World history and '76 begins with the discovery of 1492 and passes through settlement of Massachusetts Bay Colony in 1628 to the birth of John Adams and his preparation for his revolutionary destiny. The epitome of the paideuma (*LXII*), like the Homeric Nekuomanteia (*I*) for "ELEUSIS" and like the *Li Ki* (*LII*) for "KUNG," then runs through the phases of '76 to Adams's retirement from politics and a Poundian judgment of his whole career. "ELEUSIS" evolved over millennia and "KUNG" evolved over even more millennia. "JOHN ADAMS," however, evolves over a single revolutionary generation in modal repetitions of the same materials, which give the overall paideuma the four revolutionary phases while condensing a world Declaration into a first phase. Like "ELEUSIS" and "KUNG," "JOHN ADAMS" also evolves from a local context to a world context.

As always, voyage (now circumnavigation) discovers the histories and Pound brings them to life on their own ground. As Chinese revolutionary founding "KUNG" is a third episode of '76 revised for One World; its theme as a second paideuma within a world paideuma is struggle defined both personally and politically by Confucius. As a fourth episode of revised '76 "JOHN ADAMS" consummates New World history and '76 in continuing revolution; as a third paideuma within a world paideuma it adds American founding. "JOHN ADAMS" also consummates in the ten drafts the Declaration's argument against the past and a phase of world declaration.

As fifth and sixth drafts of ten "KUNG" and "JOHN ADAMS" present and amend on a world scale the cases against the executive tyranny of King George III and the justicial tyranny of "our British brethren." For this purpose the catechumen of paideuma evolved in "ELEUSIS" develops the role of prosecutor foreshadowed in *XLVI*. A first half of Canto *LII* reformulates "Such has been the patient suffering of these colonies, and such is now the necessity which constrains them to alter their former systems of government" in terms of the philosophy derived and the evidence assembled in "ELEUSIS." In the second half of Canto *LII* the *Li Ki* reformulates both for prosecution and for amendment the generalizing "The history of the present King of Great Britain is a history of repeated injuries and usurpations, all having in direct object, the establishment of an absolute tyranny over these States." As a Chinese version of the revolutionary "vision" (cf. the epitome *V*) derived from "ELEUSIS," the *Li Ki* provides an ideal revolutionary model for amending dynastic violations. It governs "Facts . . . submitted to a candid world," which prove that "A prince whose character is thus marked by every act which may define a tyrant is unfit to be the ruler of a free people." At the same time it amends the prosecution by defining ideal Confucian emperors culminating in the MANCHU.

The "Facts . . . submitted to a candid world" in *LIII–LXI*, in number twenty-seven as in the Declaration's case, are designated in a "Table" which precedes the draft. The twenty-seven items of Chinese history coming out of the *Li Ki* do not follow the Declaration's indictment point by point, but they muster against similar violations the efforts of Confucian rulers, dynasties, and officials to rule "a free people."

The keynote of "JOHN ADAMS" is the case against "our British brethren" conducted legally so that necessary separation can be followed by mutual participation in a world comity of nations:

> Nor have we been wanting in attention to our British brethren. We have warned them, from time to time, of attempts made by their legislature to extend an unwarrantable jurisdiction over us. We have reminded them of the circumstances of our emigration and settlement here. We have appealed to their native justice and magnanimity, and we have conjured them, by the ties of our common kindred, to disavow these usurpations, which would inevitably corrupt our connections and correspondence. They, too, have been deaf to the voice of justice and consanguinity.

The two cases lead to the conclusion of the Declaration's argument against the past, "We must therefore acquiesce in the necessity which denounces our separation, and hold them, as we hold the rest of mankind, enemies in war, in peace, friends." Though in Pound's handling the cases seek separation from "enemies in war," they also (for world union) amend separation by seeking "in peace, friends." This theme is emphasized in the "Table" for "JOHN ADAMS," which continues the Chinese chronology as a collective decad "LXII–LXXI" in ten topics coming out of the capitalized "JOHN ADAMS" and covering his political career. From his career evolve first revolution for separation but then peaceful international relations. The topics of the "Table" do not follow the order of the text (subjects or cantos), nor do they itemize the case. Instead they take a general prototype form to perfect the revision of '76 in a Bill of Rights and to perfect a phase of world declaration. The special form of the text will be described in due course.

In accord with the Declaration's cases the motive of "KUNG" is to "promote the general welfare" and of "JOHN ADAMS" to "secure the blessings of liberty to ourselves and our posterity"—though Adams's principle "not less of order than liberty" holds open the necessity of new union inherent in the Constitution which the Preamble introduces. "KUNG" offers a form of Amendment for the states' rights evolved in "ELEUSIS" and a new form of Presidency (following the precipitation of world Congress in "ELEUSIS") for One World. "JOHN ADAMS" offers a form of Supreme Law and a new form of Judiciary. The revolutionary form is activated by the due process of Confucian revolution and by the fair trial central to American revolution.

"KUNG" *LII–LXI*: Canto *LII*

At a turning point "Between KUNG and ELEUSIS," in a tone shifting from derivatory to didactic, a rubric sums up Eleusinian Liberty ("ONE") as fact and principle:

> And I have told you of how things were under Duke
> > Leopold in Siena
> > And of the true base of credit, that is
> > > the abundance of nature
> with the whole folk behind it.

The unifying rubric opens a summary which sets the premises derived in the four drafts against "neschek," Geryon and Usura united as "the serpent," excessive interest. In the rubric "the light of the doer" is "cleaving to" the "Great bulk, huge mass, thesaurus" of millennial history (*V*) from which it has emerged and which is continuing. A "clock tick" (*V*) in "anno seidici" of the new era elicits a modern version of the rubric, Nazi Finance Minister Schacht's declaration that credit is good only so long as it is advanced against goods needed and deliverable. In retrospect this principle has been opposing neschek since the new era began in *XVI. Cantos.*

Lives under neschek (cf. *XVII–XXX*) are brought up to date. Locally, in a paradisal landscape by a half-ruined tower where a peasant is complaining that her son has been taken for war, a Sienese intellectual has adjudged plutocracies to be less violent than fascist Italy, which has undertaken military adventures in Ethiopia and Spain. Internationally gentile vengeance retaliates against the "sin" and "vendetta on goyim" of a few "big jews" (their names censored), and a British writer confides to her "mama" (unofficially) that when not against its interests the Empire should keep its pledges to Arabs. "Thus we lived on" through the League of Nations' sanctions against Italy, through Russian manipulations at Geneva, through the profiteering of gold brokers.

Contemporary struggle turns to contemporary confirmation of lessons inherent in "Jefferson-Nuevo Mundo." John Adams attributes society's ills to ignorance of the nature of money, credit, and circulation, a remark which will focus "JOHN ADAMS." Frustration in the face of such ignorance, which allows neschek its opportunity, elicits a warning attributed (wrongly) to Franklin that America had better keep out the Jews or face the curses of succeeding generations (cf. "THE CITY OF ARARAT, *XXXIV*). A diatribe fueled by Franklin's warning (cf. Mitteleuropa, *XXXV*), and the diatribes of

"Siena-Leopoldine Reforms" requires censoring five lines. To stabilize himself the would-be prosecutor reaches for his case: "Did commit, that he did in the Kingdom of Italy..." presumably cites Napoleon; "of the two usuries, the lesser is now put down" alludes to a distinction between fornication and usury in Shakespeare's *Measure for Measure*; "that he did in the Kingdom of Britain etc/" comes to rest on the case against King George. "Between KUNG and ELEUSIS" reminds the prosecutor that the catechumen is also seeking amendment derived from mythic ideals.

The transition culminates by setting reminders of medieval art in Provence and Siena, and of medieval song in Spain and Tuscany, against the Church's failure since the Renaissance to hold against neschek. Hence the need for "KUNG." "Know then," rounding back to the opening "And I have told you," makes both the speaker and his reader catechumens of the *Li Ki* as "the clock ticks and fades out" for "again the vision" (*V*).

The *Li Ki* opens up the months and seasons of nature in a ritual English like that of the ritual cantos of "ELEUSIS." Beginning with the end of spring, the months move through the seasons prescribing symbols, sacrifices, ceremonial duties of the Emperor, and the proper seasonal occupations. Whereas the principle of the archetypal European rite, the Nekuomanteia, was revival of the past through the rites of "ELEUSIS," or renaissance, the *Li Ki* harmonizes continuous human life with the cycles of nature. Whereas "ELEUSIS" ritualized intellect and sexuality fitfully through many individually inspired minds and through heterogeneous revivals in many times and places, the Chinese calendar roots the chronological millennia of the Middle Kingdom in nature ritualized by a collective mind which has received a single Mandate of Heaven.

Having run from the end of spring through summer, autumn, and winter, the *Li Ki* modulates into three Confucian political principles. "Call things by the names," the first principle of government $cheng^4\ ming^2$, will link the three paideumas ideogramically (cf. *LI*, *LX*, and "JOHN ADAMS" *passim*). "Good sovereign by distribution / Evil king is known by his imposts" differentiates the case for Confucian rule and the case against executive tyranny (it will appear ideogramically in *LV*). "Begin where you are" brings "between KUNG and ELEUSIS" back as an analogy by being put in the mouth of Lord Palmerston, who "in the Kingdom of Britain" did not perpetuate the policy indicted by the Declaration but "began" public works in Ireland and London. Given the *Li Ki*, the lessons, and Palmerston's example, the initiate of "ELEUSIS" and catechumen of "KUNG" is ready to present his case.[2]

Serving as "REVOLUTION . . . in the minds of the people," as a Declaration, as Preambles, as a Constitution, and as a Bill of Rights in Seal/Calendar form, the *Li Ki* epitomizes the decad "KUNG." The source for Chinese mil-

2. On the sealing ideogram $chih^3$, see below p. 265.

lennia is the *T'ung Chien Kang Mu* or *General Mirror of History*, a chronicle begun in the eleventh century A.D., periodically revised and extended, and completed in 1775 by the MANCHU, with whom "KUNG" ends. The MANCHU compilation was offered to the West in the text Pound used, *Histoire Générale de la Chine ou Annales de Cet Empire; Traduites du Tong-Kien-Kan-Mou* by Père Joseph-Marie de Moyriac Mailla, a Jesuit missionary in Peking; the thirteen volumes were published, fortuitously but also in the world spirit of the time, during 1775–85. Inheriting this tradition and all its implications, Pound condenses the "prelector" Mailla and bends his work to his own purposes and to the form of '76.

Like all drafts "KUNG" has by cantos the form "to be unity" by duality, trine, and tetrad. But given major changes in Chinese history, the homogeneous chronology, and an obvious "repeat in history" within the draft, prototype form is subordinated to substantive form. Thus the *Li Ki* (*LII*) obviously stands by itself as mythic ritual embodying the historical revolution to be evolved in the rest of the draft. Ritual becomes revolution when ritual lapses (*LIII*), establishing a pattern of the old yielding to the new over and over again to the end of the draft. After *LII* and *LIII*, the latter ending with Confucius, ritual and ritual revolution become codified as "the law of Chung Ni," a name for Confucius derived from the concise style of the Confucian books; revolution by revival of the books becomes a means of evolving new dynasties out of dynasties which have "lost the law of Chung Ni" (*LIV* et seq.). Comprehensive reforms within China and a first incursion of Tartar barbarians "attracted" and themselves reformed by Chinese civilization (*LV*) look toward perfection of the *Li Ki*, of ritual revolution, and of Confucian revolution in a world context, by the Manchu Tartars (*LVIII–LXI*). Reading the draft should follow the *Li Ki* (*LII*), ritual revolution (*LIII*), and Confucian revolution (*LIV–LVII*) to the perfection of Confucian revolution (*LVIII–LXI*).

To emphasize theme and form Pound relies as always on selection, condensation, and arrangement, and on division by cantos with topical rubrics. But as the "Table" shows he has not included all dynasties and has cited among the selected dynasties certain emphatic events, individuals, objects (the Books), and peoples. He also emphasizes subjects and themes within the text by a new and more profuse use of ideograms (these constitute within the draft an overall form, to be described later). Further, he points emphases and makes personal judgments throughout while drawing analogies with "ELEUSIS" preceding and "JOHN ADAMS" to come. The overall tone is that of an initiate of "ELEUSIS" injecting "ELEUSIS" into an evolving "KUNG" while modifying the one by the other. Being an American, and having absorbed "Jefferson-Nuevo Mundo" within "ELEUSIS," he is inescapably anticipating continuation of the same activity into "JOHN ADAMS."

The homogeneity of "KUNG" results also in easily identifiable substantive themes, which have appeared before but which here achieve new and sharper focus. Dynasties are differentiated by excessive taxation, which stagnates commerce, or by circulation of money and credit, which increases commerce and yields the primary value in "KUNG," abundance. Another differentiation, coming out of the first, is promotion of war or peace. Another is infection by otherworldly, subjective Buddhism and Taoism, which results in social disorder, versus allegiance to the Confucian tradition as a means of achieving order and promoting the general welfare. These themes are related to dispersal of the civilizing power of the Middle Kingdom, versus its "attraction"; this phenomenon, illustrated by the Mongol and Manchu Tartars, is related to the "churning" of the revolutionary mind introduced by So-Shu (*II*); as a mode of colonization it anticipates the American colonist, struggler, and catechumen attracted toward high cultures, entering them, and undergoing the process that makes him a paideumatic "nuova persona." The various means of emphasizing subjects concentrates on these themes. Only an exhaustive reading of the text can disclose their prevalence. Here only a few examples can be cited in passing.

Canto *LIII*

The *Li Ki* having ritualized the cycle of nature, Canto *LIII* ("Canto" for the beginning of Chinese millennia) evolves pre-Confucian history in four phases. Beginning about "2837 ante Christum" the earliest rulers "taught men" handicrafts, improved agriculture, invented an alphabet, contrived bricks for building, introduced money, invented musical instruments, and encouraged the art of setting words to music. Following them (pp. 262–64)[3] the Great Emperors founded the first dynasty, HIA: Yao measured the heavens, Yu controlled the floods of the Yangtse and based taxation on local produce, and Chun took the spirit of heaven and the harmony of music as his ethical guides. These three are celebrated along with a fourth, Kao-Yao, in four axial ideograms (their names) which come to a focus in "abundance."[4]

When HIA was unable to cope with drought, so that grain became scarce and prices were rising, Tching Tang opened a copper mine in (fortuitously) 1760 B.C., made discs with square holes in their middles, and gave them to the people to buy grain where it was available. When the silos were empty after seven years of sterility he prayed on the mountain and came down with a pattern for ritual revolution that echoes the *Li Ki*:

---

3. From here on, for the longer cantos, page numbers indicate significant divisions. The page numbers refer to the first collected edition, *The Cantos* (New York: 1970), and to its subsequent printings.
4. Kao Yao was not an emperor but minister of crime to Chun. Needing a fourth Pound found one whose name, at least in transliteration, renewed the first emperor, Yao.

Tching prayed on the mountain and
        wrote MAKE IT NEW
on his bath tub
        Day by day make it new
cut underbrush,
pile the logs
keep it growing.
Died Tching aged years an hundred,
in the 13th of his reign.
        'We are up, Hia is down.'
Immoderate love of women
Immoderate love of riches,
Cared for parades and huntin'.
        Chang Ti above alone rules.
Tang not stinting of praise:
        Consider their sweats, the people's
If you wd/ sit calm on throne.

hsin[1]

jih[4]

jih[4]

hsin[1]

Both the text and the four ideograms for Chinese paideumatic revolution are directed against and come to a focus in the axial ideogram "Hsia," which has thereby yielded to the dynasty CHANG. Tching's motto introduces revolution and government by axioms and sayings in the style of Chung Ni, literally a man of the middle who gets it across and then stops, popularly "Confucius say . . .''; the MANCHU will perfect it in *cheng*[4] *ming*[2].

After CHANG has lost the mandate, TCHEOU (pp. 266–72) comes in with mottoes written all over walls and builds itself on sayings. Its shining light, the minister Chao Kong, fulfills four functions (pp. 267–70). He sustained dynastic continuity by calling the historians to reaffirm the charters, the ancient constitutions, and the rites. He surveyed land and promoted land reform, causing farmers to sing that Yao and Chun had returned and that "Peace and abundance bring virtue." As "the tireless" he sat in a pear grove deeming justice and measuring lands so that the grove was commemorated in folk song. In testament

Said Chao-kong: Talk of the people
        is like the hills and the streams
        Thence comes our abundance.
To be Lord of the four seas of China
        a man must let men make verses
        he must let people play comedies
        and historians write down the facts
        he must let the poor speak evil of taxes.

The testament is carried out in a renewed observation of the "RITE" of the *Li Ki* (p. 271). TCHEOU and Chao-Kong receive in their middle (p. 268) Confucius's approval of five centuries later. Confucius's judgment is sealed with the axial ideogram *Chou*[2], literally lord over the mouth contained within a squared boundary.

TCHEOU fell, however, because they neglected tradition, because subordination failed, because "were not rods in a bundle" (the fascis). Peace and order devolve into "Wars, / wars without interest / boredom of an hundred years' wars." In the state of Lou, however, a local hero had a son named Kung-fu-tseu. His name gains the catechumen's "Taught and the not taught. Kung and Eleusis / to catechumen alone," which is sealed on the right with the ideograms for the nickname derived from the style of the Books, *Chung*[4] *Ni*[2]. Kung rises from poverty up through a series of economic posts to become minister, philosopher, and finally editor of the *Odes* (pp. 272–73). As *XIII* has already implied and as the sequels will show, the philosopher's codification of the whole previous tradition laid the foundations upon which every subsequent just dynasty rose. *Canto LIII* ends with notice of Kung's heritage both familial and political:

> Thus of Kung or Confucius, and of 'Hillock' his father
> when he was attacking a city
> his men had passed under the drop gate
> And the warders then dropped it, so Hillock caught
> the whole weight on his shoulder, and held till his
> last man had got out.
>   Of such stock was Kungfutseu.

Chou

The ideogram seals not only a second phase of Chinese history but also Congress 1–53, modifying Eleusinian individualism with public responsibility. "Hillock" and Kung are the kind of men on whom destinies of all men may depend.

Confucian Revolution *LIV–LVII*

The clauses of Congress shift through the activating conjunction "So that" (cf. *I* to *II* and the first draft to the second) to the clauses of Presidency (54–65). A factive, inventive warrior covered bulls with leather masks to simulate dragons, tied poignards to their horns and torches to their tails, and so broke a siege. More generally, however, wars continued for three or four hundred years. Accompanying them the Great Wall was built and all China was united, but at the cost of burning the books because of "fool litterati." HAN begins to rise, however, and Confucian revolution to emerge, with a denial of Lenin's axiom "any cook can govern." New revolution is signaled by restoration of the Confucian books (pp. 276 ff.). Revival and incorporation of the Great Emperors and of ritual revolution draw to the central axis the framing ideogram of Tching's motto "MAKE IT NEW." But now "seepage of Buddhists" elicits the collocation (p. 281)

> war, taxes, oppression
> backsheesh, taoists, bhuddists
> wars, taxes, oppressions

As dynasties fall from these causes the rise of new ones on reestablishment of the books (pp. 278, 280, 281) draws the generalizing "halls were re-set to Kung-fu-tseu / yet again, allus droppin' 'em and restorin' 'em / after intervals" (p. 284).

War and taxes join in the rubric to *LV*,

> Orbem bellis, urbem gabellis
>
>   implevit,

which had been applied to the reigning Pope during the Siena founding. This policy is immediately countered by the policy of an emperor who threw his riches into circulation to promote commerce; the contrast is sealed by axial ideograms from the *Ta Hio* (X.20), "The humane man uses his wealth as a means of distinction, the inhumane man becomes a mere harness, an accessory to his takings" (cf. "Good sovereign by distribution / Evil king is known by his imposts," *LII*). This distinction prepares for the main subject of this second canto of Confucian revolution, the sweeping economic reforms of the minister Ngan (pp. 296–99), who repeats Kung's career and elaborates his policies. Ngan champions reform of market tribunals, the just price, tax relief, stimulation of commerce by circulating the whole realm's abundance, and social credit to farmers. Other models are the Great Emperors and Kung's political model, the TCHEOU age of Chao Kong. Ngan's reforms draw opposition, but the Emperor supports them. A history since TCHEOU is written. The reigning Emperor is lauded for renewing the Mandate of Heaven in the terms of frontispiece to "KUNG," the Rays ideogram. "Said Ngan: YAO, CHUN were thus in government."

After Ngan, however, taoism and "state usury" sap the dynasty, leaving it vulnerable to barbaric outlanders who are attracted by the promise of booty but who end up being civilized by Confucianism. This theme looks forward to the MANCHU. Here (pp. 299–300) the Turkish tartars, the Manchurian tartars, and the tartars of Ghengiz Khan are identified, but now it is Ghengiz's who enter China and found a new dynasty. Ghengiz is attracted not only by China's wealth but also by his "hearing of alphabets / hearing of *mores*." He brings a new economic idea of promoting monetary circulation, paper money, since coin was too heavy to be transported by a nomadic people. An advisor broaches the new idea of taxing the conquered rather than exterminating them. The Mongols also lay a higher tax on luxuries (wine) than on necessities.

These new ideas, introduced at the end of *LV*, formally open *LVI*, the theme of which is founding the YUEN (Mongol) and then MING dynasties. Text and ideograms recur to the Great Emperors, to "the law of Chung Ni," and to former pre-Confucian and Confucian dynasties. Ghengiz and Yuentchang, the MING founder, are linked by the thematic "No slouch ever founded a dynasty" (pp. 302, 307). Ghengiz revives policies of the Great Emperors, three of whom return ideogramically (on the right, p. 302); into prevailing dynastic chaos he came as a founder "saying nothing superfluous," i.e., in the style of Chung Ni. The Great Emperors and dynasties prior to Kung and after are summarized (pp. 303, 305) as YUEN tradition. But after Kublai (p. 304), whose reign was equivocal, the same old abuses returned (pp. 306–7). In response Yuentchang, a man of the people, rebels—not against YUEN or against Ghengiz and Kublai, but against "lice that ate their descendants" (p. 308). The Mongols fell "from losing the law of Chung Ni," which returns ideogramically on the right. Yuentchang founds MING as Hong Vou, its first Emperor. MING's tradition is sealed axially by ideograms for the Great Emperors YAO and SHUN and for the dynasties HAN and TCHEOU (p. 309).

At the end of *LVI* Hong Vou orders his mandarins to insure the succession of his son, but at the beginning of *LVII* the son's uncle sets about to unthrone him on the pretext of protecting him from the guiles of his ministers. The unthroning is completed with the connivance of Buddhists, who with eunuchs make supernatural religion responsible for the decline of MING in the canto. The decline of MING is analogized to the concurrent decline of Malatesta in Italy, but publication of new maps touches on the coming European voyages of discovery and also on the coming of the MANCHU, both of which will open up China to new influences. MING search for an elixir, for transmutation of metals, for "a word to make change" precipitates in about 1492 the ideogram *pien*[4] "change" or "rebellion," which pictures almost perfectly the

American revolutionary Eagle with a mouth on its breast, delivering words that culminate in its head.[5] *Pien*[4] foreshadows coming MING revolution.

5. Pound denominates *pien*[4] "the sign of metamorphosis" in "Mang Tsze (The Ethics of Mencius)," *Criterion*, London, July 1938.

Reference to a MING "star chamber" suggests the constellation. An anti-MING symbol is completed by a minister's diatribe of a kind that will be abjured by the MANCHU:

> To hell with the pyramid
> YAO and SHUN lived without any such monument
> TCHEOU KONG and Kungfutseu certainly wd/ not have
> ordered one
> nor will it lengthen YR MAJESTY's days
> It will shorten the lives of YR subjects
> they will, many of 'em, die under new taxes.

But MING begins to be buried under mountains of hoarded treasure until the MING heritage of Confucian revolution ends with China open to incursions from all directions.

The four cantos of Confucian revolution can be read as declaration through reestablishment of the books (*LIV*), as Confucian struggle illustrated by Ngan's reforms and by the coming of the Mongols (*LV*), as formal revolutionary foundings by YUEN and then MING (*LVI*), and as continuing revolution illustrated by MING succession (*LVII*), the failure of which is formally sealed by a foreshadowing of positive continuing revolution. Continuing revolution by the MANCHU now perfects the *Li Ki*, the four phases of ritual revolution, and the four phases of Confucian revolution not only in four cantos but also in a phasal form closer to that of '76 than any other such form in the poem. The world, not merely Chinese, context prepares for a full unfolding of '76 in "JOHN ADAMS."

MANCHU Revolution *LVIII*

An oriental version of "Nuevo Mundo" brings MING China into relations with Japan, Korea, the Christian West, and the Manchu tartars. A Japanese version of original Chinese founding goes back to "the beginning / of all things" when "order" was established in "Sun land, Nippon," first by descendants of the gods and then by a centralizing Shogun, who put an end to internal wars and confined the descendants of the gods to keep them from interfering in business. But now (pp. 316–18) external wars between Japan and Korea, the Tartars and China, recapitulate and universalize the means used in foregoing Confucian revolutions to overthrow moribund dynasties. The catechumen sums up mournfully what has happened "from the beginning of China":

> from the beginning of China, great generals, faithful adherents,
> To echo, desperate sieges, sell outs
> bloody resistance, and now the bull tanks didn't work

sieges from the beginning of time until now.
sieges, court treasons and laziness.
Against order, lao, bhud and lamas,
          night clubs, empresses' relatives, and hoang miao,
poisoning life with mirages, ruining order; TO KALON

This period of expanding wars and European infiltration, both religious and commercial, coincides with the decline of the Renaissance, which was reversed by the Sienese founding and the American colonizations. In China it is reversed by MANCHU revolution beginning in "1625/35."

Insofar as the perspective of "ELEUSIS" began with Divus's Homer in 1538 and ended with the League of Cambrai in 1508, the Eleusinian form of '76 evolved the discovery of 1492. The MANCHU form of '76 coincides exactly with the American colonial period, 1628–1771. The MANCHU make their declaration under Tai Tsong during "1625/35" (*LVIII*), prepare for rule of all China under Chun Tchi during 1644–61 (*LIX*), solidify their rule of a cosmopolitan empire under Kang Hi during 1662–1723 (*LIX–LX*), and perfect a continuing dynasty under Yong Ching during 1723–35, when it is handed on to Kien Long for his rule of 1735–76 (*LXI*).

Tai Tsong, who gave the Manchu law from China and chose learning from the Great Emperors and Kung, makes his declaration in a new form, argumentative letters and speeches addressed to his adversaries. His voice is dignified but firm. He took arms against oppression and from fear of oppression, not to extend rule. All his actions tended toward peace and he offered a peace oath to the MING Emperor, who ignored his peace gestures. As a free lord without overlord he claims the right to take such letters and laws as he likes but no orders. Not he but the MING Emperor is responsible for slaughters and for neglect of the people and of soldiers. Tai's utterances hover on the edge of the American Declaration and of Adams's revolution by lawsuit, diplomacy, and Constitutional arguments. Petitioned by the Manchu princes to assume the fallen Mandate of MING, he does so in 1635.

Between the military struggle against MING pursued at the end of *LVIII* and completed after the beginning of *LIX*, *LIX* begins with the young MANCHU Chun Tchi's praise of the Confucian *Odes* as means of preparing the character of the Emperor for rule. Chun's opinion is in the form of a "preface" or Preamble to a translation of the *Odes* into Manchu. The catechumen comments on Chun's close reading (the kind needed to make a translation) "periplum, not as land looks on a map / but as sea bord seen by men sailing." After declaration in the mode of intelligence, which comes from circumnavigation, struggle in the mode of ethics comes from colonization, or the lay of the land. This form of "periplum" will be a keynote of the second phase, *Pisan*.

The rest of *LIX* and all of *LX* consolidate the dynasty and the empire under Kang Hi in the form of the Constitutional Branches and Powers. The main subject for the Branches is demarcating borders with Russia by treaty. For the world theme the embassy (Congress) includes two Jesuits. It travels to meet the Russians under Kang's authority (Presidency), but has to return home because of wars in the outlying provinces. The next year, however, a treaty in universal Latin and in tartar and Muscovite, guaranteeing peace and prescribing boundary stones, is sworn with a prayer "to the GOD of all things" (Judiciary). Envoys of the two states celebrate the harmony, which has been made possible because the Jesuits kept the states' envoys tempers (states of mind) until they came to agreement.

In *LX* Kang Hi actively governs his empire, but most of his concerns are policies toward Europeans, first Jesuits and other Christian religionists and then European traders. Kang has to govern China amid shifting relations and policies toward the Europeans (States). They swing from complete freedom for the Jesuits because of their aid with the arts, the sciences, and politics, to almost complete proscription because of religious conversions and aggressive trade practices (Amendment). The religious theme and the necessary imperial edicts involve Supreme Law. Kang delivers his political testament (Ratification) by declaring

> 'no DYNASTY has come in with such justice
> as ours has. I have not wasted the treasures of empire
> considering them as the blood of the people;

by ordering that Yong Ching succeed him; and by offering Yong a few minor bits of advice. But the catechumen extends the political testament to the cosmopolitan cultural terms with which Kang has introduced in *LIX*. He fostered the arts, the sciences, philosophy, and universal knowledge, all with the adjuration

> qu'ils veillèrent à la pureté du langage
> et qu'on n'employât que des termes propres
> (namely CH'ing ming)

As they sealed the paideuma "ELEUSIS," the ideograms seal with Kung's first principle of government a functioning system.

Whereas MING succession had failed in passing from *LVI* to *LVII*, Tai's argument against tyranny, Chun's preparation of his human nature for rule, and Kang's establishment of MANCHU within a world context are succeeded by Kang's son Yong Ching's perfection of Chinese continuing revolution.[6]

---

6. Why Pound parenthesized (*LXI*) is open to speculation. One possibility is Yong Ching's

"Active" and "absolute," Yong honors tradition, the spirits of earth and heaven, and "utility public" as means of seeking "good of the people," for which he is "loved." He rules under law by attending in detail to all the concerns of the empire, by working with his officials, and by being a philosopher-emperor motivated by "FU," Happiness, for all. In doing so he goes all the way back to the *Li Ki* and comprehends the entire Chinese tradition.

Yong's reign is framed by the catechumen's projective rubric (p. 334) and by his summary commemoration "CAI TSONG HIEN HOANG TI be he credited" (p. 339). The focus of the rubric, before the details of his reign begin, is "No death sentence save a man were thrice tried"; the reign itself, before the final commemoration, praised Yong for "the number of bye-laws" and for "attention to detail" before expanding the opening keynote to (p. 339)

> never had death sentences such attention
> three trials, publication of details, examination,
> to poorest as for the highest

The keynote-frame accentuates due process of law in capital cases, the theme of the Bill for this fifth draft, observed by the catechumen-prosecutor and now made explicit in his materials. If this frame expresses the spirit of the Fifth Amendment, "number of bye-laws" and "attention to detail" in actually ruling the empire for "good of the people" advert to the form and function of the Bill, ten Amendments designed to turn the de jure Constitution toward de facto governing. Accordingly Yong's reign is detailed in ten passages. They do not follow the Bill theme by theme; rather they draw on the prior drafts while projecting the sequels.

Emerging into action from the rubric and the due process theme, Yong cites Chinese and universal law to justify eviction of "immoral" Christianity and prohibition of new Buddhist temples; Christian and Buddhist laws, which "stir up revolt by pretense of virtue," are false; by seeking to uproot Kung's laws and teachings Christianity disturbs good customs (p. 334). For the people he institutes public relief during famines and public works for the unemployed while clamping down on officials who try to extort graft from his programs (pp. 334–35). Yong approves a state examiner's plan for establishing tax collection, grain prices, and the food supply (p. 335); the plan is explicitly analogized to European new economics illustrated by Renaissance Mantua (*XXXV*) and to fascist policy ("AMMASSI or sane collection"). Old Manchu customs are revived (pp. 335–36) for honoring honest citizens while punishing the dishonest, and the dynastic histories are celebrated (cf. celebrations of civic harmony in Siena and celebrations of the whole paideuma "ELEUSIS").

Revival of Manchu custom and history modulates into a focus "Between

---

continuation of the spirit and policies of Kang Hi. Another is preparation for shifting from drafts to decads for a 100-canto poem.

KUNG and ELEUSIS'' on Eleusinian parliamentary and royal responsibility (Congress and Presidency) versus Chinese imperial responsibility (Presidency alone):

> 'I cant', had said KANG HI
> 'Resign' said Victor Emanuel, you Count Cavour can resign
> at your convenience.

Out of this transition between paideumas comes Yong's perfection of ''KUNG'' as a whole by governing to honor his deceased father, by urging the style of *Chung¹ Ni²* and *cheng⁴ ming²* on his administrators (''call pork pork in your proposals''), and by performing ritual plowing and harvesting ''as writ in LI KI in the old days'' (p. 336). Diplomatic honoring of European Christians without allowing them to ''spill proppergander'' or to advance suspected ''conspiracy'' with Chinese converts (pp. 336–37) looks ahead to American diplomatic treatment of Europe in ''JOHN ADAMS.''

Opening up unused land to new settlers, increasing production on already cultivated land, increasing doles, and repairing canals, all to meet increased population and rising grain prices (p. 337), look ahead to the corporate state Pound envisioned for what became *Pisan*. Yong's political philosophy, expressed in a two-part letter consisting of axiomatic principles and their application (pp. 337–38), looks ahead to the themes of what became *Section: Rock-Drill* and *Thrones*. At his death in 1735, forty years before ''our revolution,'' he passed on to his son and successor, Kien Long, the testamentary

> 'A man's happiness depends on himself,
> not on his Emperor
> If you think that I think that I can make any man happy
> you have misunderstood the FU

(the Happiness ideogram) that I sent you.

''The light descending from heaven'' (the left)[7] goes back to the frontispiece to ''KUNG,'' the Rays ideogram; the light has passed through ''KUNG'' to (and by) *one mouth* descending on a *field* (cf. Yong honoring ''spirits of fields / of earth / heaven'' in the opening rubric). Finally, the catechumen commemorates Yong for ''number of bye-laws,'' ''attention to detail,'' and due process of law (p. 339).

Kien's reign, looking ahead to ''the rise of the Adamses,'' seals Yong's

7. ''The light descending (from the sun, moon and stars). To be watched as component in ideograms indicating spirits, rites, ceremonies.'' ''Terminology,'' *Ta Hsio: The Great Digest*, 1948, 1951.

Bill, the MANCHU, and "KUNG" with four themes. A general camped outside conquered Mohammedan towns writes his Emperor advising in the economic tradition of "KUNG" that useless cannon be turned into small coinage to keep commerce going. Kien's mother, who entered Yong's court as a concubine with an amiable personality, twice became "nuova persona"— queen at Kien's birth, and, at her death, posthumous Empress. In memorial, as on her seventieth and eightieth birthdays, Kien turned new life into justice by exempting his empire from land tax for a year. Finally, Kien wrote a poem on the beauties of the Manchu's ancestral city, Mougden, and condensed the Ming histories from which the catechumen has been writing. "Literary kuss," the catechumen-reader is told—"Perhaps you will look up his verses."

Behind the main subjects of "KUNG"—the paideumatic *Li Ki* (*LII*), ritual revolution (*LIII*), Confucian revolution (*LIV–LVII*), and MANCHU perfection (*LVIII–LXI*)—can be discerned the prototype form. A revolutionary form "to be unity" is introduced by the *Li Ki* and perfected by Yong Ching's performance of the rites "as writ in LI KI in the old days." Coming out of the unitary *Li Ki*, ritual revolution and Confucian revolution culminate in liberty through MING, which rises from the people; MANCHU revolution redirects Chinese revolution toward a new union in a world context. Constitutional trine is marked by Ngan's economic reforms and by the emerging Mongols (*LV*), then by the failing MING and the rising MANCHU (*LVIII*). For tetrad revolution against a declining MING is precipitated by *pien*[4], the ideogramic Eagle (*LVII*); Tai Tsong directs a struggle against MING (*LVIII*); Chun Tchi writes a Preamble for Kang Hi's consolidating reign (*LIX* and *LX*); and Yong Ching and Kien Long perfect and seal Chinese revolution continuing on toward "JOHN ADAMS."

A new form in "KUNG," the ideograms, has been cited as accentuation of the text. The "Table" says "foreign words and ideograms both in these two decads and in earlier cantos enforce the text but seldom if ever add anything not stated in the english, though not always in lines immediately contiguous to these underlinings" (p. 256). On the other hand ten ideogram-groups run axially through the text in *LIII–LX* while four groups appear on the right. These complements and dispositions would perhaps not be noticed except for Pound's ten-part, four-phase form, for the explicit forming of ideograms of *Pisan LXXVII* into "Canto 77 Explication," and for the emphatic "rock-drill" axis amid the ideograms of *Rock-Drill 85*. A new look at certain of Pound's prose works and Confucian translations shows that he used the same device for appendixes and forewords.[8] For "KUNG" it can be assumed that the un-

---

8. Pound first experimented seriously with ideogramic designs in tabulations and notes appended to the "Ideogramic Series" edition of Fenollosa's *The Chinese Written Character as a Medium for Poetry* (London: 1936). Close scrutiny will show, I think, that a poem ("ONE") and tables and columns, sections, and columns culminating (again) in poetic lines are working out patterns to be derived from "ONE" in four phases designed to analogize cultures paideumatically. An ideogramic axis runs through "Mang Tsze (The Ethics of Mencius)," *Criterion*, London,

emphatic axis, emerging from the enlarged "Rays" frontispiece, foreshadows the "rock-drill," which symbolizes the "bust thru" on the Calendar axis and thus the Mount and Constitution; in that respect the axis makes "KUNG," otherwise the paideuma of struggle, a Constitutional phase of the four episodes amending '76. The four ideogram-groups on the right—"MAKE IT NEW" (*LIII*), Chung Ni (*LIII*), a return to three of the Great Emperors for Ghengiz's new founding (*LVI*), and again Chung Ni for MING founding (*LVI*), seem to symbolize the *Li Ki* and ritual revolution becoming Confucian revolution and then being formalized and continued.

In 1950 and 1951, in separate editions, Pound added more ideograms to "KUNG." The British *Seventy Cantos* (1950) and subsequent British collections, but never American editions, add an ideogram tailpiece to each of *LV*–*LX*, not in the classic calligraphy of "KUNG" and "JOHN ADAMS" but in a rough personal calligraphy like but also distinguished from that already used in *Pisan* (1948). The six ideograms do not translate one by one into Preamble motives, but they do "seal" the inception and culmination of barbarian incursion and "colonization," Mongol to Manchu, or Confucianization "by attraction." So too for the rough-and-ready American. The rough-drawn tailpieces stress the place of "KUNG" as a second phase of four paideumas in a poem forced from one hundred cantos in nine or ten drafts, to one hundred twenty cantos in ten drafts and twelve decades. No longer could "KUNG" end a first phase of decads while "JOHN ADAMS" became a second phase.

The same effect is achieved in American editions, beginning with a second printing of *Cantos I–LXXXIV* in 1951, by adding the rough tailpiece *chih*[3], stop, to the *Li Ki* (*LII*). *Chih*[3] indicates that in presenting the *Li Ki* to introduce the second paideuma the catechumen has observed "the law of Chung Ni." But he is also signing himself "chih in the 3rd/tone/and a radical" (*Rock-Drill 87*), a play on an element in the Chinese alphabet and on the character of a revolutionary. Translated "a gnomon," *chih*[3] is also the second of four large axial ideograms of the "rock-drill," which culminate in "THE FOUR TUAN[1]/ . . . or foundations."

Again, *chih*[3] signs the second of four paideumatic epitomes, each of which defines the revolutionary character. Pound succeeds Odysseus and invokes Aphrodite for "ELEUSIS," and signs the *Li Ki* for "KUNG." He will inherit "JOHN ADAMS" by sealing *LXII* and crying "ARRIBA ADAMS." At the end of *Pisan LXXVII* he will affirm universal paideuma to be still actively "in the mind indestructible."

July 1938. *Confucio: Ta S'eu Dai Gaku Studio Integrale* (Rapallo: 1942) is provided with an interpretive "Ideogrammario." *Ta Hsio: The Great Digest* (1948, 1951) has an analogous "Terminology." All these and the ideograms of *Cantos LII–LXXI* are preparing for the functional ideograms of *Pisan* focused by "Canto 77 Explication."

CHAPTER FIFTEEN

"JOHN ADAMS" *LXII–LXXI*

& *LXXI CANTOS*

Not less of order than liberty...
  "JOHN ADAMS" *LXII*

'Ignorance of coin, credit and circulation!'
  "JOHN ADAMS" *LXXI*

John Adams, *The Cantos'* "protagonista civile," consummates one phase in one revolutionary tradition, in one man, in one form of revolutionary justice, in one liberty. The "Table" to "JOHN ADAMS" applies the prototype ONE: 1–4, 5–6, 7, 8–9, 10 to Pound's interpretation of '76 for separation evolving into new international relations. The whole decad "LXII–LXXI" begins and is comprehended in the epitome first topic "JOHN ADAMS." "JOHN ADAMS," "Writs of Assistance," "Defence of Preston," and "The congress (nomination of Washington)" (1–4) expand the epitome to "REVOLUTION . . . in the minds of the people" in Seal-form up to the Congress of 1774, which in 1775 appointed Washington commander-in-chief for the struggle and finally turned its arguments about independence into the Declaration of 1776; the Declaration declared states' rights in America while looking toward new relations among a comity of nations ("The congress" is a first turn in Constitutional trine). "Voyage to France (not being diddled by Vergennes or plastered by Franklin)" and "Saving the Fisheries" (5–6) carry Adams's diplomatic struggle in Europe to the achievement of separation and liberty by the Peace of 1783. "Plan of government" (7), which began in 1776 with the Declaration, confirms states' rights for a unified America; by a turn from liberty to new union and by Constitutional trine it projects new relations between America and Europe. New relations are established by Adams's official embassies in "Recognition, loan from the Dutch, treaty with Holland" and "London" (8–9). As President of the new nation under the Constitution and Bill of Rights, Adams crowns '76 both nationally and internationally by "Avoidance of war with France" (10).

But the text of "JOHN ADAMS" does not unfold either by this form or by the ten-canto prototype. Both the "Table" and the decad are overarching forms for the whole as a sixth draft, but the draft is swallowed up in a working form by which "JOHN ADAMS" condenses the whole Declaration into the six drafts of the first phase. As is his wont Pound extracts from his source, *The Works of John Adams, Second President of the United States, with a Life of the Author* edited by Adams's grandson Charles Francis Adams (ten volumes, 1850–56), the phasal form of '76 already amply built into his poem. The "Life," going back to the arrival of the Adamses at Massachusetts Bay, forms with the "Works" a New World history through the revolution; begun by John Quincy and finished by Charles Francis, the "Life" makes the whole a work by three generations of Adamses turned by the successor Pound into epic poetry. Pound's radical selection and condensation follows Charles Francis's editing and classification while turning them deftly to new ends. The resultant form for *The Cantos*, as will be shown, is an historical biography of Adams coming out of universal and New World history, the diary of a "nuova persona" from personal beginnings through the outbreak of revolution to his diplomatic struggles in Europe, his argumentative theory of constitutional government complemented by his practice as an official of such government, and a testament for continuing revolution.

Biography, diary, theory of government, practice of government, and testament each goes back to beginnings, giving the effect of drafts within a draft, of concurrent phases, and of sequential phases. These five parts, joining with the previous five drafts (as their epitome, *VI*, joined with the first five cantos), condense the Declaration into the first phase. To condense the Declaration, which contains all forms, the biography is the keynote and dominant form of the whole draft, as in the "Table." The other four parts project the four drafts (in three phases) to come.

But since the theory and practice of government are complements (Branches and Powers), the form is also the four-phase form contained within the Declaration. The phasal shift thus consummates all previous four-phase subjects while projecting from the poem's first phase its four phases. As in the Malatesta cantos, the other integral "Life and Works" of *The Cantos*, objective history is the mode of the Declaration, eye-witness experience is the mode of the Preambles, justice and government is the mode of the Constitution, and testament is the mode for delivering the Bill and Seal of continuing revolution into the hands of the twentieth-century poet.

The Biography

The Biography follows the Adamses briefly from 1628 before coming to John's birth in 1735, his preparation for a governmental vocation, and his early entry into the conflicts which led up to the Declaration. This prelude emerges from universal and New World history, summarizes the previous drafts in American terms, and initiates a Seal/Calendar form while evolving

"REVOLUTION . . . in the minds of the people." The rest of *LXII* constitutes a four-phase epitome spanning Adams's career up to his retirement and
testament; his retirement, up to his death, is elaborated briefly at the beginning
of *LXIII*.

The first page (341)[1] of *LXII* condenses the spirit of '76 coming out of
world history, summarizes the foregoing drafts as the opening fragments of *VI*
summarized *I–VI*, and contains the spirit of HORUS, upon whom "the year
turns," taking form on the cycle in the feasts of ZAGREUS and PAN "of no
era" (i.e., before the revolutionary mind breaks into time).

Rearranged from Charles Francis's preface and made quasi-divine by
italics, the mythic keynote to the whole of "JOHN ADAMS" and to its
revision of '76 for new world relations—

> *'Acquit of evil intention*
> *or inclination to perseverance in error*
> *to correct it with cheerfulness*
> *particularly as to the motives of actions*
> *of the great nations of Europe.'*

—advances the mythic keynotes of "ELEUSIS" and "KUNG," the *Odyssey*
and the *Li Ki*. This theme combines and transforms the ritualization of mind
and sexuality into renaissance, and the ritualization of human nature within
general nature, into a new and higher conception of justice. The main idea
seems to be correction of Eleusinian paideuma by Chinese paideuma in the
light of the about-to-be revealed American paideuma; as such it mitigates via
Confucian ethics and American justice the charge against Odysseus which
opened *VI*, "What you have done, Odysseus, / We know what you have
done..." It is also a keynote for broaching the case against "our British
brethren" while revising it and the Declaration's whole argument against the
past. Through it the motives for states' rights will be completed to "secure the
blessings of liberty to ourselves and our posterity." Supreme Law for states'
rights will interact with Judiciary for new union. All is activated by the right
to fair trial, which both Adams and Pound observe.

The keynote is not only "ONE" within *LXII*-as-"ONE," but also the first
of four fragments preceding John Adams's birth. As the first it is a voice of
discovery of 1492 and a voice of declaration. It is followed by the address
from the Massachusetts Bay Charter, "TO THE GOVERNOR AND THE
COMPANIE," "for the planting / and ruling and ordering of New England,"
signed 19 March 1628 by "nuove persone" of the colony, among them
Thomas Adams. This fragment of colonization and struggle modifies Guil-

---

1. On the other hand Pound complained to Eliot "I rather wanted a blank page or sub title
before Canto 62 and I think I marked it in ms/ but NOT in the galleys, and it will be too expensive
and too much trouble to put it in now." 24 October 1939, Collection at Yale.

laume de Poitiers' selling out his ground rents to go on the road as a troubador (*VI*).

The results of the charter are ''(abbreviated)'' into the founding of a new plantation on and near the site of three preceding ones,

> Merry Mount become Braintree, a plantation near Weston's
> Capn Wollanston's became Merrymount.

Guillaume's poetic celebration of his sexual prowess becomes a Seal/Calendar arcanum symbolizing Constitutional Branches/Powers. In the intended translation, ''Sun Mount become Constellation, Shield planted near Weston's'' interacts with ''Eagle'n'Shield'n'Stars became Sunmount.''[2] By paideumas ''Eleusinian holiness and Chinese order have become American thinking about government'' near (cf. *Pisan* to come) ''where Pound's ancestors preceded the Adamses.'' By drafts, retrospectively, ''An Eagle's Renaissance tradition and Renaissance personae became the American Mount made Merry by ''my 'Holy City' '' Siena. Prospectively, by a new Renaissance, the paideumas of the first line may become through a new ''Capn Wollanston's'' (the *Pisan* Eagle's *Section: Rock-Drill* and *Thrones*) a new ''Merrymount'' (what became *Drafts & Fragments*).

A fourth fragment realizes Guillaume's ''The stone is alive in my hand, the crops / will be thick in my death-year...'' in dynastic continuity and in a transforming ''establishment'':

> ten head 40 acres at 3/ (shillings) per acre
> > who lasted 6 years, brewing commenced by the first Henry
> > continued by Joseph Adams, his son
> at decrease left a malting establishment.
> Born 1735; 19th Oct. old style; 30th new style John Adams
> its emolument gave but a bare scanty subsistence.

''Ten head'' of Adamses on land bought for 120 shillings is an arcanum for a prototype (*I–X*) projecting ten drafts of 120 cantos. A summary of ''ELEUSIS'' has come to a focus in an American version of ZAGREUS's wine and in a new birth on ZAGREUS's feast. Brewing alone is not, however, a sufficient vocation for a new era.

The dynastic scion does not die, like the young king in *VI*, but eschews both brewing and the study of theology, the latter because it would involve ''endless altercation'' (aimless declaration), ''to no purpose'' (empty motives), ''of no design'' (formlessness), and ''do no good to / any man whatsoever'' (fruitless ends). Brewing in Adams's mind is a political vocation for what is coming:

2. Cf. Chapter Four, p. 66. Pound's alteration of ''Captain Wollaston's'' to ''Capn Wollanston's'' is deliberate.

> not less of order than liberty...
>   Burke, Gibbon, beautifiers of figures...
> middle path, resource of second-rate statesmen...
>   produced not in Britain:
>   *tcha*
>   tax falls on the colonists.

The first three lines call for new tradition, new personae, and new philosophy. Culmination in *"tcha"* (tea) and its ideogram summarizes "KUNG." The elements of the ideogram—*grass* over *man* (which looks like a Mount) over *tree*—picture "Merry Mount become Braintree." To tax tea, the first universally accepted donation of the Orient and a word taken from Chinese into all languages, is to violate the spirit of the feast of PAN.

The Eleusinian spirit that gave birth to a new ZAGREUS will be carried through "Adams' paideuma" by Adams's political passion echoed by tags of Cavalcanti's love canzone (*XXXVI*), which philosophized the troubador love code of the epitome *VI*. The Confucian spirit focused by $tcha^2$ for a new PAN will be carried ideogramically. The ideograms of "JOHN ADAMS" form with the Rays ideogram frontispiece to "KUNG" and "JOHN ADAMS," which contains radicals meaning bright bird feathers, and with the ideogram axis of "KUNG" guided on the right by Chinese revolution, an arrow. For the arrowhead $tcha^2$ on the right moves to $ching^4$ in the middle (*LXIII*) to $ching^4$ $ming^2$ in the middle (*LXVI*) to $ching^4$ on the left (*LXVII*); $ching^4$ then moves back to $ching^4$ $ming^2$ in the middle (*LXVIII*) and the whole comes to a central focus in Adams's Constitutional ideogram $chung^1$ (*LXX*), a vertical axis passing through mouth, Englished "I am for balance":

> *tcha*
> *ching*
> *ching ming*
> *ching*
> *ching ming*
> *chung*

As Cavalcantian Amor exercizes the passions while controlling them, the ideograms substitute for "middle path, resource of second-rate statesmen" a dynamic swing between extremes until the whirling revolutionary mind, sustaining an "unwobbling pivot" rooted in earth and touching heaven, hits the bullseye.

Page 341 has summed up five drafts of two paideumas in discovery and colonization and in the two feasts "of no era." Revolution itself emerges with the Boston Massacre, which focuses the case against "our British brethren," the motive toward liberty, constitutional questions in the mode of Judiciary/ Supreme Law, and the question of fair trial in criminal law. Within these modes the argument behind the Declaration evolves (pp. 342–45) until the

Declaration itself formalizes its argument against the past in separation (p. 345). As we shall see the whole period leading up to the Declaration also embodies four-phase "REVOLUTION . . . in the minds of the people" beginning with Adams's formation of a new tradition from discovery and colonization and his emergence from them as a new persona (p. 341).

Prime Minister Lord North and the "Louses of Parleymoot," blinded by mercantile interests to "the rights of a continent" which "no longer saw redcoat / as brother or as a protector," and where habits of freedom ("the minds of the people") had formed, resorted to force in a matter of right by sending troops to Boston; Boston is analogized to the new cradle of liberty, Pound's Rapallo. The troops fired on a citizenry motivated by liberty (the Sons of Liberty). The case for the troops is taken by Adams, already a legal advisor for the patriots, who argues that until abandonment by the British administration and outrage by the soldiery should break "the bonds of affection," criminal cases should be given fair trial under a law not bent to the passions of the times. In argument against the Governor of Massachusetts Adams broadens the political case against Britain into constitutional questions by challenging the King's right to seize lands as colonies and by disputing control over the colonies by Parliament, by the King, and by the King's judges. Again Britain is guided by a "Mercantile temper" rather than by justice. Adams prefers to rely on just interpretation (by Judiciary) of the British constitution (Supreme Law) "without appeal to higher powers unwritten"; at this point he gets it in a formal impeachment of the King's Chief Justice in Massachusetts. Pound marks a phase of justice (pp. 342–43) for "REVOLUTION . . . in the minds of the people" by interpreting the theme and symbol for revolutionary founding,

> These are the stones of foundation
> J. A.'s reply to the Governor
> Impeachment of Oliver
> These stones we built on

The arguments broaden further during the Congress of 1774 (pp. 344–45) until Lexington precipitates from them the still broader arguments and acts which result in the Declaration. At the same time, for a fourth phase of "REVOLUTION . . . in the minds of the people," Adams frames the arguments right up to formal declaration with letters to his Providence, his wife Abigail. He writes from Congress first that he doesn't receive a shilling a month, but "[I] mope, I muse, I ruminate" (poetically) elicits the practical/ poetic "Cut the overhead my dear wife and keep yr / eye on the dairy." Just before the Declaration is formalized he belittles to Abigail the final speeches and prefers "Providence in which, unfashionable as the faith is, I believe."

The arguments in Congress and in Adams's polemical writings tend more and more toward independence until Lexington moves both arguments and acts toward their inexorable end. While preparing the funding of the war and

urging a navy Adams "Guided pubk mind" with constitutional arguments
and helped frame state constitutions. Always in his mind, as well as states'
rights, was the need for a central authority to govern war, trade, and disputes
between states (cf. "not less of order than liberty"). Independence emerges
as much from practical acts as from arguments, though the case against
Britain is not forgotten, until the Declaration is celebrated "with pomp bells
bonfires on the 2nd day of July," 1776. Continuing revolution "in the minds
of the people" (the form for which is the Bill and the Seal) has become the
beginning of formal revolution. The separation is summed up as a more far-
reaching act than any social community has yet carried out. Still, despite
Britain's inadequate concessions, her always being too late, and her action
from "Cavalier" sentiment rather than from principle, it is reasonable only
by geography.

The epitome (*LXII*-as-"ONE") and the Biography (*LXII–LXIII*) are dominated by the Declaration as the document of universal history resulting through
"REVOLUTION . . . in the minds of the people" and through "Clearest
head in the Congress" in formal revolution. Within *LXII* pages 341–45
present the Declaration as a document for "Birth of a Nation" (p. 344) by
separation while the rest of *LXII* unfolds the rest of the Declaration. As always
the other phasal documents are moving concurrent. By phases, however,
pages 341–45 evolve the Declaration from New World history and project the
Biography (*LXII–LXIII*), while three subsequent themes of *LXII* project the
Diary, Governmental Theory and Practice, and the Testament.

"Clearest head in the Congress / (John's was)" turns through "THUMON,"
heart, passion, or life, to Adams's character seen in a brief sketch of his
diplomatic struggles in Europe (pp. 345–47). "We want one man of integrity
in that embassy" (to France) expresses the will of "WE the People." The
problem in the French embassy is "the ethics, so-called," of Franklin, which
draw the remark that moral analysis is the purpose of historical writing. In
Holland, Adams achieves "Birth of a Nation" not by separation but by recognition as a nation among nations, and negotiates a loan and a treaty of
commerce—these without arts, disguises, flatteries, or corruptions by a man
"who to the age of 40 years / had scarce crossed the edge of his province." In
London his observations range from the venal ethics of the British press to
England's penchant for making gain out of her neighbors's troubles, while the
now experienced statesman shows "fundamentals in critical moments." The
passage involves local and cosmopolitan, liberty and union. Its subjects will
be elaborated in different perspectives in the Diary and in the Practice of
Government.

Adams returns to America on the wings of "AS of a demonstration in
Euclid: / system of government" (p. 347), which projects the Theory of
Government as the Branches of the Constitution. Election under the Constitu-
tion to the offices of vice-president and president (pp. 347–49) projects the
Practice of Government as the Powers. He is uncomfortable in both offices

because of a growing financial power, an increasing national debt, intensifying faction, and insufficient public responsibility; only "a love of science and letters" and "a desire to encourage schools and academies" can "preserve our Constitution."

He retires from public office with a keynote projecting the Testament, "Not vindictive that I can remember / though I have often been wroth" (p. 349). These lines elicit final judgments from Charles Francis, through Pound (pp. 349–50), that he staved off war, left the country prepared should it come, pardoned those convicted of opposing direct taxation, and out-maneuvered the Hamilton faction's effort to embroil us in Europe; the opening self-characterization is seconded "wont to give to his conversation / full impetus of vehement will." Finally Pound, who on the authority of "ego scriptor cantilenae" has anathematized Hamilton and signed himself (11th Jan. 1938, from Rapallo)," seals and delivers the epitome of New World history evolving '76

> But for the clearest head in the congress
> > 1774 and thereafter
> > pater patriae
> the man who at certain points
> > made us
> at certain points
> > saved us
> by fairness, honesty and straight moving
> > ARRIBA ADAMS

Axial phrases hold a single revolutionary life firm in the middle through four phases (cf. the arrow-shaft of "KUNG") as judgment moves from left to right (cf. the arrow-head evolving in "JOHN ADAMS"). "ARRIBA ADAMS" celebrates the mind, character, constructivity, and crowning achievement of the culminating traditional "protagonista civile" of "a poem containing history."

The Diary

After the Biography has continued at the opening of *LXIII* to Adams's death and memorial, Adams comes to life like Malatesta in the Diary. Beginning '76 again with "Vol Two (as the protagonist saw it)," this longest of the five parts divides between Adams's evolution in America up to separation by the Declaration (*LXIII–LXIV* and the first half of *LXV*, pp. 352–68), and his diplomatic efforts in Europe to enter the new nation into a comity of nations (the second half of *LXV* and the opening of *LXVI*, pp. 368–81). The halves are obviously the halves of the Declaration evolved to the Preambles, liberty to new union. But the mode, unlike that of the first phase (and the third to come), is not entirely political. Instead a New England character vividly aware of persons, places, nature, customs, etc., and strongly motivated toward liberty and justice, evolves in America through study and practice of the law while entering the politics of the revolution; the evolution continues in cosmopolitan Europe with no diminution of nonpolitical interests while he is executing his political tasks. Interpenetrating each other, personal and public form a revolutionary personality, the form of the constellation symbolizing at once a new life and a NOVUS ORDO SECLORUM.

Adams began a study of the law by remarking that the "design" of one of his editions is "exposition [axial *ching*^{4}] / of technical terms" (*LXIII* p. 352). Ideogram has moved from *tcha*^{2} on the right to *ching*^{4}, right, in the middle, preparing for *ching*^{4} *ming*^{2} in the middle when Adams enters the constitutional arguments of his Theory of Government (*LXVI*). Adams complements intellectual study with physical exercise and character building, which are underlined with tags from Cavalcanti's love canzone (p. 353): *"in quella parte / dove sta memora"* links activity, inspiration, will, and memory; having read Shakespeare's *Timon of Athens*, "the manhater," Adams comments (with the catechumen) "must be (IRA must be) aroused ere the mind be / at its best / *la qual manda fuoco.*" Intimations of the revolution enter at the end of *LXIII* with the Writs of Assistance, on which Adams and other colonial lawyers comment "a contest appeared to be opened."

Adams's development continues (*LXIV*) as the revolution begins to focus on taxation without representation, which brings British troops and the Boston Massacre. From devotion to justice he undertakes the defense of Captain Preston and his men. Canto *LXIV* ends with the Boston Tea Party, to Adams only an attack on property, and with the impeachment of Chief Justice Oliver, to Adams a much more important constitutional question. Although (as in *LXII*) Adams would be glad "if constitution cd carry on / without recourse to higher powers unwritten," he must now confess that "irregular recourse to original power" for impeachment by the House before the Council was "necessary, absolute, indispensable."

Accordingly Congress assembles and evolves out of its arguments the Declaration (*LXV* pp. 363–68). Adams is immediately aware (with Patrick Henry, who calls himself not a Virginian but an American) that his arguments tend toward independence. Arguments in Congress involve such concepts as "Bill of Rights," "law of natr/Brit. constitution," and "American legislature." Washington is nominated after Lexington. "John Adams as seen by John Adams, squabbles in congress" are concerned more with a new government-in-the-making's efforts to provide for war both militarily and economically than with making the Declaration, which here receives little more than an aside or a footnote (p. 367) amid the flurry of trying to respond to events. Separation comes to a focus instead, in a mode appropriate to this personal phase, in Adams's request to Lord Howe, in parley, that he be addressed " 'In any character yr/ Lordship please *except* / that of a British subject'' (p. 368).

The second half of the Diary vividly records a tumultuous voyage to Europe and life in France, Spain, Holland, and England, all as background to the embassies introduced only narratively and politically in *LXII*. Adams struggles against French self-interest, against Franklin's easygoing political morality and francophilia, and against Europe's efforts to work the new nation into its balances of power. From the Dutch he gains recognition, a loan, and a treaty of commerce. All leads ultimately to a just peace, which saves the local fisheries while formally establishing the United States as a separate and equal member of the world comity of nations. Peace having been made, it becomes expedient that intercourse and commerce be opened with the old enemy, England. It is. The Diary thus ends with Adams's ambassadorship to England, which gives ''pater patriae'' an opportunity, though ''there is no drop not American in me,'' to enjoy the ''poetic'' beauties of the mother country.

The Theory and Practice of Government

The Diary ends with a jump from England about 1785 to Adams attending to his farm and homestead in the eve of the 1796 election (*LXVI* p. 381). The Biography having subsumed ''ELEUSIS'' and Congress by emphasizing Adams's work in the Continental Congress culminating in the Declaration, and the Diary having subsumed ''KUNG'' and Presidency by emphasizing Adams's personal struggle, the occasion of the presidential election of 1796 is opportune for turning from Presidency (clauses 54–65) to show Adams's qualifications for that office in the modes of Constitution and Judiciary (clauses 66–71). To show how Adams ''made us'' Pound arranges his *Essays and Controversial Papers of the Revolution* (1765–74) and his *Works on Government* (1776–89) into his Theory of Government (*LXVI* p. 381–*LXVIII* p. 396), and, through a new beginning with the new government declared in 1776, arranges his *Official Letters, Messages, and Public Papers* of 1777–1801 into his Practice of Government (*LXVIII* p. 396–*LXX* p. 410). He arranges the Theory so that its main subjects reflect the evolution of the Branches, and repeats the embassies again so that they fall roughly into the amending process of the powers.

''WHERETOWARD THE ARGUMENTS HAD BEEN / as renouncing the transactions of Runing Mede?'' (*LXVI* p. 381) invokes as a guarantee of the rights of the people of the colonies the Magna Charta, the constitutional foundation of the British Parliament (Congress) in relation to the crown. The rest of *LXVI* argues against parliamentary imposition of taxation without representation and for a judiciary independent of the king and of the people wherever the British constitution applies. Against British interpretations the "real" constitution, which is not "of wind and weather," is sealed in the middle by *ching*⁴ *ming*² (p. 382), which extends the *ching*⁴ of Adams's earlier legal studies (*LXIII*) to Confucius's first principle of government. *Ching*⁴ *ming*² now links the three paideumas, constitutionally Congress, Presidency, and Judiciary.

The first half of *LXVII* (pp. 387–91) evokes "folcright" against undue expansion of royal prerogatives (Presidency). Emphasized is an argument against the right of the king to claim all lands his subjects could find and his power either with or without Parliament to control their internal affairs. "NOVANGLUS" (The New Englishman) continued the argument almost until hostilities broke out at Lexington in 1775, after which several other papers written and sent to the printer were probably lost amid the confusion.

Lexington and the imminent Declaration precipitate from a well-prepared constitutional mind, "on sudden emergency" beginning " '76 or '75" from Philadelphia, a "PLAN OF GOVERNMENT," "legislative, executive and judicial." Though some forms are better than others, KUNG, Zoroaster, Socrates, Mahomet and other authorities "really sacred" agree that the aim of all is the happiness of society. Every government is founded in some principle or passion of the people "*ma che si sente dicho,*" Cavalcanti's elevation of intention over reason. The best British political philosophers have argued for an empire of laws, not men. As a constitutional theorist (Judiciary) Adams thinks out the functions of legislative, executive, and judicial Branches, concluding

> The colonies under such triple government wd/ be
> Unconquerable by all the monarchs of Europe
> few of the human race have had opportunity like this
> to make election of government, more than of air, soil or
>   climate
> When before have 3 million people had option
> of the total form of their government?

His thinking continues through the discussion about the Declaration and through his work on the Massachusetts Constitution to a more general review of constitutions ancient and modern leading toward the Constitution itself. He concludes, about 1787, that there should be orders of officers, not men, in America, and that there has been "no distinct separation of legislative, executive and judicial / heretofore save in England."[3]

The rubric to *LXVIII*, "The philosophers say: one, the few, the many," raises the question of relations between people (States) and any government. The one and the few have too often ended up using the people as "mere dupe," as "underworker," as "purchaser in trust" for some tyrant, "dex-

3. A remark to W. H. D. Rouse during *The Fifth Decad* and three years before "KUNG" and "JOHN ADAMS" may mean more than it seemed: "I think by, perhaps 67 the reader may see WHY I am doing it, and instead of padding what's there, the later cross weave will fill in what you now have." March 1935, *Letters*.

terous in pulling down, not in maintaining.'' The form of government must mitigate ambition high and low by taking a definition of commonwealth for a definition of liberty so that no branch ''by swelling'' should overwhelm any other. The final check on centralized Branches is continual thinking about ''CONSTITUTIONS'' (plural), which would preserve liberty, assure that authority comes from a proper constitutional source, prevent the misery of slavery where the law is allowed to wobble, and allow varied ''states of mind'' to exert their influence. Theory comes back to the principle that primitive man was gregarious, with passions, appetites, and predilections to be observed, commended, and esteemed. Adams touches on four-Branch government by asking if every colony (State) did not have a governor (Presidency), a council (Judiciary), and a senate and house (Congress) ''none of which went by heredity?''

Theory (culminating in the Branch States) turns to the Powers (beginning with the Power States) through a rubric *''Emissaries of Britain and France* cd/ speak and hold caucuses / Commission to France '77'' (*LXVIII* p. 396). In the new mode of official documents the Practice repeats again, with loose relevance to the specific Powers, the embassies to France, Holland, and England culminating in Adams's return to America to assume Constitutional offices. Negotiations with France (*LXVIII* pp. 396–400) try to preserve the new State's independence of the European power struggle, in which no argument is respected but force. Return of *ching*[4] *ming*[2] to the middle (p. 400), accentuating the need ''to show U.S. the importance of an early attention to language,'' shifts from France to Holland. Recognition, the loan, and the treaty of commerce, proposed in *LXVIII* (pp. 400–402) and executed in *LXIX* (pp. 403–6), amend the foregoing state of affairs.

England (*LXIX* pp. 406–7) provides little matter for Supreme Law, so Lafayette writes to Adams in 1787 that within a few years France will come to ''a pretty good constitution,'' and Adams writes Jefferson of their respective fears of Constitutional imbalance, '' 'You fear the one, I the few.' '' Pound proves Adams right by going outside Adams's works to one of the first acts of Congress under the Constitution, redeeming at full value the now worthless ''Continentals'' issued during the struggle to pay the soldiers. That members had bought up notes in anticipation of the redemption evokes from Pound a neo-Dantean diatribe condemning to Hell ''the betrayers,'' ''advance guard of hell's oiliness,'' whose progeny have shown no repentance. Madison and others tried to block the swindle, but failed. That the Supreme Law of the land was betrayed from the very beginning puts Adams on the defensive for the rest of the draft.[4]

Ratification is presented through a brief sketch of Adams's defense of ''our constitution'' during his Presidency (*LXX* pp. 409–10). His main achieve-

---

4. ''52/61 China; 62/71 John Adams, pater patriae U.S.A.—more than Washington or Jefferson, though all three essential and all betrayed by the first congress.'' To Katue Kitasono, 3 March 1939, Collection at Yale.

ment is forestalling European and American intrigues (some within his own administration) to involve America in European balances of powers and wars. By unmasking the intrigues he is able to maintain peace. He executes his office by affixing his official signature and the Seal to his acts. After defeat in the 1800 election he exhorts perpetual neutrality in all European wars and leaves a state with its coffers full.

The Testament

The rubric "And in the mirror of memory, *formato loco*" modulates at the point of Adams's retirement from public life into a culminating mode of continuing revolution and poetry excerpted from the *General Correspondence* to form a Testament. The rest of *LXX* (pp. 410–13) looks back upon '76 as a destiny and a tradition. Moving on from the retirement of 1801, *LXXI* unfolds phases of continuing struggle (pp. 414–15), continuing study of government (of constitutions, pp. 416–19), and continuing effort to turn '76 into epic poetry (pp. 419–21). Each of the four phases of the Testament goes back to beginnings and comes through the Congress of 1774 (which wrote the Declaration) to a point in Adams's life of continuing revolution (1801, 1813, 1815, 1818). An overarching chronology from the Boston Tea Party of 1773 to 1818 has the form of the "Table." Each of the phases has the theme and form of its respective theme in the whole draft, so that the draft, having unfolded the epitome (*LXII*) and the Biography (*LXII–LXIII*), comes to a focus in a final consummating transformation. Since the Testament is even more tightly organized than the opening of *LXII*, it demands closer attention than the foregoing phases.

"In the mirror of memory" recalls Van Buren looking back on the bank war (*XXXVII*), which turned political revolution economic. "*Formato loco*" evokes "that formed trace in the mind" into which Amor directs a man to look for inspiration (Cavalcanti's love canzone). Formed memory is a source of lessons from the past, for the future, in the form of revolutionary poetry. "In the mirror of memory, *formato loco*" looks through Adams's Testament toward forming a world paideumatic "nuova persona" by "thinking in poetry" in *Pisan*, where a mind informed by the world paideumas will use its own "mirror of memory" and '*formato loco*" to unify a world revolutionary paideuma.

Beginning with Cavalcantian Amor and with the idea of a poem about the Boston Tea Party evokes from *LXII* the Eleusinian opening and the first ideogram, $tcha^2$; ideogram and Amor will focus the first phase of the Testament, and the idea of a poem of '76 will dominate its fourth phase. The first phase, coming out of the Boston Tea Party, comprehends all four phases chronologically. First the Congress of 1774 is anticipated as "a nursery / for American statesmen" where new ideas about government are entertained and discussed; in retrospect it appears that "our trouble is iggurunce / of money especially."

The military struggle in America (for liberty) and the diplomatic struggle in Europe (for new union) focus now on shaping public opinion, or the will of "WE the People." England tried to deceive the public by spreading false news about the progress of the war in America. Adams's tie to local New England nature (the mode of struggle) precipitates by parenthetical interlineation France's policy of making the emerging nation only strong enough to further her own international aims; cited is popularizing Jefferson while depopularizing Washington. Returning from his experience with the "divine science of politics" in Europe, Adams regrets that after a "generous contest for liberty" the American people have forgotten of what it consists; they would profit by remembering "the struggle" of the 1760s to 1780s. The international peace of 1783 again emphasizes the local fisheries, which many Americans ignored or were inclined to give away.

Jumping beyond the Constitution of 1787, Adams considers constitutions and the study of government in general. France's Constitution is an experiment by which she cannot long be governed. Regrettably few in any nation understand any system of constitution or administration and these few do not unite. But against Americans' unexpected disposition to corruption in elections, he brings the ideogramic arrow to a bullseye with

I am for balance

and know not how it is but mankind have an aversion
to any study of government

Chung[1], middle, an ideogramic form for the Constitution, passes through Adams's defeat in the 1800 election to retirement into continuing life and revolution. His determination "WHILE I BREATHE" ("DUM SPIRO") not to commit the lamb to the wolf (those who are "against any rational theory") expresses the Bill and is sealed "DUM SPIRO AMO" (WHILE I BREATHE I LOVE). Eleusinian "AMO" illustrates the meaning in *Rock-Drill 94*, "Beyond civic order: / l'AMOR" (poetry).

The first phase having defined a tradition of continuing revolution at the point of Adams's retirement from public life, the second (*LXXI* pp. 414–16) draws lessons from that tradition and applies them to continuing struggle. The complementary halves of the second phase—liberty and union, local and international, independence and dependency, private and public—oppose and balance repeated subjects in halves formally marked by a break in the text (pp. 414–15, 415–16). Again struggle generates a public opinion, again often at odds with Adams's.

Looking into "the mirror of memory" reveals that the past was indeed
"formato," the intellectual realization of the first phase. The intellectual
rubric "And in the mirror of memory, *formato loco"* is succeeded by two
ethical rubrics, one private and one public: a German ambassador once told
Adams he couldn't stand the sexual ethics of St. Paul; dismissed to the joy of
both parties, Adams does not curse the day he entered public affairs. The
main subject of the phase, public opinion, is introduced by going back to the
first year before the Congress of 1774 when Adams overheard a yeoman in a
barroom speculating to others that if the British could take Hancock's wharf
and Rowe's wharf they could take "my house and your barn." Another's
"Rebel!" disgusted Adams, who would meet rebellion when British governors and generals should begin it by rebelling against principles of the constitution (cf. motives of the Preamble). This recollection precipitates Adams's
resentment of present injuries from England and France, his readiness "as in
the beginning" to fight whichever should first force America into a war, his
recollections of British ingratitude and injustice before the Writs of Assistance, and warnings about guarding independence against new British and
French interference. In the middle of the first half a new and even direr an-
tagonist emerges, "swindling banks" which have ruined the currency by
issues against gold or on nothing. Another swindle has been circular letters
designed to impress on Congress so-called public opinion. After opposing any
division of "the Union" in the face of British and French threats to "independence," Adams rounds back to the public opinion of 1773 with the principle
that government can be rightly carried on "When public opinion is rightly informed, as it now is not." For, British policy and French interference go so far
as to hire American papers. And, as Vergennes had remarked, "Mr Adams,
newspapers govern the world."

Constitutional principles are elaborated in France's untested appropriation
of British and American models for local conditions, and in the suitability of
the English constitution *"for* / a great nation *in* / Europe"*; accordingly al-
liance with either France or England would end "our system of liberty"
(liberty ordered). Conversely merchants would interpret liberty as the right
"to do as they please," and would have united with England or France rather
than lose free use of the Mississippi. Sexual ethics return in Adams's reluc-
tance to inculcate fidelity to the marriage lest he be thought motivated by
resentment against Hamilton; in a story of four girls to be hired in England by
General Pinckney for Adams and himself; and in the impossibility of trying to
suppress the oldest human profession, prostitution. "You may as well preach
against rum to / Indians" modulates into a locus for a later will of "WE the
People," an Indian chief's petition to President Adams that he prohibit rum
before it should sweep away the whole Indian way of life. As a mediating
locus extending a similar locus of the first half, however, Adams trumps
ignorance of government, international relations, sexual license, and rum

with the newer, more pervasive villain: though it would be "romantic" to abolish all funding and banks in the present "state of the world," nevertheless

> Every bank of discount is downright corruption
> taxing the public for private individuals' gain
>   and if I say this in my will
> the American people wd/ pronounce I died crazy.

Again Adams's will and the will of the people are at odds, but his is supported by the fact that commerce (more than rum) is drawing young Indians away from their idyllic way of life (with which Adams has been entertained). Dependency or independency culminates in the fact that while "we feel like / colonists" we will be dependent on France or England, versus the fact that natural resources to support a war enable "a nation" to "do what it please" (cf. the merchants, above). Taxes must be laid and the War of 1812 must be supported. The question of a public mind culminates with indignation against annihilation, interpolation, or prohibition of histories, which inform "WE the People" (cf. *XXXIII*), and with irony directed against what "our 'pure uncorrupted uncontaminated unadulterated' " public mind has become.

A projected history of the colonies under Britain, which would presumably revive the "generous" public mind of '76, serves as a Preamble to the governmental rubric "THEMIS CONDITOR," Adams as founder of the law. The colonial period comes into the Congress in 1774 through Patrick Henry, who alone sensed the precipice and dared face it. The Declaration is glanced at as the source for the kind of "rational theory" that would oppose "spirit of party," "ecclesiastical bigotry," and "aristocratical and democratical fury," all abjured in Adams's Constitutional theory (e.g., *LXVII* pp. 393–94). The peace of 1783 is repeated in the imminent peace being negotiated after the War of 1812. Both efforts are sealed in the middle of this third phase of the Testament by a pictured Mount,

> JOHN ADAMS
> FOR PEACE
> 1800

So Adams "saved us" once and so the lessons of his Testament can save us again.

The Mount divides the phase symbolically into Branches and Powers. Against the Constitution as written and operating are educed the circular letters, more religious fanaticism, and the crisis of the 1800 election. Adams queries ironically if anyone believes South America capable of free government, then universalizes

No people in Europe cares anything
about constitutions, 1815, whatsoever
not one of 'em understands or is capable of understanding
any consti-damn-tution whatever

The last major subject of the phase is the reconciliation of Adams and Jefferson via their letters, already presented (*XXXI–XXXIII*) as a locus for thinking about government and continuing revolution.

The Testament and the draft end proposing '76 as a poetic tradition, offering a persona for a revolutionary poet, affirming a revolutionary poet's inheritance of tradition and persona, and climaxing the whole with poetry itself. As tradition Adams assembles the men of Boston. He credits James Otis with a great part of his own argument against the illegality of destroying the charters. Sam Adams provoked the sending of the "Poor soldiers," who "knew not what sent 'em." Adams himself imported the only set of *State Trials* into America. If John Hancock was vain, so was Adams, nor was Hancock affected by inherited wealth: a thousand families depended upon him, the people elected him, and both Adamses approved their intelligence. Without knowing the actions of the men of Boston one cannot know what made "our revolution." Their acts were "magis decora poeticis fabulis," more worthy than poetic fables.

The catch-phrase "Credit Otis with a great part of my argument" modulates through the Latin into "Otis wrote on greek prosody." Adams published what Otis had written on Latin and begged to print the Greek prosody, but Otis said there were no greek types in America and that if there were, no typesetters could use them. This was one reason why America was not ready to produce an epic of '76 in its neo-Renaissance spirit (cf. *XXX*). Another was that Otis burnt his papers in melancholia after having resigned his post as Advocate General and being beaten up by coffeehouse bandits "in good looking clothes." Like the betrayal of the Constitution by the First Congress, Otis's fate (he died in 1783) gives the impression of a revolutionary civilization being betrayed before it had been completed.

Undaunted by Otis's fate, Pound accepts him as the catalyst of all '76 constituted of Adams's public life from 1760–1800 (the form of the "Table," here also the Branches):

Otis against the writs, J. A. versus judiciary,
Defended Preston, defended the soldiers;
Fisheries, peace, nomination of Washington, kept peace with
France 1800.

Beyond this tradition lies the problem of money; in Destutt Tracy's words gold and silver ought never to have been stamped save by weight, since they are but commodities like wheat or lumber; stamping them joins material greed with political power. For the Powers Adams comes back in his own voice, first for his familiar "Keep out of Europe" and then for his less known anticipation of the revolutionary sociology of Karl Marx ("Charlie Mordecai"): plantation slaves shouldn't be freed to a worse wage slavery, but at the same time plantation owners who make that argument should be laughed out of court. Adams's last words focus the most penetrating insight of his Testament, which frames the cases (cf. *LII*) and focuses all the foregoing, " 'Ignorance of coin, credit and circulation!' "

A sixth draft, a revision of '76 in four episodes, an assembly of three world paideumas, and a phase of tradition which also condenses the whole Declaration, end with the Hymn of Cleanthes, its Greek type remedying what Otis lacked. "Glorious, deathless of many names" apostrophizes a polytheistic "mind of heaven." "Zeus aye ruling all things" singles out the "God who made it." "Founder of the inborn qualities of nature" celebrates "the laws of nature and of nature's god." "By laws piloting all things" evokes a triumphant ship of state focused in the Greek "*κυβερνῶν*," helmsman and political leader. The prayer unites voyage and declaration while voicing E PLURIBUS UNUM for "the first phase," MDCCLXXVI for world paideuma, and ANNUIT COEPTIS for the revision of '76.

It also focuses a convergence of drafts, episodes, paideumas, and phase with clauses 1–71, precipitating world paideumatic Branches. The convergence of drafts and clauses precipitates six draft-Articles of a states' rights Constitution ready to be ratified: states' rights' Branches having been defined by Renaissance city-states and by American geographical states, Siena has introduced the corporate state while activating corporate amendment, which has been carried through Confucian China to a Supreme Law defined in "JOHN ADAMS." Simultaneously and by paideumatic amendment, "ELEUSIS" *I–LI* modified by examples of "KUNG"—the *Li Ki* (*LII*) and Chinese ritual revolution sealed by Confucius (*LIII*)—has realized a form of world Congress 1–53. The Chinese emperors culminating in the MANCHU (*LIV–LXI*) and modified by Adams the "protagonista civile" of tradition (*LXII–LXIII*) and self-reporting diarist (*LXIII–LXVI*) have realized a form of world Presidency 54–65. Adams the constitutional lawyer, legal theorist, founder, Constitutional statesman, and testator (*LXVI–LXXI*) has realized a form of world Judiciary 66–71. Return to origins "In the mirror of memory, *formato loco*" recovers the original purpose of '76, states' rights, which in *Pisan* will be completed by clauses 72–84 while projecting through the emergent world Branch/Power States a world amendment.

Prototypic unity, duality, trine, and tetrad are swallowed up in "JOHN ADAMS" by the convergence of archetypal revolutionary form with its complete historical realization. Circumnavigation perfects discovery and settling a new continent perfects colonization; Adams's biography, his diary of the struggle, his thinking out a sane state while implementing it, and his last will and testament catch the mind of '76 in full flight. Adams's growth in America, his work in Europe, his constitutional activities—research, legal argument,

proposal, and defense—and his adumbration of revolutionary poetry, provide
an explicit model for Pound's revolutionary tradition, for his own struggle on
two continents, and for the world scope of his justicial and poetic mind. The
biography outlined in the "Table" finds in Adams's life and work verifying
analogies for what Pound has done in the foregoing drafts and for what he will
do in their sequels. Adams's revolution in America up to "The Congress
(Nomination of Washington)" foreshadows Pound's revolution in Europe
("ELEUSIS") and his "nomination" of Mussolini. Adams's diplomatic voyages to Europe to secure recognition and to protect American economic interests foreshadows Pound's voyage to Cathay and America on behalf of
Europe. Adams's "PLAN OF GOVERNMENT," which was precipitated
"on sudden emergency" during 1776 or 1775, projects a culmination of
"thinking out a sane state"—amending the Renaissance and American states
for the corporate ideal—which Pound intended to perfect in what became
Pisan. Turning the attention of the new nation wholly to relations between
America and Europe projects Pound's effort to bring independent cultures
into a new world order.

The modal phases of "JOHN ADAMS" clinch all previous four-phase
subjects up to the episodic revision of '76 while projecting the consummation
of paideumas and phases. For the paideumas the biography subsumes the
tradition evolved in the four drafts of "ELEUSIS," the diary subsumes the
struggle followed through "KUNG," theory and practice is the heart of
"JOHN ADAMS," and the testament projects the catechumen's inheritance
of paideumas as constituents of a world paideuma. For the four phases the
biography projects a completed first phase, the diary projects Pound's mental
diary at Pisa, thinking about government and implementing it project the
halves of a seal that will constitute *Los Cantares,* and the testament projects
the testament of *The Cantos* and *The Cantos* as a testament, what will become
Drafts & Fragments as ill-fated as the unfinished work of James Otis.

Pound leaves out of Adams's version of '76, probably in part because of
Adams's antipathy, an analogue of Otis, Tom Paine, the cosmopolitan revolutionary par excellence on whom Pound modeled his historical imagination and
life almost as silently as he did on Columbus's. When Adams's biography first
shifts to the Congress of 1774 (*LXII*) Pound is careful to specify the Massachusetts delegation "Bowdoin, Cushing, Sam Adams, John A. and Paine
(Robert)." At the other end (*LXXI*) he carefully omits "Thomas Paine's"
from "Took Matlock, Cannon and Young's [and Thomas Paine's] constitutions / believing them Franklin's, they, / Beaumarchais and Condorcet, have
paid. They did not like mine." In the second hemicycle Paine will become an
imaginative model for a new protagonist under PAN just as, in the first hemicycle, protagonists from the past have been reborn under ZAGREUS through
the imaginative model Columbus.

Otis stands in for Paine as the first phase looks toward the second. The legal
arguments against British policy, for the unwritten constitution common to the

home country and the colonies, had been won before Lexington but had failed to prevent resort to arms. Adams's "Avoidance of war with France" led Pound to hope that having become through *The Cantos* a medium for the lessons of history he could "stave off war" in 1939 by talking to American leaders in Washington; the revolutionary precedent both in Adams's generation and in his own were the alternatives at the end of the Declaration's revolutionary argument, "We . . . hold them, as we hold the rest of mankind, enemies in war, in peace, friends." On the other side his hurry to get Adams into his poem as world peace was deteriorating appears in a letter to his old teacher at Hamilton College, J. D. Ibbotson: "AND I have damn well got to get a copy of Johnnie ADAMS' letters QUICK, and some how. NO use in the boss quoting Gustav le Bon when he might just as well be quoting J. Adams (père).''[5] Gustave le Bon was an historian and theorist of the psychology of crowds in a new revolutionary era. "The boss," of course, is Mussolini.

But the melancholy example of Otis, Adams's eulogy notwithstanding, boded "The 'repeat in history' " not only of 1775–83 but also of World War I. Otis's fate foreshadows a possible fate for Pound at another "crisis point of the world." Like Elpenor and Divus, Otis is *"A man of no fortune, and with a name to come."* For Odysseus/Adams he is an avatar of "our friend Elpenor,'' who instigated "REVOLUTION . . . in the minds of the people''; for Pound the inheritor he is an avatar both of Elpenor and of Divus, who instigated *The Cantos* and to whom Pound gave a revolutionary name. "Otis" suggests Odysseus's collective name for himself, "ΟΥ̓ ΤΙΣ'' or No Man, the name adopted in *Pisan* for the collective persona "Odysseus / the name of my family'' (*LXXIV*); "ce rusé personage, Otis'' (*LXXVIII*) unites with "no man'' of the *Odyssey*, via the unsung hero of '76, with the revolutionary initiate all but lost among "the voiceless'' in the Pisan stockade. Fancy can play with how prophetic Pound may have been of his own plight. In any case the events of 1939–45 almost ended Pound and his poetry while peace was being made. In Circe's swine-sty Pound became *"A man of no fortune"* indeed, leaving *"with a name to come"* dependent upon how he might react to the historical and personal debacle.

5. 9 January 1938, Collection at Yale.

CHAPTER SIXTEEN

ON SUDDEN EMERGENCY

"I am still fighting the Revolutionary War . . . at odd moments."
Broadcast, 14 March 1943

The Cantos was conceived and composition began before World War I, peri-odical publication began during World War I, and the definitive publication was "an act of emergence" from World War I. The necessary and actual condition for the first phase was world peace. Pound's minimum hope was that the total expression of the "revolt of intelligence" consummated in *The Cantos* would help preserve peace. Research disseminated through vari-ous ABC's, political polemics, and expanding analogies between twentieth-century and previous revolution were intended to cause world enlightenment "by attraction" on the ideal level of poetry. Even if such a method were practicable, Pound was too late. Overtaken by events, and more obviously overcome by incredible misunderstandings of what had been shaping twen-tieth-century history, he found that the meliorating continuity on the surface of his poem had broken down. After *LXXI Cantos* the poem reflects that break-down, though the dream, the motive, and the form persist.

Pound had been thought anything from eccentric to mad ever since his arrival in London. Wyndham Lewis, his collaborator in *Blast* (1914), later designated the American exile who had passed through London and Paris to settle in Italy "a man in love with the past" and "revolutionary simpleton" (*Time and Western Man*, 1927). Those who either received or followed his spates of letters and polemics could think him tedious, superficial, obsessed, or insane, particularly when he set himself up as an economist. As the tension of the 1930s increased and the pressure to take a stand for democracy, com-munism, or fascism became almost unavoidable, Pound's deliberate align-ment with Italy, Mussolini, and the fascist revolution turned suspicions into certainty and revulsion. The Rome-Berlin axis denigrated his position further, especially since an early contempt for Hitler and nazism began to turn to apologetics and even support. Anti-Semitism began to color his utterances more luridly and Nazi anti-Semitism amplified brutally whatever racist terms he might use. How could this square with the self-proclaimed Jeffersonian Democrat and Confucian? What about his claim to be using accurate facts against those responsible for "the historic blackout"? To be an impeccable eye-witness who demanded the test of experience? To be an intellectual re-

sponsible for keeping the language clean so that *cheng¹ming²*, the first principle of government, could serve lawmakers? What about the poet responsible
not only for the language but also for the insights that deliver the original
"poetic fact" necessary for "the antennae of the race"? How could he "voice
the general heart" in "the tale of the tribe"?

Pound always made the simple assumption that perverters are criminal and
evil. "Criminals have no intellectual interests." They deny human nature
and one of its most important faculties, the mind. By having lost "il ben
dell'intelletto" they reduce themselves below the level of Circe's swine to the
scatological level of Hell *XIV–XV*, "without dignity, without tragedy." Another danger follows Niccolò d'Este's execution of his second wife and his
son (*XX*): madness. Niccolò's delerium (cf. also Cabestan's lady and Actaeon-
Vidal, *IV*) illustrates the "clear shapes, / Broken, disrupted," the "Wilderness" and "confusion," "source of renewals," to which Pound had to submit
himself supported only by the faith that such chaotic "states of mind" would
reveal themselves to be "the discontinuous gods."[1]

Toward the end of the 1930s Pound began to sense an impression he might
be making:

> A man working on a large project may often seem a bit mad. He
> speaks in large terms at one moment and in the next is discussing minute
> details which, on the surface, have little to do with the main problem. A
> man whose mind moves faster than a snail finds it tedious to have to
> explain the connecting links of his thought. If he has had the patience to
> do it once in, say 1923, it is hard for him to realize that his reader of
> 1937 may have no idea of what he has been driving at for more than a
> decade. . . . A man lives in his own time: present, past, or, in the case
> of genius, even in tomorrow. For international Verkehr tomorrow is as
> good a sportsfield as we can choose.[2]

There was the strain of finding the right matter for *The Cantos*, not only new
economic theory but even twentieth-century protagonists. His mind had to
become a delicate instrument capable of containing vast quantities of data
while relating "everything to everything else" by refined analogies and perceptions. It had to achieve freedom and calm even under the pressure and
chaos of external events in which he had perforce become involved. It had to
sustain the effort, given such complexities, to achieve the simplicities of

1. Vanni Scheiwiller, Pound's Italian publisher, told me that Pound had shown an unusual
interest in madness; he cited Pound's translation in 1941 of a part of Enrico Pea's *Il Moscardino*
and his interest in *I Tetti Rossi: Ricordi di Manicomio* by Corrado Tumiati, 1931, which resulted
in the title of an article on the "manie" of American and British economic policies ("Tetti
Rossi," *Meridiano di Roma*, 16 March 1941). He also reviewed Phyllis Bottome's *Private
Worlds* (*New English Weekly*, London, 1935).

2. "Totalitarian Scholarship and the New Paideuma," *Germany and You*, Berlin, 25 April
1937.

"reading matter, singing matter, shouting matter, the tale of the tribe." It had to persist in "the poet's job . . . to *define* and yet again define till the detail of surface is in accord with the root in justice . . . LUCIDITY."[3]

Pound was not merely "a man in love with the past" and a "revolutionary simpleton" but a man trying to live within a Chinese box or in concentric "curves of time": to live in several pasts that foreshadowed their sequels, to live between past and future in a present that would synthesize the pasts, to live in a future that would subsume not only the forms but also unforeknown historical events, and to live in a timeless duration with which all these dimensions could harmonize.[4] It is no wonder that during 1939–45 Pound's experiences resulted in something like madness. What is remarkable is that he had built contingency into his form so that it could absorb catastrophe. The seventh draft and second phase was to consummate a revision of '76 in world paideuma and to ratify the corporate state under Mussolini. History imposed ruin, tragedy, nostalgia, and elegy for the timeless vision, for "300 years culture," for "20 years of the dream," and for "the companions." Yet by confession, rectification, and a resurgent effort, both poet and poem endured the dark night of the soul in a tragic mode until new light promised the possibility if not the certainty of carrying on.

Having finished *LXXI Cantos* in 1939 Pound was thinking of a 100-canto poem based on the assumption that the fascist revolution and corporate state could become contemporary world models. He had "got to the end of a job or part of a job (money in history)"[5] in a first phase; with "29 canters to write" he was "at about the end of the Purgatorio or chronology plus hestorik process part."[6] "Purgatorio" refers to the middle four drafts of trine, the three paideumas and synthesized world paideuma to come; "chronology plus hestorik process part" refers to the same six drafts plus one draft in tetrad, a first phase and a coming second. He also needed "for personal ends" (a reference to paideumas culminating in personality) "to tackle philosophy or my 'paradise,' "[7] which as a final third of trine would modulate out of the end

3. To Basil Bunting, December 1935, *Letters.*

4. "The contemporary world doesn't exist. For nothing exists which is not in rapport with the past and future. Thus the world of today exists only as fusion, as a curve of time"—Grazia Livi, "Interview with Ezra Pound," *Epoca*, Milan, 24 March 1963, translated by Jean McClean in *City Lights Journal*, Number Two, San Francisco 1964. In "Patria Mia" VI, 10 October 1912: "One wants to find out what sort of things endure, and what sort of things are transient; what sort of thing recur; what propagandas profit a man or his race; to learn upon what arc are the forces, constructive and dispersive, of social order, move; to learn what rules and axioms hold firm and what sort fade, and what sort are durable but permutable, what sort hold in letter, and what sort by analogy only, what sort by close analogy, and what sort by rough parallel alone." The word "arc" has been omitted ever since 1912, probably by mistake. The omission obscures Pound's conception of eras as "curves of time" and as expressions of the Calendar cycle.

5. To George Santayana, 8 December 1939, *Letters.*

6. To T. S. Eliot, 18 January 1940, Collection at Yale.

7. To Santayana, ibid.

of "Purgatorio." He would continue composing by decads—"have 72/81 to think of."[8] Such composition, drawing on the revision of '76 and the world paideumas via Adams's Testament, would make the Renaissance new according to the design of the bill of lading, which condenses decads into a Seal/ Calendar form for building horizontal slabs up to vertical columns. Building by the four phases of the bill of lading would subordinate and condense drafting.

Pound's simultaneous application and revision of the Declaration's revolutionary argument reconciled European and American revolution in the ritualized "ELEUSIS" and found correctives in the didactic "KUNG" and the equitable "JOHN ADAMS"; all seek in mutual independence a basis for reconciliation on new paideumatic principles. Consummation of the first phase with a prayer to Zeus, god of all men, stresses this conciliatory side of "We must, therefore, acquiesce in the necessity which denounces our separation, and hold them, as we hold the rest of mankind, enemies in war, in peace, friends." When Pound finished his first phase war had not yet broken out; he assumed that the argument evolved in his poem might prevent it by directing "the opinions of mankind" against Geryon and Usura in behalf of a world accord on foundations free of their tyranny. So, "1918 Began investigation of causes of war, to oppose same" and "1939 first visit to U.S. since 1910 in endeavour to stave off war"[9] frame a "better tradition" that had qualified its initiate to be a demonstrator of self-evident truths and a declarer of causes to those responsible for the opinions and well-being of mankind. So enlightened, a world mind would be open to evolution in the spirits "ELEUSIS," "KUNG," and "JOHN ADAMS" as Pound's poem had discovered them.

His effort failing, he separated at the outbreak of war in Europe according to the declaration "We, therefore, the representatives of the United States of America, in general Congress assembled, appealing to the Supreme Judge of the world for the rectitude of our intentions, do, in the name, and by the authority of the good people of these colonies, solemnly publish and declare, that these united colonies are, and of right ought to be, free and independent states." Like his predecessor Adams he had to carry out the revolutionary struggle for which he had become a personal medium during war, not on two continents only but in the whole world. His method was less diplomatic, like Adams's, than polemical, like the penman Tom Paine's—by essays, pamphlets, books, and Confucian translations in Italy, and by radio to England and America. His personal struggle evolved through four phases of World War II and resulted in two false starts on the next draft of *Cantos*. The first phase, beginning with the end of *LXXI Cantos* and the outbreak of war in 1939, ran to America's entry in December 1941. The second ran to the fall of Mussolini in July 1943 and Italy's surrender in September. The third com-

8. To Henry Swabey, 1 August 1939, Collection at Yale.
9. "Autobiography," *Selected Poems* 1949.

prised Pound's efforts to contribute to the founding of the nazi-sponsored
north Italian Repubblica di Salò under a liberated Mussolini, from early 1944
until the collapse of Italy and Germany in late April 1945. The struggle
culminates and is reflected in *The Pisan Cantos*, which begins with the execution of Mussolini in April 1945 and runs during Pound's imprisonment at Pisa
(May to November) through the end of world war in August and on into the
subsequent peace conferences. The overall pattern is the same as that begun in
1760 and passing through Lexington and 1776 to the peace conference of
1783.

Having since 1930 carried on "continual polemic in two languages,"[10] first
literary and cultural, then economic, in 1939 Pound expanded the Italian side
in *Il Meridiano di Roma*, a literary and political weekly. He began contributing before his trip to America "to stave off war" and after his return
contributed regularly until Mussolini fell and Italy surrendered. To prepare for
a new phase of his poem he began new translations of Confucius, now taking
account of ideogram. With the coming of war a new medium entered: radio.
Having shown a growing awareness of radio communication and radio style
for a number of years, he now saw it as an opportunity for continuing his
polemic in the only medium which could maintain contact with his own
language and with his necessary audience in England and America. Radio
was imperfect in the sense that he could not receive communication, for
which he excoriated the British and American governments. But radio polemics would complement polemics written for Italy in the spirit of Tom Paine.
His premise was "that free speech without free radio speech is as zero"
(*Pisan LXXIV*).[11]

By March 1940, before Italy entered the war, Pound had already begun to
broadcast over Rome Radio, directly to England but indirectly to America.[12]
He formulated the essential theme of all his World War II polemics, written
and spoken, in "Nego,"[13] an article later retitled "Carta di identità di Ezra
Pound: Nego" and used as an introduction to his collected essays from *Il*

10. Ibid.

11. Pound had used almost the same phrases in "The Damn Fool Bureaucrats," *New Masses*,
New York, June 1928. He wrote his father on 29 November 1924 (Collection at Yale): "As to
Cantos 18–19; there ain't no key. Simplest parallel I can give is radio where you tell who is
talking by the noise they make. If your copies are properly punctuated they shd. show where each
voice begins and ends. It is NOT a radio. You hear various people letting cats out of bags at
maximum speed. . . . Mostly things you 'oughtn't to know,' not if you are to be a good quiet
citizen."

12. The British Library of Information has recordings and transcriptions (Gallup B 50) but I
have not consulted them. The FCC began to monitor and transcribe just before Pearl Habor. Since
this writing Leonard Doob has edited from Pound's papers *"Ezra Pound Speaking": Radio
Speeches of World War II* (Westport, Conn.: 1978). In my view the FCC versions, though
incomplete and often mistranscribed, tell the story. They have served the purpose here.

13. *Giornale di Genova*, Genoa, 13 April 1940.

Meridiano.[14] "Nego" denies that the white people of Europe, Nordic or Mediterranean, are ready to give up to usurers, Jewish or Aryan, a nation's primitive right to control money and purchasing power. It warns that the term "Federal Union" is usurers' propaganda for a Europe different from "fascist total Europe"; all radio stations should concentrate against it. It challenges H. G. Wells's liberal "Rights of Man" with "Il diritto di non indebitarsi" (the right not to put oneself in debt), a kind of Poundian Eleventh Amendment.

At the same time as "Nego" he defined his role "As a writer" seeking outside America (as he had done in *The Cantos*, especially in "Jefferson-Nuevo Mundo" and "Siena-Leopoldine Reforms"), a living version of '76. In "Antifascisti,"[15] having criticized inertia within the fascist revolution, he signed himself modestly (I translate) "a Mazzini in search of a Cavour," with the qualification that Mazzini did not have the good sense to value Cavour as Pound could "in the light of the past." "The light of the past" is *LXXI Cantos*. Mazzini : Cavour :: Pound : Mussolini. Mussolini, supposed to be Jefferson revised or a new Adams, was to be subsumed in a revised Washington supported by a new Tom Paine. To explain Pound looked back to America's Manifest Destiny and even to "one who in 1770 wrote on Greek metric" (Otis). Now, Otis : Adams :: Pound : Mussolini. The Otis analogy continues through the growing plutocracy. Artists like Henry James, Whistler, Henry Adams, and Pound sought Europe simply to survive. A laboratory in which to analyze "usurocracy" did not exist. It was necessary to create one. Such is the mind of *The Cantos* and the poem itself, from Aristotle through Adams to date. Adams created the American system, which is still valuable and worth reviving. It is not the Italian system, but both are parts of the same historic process.

Suddenly, however, as the argument is bringing America and Italy together "nell'anno XVIII dell'Era *Nostra*," the analogy and the balance break down: "Il vostro problema è vostro (Duce B. M.), il mio è mio, god damn it, e non vedo che si possa finirlo in dieci minuti ne anni. Ma nel 1940 io so onorare la vostra rivoluzione, come nel 1840 Zobi seppe onorare la nostra, (dal 1776 al 1826 e continua) e con questo rimango vostro dev. mo etc. etc."[16] Frustration and exasperation are obvious. One suspects an intellectual crisis brought on

14. *Orientamenti* (Venice: 1944). He took the other part of the title from *Carta da Visita* (Rapallo: 1942), his introduction of himself to Italy as a pamphleteer who, after America had entered the war, decided that he would contribute to the Italian war effort.

15. *Meridiano di Roma*, 14 April 1940.

16. "Your problem is yours (Duce B.M.), and mine is mine, god damn it, and I don't see how it can be solved in ten minutes or years. But in 1940 I know how to honor your revolution, as in 1840 Zobi knew how to honor ours (from 1776 to 1826 and continuing) and with this I remain your most dvtd. etc. etc."

by the outbreak of the war that Italy was about to enter by declaring war on
crumbling France.

One may conjecture the sentiments of the oddly impersonal rehearsal of the
30 January 1933 meeting which made Mussolini the twentieth-century protagonist (cf. *XLI*): "In the year XI E. F. to a high personage who asked me:
'What do you want?' I answered: 'Peace, to finish my poem.' " He almost
apologized for his preoccupation with art: "Today I am seven years older; I
haven't remained in that shell. The poem goes forward and I have more
mature desires, to raise myself to which I have had a not alien example.
[Dante?] No American from 1900 to 1910 imagined the possibility of a world
not dominated by fat and dirty plutocracy, by mercantilist vulgarity and by the
swinish power of gold. I have gone to school for 32 years in Europe, of which
the last sixteen have been the most, let us say, interesting." As for the poem,
he asked "the critics of the drawing-rooms" not to think that he found "the
cantos of the 'Paradiso' unworthy of human attention." Pound seems to have
had to screw up his will in order to reconcile reaffirmation of his political
choice, the war, and postponement of the "Paradiso" at whose threshold he
thought his poem had arrived. The struggle and conflict find their place in
Pisan. Mussolini's challenge and Pound's answer are postponed to *Section:
Rock-Drill*.

As to the analogy between '76 and fascism, Pound would go on in his
writings and in his broadcasts to link the culmination of the Declaration's
theory of revolution, "it is their right, it is their duty, to throw off such [read
"usurist"] government and to provide new guards for their future security,"
with Mussolini's "Liberty is not a right but a duty" and with economic
"autarchy" joined to Renaissance individualism. "Fascist total Europe" was
repeating the thirteen colonies' confederation to resist England. British colonial policy appears to have been born with the Bank of England in 1694 (cf.
XLVI) and to have precipitated the Revolution by suppressing Pennsylvania
paper money in 1750. Current British usury had captured American policy:
the Atlantic Charter and the exchange of American destroyers for British
bases had made England actually and America potentially a machine for
imposing colonialism's heir, imperialism, first on the old continent and ultimately on the world. It was one of a series of "repeats in history."

To this first phase belongs the first start of what became *Pisan*, "Canto
Proceeding (72 Circa)"[17] and "Lines to go into Canto 72 or somewhere."[18]
Coming out of *LXXI Cantos* and as yet undisturbed by events, both were
composed before the entries of Russia, Japan, and America made a second
world war more universal, absolute, and wholly revolutionary than the first,
and before the broadcasts had turned from diatribe to vituperation. The frag-

17. *Vice Versa*, New York, January 1942.
18. To Katue Kitasono, 12 March 1941, *Letters*.

ments were witheld from the poem until being added under *Fragments of Cantos* (1968) as "Addendum for *Canto C*" dated "Circa 1941," indications that they are vestiges of the 100-canto alternative just as the other *Fragments*, "Notes for *Canto CXVII* et seq.," signify failure of the 120-canto recourse. The complementary themes of the two fragments are tradition and nature. First, realizing prophecy, a diatribe looks back on the villain of "money in history," neschek (*LII*), in a tone now more elegiac and mythic than angry; an invocation from "the labyrinth" to Aphrodite as pure light, crystal, and clarity looks ahead to a new mode. In the new mode, second, inspired epiphany finds a "paradiso terrestre" in the Rapallo landscape; almost all its images will appear in *Pisan*; the letter from which the fragment was recovered comments "All of which shows that I am not wholly absorbed in saving Europe by economics." The fragments can plausibly be regarded as relics of an intended peaceful struggle pointing toward the 100-canto consummation of which they serve now as retrospective reminders.

Meanwhile the life and thought that had evolved out of 1939 and out of *LXXI Cantos* was pouring into "Europe calling, E. P. speaking," a voice that would find itself properly in *Pisan*. Pound later claimed of the broadcasts made both before and after Pearl Harbor: "1940 after continued opposition obtained permission to use Rome Radio for personal propaganda in support of U.S. Constitution, continuing after America's official entry into the war only on condition that he should never be asked to say anything contrary to his conscience or contrary to his duties as an American Citizen. Which promise was faithfully observed by the Italian government."[19] The theme of struggle gives a coherent motive both to the broadcasts and to the prose polemics addressed to Italy. But this tone is misleading. It is overwhelmed by blatant support of the Rome-Berlin axis and of Mussolini and Hitler; by vituperation against England and Churchill, America and Roosevelt, Russia and Stalin; by virulent attacks on alleged international usury colored with a fanatical animus against Jewry—against "kikery," "Judiocracy," and the perverted freemasonry revealed in and responsible for the notorious *Protocols of the Learned Elders of Zion*.

Still, along with speech of the bourgeois gutter (Pound later regretted the anti-Semitism as a "suburban prejudice" derived from his upbringing in the 1890s), and along with a mind distorted by an obsession, the wracked mind of a man of goodwill remains dedicated to justice precisely because he had elevated the American ideal into an epic vocation. Pound had become the creature of what he took, during a crisis partly chosen, partly fallen into, and partly imposed upon him, to be right and justice. He never repudiated the episode or the error. Doing so would have precluded expression of "The enormous tragedy of the dream," if not "in the peasant's bent shoulders"

19. "Autobiography," *Selected Poems* 1949.

then surely in his own person. It would also have violated the integrity of the poem whose medium he was. Instead he incorporated the episode along with other elements and other realizations.

The first phase of World War II passed into the second with the attack on Pearl Harbor. Pound's risks increased and he knew it. After a broadcast on 7 December, still directed more toward England than America, he fell silent. Apparently the crisis undergone in 1940 recurred. He returned on 29 January 1942 with an elaborate introduction designed to assure legality under a Constitution that did or should allow revolutionary activity: "The Italian Radio, acting in accordance with the Fascist policy of intellectual freedom and free expression of opinion by those who are qualified to hold it, following the tradition of Italian hospitality have offered Dr. Ezra Pound the use of the microphone twice a week. It is understood that he will not be asked to say anything whatsoever that goes against his conscience, or anything incompatible with his duties as a citizen of the United States of America." In his talk on 29 January he explained that after 7 December he had retired to Rapallo "to seek wisdom of the ancients."[20] He spent a month trying to "figure things out," "to make up my mind about some things." He had a perfectly good alibi if he wanted to play things safe, that he was "officially occupied" with a new translation of Confucius. But he defined his duty as an American citizen by the fact that the United States had been illegally at war for months because of "the criminal acts of a President whose mental condition was not, so far as I could see, all that could or should be desired of a man in so responsible a position or office." Roosevelt had broken his promises to the electorate and violated both the presidential oath of office and "the oath even the ordinary American citizen is expected to take every time he gets a new passport."

Confucius and Mencius had both been up against similar problems, both had seen empires fall, both "had seen deeper into the causes of human confusion" than most men ever think of looking. Despite his need to compare the terminologies of Chinese and Greek philosophy, and both to the terminology of medieval Catholic philosophy "to keep my own work in progress progressing" (cf. the coming synthesis of world paideumas), he decided that a complete break in "self communication" between "the calm and men of the Jewish hemisphere" was not to be desired. The "calm" is the mind of *The Cantos*.

Not only his Italian polemics but also the broadcasts make it clear that his seemingly insane activities and monumental egoism were directed by his deliberate effort to live inside the revolution of '76 while bringing his American heritage to the Italian (or Eleusinian) struggle. He was "still fighting the Revolutionary War . . . at odd moments" (14 March 1943). Jefferson writing

20. This and the following quotations are from the FCC transcriptions.

to Madison that the French constitution, then being drafted, ought to limit
debt on the principle that "the earth belongs to the living," elicited for
his own effort "to think out a sane state" (27 April 1943). "It is much
easier . . . to conceive a state wherein all men are slaves, and no man has any
right for whatever life and liberty and where even pursuit—marvelous phrase
that pursuit of happiness—would be illegal, or at least regarded as a grave
misdemeanor." On 1 June he accused America of having betrayed the national founders by not using the machinery they set up. "You have not kept
the Constitution in force. You have not developed it according to its own
internal law. You have not made use of the machinery provided in the Constitution itself to keep the American government modern. The main protection
of a whole people is in the clause of our Congress issuing money. But that is
not the whole of the Constitution. There is nothing in it to prevent an adjust-
ment of or progress from local articulation, [or] administration divided by
geographic divisions, [to] articulation by trade and professional organizations." On 25 May he had said that if adopted the corporate state would
improve his representation by "both articulations," viz., as a member of a
"confederation of artists and professional men" and as a "citizen of Mont-
gomery County." "Its own internal law" suggests Branches and Powers
in their mutual relations. "Articulation" suggests "THE STATE SHOULD
MOVE LIKE A DANCE," Pound's poetic idea of a body politic.

Pound was in Rome in September 1943 when the Badoglio government
capitulated to the Allies. Unable to get back to Rapallo he walked most of the
way to Gais in the Italian Tyrol where his daughter lived with her foster
parents. From there he made his way back to Rapallo and threw himself into
the fascist revolution continued under a restored Mussolini through the Fascist
Socialist Republic established in North Italy under Nazi sponsorship; this
would be "the Republic . . . dreamed" in the pamphlets and in *Pisan*.

In one sense Pound had to start all over again after Mussolini's fall. But,
given the opportunity of a new republic in process of being formed, he
sustained thematic and formal continuity. His principal publications during
1944–45 were Confucian translations; the pamphlets *L'America, Roosevelt
e Le Cause della Guerra Presente, Oro e Lavoro*, and *Introduzione alla
Natura Economica degli S.U.A.* (Stati Uniti dell'America); his essays from *Il
Meridiano* collected as *Orientamenti*; and *Jefferson e Mussolini*, an Italian
revision of his 1933–35 correlation. He also published in a number of small
northern papers, regularly in the rabid *Il Popolo di Allesandria*, as one of the
"Scrittori di Tigullio." Mixed with inflammatory notes that fit the general
tone of the paper were also notes and quotations from Confucius. (It has been
reported that some of Pound's Italian friends could forgive him everything but
contributing to *Il Popolo*.)

During the Salò effort Pound wrote and sent to Mussolini, in Italian, new
versions of *Cantos LXXII* and *LXXIII*, with the proffer "Duce, my talent is at

your service. I hope at least Canto 73 can be of use.''[21] In Canto *LXXII*
various figures from Italian history, past and present, justify Pound's use of
poetry instead of enlistment to rally the latter Italian war effort. Canto *LXXIII*
poetizes melodramatically a patriotic martyrdom earned at Malatesta's Rimini
and praised by Guido Cavalcanti. Neither of these tasteless effusions is relevant to the tone of *Pisan*. Both are blessedly omitted, leaving a noteworthy
hiatus for this particular episode of the personal struggle. The hiatus reflects
definitively the shift from 100 to 120 cantoes; it is otherwise filled, as will be
seen, by adjustments in the ultimate *LXXIV* and *LXXVI*.

The fourth and last phase of World War II, as far as Pound and his poem
were concerned, was the final collapse of "the effort" since 1922 to realize
the historical corporate state, and the execution of the historical protagonist
and "nuova persona" Mussolini. Pound himself was taken from his Rapallo
residence in May 1945 by partigiani and turned over to American authorities, who remanded him under indictment for treason to the Pisan Disciplinary
Training Center (DTC). After his health broke down from solitary confinement in the "gorilla cage" under exposure to the elements and he had recovered in the camp hospital, he wrote *The Pisan Cantos*. Deprived of libraries
for the first and only time during his work in progress, he had to rely on his
memory and on his immediate environment. But tradition remembered, personal memory, nature, and personal epiphany had already been prepared by
the epitome for *Pisan*, *VII*. The poem was ready to accommodate either
historical success or historical debacle while its argument, its motives, its
forms, and its ends continued. It simply moved into "the stillness outlasting
all wars" and into "the timeless air" where passage through a nightmare of
history could be reflected by passage through a dark night of the soul. As
Pound wrote to the Base Censor of the DTC, disclaiming cipher or intended
obscurity, "The form of the poem and main progress is conditioned by its
own inner shape, but the life of the D.T.C. passing OUTSIDE the scheme"
(he might have added the contemporary history beyond the barbed wire)
"cannot but impinge, or break into the main flow."[22]

Pound had long since prepared a mythic background or "Paideuma" for
transforming prophetic revolutionary tradition formed in the mind into a
struggle carried out in the mind (and heart). He would consummate and
synthesize the three world paideumas through the phase of personal struggle
in the mode of a "New Paideuma," which he saw emerging frm the tyranny
and chaos of modern history. Pound took the term "Paideuma" from the
German anthropologist Leo Frobenius, who had evolved from his field studies

21. These versions and the proffer were discovered by Professor Daniel Susmel among papers
of Mussolini seized by the U.S. Government. The Pound family published them in Washington in
1973 to secure copyright.
22. "Ezra Pound: A Prison Letter," *Paris Review* 28.

of African cultures a theory of the rise and fall of cultures analogous to the four ages Creative Childhood, Youth, Maturity, and Old Age.[23] Frobenius's scientific handling of the origins of myth and magic rationalized for Pound his own youthful view that the powers of the mind and of poetry could help "cure" or "resanitize" the ills of culture and change the world.

By 1938, in "For a New Paideuma," Pound defined paideuma not as "Zeitgeist or Time spirit," which "might be taken to include passive attitudes and aptitudes of an era," but as "the active elements in the era, the complex of ideas which is in a given time germinal, reaching into the next epoch, but conditioning actively all the thought and action of its own time."[24] Elsewhere he added to an epoch "un popolo" (a people) and to an impersonal "complex of ideas" the personal challenge "One can die of it, or one can collaborate and adjoin a force of one's own will to this complex."[25] In "For a New Paideuma" Pound elaborated that Frobenius has "left the term with major implications in the unconscious (if I understand him aright)," but did not think the anthropologist would "necessarily limit it to the unconscious or claim that the conscious *individual* can have no effect in shaping the paideuma, or at least the next paideuma." He took it that " 'the indifferent have never made history'." Paideuma, conversely, does.[26]

In going back to the unconscious in the individual Pound was, like Frobenius, going back to the collective racial myths of prehistory and to its magical view of the world. Pound's early poetry abounds in "states of mind" attributed to the inspiration which precedes poetry, an individual analogue to the mythic perceptions which precede history. These take the form of metamorphoses, of inspired prophecies, of "the vision" of Platonism or Neo-Platonism and of the effort to "gather the Limbs of Osiris." "Psychology and Troubadours"[27] turned into mythic archetypes *The Spirit of Romance: An Attempt to Define Somewhat the Charm of the Pre-Renaissance Literature of Latin Europe* (1910). A complement to "Imagism," mythified individual perception, was Jules Romains's "Unanimisme," a myth of the psychological

23. "Pound and Frobenius" are treated by Guy Davenport in *Motive and Method in The Cantos of Ezra Pound*, English Institute Essays, ed. Lewis Leary (New York: Columbia University Press), pages 33–59. On the stages, see below.

24. "For a New Paideuma," *Criterion*, London, January 1938.

25. "Significato di Leo Frobenius," *Broletto*, Como, April 1938. For Pound's Italian writings I give the title in Italian and then translate when quoting.

26. Pound set Frobenian paideuma against "Freud, or Freudianism," which is not a "culture" but a "pathology . . . devoted to taking or trying to take something *out* of a diseased or infirm mind. Fascist culture is at the opposite pole; its system is to put something *into* the mind; a battery, a nutriment. It seeks not to combat a particular malady but to produce a state of health impermeable to disease" ("Totalitarian Scholarship and the New Paideuma," *Germany and You*, Berlin, 25 April 1937).

27. *Quest*, London, October 1912. In *Prolegomena 2* (1932), a vestige of a planned "Complete Prose Works," it was added as Chapter V to *The Spirit of Romance*.

forces latent in the modern urban crowd.[28] "Vorticism" pushed his own lyric poetry into the archetypal "In a Station of the Metro"; he selected as the focal Vorticist manifesto the sculptor Gaudier-Brzeska's "Vortex," which went back to prehistoric origins of sculpture and carried mythic spirits through peoples and epochs to the moderns.[29] He reviewed enthusiastically the books of Allen Upward on Christianity as divine revolution[30] and on mythic interpretations of language[31]; Upward's imitations from the Chinese and translations of Confucius prepared Pound for the Fenollosa papers.[32] Out of Fenollosa, received in late 1913, came Pound's own Chinese translations, *Cathay* (1915) and the Noh plays (1915–1917),[33] and his sponsorship of Fenollosa's "The Chinese Written Character as a Medium for Poetry,"[34] which by corroborating and enriching (mythifying) Pound's Imagism and Vorticism laid the grounds for the "natural language" of *The Cantos*.

At a meeting of the Aristotelian Society during the 1910's when the Neo-Platonist G. R. S. Mead, the "old man" who with Yeats ("Lusty Juventus") explains his Neo-Platonism in *XXIX*, wondered what Pound was doing there, T. S. Eliot replied, "Oh, he's not here as a philosopher. He is here as an *an thro pologist.*"[35] Pound's interest in modern scientific anthropology began to surface through his association during 1930–1931 with the journal *L'Indice*, Genova. For his page "Affari Esteri" he introduced "Romains Parla di Se Stesso" with the note "A live group existed in Paris from 1910 to 1912 and the livest was Romains, who promulgated 'Unanimism'."[36] He introduced "Bruhl e i selvaggi: Les fonctions mentales dans les sociétés inferieures"

> (These essays of Levy-Bruhl, and others by divers authors to be presented later (Fenollosa, Frobenius and also Hudson) have a bearing on the problems of "language," and are not chosen for the general aim of chatting about philosophy at large.)[37]

28. "Monsieur Romains, Unanimist," "The Approach to Paris" III, *New Age*, London, 18 September 1913.

29. "Vorticism," *Fortnightly Review*, London, 1 September 1914. "Vortex" in *Gaudier-Brzeska: A Memoir*, 1916, and later in *Guide To Kulchur*, 1938.

30. A review of *The Divine Mystery: A Reading of the History of Christianity Down to the Time of Christ* (sic) (London: 1913), in *New Freewoman*, London, 15 November 1913.

31. A retrospective review of *The New Word: An Open Letter addressed to the Swedish Academy in Stockholm on the meaning of the word IDEALIST*, 1907.

32. Upward began publishing on Chinese in 1900; he contributed many adaptations and translations to *The New Freewoman*, *The Egoist*, and *Poetry* (Chicago) during 1913–14, with and through Pound. In 1937 Pound guessed himself to be "the sole reader of all Upward's books, now surviving." To Michael Roberts, July 1937, *Letters*.

33. *'Noh,' or Accomplishment: A Study of the Classical Stage of Japan*, by Ernest Fenollosa and Ezra Pound, 1917.

34. *Little Review*, New York, September, October, November, December 1932.

35. To George Santayana, 8 December 1939, *Letters*.

36. *L'Indice*, 25 June 1931.

37. *L'Indice*, 30 July 1931. Pound's letters of the 1930s associate Frobenius and Fenollosa.

He had more to say in "Nota preliminare" to a longer extract from Frobenius, "Miti dei Primitivi."[38] Frobenius's challenge is "But what is their 'Weltanschauung?'," which Pound translates "What is the disposition of their sensibility toward the world?" Frobenius does much more than ask about a certain "stato di animo" or discuss an "idea." He discusses "the survival of totemistic ideas in the mind already invaded by the solar disposition of the sensibility." Elsewhere he discusses tendencies among agricultural peoples, who are disposed to consider space as a closed edifice, in contrast with those of nomadic peoples who feel it open and extended. Another fundamental contrast is that between peoples disposed to create material splendors and individuals ragged in appearance but hiding under the most sordid rags a formidable culture: "A dirty arab, full of botanical science"; "Throughout Africa here and there relics and fragments of Byzantium, of medieval chivalry, etc. etc." Pound elaborated his interest in local spirit of place in "Terra Italica"[39] and used Frobenian perception in *Jefferson and/or Mussolini*[40] to evaluate the health or decadence of cultures (with particular reference to the index of usury) by their art forms.

In 1936, in *The New English Weekly*, London, to which Pound was a regular contributor, a collaborator with Frobenius and with Pound, Douglas Fox, probably at Pound's instigation, published "Frobenius's Paideuma as a Philosophy of Culture" I–VI.[41] Fox's rubrics were "The Dominants Time and Space" (I), which led into an epistemology of sudden seizure or epiphany á la myth or á la Imagism (II); "Mysticism and Magic as the expression of the Dominants, Space and Time" (III); "The Meaning of 'World History'"

E.g., to T. S. Eliot, 1 February 1940, *Letters*:

> There is, so far as I know, no English work on Kulturmorphologie, transformation of cultures. Can't use a German term at this moment. Morphology of cultures. Historic process taken in the larger.
>
> I know you jib at China and Frobenius cause they ain't pie church; and neither of us likes savages, black habits, etc. However, for yr. enlightenment, Frazer worked largely from documents. Frob. went to *things*, memories still in the spoken tradition, etc. His students had to *see* and be able to draw objects. All of which follows up Fabre *and* the Fenollosa "Essay on Written Character." . . .
>
> Not that I shd. claim to get on from where Frobenius left off, in that his Morphology was applied to savages and my interest is in civilizations at their *most*.

"Civilizations at their most" describes the paideumas "ELEUSIS," "KUNG," and "JOHN ADAMS." "Memories still in the spoken tradition" applies to their transformation and synthesis in *Pisan*.

38. *L'Indice*, 25 July (I. Times and Forms of culture, II. Essence and development of mythological figures), and 10 November 1931 (3. A critique of the old vision of the world, 4. The common bases of all the mythologies, 5. The myths of the diverse regions, 6. The three modes for considering method).

39. *New Review*, Paris, Winter 1931/1932.

40. *Jefferson and/or Mussolini*, 1933/35, Chapters XIII, XXII, XXVII.

41. *New English Weekly*, London, 10, 17, 24 September and 1, 8, 15 October 1936.

and "Sun and Moon as Tutors of the Irrational" (IV); "The Birth of Destiny" and "The Birth of the State" (V); and "The High Religions, Summary" (VI). Pound probably collaborated. A table of accruing steps relating four "Paideumatic Stages of the High Cultures" to four ages of man and building "ply over ply" by metamorphosis of accruing "mass relations" has the same form as do the phases in *The Cantos* (see figure below). They illustrate Pound's use of the Pythagorean tetraktys.[42] Fox cites Fenollosa and explains epiphanic seizure by sun and moon and number (IV). In the manner of Pound's "halves of a seal," most succinctly imaged in the Seal/Calendar arcanum at the end of *Rock-Drill 88*, sun and moon provide two polar mythologies which permeate and fructify each other to produce something new (V). Finally (VI), it is paideumatic law that all temporal growth is connected with a movement

THE PAIDEUMATIC STAGES OF THE HIGH CULTURES

1	2	3	4
			MATERIALIZATION (Old Age) Predominance of spatial tendencies, world economics, specialization, Machine Age, man "ruler of future."
		HIGH PHILOSOPHY (Maturity) Logic, common sense, emphatic "I" feeling, man has become a critical *subject* of existence.	Philosophy articulated, no philosophy obligating, "History of Philosophy," demetaphysication of thought, "the free spirit," lack of connexion.
	HIGH RELIGION (Youth) Anastrophe, man as the son of God, favoured object of creation, highest transcendentalism.	Religion articulated, state church, division of creeds, formation of sects, separation of art from religion.	Religion utilized, Bible criticism, liberal theology, religion a decoration for political ends, art "for this world," l'art pour l'art.
HIGH MYTHOLOGY (Creative Childhood) Spontaneity and isolation, "we" feeling man as "Objekt des Geschehens," estate as "idea," nothing profane.	Mythology, articulated, the profane enters the State, state for the utilization of power.	Mythology utilized (as a subject for artistic representation), state as a system of order.	Mythology worn out (material for scientific research), democracy the ideal of the weak state, state of social service, private means and political parties.

42. See the discussion of "gnomonic growth" and Pythagoreanism in "The Mathematical Symbolism," pp. 29–33 and 39–41.

through space; thus geographical shift is necessary for the development of cultures; thus too the need for actual or imaginative traveling.

Fox closes with a motto of Frobenius from Goethe: "though the world as a whole progresses" (more strictly "moves," Fox comments) "youth must ever begin at the beginning and, as an individual, go through the epochs of world culture for itself." In *The Cantos* Pound begins at both ends (Frobenius's Materialization and Old Age, High Mythology and Youth) and seeks to reinstill the old cultures with the spirits of their origins. The desired result of a simultaneous descent (into the past) and ascent (into the future) is a consummation, a fusion, and a focus which makes new and keeps alive all phases of the historic process. To do so is to live at once historically and mythically, or as if divinely.

In 1936 Pound extended his adaptation of Fenollosa's "Chinese Written Character" as an *ars poetica* for world poetry by digging into the theory and practice of ideogram; in "Notes by a Very Ignorant Man" appended to a new "Ideogramic Series" edition[43] he began his practice of reading ideograms more personally and mythically than lexically and linguistically. He also began his custom of laying them out in lines, columns, and tables for special symbolic visual meanings and effects, a version of what he had long been calling "the ideogramic method" (more on this below).

"Totalitarian Scholarship and the New Paideuma,"[44] written by Pound and "Edited by Douglas Fox," found Frobenian symptoms of a new paideuma in the Vorticist art of the 1910s and rejected Spengler's gloomy theory (also derived from Frobenius) of the decline of the West. Pound asserted "most positively the mutual need of the different racial vigours in our Paideuma" and "absolutely the need of a new methodology" (like Frobenius's field research and his own ideogramic method).

> I assert most positively that we must PUT OFF the vanity of weak races which dare not separate their true donation to mind and thought from their secondary donations.
>
> To World Literature each nation can give its valid part and receive in turn the primal and valid donations of the other races. Italy can give its Cavalcanti and Dante, but must not ask us to accept a trail of inferior writers without worn reputations.

As to Time and Space, "A man lives in his own time: present, past, or, in the case of genius, even in tomorrow. For international Verkehr tomorrow is as good a sportsfield as we can choose."

"The Jefferson-Adams Correspondence"[45] measured the level of civiliza-

43. *The Chinese Written Character*, by Ernest Fenollosa, An Ars Poetic with a Foreword and Notes by Ezra Pound, "Ideogramic Series" (London: 1936), pp. 39–52.

44. *Germany and You*, Berlin, 1937.

45. *North American Review*, New York, Winter 1937/38; revised as "The Jefferson-Adams

tion in America during their lifetime by the paideuma from which it had emerged, "ELEUSIS," and by Frobenian standards. At the same time he added squibs on different forms of government which had arisen from different peoples and paideumas and so were native to them and only limitedly exportable.[46] (He hoped, however, that all nations and cultures were evolving toward some form of the anti-usurist corporate state.)

Among Pound's canonical prose books deployed as focal glosses for phases of *The Cantos*—*The Spirit of Romance* (1910) to *Make It New* (1934) and *Polite Essays* (1937) gloss "ELEUSIS" (and the first phase); *Impact: Essays on Ignorance and the Decline of American Civilization* (1960) glosses "JOHN ADAMS" (and the third phase)—*Guide To Kulchur* (1938) and Pound's version of the Confucian four books[47] gloss "KUNG" (and the second phase, *Pisan*). Thus *Guide To Kulchur* is Pound's most personal book, keyed by his "Digest of the Analects, that is, of the Philosophic Conversations" into the "one principle" text on its first page, the ideograms *i i kuan chin*. Pound finds in the ideograms an analogy to his own "one" tradition remade "by" himself and "passing through" transformation into symbol until the whole "emerges" live and fructive:

> In the "ONE PRINCIPLE" text we have four common signs: *one, by, passing through, emerging.* . . . The second sign is said to be the reverse of fixed, or stopped, in the third sign we have the string passing through the holes in the coins, in the fourth we have the earth, the stem and the leaf.[48]

In "Zweck or the Aim" Frobenian "New Paideuma" is defined as in "For a New Paideuma" and sealed with Kung's "first principle of government," ideogramic "CH'ING MING," the right or exact word.[49] In "KUNG" "Kung is modern in his interest in folk-lore. All this Frazer-Frobenius research is Confucian." "THE LESSON of Chinese History" is "recurrence" of beneficent dynasties by a return to Confucianism (see "KUNG" *LII–LXI*). "Recurrence" is different from "innovation," which is to be found in "the U.S. Constitution" (see "JOHN ADAMS"). The lessons of the paideumas are

---

Correspondence as a Shrine and a Monument," *Impact: Essays on Ignorance and the Decline of American Civilization*, 1960.

46. Chief instances are "Race," *New English Weekly*, London, 18 October 1936; "Our Own Form of Government," dated 1936 but not published until *Impact* (1960); "The Jefferson-Adams Correspondence" (written in 1936); and "National Culture: A Manifesto" (1938), presumably written in conjunction with Pound's joining the National Institute of Arts and Letters to rouse it to his "endeavour to stave off war," but not published until *Impact*.

47. Pound began publishing translations of Confucius in 1928, but the definitive canon is constituted of *Ta Hsio: The Great Digest* (1948, 1951); of *Lun Yu, Confucian Analects* (1951); of *Chung Yung, The Unwobbling Pivot* (1948, 1951); and of *Shih Ching, The Odes, The Classic Anthology Defined by Confucius* (1954).

48. *Guide To Kulchur*, Chapter 1.

49. Ibid., Chapter 5, pp. 57–59.

available now ''(1938)'' for an intended synthesis of world paideuma for a world corporate state.[50]

The manifesto ''For a New Paideuma,'' already cited, sums up the foregoing with emphasis on the Chinese component of a world culture. ''Significato di Leo Frobenius''[51] stressed Frobenius's having shown that ''when art is sick the illness isn't there only. It can be the revolt of a superior man against whatever conditions, or the submission of a weak and unconscious man to given contingencies, but it shows the state of mind (and body) circumstanding and inhering.'' ''Il Geheimrat'' Frobenius had created a whole education of perception and thus revealed ''a fountain of miracles'' of insight and intuition. He had revealed ''the crisis *of* and not *in* the system.'' ''And to us, who have not the benefit of his instruction, he furnishes collateral for the new totalitarian philosophy. The totalitarian state creates from it, but in the state there are elements active and elements sluggish or only passive (bromides).'' More important Frobenius offers ''the instruments for totalitarian researches and a great part of a method for the intelligent study of history. Beginning with the primitives, who alone conserve today the keys of the distant past which serve to open for us cultural elements fostered in the most advanced civilizations, his system would serve for the study of all history.''

Pound found too in the Frobenian drawings of primitive rock painting his own method of ''palimpsest'' or ''ply over ply'' (cf. ''Paideumatic Stages of the High Cultures''). He illustrated it with a cave painting from the ''Grottoes at Makumba (Southern Rhodesia) Rock Drawings,'' ''Strata ply over ply'' and ''designs divided into divers strata.'' A concluding footnote called attention to *African Genesis*, newly published by Frobenius and Fox, a collection of African fables more simple than Aesop's, often without obvious moral but sometimes carrying a moral ''profound as the process of nature herself.''

Close scrutiny of the 1936 ''Chinese Written Character'' will show, I think, that a poem (''ONE'') and tables of columns, sections, and columns culminating (again) in poetic lines are working out patterns derived from ''ONE'' in four phases and designed to analogize cultures paideumatically. An ideogramic axis with a meaning allied to the text but also integral in itself runs through ''Mang Tsze (The Ethics of Mencius).''[52] This axis anticipates the axis begun with tail-feathers in the ''Rays ideogram''-frontispiece of ''KUNG'' and ''JOHN ADAMS''. All these anticipate an interpretive ''Ideogrammario'' at the end of *Confucio: Ta S'eu Dai Gaku Studio Integrale* (Rapallo 1942) and an interpretive ''Terminology'' preceding *Ta Hsio: The Great Digest* (1948, 1951). All prepare for the functional ideograms of *Pisan* focused by ''Canto 77 Explication 1–10'' and of *Los Cantares* focused by the ''rock-drill'' of *85* and by the Seal/Calendar arcanum of *88*.

50. Ibid., Chapter 49, pp. 272–75.

51. *Broletto*, Como, April 1938.

52. *Criterion*, London, July 1938.

In "Orientamenti"[53] (which would become the title for his collected Italian writings in *Il Meridiano di Roma*, 1939–1943) Pound applied the ideogramic method in "four chapters" of a single ideogram. The first cited symptoms of "new Paideuma" in the novelistic diagnoses of nineteenth-century society, which had perfected itself in the *avant garde* art of the new century. Second was Homer's preoccupation with the means of life—how Odysseus could eat on his raft and how his swine were preserved—and Dante's and Shakespeare's moral preoccupation with ethics and economic justice. Third, there had been two great founts of millennial civilization, *"Roma"* (for Pound a sacred concept—see below) and the Chinese empire; between had stretched a zone tartar and barbarian, which impeded communication between the great civilizing centers of Asia and Europe. Fourth, every time a durable dynasty established itself in China, it based itself on the sanities, the honesties, codified and meditated by Confucius. Pound also touched a keynote of the coming *Pisan*, "Le Paradis n'est pas artificiel," in the basis of his "pragmatic idealism": *"when* the idea is complete, it enters into action. The imperfect (immature) remains in the shell of the 'private world.' The great genius does not create a 'paradiso artificiale' but a world that will come, that will exteriorize itself with more or less velocity."

On 7 August 1939, after having completed in *The Cantos* the three paideumas "ELEUSIS," "KUNG," and "JOHN ADAMS" with the assumption that he had provided materials for a "New Paideuma," and after having returned from a trip to America "in endeavour to stave off war" (he got as far as anti-Roosevelt senators and Secretary of Agriculture Henry Wallace), Pound threw together as if "on sudden emergency" what he took to be the crucial elements of a "European Paideuma" and sent them to Fox in Germany in hopes of having them published there. They were not. The scrawled manuscript (in the form of a letter) is at the Humanities Center at the University of Texas in Austin.

In 1938 or 1939, probably in conjunction with "Significato di Leo Frobenius" and "European Paideuma," Pound prepared and sent to Fox, presumably to be published in Germany, a mythic background for transforming prophetic revolutionary tradition formed in the mind into personal struggle carried out in the mind (and heart). Behind his polemics of 1939–1945, for a projected phase of struggle in *The Cantos*, lies the unpublished paideumatic parable and neo-mythic manifesto "ORIGO."[54] "ORIGO" focuses all Pound's anthropological studies and paideumatic writings into and through a fragment of earliest epic poetry transmitted by word of mouth to Frobenius in Africa, *The Lute of Gassir*.[55] A tale of passage from a warrior culture to

53. Venice, 1944–XXII.

54. At the Humanities Center of the University of Texas at Austin, published here by permission.

55. *The Lute of Gassire* appears in *African Genesis* by Leo Frobenius and Douglas Fox (New York: 1937). *Leo Frobenius: Il Liuto di Gassire, Legenda Africana con una nota di Ezra Pound,*

high civilization (cf. the *Iliad* to the *Odyssey*), it tells about an ideal city, Wagadu, lost through the vanity of a king's son who sacrificed everything for the immortality ascribed to song. By doing so, however, Gassir initiated an historical process whereby Wagadu, which exists in the human heart, would be finally fixed there never to be lost again. This manifesto of pure paideuma goes back behind all origins, including those of "ELEUSIS," "KUNG," and "JOHN ADAMS." Out of it, through a "stillness outlasting all wars" and "the timeless air," will come at Pisa a city "now in the heart indestructible."

Beginning with the hortatory refrain of *The Lute of Gassir* "ORIGO" puts into personal terms the well-known fugal form for the narrative of events which Pound sent his father in 1927: coming out of "Proposition #1" a three-part "Proof" modulates into a culminating fourth (cf. "Gods, etc.," poetic "states of mind").[56]

ORIGO

Hoooh! Fasa!

Proposition #1: the next 3000 years is hatched. The egg of chaos has labored. And the bird is out.

Proof. 1 I dreamt last night I gathered a bunch of sticks and put them aside under a bush to make a fire with. I have still the feeling in my arms of the awkward bundle against my chest.

2 Some eyes are no longer confused. They have lost the look of stone, its edge. Or of wood, the rot and watery part.

3 Of late a President had a poet at his side. It was the President who was the juggler, and the tumbler. The poet was the severe one, shy. And if he was jester, the play was in his language. Events he played straight, a civil war there, how fake a leader was rising in the state next to that war, precisely what is clear in the intent of a people, here.

So that you will not think these cards I show you are obscure, I would tell you a story. I got it from the people, old ones in the neighborhood. It has to do with origin, us. It is called WHEN THE WORLD WAS NEW ....(Hopi)

I should like to call this story ADAM AND EVE, THEIR SONS AND MOST REMARKABLE DAUGHTERS, but it doesn't matter. The people from whom I learned it had their eye on something else, the radical, the root underneath the tree. IN THE BEGINNING....

was published in Milan (1961) in a translation by Pound's grandson Siegfried Walter de Rache-wiltz. Pound's note was "Il Significato di Leo Frobenius" from *Broletto*, 1938.

56. 11 April 1927, *Letters.* See the interpretations in "The Mathematical Symbolism," p. 12.

..... Perhaps Gassire took a new path not because he could not wait to be king but because he had to sing. Perhaps Wagadu had to be lost in order to be Wagadu. And there, perhaps, is the meat of our egg.

So, before / I can tell you about Gassire you must know about Wagadu, of which Gassire was a child. For the story as I got it from Douglas Fox who got it from Leo Frobenius who got it from a people who, in their turn, remembered it from their fathers' fathers, makes it quite clear that Wagadu gained in splendor from what Gassire, in his vanity, did. So you must know, and recognize, Wagadu, of which we, too, are children:

Four times....... (with breakups to follow)

"ORIGO" projects from the 5000-year past of *LXXI Cantos* (both pre-history and history) a 3000-year future or NOVUS ORDO SECLORUM. "Proposition #1" subsumes a new view or interpretation of *LXXI Cantos* in the new paideumatic light. The Odyssean Eagle having emerged E PLURIBUS UNUM with a prophecy of the future E PLURIBUS UNUM, the mode passes to the complementary Elpenor, archetypal source of epiphanies and dreams. A premonition of the fascis (Proof 1), symbol of the Italian corporate state, symbolizes historical facts or "limbs of Osiris" unified in the shield on the Eagle's breast and ready to give new life. The stellar vision of NOVUS ORDO SECLORUM has come to life through ethical clarity (Proof 2). The dreamer casts himself into the political role taken by Elpenor vis-à-vis Odysseus and by Pound vis-à-vis American presidents and leaders of his own time both in *The Cantos* and out. With reference to the present a voice of MDCCLXXVI is relating itself negatively to Roosevelt and positively to Mussolini. The symbol is the Mount.

"Proposition #1" is prophetic history looking toward the emergence of a "nuova persona." The three-part "Proof" has shifted to personal narrative for personal struggle in the modes of dream and memory. To illuminate the revelations and refer them to race memory, the narrator goes back to world origins and a mythic form of New World history in the voice of ANNUIT COEPTIS. The form is Pound's fundamental form of New World history, discovery and colonization "busting thru" into four-phase revolution. Like a fortune teller referring to the Seal/Calendar arcanum ("these cards") he opens with a Hopi myth (I can't find which one) applied to original discovery of the world. Mythic tradition passes for colonization to mythic personae, presumably those of the Biblical story up through Noah (*Genesis* 1–9). The two creation myths lead into a story of four-fold revolutionary change in which the speaker casts himself as the innovating Gassir.

Wagadu, a symbol for the motive "To build the city of Dioce whose terraces are the colour of stars" (the sun-temple), was lost four times. Of Gassir's vanity the fruit was epic song. Of infidelity the fruit was a rain of gold and pearls. Of avidity the fruit was writing. Of discord the fruit will be "the capacity of enduring like the sands of the south and the rocks of the Sahara, because every man will hold a Wagadu in his heart and every woman will have a Wagadu in her womb." The spirit, form, and paideumatic mode of this myth for the origins of epic poetry and its renewal by struggle prepare for a synthesis of new paideuma by a "nuova persona" who will rely not on history books but on the oral tradition—on what remains "in the mind" and "in the heart indestructible."

Pound's "Serious Artist" of his 1913 essay had become the "serious character" of Vorticism, who in his turn became the paideumatic artist acting "sul serio," a catchword in the paideumatic essays. In 1940 Pound published in *Il Meridiano di Roma*[57] "Sul Serio," a glorification of the Roman Catholic Church for having preserved against Hebrew and Protestant negations "the divine and eternal principle inherent in grain, in the seed; the spirit, in sum, of illuminating fecundity." He clinched or "focused" his essay with an Eleusinian manifesto coming out of a Confucian saying in American form:

> Ma "sacrificare ad uno spirito che non il
> il vostro" presenta degli inconvenienti. In
> quanto Romana ECCLESIA FLOREAT.
> Amor deus est. Roma dea est. Deus est
> Amor.
>
> ROMA
> O   M
> M   O
> AMOR
> Granum Europae Salus.
>
> **Ezra Pound**

The personal assertion will become the upper right column and horizontal axis of the ideogramic "Canto 77 Explication." The subject is European in four phases. "Insofar as it is Roman may the CHURCH FLOURISH" declares a universal tradition. "Love is a God. Rome is a Goddess. God is Love" identifies the personae of struggle by male/female dichotomy (cf. the Eagle and Providence and Pound's Calendar cycle). The palindrome transforms and balances (cf. the Mount and the Seal/Calendar arcanum). "*Grain is the well-being of Europe*" consummates the whole. Inscribed is a civilization of liberty and abundance.[58]

57. Roma, 1 September 1940.
58. Documentarily the four symbolize the Declaration, the motives of "WE the People" forwards and backwards, the Constitution, and the Bill of Rights.

CHAPTER SEVENTEEN

THE PISAN CANTOS LXXIV–

LXXXIV & LXXXIV CANTOS

OὟ ΤΙΣ, OὟ ΤΙΣ? Odysseus
                    the name of my family.
   Pisan LXXIV

I surrender neither the empire nor the temples
                                        plural
nor the constitution nor yet the city of Dioce
each one in his god's name
   Pisan LXXIV

John Adams, the Brothers Adam
            there is our norm of spirit
   Pisan LXXXIV

As a seventh draft extending the concurrent documents of '76 from a tra-ditional first to a personal second phase, *Pisan* had been projected by the epitome in the prototype decad, *VII*, where Pound inherited in his own person a confining, moribund tradition but broke out of it by asserting natural pas-sion, personal epiphany, and "passion to breed a form" of "New Eros," until he emerged with "the live man out of lands and prisons" to reassert the "more live" Renaissance tradition evolved in *I–VI*.

For its prototypic Eagle (from *I*-as-"ONE") *VII* had drawn through Odys-seus the personality representing all the dead, Elpenor, who had focused the general human condition in his account of his death at Circe's and in his request for a new life. From "Seal sports" (second of the Seal prototype *I–IV*) it had drawn personalities focused by a mind churning forms out of historical and natural phenomena opened by epiphanies, which revealed meta-morphoses of the gods in the form of the constellation. From these, through *VII*, the prototype draft had revealed the historical victim Malatesta (*VIII–XI*), who nevertheless transmitted from his disasters not only material achieve-ments but also still living form and spirit inheritable by a later revolutionary. Pound's chief models in the Pisan camp are Odysseus-Elpenor in Circe's swine-sty, Acoetes at the mercy of his crew and King Pentheus, himself imprisoned in a tradition represented by life in modern London and Paris before, during, and after World War I, and Malatesta shut within the conditions of his time.

These projections or prophecies of the general human condition evolve from the Eagle vision epitomized in the first draft, which becomes the first of the four Seal-drafts of "ELEUSIS." The second Seal-draft (*XVII–XXX*), elaborating "Seal sports," seeks a stellar "nuova persona" within the Renaissance decline and its result, a modern world similarly dominated by war. Efforts to evolve a "better tradition" out of the destructive tradition culminate in "JOHN ADAMS," which projects through Adams's diary a declaration of independence stressing legal argument rather than the argument of war implicit or explicit in the struggles of Elpenor, of Acoetes, of Pound, of Malatesta, and of the "nuova persona" passing from these through the subsequent drafts toward full emergence in what became *Pisan*. But war appeared to have destroyed the "better tradition" along with its putative twentieth-century inheritors. The dream, the fascist revolution, the corporate state, and Pound himself appeared to be shattered.

Pound had hoped that the argument of *The Cantos* could "stave off war." Still, though, his poem was ready for war and its consequences as Adams had been ready on the "sudden emergency" of Lexington to continue his arguments about the constitutional tradition into a formal "PLAN OF GOVERNMENT." In *Pisan* Pound would adapt the struggle of '76 as it occurred historically. War passes to peace and a dark night of the soul would pass to new light; out of chaos both public and personal would come a motivation first from the Declaration, union to liberty, and then toward the Constitution, achieved liberty to new union. The tradition and the self would be synthesized and resynthesized in memory by new epiphanies and new affirmations of destiny until a process of regeneration had been validated in lyric song.

More generally, continuing voyage extends the eastward circumnavigation of the first phase to a paideumatic circumnavigation from "ELEUSIS" via "KUNG" and "JOHN ADAMS" to Pisa, a "poetic" Italy where he would incorporate the history of 1939–45 while synthesizing world paideuma in a context dominated now by nature. At the same time "the great periplum" of the sun would "bring in the stars to our shore" for a coastal "periplum" aimed at bringing the matter of a second hemicycle to life through a definitive colonization on Pisan local (later Phaeacian and Ithacan) ground. (For "periplum" cf. Hanno's colonizing voyage along the coast of Africa, *XL*, and Chun Tchi's metaphor for careful reading in his preamble to the Manchu translation of the *Odes*, "periplum, not as land looks on a map / but as sea bord seen by men sailing.")

Continuing '76, Pound the declarer sums up the Declaration's six-part argument against the past by declaring independence from a usurist tradition in behalf of a personally reaffirmed "better tradition." The emergent "nuova persona'' for ''WE the People'' ordains the six motives from union to liberty for states' rights while turning the motives from reaffirmed liberty toward new union. Pound's ''states of mind'' sum up six draft-Articles in Ratification of a Constitution for a model corporate state, ideal if not actual, while his synthesizing of three paideumas (in six drafts) is projecting the ideal model through the world Branch/Power States. Pound applies the Bill's common law rights (Seventh) interpreted to be the common laws of nature, of human nature, and of nations.

Canto by canto the seventh draft of concurrent documents continues the form of every draft, an Eagle epitome (*LXXIV*-as-''ONE''), a Seal-form (*LXXIV–LXXVII*), and a decad ''to be unity'' via duality, trine, and tetrad to a ''sea-change'' (*LXXIV–LXXXIII*); in reversion from the perfect decads which focused and embodied the paideumas, a coda (*LXXXIV*) completes the draft.

In the shift to the second phase, however, the Eagle epitome and the Seal-form are rederived from Pound's personal life by epiphany as Eagle *I* and Seal *I–IV* were derived by opening up a Renaissance poetic tradition. Moreover, as *IV* projected the Calendar toward the prototype decad and draft, *LXXVII* and the coda ''Canto 77 Explication'' precipitate the Calendar form ideogramically and project it toward the decad and draft of the new phase. A symbol for epiphanies churned up from memory and nature by the whirling stellar mind, ''Canto 77 Explication'' draws all '76 into the form of the Preambles suffused and mediated by the personal ''To sacrifice to a spirit not one's own is flattery (sycophancy),'' for the new life of a NOVUS ORDO SECLORUM evolving from union to liberty and then from liberty to union. It is the locus for this meaning carried by ideograms which punctuate the draft-phase from beginning to end. Derived from four cantos through a single canto and rearranging the ideograms enumerated ''1–10,'' the form applies to a single canto, to all Seal-forms, to the draft-phase, and, through these, to the whole poem being drafted and built. More particularly, the forms churned up in Seal *LXXIV–LXXVII* and carried by ideograms prepare for the gradual emergence of a sustained song of liberty in a first hemicycle (*LXXIV–LXXIX*), then for a series of sustained songs (*LXXX–LXXXIII*) which reintegrate Pound's mind in a new union with itself and with ''now my world.''

The narrative in *Pisan* is carried by a symbolically enforced stream of consciousness (''PANTA REI,'' all things flow). The flow carries memories being brought to life in Pound's mind while being given form. A passage in *LXXIV* refers to ''intaglios . . . left us'' by Malatesta's artists

> for roll or plain impact
> or cut square in the jade block

Fragments of a shattered tradition being gathered (by discovery) and brought to life (by colonization) take form as memories on a roll (Declaration), as epiphanies received from the immediate surroundings (Preambles), as these arranged in new and definitive form (Constitutions), and as new form perfected in art (the Bill and Seal). Such, we shall see, is the pattern for deriving Seal *LXXIV–LXXVII* and "Canto 77 Explication" as forms for the perfecting songs of the latter cantos of the decad.

One other formal feature is the Constitutional matrix for building in the second phase. Clauses 1–71 of the three federal Branches having provided a matrix for six draft-Articles and three paideumatic Branches in the first phase, clauses 72–84 of the states' rights and amending half of the Constitution, Pound's newly active, personal "states of mind," provide a matrix for a seventh draft-Article and for the paideumatic Branch/Power States. The complement of clauses not only inheres in the hiatus for 72–73 and the unfolding to 84, but is also marked by formal divisions (dots across the page) of *LXXIV* (p. 442) and *LXXVI* (p. 458); by the latter clauses 72–76 are comprised in *LXXIV–LXXVI* in preparation for synchronicity from the end of Seal *LXXIV– LXXVII* to the end of the draft. Seven draft-Articles converging with 84 clausal cantos complete states' rights for a corporate state, ideal if not actual, as a world model enriched by world paideumas; the seven drafts also build the Mount of the whole poem to this juncture. Succeeding the three world paideumatic Branches, the world Branch/Power States derives its function as a Power from its incorporation of the clauses of the whole amending process (States 72–78, Amendment 79, Supreme Law 80–82, Ratification 83, and memorializing, signing, sealing, and delivering 84). While the prototype cantos are subsuming the foregoing drafts and projecting the drafts to come, the paideumatic Branch/Power States is projecting the coming drafts also through the clauses of Amendment, Supreme Law, and Ratification.

Finally, it seems that Pound had in mind a "repeat in history" of episodes from the life of Tom Paine. The polemical voice of 1939–45 and the poetic voice of *Pisan* both have behind them the famous opening lines of *American Crisis* by "COMMON SENSE," written during the dark days before Trenton (cf. Malatesta's postbag):

> THESE are the times that try men's souls. The summer soldier and the sunshine patriot will, in this crisis, shrink from the service of their country; but he that stands it *now*, deserves the love and thanks of man and woman. Tyranny, like hell, is not easily conquered; yet we have this consolation with us, that the harder the conflict, the more glorious the triumph. What we obtain too cheap, we esteem too lightly: it is dearness only that gives every thing its value. Heaven knows how to put a proper price upon its goods; and it would be strange indeed if so celestial an article as FREEDOM should not be highly rated. Britain, with an army to enforce her tyranny, has declared that she has a right (*not only to* TAX) but "to BIND *us in* ALL CASES WHATSOEVER," and if being *bound in that manner*, is not slavery, then is there not such a thing as slavery upon earth. Even the expression is impious; for so unlimited a power can belong only to God.

Ideogramic macaronics in ''Canto 77 Explication,'' juxtaposing columnar ''TOM PAINE'' with columnar ''WASHINGTON'' and coming to a focus through initials of the men of '76 in ''EP,'' have already been noted (p. 103) and will be again.

Another episode, not Paine cooperating with Washington during the struggle but President Washington's seeming abandonment of the international revolutionary to his fate when Robespierre had consigned him to the Bastille and to death, elicited Paine's famous epigram on Washington the ''marble-hearted'' (cf. Pound and the leaders of his time). But it also brought comfort from a lady who wrote to the imprisoned Paine under the name ''The Little Corner of the World.'' Paine replied with a poem ''From the Castle in the Air to the Little Corner of the World'' in which his Castle of Fancy, built in a heavenly paradise, is blown away by a storm while its inhabitant slept. Traversing the world it passes over a beautiful garden spot, feels an attraction, and is drawn down to earth. There the voyager finds a solace and delight from which he and his castle re-ascend refreshed for new flight.[1]

Not only the situation but the imagery of the poem suggest *Pisan*. Moreover, Pound seems to have recalled them for his epiphanies of ladies who bring comfort and new inspiration. Into the dark night of the soul comes Cunizza ''al Triedro,'' in the (little) corner, along with other ladies (*LXXIV*, *LXXVI*, *LXXVIII*). They help confirm that ''Le Paradis n'est pas artificiel'' but exists only in ''fragments.'' They are associated with the ''castellaro,'' ruined castle, whereof there is ''no vestige save in the air.'' The whole passage on the dark night of the soul (*LXXIV* pp. 436–38), involving imprisonment among comrades in misery and enslavement to usury, echoes both ''These are the times that try men's souls'' and the ease brought by female solace and by thus inspired lyricism. The ladies precipitate at the beginning of *LXXVI* ''from il triedro to the Castellaro,'' the ''Little Corner's'' form of address to the beleaguered ''Castle.'' Pound's ladies join with other omens and inspirations to prepare for the saving lyrics of the latter half of the draft/phase.[2]

LXXIV-as-''ONE''

In *LXXIV* Pound defines ''the minds of (WE) the people'' through ''Odysseus / the name of my family,'' or through his Eagle-personae. He subordinates

---

1. See Appendix C.

2. The French in *Pisan*, a medium for expressing grief and remorse, apparently echoes another prison poet, Villon. In ''Montcorbier *Alias* Villon,'' *The Spirit of Romance*, 1910, ''Dante reaches out of his time, and by rising above it escapes many of its limitations,'' while ''Villon in some way speaks below the voice of his age's conventions, and thereby outlasts it.'' Versus Whitman's self-consciousness, ''Villon's greatness is that he unconsciously proclaims man's divine right to be himself, the only one of the so-called 'rights of man' which is not an artificial

Odysseus to Elpenor, however, opening up Elpenor's role and voice as they were opened up in the Seal-epitome (*II*) and in the decadal epitome (*VII*) for *Pisan*. Each of four phases is a four-phase whole, each sequel transforming its predecessor(s), while the four together are constituting (like *I*-as-"ONE") a ten-part, four-phase whole plus coda. Anticipating all four roles, the Odyssean voice abbreviates in a six-part passage (pp. 425–26) the apparent fate of the tradition defined in the six drafts of *LXXI Cantos*. The Elpenorean voice, opening up the lengthy middle of four formal phases (pp. 426–42), draws all roles of the archetypal Eagle personality into the second phase on Pisan ground. The Tiresian voice (pp. 442–47) resurveys the lifetime destinies of the "man of ill star" and the "man of no fortune" as forms revealing a definitive predestined form and its aim. Emerging through the three Eagle voices Pound sketches his own fourfold destiny as his own Divus (pp. 447–48). A coda (p. 449) celebrating a mind still integral, still able to educe form, and still able to create, transforms the invocation of Aphrodite while affirming Pound himself to be the comprehensive living Eagle.

As in *I*-as-"ONE" Odysseus projects a ten-part, four-phase whole, here by projecting "my family." Odysseus's six-part summary is extended to a whole by Elpenor's four formal phases. The Tiresian phase is written as three parts projecting a fourth and as halves two by two. When it is added, Odysseus's six plus Elpenor integrated into one plus Tiresias's three constitute a whole. Pound's voice consummates Odyssean six, Elpenorean unity, and Tiresian halves in a fourfold unity which completes a final whole of ten parts in four phases.

The voice of "Odysseus / the name of my family" faces the historical situation and affirms the "better tradition" against it by summation. A general rubric for the whole phase,

The enormous tragedy of the dream in the peasant's bent shoulders,

strikes a keynote for the millennial struggle of "WE the People," which is brought up to the execution of Mussolini, twice-crucified instead of twice-born ("DIGONOS"), in April 1945. The fate of Mussolini and his mistress symbolize the fate of the revolutionary Eagle and Providence. Undaunted, however, Pound differentiates the fascist effort from the enervation of T. S. Eliot's hollow men by bringing the dream round to the honorable motive (for the whole poem in terms of its personal phase), "To build the city of Dioce whose terraces are the colour of stars."

This contemporary condition of millennial revolution summarizes *XVI. Cantos*. Providential justification and ethical purgation by the soothings and beauties of "the way" and "the process" of a universal nature, immaculate in its "candor," summarize *XVII–XXX*. The "great periplum" of the sun carries

---

product." Paine, Villon, and a newly respected Whitman constitute a principal complex of precedents for Pound's voicing of the present plight of "WE the People."

the stars, including the rebel (but light-bearer) Lucifer, to the New World ("Jefferson-Nuevo Mundo"); placed here "ΟΫ ΤΙΣ, ΟΫ ΤΙΣ? Odysseus / the name of my family" evokes the men of '76 arranged in *Canto XXXI* and to be echoed ideogramically in this phase (cf. "Canto 77 Explication"). Despite a hostile god and the stupidity of the populace, Renaissance art and politics have transmitted "a precise definition" to "our time" ("Siena-Leopoldine Reforms"). From "DIGONOS" through rain, sun, stars, wind, and moon these passages have been interpenetrated by mythifying natural symbols for a cosmic revolutionary process, the phasal version of the myth behind "REVOLUTION . . . in the minds of the people" (the Seal-vision, the Declaration's premises, "ELEUSIS," etc.).

Getting down to unmythified cases, the lessons of T'ang history ("KUNG") still expose economic manipulations in modern China, in British imperial India, and in the British Empire as a whole. Further ("JOHN ADAMS"), a revolution need not take over the means of production but can be accomplished by adjusting money and credit to work needed and done inside a system, which then need not adopt the kinds of make-work policies characteristic of the depression years. But denial of the "better tradition" and of the principle "that free speech without free radio speech is as zero" (cf. Adams on liberty) have brought Odysseus/Pound to the death cells. That militarism is progressing westward, that despite Germany's surrender in the west (on 7 May) peace is only absence of war as in 1918 ("im Westen nichts neues"), that the Constitution is still in jeopardy, and that "that state of things" is "not very new either," rounds back to the opening tyranny by abbreviating the rest of the revolutionary form as declaration (cf. "JOHN ADAMS").

The Elpenorean expansion (pp. 426–42) opens up the chief persona of the second phase (and seventh decad/draft). Its four phases personalize the foregoing summarized tradition, focus personality, and project prophesied destiny and its realization. To tradition as memory on a "roll" it adds direct observation of the immediate setting, or "plain impact." The drive forward of the Odyssean argument against tyranny and for liberty becomes the churning of fragments of memory, which embody the quest for liberty, with immediate perception, which seeks new union, until the duality unites in epiphanies. Resultant formal epiphanies of tradition, personality, destiny, and poetry, when added to the Odyssean summation, constitute a dual whole.

Elpenor speaks "4 times to the Song of Gassir" (see pp. 317–18). The pattern for the epiphanies is the ideal city of Wagadu, "4 times . . . rebuilded" until it becomes "now in the mind indestructible," and affirmation of the stellar mind voiced NOVUS ORDO SECLORUM as "Odysseus / the name of my family" affirmed the traditional mind (the shield voiced E PLURIBUS UNUM). Its four towers and four gates travestied by the DTC, Wagadu is a locus for other such ideal cities as Zion to be redeemed with economic justice, the city of Dioce to be built, and "Italia tradita," an ideal Italy still in Pound's mind, to be resurrected. This whole mental process of epiphanic focus takes place in acutely suffered history and in vividly rendered nature, under Pisan mountains in the sight of the Tower of Pisa. The natural and civic "Mounts" evoke an envisioned oriental sacred mountain, Mt. Taishan, toward which the stellar plan in the mind aspires. A whole human scene under the heavens aspires toward realization of the envisioned Mount (Elpenor's plan) and its consummating solar epiphany.

After a textual break from the Odyssean summation and a rubric which identifies (Odysseus) Elpenor in bed at Circe's— " 'of sapphire, for this stone giveth sleep' " (cf. "her bedposts are of sapphire," etc., *LXXVI*)—each Elpenorean phase begins with a topical rubric, churns up memories and perceptions, and comes to an epiphanic Seal-focus followed by a textual break and a new beginning. The rubric for the first phase (pp. 426–29) differentiates Elpenor's digging into the earth from Odysseus's in terms which will come to apply to the whole decad:

> not words whereto to be faithful
>> nor deeds that they be resolute
>>> only that bird-hearted equity make timber
>>> and lay hold of the earth

The beginning of the world according to the Gospel of St. John ("in principio verbum") and the Christian paraclete (the Holy Ghost as comforter, with asides to the Pentecostal gift of tongues) become the personal "verbum perfectum: sinceritas." "A lizard upheld me" and "the air was made open" bring epiphany as Eleusinian light sealed by a first ideogram, *hsien*[3], meaning epiphany;[3] it is elaborated as "the paraclete . . . the precision" present in the Chinese Great Emperors on Mt. Taishan and "in the hall of the forebears / as from the beginning of wonders."

The first phase having epiphanized tradition, the second (pp. 429–32) epiphanizes the man and his comrades as collective Tovarisch, who "blessed without aim" and "wept in the rain ditch at evening." The rubric surrounds Pound with the DTC's parody of Wagadu, "4 giants at the 4 corners" ("the guard roosts"), but also with the charity of

> three young men at the door
> and they digged a ditch round about me
>> lest the damp gnaw thru my bones

Charity suggests "to redeem Zion with justice," but that does not prevent a fellow prisoner from being hung for murder and rape to the second ideogram of the draft, *mo*[4], which looks like a man being hung and is translated, from its elements, *man* under *sun* under *grass*, "OÝ TIΣ / a man on whom the

---

3. *The Pisan Cantos* (1948) and the first printings of *LXXXIV Cantos* had *ming*[2], the sun-and-moon ideogram; *hsien*[2] was substituted in the sixth printing of *LXXXIV Cantos*. *Hsien*[2] thus looks toward *ming*[2] (*LXXXIV*) as the constellation anticipates "the total light process" breaking through the clouds.

sun has gone down.'' But the following text, though it reiterates "a man on whom the sun has gone down," reverses the mood so that a *man* with a *sun*-mind also grows *grass*, or, symbolically, would rebuild Wagadu (and "Italia tradita" and the city of Dioce). His motive makes its four corners, four gates, and "a terrace the colour of stars" "now in the mind indestructible." His churning stellar mind is imaged "in a dance the renewal" (cf. the dance, *LXXVII*). But "between NEKUIA where are Alcmene and Tyro" (a first phase) and "the Charybdis of action" (a third) he must, as here, retire to "the solitude of Mt. Taishan," where *mo*[4] looks like "sun dragging her stars" in periplum and where earth's waters follow the sun and moon. Since panthers die in captivity, a personality rising from death follows Circe's or Dionysus's "It is consummated, Go" (in Latin) to where, surrounded now by his fellow prisoners as "herds" and "cohorts" (cf. the young men at the rain ditch), he looks on Mt. Taishan.

A third phase (pp. 432–37) epiphanizes destiny, justice, and form. A parodistic epiphany anticipates Pound's destiny. In Tangier, about 1904, "I saw" the Tiresian blood-rite and prophetic tongue of fire (the paraclete) enacted when a fakir ignited dead straw by putting it into his mouth after a snakebite had drawn blood from his tongue. This prophecy introduces an elegy for artist comrades of his own generation, all of them in the same boat (of death). On "this day" recollections of a lost world cloud the sun.

But reading from a monument the anniversary of the French Revolution (cf. the Mount of MDCCLXXVI) while the hill north of Taishan is "ablaze" introduces a mediating epiphany of justice. The redemptive theme passes through a visionary halves of a seal ("cloud over mountain, mountain over the cloud") to a "cut square" focus in the very middle of the phase (p. 434),

> I surrender neither the empire nor the temples
> plural
> nor the constitution nor yet the city of Dioce
> each one in his god's name

Governmental forms of the three paideumas emerge from the wreck of the revolutionary effort and culminate in the symbol for world paideuma and for the stellar phase. Each state of mind receives the positive sanction of a Biblical version of *Pisan*'s revolutionary theme, "To sacrifice to a spirit not one's own is flattery (sycophancy)." The evolving epiphany receives the further sanction of Aphrodite seen rising again from the sea and taking her place at her shrine.

Out of the destinies of fellow artists, through the mediating justicial epiphany, come the dark night of the soul and the destinies of Pound and his present comrades in misery: all are slaves in a slave ship (of state), swine in Circe's sty (which now even Odysseus/Pound has entered), and victims in a body politic poisoned by usury without even the consolation of Circe and her attending beasts. Epiphanies of destiny and justice are generalized into an epiphany of form. Through a dead comrade's "seal"[4] come Malatestan "intaglios . . . left us"

> for roll or plain impact
> or cut square in the jade block

The form is the same as that of the mediating epiphany of justice. In the overall Elpenorean phase it refers to data given form on a "roll" of memory, to the "plain impact" of epiphanies with or without ideograms, and to these forms revealing "cut square," as they have in this third of the Elpenorean phases. The forms so far revealed will be perfected "in the jade block" of a fourth phase. The overall form can be extrapolated from here through various larger manifestations to the whole poem.

The fourth Elpenorean phase (pp. 437–42) irradiates "nox animae magna from the tent under Taishan" with delights ranging from Cunizza "al Triedro" and the ladies to physical pleasures to illuminated song. The keynote, "Le Paradis n'est pas artificiel," will key also the fourth phases of *LXXVI*, of *LXXVII*, and of the decad (*LXXXIII*). Illuminations come mainly from the paraclete of the Chinese Great Emperors in flashes of wisdom and in "the sharp song with the sun under its radiance" raised to "the compassionate heavens" (cf. "a man on whom the sun has gone down"). The paraclete is explicit in "master of utterance / who turneth his word in its season and shapes it." Elpenor's epitaph "of no fortune and with a name to come," which was granted to Divus, makes the persona unmistakable. "From the law, by the law, so build yr/ temple" recalls his tomb and the repeated "each in the name of its god" his individuality. Elpenor/Pound ends his fourfold second phase by affirming what it sought,

> "I believe in the resurrection of Italy   quia impossibile est
> 4 times to the song of Gassir
> now in the mind indestructible

> .   .   .   .

The formal dots accommodate States 72 and 73 formally if not substantively within *LXXIV* (the Constitutional fragments are more matricial than thematic)

---

4. Allen Upward's "seal Sitalkas" (cf. also *Thrones 107*) was embossed on the cover of his *The Divine Mystery: A Reading of the History of Christianity Down to the Time of Christ* (London: 1913), a book that reinforced and contributed greatly to Pound's millennial revolutionary vision. Upward's seal, an ancient Greek sardonyx, green with red spots, was engraved with a figure associated in his chapter "The Savior" with the Mediterranean grain gods, with John Barleycorn in folklore and in Burns's ballad rendition, and with Christ. Of it Pound wrote Harriet Monroe (20 January 1914, *Letters*) that while a resident in Nigeria Upward had performed at least one miracle by means of a "gnostic gem" (cf. Frobenius the rainmaker *XXXVIII*, *LIII*, and *Pisan, passim*).

while dividing the Odyssean summary and the Elpenorean expansion from Tiresian prophecy, Poundian realization, and the coda.

The Tiresian phase (pp. 442–47) is introduced by naming the queen of the underworld, "KOPH," and citing Tiresias by epithets, "ΑΓΛΑΟΣ ΆΛΑΟΥ," famous for blindness: Kore granted that of all her subjects Tiresias could keep "his mind entire" and so could continue the compensatory gift of prophecy granted by Zeus. The mode is neither Odyssean derivation of a tradition nor Elpenorean epiphany, but prophecy derived from knowledge of past and present. The phase is halved two and two by affirming that the roles of the "man of ill star" (p. 443) and the "man of no fortune" (pp. 443–46) are roles of destiny, and then by deriving from them a form (p. 446) and its aim (pp. 446–47). Trine is symbolized by a tag for the Mount between the two halves and realized by truncating a fourth phase (cf. Anticleia in *I* and the ruins at the end of *III*).

The "man of ill star" inheres in a British ship captain treading water because he fell from his ship with an unsecured section of taffrail. The "man of no fortune" inheres in Silvio Gesell, the theorist of stamp scrip and of the Natural Economic Order, who fell with a short-lived government but was acquitted as an innocent stranger. Tiresias/Pound appears as an old man, still active, "serving small stones from a lath racquet" (the golden wand); he is also associated with Pontius Pilate, the judge of Christ, and stands in sight of two red cans labeled "FIRE" (cf. the tongue of fire). He first (p. 443) carries snatches of Odysseus's destiny from the time he left Ithaca until after the shipwreck that destroyed his crew and left him on his raft to be driven "as the winds veer in periplum." Ahead lie landfalls on the cliffs above Charybdis, at Calypso's island, and at Phaeacia, before destined return to Ithaca. Pound's first landfall is Pisa, where a "periplum" of colonization and struggle is being guided by the epiphanic ideogram-groups.

Elpenor (pp. 443–46) is found under the Tarpeian Rock, from which Roman criminals were hurled to their deaths, drunk with wine and uttering " 'in the name of its god' " and " 'Spiritus veni' " (I came a spirit, cf. "The soul sought Avernus"); he did not come to a "schema," however, for (says Aristotle/Tiresias), philosophy is not for the young. Still, Elpenor's vision of beauty (inspired by Circe) and his plan for a tomb associate him with Pound's Mauberley, who sought "to carve Achaia" in cameo profile, through Aubrey Beardsley, probably one of the models for the ill-fated Mauberley. Beardsley's repeated "Beauty is difficult" complements Odyssean "periplum." Elpenor's future destiny is clinched " 'and with a name to come.' "

The symbol for trine, formally halving the Tiresian phase, is the one line "aram vult nemus," the grove wishes an altar (p. 446), or a Mount for Elpenor's tomb and Tiresias's prophecy of form.

Third and formally (p. 446), Tiresias affirms that "the form" has inhered in Odysseus's " 'ghosts move about me' 'patched with histories' " (from

Ur *I*) and in Elpenor's preparation (from natural forms) to face his challenge "Beauty is difficult." These forms are subsumed in Tiresias's "mind entire" by "the form beached" at Pisa but now illuminated by the sun. "La purezza," the "paraclete or the verbum perfectum: sinceritas," causes the form, which is potentially the churning revolutionary mind, to act ("funge"). Tt acts on certain images formed in the Cavalcantian mind (*"formato loco,"* as in Adams's testament) "to remain there" and become, with action, resurgent "ΕΙΚΟΝΕΣ." The Providence for Pound's artistic destiny is the spider on his tent rope ("Arachne mi porta fortuna"). The aim (in a four-line fourth phase, pp. 446–47) is, with Divus, "to forge Achaia."

Pound comprehends all the destinies in his own by finding a destiny in his own life from about 1900 in America to the present 1945. Periplum in New York City and items of tradition (including alabaster model "Towers of Pisa") prepared for periplum to Europe (beginning in 1906). Gibraltar and the Pillars of Hercules interested him (in 1908) not only for Odyssean background but also for the details of his own life there, including beer served to sailors (cf. Elpenor); appreciation of art in Italy was Elpenorean.

In 1912 occurred a Tiresian omen: at the "Trattoria degli Apostoli (dodici)" in Verona a head waiter announced "Ecco il tè" (Here's the tea) and explained its "mysteries" to a young boy. The waiter spoke as with a tongue of fire. Evoked for turning personal destinies into universal revolutionary poetry are the twelve of the Calendar cycle, OSIRIS explaining to HORUS, or Tiresias explaining to Odysseus or Elpenor.

This omen evolves more literally into a Tiresian contrast between world cultivation and trade in tea, coffee, peanuts, soy beans, and maple syrup, and world war, which has cast down "stone after stone of beauty" (cf. "you cannot yet buy one dish of Chinese food in all Italy / hence the débacle," p. 507). Against a final cause of war, the commercialization of art, is set the fact that in 1945 Tyrolese artists still carve wood "in the tradition" and cut intaglios in the manner of the Malatestan artists. This analogue to Divus and Pound projects the end of the epitome to the end of the decad.

The coda (p. 449) celebrates the foregoing canto as a stellar mind in the form of a crystal ball of water upheld by the jet of a fountain. This upwardly directed stream of consciousness has lifted the Odyssean mind out of the dust of Hell to Elpenorean reverie in the soft winds under Taishan. The liquid is not an "accident" but a "property" and an "element" in "the mind's make-up"; as the Tiresian form it is active and functions, else the dust would remain inert in the fountain's basin. Imagination turns the dust into iron filings and, like a magnet, gives them the form of a natural rose. A concluding "we who have passed over Lethe" bespeaks not only the "family's" passage out of Hell but also its retention of memory so that matter of the past may remain for a new "mind's make-up." The crystal ball will derive from the past, via the present, what is to come.

Seal *LXXIV–LXXVII*

As the four archetypal events of *I*-as-"ONE" projected in Seal form a tradition of revolutionary poetry, the four archetypal personae for "the mind of (WE) the people" project in Seal form a personal medium for envisioning the form of "REVOLUTION." "Odysseus / the name of my family" becomes the inclusive figure for the shield voiced E PLURIBUS UNUM (Seal *LXXIV*) while the other personae project the sequels. From a dichotomy of individuality (for liberty) and collectivity (for union) manifested in his own life, Pound rederives the Seal/Calendar form in the personal mode. This rederivation contains the forms—most overtly sheet music and ideogramic arrangement—for Liberty *LXXIV–LXXIX* and subsequent New Union.

If Seal *LXXIV* transforms Seal *I* to a mode of memory, Seal *LXXV*, like Seal *II*, is all emergent personality, epiphany, and metamorphosis. As suddenly and unexpectedly as Elpenor from the dead or as epiphanic personae from history (*II*), Pound's musician friend Gerhart Munch issues from World War II ("Phlegethon") with classical sheet music in his satchel. From it Pound singles out a musical score "not of one bird" (Eagle and shield) "but of many" (Eagle-stars), a Renaissance "Canzone degli Uccelli" reset a century later and now, "per metamorfosi," reset by Munch for violin.[5] Munch focuses personality and the score epiphanizes the Elpenorean form "now in the mind indestructible." The few lines of text and the dominant epiphanic score, like text and ideograms, constellate duality: Munch's liberation from Hell has brought a renewed union of the many for a NOVUS ORDO SECLORUM. Staff, notes, parts, and whole provide a pattern for the coming ideogram-score, for that score taking the form of nature's birds in the prison camp wires, and for consequent redemptive song.

Seal *LXXVI* brings up to date, through the Tiresian voice, the justices, destinies, Mounts, and ruins of Seal *III*. A fourfold Seal-form received at the beginning (pp. 452–54) stimulates the motive "Why not rebuild it?" and projects the whole canto as halves of the Seal.

Inspiration descending from the sun hidden in a cloud bank but coming through its edge stirs Cavalcantian memory, which recalls in a voice of MDCCLXXVI a lady friend's prediction that the war would break Mussolini's political but not economic system.

Both have been broken, but the prophetic lady turns epiphanically into inspiring women who descend from "the high cliff . . . in the timeless air," opening up the bird canzone. Explaining as "from il triedro to the Castellaro" that they have been brought (as a "fleet" of stars) by "the sun in his great periplum," the ladies complain about the broken dream but reassure that they still have "the mould."

---

5. "I spose Faber will give me a FEW musical illusions in next vol? One fer Canter XX. shall want I think four in whole poEM." To T. S. Eliot, 1 June 1940, Collection at Yale.

The Tiresian mind surveys the destiny of the broken world and adjudges "progress, b . . . . h yr/progress." Furthering the judgment Pound adduces "the form" as Confucian revolution:

progress, b . . . . h yr/progress
la pigrizia   to know the ground and the dew

but to keep 'em three weeks   Chung
we doubt it

and in government not to lie down on it

the word is made

perfect

better gift can no man make to a nation
than the sense of Kung fu Tseu
who was called Chung Ni
not in historiography nor in making anthologies

(b . . . . yr/progress)
each one in the name of his god

Phases of knowledge, personae, government, and perfected word are spanned by "Chung"[6] and the sketched "*ch'eng*[2],"[7] the consummating form to be rederived in *LXXVII*. Here it leads back to memory and through the idea of a just Zion, Wagadu, etc., to the self-motivating "Why not rebuild it?"

His own destiny and the world's since "the dream" began in Venice (*III*) evolve in memory until the inspiring women reappear as goddesses in Pound's own crystal ball (cf. "Gods float," *III*). Their appearance enables him to extend Cavalcantian memory to

nothing matters but the quality
of the affection—
in the end—that has carved the trace in the mind
dove sta memoria

(Cf. the "formato loco.") Revision and reaffirmation transport him to "the cliff's edge" whence the ladies had descended, where he finds familiar beasts ("ferae familiares") in the "gemmed field" of the constellation. It is not yet

6. This *chung*[1] from the 1970 edition replaces a rougher orthography of previous editions. Both are distinctively Poundian (cf. *chung*[1] in "JOHN ADAMS" *LXX* and *Los Cantares* for classic versions); this one suggests a vortex moving toward a focus.

7. In "Terminology" for *Ta Hsio: The Great Digest* (1948, 1951) Pound rendered *ch'eng*[2] " 'Sincerity.' The precise definition of the word, pictorially the sun's lance coming to rest on the precise spot verbally. The right half means: to perfect, bring to focus."

a paradise perfected beyond justice by "*atasal,*" union with the divine, but on "the mountain" and in "the shut garden" of Aphrodite (cf. the first song, *LXXIX*) he "rested." "Memora" (the shield) and "the gemmed field" have framed a first half (pp. 452–58) marked off by the formal dots which will at last bring Constitutional clauses (States 75 and 76) into synchronicity with cantos.

A second half (pp. 458–63) is halved and framed by symbols of the Mount and the sun-vision. First (pp. 458–59) the punishment threatened against abettors of My Cid is echoed by a Tiresian blindness and by Pound's emergence as a lone ant from "a broken ant-hill," the wreckage of Europe, bearing its destiny and his own. The parts must be reassembled as after World War I. His "mould" is still the crystal ball filled with ladies in the mountain garden, but now it begins to open up more personal "sequelae."

The keynote of the fourth Elpenor phase of *LXXIV* (and of the fourth of *LXXVII* to come), "Le Paradis n'est pas artificiel," opens up the sun-vision (pp. 460–63). It generalizes the previous "fragments" to "States of mind are inexplicable to us" (and so can be only imaged); the keynote also deepens through grief and through "J'ai eu pitié des autres / probablement pas assez, and at moments that suited my own convenience" to "l'enfer non plus." The apparent wreck of the dream (cf. the ruins, *III*) takes him back to Venice for a reexamination of his poetic destiny and vocation. While recalling how he almost chucked it all into the canal (and might again), he bids a spider, who brings him fortune, to spin a new form (cf. "Chung," *ch'eng*) on the rope of his tent (a fragile Mount). A butterfly (a fragile Eagle) flies out through his smoke hole toward the sun.

Recapitulation of "ends and beginnings" (to be elaborated to date in *LXXVII*) ends, despite further weeping, with images of usury's constructions and destructions versus his own constructions, Aphrodite's, and the butterfly's; despite destruction "cameos" and "fragments" remain ("for roll or plain impact / or cut square in the jade block," *LXXIV*). A final rededication to his destiny comes through recognition of the destinies of poor devils, the slaves of usury, sent by change ("ΜΕΤΑΘΕΜΕΝΩΝ") of the currency to the slaughter, there to eat or be eaten like Odysseus's crew or the cattle at the sun-god's beautiful island ("ΝΗΣΟΝ ᾽ΑΜΥΜΟΝΑ"). Revolutionary destiny is reaffirmed by the justicial "woe to them that conquer with armies / and whose only right is their power." The Greek tags make "the word . . . perfect" (*ch'eng*[2]) while they and the judgment restate the focus of Seal *III*, "Nec Spe Nec Metu."

From Abner to Zagreus textually and from *chung*[1] to *ch'eng*[2] ideogramically, Seal *LXXVII* consummates the personal Seal *LXXIV–LXXVII* by re-deriving from a personal text an ideogramic form of the flexible prototype ONE: 1–4, 5–6, 7, 8–9, 10 plus a coda. The ideograms have this flexible form for all the documents of '76 and for the Seal when taken by themselves. The text arranges them into four phases as irradiating sun-rays of a Seal-canto consummating its antecedents in the same form as Seal *IV* and in the same voice, ANNUIT COEPTIS. Rearranged into "Canto 77 Explication," which adds the halving horizontal axis, they draw all forms into a stellar plan and Seal/Calendar arcanum for a second phase.

A four-phase rubric subsumes the foregoing and projects the consummation (cf. the fourfold invocation of *IV* and the four-image modulation into "Siena-Leopoldine Reforms"). On "this day" Abner-Pound, instead of watching to see if it would act by itself, lifted a shovel (the shield) to dig up the remembered dead. A sailor warned against the Sirens (seductive stars).[8] An official tried to get Pound onto a justicial commission to inspect the mass graves (a parodied Mount) at Katin. These evolve a statement that the beau monde governs, or at least is a level to which things tend to return, symbolized by

>   Chung
>
>   in the middle
> whether upright or horizontal

That the beau monde appropriates advantage and privilege, however, and will stop at nothing to retain them—so Kung charges—makes "Chung" into continuing revolution. "Upright or horizontal" looks from the comprehensive symbol to the stellar "Canto 77 Explication."

Out of "Chung" (ONE/1) come ideograms elaborating the "process" as "what precedes" (2) and "what follows" (3). On arriving at Hamilton College in 1904 Pound entered a store "preceded" (2) by the crash of his "huge gripsack or satchel" (cf. Munch's) into the glassware. The crash and the query "WOT IZZA COMIN'?" were "followed" (3) by Pound answering "Sochylism is a-comin'." Ascribing his revolutionary (or counter-revolutionary) vocation to 1904 is "somewhat previous," but his American heritage in his satchel (and in his mind) made the omen "effective for immediate scope." If "things have ends (or scopes) and beginnings," "what precedes" and "what follows" is "process," not mere sequence. The then potential form of '76 is "now in the mind indestructible" as Munch's satchel carried the bird can-zone. It was in the "zaino" (knapsack) he carried from Rome to the Tyrol in 1944 (*LXXVIII*). It was in a safe a fellow prisoner stole but couldn't open because he lacked the combination of the coming "Canto 77 Explication," here anticipated "2,   7,   hooo . . . Fasa!" for opening up the city of Wagadu "now in the heart indestructible." Freed by Abner's digging and the "process," men bring from the underworld and Wagadu paired ideograms for " 'How is it far, if you think of it?' " (4), which completes the ideo-

8. The German Admiral Von Tirpitz sent his daughter to school in England with the warning " 'not to be taken in by the English charm.' That came out as I was speaking of Hull and the 'Pilgrim's dinner,' etc. and how every sucker falls for it once." To J. D. Ibbotson, 20 April 1936, Collection at Yale.

grams to be numbered "1–4" of "1–10." Opening up Wagadu completes
"REVOLUTION . . . in the minds of the people" for the Seal cantos of the
second phase.

The next two ideograms turn from "REVOLUTION . . . in the minds of
the people" to an external "next day." "Bright dawn" (5) comments on justice by casting the shadow of the gibbets on the "sht house."⁹ Reaffirmation
of Cavalcantian affection opens up the sun (6) as god's mouth, which completes a first hemicycle and phase concluding with memories of World War I
London and the Odyssean tag "periplum." A three-line shorthand condenses
the whole into the first phase, or projects the succeeding phases (cf. the condensation in "JOHN ADAMS"). That the stellar dance is a "medium" (with
a pun on "middle," *chung*¹) looks ahead to the second ideogramic phase.
" 'To his native mountain' " looks to a third. A Greek motto from Epictetus
("the soul carrying the dead body") looks to a fourth.

Accordingly a dance from the time of Justinian (cf. "in a dance the renewal," *LXXIV*) illuminated the meaning and performance of the Mass for a
Spanish priest friend of Pound's whom a deluxe car carried over a precipice in
the manner of "*sumne fugol othbaer*," a bird carrying a soul (cf. Elpenor and
the bird canzone). Elaborating the textual-visual duality of *LXXV*, a text on the
left translates the foregoing ideograms (the upper left of the coming "Canto
77 Explication," "1–6"), while an untranslated ideogramic sentence (the
upper right of "Canto 77 Explication," "7," there to be translated and then
Englished as a horizontal axis) runs down the right. The pure, epiphanic right
guides translation of "Chung" into "the Mass," of "precede" into pagan
rituals incorporated into it, of "follow" into news "in the s.h." and on Mt.
Ida that World War II had ended, and of "How is it far, if you think of it?"
into the rituals of the sacred grove at Nemi, where the priest defends himself
as "day comes after day." The shift to diurnity turns "dawn" into a contrast
between the war-ending atomic bomb and justice, which raises the question
whether a bomb can be put together again "as the two halves of a seal, or a
tally stick?" "God's mouth" (the "sun") answers that the wills of two Chinese kings thousands of years and miles apart were "as the two halves of a
seal / ½s / in the Middle Kingdom." Rounding back to another "Middle"
(*chung*¹), the juxtaposition completes a duality in two phases while introducing the theme and ideograms of a third of trine and of a third phase.

The ideograms of the first phase (pp. 464–66) were scattered in the text.
Those of the second (pp. 466–67) formed a Chinese sentence juxtaposed with
the text. The three ideograms of the third (pp. 467–68) move back into the
text but keep the closely associated vertical form of the sentence. The first

9. For the symbolized draft "KUNG" as a new "dawn," cf. "The romantic awakening dates
from the production of Ossian. The last century rediscovered the middle ages. It is possible that
this century may find a new Greece in China," "The Renaissance" I: "The Palette," *Poetry*,
Chicago, February 1915.

unites the two sages in one "directio voluntatis," or "lord over the heart" (here eighth, in "Canto 77 Explication" ninth). " 'Halves of a seal' " (here ninth, in "Canto 77 Explication" eighth) join the destinies of Lord Byron and Kung, of Pound and Voltaire, before releasing its real subject, the distributive function of government from '76 in China ("1766 ante Christum," Tching T'ang's distributist revolution, *LIII*), through Greece, Siena, and American '76 (Jefferson's " 'the earth belongs to the living' " and Adams on the iniquity of banks of discount), to the charge that changing the value of money ("METATHEMENON") manipulated World War II. The ideograms for "halves of a seal" are supposed to alert us to the initials "T J," "J A," and "T P" culminating in "E P," and so to enforce the end of this phase with '76 while preparing us, when "Canto 77 Explication" puts all '76 together, for further macaronics. "METATHEMENON" ends this phase as it ended *LXXVI*. The three ideograms and the substantive finality of "halves of a seal" make the three phases (trine) anticipate a whole, as will the similarly concluding, ten-ideogram, left column of "Canto 77 Explication."

The third phase passes to a fourth (pp. 468–75) through a passage framed by the expected "Le Paradis n'est pas artificiel," between invocations which foreshadow the concluding "focus":

      Le Paradis n'est pas artificiel
$Κύθηρα$, $Κύθηρα$,
Moving $ὑπὸ$ $χθονὸς$ enters the hall of the records
    the forms of men rose out of $γέα$
    Le Paradis n'est pas artificiel

Living and dead join between the frame, through the invocations. Having brought grief in Seal *LXXVI*, the "Paradis" rubric here brings acknowledgment that the bird does not fly in tempest as in calm air but that the arrow must fly straight even under bad government. Needed is Confucian self-correction: " 'Missing the bull's eye seeks the cause in himself,' " and " 'only the total sincerity, the precise definition.' " Self-correction, to be evolved in the rest of the decad, here goes back to 1912, when he was challenged for having no political passions. The debate with history continues in the perspective of the collapse of 1945, without ideograms but dominated by poets and poetry, by flashes of divine presence, and by comparison of the prisoners and the camp fence (cf. the bird canzone, the ideograms, and the coming birds on the wires) to the Schifanoia calendar.

Memories and observations finally accelerate into ten focusing images (pp. 474–75). They include a prisoner's can-lid with his name on it (Seal and Calendar cycle), reiteration of the Schifanoia calendar, a recall from *XIX* of bargaining for "ten bob's worth of turquoise" (the Calendar cycle and the ideograms), "mind come to plenum when nothing more will go into it" (for Seal *LXXIV–LXXVII*), the apparently mad prophetess Cassandra, and finally, in a snatch of folk song, "Sister, my sister, who danced on a sequin" (*chung*[1] churning up its revolution against monetary injustice).

Through the dance the images "focus" the canto between columnar, horizontal ideograms (10) onto the vertically emergent god of Pound's birthday and "of no era":

 bringest to focus

ch'êng   *ch'êng*

Zagreus

Zagreus

"Canto 77 Explication" is a comprehensive Seal/Calendar arcanum for '76, as described in Chapter Three. As Seal *I–IV* derived a traditional form in the spirit and matter of "ELEUSIS," Seal *LXXIV–LXXVII* derives a personal form in the spirit and matter of "KUNG." The horizontal axis emphasizes hemicyclic Preambles for a second phase. The personal orthography with heads tipped leftward gives the ideograms the look of birds; as transformations of forms "now in the mind indestructible," of "not of one bird but of many," and of the ladies on the high cliff and goddesses within the crystal ball, they are bird-stars constellated into a new musical score to which to replay and continue playing '76. Viewed together and in relation in "Canto 77 Explication," the ideograms set against Yankee Doodle's macaronic spelling of "WASHINGTON" culminating in the initials of the other men of '76 and his own (left column), "TOM PAINE" culminating in Paine's initials and his own (right column).[10] In constellating the struggle the ideograms form a single *chung*[1] with an axis "horizontal" (the constellation) instead of "upright" (the whole edifice from shield to sun-vision, which will be revealed by addition of the ideogramic axis of *Rock-Drill 85*). The epiphany ideogram *hsien*[3], the epiphany of personality *mo*[4], the epiphany of form *chung*[1] (*ch'eng*[2]), and this constellated *chung*[1] metamorphose the bird canzone for the coming new music. The four ideogram groups are the first of the twelve guiding the more local, personal "periplum."

In a larger structural sense the ideogram-irradiated text consummates the epitome and the four Seal-cantos as "REVOLUTION . . . in the minds of the people" while "Canto 77 Explication" rederives the Calendar from the Seal and projects it to the decad/draft. "Canto 77 Explication" also changes "mass relations" so that the cantos of Seal *LXXIV–LXXVII* take their places

10. I feel entitled to a *jeu d'esprit* here. Yet in fact I *do see* the calligraphy to be intended, and would so argue if I had the descriptive space, should write an essay, or could contend *viva voce* and gesticulatively. In any case note the evidence that leads into the WASHINGTON-PAINE duality—in fact focuses that duality via trine into tetrad and new unity.

in the seventh Calendar decad projected "1–10." All cantos also take their places in a second phase, cantos "1–6" of which are transforming and condensing the previous drafts, canto "7" of which will condense *Pisan*, and cantos "8–10" of which will project the subsequent drafts.

Liberty *LXXIV–LXXIX*

With "Canto 77 Explication" all the personae, kinds of materials, and forms of *Pisan* (the seventh draft and second phase) have been made explicit as "REVOLUTION . . . in the minds of the people" projecting revolutionary implementation; it remains only to apply the forms to the matter toward the ends of declaration, liberty, states' rights, and common law in the seventh draft, and toward the ends of liberty and new union in the second phase. Seal *LXXVII* and "Canto 77 Explication" plainly group the guiding ideograms prototypically: "1" as "ONE" projects *chung*² to the whole, "1–4" are grouped for a revolutionary philosophy coming through "REVOLUTION . . . in the minds of the people," "5–6" are paired (for cases), and "1–6" sum up a first hemicycle and phase; "7," evolving in "1–6," sums up, transforms, and extends "1–6" while changing hemicycle and phase and projecting the sequels; "8–9" ("9–8" in the text) are paired in another change of phase as realizations of form and motive; "10" perfects or focuses the whole in a fourth phase.

The substances of the ensuing cantos show the prototype themes and the themes of the ensuing Constitutional clauses. But the overlying form, projected by "Canto 77 Explication," is a song of liberty being "churned up" in *LXXIV–LXXIX* and complementary songs of new union being "churned up" in *LXXX–LXXXIII*. For this dominant theme the narrative of memory (for the prototype) and the emergent epiphany (for the second phase) constellate a basic duality. The epiphanic personal emphasis is "sealed" by ideograms and the bird canzone rising to Seal *LXXVII* and "Canto 77 Explication," and from there carried ideogramically to the end. The substantive epiphanies, however, are the sustained songs of liberty and union. While what follows subsumes the prototype and clausal themes, it emphasizes the dual theme of the second phase.

"The minds of the people" projecting "REVOLUTION" and its implementation having coalesced in *LXXIV*-as-"ONE," and "REVOLUTION . . . in the minds of the people" having emerged in Seal *LXXIV–LXXVII*, these become in the decad the premises and their concomitants. While the four-phase *LXXVII* consummates the premises emerging from the Seal, however, the epiphanic ideograms of "Canto 77 Explication" are transforming premises ("1–4") and the coming cases ("5–6") into motives so that "1–6" may precipitate the evolving epiphanic song of liberty.

Cantos *LXXVIII* and *LXXIX* are paired as cases against victorious usury through which the evolving song of liberty finally comes. Canto *LXXVIII* weighs a Varchian case (*V*) setting the collective military victors, "40 geese" who have assembled to make peace but really to continue "the economic war," against the individual case of Mussolini, whose corporate state, ideal if not actual, is claimed to have sought real peace through economic justice. Mussolini has followed Lorenzo dei Medici (pp. 477–78) as peacemaker and stylist who shared with Pound the effort "to dream the Republic" (of Salò). Pound recalls Mussolini's principles (p. 479) and his own explanation of the principles of social credit (pp. 481–82), probably in 1933; Mussolini said then that he would have to think about it, but was hung up by the heels before his thought could come into action efficiently. Vindication of the corporate ideal culminates States 72–78.

The ideal of the corporate state remains in Pound's mind supported by the epiphanic forms evolved in Seal *LXXIV–LXXVII* ("again the vision," *V*). The rubric to *LXXVIII* includes, against collective usury, foreshadowings of the supportive epiphany. Music leading toward the presaging ladies is keyed by "little sister who could dance on a saxpence" and by her more formal *"Sobr' un zecchin'!"* (from *LXXVII*), leading into a Cassandra with "eyes . . . like tigers." Against the "40 geese," to help "dream the Republic" and found it, Pound carried his bird-stars northward in his "zaino" (knapsack) as Aeneas carried his "gods" from fallen Troy to Italy. Insect music, folk song, and news that the Mozart festival has reopened in Salzburg, emerging in the middle of *LXXVIII*, look toward a crescendo in *LXXIX*; "Aram nemus vult" (from *LXXIV*) looks toward a final focus of *LXXIV–LXXIX* while "as under the rain altars" looks beyond toward *LXXX–LXXXIV*. *"Sobr' un zecchin'!"* takes ideogramic form in *tao*³, the way, a music accompanying Pound's monetary advice to Mussolini.[11] Toward the end of *LXXVIII* Odysseus's amorous escapades bring a further elaboration of the ladies, including tiger-eyed Cassandra, who circle about Pound's mind unperceivable by his captors, presaging *LXXIX*. Canto *LXXVIII* ends with a silent moonscape waiting for something to happen and with final judgment from natural spring and autumn and from Confucius's *Spring and Autumn*,

there

are

no

righteous

wars

Lunar peace and the "benediction" passing white oxen mock the peace being sought by victorious usury. The Varchian case is clinched in a Confucian version of the Eleusinian "focus" "Zagreus / Zagreus" of *LXXVII*.

---

11. *Tao*³ is translated in "Terminology," *Ta Hsio: The Great Digest* (1948, 1951), "The process. The footprints and the foot carrying the head; the head conducting the feet, an orderly movement under the lead of the intelligence."

The expectant moonscape and the hinging judgments open onto a still expectant moonscape in *LXXIX*. Self-justification for Odyssean love of the ladies (cf. Odysseus and the troubadors, *VI*)—

> think not that you wd/ gain if their least caress
> were faded from my mind
> I had not loved thee half so well
> Loved I not womankind''

—opens up the case for and against many individuals (enemies and brethren). For the coming epiphany, the musical rubric picks up the musical middle of *LXXVIII* ''So Salzburg reopens,'' which ''lit a flame in my thought.'' Amorous changeability keynotes Amendment 79.

The narrated case of *LXXIX* considers such instances as a brother prisoner's musical talent, a certain Goedel's aid during the walk north, the trial of Maréchal Petain, the camp band's music versus Beethoven's, the unprovoked attack on Ismarus of the Cicones by Odysseus and his crew on their home voyage, perverters of the Constitution, Athena's insufficient sex appeal, the atom bomb and the slaughter ''(on both sides),'' munitions profiteers, and the ''pejorocracy'' of Yeats's ''pragmatic pig'' of a world ''½'' (or even ''2 thirds'') ''dead at the top.'' Epiphany is augured as birds begin to form musical notes on the camp wires. Nature joining in Pound's eye with artifice elicits a vindication of his own style sealed $t'zu^2\ ta^{24}$, clear words:

     4 birds on 3 wires, one bird on one
   the imprint of the intaglio depends
     in part on what is pressed under it
  the mould must hold what is poured into it
          in
         discourse
            what matters is
to get it across e poi basta
     5 of 'em now on 2;
     on 3; 7 on 4

His matter is affecting (via his informing mind) his art. His informing mind is seeking to hold its matter. In discourse matter and form should converge in communication, a proof imminent in the epiphanic songs. Meanwhile he is the chattering yellow bird who must come ''to rest'' in such songs: after $t'zu^2$ ta^{24}, the sixth ideogram-group in the sixth canto, nature's birds take the form of three tiny, sketched ideograms for ''the yellow bird / to rest'' signed ''(auctor)'': HORUS (as central star) mediates six foregoing ''periplum'' ideograms aimed at liberty and six (to come) aimed at new union.

Before the cases end, out of the opening moonscape and erotic rubric, out of the apparitional birds, and out of ideogramic vindication of style and identification of voice, invocation of epiphanic song begins. Pound invokes

"O Lynx, my love, my lovely lynx" that it keep watch over his fermenting wine-pot mind and guard close his mountain still "Till the god come into this whiskey" (cf. Amendment 79). Though the matter of the epiphany will be Eleusinian, the spirit of his moonshine will be American and Indian: "Manitou, god of lynxes, remember our corn" runs from the Indian god to American style (cf. '76 and Dos Santos's "did it on water-soaked corn," a parody of Whitman's style, *XII*). As the invoked epiphany seeks to work itself free from narrated memory (pp. 488–89) Pound ends his cases with a self-vindication which turns the moonscape to dawn:

> The moon has a swollen cheek
> and when the morning sun lit up the shelves and battalions
> of the West, cloud over cloud
> > Old Ez folded his blankets
> Neither Eos nor Hesperus has suffered wrong at my hands

Or he ends with a play on a brother prisoner's name and "sweet land of liberty," "Sweetland on sick call."

The lynx litany invokes a ritual dance of demigods (the constellation) in a mountain forest filled with light, "in the close garden of Venus," where each lies under his fig tree (cf. "each in the name of his god") free of the dust of Hell. Priapus, Bacchus, and Aphrodite (a Holy Family analogous to HORUS, OSIRIS, and ISIS) are worshipped as "having root in the equities." As epiphany breaks free of memory (p. 489) the lynx and Manitou are bid keep watch on the epiphanic flame until the fermenting mind begins to reveal fire-bearing fruit (pp. 489–90), a transformation of the crystal ball. The fruit modulates into "The rose in the steel dust" taking natural form amid a stir of dust from old rose leaves of memory (pp. 490–91). Finally (pp. 491–92) the dance of the demigods draws forth ladies and goddesses leading in triumph Aphrodite, goddess of love and liberty, "terrible in resistance" but a petal lighter than the sea-foam from which she was born. The epiphany of liberty focuses (from *LXXIV* and *LXXVIII*) nature's desire for a shrine,

> aram
>
> nemus
>
> vult

Canto, cases, and hemicycle end apostrophizing New World associates of the lynx, the puma and Cimbica, sacred respectively to Hermes and Helios.[12]

Revealed liberty completes an epiphany introduced in lesser epiphany by the birth of Venus in *LXXIV* and evolving through other epiphanies enforced by symbolized music both artificial and natural. It reveals against the "pax

---

12. Professor John Espey informed me that "Cimbica" is an Indian name for a California wild cat.

mundi'' being arranged by triumphant usury in the cases (*LXXVIII–LXXIX*) a basis for real world peace in harmony with a tradition of nature and her goddesses made new in renewed traditional song. It justifies a liberal love of the ladies, without which such a vision of liberty would have been impossible. The focuses ''Zagreus / Zagreus'' for renaissance (*LXXVII*), ''there / are / no / righteous / wars'' for natural ethics (*LXXVIII*), and ''aram / nemus / vult'' for founding (*LXXIX*) drive home in Seal symbolism the spirits of the three paideumas condensed in the respective cantos. Within the second phase under PAN, the hemicycle ends under KUPRIS keynoted by the libertarian PRIAPUS and prepares for a second hemicycle under JUNO, whose feast is EPITHALAMIUM for new union.

New Union *LXXX–LXXXIV*

As a seventh canto (cf. *VII*) *LXXX* sums up its predecessors to declare independence and ordain through liberty states' rights; as a second phase it turns from liberty toward new union. In the form of *VII*, which summed up a tradition and projected a new tradition, and of *LXXIV*, which summed up tradition while projecting a personality for ''WE the People,'' *LXXX* sums up personality directed toward liberty and projects personality directed toward new union. Personality directed toward liberty (pp. 493–500) comes through a six-part recapitulation of the struggle for liberty in *LXXIV–LXXIX* as six drafts come through the Odyssean opening of *LXXIV* and as ''7'' comes through ''1–6'' in ''Canto 77 Explication''; a struggle from achieved liberty emerges like ''7'' on the horizontal axis (pp. 500–14), and projects the rest of the decad as ''halves of a tally stick'' directed by ''one's will'' toward the ''focus'' (''8–10'') of a new union (pp. 514–16). The dichotomy will be phrased as a marriage of ''man, earth; two halves of the tally'' (*LXXXII*) before being focused as a culminating union with ''now my world'' (*LXXXIII*).

A fellow prisoner's ''Ain' committed no federal crime, / jes a slaight misdemeanor','' reflecting on ''the vagaries of our rising θέμις'' (and on the treason charge against Pound for his self-styled defense of the Constitution), provides a rubric for Supreme Law 80–82 in *LXXX–LXXXII*. In the six passages the personality confirmed by the epiphany of liberty affirms his struggle against death and destruction.

The rubric for the first and for the whole, ''Amo ergo sum, and in just that proportion,'' introduces interlineations which set a pattern for personal emergence. The first (pp. 493–94) sums up in the deaths of friends and in lost customs and manners ''eras'' that have ended since the beginnings during the 1910s. Through it come ''senesco sed amo,'' a regret that the ''eucalyptus bobble'' of memory is missing, but relief that ''the mortal fatigue of action postponed'' is over. The ''eras'' evolve to ''Turgenev (Tiresias)'' 's ''Nothing but death is irreparable,''[13] which elicits the affirmation (of memory) ''Still hath his mind entire'' (cf. *LXXIV*).

The second (pp. 494–95), which contains an analogy between calligraphic style and an ability to draw down birds from the trees (cf. *LXXV*), views the victims of political and literary collaborations (including those with the Axis during World War II) through a refrain which admits an inexorable ''warp and woof'' (the constellation) ''from heaven.'' The stellar destiny is epiphanized by Old Glory at once etched against the sky (the stripes) and melting into it (the blue field). The result is a ''law of discourse'' at once intellectually functional (''To communicate and then stop, . . . To go far and come to an end'') and aesthetically attractive (like Circe's hair or like bird-charming calligraphy).

The third (pp. 495–96), raising the question of the Italian succession after the betrayal of ''poor old Benito'' (and his systems, *LXXVI*), theorizes that revolutionary success or failure depends on what can be done with the gunmen and (replying to Yeats) that a man must occasionally sit in a senate if he hopes to pierce the ''darrk'' senatorial mind.

The fourth (pp. 496–98), confessing ''action somewhat sporadic,'' wonders about destructions and restorations in the ''Holy Cities'' Siena and Rimini and about resurrection of the revolutionary spirit (cf. *LXXVII*). The spirit remains in the memory to be drawn forth by the ''eucalyptus bobble,'' ''cat-faced, croce di Malta, figura del sol'' (a star), which is sealed with the ideo-grams for ''How is it far, if you think of it,'' the fourth of *LXXVII* and ''Canto 77 Explication.''

Confirming ''to each tree its own mouth and savour'' modulates into (fifth, pp. 498–99) the cadence count of the camp trainees, *''Hot hole hep cat,''* and into the camp's loudspeaker music. These, along with ''Prowling night-puss'' 's rummaging among Pound's effects, threaten the self-inspiring mind (cf. *LXXVIII*); but it protects ''the cat-faced eucalyptus nib'' by appropriating from the camp's ''radio steam Calliope'' (the Muse of epic poetry) and from its Battle Hymn of the Republic ''mi-hine eyes hev'' (seen the glory of the coming of the Lord)—and seen a good deal of the republic, which is ''fairly tough and unblastable.'' As to the hymn, well, in contrast to ''the *god*-damned crooning / put me down for temporis acti.''

At the other end from the ''eras'' (sixth, pp. 499–500) ''Amo ergo sum'' is confirmed beyond time by the self-identification ''ΟΥ ΤΙΣ / ἄχρονος / now there are no more days.'' Moon, stars, and dawn converge (cf. the atmosphere of the epiphany of liberty, *LXXIX*) as the libertarian role is found in the con-stellation of Orion and its dog-star, which receives the ideogram *ch'üan*[3], in its elements a man (cf. *mo*, ''a man on whom the sun has gone down,'' *LXXIV*)

---

13. ''Turgenev builds a whole novel into the enforcement of some one or two speeches, so that we have, as the gaunt culmination, some phrase about 'the heart of another' or the wide pardon in Maria Timofevna's 'Nothing but death is irrevocable.' '' ''The Rev. G. Crabbe, LL.B.,'' *Future*, London, February 1917.

led by a dot (a star). Emergence from the destructions and from the descent into Hell, and acknowledgment that things must be taken as they come, confirm a freedom to continue writing. The style is "dialog" between old and new symbolized by Old Glory precipitating NOVUS ORDO SECLORUM. The new aim will be to bring the reader by the "law of discourse" (cf. *t'zu²* *ta²⁴*, *LXXIX*) to "the gist of the discourse," a new union within the self and between the self and "now my world."

A large break and a rubric of successive beginnings open up a formal, nostalgic autobiography, the main body of the canto (pp. 500–514). A brief Odyssean opening recalls departures from America in 1908 with eighty dollars, from England in 1921 with a letter of Thomas Hardy's (on the primacy of subject matter), and from Rapallo to the DTC with one eucalyptus pip. A longer Elpenorean passage envisions a boy nailed to the earth above Rapallo beneath a changing moon goddess who governs suffering, death, truth, "the paraclete," the joy of birds, and fatal beauty. The young Dumas, author of comradeship (*The Three Musketeers*), weeps as "Death's seeds move in the year"; but, like the eucalyptus, they are "semina motuum," seed of motions. Larks rise at Allegre, above Rapallo. Changing fate comes to a focus in Chinese, Latin, and Greek for the Three Graces, consoling caretakers of the weeping Tovarisch and Elpenor.

The prevalence of bad government, which brings fog from the marshland and claustrophobia of the mist, gives the impression that "beyond the stockade there is chaos and nothingness," that only the DTC and the mind within it are real (cf. "we alone having being," *VII*, and Wagadu "now in the mind indestructible," *LXXIV*). With almost no reference to present circumstances, a long memorial periplum passes back to London and Paris before, during, and after World War I (pp. 501–7), then to New York of 1910–11 and earlier (pp. 507–8), and then to mixed recollections of London, Provence, and Venice (pp. 508–10). His friends' works are like cobwebs when the spider is gone (p. 501). "Les moeurs passent et la douleur reste" (p. 504). He adjures a girl (his daughter) that when she is old she remember and pass on that "there can be honesty of mind / without overwhelming talent / I have perhaps seen a waning of that tradition" (p. 506). Recollection gradually intensifies the feeling for what has been lost until Aphrodite's appearance in "the moon's barge" (p. 510) portends KUPRIS passing to a sterner JUNO. Elegy deepens further (p. 511) with Elpenor's tag "Beauty is difficult" and with presages of coming epiphanies (esp. *LXXXI*) until debacle breaks through former beauty and serenity (pp. 511–12) in a reprise of Odyssean (pp. 512–13) and Elpenorean destinies (pp. 513–14).

Odysseus, the Axis, and Pound are joined in "care and craft in forming leagues and alliances" and in "the folly of attacking that island" (Ismarus and England), all "against the decree" of fate. On the other side is Zeus's justification of Odysseus, "with a mind like that he is one of us." But despite a benign wind now favoring the periplum Pound finds himself at the gates of death; only Whitman and Lovelace found in a cheap anthology on "the jo-house seat" (cf. Leucothoe's "bikini," *Los Cantares*) saved him as the raft broke and the waters washed over him (at "the Charybdis of action," before Calypso's, Phaeacia, and Ithaca). "For those who drink of the bitterness" he invokes the Mass and the saints, begs repose from the eternal process of the "saeclorum" ruled by the Queen of Heaven (Mary cum JUNO), and ends with an Odyssean confession (in Villon's French)

> Les larmes que j'ai creées m'inondent
> Tard, très tard je t'ai connue, la Tristesse
> I have been hard as youth sixty years

A breakdown of Odyssean inflexibility in the face of error brings reiteration, in this new mode under a stern JUNO, of entry into Circe's swine-sty. In calm after tempest "the ants seem to wobble / as the morning sun catches their shadows"; so do the shadows of men of no fortune being mustered by name for their daily duties. Out of Hell, in a wind so light that "the day moves not at all," they earn Elpenor's "men of no fortune and with a name to come." Pound becomes Elpenor. Elpenor himself is granted a tomb under Zoagli where he can count the shingle. By identifying his fate with the prisoners' Odysseus/Pound has laid Elpenor's ghost to rest.

So Pound reconciles himself to his present condition and his nostalgia. He reconciles himself to England epiphanically in two groups of lyric imitations ("8–9") and in a focusing lyric ("10"). The first of two (pp. 514–16) begins with a boisterous economic takeoff on the self-exiled Browning's nostalgia, "Oh to be in England now that Winston's out": now, "if money be free again," the bank may be the nation's, the old charters may be revived, and the old terrace may come alive again. Snatches of older lyrics recall the ghosts of a still older England as Pound had elicited them on their own ground decades earlier; they end with a snatch from Bertran De Born's elegy for the death of the youthful heir to the English throne, with which Born had tried to reconcile himself to the father Henry II (cf. Pound's "Planh for the Young English King," *Personae*, and *The Sixth Canto*).

Elegy modulates into the second of two (p. 516), "Tudor indeed is gone and every rose," a sorrowful takeoff on the Victorian *Rubaiyat*. Ancestral hatreds dating back to the War of the Roses continue to victimize artists like Edward Fitzgerald and Pound and to prevent reconciliation with France. Careless even of exact ancestries, the hatreds are careless too whether "a rational soul" might be stirring within the rose's "stem or summer shoot" to advance contrition and, if not seeking France's forgiveness for past wrongs, seeking at least their oblivion. "A rational soul" may suggest Tom Paine seeking reconciliations (with Washington, England, and France), as in the calligraphic macaronics of "Canto 77 Explication."

In any case "a rational soul" tries to save a "green midge half an ant's size" by advising it to stay on the safe side of the rain ditch lest it become the

"T-bone" of a "puss lizard" (p. 516). The little vignette holds some promise that Kensington Gardens in "our London / my London, your London" may have remained as unchanged as the Pisan field and as susceptible to such protection. If the lyrics beginning "Oh to be in England" project the self-catechizing epiphany "What thou lovest well" (*LXXXI*), and if "Tudor indeed is gone" projects the epiphanic "connubium terrae" (*LXXXII*), then reconciliation of London and Pisa project coming union through a wasp family with "now my world" (*LXXXIII*). A final reconciliation, "sunset grand couturier," may project prior codas (the fountain mind, *LXXIV*, and "Canto 77 Explication") toward the affirming coda *LXXXIV*.

"Sunset grand couturier" having brought back the night, the rubric of *LXXXI* catches Zeus lying "in Ceres' bosom" before sunrise while Taishan is "attended of loves" under Venus (the morning star) in preparation for JUNO's EPITHALAMIUM. Self-catechesis (*LXXXI*) and marriage with the earth (*LXXXII*) are linked like the phase as "man, earth: two halves of the tally" while continuing the evolution toward new union. Or, the man speaks in both *LXXXI* and *LXXXII* in response to the call of the earth through the magic jynx-wheel, named after the jynx-bird, with which a woman draws her lover: she intones a Greek tag from Theocritus in each canto. Not only man but also mind and heaven will marry the earth. New union evolving through new personality derives from the Malatestan drive toward a new revolutionary tradition (*VIII–IX* in *VIII–XI*). It subsumes the relevant projections of new union by the Declaration (de facto independence and sovereign powers) and by the Constitution (Amendment and Supreme Law), activated by the Bill's political rights. The two cantos project *Section: Rock-Drill* and *Thrones*.

Both *LXXXI* and *LXXXII* have very formal four-phase forms (cf. Branches/ Powers in the dead) for the dual memory and epiphany. After the rubric the first half of *LXXXI* (pp. 517–19) consists mainly of remembered revolutions and revolutionaries, violent and peaceful, right and wrong, into which comes the Greek "Jynx . . . bring my lover to my house." In the middle "AOI!" introduces epiphany with a "*libretto*" (pp. 519–20) of neo-Renaissance English lyric aimed at tempering the instruments, fashioning "so airy a mood / To draw up leaf from the root," and so turning cloud to spirit. The eyes of Chaucer's merciless "beauté," modulating into the light murmur of birds or insects, brings "new subtlety of eyes" into the tent, "whether of spirit or hypostasis" (p. 520). The new eyes show no anger but what the blindfold (of justice) hides, a "stance between the eyes," color, "diastasis" (rest), carelessness, and unawareness. They do not fill the tent with the "full Ειδὼς" (vision) but "interpass, penetrate" with Pound's eyes (cf. the interpenetrating constellation) as his voice chants

> sky's clear
> night's sea
> green of the mountain pool
> shone from the unmasked eyes in half-mask's space.

Mystical justice educed by lyric song and chanted into stellar vision elicits from him who has been prepared the famous self-castigating litany "What thou lovest well remains, / the rest is dross" (pp. 520–22).

Remembered revolution included parenthetically the poetic revolution "To break the pentameter, that was the first heave." "Oh to be in England now that Winston's out" and "Tudor indeed is gone and every rose" returned to pentameter for reconciliation with the English tradition, though the first goes on to stretch even the energetic Browning's rhythms and rhymes, the second stiffens the languid *Rubaiyat* stanza, and both have a distinct Poundian *robustezza* of tone and movement. The shorter lyric lines of *LXXX* are virtual quotations and the midge-lyric is Poundian free verse. The *"libretto"* of *LXXXI* refashions quatrains and couplet refrains in a virtuosity of trimeters and tetrameters using iambs, trochees, anapests, and dactyls. "What thou lovest well remains," after the Chaucerian pentameter adapted from French syllabics, reconciles Pound to the tradition of French syllabics crossed with English accentuals which produced the traditionally most serious English form, blank verse. For his serious moral subject he echoes or subsumes "ply over ply" the blank verse of every period of English, again varying it so that it is unmistakably twentieth century and his own. Moreover the litany consummates the four-phase canto in four stanzas: historical tradition, aesthetic tradition, moral tradition, and poetic tradition affirmed.

A stanza of historical tradition repeats in five of its eight or ten lines (depending on line breaks) that "What thou lovest well remains," that it "shall not be reft from thee," and that it "is thy true heritage"; the second and third assertions (lines two and three) are reversed in the last two lines, so that "What thou lovest well" frames the stanza doubly and triply. If apparently broken lines are rejoined, all lines are blank verse except for two echoes of French alexandrines. Between the heavy declaratory frames, in stretched pentameter, occur the challenge of *Pisan*, "Whose world, or mine or theirs / or is it of none," and the succession of phases into *Pisan*, "First came the seen, then thus the palpable / Elysium, though it were in the halls of hell."

A stanza of aesthetic tradition, except for one broken line almost perfect blank verse, opens with all English imagery extended in Pound's own kind of symbolism or imagism, "The ant's a centaur in his dragon world." Pound makes it a rubric for a new refrain, "Pull down thy vanity," here directed at human presumption that it "Made courage, or made order, or made grace." Man must "Learn of the green world what can be thy place / In scaled invention or true artistry" (terms for Pound's own schema and spontaneity); for, framing with the first line, "The green casque has outdone your elegance."

" 'Master thyself, then others shall thee beare,' " going back to the Chaucerian moral tradition, introduces a diatribe against human pride. "Pull down they vanity" frames a reduction of assumed human grandeur to "a beaten dog beneath the hail" and "A swollen magpie in a fitful sun," "Half black half white / Nor knowst'ou wing from tail": while divided pentameters reflect moral urgency, framing rhyme (''Hail/tail'') and a framing ''Pull down thy vanity'' bind the diatribe. Diatribe by natural image passes through a mediating ''Pull down they vanity'' to direct moral diatribe in the same rhythms but now virtually all rhymed:

> Pull down thy vanity
> > How mean thy hates
> Fostered in falsity,
> > Pull down thy vanity,
> Rathe to destroy, niggard in charity,
> Pull down thy vanity,
> > I say pull down.

The three stanzas have sought through historical, aesthetic, and moral tradition grounds for new poetic action. A fourth stanza affirms what Pound has done in the same substantive terms but in a comparably humble free verse. The claim ''But to have done instead of not doing / this is not vanity''[14] is supported by his having ''with decency, knocked / that a Blunt should open.'' (Before World War I Pound and others formally called on Wilfred Scawen Blunt, a blunt man and a poet of the tradition, to honor his career). The gesture revered shared tradition and shared humanity: ''To have gathered from the air a live tradition / or from a fine old eye the unconquered flame / This is not vanity.'' Through the overall epiphany, a purgation, tradition has accepted its latest spokesman so that he can justifiably say ''Here error is all in the not done, / all in the diffidence that faltered'' and traverse the ellipsis toward the ''connubium terrae.''

The rubric to *LXXXII*—

> When with his hunting dog I see a cloud
> > ''Guten Morgen, Mein Herr'' yells the black boy
> > > from the jo-cart

—presumably personifies Pound as the clouded constellation Orion being led by the dog-star (cf. *LXXX*), and as the accused traitor being led by his nose, toward the painful ''connubium terrae'': pentameter mitigates the cloud, however, while camaradarie mitigates the smell. Complementing *LXXXI* (Branches) in the decad, *LXXXII* has its memories and epiphany extended to four for the Powers. The memories (pp. 523–25), in the light of the nostalgias and poetic epiphanies of *LXXX* and *LXXXI*, gather recollections of the London poetic scene before World War I around the general idea ''But given what I know now I'd have / got thru it somehow.'' The memories come to a focus in

---

14. Voltaire, when he was being sculpted by Pigalle at 76 years old, in a letter to Mme. Necker, Ferney, 19 juin 1770: ''Ma statue fera sourire quelques philosophes, et renfrognera les sourcils éprouvés de quelque coquin d'hypocrite ou de quelque polisson de folliculaire: vanité des vanités! Mais tout n'est pas vanité; ma tendre reconnaissance pour mes amis et surtout pour vous, madame, n'est pas vanité.''

"the idea that CONversation," a principal medium of revolution, "should not utterly wither," attributed to Yeats and Ford Madox Ford. Yeats is singled out for his "choice / and / perfect / lyrics" and for his anecdotes, but Ford's conversation consisted in "*res* non *verba*" and he never "dented an idea for a phrase's sake," revealing thereby more "humanitas" or "jen" (the ninth ideogram).

Epiphany begins to come through memories in references to the murder of Agamemnon by Clytemnestra, to Greek moulds in the margins of Basinio's manuscript epic about the Malatesta, and to the works on Greek prosody by Otis (cf. *LXX*) and on Greek types by Soncino (cf. *XXX*); all elicit a mournful "The 'marble men' shall pass into nothingness." As in *LXXIX*, however, birds on the wires herald epiphany in another mode. Lyric (p. 525) begins to emerge through a reappearance of Cythera from the liberty hemicycle and from *LXXX* ("in the moon's barge"), through a snatch from Landor ("With Dirce in one bark convey'd," cf. the lyrics of *LXXX*), and through "Be glad poor beaste, love follows after thee" (cf. the litany, *LXXXI*). These modulate into the spontaneous "Till the cricket hops / but does not chirrp in the drill field," which opens up a wedding invitation:

8th day of September
    f   f
      d

        g
        write the birds in their treble scale

The song, however, is "Terreus! Terreus!," a bird-cry of rape, death and metamorphosis.

The epiphany expands (pp. 525–26) through the recurrent judgment of Confucius's *Spring and Autumn* (cf. *LXXVIII*) that there are no righteous wars, here elaborated to mean total right on either side. News of war's end (an epiphany), which takes a long time to traverse the ignorance of locality, traveled quicker (more epiphanically) when they conveyed the fall of Troy to Greece by lighting fires on a string of mountain tops. So Whitman remains "exotic, still suspect" four miles from Camden while "in Tdaenmarck efen dh'beasantz gnow him."

The song of the brown bird bereaved of his mate in Whitman's "Out of the Cradle Endlessly Rocking" announces a four-phase "connubium terrae." The chantlike free verse adapts Whitman's New World cadences to new circumstances, as has (in one sense) Pound's whole poem. A wooer intones the power of "GEA TERRA" to draw until one sinks into her "by an arm's width / embracing thee" and so recognizes that "Wisdom lies next thee, / simply, past metaphor."

A bridegroom asks that herbs flower from the spot where he lies, as he imagined they did from Niccolò d'Este's body buried naked by the Po (*XXIV*). The wind draws like the jynx-wheel until he imagines that he lies in the earth "to the breast bone, to the left shoulder / . . . to the height of ten inches or over" (a measure of '76). The consequent "man, earth : two halves of the tally" is Whitmanian.

The wisdom of coming rebirth, "but I will come out of this knowing no one / neither they me," brings the "connubium" itself, not an Agamemnon-like death but immersion in the "mysterium" of "fluid XΘΟΝΟΣ" until he is drunk with its "'IXΩP."

Finally "but that a man should live in that further terror ["the undertow / of the wave receding"], and live" introduces a climax to the dark night of the soul,

the loneliness of death came upon me
(at 3 P.M., for an instant)   δακρύων
                                                                  ἐντεῦθεν

Out of the Greek "I weep therefore" comes the "I am" of the spirit of '76 set to neo-Whitmanian music,

three solemn half notes
                         their white down chests black-rimmed
on the middle wire
                         periplum

The Requiescat In Pace of *p'i*[1] *san*[1], three great, a pun inherent in the title of the draft,[15] affirms through the culmination of the "periplum" a rebirth of Odysseus/Pound through "my family," the myriad dead, Elpenor, and Tiresias, and of a new Tom Paine through "my family" Jefferson, Washington, and Adams.

Canto *LXXXIII* "focuses" ("10") the decad of the seventh draft, fourth paideuma, and second phase. As in the previous cantos of *Pisan*, however, the themes of the second phase (liberty and new union) subsume the decadal themes in a tenth canto, which in the several documents are anyway new union activated by the reserved powers of the Bill. They also subsume the themes of the seventh draft and fourth paideuma, which will be summed up in the coda *LXXXIV*. Further, its clause 83 "ratifies" the 83-clause, seven draft-Article states' rights Constitution, which is converging with the themes of the seventh draft and fourth paideuma; convergence will be completed by the clause of memorializing, signing, sealing, and delivering, 84 in *LXXXIV*. Canto *LXXXIII* is to be read primarily within the evolving second phase, but the other themes show through.

The mind's flow and the poet's breath, art, and imagination converge with nature's flow, the breath of the process, nature's art, and the world's eyes, sun and moon. The epiphanies of union are "focused" but also tested by the

15. Cf. "Our dynasty came in because of a great sensibility" (*p'i*[1] *ling*[2]), *85*, and the *San Ku*, three orphan (ministers), *87*, *90*.

sense of a lost world perhaps never to be seen again, and by the theory and practice of another kind of symbolist poetry; only then do the universal eyes and the poet's eyes focus in "my world." Ten irradiating parts achieve all "focuses" substantively while perfecting the ten-part epitome (*LXXIV*-as-"ONE"), "Canto 77 Explication," and the draft/phase locus (*LXXX*), and while consummating the ten cantos of the decad. Personal convergence of the living revolutionary persona with nature transforms convergence of the historical Malatesta with the historical Eagle (*X*).

Unlike its predecessors, this culminating epiphany begins at the beginning, first to consummate the epitome (*LXXIV*) and then to consummate the Seal-vision (*LXXIV–LXXVII*). Its rubric cites the epiphanic theme of the decad's stream of consciousness, "ὕδωρ," and extends it to a political motive, "HUDOR and Pax." Further, it elaborates epiphany to Gemisto Plethon's Neo-Platonic philosophy, which "stemmed all" (cf. PAN) "from Neptune," inspiring thereby the bas reliefs in the Tempio Malatestiano (which included a zodical calendar); also to the remarks of "Mr Yeats (W. B.)": " 'Nothing affects these people / Except our conversation,' " for Pound the only true mode (the artist's) of effecting "REVOLUTION . . . in the minds of the people."

Past history (the shield) yields the philosopher of light and of "the virtue *hilaritas*," Scotus Erigena (cf. *LXXIV*), caught putting Greek tags in his verses (cf. Pound's ideograms) while the queen of France is stitching her husband's shirts. The homely scene introduces a pervading family theme, which consummates "Odysseus / the name of my family." The passage focuses "Le Paradis n'est pas artificiel," the theme of Pound's "paradiso terrestre" (cf. Elpenor in *LXXIV*, *LXXVI*, and *LXXVII*).

"Uncle William" Yeats's epiphany, on the other hand, consisted in admiring "the symbol" with the object (here Notre Dame Cathedral) "standing inside it." Epiphany beginning and ending in the mind (the form is the constellation) is countered by Pound's admiration of actual churches and by his "sered eyes," which in the quiet of his drenched tent see a rain the color of feldspar and "blue as the flying fish off Zoagli." Elicited by an experience of "pax" and "HUDOR," the fragment of wisdom "the sage / delighteth in water / the humane man has amity with the hills" recalls the differentiation between Yeats and Ford (*LXXXII*) and looks forward to a climactic amity with a wasp family. Recollections of grass growing by weirs, on a roof, and up to windows (is Whitman lurking here?) are set against "thought Uncle William," until a face worn in a "family group," repeating a face in a fresco painted two centuries earlier, illustrates how nature, the source of art, makes art new in new life. Pound's stream of consciousness is generalized "πάντα 'ρει," which Yeatsian symbolism abhorred.

The general theme places the sage below the altars of the rain spirits (cf. "aram nemus vult" and the Mount), which have filled all hollows so that vision moves forward to "the phantom mountain above the cloud" (the

Mount seen in and from the constellation). First, however, evidence of human injustice is read in the eyes of a caged panther, which say " 'Nothing. Nothing that you can do...' ''; Pound responds from his own case

> Nor can who has passed a month in the death cells
>> believe in capital punishment
> No man who has passed a month in the death cells
>> believes in cages for beasts

But the eyes of a dryad are like clouds over Mt. Taishan in the middle of a rainstorm. Rain penetrating to the roots draws ''the hidden city'' upward under the bark. Chinese Taishan joins with American Chocorua at Eleusinian Pisa. A new moon faces Taishan, so that one must count by the dawn star (Lucifer, but also Venus). The dryad's peace is like water as September sun strikes the pools. Heliads (sun-rays) lift the mist from young willows until no base is seen under Taishan, only the brightness of '' *udor* ὕδωρ.'' Poplar tips float in the brightness until the justiceless DTC vanishes. Only the stockade posts stand: Wagadu, before ''in the heart indestructible,'' remains for the eyes.

The dawn sun having ''trapped their shadows'' so that ''the ants seem to stagger,'' the evolving Seal epiphany is articulated like its predecessors as wisdom. A universal breath, coming through the poet, harmonizes Anglo-Saxon monosyllables and Romance polysyllables with a Confucian formality. The breath ''wholly covers the mountains,'' ''shines and divides,'' ''nourishes by its rectitude,'' ''does no injury''; ''overstanding the earth it fills the nine fields / to heaven.''

> Boon companion to equity
>> it joins with the process
>>> lacking it, there is inanition

''When the equities are gathered together / as birds alighting'' (cf. Elpenor's ''that bird-hearted equity make timber / and lay hold of the earth,'' *LXXIV*) ''it springeth up vital.'' ''If deeds be not ensheaved and garnered in the heart / there is inanition.'' ''That he eat of the barley corn / and move with the seed's breath'' rounds back to the beginning. The ''sered eyes'' and the eyes of panther and dryad focus in ''the sun as a golden eye / between dark cloud and the mountain,'' which awaits a coming moon's eye.

Testing the Seal epiphany, the next two passages result in homely focuses of *LXXVIII* and *LXXIX* culminating in a humble family version, objective rather than mental, of evoked Aphrodite. Admonition to let the process grow naturally, recalled from a Venetianess and sealed Confucianly ''don't work so hard'' (the tenth ideogram group in the tenth canto), causes eyes to picture places in the Venice of their youth and the ''family eyes'' of an old gondolier reflecting the Adriatic over three generations. The eyes weep.

But the same eyes catch ''Brother Wasp'' (cf. the brotherhood of the second case) building of mud, by the "swallow system," a neat four-room house shaped like a squat Indian bottle (cf. Pound in a bottle and the American Indian theme, *LXXIX*). Minutely observed fact restores the past as dream and the present as *hilaritas* ("It comes over me that Mr. Walls," a prisoner who lent him a razor, "must be a ten-strike / with the signorinas"). Accordingly, as a consequence of the "connubium terrae," warmth after chill sunrise" brings "an infant, green as new grass" to the opening of "Madame La Vespa's bottle." With the new birth the poet's spirit springs up again as mint or as had clover "by the gorilla cage / with a four-leaf." He knows that "When the mind swings by a grass-blade / an ant's forefoot shall save you"; to one saved "the clover leaf smells and tastes as its flower." Through this neo-Whitmanian gist the infant wasp has descended from the mud on the tent roof like Odysseus or Elpenor from Circe's. "Like to like colour he goes amid grass-blades" greeting and carrying "our news" to those that dwell under the earth. There, begotten of the air of the process and of Pound's breath, the scion of the insect family "shall sing in the bower / of Kore" and "have speech with Tiresias, Thebae." As Pound saved the midge (*LXXX*) this persona saves Pound. "Cristo Re, Dio Sole" focuses the new epiphany. The wasp has made her "adobe," the "tiny mud flask," in "about ½ a day"; her lesson and Pound's "and that day I wrote no further" halve the canto, union to liberty.

The rest of the canto stresses liberty coming to a focus in new union. "There is fatigue deep as the grave" echoes "the mortal fatigue of action postponed" (*LXXX*). In the aftermath of the "connubium" "sun rises lop-sided over the mountain" prepares for a focus of new union, but first a recollection of Yeats composing while he and Pound were sharing a cottage in Sussex before World War I tests the epiphanic lyricism introduced in *LXXX*. Pound imitates comically a noise in the chimney which turned out to be "Uncle William" composing "a great Peeeeacock / in the proide ov his oiye." Yeats's bird was "perdurable" and "aere perennius"; but the symbol of pride, the pride of the poet's eye (too much eye?), the pressure of composition, and the primacy of "*verba*" over "*res*" fly in the face of Pound's revelations. The test of grief has been answered by the wasp family, recreation of which has provided a measure for testing Yeatsian poetic practice. The rest of the Yeats anecdote brings out further his preference for an art removed from nature in both origin and end.

Countering Yeatsian symbolism, "clouds lift their small mountains / before the elder hills" releases a focusing of new union in the terms of *LXXXI*. "Sun rises lop-sided over the mountain," which introduced the Yeats anecdote, is joined by "A fat moon rises lop-sided over the mountain," so that the eyes of *LXXXI* become the world's eyes for the "full Εἰδὼς." This time it is "my world" as the eyes "pass and look *from* mine / between my lids" in "*atasal*," union with the divine (cf. *LXXVI*). The stellar form of *LXXXI* and of the second phase returns

    sea, sky, and pool
    alternate
    pool, sky, sea

so that "morning moon against sunrise" ("halves of a seal") looks like "a bit of the best antient greek coinage" (a unified seal).

Uniting nature with art and the poet with both brings back the "connubium terrae" and a decadal frame from the end of *LXXIV*. German "und" precipitates an anacreontic lyric in German ("The ladies tell me 'You are old, Anacreon' ''), which echoes the taglied "Guten Morgen, Mein Herr" and the connubium (*LXXXII*). The lyric recalls the Bacher family of the Tyrol, from whom Pound learned (at the end of the epitome, *LXXIV*) that a "Madonna novecento" could be as a "Madonna quattrocento," and as "perfect." Emphasis here on the Madonnas, and a shift from Tyrolese masks to Tyrolese architecture, measure a distance traveled from personae to shrine.

The end of *LXXXIII*, an anecdote about the American Congress and the States of the Union during the century leading up to the present, is unexpected. It focuses the work on the clauses of a states' rights Constitution ironically with Ratification 83. Pound recalls his own family tradition of sitting in the Senate gallery or House gallery to hear "the fire-works" (as he himself once witnessed "a very poor show" in Westminster). "But if Senator [Ninian] Edwards [Illinois, served 1818–24] cd/ speak / and have his tropes stay in the memory 40 years, 60 years?" Art for a possible continuing revolution and NOVUS ORDO SECLORUM measures a descent advantageous neither to the Senate, nor to "society," nor to the people. Presumably since Pound "went down to the ship," "The States have passed thru a / dam'd supercilious era" (an era to raise eyebrows above the "dark eyelids" of Providence). The lyric

    Down, Derry-down /
        Oh let an old man rest

ends work on a seventh revolutionary decad, on the decad of a fourth paideuma and second phase, and on the draft-Articles of an 83-clause states' rights Constitution.

The coda *LXXXIV* uses the form ten-plus-coda to reconsummate the struggle of 1939–45 for the architectural draft culminating states' rights (seven draft-Articles in 84 clauses), for world paideuma (fourth) adding the world Branch/ Power States, and for a fully completed phase of struggle focused by the final two periplum ideograms. For the Constitutional culmination and middle it elaborates in mainly political and economic terms, mainly American, what could not be elaborated in the tenth of the decad. The first three passages, all American, and the second three, paideumatic, refer mainly to the 84 clauses and states' rights. The struggle for liberty and new union is focused ideogramically in the third three by "WE the People" in the spirit of '76. The last gives an American cast to the concurrent themes of the seventh draft of continuing revolution.

The opening "8th October" memorializes both the completed Constitution and, with snatches of Provençal elegy, the death of the poet J. P. Angold. The first passage goes back to Pound's prewar visit to Washington, where states' rights senators discussed with him Roosevelt's "eastern idea about money" and the state of the country, but could not think "what a man like you / would find to *do* here." Hence the struggle in Italy and consequent imprisonment at Pisa, which is memorialized to the tune of "ye spotted lambe / that is both blacke and white / is yeven to us for the eyes' delight" as fellow prisoners are checking out. For writing on currency "We will be about as popular as Mr John Adams" (a signature for mutual work) "and less widely perused"; he (and perhaps the reader) will be like a leopard remembered lying on its back in Rome zoo playing with straw "in sheer boredom."

But the paideumas remain. Incense to Apollo opens a glimpse of an Italian mountain paradise and of gorges between sheer cliffs threaded by troubadors when they sought the roots of Romance lyric in Spain (*VI, VIII*). "The old Dynasty's music" opens a glimpse of a Chinese fountain paradise, though elsewhere a whole town was destroyed for hiding a woman. Americans' apparent waste of money and time in risky ventures and in travel have yielded an equivalent either in "experience" or in "a run for her money," even "perhaps more than was in it." For Pound it has been "Under white clouds, cielo di Pisa, / out of all this beauty something must come."

The Pisan moon, "my pin-up, / chronometer," measures ethically states-men from ancient China to the present. The dynasty of Tching T'ang (YIN), who introduced revolution in "1760 ante Christum" (*LIII*), bequeathed three men full of "humanitas (manhood) / or jên^2" who resisted tyranny. Similar are a Renaissance Alessandro (dei Medici?), an unidentified Fernando, and "il Capo" (Mussolini); also Pierre Laval, Vidkun Quisling, and Phillipe Henriot. World War II collaborators are unsavory. But who tried to cut his losses by going out of industrials into government when "the slump was in the offing?" Versus who, "prepense, got OUT" of industrials "so as not to be nourished by blood-bath?"

This challenge of the ethics of the 1930s and 1940s is based on Dantean ascent by "ἠθος gradations" to "distinctions in clarity" sealed by *ming*^{2}, sun and moon, the universal eyes.[16] Universal halves of a seal signify "John Adams, the Brothers Adam," individual and collective ("Odysseus / the name of my family"). Duality comes to focus in "there is our norm of spirit . . . / whereto we may pay our / homage" sealed by the twelfth and last landmark ideogram, *chung*^{1}, Adams's ideogram for "balance" (*LXX*), and the pattern

16. "The sun and moon, the total light process, the radiation, reception and reflection of light; hence, the intelligence." "Terminology," *Ta Hsio: The Great Digest*, 1948, 1951.

governing "Canto 77 Explication" ("Chung . . . horizontal").[17] The religious expression of the states' rights theme of *Pisan*, "Saith Micah: / Each in the name of... ," opens onto a final definition of "his god."

Micah's declaration of independence opens through "So that" four declarations which turn the motives, states' rights, and activating common law toward world union. In present 1945, at the Potsdam Conference, where the Allies were seeking to lay the groundwork for world peace and new world order, "Kumrad Koba" (Stalin as a new Tovarisch), looking at Churchill— "the sputtering tank of nicotine and / stale whiskey / (on its way out)"— remarked "I will believe the American" (Truman). More personally, when Pound asked a Circean "pastorella dei suini" (his daughter) at the barbed wire whether the American soldiers had conducted themselves better or worse than the Germans, she answered "uguale"; Stalin's remark and her answer suggest that the vision of world order is neither in Berlin nor in one nation, but at Pisa in a mind that has affirmed the lesson of "John Adams, the Brothers Adam."

Accordingly Lincoln Steffens's observation that nothing can be done with revolutionaries until they are "at the end of their tether" applies to all adduced, including Pound of *Pisan*. Pound himself remarks sadly of modern statesmen "that Vandenberg has read Stalin, or Stalin, John Adams / is, at the mildest, unproven." Hence the debacle. But looking beyond war and beyond the dark night of the soul, through the American Thanksgiving, toward a new beginning, the consummating canto ends as it began with a snatch of song, now a personal memorial:

> If the hoar frost grip thy tent
> Thou wilt give thanks when night is spent.

Although *Pisan* is a seventh draft of a projected ten and a second phase of a projected fourth, Pound had good reason to think during the writing in 1945, if not so much at the time of publication in 1948, that, given his mental, physical, emotional, and legal conditions, and the state of his creative powers, *Pisan* might be the last of *The Cantos* that he would ever write. He was close to possible death either natural or justicial. The Pisan dark night of the soul reflects his sense of a narrowing "life vouchsafed." He therefore built into *Pisan* the summary by cantos *LXXIV–LXXIX* of the former drafts, the summary of ongoing *Pisan* (*LXXX*), and the projections of prospective drafts (*LXXXI–LXXXIII*) and coda (*LXXXIV*) to which attention is called by "Canto 77 Explication." To be sure the poem had always projected the whole formally and thematically. Now, however, it had to project the whole substan-

17. The 1970 edition made the same change for a rough *chung*[1] to a vorticial *chung*[1] as in *LXXVI*. It also added a transliteration.

tively and tonally as well, since the chooser of subjects and recorder of tones was in jeopardy.

The collection *LXXXIV Cantos* published simultaneously with *Pisan* thus had not only the significance of a gathering by "mass relations" of four paideumas in two phases for possible continuity, as *Seventy Cantos* of 1950 would gather in one phase '76 revised in four episodes for world revolution; it also stood as a possible surrogate for all that Pound would be able to do. In seven drafts and two phases it projected through its final epiphanies for new union in the several concurrent modes the themes and symbols of eighth, ninth, and tenth drafts and of third and fourth phases. The realizations and projections built a single Constitutional form of 84 clauses into a single newly inspirited and at least newly adumbrated Statue of Liberty. If he could do no more, then the poem to that point would show his contemporaries and posterity not only what he did do but also what he would have done had such been his fate.

CHAPTER EIGHTEEN

SECTION: ROCK-DRILL DE

LOS CANTARES 85-95 &

LOS CANTARES 85-109

"Live up to your line . . . and the constitution"
  Rock-Drill 86

At the end of January 1946, having written *Pisan* more than two years before it was published, Pound cried from the "Dungeon" of St. Elizabeths "mental torture / constitution a religion / a world lost / grey mist barrier impassible / ignorance absolute / anonyme / futility of might have been / coherent areas constantly invaded / aiuto."[1] The key phrase amid this mental panic is "constitution a religion." He had written a first phase dominated by Mediterranean polytheism (cf. the closing Hymn to Zeus), which had drawn into it Chinese pantheism and American "constitution a religion." *Pisan* had drawn Mediterraean polytheism into Chinese pantheism while projecting "constitution a religion." He would now save his mind and himself by drawing polytheism and pantheism into "constitution a religion." All religions were pointing toward realization of a world religion like that delineated in the Calendar. He would be saved by continuing his poem, in which "the beauty is not the madness" but "beauty under the elms— / To be saved by squirrels and bluejays" (*CXVI*).

In 1955, still confined under indictment for treason but adjudged mentally unfit to stand trial, Pound had the two-colored deluxe quarto *Section: Rock-Drill 85-95 de los cantares* published in Milan, Italy.[2] The eighth draft not only advanced toward an intended ten but also, as indicated by its ending and by the projected form of the poem, added the first of "halves of a seal" designed to constitute a third and Constitutional phase. An eighth draft had

1. Julien Cornell, *The Trial of Ezra Pound, a documented account of the treason case by the defendant's lawyer* (New York: 1966).
2. *Section: Rock-Drill* and *Thrones* are complements in every respect, including format. A "Note" in each accentuates meticulous formality: "This volume has been printed in conformity with the typographical instructions given by the author."

the complement of its seven predecessors, "ONE, ten, eleven, *chi con me* 曰 tan?," with the appropriate themes and forms of the argument, the motivation, the justicial form, and the activating rights and powers. It also added, not to be discoverable until the third phase would be completed (if it were), Sections i–xi as a Constitutional matrix for what would become Sections i–xxv in the whole *Los Cantares 85–109*.[3] Not only the Constitutional Sections, however, but also the prototype of the decad/draft are subordinated to other more self-evident forms. The most evident is dictated by what appears to be a still persisting apprehension that either Pound's life or his inspiration or both were in jeopardy, so that as with *Pisan* he had to write as though this draft might be all he could do.

The expected themes are asserted independence, to provide for the common defense, (Presidency)/Amendment, and freedom from cruel and unusual punishments. But decadal organization is merely acknowledged by symbolic forms like the "rock-drill" axis of oversized ideograms running through the epitome *85*-as-"ONE," or like the Seal/Calendar arcanum at the end of what ought to be Seal *85–88* organized by subjects, or like a decad/draft *85–94/95* seemingly projected by both. All the apparent prototype forms apply both less and more than expected.

What are self-evident, subordinating all other forms (at least until the phase has been completed), are three dominant paideumatic subjects of about equal magnitude. The first is dominated by the Chinese *Shu Ching* or *History Classic*, asserted to contain "the basic principles of government" and accentuated by ideograms, mainly axial (*85–87*). A second is dominated by Senator Thomas Hart Benton's *Thirty Years View* of the operation of American Constitutional government during the Jackson era, here centered in the Bank War and accentuated by the Seal/Calendar arcanum (*88–89*). A third is constituted of a series of epiphanies of Eleusinian Amor received through several personae and experienced directly by Pound himself (*90–95*). These subjects reseparate, in the mode of justice, the world paideuma synthesized in *Pisan* from "ELEUSIS," "KUNG," and "JOHN ADAMS"; accordingly the personal *Pisan*, like "ELEUSIS," inaugurates from its Eleusinian ground a fourfold circumnavigation passing through Chinese justice and American justice to an Eleusinian culmination, not only justicial but patently poetic. The result is not only an eighth draft introduced by the *Shu* but also projection from Benton and from Amor, substantive and tonal as well as formal and thematic, of a ninth and tenth—which Pound might not be able to write. This possible ending in mid-third-phase was canonized after a third phase had been completed by the collection *The Cantos* (*1–95*), entitled parenthetically to indi-

---

3. *Cantares* presumably commemorates the auspices under which Columbus sailed. Cf. the Constitutional Seal *III*, with Myo Cid, and the American Constitutional draft "ELEUSIS" subtitled "Jefferson-Nuevo Mundo."

cate both its first meaning as a possible abortive ending and its new meaning as a transition to what had come.

By the three subjects the *Shu* asserts with ideograms of varying boldness "basic principles of government" inherent in independence, Benton asserts sovereignty independent of the money power, and Amor unites epiphanic visionaries under revealed Providence in a Poundian pledge. Amor culminates three paideumatic motivations toward new union. The theme of *Shu* is amendment, Benton upholds and exercises the Constitution as Supreme Law, and Amor focuses a Constitution for world union in Ratification. Through *Shu* comes Pound claiming his political rights against the cruel and unusual punishment of a "Bellum perenne" against usury, which threatens to make him one of the "Old crocks to die in a bug-house." But with Benton he exercizes rights retained by the people to validate the amending process coming from the *Shu*. Amor validates the whole with powers (imaginative and poetic) reserved to the States or to the people.

Overlaying these major subjects and themes upon the decad, which contains many of them paradigmatically by cantos, requires that the style of *Section: Rock-Drill* be unique. It is—not only for these single overlays, but (as we shall see) for much more intricate and complex ones. That is the reason for grouping cantos by subjects both here and in *Thrones* to come, and, as we shall also see, for organizing still other canto-groupings formally into fourfold forms indicated by "THE FOUR TUAN . . . / or foundations" (*85*), by the Seal/Calendar arcanum (*88*), and by "the whole creation concerned with 'FOUR' " (*91*).

Further indication is a uniquely functional use of varied pictorial images: ideograms of varied sizes, placings, and arrangements, principally for axes; the four suits of the Seal/Calendar arcanum; plainsong musical notation; a hieroglyphic picture, motto, and repeated seal; and a Sumerian seal visibly suggesting the American. (The pictures will culminate in *Thrones* in a picture of the temple and in raw materials out of which the Sumerian seal was constituted.)

The rock-drill axis, for instance, not only cuts Golden Sections, inscribes them MDCCLXXVI, and constitutes them for building *Thrones*, it also constitutes with the text the vertical axis of a *chung*-form (axis + mouth) whirling between left and right columns (cf. "Canto 77 Explication" with an axis "upright" rather than "horizontal"); it thus churns up new forms for amending the Constitution. The Seal/Calendar arcanum condenses the same form into the dynamically interacting Branches/Powers, which draw the text from the left margin onto the symbolic axis and transform it into the Calendar phrase on the right. These forms apply, as we shall see, not only to the cantos in which they appear but to the dominant groupings in both *Section: Rock-Drill* and *Thrones*.

These new forms, along with such expected formal and stylistic devices as cantos, rubrics, frames, key thematic lines, and recurrent words, lines, and imageries, make possible the other varied groupings of *Section: Rock-Drill*, which are designed to constitute with *Thrones* a formal balancing of two drafts as Constitutional "halves of a seal," Branches interacting with and followed by Powers. More functionally, however, they are designed to constitute ten drafting subjects in the process of constituting and building xxv Constitutional Sections into an overall amendment of the Constitution for a world corporate state and for a new world union of such states. This would draw the Constitutional mode of the whole poem into the third phase as the Declaration and Preamble modes were drawn into the first and second, and as the mode of the Bill would be drawn into a possible fourth.

We are now speaking from the perspective of *Thrones* achieved but a final draft and phase still uncertain. *Thrones 96–109 de los cantares*, like its complement *Section: Rock-Drill*, was published in Milan as a two-colored deluxe quarto, in 1959. It was not only a ninth draft realizing what was projected by Benton *88–89* and so completing a third phase, it also commemorated Pound's freedom from confinement so that he could return to Italy and re-establish his residence there. In the manner of *Pisan* and *Section: Rock-Drill*, the end of *Thrones* projects from Amor *90–95* an Odyssean return, but realization would have to await a still only possible (though now seemingly more feasible) last draft and phase.

Reading *Section: Rock-Drill* by itself draws us to the three major subjects. When *Thrones* is read, however, we see from its subjects not only what *Section: Rock-Drill* prepared but also how it did so. *Thrones* is constituted of four paideumatic constitutions, both explicitly and implicitly. With allowances for source and consequence, in *96–97* a medieval Byzantine law code grows out of the relics of the western and eastern Roman Empire until it is confirmed by world monetary history and Eleusinian Amor as a model for the corporate state intended but not delineated in *Pisan*. The Manchu *Sheng Yu* or *Sacred Edict* is amended in four voices in *98–99*. In *100–106* the VII Articles of the American Constitution, a Supreme Law informing the amending mind, are applied to an amendment of nineteenth- and twentieth-century American and European history in the light of world paideuma. In *107–109* Pound joins Sir Edward Coke in all modes for Ratification of an amended world Constitution by the English constitution assembled in Coke's *Institutes*, from the Magna Charta and appended charters up to the laws of Elizabeth I. He carries the English constitution to the New World and toward the Constitution of '76 by appending the Connecticut Charter, which his ancestor Captain James Wadsworth hid in the Charter Oak in Hartford when crown officers tried to repossess it. So Pound has hidden the Constitution of '76 in his own mind— not only to save it but also to amend it for his world vision, and, incidentally, to conduct the trial for treason denied by him by the sitting custodians of the Constitution.

The three major subjects of *Section: Rock-Drill* by itself are so written that

Amor *90–95* is also divided into a vision at Castalia on Mount Parnassus (*90–93*) and an application of that vision to intercultural "Brederode" or Brotherhood (*94–95*). By that division *Shu 85–87* becomes Congress, Benton *88–89* becomes Presidency, Parnassus *90–93* becomes Judiciary, and Brotherhood *94–95* becomes States as a Branch. Eleusinian constitution then focuses the Power States, Chinese constitution carries out Amendment, the American Constitution is applied as Supreme Law, and the English constitution (with its extension to Connecticut and beyond) effects Ratification. Here the themes are only specified for larger proportions; detailed application will be described later.

These Branches, ideal like "basic principles of government," complement the Powers of *Thrones*, which result in the actual constitutions. But a working form is prepared within the Branches. *Shu 85–87* is divided into *Shu 85*, an impersonal historical epitome for all *Los Cantares* accentuated by the "rock-drill" of enlarged ideograms, and Bellum *86–87*, a personal application of "the basic principles of government" to continuation of the "Bellum cano perenne" (*86*) "between the usurer and any man who / wants to do a good job" (*87*). Benton *88–89* remains a third subject. Amor *90–95* having already been divided into Parnassus *90–93* and Brotherhood *94–95*, Parnassus *90–93* divides further into two Castalian visions, a vision of intellectual Amor received visually at Fount Castalia (fourth) and a vision of ethical Amor (fifth) received more intimately from Parnassus as Flora Castalia wafted and taking root in fertile ground. Brotherhood *94–95* then becomes a sixth subject, intellectual and ethical Amor extended to social Amor in the root sense of brotherhood and friendship, or Amor political and justicial. A culminating religious Amor will end the seventh subject, an Eleusinian corporate state emerging and being projected to the world (*Thrones 96–97*). The remaining subjects of *Thrones*—Chinese (*98–99*), American (*100–106*), and English (*107–109*) constitutions—complete the ten working subjects of the phase.

As ten subjects (drafts and parts of "JOHN ADAMS") of the first phase condensed the Declaration while projecting the coming drafts and phases; and as *Pisan* condensed the Preambles while subsuming the previous drafts and phases, condensing the seventh draft and second phase in progress, and projecting subsequent drafts and phases; so the ten subjects of *Los Cantares* condense the overlapping Constitutions while subsuming the previous drafts and phases, condensing the eighth and ninth drafts and third phase in progress, and projecting a tenth draft and fourth phase. This is a way of projecting all from the Declaration, drawing all motivations from other phases into a second, drawing all Constitutional forms from other phases into a third, and consummating all rights from other phases into a fourth. These condensing transformations will be cited later.

The working decad for drafting the third phase, constituted of the ten subjects, subsumes the Declaration and the Preambles in the Constitutions while projecting the Bill of Rights and the perfecting Seal. *Shu 85*-as-"ONE" is the epitome. *Shu 85*, Bellum *86–87*, Benton *88–89*, and Fount Castalia *90–91* constitute "REVOLUTION . . . in the minds of the people" as a Seal-vision. Out of the epitome and the Seal comes the Declaration "to be unity"; its premises emerge from the Seal-vision, its argument against the past inheres in the six subjects of *Section: Rock-Drill*, and the four constitutions of *Thrones* declare independence for states' rights while projecting new world union. The six subjects of *Section: Rock-Drill* culminate in Amor for liberty and the constitutions of *Thrones* turn from liberty toward new union.

Both "to be unity" and duality are, however, subsumed in Constitutional trine, histories modulating into epiphanies modulating into constitutions. The histories—*Shu*, Bellum, and Benton culminating in Amor—embody states' rights Branches. Modulating out of the histories via Fount Castalia into epiphanies of the several kinds of Amor, Fount Castalia, Flora Castalia, and Brotherhood culminate in the constitution for an Eleusinian corporate state and in the religious Amor at the end of *96–97*. They embody states' rights Powers through which are emerging world Branches; while the epiphanies are dominated by Amor, they are drawing on *Shu* and Benton for Chinese and American paideumatic forms, which are continued in the eclectic textures. Out of the epiphanies modulate the four constitutions for the four world Powers.

Inherent tetrad is undergoing a "sea-change" to new unity. A tradition of Amor carrying "basic principles of government" and incorporating Chinese and American counterparts, the Eleusinian Amor defined by the early medieval philosopher Richard of St. Victor, emerges from within previous subjects to a focus in Amor *90*, whence it unfolds its intellectual, ethical, and social aspects (correspondingly Eleusinian, Chinese, and American) to a tradition culminating in the sixth subject (see "LOVE, gone as lightning, / enduring 5000 years," the rubric to *95*). The activating themes are the private and legal rights of the Bill (First–Sixth) focused in the shield voiced E PLURIBUS UNUM. A plan for new government inheres in the Byzantium guild code of *96* and a new personal Amor in the religious love of *97*; they adapt the common law (Seventh) focused by the constellation voiced NOVUS ORDO SECLORUM. New form and new Amor are applied to amendment of the Manchu *Edict* through personae and to extension of the American Constitution by Pound himself; the activating themes are the political rights (Eighth–Ninth) focused in the Mount inscribed MDCCLXXVI. Amor and the governmental forms culminate in Coke's and Pound's uses of the reserved powers (Tenth) focused by the sun-vision voiced through Providence ANNUIT COEPTIS.

It seems evident that initially Pound intended *Section: Rock-Drill* to be read by itself as an eighth draft constituted of three subjects, the first two projecting eighth and ninth drafts and a third phase, and the third projecting a tenth draft and fourth phase. The addition of *Thrones*, however, precipitated from *Section: Rock-Drill* its four Branches balancing four Powers of *Thrones*, and its six drafting subjects followed by the four drafting subjects of *Thrones*.

It is clear from the form of each of the ten subjects that once *Thrones* had been added, *Los Cantares* was to be read according to its ten drafting subjects, to which all other forms would be firmly subordinated.

It can be seen that all but the first, ninth, and tenth of the ten drafting subjects are constituted of two cantos, "halves of a seal" symbolizing in the third phase the Branches/Powers dynamic. But in fact the phasal epitome, *Shu 85*, consists of one revolutionary tradition, constitutional in mode (as symbolized by the enlarged "rock-drill" drawing from the text "the basic principles of government"), shared by successive Chinese dynasties, CHANG for Branches and CHOU for Powers. The ninth, *100–106*, spreads the Branches over *100– 103* and the Powers over *103–106*. Coke *107–109* deploys over three cantos four phases each informed by its respective Branch/Power. In each subject the Eagle Pound's justicial revolutionary mind, informed by and informing its matter, churns its subject between Branches and Powers into a manifest form. The axis mediating and activating the extremes is subsuming drafting and building from the shield via the constellation into the Mount, while projecting the whole toward the sun-vision and the temple of Providence.

The fourfold Branches/Powers dynamic is variously distinguished. Single Chinese revolution stretching over two dynasties is constituted of four phases containing and informed by the "basic principle" "THE FOUR TUAN . . . / or foundations," which with the text groups into both revolutionary and Constitutional "FOUR" the thirteen axial ideograms. (As we shall see the ideograms also symbolize stripes and stars transformed into stones and projecting sun-rays, the "bust thru" from the Calendar cycle to the axial Mount, and clauses 72–84 of the Powers working within a text embodying the Branches.) The "FOUR" of Bellum *86–87* is accentuated by several ideogram axes. Benton *88* has four obvious divisions for the Branches culminating in the focal symbol for Branches/Powers in the phase, the Seal/Calendar arcanum; this modulates into Benton *89*, the Powers, through a fourfold thematic rubric. Fount Castalia *90–91*, Flora Castalia *92–93*, and Brotherhood *94–95* are marked by varied means, most obviously canto divisions, pictorial symbols, and substantive thematic shifts. Eleusinian constitution uses four subjects. Manchu revolution and constitution, projected from the *Shu*, are presented in four voices. American Constitution, working through Benton's mind informed by Articles I–IV and IV–VII in two cantos, becomes American Constitution working through Pound's mind informed by Articles I–IV and IV–VII in seven cantos. Coke *107–109* imposes upon three cantos Constitutional gathering, personal struggles, amendment, and extension to continuing revolution.

This Constitutional "FOUR," a third-phase locus for all "FOUR"'s, does not, however, apply only by these formal divisions. Rather Constitutional "FOUR" is a bounding form within which voices of tradition, personality, justice, and poetry may move freely and so, in effect, concurrently. In the Seal/Calendar arcanum the four suits are formal divisions while the Calendar phrase spreads throughout its scope concurrent divisions of one year (365 days and twelve months implicitly, "fifty / 2 / weeks" and "4 / seasons" explicitly). The opening up of the Seal/Calendar arcanum in the rubric to *89*—

To know the histories

to know good from evil

And know whom to trust.

Ching Hao.

Chi crescerà

(Paradiso)

"of societies" said Emanuel Swedenborg.

—articulates the revolutionary themes in Branches/Powers form. "The histories" are projected "to be unity" throughout by the axial *Shu Ching*. For duality "the histories" are balanced with persons ("whom to trust," "Chi crescerà," and " 'societies' "). Histories, persons, and justice ("(Paradiso) / ' "of societies' ") constitute trine. Symbolic names—*Shu Ching*, "Ching Hao" (an historical person and "Classic love"), "(Paradiso)," and "Emanuel Swedenborg"—constitute a thematic tetrad given a "sea-change" by an ultimate poet. The arcanum-opening arcanum reads both sequentially and concurrently, from forms on the left to realizations on the right. Concurrency is also effected as always by a sequence each unit of which contains all themes— contains them in formal order but in effectual freedom.

So we follow revolutionary histories being focused by *The Cantos*, a revolutionary history. We follow revolutionary personae who bear the will of "WE the People" being focused by Pound, the person caught in our history. We follow revolutionary forms of justice being focused by the Branches/ Powers dynamic (most obviously the Seal/Calendar arcanum). We follow revolutionary poetries and poets being focused by the new poet who is doing all the talking. This simultaneity will become especially evident in *Shu 85* and in Benton *88–89*, where histories, personae, pictorial symbols, and poetic focuses, working with and within discrete, sequential Branches/Powers, churn historical dust and natural elements into Sections of the law to be drafted into a Constitution on paper and built into a Mount of tiered stone.

Little has been made of the Constitutional Sections i–xxv, a main effect of which is a phasal amendment of the clausal states' rights Constitution by condensing clauses into phases in a third phase added to the first two.[4] Another

4. Presumably designation of each canto "Canto" reflects the Constitutional matrix and formality of the phase. So does arabic, not roman, enumeration. The British *CIX Cantos* (1964) homogenized arabic to roman without the designation "Canto," perhaps expressing that by 1964 Pound knew he could complete only three phases. *Drafts & Fragments* recurred to roman

effect, enforced by the heavily pictorial red-and-black deluxe quartos (which will be extended by a red-and-black deluxe folio for *Drafts & Fragments*), is recollection of the illustrated, red-and-black deluxe folios *XVI. Cantos* and *The Cantos 17–27*, which were subsumed in the deluxe monocolored quarto *XXX Cantos*. The first two drafts and three volumes completed the Renaissance planned by the Malatesta bill of lading. The last three drafts in three volumes try to "make it new." The matrix of *Cantos 85–109* formed from Sections i–xxv provides "One: ten slabs best red" for *Cantos 85–95* of *Section: Rock-Drill* and "Eight ditto" and "Six of same" for *Cantos 96–103, 104–109* of *Thrones*. These three divisions, which are demarcated by the text, are not complete in themselves, but prepare for a fourth phase and final draft with a matrix of "Eight columns" for Articles I–VII(VIII), modulating into "etc . . . with carriage, danars 151" for four Branches/Powers. This remaking of the Renaissance in a 120- instead of a 100-canto poem was restated and prepared in "Canto 77 Explication," where the renewal after *Pisan* was symbolized by four ideograms enumerated for three drafts "8-halves of a tally stick" and "9-direction of one's will" (reversed from the text of *Pisan LXXVII*) culminating in "10-perfect or focus."

The following analyses subordinate the preliminary and ideal forms of *Section: Rock-Drill*, the decadal form of each draft, and the cantos of *Los Cantares* to the ten working subjects. The purpose is to clarify the inclusive subjects through their specific matters, through their Branches/Powers forms, and through those aspects of texture which distinguish a particular subject from all others. It should be kept in mind that themes and forms may be mixed in these extraordinarily diffuse cantos, and that quarrels could easily arise about emphases. One can only claim long living with the texts bolstered by the rather self-evident or at least persuasive formal divisions into fourfold subjects, and bolstered too by the formal, thematic, and stylistic norms of the poem, with allowance for plausible transformations due to change of phase. One must remember too that themes may be as much in the Constitutional mind of each subject and of the phase, to be discerned as much or more with what the mind is doing with the subjects, through pure form, and through relations of one subject to another, as through literal materials. The literal is always there, but it must be found and brought forward to square with the symbolic, be the latter formal, verbal, or pictorial. The text is Pound's "arcanum," which is "his own" (Constitutional) "mind to stand by him" (*91*), and " 'the sort of thing that... / that does go on in one's mind'," the catch being "Whose mind?" (*95*). The mind of the Constitution is seeking to derive from the several cultures a corporate state for states' rights and economic jus-

---

numeration, with "Canto" titles. The 1973 American collected *Cantos* (posthumous) regularized all titles simply to roman numerals. For reasons clearly evident by now, I retain the conventions of Pound's last still-evolving text. From that one, I assume, he would be looking back from a 121st "triangular space" beyond his Mount.

tice, and to project it to a world Constitutional order. With these considerations in our minds we shall describe at least the major aspects and outlines of each subject of the phase.

Shu 85

From the revolutionary events, personae, prophecies, and symbols of the epitome *I*-as-"ONE," the text and the "rock-drill" of the epitome to *Los Cantares* draw the prophecies and forms of justice summed up in those of the universal seer Tiresias, whose golden wand transforms mast, sword, and oar while anticipating the poet's pen and Aphrodite's golden bough. From Seal *I–IV* they transform Pound presiding over and following the steps and stones of the law from Venice through the aboriginal gods and My Cid's quest for justice to the Renaissance ruins (*III*), the form for which is the Branches/ Powers dynamic and the symbol the Mount of MDCCLXXVI. From the Renaissance revolutionary mind (*I–X*) they transform Malatesta's history opened up by "These fragments you have shelved (shored)" and a broken seal (*VIII*), and Sigismundo's effort to build the Tempio according to the plan in the bill of lading (*IX*). From world revolution they transform the arena vision of world cultures extended from the Renaissance to America viewed from the steps of the "arena Romana" (*XII*), and to China introduced by Kung's emergence from the dynastic temple (*XIII*). The text and the rock-drill also condense the themes of the foregoing drafts and project the themes of those to come; from these they epitomize and project the ten subjects of *Los Cantares*. From these world sources comes the plural rubric "Our dynasty came in because of a great sensibility."

The single subject is "the Shu, the History Classic," in which are "found . . . the basic principles of government" focused by the enlarged ideograms. Canto 85 records the tradition established by the first Chinese revolutionary emperor, Tch'ing T'ang of "1760 ante Christum" (*LIII*) who founded the CHANG dynasty. T'ang's tradition is handed on within CHANG until CHANG loses the mandate (pp. 543–51), at which point it is picked up and renewed by what becomes Kung's dynastic model, CHOU (pp. 551–59). These halves are further divided in "FOUR": the minister Y Yin formulates the CHANG legacy and successfully transmits it to T'ang's son (pp. 543–48); centuries later a CHANG emperor revives it but CHANG finally loses it (pp. 548–51); new revolution, claiming the legacy as its own, founds on CHANG's principles the CHOU dynasty (pp. 551–57); finally CHOU perfects it for continuing revolution (pp. 557–59).

"The basic principles of government" found in this process ideogramically by the "great sensibility" enforce this Constitutional "FOUR" for Branches/ Powers while deriving from it (or accompanying it with, or imposing upon it) an ideogramic paradigm for revolution as a whole. Separate from the text and as a whole the ideograms focus the thirteen of each Seal symbol into the stones of the Mount and symbolize the "bust thru" from the Calendar cycle to the Mount. Separate from the text and divided and grouped to symbolize the clauses of the "FOUR" Powers (States 72–78, Amendment 79, Supreme Law 80–82, and Ratification 83/84), they interact with and amend "FOUR" textual Branches. Grouped with the text (as "found" in it) they manifest in Constitutional terms an ideogramic prototype. For concurrency the text provides tradition and personae, and the ideograms emerge as forms of justice; as per the concluding "NOTE," "Kung said he had added nothing," Pound translates, arranges, unifies, and consummates the other dimensions in poetry.

Phase, draft, canto, and axis begin with doubly oversized LING², spirit, as axial epitome "ONE":

LING²

Our dynasty came in because of a great sensibility.

All there by the time of I Yin

All roots by the time of I Yin.

Galileo index'd 1616,

Wellington's peace after Vaterloo

The first impacts are purely sonantal, like a (Liberty) bell, and visual. The issuing text identifies the all-containing source and cause of CHANG continuing revolution, cites its "sensible" persona, and includes all the coming "basic principles" in the originating LING²; Y Yin's ideograms comprise Pound's condition as if during a counter-Renaissance and counter-Reformation, and the state of the world as if after a counter-revolutionary war whose reconstitution of peace is merely "the economic war has begun."

The "great sensibility" enables those who can to see in LING² an axis rooted in heaven and passing through four raindrops or clouds, three mouths, and two human figures inside a workshop, to become rooted in earth. Conversely it builds up to heaven. It symbolizes the Mandate of Heaven delivered in the form of the four suits to be realized by the Calendar phrase. As such it symbolizes the front of the Seal overlaying the back and the Branches overlaying the Powers.

Its counterpart, back overlaying front and Powers overlaying Branches, is doubly oversized CHEN⁴, shock or startle, which will first appear off the axis in *86* under a Providence ("La donna che volgo"):

In *91* a small *chen*[4] will be translated "timing the thunder," i.e., ordering change. CHEN[4]'s upper half, an alternative to LING[2]'s clouds, transforms raindrops to sun-rays. Its lower half, replacing "the three voices," the work-shop, and the human figures, is *ch'en*[2], portion of time. The lower horizontals picture tiers of the Mount while the rest stands for the constellation and the shield. CHEN[2] shows "T P" and "E P."

After the Gaudier-Brzeska profile of Pound (the Eagle looking left) had appeared in red on the cover of the Italian *Section: Rock-Drill*, and after doubly oversized LING[2] had headed the "rock-drill" axis of the epitome *85* and doubly oversized CHEN[4] had appeared on the right in the ensuing *86*, LING[2] and CHEN[4] took the form of the Seal/Calendar arcanum (*88*). Thence they appeared as complementary symbols, in the same order and reversed, on and in *Thrones*. LING[2], on the front cover of *Thrones*, moved toward the text in a complement to the cover of *Section: Rock-Drill*, the ideograms *pao*[3] *en*[1] *te*[24]—lexically "protect grace virtue" and macaronically "Pound"—in red, in a vertical cartouche, in the middle, on the title page. CHEN[4] then appeared in the middle in the draft epitome *96*, and LING[2] appeared on the right in the ensuing *97*. Finally, completing this symbolism, CHEN[4] appeared on the back cover, lower right. Disposed thus LING[2] and CHEN[4] symbolize "halves of the Seal" symbolizing the two drafts as Branches/(Powers) and (Branches)/ Powers. First the guiding Branches are being amended by the active Powers, then the Branches are guiding the amending Powers.

LING[2] introduces ideograms 1–4 marking Y Yin's ideal principles, ideo-grams 1–6 carrying them into action, and ideograms 1–7 (the CHANG ideo-grams) passing into a second phase while marking States 72–78; it mediates between *XVI. Cantos* and *Shu 85*.[5] Y Yin's second ideal principle, CHIH[3], stop, is translated "a gnomon" (an epitome or a sundial pointer) for "Our science is from the watching of shadows"; described at the head of an ideo-gram axis in Bellum *87* "chih in the 3rd/ tone / and a radical," it symbolizes the revolutionary persona mediating between *XVII–XXX* and Bellum *86–87*. Y Yin's third ideal principle, set against those who "scatter old records" and "jump to the winning side" during "turbae" (wars), is HSIEN[2], virtuous, called a "form" (of government) and containing the radicals statesman, loyal, and valuable; touching on Pound's defense of the Constitution (especially

5. The themes of '76 will not be restated here; they will be restated from the foregoing prototype and drafts for the ten subjects projected from these through the ideogramic "basic principles."

during World War II), it mediates between "Jefferson-Nuevo Mundo" and Benton *88–89*.

Y Yin's fourth ideal principle turns toward new action and Constitutional trine by instructing "have scope and beginnings" and by constituting elements and meanings of the "Confucian Four TUAN" (Love, Duty, Propriety, Wisdom) into their enlarged ideogram TUAN², principle. Instructions for liberty and union frame a complex arcanum which reads at once horizontally and vertically (cf. "Chung . . . in the middle / whether upright or horizontal," *Pisan LXXVII*):

II. 9.   have scopes and beginnings   tchōung

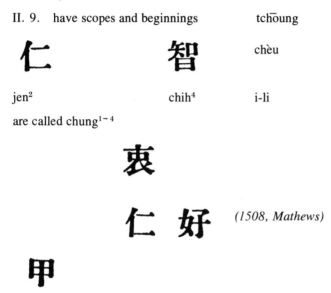

jen²   chih⁴   i-li

are called chung¹⁻⁴

(1508, Mathews)

no mere epitome without organization.

"Tchoung" carries "scopes and beginnings" to an "end." The first and last ideograms of "THE FOUR TUAN" point to a new beginning ("chèu⁴"); they are transliterated with the middle two, "i-li," added, but added so that they refer to the four drafts of "ELEUSIS" *I–LI*. "THE FOUR TUAN" are summed up in "chung¹⁻⁴," which ranges from *chung²* ("in the middle") to *chung⁴* "gain an end" (cf. "tchoung"). The various "FOUR"'s are in the process of being elaborated in four lines of ideograms: the Four TUAN are opened up by a central *chung²*, inner man, by *jen² hao³⁴* (love accentuated with the implication of male and female), and by *chia¹⁴*, the first of The Ten Celestial Stems, which pictorially focuses a fourfold field in an emerging root (cf. LING²).

The "Four TUAN" are opened up through "the sun under it all" (cf. *chih⁴*) as "Justice, d'urbanité, de prudence" culminating through "wei heou" (make thick) in "Σοφία," Wisdom, which is glossed "the sheltered grass hopes, chueh, cohere.'' Arcanum and translation then come to a focus through the insistence "Not led of lusting, . . . not of the worm, contriving," "but is as the grass and tree / eccelenza," in

THE FOUR TUAN[1]

or foundations.

Hulled rice and silk at easter
    (with the *bachi* held under their aprons
From T'ang's time until now)
That you lean 'gainst the tree of heaven,
    and know Ygdrasail

The ideogram mediates between "Siena-Leopoldine Reforms" and Amor *90–91*, drawing on the rites of both and the universal Ygdrasail of the latter while summing up the "basic principles" of T'ang's legacy. The conceptual meaning of the ideogram, principle, draws in the natural "All roots," the justicial "foundations," and the religious "tree of heaven," which phrases the visual LING[2] (cf. the Seal/Calendar arcanum).[6]

"THE FOUR TUAN" are symbolized by three radicals constituted into two halves and one ideogram, another form of LING[2] and the Seal/Calendar arcanum. The left radical, the verb "to set up or stand," builds a right half constituted of two radicals, the noun "mount" over the conjunction "and." The left pictures the Eagle spread over the whole Seal; the right pictures the striped shield rooted in the earth and passing through the constellation to the Mount culminating in a sun-temple raised by columns as in the Sumerian seal (*94, 97*) and in Pound's own drawing of the temple (*97, 100*). The left symbolizes the Seal-builder and the Branches (cf. LING[2]), the right symbolizes the Seal-edifice and the Powers (cf. CHEN[4]). Enlarged TUAN[1] will appear axially in each of the first three subjects of *Los Cantares* (and in the Seal/Calendar arcanum) before being absorbed into Amor *90–91*. Thence it will be transmitted to the last canto of the phase to focus "Ten families in pledge" constituting "a chief pledge" (a Declaration in the form of a Constitution) for "a city." Thus the ten subjects are framed and thus "Ten," tetrad, trine, duality, and unity are equated.

Having formulated T'ang's legacy for the heir, Y Yin bids him apply it by the "process" TE[2], virtue, "plus always *Τέχνη*," and from *Τέχνη* back to oneself (Pound defined TE[2] as "the action . . . resultant from . . . looking

---

6. Cf. Pound's explanation of "The Confucian Four TUAN" as "Places you start to build from, principles, or, if analyzing, clues." See p. 73.

straight into the heart. The 'know thyself' carried into action. Said action also serving to clarify the self-knowledge").[7] TE[2] refers to "THE FOUR TUAN" moving from Love to Wisdom (cf. Congress to States) while *Τέχνη* is moving from Wisdom to Love (cf. States to Ratification). TE[2] elicits an analogy to the superior process of Richard of St. Victor, " 'Cogitatio, meditatio, contemplatio' " (*87*), the source of poetry.[8] Richard's lies behind the European process act, observe, and believe culminating in Amor. Both are subsumed in the American process of '76. That Y Yin sent the young king into seclusion by T'ang's tomb to think things over elicits for our time "that they make total war on CONTEMPLATIO." TE[34] mediates between "KUNG" and Amor *92–93*.

From TE[24] the young king evolves a series of maxims which make him "one virtuous man" ("i jênn iuên") ready to carry the legacy into "use," I[3], which mediates "JOHN ADAMS" and Brotherhood *94–95*. Accordingly Y Yin turned the governments over to a new emperor whose eye was directed toward the future ("chên"), whose character was as upright as "the pivot" (the axis) perceived by Y Yin, and whose mind was so "simplex" that the different clans say "Bigob! He *said* it . . . Right here is the Bill of Rights." This end of a first hemicycle and phase is elaborated by ideograms accepting the emperor's duty to make sure that each man and woman has the freedom to use all his or her talents for a common good. The Bill and continuing revolution last 300 years (ideogramically) before decline requires a CHANG revival.

CHANG decline is reflected by the decline of the West from the Crusades to World War II, but an emphasis on an America "UBI JUS VAGUM" (where the law wobbles) is offset by Alexander the Great paying the debts of his soldiers on the principle of the prior personal TE[2] adapted to the public "Not serendipity / but to spread / [TE[24]] / tê thru the people." TE[24] marks the end of States *72–78* and, with an ideogram to come, duality for a second phase mediating *Pisan* and *Thrones 96–97*. For a revival of CHANG it marks the aim of Emperor Kao Tsong, who, "Wishing to bring back T'ang's state of awareness" (LING[2]), restudied the legacy as a personal performance of rites until the epiphany ideogram *hsien*[3] (keynote of *Pisan*) opens up Y Yin's TE[24] and I[2] (fifth and sixth) as a *chung*-form reminiscent of the columnar "Canto 77 Explication":

½ research	and ½	*Τέχνη*
½ observation,	½	*Τέχνη*
½ training,	½	*Τέχνη*
		Tch'eng T'ang for guide.

Hinted too is a dichotomy of European and Chinese processes in American

---

7. "Terminology," *Ta Hsio: The Great Digest*, 1948, 1951.

8. On further details of St. Victor's process and on its relation to Aristotle's "kinds of knowing and Confucian process," see Appendix D.

form. T'ang's guidance is sealed by the same "chên" as was TE^{24}-I^3. Two hundred years later, however, CHANG declined irretrievably so that to leave the country was the only politic advice. The adviser, however, says in English, Latin, and ideograms, that after having inherited the CHANG legacy he is not a slave. So, despite World War II and the destruction of the corporate effort, Pound did not go "into Corea" to preserve the line but remained in Italy "to dream the Republic" in his envisioned tradition.

In the manner of preparing to write the Constitution the CHOU half of *Shu 85* subsumes the CHANG half before manifesting the Constitution itself and its sequel. CHANG decline precipitates a rising by a family descended from Shun and King Wan, the exemplars of "halves of a seal" in *Pisan*. Assembling their troops, they quote T'ang's " 'Our dynasty came in because of a great sensibility' " and small *ling*^{2} as keynote for their declaration, which asserts "Heaven and earth begat the perceiver, / 'ch' e' ditta dentro' "; accuses the CHANG emperor Cheóu of losing the Mandate of Heaven by inflicting hardships; and justifies revolt by focusing Y Yin's LING^2-I^3 "Gentlemen from the West, / Heaven's process is quite coherent / and its main points perfectly clear."

The Preambles emerge from the longer struggle consisting of battle orders (for liberty) and of ethical principles for leadership (union), mostly in ideograms, delivered by the leader Wu. Wu leaned on his yellow halberd (cf. the axis) and delivered the battle orders " '6 steps or 7, reform,' " a preamble of six motives leading to an enacting motive, and " '4, 5, 7 strokes, reassemble,' " action upon the preamble citing the turn and the Chinese Amendment of a states' rights Constitution. (This is the seventh part and second phase of *Shu 85*; Pound altered his source by dropping "6" from strokes and adding the distinction "reform" and "reassemble.") The battle order ends " 'do not chase fugitives' " (i.e., give them their liberty).

Ethical justification of leadership begins with the rubric " 'Liking some, disliking others, doing injustice to no man.' " Wu applies it mostly with untranslated ideograms until his own "There be thy mirrour in men" and, issuing from the ideogram for friend, his own and Pound's "Odysseus 'to no man,' " a play on the protagonist's name (cf. *Pisan*) and his relation specifically to Elpenor. The ideogram for fire ("tcho") then precipitates from Wu's Preamble for new union the large ideogram CHING^4, reverence or pray, to be applied in *88* to "all-men," to "the vegetal powers," and to " 'life however small.' "^{9} The result of CHING^4 is "that you can know the sincere," which enabled T'ang to unite the empire for benefit; the present CHANG is "neither watching his / own insides, nor respecting the workings." CHING^4 symbolizes Amendment 79. With the public TE^{24} of CHANG it constitutes duality for

9. The frontispiece to Pound's translation of the Confucian *Analects (Lun Yu)* translates *hsin*^{4} "man standing by his word" and CHING^4 "respect for the kind of intelligence that enables grass seed to grow grass; the cherry stone to make cherries." *Hudson Review*, New York, Spring 1950.

a second phase of the canto (CHANG/CHOU pp. 548–55). TE²⁴-CHING⁴ also mediate *Pisan* and *Thrones 96–97*, the Byzantine constitution for a corporate state extended to the world and sealed by Amor.

CHOU founding, a third phase, returns to the rubric "Our Dynasty came in because of great Ling²" sealed with repeated LING² (now only enlarged); in close proximity it seals "The arrow has not two points" with ERH⁴, not, and "O nombreux officiers / Imperator ait" with I⁴, city. Wu, now emperor, unites LING² mediating the ongoing *Section: Rock-Drill* and *Sheng Yu 98–99*, with ERH⁴-I⁴ projecting *Thrones* and the American Constitutional Branches *100–103* and Powers *103–106*. Through "Iterum dico" he closes the phase with three exemplary CHANG emperors who levied "naught above just contribution." The three ideograms symbolize Supreme Law 80–82. They symbolize trine by subsuming the Calendar hemicycles in the axial "bust thru" to the emerging Mount. They look like and express tail-feathers directing an arrow-shaft to an arrow-head and a bulls-eye (cf. the arrow axis of "KUNG"/ "JOHN ADAMS," rays via a shaft to the first principle of government, *cheng⁴ ming²*, hitting the bullseye with the Constitutional *chung¹* "I am for balance"). LING², the sensibility-ideogram, and ERH⁴, an epiphany-ideogram containing the radical "arrow" for the axis, culminate in the founding-ideogram I⁴. A consummating poetry-ideogram is to come.

The foregoing phases of the canto (and of the poem?) focus Pound's economic ideal through "invicem docentes"—mutually teaching signed with Poundian initials

—upon CHIAO¹⁻⁴, as noun "doctrine" and as verb "to teach," translated "Sagetrieb," German "speech-power" but Yankee Doodle's "tale of the tribe." Ideograms for implementing a poetic consummation open up LING² for continuing revolution. "Awareness" must be daily maintained and respected. Fit men must be trained to see that the Mandate of Heaven extends to the people's welfare. "Get the mot juste before action" because "Awareness [is] restful & fake is fatiguing." Not all things are from one man, "That is, in some cases, charity," or "awareness extended." "The 5 laws"—the Wu Chang or Five Constants, The Four Tuan consummated in *hsin²*, faith, the man standing by his word—"have root in an awareness / *che funge*," *that acts*.[10] CHIAO¹⁴ symbolizes Ratification 83. It awaits a repeated CHIAO¹⁴ for

10. Fenollosa describes how the Wu Chang inform one of the Ban-Gumi or series of Noh plays: "Fifth comes a piece which has some bearing upon the moral duties of man, Jin, Gi, Rei, Chi, Shin; that is, Compassion, Righteousness, Politeness, Wisdom, and Faithfulness. This fifth piece teaches the duties of man here in this world as the fourth piece represents the results of carelessness of such duties." Ernest Fenollosa and Ezra Pound, *'Noh,' or Accomplishment: A*

memorializing, signing, sealing, and delivering 84 and for projection of Coke *107–109*.

A last page consummates a consummation in a fourfold coda. Historically an artist's awareness acts through the sculptor Brancusi's sense of a paradisal day and through Pound's awareness of murder protected in his own time; of jury trial founded in Athens but denied to him in America; and of tyrants resisted. Through "Tyrants resisted," and not by the cowardice of the vile (in Greek), these contemporary anecdotes modulate back to a King Owen who "had men about him." Anecdotes and personae precipitate the thirteenth and last "principle," another CHIAO[14]. The foregoing "Sagetrieb" is delivered "as the hand grips the wheat" to the successor Pound, who ideogramically grips a sheaf of principles on an axis (cf. the golden bough at the end of *I*). Having already "Risked the smoke to go forward / . . . aperiens tibi animum:" (cf. the colon at the end of *I*), he will now risk it in constitutional light. A mind now containing "the basic principles of government" will find those principles elaborated and will apply them in the ten subjects to come.

From its rubric of tradition "Our sensibility," *Shu 85* has been presented as a whole formal revolution; it could be analyzed as such through its text, which contains tradition, personae, and poetry organized by its ideograms. In a first subject of ten activated by the freedoms of religion, speech, and assembly, declaration of a revolutionary destiny and the motive from union toward liberty have been focused in the dynamic form Congress/States. For the Branches/Powers dynamic Y Yin handing on a tradition has been a figure for Congress. Kao Tsong reviving the tradition ritually has been a figure for Presidency. In this Constitutional phase Wu has subsumed the foregoing for Judiciary. Pound-as-poet (cf. *I*) has subsumed these figures and their forms in Ratification while being the agent of the amending Powers. Overall Pound has derived and employed Congress/States.

Bellum *86–87*

The second subject addresses itself to the natural rights of man and men—one, few, many, and all—politically, ethically, philosophically, and religiously, the categories for Branches/Powers within each subject and for the ten subjects evolving by Constitutional trine. The medium for natural rights is the text while the medium for the right to bear activating arms (of feeling and imagination) is ideogramic axes which halve *86* and inform the second half of *87*. Text reflects the Branches and axes reflect the Powers, all four within en-

---

Study of the Classical Stage of Japan, 1917. Fenollosa's transliterations are Japanese forms of Jen, I, Li, Chih, and Hsin.

compassing Presidency/Amendment. The substantive expression of this dichotomy is the actual history of nineteenth and twentieth century "Bellum
perenne" being interpenetrated by an amending text-and-ideograms of the
corrective *Shu*.

The rubric for the whole subject, Presidency/Amendment (*86–87*), and for
Congress/States (*86*: pp. 560–64) within it, is Pound advancing through the
smoke "WITH solicitude"—for all men and for peace—"that mirroured
turbationem," the states of mind that cause "bellum perenne." Pound succeeds both the personae of the *Shu* (who speak through him) and such defenders of European peace and order as the ministers Bismarck and Talleyrand,
counterparts of Chinese ministers, for Congress; for States he quotes an artist
like Brancusi. Opposed are those who have "forgotten" the ideal, who have
"Lost the feel of the people," who have made the way "not clean, noisy"
with "hearts loveless," who have been "lost to all i⁴," duty, the second
TUAN.

An axis headed by *hsü*⁴, solicitude, dominated by enlarged TUAN² for the
Branches/Powers, and culminating with *i*⁴, duty, can be paraphrased along
with the text it interpenetrates thus:

> With one man's solicitude . . . for the feel of the people . . . using
> the Constitutional TUAN² in a single mind . . . to make edicts substan-
> tial and concise . . . with the whole heart . . . , and receiving from a
> King Mou Wang instructions in the virtues of ministers whose names are
> recorded in the Great Register of the Great Historian . . . ; I may live up
> to my line (the men of '76 and my grandfather Congressman Thaddeus
> Coleman Pound) and to the form of the Constitution and so become
> the kind of single man on whom it may all depend . . . because he is
> devoted to Duty, the second TUAN.

The Branches and Powers are pictured by " 吕 ," *lü*³, musical pipe or
backbone, mouth over mouth, translated "habitus" (form).

The meaning of the axis brings back an extension of the nineteenth- and
twentieth-century struggle culminating in a Parliamentary betrayal and in
acceptance of "All, that has been" as a destiny. But it raises the final question
"what will they trust in / 信 now," the man standing by his word, culmination of the Four TUAN in the Five Constants, here the one man and the
Constitution. *Hsin*⁴ answers "what" as order achieved by the Constitution,
which has also been referred to by pronoun in "It may all depend on one
man" and "It can't all be in one language."

Presidency/Amendment (*86*: pp. 564–68) opens with efforts against economic tyranny during wartime by Mussolini and Alexander the Great. But
instances from "THEY LIED" to murder are focused by a communication
from an American historian about Rooseveltian egoism, an aggravation of
"turbationem" which precludes his hearing any advice:

"Don't write me any more things to tell him
(scripsit Woodward, W. E.)
"on these occasions

talks." (End quote)

This negative locus for Presidency / Amendment frames another return to positive nineteenth- and twentieth-century efforts. A negative-positive axis begins in verbal disturbances, is dominated by CHEN[4] for (Branches)/Powers, and ends in a tranquilizing (via CHEN[4]) of disorderly Amendment. The interpenetrating text-and-axis can be paraphrased:

> not gifts of litigations . . . which simply enforce the shocks (CHEN[4] transliterated on the axis) of Man under his tyranness Fortuna . . . as in the case of a king of the CHOU decline who was killed by barbarians . . . but (from the ideogram CHEN[4] on the right) the example of a minister motivated by duty (the second TUAN) to defend the emperor by turning the shocks of Fortuna into harmony and peace (as in the orderly amending process of the Powers) and so meriting ritualized gifts . . . or the example of an emperor of the CHOU heyday (chosen by KUNG as his political model, *LIII*) who moderated necessary suppression of insurrections while ordering that the peoples' animals and fields not be plundered or ravaged.

Inflated "HE," returning, imposes his verbal "turbationem" on a Senate containing at most twelve literates (as reported to Pound by one of its members) and on the House Foreign Relations committee, so that by 1939 "hysteric presiding over it all" was rushing the world and America into Pound's predestined theme, "Bellum cano perenne . . . ".

"Bellum cano perenne . . . ," articulated at the turn between *86* and *87* for the whole second subject, modulates into *87* and Judiciary/Supreme Law (*87*: pp. 569–70) through ". . . between the usurer and any man who / wants to do a good job," a cause of "Bellum" itself. Judiciary/Supreme Law, without ideograms, adjudges between "any man" and "usurer," "good job" and bad, "an honour roll" of "clean values" versus "total dirt" and "farce," all in a context of "paideuma fading" and "Infantilism increasing till our time." The justicial loci are Antoninus's "Law rules at sea," the principle of an equitable State that does not benefit from private misfortune, and precision in economic terminology: all culminate in Richard's "Cogitatio, meditatio, contemplatio," a "Centrum circuli" for the mythologies and for "clean values." But Europe was exhausted by World War I, by "The pusillanimous wanting all men cut down to worm size" (from *85*), and by the decadence of the vile, "*κακοῖσι*" (in *85*, *86*, and *87*). Pound continues his belief in Constitutional justice, however, "quia impossibile est" (cf. "I believe in the resurrection of Italy quia impossibile est," *Pisan LXXIV*).

In each subject States/Ratification emphasizes arcanum, as doubled CHIAO[14] for "Sagetrieb" and "Awareness extended" in *Shu 85*. Here (87: pp. 571–76) Pound assembles his own axis of ideogramic loci for the arcanum-bearing "Men's mind" of "all men" moving from civil justice to economic justice measured by just "interest."

"Ver novum" (new spring) for new "states of mind," and "hic est medium" for mid-canto, for the medium Pound, and for the medium poetry, open up an axis-framing *chih*[3], the second ideogram of the "rock-drill," there translated "a gnomon" for epitome and for "the watching of shadows" and here translated "chih in the 3rd/ tone / and a radical" (both a Chinese alphabetic character and the revolutionary visionary). *Chih*[3] opens up civil justice, which in mythic Athens needed Athena's divine intervention to break the tie of "6 jurors against 6 jurors" (cf. the Calendar cycle) and so turn old law to new. All "Right" was under CHANG save what came in Athens, and Y Yin's philosophy anticipated medieval Platonism's " 'All things are lights.' " These ideals modulate through Justinian's civil codes, which were "inefficient" in dealing with economic justice, into the corrective corporate state (the locus of States/Ratification) explained by Mussolini " 'We ask 'em to settle between 'em. / If they can't, the State intervenes.' " All the foregoing are focused in the philosophy of light given the form of Chinese revolution, *jih*[4] *hsin*[1], to be translated at the end of *94* "To build light."

Such a motive and plan illuminate the fact that "gold-bugs" are against "ANY order" and that "the squirmers" know how to "plunder men's mind, / wanting all men cut down to worm-size." *Chih*[4] ("directio voluntatis") makes money more "An instrument of policy" than "a measure." A few who understand such arcana, not only technically but also aesthetically, are "causa motuum," cause of movements, as "pine seed splitting cliff's edge," as the roots of sequoias moving the earth and teaching " 'Slowness is beauty.' " Such were the *San*[1] *Ku*[1], the Orphan Ministers, who advised the emperor on relations between the Mandate of Heaven and the laws of the state. Through a tower-room at Poitiers, so constructed that one can stand in it without casting a shadow, the *San*[1] *Ku*[1] are analogized to the keepers of the mysteries of the Golden Section, "the proportions," which may have been behind a policy of lending without interest. Such mysteries and motives would have come from a concrete sense of natural phenomena containing "signatures" and so "needing no verbal tradition." Rooted in *hsin*[1], the heart, such perceptions prove that "the cosmos continues," which is elaborated in varied kinds of vision exhibited by "all men." The locus of the varied visions is *tê*[24], translated "interaction" for an image of light casting the shadow of a water-bug onto the bottom of a puddle in the form of a flower, or interaction of light, object, and shadow symbolizing interaction of mind, act, and virtue.

Perception of a mathematical construction of shinbones, illustrating the problem of using "Speech as a medium" for achieving order, introduces Mencken's pessimism about getting an economic idea into "all men" and Mencius's idea, in his "great chapter," *shang*[4], of taxing by share rather than by fixed charge so as to eliminate *li*[4], the profit motive. Leaving the sun out of *chih*[4], the fourth TUAN, and dancing girls out of religion, introduces such omissions as "focus," "use of process," and "true editions" from matters intellectual. "That fine old word . . . 'An independence' " (an independent income) has disappeared from personal economics.[11] Amounts of "coherence" and "endurance" are used (rightly) to measure literary works like *The Cantos*, but the novelistic "dissolving view" coined by Henry James should be "registered." All should be registered along with "Chiefs' names on a monument"; but "Seepage" having subjected "the élan, the block" to "dissolution," the focusing *chih*[3] now adds its lexical meaning "stop."

But *chih*[3] the "radical" continues. Beyond the axis he quotes James again that his time has arrived at an opaquely phrased "ubicity, ascertaining." Were the keepers of the Golden Section making loans without interest, which bumbling fanatics (church councils) do not understand? Justice and directio voluntatis are functions of Richard's contemplatio. But left among "Old crocks to die in a bug-house" the radical mulls over London loans to Tibet, an old colonel who turned against masonry, and what someone "saw in the Treasury . . . / probably nothing." Bellum *86–87* ends mythically but gloomily "Tigers mourn Sikandar" (Alexander the Great?).

Benton *88–89*

Benton *88–89* consists principally of Pound's condensation and arrangement of Senator Thomas Hart Benton's *Thirty Years View; or, a History of the American Government for Thirty Years, from 1820 to 1850 Taken from The Congress Debates, the Private Papers of General Jackson and the Speeches of Ex-Senator Benton, with his Actual View of Men and Affairs* (1856). Pound takes the Congressional and Presidential sources directly and adopts Benton's constitutionally grounded "*Speeches*" for Judiciary, his "*View of Men and Affairs*" for States. Benton *88–89* elaborates the Constitutional "Jefferson-Nuevo Mundo" via the mediating "hsien form" (HSIEN[2]) of the rock-drill. Government by consent activated by lawmakers in the halls of government and by actual soldier lawmakers (President Jackson and General John Frémont) are subsumed in the dynamic Judiciary / Supreme Law by which "*the Working of the American Government*" is tested constitutionally. The ideogramic axis disappears from *88* but is transformed into the consummating Seal / Calendar arcanum, through which a new ideogramic axis is precipitated in *89*. Canto

---

11. "The fine old word 'an independence' meaning *not* to be a slave to controller of credit." To Joseph Gordon MacLeod, 28 March 1937, *Letters*.

88 is divided into four discrete subjects for the Branches consummated in the four suits. In *89* the Powers evolve in concurrent formal modes opened up by the rubric to *89*.

April Fool's day, the Senate not then being in session, sets the stage for preparing the duel between Senator John Randolph of Virginia and Senator Henry Clay of Kentucky; Benton was drawn in as Randolph's friend and Mrs. Clay's blood relation. The cause, a matter of honor from the Senate floor, and the result (neither was hurt, Randolph at least intending to inflict no injury), are subordinated to Randolph's distinction between the value of gold, "My MONEY!,'" and the paper of the National Bank. Within the overall Judiciary/Supreme Law the limitation to Congress (*88*: pp. 577–79) transforms *Shu 85*: against a vestige of the military methods used by CHANG and CHOU (duelling), Randolph illustrates the monetary "LING^2" needed for the new kind of revolution "to be unity" in the third subject. The duel proceeds to its ground, where it and the monetary theme modulate into Pound's financial "Bellum perenne."

"Bellum perenne" (for Presidency/Amendment, *88*: pp. 579–82) brings out Pound's struggle of Bellum *86–87* in more explicit monetary terms. "Bellum perenne" for monetary liberty goes back to the founding of the Bank of England and to suppression of colonial paper in 1750, which are countered by Lexington, by Lincoln's greenbacks, and by Pound's congressman grandfather's effort to keep part of the interest-bearing national debt "in circulation as currency"; the results "in our time" are blood, fatigue, and deprivation of Pound's rights ("benefit of . . . peerage" and a scholar's access to books). The broader "Histories" of the "distributive function of money" are touched in Tch'eng T'ang's revolution, in Antoninus's lending policy, in Pound's grandfather's effort, and in Mencius's tithing system.

The struggle for monetary liberty turns on a culminating "PERENNE" through "Cano perenne" to Pound's positive beliefs in the Confucian *Great Learning* ("Dai Gaku"), in "thrones" of justice, and in varied individual perceptions, all aimed at benefitting "the all-men" as well as the Emperor in the spirit of *ching*[4], "To respect the vegetal powers / Or 'life however small.'" The unifying perceptions culminate in a chorus of warnings about banks, currency manipulation, and resultant economic war by such "chiefs" (cf. the end of *87*) as John Adams, Major C. H. Douglas, and Anatole France.

Judiciary/Supreme Law (*88*: pp. 582–89) is introduced by "Old Bullion's" argument against exclusion of foreign currency, "A currency of intrinsic value FOR WHICH / They paid interest to NOBODY," as "unconstitutional fraud." As an heir to Jefferson and Adams ("OBEUNT 1826, July 4"), Benton argues for financial justice in three major policies ("trine"), free currency, low tariff, and credit control by the government instead of by the national bank. All his arguments are cast in constitutional terms in an effort to promote prosperity by balancing federal union and states' rights. His culminating argument against renewing the national bank's charter rings changes on the intention of the Constitution and on all Branches and Powers, all of which the bank has either undermined or is threatening. His final indictment is read to the Senate by his colleague Senator Clay in the same way that Pound is voicing universal revolution: "from a narrow strip of paper, rolled round his finger," the persona voices his data "so that the writing shd not be seen," the persona "not having had leisure to copy and amplify" the revolutionary document(s) in his own form and manner.

But that is exactly what Pound has done to transform histories, personae, and justicial documents into his own poetry. The Seal/Calendar arcanum subsumes the foregoing phases and Branches in continuing revolution and States/Ratification:

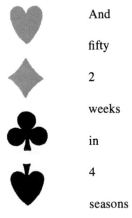

And

fifty

2

weeks

in

4

seasons

Using fragments of Liberty and Constitution "for roll or plain impact / or cut square in the jade block" (*Pisan LXXIV*), the "roll" of data has come through the "plain impact" of the struggling persona's voice into the "cut square" of the four suits, which in Pound's poetic voice will inform the "jade block" of the Calendar cycle and tabulation. The Seal/Calendar arcanum not only consummates the Branches of *88* and will inform the Powers of *89*, it also projects LING[2], "THE FOUR TUAN[1]," and Richard's portended Eleusinian Amor toward the Seal/Calendar culmination (by subjects) Amor *90–91*.

As explained earlier the rubric to *89* turns the discrete suits and the concurrent "4 / seasons" into the substantive terms tradition, personae, forms of justice, and consummating poetry:

To know the histories

to know good from evil

And know whom to trust.

Ching Hao.

Chi crescerà
>> (Paradiso)
>>> "of societies" said Emanuel Swedenborg.

Constitutionally discrete Branches guide concurrent Powers of the amending process. Over the whole canto Benton's history differentiates "good from evil" for initiating States, personae "to trust" promote Amendment, an ideogram axis carries a "Paradiso" of Supreme Law, and Pound's interpolations carry a Ratification "of societies."

The opening rubric contains in States all "to be unity." At about mid-canto Randolph, Benton, and Van Buren are focused in

>> he, Andy Jackson
>> POPULUM AEDIFICAVIT
> which might end this canto, and rhyme with
>> Sigismundo.

These two soldier-lawmakers yield for duality to an image of Columbian voyage through which comes the soldier-persona General John Frémont, Benton's son-in-law. His wife did not forward dispatches ordering him not to proceed against the Mexican Pacific coast,

>> so Frémont proceeded toward the North West and
>>> we ultimately embraced Californy

Amendment as Manifest Destiny recurs throughout the second half of Benton's history until Pound includes it in his ending.

The ideograms enforce "basic principles of government" coming (again) out of the opening *Shu Ching*. About three-fourths of the way through the canto the locus of the axis accentuates the applied Branches/Powers:

>> "Neither by force nor by fraud, that there be
> no coercion, either by force or by fraud,
>> That is law's purpose, or should be.
> Ἀθήνη swung the hung jury

 tuan, there are four of them.

 chen, beyond ataraxia

"Beyond passionlessness" makes small *chen*[1], virtuous, nearer to Italian *virtù*, power, for enlarged TUAN[1] as the Supreme Law of the amending Powers. The last ideogram, for "semina motuum," is *chi*[1], changes like those originating in the moving power of the universe. Enlarged TUAN[1] has appeared on axes in all three subjects; its spirit will be subsumed in Amor *90–91*, which will project from states' rights Branches (*85–91*) states' rights Powers evolving Branches for a new union (*90–97*) and thence Powers of a new union (*96–109*).

Poundian interpolations appear in these loci and throughout. After mid-canto they become more frequent and more mixed with the other dimensions, bringing back Pound's continuing revision of nineteenth- and twentieth-century history (of which Benton is a locus) in millennial light. All modes come to a focus in a Poundian comment on the Senate's expunging of its censure of President Jackson, a part of the overall "parliamentary history / dull or not, as you choose to regard it." Address to the reader makes both him and Pound their own personae. "I want Frémont looking at mountains," a poet's choice, is a verbal ideogram (free, mount, mountains). "Or, if you like, Reck, at Lake Biwa" shares with a reader-poet an American friend's name adapted (Reck, reckon) to absorption of the spirit of Ernest Fenollosa, American pioneer in the Orient, at his mountain grave or shrine in Japan. Further west, however, lie Mount Parnassus and Eleusinian Amor.

Amor *90–91*: Fount Castalia

Amor *90–91* condenses "Siena-Leopoldine Reforms," which consummates "ELEUSIS," via the "great sensibility" LING[2] and its axes, via the axial TUAN[1] which appears in each prior subject, and via adumbrations of Richard's Amor. It focuses a Seal-vision ("the histories" *Shu*, Bellum, and Benton) while modulating into the middle epiphanies of the trinal Constitutional phase. Through new inspirations, the theory of continuing revolution activated by the right to privacy (except under specific warrant, here Richard's opening of the heart) is subsumed in States/Ratification for states' rights, which precipitates through the "new" not only the beginning of the states' rights amending process but also Congress initiating a Constitution for new world union. Accordingly the elegiac tone of "the histories," colored as they are by the plight of justice and its proponent, continues through Amor *90–91* until, for the epiphanies emerging from the histories, Amor *90–91* ends "That the tone change from elegy" because of the "experience" actually undergone.

Before becoming the Congress/States phase of Amor *90–91*, *90* by itself is the most perfect epitome in the poem for a Seal-vision evolved from a priori historical inspiration unfolding through mental activity until it reveals its spirit. The text emerges from an epigraph (from Richard) which defines the relation of the human mind or heart to Amor. Beginning with a rubric for a fourfold Seal-vision (cf. the invocations of Seal *IV*), it evolves a fourfold Seal-vision (cf. Seal *IV*) which results in an Englishing of the Latin epigraph. The revelation, which articulates Amor intellectually, itself elicits through another Latin line from Richard, planted earlier in the text, a personalized, macaronic celebration of the poet and his Providence.

The Eleusinian rubric—

"From the colour the nature
        & by the nature the sign!"
Beatific spirits welding together
      as in one ash-tree in Ygdrasail.
      Baucis, Philemon.
Castalia is the name of that fount in the hill's fold,
      the sea below,
               narrow beach.
Templum aedificans, not yet marble,
      "Amphion!"

—transforms pictorial LING^2 and TUAN^1, the Seal/Calendar arcanum, and the articulation that opened *89*. Sensibility derives the sign. The tree of the universe, in *85* a fusion of LING^2 and the foundational, articulating TUAN^1, unites heavenly spirits blessing (by metamorphosis) human spouses. Parnassian Castalia inspiring Amphion's temple-building music renders TUAN^1. The four passages are realizing the four suits by the Calendar phrase. The themes are history, persons, paradisal forms, and temple-building song.

The rubric modulates through the San Ku (with ideograms) and the room at Poitiers into an affirmation of "Sagetrieb, / that is tradition," here the Golden Section proportions. Latin tags from Richard make Aphrodite the inspiration of the eye, useless thinking a waste, and images found in the mind likenesses of the divine. The inherited traditon has been for revolutionaries like Pound, who are "not arrogant from habit, / but furious from perception" (they include Perón and Hitler), the seed of movements, "semina motuum" (cf. *chi*^{1} at the end of *89*). Reviving rain on Parnassus brings now to "parched grass" what Sibylline prophecy and the favor of "Isis Kuanon" brought when Pound was in "Erebus, the deep-lying." The litany "m'elevasti" recalls how he was lifted "from under the rubble heap," "from the dulled edge beyond pain," "from the dulled air and dust," "by the great flight."

Stasis and dust modulate into movement and water through serpents symbolizing rebirth, which is ritualized by the Adonis rite of "Siena-Leopoldine Reforms" (*XLVII*). The dark of Erebus turns to light rising through Fount Castalia (cf. the fountain mind of *Pisan LXXIV*) to an altar in a temple of elms while Chinese rivers are "rushing together" (cf. spirits "welding together"). The waters (of the mind) carry fish, flotsam, and torn boughs, but are "clear with the flowing." "Out of heaviness where no mind moves at all" (stasis) have come " 'birds for the mind' / said Richardus" (movements); to come (as he also said) are " 'beasts as to body, for know-how.' " One recognizes conditions and symbols of *LXXI Cantos*, of *Pisan*, of the now evolving *Los*

Cantares. "Body, for know-how" refers to the Mount, symbol of the Constitution. But first a Preamble is symbolized by "Zeus with the six seraphs before him." Six has so occurred and will recur; "Zeus" focuses "the Divine Mind"; the "seraphs" will become blue-jays under the elms at St. Elizabeths.

"The architect from the painter" modulates movement and water into building and stone as an edifice begins "Taking form now . . . in the air." Its bas-reliefs assemble beasts and birds from a woodland beyond the dead (*"ἐπὶ χθονί"*) in a sculptured landscape of sward Castalia. Dionysian rites of rebirth draw "furry assemblage" and avian voices "For the procession of Corpus," waiting for the reborn to appear.

Banners, flute tone, and flame on the altar bring the dead out of Erebus, through "the crystal funnel of air," to "new forest," "free now," "the delivered." Free they are "no shades more" but "lights," though "the dark shade of courage" Electra remains "bowed still with the wrongs of Aegisthus." Referring back to the rubric (Ygdrasail) and to the trees of "new forest," "Trees die & the dream remains."

The rendered dream opens up the epigraph

> Not love but that love flows from it
> ex animo
> & cannot ergo delight in itself
> but only in the love flowing from it.
> UBI AMOR IBI OCULUS EST.

A revealed tradition of intellectual Amor (*90*) modulates through a plain-song epigraph, the focal symbol of Amor *90–91*:

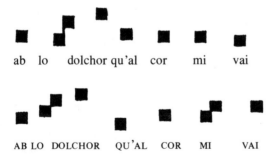

ab   lo   dolchor qu'al   cor   mi   vai

AB LO DOLCHOR   QU'AL   COR   MI   VAI

"From the sweetness which goes into my heart"—from a canzone by Bernart de Ventadour a line of which appears in each phase of *The Cantos* (see *Fragments of Cantos*, chapter 20)—activates Richard's Amor personally. For Branches/Powers Sir Francis Drake focuses personae, Pound judges himself, and through Odysseus Pound reveals an arcanum of intellectual Amor.

A continuing rubric—"that the body of light come forth / from the body of fire"—modulates *90* into all *91* while "And that your eyes come to the surface / from the deep wherein they were sunken, / Reina—for 300 years"

opens up Presidency/Amendment (*91*: pp. 610–13). Eyes that inspired philosopher, mystic, and lawgiver with "The GREAT CRYSTAL" (ball of
prophecy, cf. *Pisan*) focus in the eyes of Queen Elizabeth inspiring Sir Francis
Drake to the destruction of the Spanish Armada, which he saw as "Crystal
waves weaving together toward the gt/ healing," or ritual protection against
violating the sacred. The Adonis rite of "ELEUSIS" *XLVII* returns to be
Anglicized in a song by Drake to Diana (Elizabeth mythified) that she aid his
enterprise. As Actaeon he spread a deer-hide near Diana's altar. As Lear laid
in Janus's temple (of war and peace) he turned *chen*[4], the ideogram for "Man
under Fortuna," into "timing the thunder," the orderly amending Powers.
The Anglo-Saxon voice, ever approaching Pound's own, recalls in song the
birth of Merlin, whose "fader was known of none," so that magician, son of
God, and poet seem to merge. Finally Pound applies all these personae and
rituals to his own burial "by Aurelie, at the east end of Stonehenge" (a sun-
Calendar) "where lie my kindred." His immersion in Anglo-Saxon myth and
history culminates in a flow of light "Over harm / Over hate . . . whelming
the stars." Light focuses Athelstan's setting up guilds before 940 A.D. (cf. the
Sienese model for a corporate state and for world Congress) and a shared
heritage ("So hath Sibile a boken isette").

Judiciary/Supreme Law (*91*: pp. 613–15) opens with self-judgment, dis-
tanced by italics, of how Pound has implemented his own destiny and adjudged his own Armada:

> *Democracies electing their sewage*
> *till there is no clear thought about holiness*
> *a dung flow from 1913*
> *and, in this, their kikery functioned, Marx, Freud*
> *and the american beaneries*
> *Filth under filth,*
>   *Maritain, Hutchins,*
> *or as Benda remarked: "La trahison"*

Having freed himself of such diatribe he would like, "damn all" (a characteristic colloquial judgment), to see Verona again, to eat in the restaurant
which recalls his Calendar, to sit again in the arena (a Mount). But the violent
deaths of persons actually known re-enforce his commitment to a vocation
less chosen than imposed. Accordingly the birth of Merlin brings back the
refinement "from fire to crystal / via the body of light," assembly of "the
gold wings," and protection of the inspiress by lions and by encircling lights.
So re-inspired or always inspired, the "Bright hawk whom no hood shall
chain," a Yeatsian symbol for the mind of those whom Pound makes "skilled
in fire, / shall read 旦 tan, the dawn."

"Waiving no jot of the arcanum / (having his own mind to stand by him)"
opens States/Ratification (*91*: pp. 615–17). A predestined mind tells Pound

as Leucothoe told Odysseus in the waves off Phaeacia "get rid of the parapernalia" (*sic*) because he had to endure what had to be endured ("TLEMOUSUNE") and because " 'my bikini is worth your raft.' " Odysseus entering Phaeacia, a symbolic "Holy City" of justice, will persist from here to the end of the world Constitution. Accordingly, for both states' rights and Congress (fourth phase of the fourth subject), new epiphanies are confirmed by mystical philosophers, by the mind's new activity, and by love insuperable ("charitas insuperabilis"). "If honour and pleasure will not be ruled" a mind "stirring and changeable / 'light fighting for speed' " will "come to that High City" where "Formality" (the Seal-vision) will confirm "the whole creation concerned with 'FOUR.' " In "new forest," under "NUTT overarching,"[12] " 'Ghosts dip in the crystal, / adorned." "That the tone change from elegy" is justified by the case of Joan of Arc; the triumphant martyr enables Pound to answer "A lost kind of experience?" with "scarcely" and to familiarize "UBI AMOR IBI OCULUS" into "O Queen Cytherea, / che 'l terzo ciel movete."

We recall that before the addition of *Thrones Amor 90* introduced a third subject (Eleusinian Amor *90–95*) added to *Shu 85–87* and Benton *88–89*. We recall that after *Thrones* was added ideal *Shu 85–87*, Benton *88–89*, Parnassus *90–93*, and Brotherhood *94–95* (Branches) balanced Thrones (*Powers*) while the working subjects *Shu 85*, Bellum *86–87*, Benton *88–89*, Fount Castalia *90–91*, Flora Castalia *92–93*, and Brotherhood *94–95* evolved sequentially toward *Thrones*. Its mode of poetry makes Fount Castalia *90–91* States/ Ratification consummating the four-phase Seal-vision and revolutionary philosophy; poetic "states of mind" are obvious. Its mode of tradition—an intellectual Amor inspired from without which brings things "together" for the "new"—makes it Congress/States initiating an amending process and new Branches. Its loci for Congress are intellectual Amor, Drake inspired by Queen Elizabeth, the Branches/Powers dynamic, and the symbolic "new forest" into which come the reborn dead. As we shall see each of the middle epiphanies has analogous forms and figures appropriate to its aspect of Amor.

Amor *92–93*: Flora Castalia

Ethical Amor is inspired from within, its persona is Egyptian King Kati, and its end is "nuova vita." Its phasal loci are honor, Kati's motto "A man's

---

12. "NUTT," the night sky (giving birth to the sun), the waters of the heavens, and the mother of all life, is the mother of the newer gods and so of OSIRIS (and ISIS and HORUS). Pound may have had Egyptian deities and American poets in mind when he called Whitman "a hard nutt" and the *Leaves of Grass* "the book," which it was "impossible to read . . . without swearing at the author almost continuously"—to his father, 3 June 1913, *Letters*. For Whitman as father see "What I Feel About Walt Whitman" and "A Pact"; for Whitman as mother see the Americans of *XII* and macaronic "chih$^{2-5}$ ma set out hemp" (*Thrones 99*).

paradise is his good nature," distributive justice, and the individual poetic imagination. The case against executive tyranny becomes a case for human "good nature" versus a nature exemplified by usury; the workings of Amor provide an activating due process of law; case and process are subsumed in states' rights Supreme Law interacting with world Judiciary. The phasal loci evolve from the case worked upon by recalled Castalian inspiration, which unfolds from seed to petals to named Flora Castalia until (at the end) Pound apostrophizes Flora Castalia grown from the initiating seed. "KUNG" is condensed via TE^2 of the rock-drill, the Confucian "process" of self-correction from within.

A four-phase rubric opens Congress/States (*92*). From Parnassus seed is blown toward soil where it may grow. It is appropriate to the mind as certain seeds are to birds and animals. The alchemical version of the Seal-vision defines mental form and undergoes its "sea-change" into the challenge "And honour?" Examples of honor culminate in Guicciardini's "A chi stima . . . l'onore assai" (cf. "nothing impossible to him who holds honour in sufficient esteem" at the end of the translation of *Chung Yung*, 1948, 1951).

Honor as ethical love reopens Castalian vision, which culminates in the personal "Le Paradis n'est pas artificiel" (cf. *Pisan*) but is "jagged" and comes in flashes between agonies: Hilary (cf. "hilaritas") "stumbles," but "the Divine Mind" is "abundant / unceasing / *improvisatore* / Omniformis / unstill." Affirmation of process is set against the degradation of holiness and of sacraments by usury, Pound's "armada," against which he reasserts his own honor. He has seen degradation and its cause and effect, desensitization, for forty years, or for twenty-five hundred. The negation of LING^2 and Amor, desensitization (repeated four times in four lines) blots out all but "a little light from the borders."

The seed blown from Parnassus finds soil through the opening of *93*.

After linking Kati's motto as "two ½s of a seal" first with another Egyptian king's "angelic bread" and then with Odysseus "having his own mind to stand by him," Presidency/Amendment (*93*: pp. 623–27) swings back to the case, the crux of which is "Some sense of civility." The Ureus, the Egyptian sacred snake symbolic of sovereignty, reopens the process of Amor, which comes with the passion (suffering) of Tristan and Isolde in song wafted by petals and rain from "sward Castalia again." "Out of the Ureus" come courtesy, honesty, and "Nine knowledges about *chih*^{3}," the ideogram for individuality and for ends and beginnings; the two knowledges cited suggest a differentiation of *Section: Rock-Drill* and the projected *Thrones*; the eighth is natural science and the concrete ascribed to the natural scientist Agassiz and symbolized by the fixed stars; the ninth is moral and "the agenda" ascribed to Kung and symbolized by "the crystaline." The Ureus also yields via incense to Queen Nephertari and Isis, in Dantean Italian, the "good nature" described by "this uniting which is within the mind, seeing without that which it loves." Castalian eyes open up Dantean elaboration.

Dante's *Convivio*, his banquet of philosophy, particularizes Kati's claim that paradise is man's good nature and Pound's experience that paradise is intermittent and "jagged." Love makes one beautiful. It is the form and shape of philosophy. Men are naturally friendly. Beauty and morality are equivalents. Love delights only in loyalty and in hearing "both of ancient times and our own," a Malatestan *Convivio* (*XI*). That man is a "compagnevole animale" is signed with Kati's hieroglyphic name,

"compagnevole animale"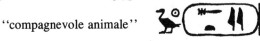

making Dante and Kati "two ½s of a seal." All such qualities enter Pound's reply to Mussolini's question why he wanted to put his ideas in order, "For my poem," and his seeing beauty seated on three sacks of laundry. They come to a focus in effulgent honesty and in "Dio, la prima bontade," prime goodness as the source of man's. Divine goodness can be written i^4, Duty, whence Augustine (of *The City of God*) joins Dante and Kati.

For Judiciary/Supreme Law (*93*: pp. 627–31), as Dante put it in the *Convivio*, distributive justice adorns goodness; the method is "'Know agenda, / to the utmost of its virtu, / of its own'"; Shakespeare also mentioned the subject, and Kati seals it. Recurrence of the negative case is countered by a further expansion of vision. As "The autumn leaves blow from my hand," in the face of Tristan and Isolde's passion, Pound prays to blessed ladies for compassion: though he has not pitied others enough he has sought nothing for himself, only that the child "walk in peace in her basilica, / The light there almost solid"; ideograms for "holding that energy is near to benevolence" affirm both distributive justice and his own motive. Asleep in Castalian forest, awaiting rebirth, he affirms his Odyssean quest for the new and "the soul's job," to "Renew" accented by the ideograms for Chinese revolution "Plus the luminous eye" of personal epiphany. In such sleep, wafted by song, came Flora Castalia, now named. The epiphany ideogram *hsien*[3] confirms an enflamed (inspired) "nuova vita"; the whole experience of adorning goodness for distributive justice is sealed by Kati's seal.

For States/Ratification (*93*: pp. 631–32) within Presidency/Amendment, the mind turns to a meticulously dichotomized arcanum of its own process. A first half begins with "the trigger-happy mind" amid stars, dangers, and abysses "going six ways a Sunday," union to liberty; a second half, introduced by mental velocities seeking "duration," ends "going six ways to once / of a Sunday," liberty to union. The case in the first half is against philologers, who will be baffled by the mind's working, and against biographers, for whom *The Cantos* will be a "butcher's block"; neither will understand "quidity" or that there must be "incognita." The case in the second half is against the stupidity of a friend of Yeats's who couldn't think unless a cannonade were going on, and against "malevolence," to be exposed by the mind's "antennae" (cf. "Artists are the antennae of the race").

In the first half "incognita" is illustrated by "un lume pien' di spiriti" (d'amore) and "of memories," which raise the ethical question "Shall two know the same in their knowing?"; the ethical question in the second half extends knowledge to character: "Without guides, having nothing but courage / Shall audacity last into fortitude?" Respective codas addressing the poem itself state the same theme using line reversals and chiasmus:

> You who dare Persephone's threshold,
> Beloved, do not fall apart in my hands

and

> You are tender as a marshmallow, my Love,
> I cannot use you as a fulcrum.
>   You have stirred my mind out of dust.

Dichotomous States/Ratification turns on a mediating dichotomy which sets Dantean Paradiso and Swedenborg's societies of angels (cf. the arcanum opening Benton *89*) against Hell and the way out of it: those "chi crescerà" would be individuals, and angelic societies would be formed "by attraction"; from the " 'Blind eyes and shadows' " of Hell, the labyrinth, the mind would emerge by a path "wide as a hair / . . . to enter the presence at sunrise." Dichotomies end with thanks to the petals of Flora Castalia, now directly addressed, which drift through an air "½ lighted with pollen" (cf. the opening "blown / seed"); and to a deliberately opaque Monna Vanna (cf. Mona Lisa?) who makes him remember ("tu mi fai rimembrar").

Brotherhood *94–95*

Social Amor is built up from wide experience, its persona is the neo-Pythagorean philosopher Apollonius of Tyana, and its end is "the new law . . . from affection alone." The scope is notably cosmopolitan, deliberately "rhyming" varied cultures and languages; a pervading entity, a functioning government, is embodied in a city (the Mount) symbolized by ideograms and a seal, the media for justice. This subject is reversed from Amor *90–91* and *92–93*: the end is defined at the beginning and the phases of persona and justice occupy the rest of *94* so that *95* can end both a sixth subject and a draft with Pound's own situation and with a transition to *Thrones*. The case against usury is continued while "Brederode" is amending the case against "our British brethren"; Pound is giving fair trial to Apollonius on the grounds of

"Brederode" while fair trial is being denied to himself; case and method are subsumed in states' rights Supreme Law interacting with world Judiciary. "JOHN ADAMS" is condensed via TE², the ethical "process," put to use by I³, the means of preparing "one man" for governmental office.

The comprehensive rubric "Brederode," from Adams's correspondence with Benjamin Rush after '76 and his retirement from the presidency, names one of the founders of the Dutch republic; as pseudo-Anglo-Saxon "Brotherhood," however, it restates the rubric to "JOHN ADAMS," *"Acquit of evil intention"* (cf. also the consequence in *Pisan*, "John Adams, the Brothers Adam"). "Brederode" is completed with Adams's limitation of relations between governments to "treaties of commerce only," which opens up a four-phase thematic rubric. After the historical "Brederode," Pound invokes his inspiring "Blue jay, my blue jay / that she should take wing in the night" to whatever parts of the world, a foreshadowing of Apollonius's travels. Axial ideograms for the Kingdom of T'ai Wu Tzu, sonantal macaronics for the city of Dioce, introduce the theme of justice in its symbolic medium.[13] Culminating "Brederode." Adams alludes to the funeral of his friend Lincoln.

The rubric introduces Congress/States (*94*: pp. 633–35) within the overall Judiciary/Supreme Law. Adams's remark on treaties of commerce is elaborated to his perception that depreciations of the currency are "to the favor of the whole people" (a tag linking *94* and *95*) and to his understanding of "the bank hoax" and its result, "the corruption of history." But here the inspirational side of Adams's passion for justice, "DUM SPIRO AMO" (*LXX*), looks from previous Amor through "Beyond civic order: / l'AMOR," to Apollonius. The transition is carried by inspirational perceptions culminating in Justinian's Corpus of Roman Law, in which "the new land" is said to come "from affection alone." In culmination Pound gathers a Congress of Kung, Mencius, Dante, and Agassiz "for Gestalt seed" (cf. Castalian seed), grants pity to the infected (while maintaining "antisepsis"), and bids "let the light pour."

Apollonius and his philosophy, which have been hinted since Amor *91*, unfold Presidency/Amendment (*94*: pp. 635–40). His version of "Brederode," peace with the animals under a common natural law, cited in Amor *93*, extends here to "no blood on the Cyprian's altars." Before Apollonius's life and philosophy unfold, however, Pound's emissary bluejay takes the form of the antecedent hawk-king Sargon of the first dynasty of Egypt and Sumeria,

---

13. T'ai Wu Tzu "as mentioned in Rollin" refers to Charles Rollin, *Ancient History* (Paris: 1730–38), Book III, "The History of the Assyrians," Chap. 3 on the city of Dioce. Noel Stock records that Pound wrote into a copy of *Cantos LII–LXXI*, near the date 11 February 1940:

To build up the city of Dioce
    (Tan Wu Tsze)
whose terraces are the colour of stars.

(*Reading The Cantos: The Study of Meaning* [New York: 1966]), p. 72.

whose seal (bird above shield containing Mount and temple) anticipates the American:

Sargon's capital echoes the city of Wagadu (cf. *Pisan*); his range extended to Cornwall, a source for tin.[14]

Apollonius's symbolic keynote is Mencius's advice to a King Huey in ideogram, about how to govern (I translate): "Make riches grow, don't hoard jewels." Chinese advice given by an Eleusinian is "rhymed in Taxila," an Indian sun-city. Pound presents Apollonius's travels in India, Greece, the Roman Empire, and Egypt in the Greek of Apollonius's biographer Flavius Philostratus found in the Loeb Classical Library edition of F. C. Conybeare, the "prelector"; in his own English aided by Conybeare's; and in ideograms. This method gives Apollonius fair trial against the historical judgment that Apollonius was a charlatan, which is supported by Conybeare's judgment that his life is "lightly written." Pound interpolates that "no theologian touches it," not even Richard; he groups Apollonius with the chief of the Brahmins visited by Apollonius in India, with Richard, and with Swedenborg.

Apollonius's philosophy, derived from a tradition and from his own perceptions, is elaborated from experience in a way that Drake's inspiration and Kati's insight are not. The heart of his philosophy (I translate the Greek) is that the life of the cosmos engenders all things and is knit together by love. He derives this philosophy from observation of natural phenomena and expounds it in India. He tells the Greek middle East that it consists more of Homeric "many ideas" than of religion fixed in stone. In Greece he awakens the Greek heroes as did Odysseus, but without blood-sacrifice. He carries his advice to make riches grow to Rome, where, under the ideogram for balanced government *chung*[1] (of the *Chung Yung*), he makes a convert of Vespasian, who, about to seize absolute power, wants to be upright and to remain true to himself, to Roman tradition, and to the gods; Pound interpolates that Vespasian formed "neuvos archivos" (cf. "the new law") but did not show good sense in Greece. In his advice, considering that his life is governed by the gods, Apollonius is "not particular about theoretical organizations" (constitutions) but that i^1 jen^2, one man, should be $wang^2$ $wang^2$, king king. Bidding his opponents in the discussion with Vespasian to "Set it to music" (cf. Pound and '76), he departs for Africa, where he finds Egyptian economics superior

---

14. Pound took his evidence for Sargon's sovereignty over the tin mines of Cornwall from L. A. Waddell's *Egyptian Civilization: Its Sumerian Origin & Real Chronology and the Sumerian Origin of Egyptian Hieroglyphics* (London: 1930), pp. 13, 66 (hereafter cited as *Egyptian Civilization*).

to Greek. His philosophy culminates (though he will return) by setting the immortal soul above life.

In the source, what follows includes a general discussion of the nature of justice. Pound shifts, however, to an ideogramic rubric for Judiciary/Supreme Law (*94*: pp. 640–42), *pen*³, root, which looks like a rooted Mount—

—expounded "That it is of thrones, / and above them: Justice." For text he echoes Eleanor of Aquitaine and her kings (the sixth canto of the prototype) with Edward I of England and his Queen Eleanor, who nursed him back to life when he was wounded during a latter Crusade and brought luck to his reign, so that he added Scotland to his realm and brought the Stone of Scone, a symbol of imperial unification (a Mount), to London. His epitaph, "PACTUM SERVA," meaning "Be Traist" (true) to his federation, modulates back into Apollonius through "As against anyone who takes his blessings into a corner." Apollonius places imagination, which because it conceives and is ruled by its ideal is "not baffled by terror," above imitation, which because it copies what it has seen often is so baffled. Repeated *wang*² *wang*², that Sparta should be kept Sparta and that "the king . . . shd/ be king" to avoid "a melting pot," clinches his governmental advice. Judiciary/Supreme Law within Judiciary Supreme Law (and a decad) ends with an Eleusinian translation of Chinese revolution in American Seal/Calendar form:

"To build light

日   jih

新   hsin

said Ocellus.

The beginning of a fourfold rubric for States/Ratification (*95*) within Judiciary/Supreme Law and for the coda to the decad—

LOVE, gone as lightning,
        enduring 5000 years.
Shall the comet cease moving
        or the great stars be tied in one place!

—sums up LING² (with CHEN⁴ behind it) and Amor. The English is completed with a Latin phrase for "LOVE," "Demonstratress of consonances," ascribed to the Anglo-Saxon Venerable Bede, who will appear in *Thrones 96*. Three more Latin phrases, also seemingly by Bede but probably contrived by Pound, fill out a cosmic rubric culminating in a personal condition. For a cosmic persona, "God is the soul of the world, the best animal" (cf. Apollonius's animals) "and eternal." Eternity is defined "Time is everywhere" (spatial), "it is not movements, in the prayers of the world." "I awoke in a marriage bed" augurs celebration, but idealizing Latin returns to actualizing English in the gloomy "Mist weighs down the wild thyme plants." The overall rubric looks toward informing recurrences of the Leucothoe arcanum, which entered in Amor *91* and which at the end of *95* will bring Odysseus to shore in Phaeacia.

In consummating the phases and linking *94* and *95*, the rubric modulates into Adams's tag on depreciating currency "In favour of the whole people" (thrice). It also defines the term "political." In the spirit of "Brederode" man is not a political animal but Dante's "compagnevole animale," even if some do "coagulate" into cities, the Greek root for politics. In the modern state, mocked Remy De Gourmont, man is but reproducer and contribuable. Paradisally, however, and again etymologically, city comes from the Greek verb "to plow" and "polis" finds a homonym in polyglot, mythically "many sounds in that oak-wood." An honor roll centered by Adams's tag illustrates such ideas.

The rest of *95* elaborates injustices to the defenders of Pound's time but compensating interventions of the providential Leucothoe. A prayer to "Queen of Heaven" for repose, answered by Leucothoe as a sea-gull bringing light from the white foam, precipitates an honor roll of "men even in my time" whose "energy near to benevolence" (by ideograms from Amor *93*) tried to churn the crystal wave to "flood surge" and solidity. The problem is the Great Emperor Yao's worry, to find a successor (accentuated by ideograms for one man). Nevertheless, though in prison reliving the *Pisan* "periplum," "Elder Lightfoot" is not "downhearted," "He observes a design in the Process." Here (as in *Pisan*) "the Process" is confirmed by "men even in my time" and presided over by the Muses, the daughters of Memory, who govern "the sort of thing that . . . / that does go on in one's mind." The challenge "Whose mind?," however, brings the accusation "Among all these twerps and Pullizer sponges / no voice for the Constitution, / No objection to the historic blackout." Pound's defense of the Constitution from the beginning, during World War II, at Pisa, and now is set against acquiescence in his legal confinement.

Leucothoe's "My bikini is worth yr/ raft" and a celebration of her beauty (in the mind) turn "The immense cowardice of advertised litterati" upon the cases of other victims. One, "driven nuts" by bearing the burden of "non-acquiescence" in Manhattan during World War I, uttered several Cassandra-like prophecies. Other prisoners had "a nice way with children." Another spent a night in the air caught in mooring ropes.

A lone rock for the sea-gull, who can rest in water, carries tradition, personae, and justice to a religious climax. To Beddoes's "O World!" and Santayana's "Something *there*," having to play under Fortuna "a hand" (of four suits) "without face cards" against "the enormous organized cowardice," Pound nevertheless replies "Not stasis/ / at least not in our immediate vicinage." There is "something decent in the universe" (cf. a design in the [ethical] "Process") if he can "feel all this" for the thousandth time "At the age of whatever." St. Hilary saw it in an oak-leaf or vine-leaf, San Denys is spelled "Dionisio," and Dionisio and Eleutherio (gods of Liberty) were never blacked out by Calvin. Such affirmations sustain this Odysseus until the waves tore him from his raft, smashed it, and drew him under.

> Then Leucothea had pity,
> > "mortal once
> Who is now a sea-god:
> > νόστου
> γαίης Φαιήκων. . . ."

Through his Providence he will be able to extend his nostos as far as the land of ideal justice. The dots anticipate a new awakening on a shore where "Mist weights down the wild thyme plants"—if he can write *Thrones*.

CHAPTER NINETEEN

THRONES DE LOS CANTARES

96–109, LOS CANTARES 85–109,

& 109 CANTOS

Pugno pro patria.
  Canto 97

If *Section: Rock-Drill* had been the last draft, *Shu 85–87* would have asserted independence activated by protection against cruel punishments while adding world (Presidency)/Amendment. Benton *88–89* would have declared sovereign powers activated by retained rights while adding world (Judiciary)/ Supreme Law. Amor *90–95* would have made the pledge activated by reserved powers while adding world (States)/Ratification. With *Thrones* added, *Section: Rock-Drill* declares independence activated by protection against cruel punishments while adding world (Presidency)/Amendment.

The paideumatic constitutions of *Thrones* make the declaration ''that, as free and independent states, they have full power to levy war, conclude peace, contract alliances, establish commerce, and to do all other acts and things which independent states may of right do.'' The argument is activated by use of the rights retained by the people (Ninth Amendment) to continue the amending process with the motive to ''insure domestic tranquility'' and to accord the process with (Judiciary)/Supreme Law, or the Constitution itself. If the assumption of independence activated by protection against cruel punishments stressed separation, sovereignty activated by retained rights stresses new union. A founder is also using the sovereign powers of world cultures and rights retained by the people to reinterpret the Constitution that has confined him; by this means he argues the treason charges instead of leaving their resolution to psychiatric diagnosis.

The projections of phasal form have already been noted for the first draft of the third phase, *Section: Rock-Drill*. More locally, however, Tiresias's prophecy (*I*) carries Odysseus as far as Phaeacia. The "Thrones" are projected by the stones of the law which Pound and Myo Cid climb toward new justice, but which crumbled into Renaissance ruins (*III*). Pound seeks justice as he sought it for Malatesta and builds as Malatesta built the Tempio (*IX*). The world justicial aim is Confucian law and order (*XIII*).

As pointed out earlier the overlays are made possible by deploying each of the ten subjects as a Branches/Powers dynamic. A special overlay is *Thrones 96*, as epitome of the ninth decad/draft a unity but as half of the seventh subject *96–97* a unity halved. Canto *95* thus epitomizes all themes subsumed in the ninth and, as "FOUR," all Branches/Powers; with *97* it condenses all themes into a seventh subject to which it contributes two phases of Branches/Powers.

As epitome for the ninth draft *96* first presents (pp. 651–58) Paul the Deacon's Lombard history of Lombard "colonization" of an exhausted Italy, between remnants of the Roman Empire to the west and east, and their establishment there during the sixth and seventh centuries of an independent state centered in its cities, forerunners of the free cities of the latter Middle Ages and the Renaissance. The general history (of the world at that time) is followed in what has the effect of a consequence by Pound's threefold presentation of *The Book of the Eparch*, a code of rules governing the guilds of imperial Byzantium promulgated about 900 A.D. Pound's presentation of a model constitution for a model corporate state analyzes its "refinement of language" (pp. 658–60), expounds rules for the varied trades randomly (pp. 660–64), and finally perfects the *Book* formally (pp. 664–67). The four phases carry argument from tradition, struggle (the "haggling" of tradesmen), founding, and (if not exactly continuing revolution) perfection of a revolutionary founding process. Branches/Powers inhere.

For a seventh subject of *Los Cantares* the Lombard history and the Byzantine constitution (halves of *96*) are augmented by halves of *97*, the economics of Lombardy and Byzantium extended to a monetary history of the world and a completion of the epiphanic Amor of the middle four subjects of the phase. Colonization is carried into *96* by the Odyssean entry into Phaeacia and is sustained by interpolations. Local exercise of sovereign powers in Italy, within an empire, declares independence and states' rights; so does the code for a corporate state within the imperial city of Byzantium. Lombard laws, the Byzantine code, and the culminating epiphanies ratify states' rights while providing models for world States. The epiphanies manifest an activating, ratifying common law. As a seventh subject *Thrones 96–97* condenses *Pisan* via TE^2 and CHING^4 of the rock-drill, the ethical "process" spread through the people in a spirit of reverence so that "you can know the sincere." The Byzantine corporate state supplies the model intended for *Pisan* but destroyed before it became usable.

Thrones 96–97

The opening of 96 focuses themes of draft, epitome, and subject into a comprehensive arcanum, which then unfolds through four themes into the Lombard history.

> Κρήδεμνον . . .
> κρήδεμνον . . .
> and the wave concealed her,
> > dark mass of great water.

formalizes the "bikini" that brought Odysseus ashore as the Homeric head-dress, a mantilla or veil with lappets. In the plural the word became meta-phorically the battlements that crown a city's walls, as the kredemnon appears to crown the wave-hidden goddess here. The plural will occur in black shawls modeled on Demeter's gown and still worn in Venice during Pound's earliest visit (98, 102, 106). Hence such lines for the continuing "Bellum perenne" as "Pugno pro patria" (97), "The temple 川 is not for sale" (lappets and battlements are pictured, 97, 100), and "must fight for law as for walls" (98). The bikini, the kredemnon, and the shawls hint at the unclothing and re-dressing of the Statue of Liberty sought from the beginning (cf. "Patria Mia" and *1*); or, with reference to the Seal, hint at a new Mount and a new temple to be roofed and crowned with sun-rays.

The comprehensive kredemnon opens up first the contemptuous "Aesthe-ticisme comme politique d'église, hardly religion," which looks back to "Among all these twerps and Pullizer sponges / no voice for the Constitution" (95) and forward to the coming "constitution a religion" (Supreme Law derived from divine law). Phaeacian rites to HESTIA, goddess of the hearth, introduce the rise of the mind to the "Thrones" of Paradiso:

> & on the hearth burned cedar and juniper. . .
> > that should bear him thru these diafana

The sources of ideal justice are formulated

> Aether pluit numismata
> Tellus vomit cadavera,

—The aether rains laws (also customs and currencies) and the earth vomits cadavers recalls the upper and lower halves of LING² and CHEN⁴, symbols for Branches and Powers. That Tuscany in the former province and city of "ROMA" was named for the sacrificial incense modulates into Paulus's history.

Pound adapts Paulus's history in the form Congress/States (*96*: pp. 651–58) both for the epitome and for the seventh subject (states' rights Ratification and world States). The history illustrates within its theme of Lombard indepen-dence and sovereignty such constitutional principles as "laws written down," "all italian 'reip[ublicae].' under law," "Laws aim? is against coercion," and "ruin'd by vicarious government"; also, awareness of currency control and of economic justice, as in "there is no local freedom / without local control of local purchasing power."

Pound's interpolations include CHEN[4] for the Powers. CHEN[4] governs the climax of Paulus's history with "the crux of one matter," the Moslem Caliph Habdimelich's decision in 691, after the Byzantine emperor had broken a peace treaty, to begin striking his own coins with his own effigy and inscriptions; having done so he set himself to building a temple, for which he sought columns (cf. bulding the Tempio). According to Paulus the Caliph was "satanically stimulated" to this radical declaration of independence and assumption of sovereign powers. Paulus's Latin rendition will be Englished by Pound to link it with promulgation of the Byzantine edict; it will open 97 to link the two cantos.

The major achievements of Byzantium leading up to the *Book of the Eparch* (and the *Book* itself) have occurred in or been interpolated into Paulus's history: distributive justice, Justinian's Corpus Juris Romani, St. Sophia, and a "hand out" for the people. The argument for law brought out of Paulus's history continues in Pound's multilingual argument with the nineteenth century discoverer, editor, and commentator of the *Book of the Eparch*, Professor Jules Nicole.[1] The mode of the first constitution is thus that of the Declaration. The others will be presented in the appropriate consequent modes.

Within Presidency/Amendment of the seventh subject (*96:* pp. 658–67) Pound arranges his materials to constitute the epitome. For struggle (pp. 658–60), rules for silk-dressers having shown that the idea of the just price underlies "the haggling" somewhere, Pound lays out "the haggling" in a four-column multilingual demonstration of a rule against faking purple and then trying to vend it with a hard sell. The four columns consist of four Greek terms, of Pound's comment on each in English, of four ideograms, and of the ideograms transliterated. The ideograms do not translate the Greek but quote "the way purple spoils vermillion," Confucius's illustration for "I hate the way Chang sonority confuses the music of the Elegantiae, I hate sharp mouths (the clever yawp, mouths set on profits) that overturn states and families."[2] The transliterations enable one not familiar with ideograms to complete original, comment, and ideograms by going to a Chinese dictionary. After further text has affirmed the authority of the Eparch's seal, Pound comments on "refinement of language" and adds the note

> *If we never write anything save what is already understood, the field of understanding will never be extended. One demands the right, now and*

---

1. Pound doubtless sees in "Eparch" "E P" + "ARXON," justicer; Paul the Deacon, the Eparch (with his seal), and the monetary historian Alexander Del Mar (*97*) are candidates for Pound's personae in *96–97.*

2. *Lun Yu*, Book Seventeen, xviii.

> *again, to write for a few people with special interests and whose*
> *curiosity reaches into greater detail.*

He claims for the closer philological scrutiny of *Thrones* sovereign powers, under Supreme Law, activated by retained rights.

Some pronouncements on coinage, hoarding, and house rent modulate into a random presentation of regulations governing various guilds (pp. 660–63), the *Book* still not having been formally introduced. Interpolated are Wyndham Lewis calling Constantinople "our star" and Yeats's "Byzantium," and a reference to building St. Sophia; as with Siena, Pound's "Holy City" is not a symbol but a place where people may live. This phase of founding ends (pp. 663–64) with a paean to the sun, "whom the ooze cannot blacken"; with the Englishing of Habdimelich's coinage and his need of columns for his temple; and with a passage on justice, than which nothing is more ancient.

At last, "Under Leo" (ruled 886–911), "ΕΠΑΡΧΙΚΟΝ ΒΙΒΛΙΟΝ" is formally introduced from Leo's preamble: " 'Following God's example Our Serenity," "to stop trampling by one on another," has codified a body politic. Formal presentation (pp. 664–67) proceeds to a culmination in silversmiths and goldsmiths, with punishments for defacing coins and counterfeiting, until the Eparch's edict and Habdimelich's coinage come to a focus in the major aim of constitutions, "pacem." The persona for Presidency/Amendment within States/Ratification has been less Leo than his Eparch.

Together the Lombards and Byzantium illustrate the development within a larger imperial union of a model for a corporate state. Judiciary/Supreme Law (*97*: pp. 668–75) draws on and brings up to date Alexander Del Mar's *History of Monetary Systems: Record of Actual Experiments in Money made by Various States of the Ancient and Modern World, as drawn from their Statutes, Customs, Treaties, Mining Regulations, Jurisprudence, History, Archaeology, Coins, Nummulary Systems, and other sources of information* (1896). Del Mar illustrates how a state's control of its coinage, its ratios between precious metals, and its rate of exchange have been signs of its independence and how that control, though sporadically exercized, has remained in the hands of central authorities, public or private. Del Mar's analysis of Habdimelich's policy, which links his historical study with Paul's chronicle history and with Byzantium, is in Pound's handling the crux of Del Mar's monetary interpretation of history. Pound brings control of coinage and promotion of the economy together by commenting "But Mr Del Mar does not, at this point, / connect issue with backing, / though he is all for a proper total proportion / between total issue and buyables." In our time "Ike, '55, had got that far." Such lessons are preparing for the emergence of a statesman's effort to extend his purview from the foundations of an independent corporate state to a general consideration of legal and economic precedents for a new world system of civic and economic justice.

Except for a few accentuating ideograms, only axial CHEN[4] and the ideograms used to "seal" the style of the Eparch's edict have so far been formally functional. Ideograms and symbols break out again in States/Ratification (97: pp. 675–83), however, to culminate States/Ratification as a seventh subject and to consummate four epiphanies of Amor (*90–91, 92–93, 94–95, 96–97*). Culminating "new forest," "nuova vita," and "new law," "New fronds, / novelle piante" break out with the revolutionary building ideogram *hsin*[4] worded "what ax for clearing?" Ideograms disposed across the page (I translate)—

        love   dawn   love

—and glossed in Greek "wine-dark eye," symbolize the opening of a providential eye in the form of a three-column temple about to appear. The text goes back via the intellectual love envisioned by Drake/Pound in their common destiny, and thence via "That this colour exists in the air / . . . & from the nature the sign," to the rubric that opened the four epiphanies, " 'From the colour the nature, / and by the nature the sign' " (*90*). It goes back further to the rubric for all *Los Cantares*, doubly oversized LING[2] (*85*), here on the right to symbolize Branches guiding the Powers CHEN[4] and the culmination of the seven subjects of states rights (*85–97*).

LING[2] translated "Out of ling / the benevolence" also expresses Kati/Pound's ethical love, "A man's paradise is his good nature." A more elaborate disposition of ideograms (again I translate)—

        benevolence   makes   love
        love   riches   makes

—transforms Apollonius/Pound's social love while further foreshadowing the temple. The rest of the text elaborates the conditions of CHEN[4], "Man under Fortuna," but the eye affirms its epiphanies with visual symbols both read from nature and constructed from signs. Poundian religious love consummates the foregoing aspects by turning "Templum aedificans" (*90*), kredemnon, and the foregoing ideograms into the top of city walls in four affirmations that

        The temple   山   is holy,
            because it is not for sale.

Other Seal/Calendar arcana are interspersed to the end of the canto.

CHEN[4] on the right in *86* appeared bluntly as "Man under Fortuna," who turned a mere fortune wheel. In *91* small *chen*[4] was translated "timing the thunder." In *96*, with axial CHEN[4] as a symbol for the Powers in *Thrones*, Fortuna received through the experience of the epiphanies the new attribute "eyes pervanche." Now new growth and the renewed eye reveal her to be a goddess of earthly splendor with "eyes pervanche," "hidden as eel in sedge." While above the moon there is order, beneath there is chance. Whether blessed or cursed she joys in the Lord of each sphere and in "ever-shifting change" (cf. the Calendar cycle and its divinities). Even Aquinas could not demote her as she joyed blessedly in "plenilune" and in "phase over phase." Understood, she governs the prototype of the revolutionary cycle and revolutionary building,

> ONE, ten, eleven, *chi con me* 旦 tan?

A warming worshipper asks her (in Italian) "Benign light, in your eyes, what I want, do you want?" He answers for her "You want it." More jocularly he ends his praise

> May 4th. Interruption
>> mid dope-dolls an' duchesses
>>> tho' orften I roam,
>> some gals is better,
>>>> some wusser

The formula for the revolutionary prototype and the third affirmation of the temple precipitate the elements from which were made Sargon's seal, first used to introduce Apollonius (*94*):[3]

Present are bird, shield, temple, Mount, foundation, branch, a grid (of stones), and a wing, all from a thousand years before Tang, the first Chinese revolutionary, or from about the time of the Great Emperors. The elements are common to European, Chinese and American symbolism. After the fourth affirmation of the temple, Sargon's seal in its perfected form (as in *94*) introduces an end of the four epiphanies as they began, with Eleusinian rites.
   From the locus—

> Flowers, incense, in the temple enclosure,
>> no blood in that TEMENOS
> when crocus is over and the rose is beginning

—the vegetal figure for the laws will evolve to Coke's opening up of the English charters. To frame *96–97*, Paul relates North European and Mediterranean pagan temples and their gods. Sargon's seal is linked with Frederick

---

3. For Sargon's seal and inscriptions, see Waddell, *Egyptian Civilization*, pp. 19–26.

II of Sicily's book on falconry. Justinian's Code and St. Sophia are "of the Wisdom of God" ("Sapientiae Dei") like the ideograms *cheng⁴ming*,² the first principle of government and macaronics for "E. P." "Wanting the right word" is equated with "seeking the god's name" (cf. the *Pisan* theme "each one in the name of his god"). Various rituals culminate in Athelstan's setting up guilds (cf. *91*), which clinches both the epiphanies and the first constitution of *Thrones*. A closing "not lie down," sealed by its ideograms, looks toward the Manchu *Sacred Edict*.

Sheng Yu 98–99

Chinese government was introduced by Confucius in *XIII*, its place was defined by the Chinese folk in *XLIX*, and its operation was followed in "KUNG." The *Shu Ching* revealed the basic principles of government being derived and codified from the first Chinese revolution in *Rock-Drill 85*, the epitome of its draft and of *Los Cantares*. Now the Manchu *Sheng Yu* or *Sacred Edict*, promulgated by Emperor Kang Hi as he was transferring the empire to his son Yong Ching (Canto *LX* to Canto *LXI*), manifests a Chinese constitution as " a reassumption of the Confucian ethic, put into action and practice by the stupendous Manchu administration as Statal teaching."⁴

The *Sheng Yu* was promulgated in sixteen maxims in classic style ("Uen-li") by Emperor Kang Hi. Yong Ching expounded his father's maxims in an urbane middle style. Wang Iu-Puh, a salt commissioner of Shensi Province, took the edict "down to the people" in "volgar' eloquio" or common speech. Pound translates the three versions, taken to constitute an amending process, into American epic English. But Pound amends the evolution for his own revolutionary purposes. Like the eighth subject of *Cantos (1–95)*, *Shu 85–87*, this eighth of *Los Cantares* takes the form of revolutionary vision, symbol, phases, and documents at once yielding and being amended by the Branches/ Powers. Pound draws upon Wang's version in an argumentative voice for a Declaration yielding Congress/States and on Kang's maxims in an authoritative voice for Preambles yielding Presidency/Amendment. Yong's *Preface* or preamble to his rendition modulates Kang into a further expansion of Wang's version for explicit constitutional amendment yielding Judiciary/ Supreme Law. Yong's version then embodies the spirit of an urbane Bill of Rights yielding States/Ratification for a theory of a state directed by continuing amendment (or revolution) toward perfection.

Having cast the *Book of the Eparch* in an argument about its language, Pound casts this second constitution of the draft in the voices of amending personae focused by and in himself as a medium of "REVOLUTION . . . in

---

4. "The Green-Room," *Virginia Quarterly Review*, Charlottesville, Summer 1958, in a letter concerning first publication of "Canto 99."

the minds of the people'' for revolution and of ''WE the People'' for the Branches/Powers. He does so by opening in his own voice, which carries what has to be amended, and then gradually converging with his personae. He opens *98* with a need and the materials for amendment, then modulates into Wang's voice of Declaration and of Congress/States. Affected by Wang's he returns in the middle of *98* in a more popular voice, which modulates into Kang's voice for the Seal generating Preambles and for Presidency/ Amendment. From the end of *98* into the beginning of *99*, affected by Kang's, his voice modulates into Yong's *Preface*, which in turn modulates into Wang's voice of Constitution and of Judiciary/Supreme Law. Finally, with but two lines and a complete disappearance of his own interpolations, Pound's voice is absorbed into Yong's voice of continuing revolution (Bill and Seal) and of States/Ratification. So ''the people'' converge with rulers who deserve it.

It should be evident that the theme is formal assumption of independence activated by personal freedom from cruel punishments (though amending is painful), subsumed in Presidency/Amendment, which is generating Amendment for new world union. Promulgating and amending the *Sheng Yu* condenses *Shu 85–87* of *Cantos (1–95)* and *Section: Rock-Drill* via the recurrence of LING², the Amendment ideogram, to reintroduce CHANG's ''Our dynasty came in because of a great sensibility'' for CHOU founding; LING² is first realized by the rock-drill itself, the single aim ''The arrow has not two points'' (ERH⁴).

''REVOLUTION . . . in the minds of the people'' (*98*: pp. 684–86) derives government from LING² and from Eleusinian Amor. An opening ''palette'' practically constitutes LING² from previous perceptions:

> The boat of Ra-Set moves with the sun
> ''but our job to build light'' said Ocellus:
> Agada, Ganna, Faasa
>
> 新 hsin¹
>
> Make it new
> *Τὰ ἐξ Αἰγύπτου φάρμακα*
> Leucothea gave her veil to Odysseus
> *Χρόνος*
> *πνεῦμα θεῶν*
> *καὶ ἔρως σοφίας*
> The Temple (hieron) is not for sale.

Seal symbols and the Calendar cycle building the tabulation (the Temple) are hinted by Greek (I paraphrase) for ''The out-of-Egypt magic / . . . Time / spirits of the gods / and love of wisdom.'' The meaning is something like ''Revolutions succeed and constitutions come in because of a great sensibility.''

The palette passes through Odysseus ''Getting the feel . . . of his soul'' during the Trojan War (an archetype for constitution succeeding struggle) to an alternation of elaborated ''awareness'' with its justicial consequences.

"Awareness" resulted in Greek mitigation of slavery, in state economic enterprises, in the Byzantine guild system, and in "ius Italicum," though black shawls (the kredemnon) are no longer worn for Demeter among the people. Nothing but "awareness" resulted in low Byzantine interest rates or in the coming Manchu *Edict*. Elusinian philosophers defined the awareness as some incarnate, some remaining spirit; as Platonic idea containing "The body"; and as "Gods by hilaritas" and by "their speed in communication." "Awareness" is god in us ("deus in nobis"), inspiring us with the kredemnon to "fight for law as for walls." Such criteria show that perceivers like Yeats, Eliot, and Wyndham Lewis, "had no ground beneath 'em," no pu^2-ideogram (lexically "no," pictorially a root). The United States Senate had only the twelve literates. No one could speak efficiently to the crowd but Mussolini, and he got out of hand. Hence the need for voices of more fundamental "basic principles of government" and "foundation" ("THE FOUR TUAN[1]") to amend western corporate theory and practice.

Wang's Declaration in a voice of Congress/States (*98*: pp. 686–89) is introduced by Yeats taking two months to amend ten lines of Ronsard and Pound working with Wang "in the salt works." Wang's voice comes out of "an awareness" in the form of a Declaration accented by ideograms, which affixes a form lacking in the presentation of the *Book of the Eparch*. Commissioner Wang Iu-Puh's ($iu^4 p'uh^{23}$) "volgar' eloquio" unites the whole people under the King, whose job, "vast as the swan-flight," is to build thought on "Sagetrieb." For natural rights he proclaims ($hsüan^1$) "a filiality that binds things together"; for forming government by consent he proclaims "pen yeh [pen^3] / then $τέχνη$ [yeh^4]" or root patrimony (cf. Pound's heritage of '76). For necessary revolution a fiery argumentative tone castigates Taoist and Buddhist supernaturalism (fo^2) for disrupting social order.

In a first case they "provide no mental means for / Running an empire" and destroy "the 5 human relations," so that even Buddha himself, from the horse's mouth, "*ch'i'd* 'em or *shed* 'em"($ch'i^1she^3ma^{13}$). In a second case it is inconceivable that "The celestial" is such a small man ($hsiao^3 jin^2$) that he wants idols, prayers, money, and the language of their "classics," and bears a grudge if he doesn't get them. The premises and cases end "If you don't swallow their buncombe / you won't have to drive 'em out."

Wang's reiterated name (*Wang*^{2} *Yu*^{4}) makes his version a declaration taking "the sense" of the *Edict* "down to the people" in "*volgar' eloquio*." Declaration challenges all who "display no constructive imagination," who use no "connection," no "grits in the mortar," no "impediments," to seek new union; "You, I mean *you* should know why, / and start new after an inadvertence" touches Pound himself.

The root and spring of independence is an intense awareness of duty "under cover on the inside" ($i^4 shên^1li^{3-4}yüan^2$) of individual character; sovereign powers constitute an equilibrium ($t'ai^4 p'ing^2$) by which the Empire "grips the earth in good manners." Since "Earth and water dye the wind in your valley," if the Emperor's feelings have "the colour of nature" then the local and the imperial will all share together (*feng*[1] *en*[1] *ch'ing*[2]).

A Poundian summary (pp. 689–91) popularizes the opening Eleusinian summary further for "WE the People" and links Kati and Kang Hi ideogramically as "two ½s of a seal." Before introducing Kang's maxims he points out that the gods appointed popular "john barleycorn" to be the people's "Je tzu," reiterates that "Thought is built out of Sagetrieb," and acknowledges his debt to his source, Baller, and to "*volgar' eloquio*." Wang was a stylist for having taken Kang's and Yong's languages "down to the people," who think and speak in quotation and repetition. For a ritual style (and it goes for *The Cantos*) "There is no substitute for a lifetime."

Kang's maxims are introduced by a phrasing of "REVOLUTION . . . in the minds of the people" voiced by "WE the People," "The meaning of the Emperor, / ten thousand years heart's-tone-think-say." His version takes the form of ideograms (the Seal) generating maxims (motives of the Preamble) in the mode Presidency / Amendment (*98*: pp. 691–93).

Almost a page of ideograms for reverencing order, raising one's son to be a gentleman, and avoiding family squabbles about land and money, all derived from Kung, apparently represent an emerging first maxim for II–VI are then enumerated and framed back to the ideograms. After a Poundian interpolation maxims are enumerated VII–X (with X, *pen*[3] *yeh*[4], given ideograms), XV–XVI (with XV, "Not a fixed charge," assigned by ideogram to Mencius), and finally XII. There seems to be no reason for this idiosyncratic arrangement and numbering but to square the maxims, at least in form if not in substance, with the Seal generating Preambles for liberty and union.

The introduction of Yong's *Preface* at the end of *98* proffers the *Edict* to be rehearsed yearly and publicly in "Deliberate converse," "with the colour of Nature," "by the silk cords of the sunlight." The ritual is a process of continuing revolution aimed at social and political unanimity:

> "Each year in the Elder Spring, that is the first month of it,
> The herald shall invite your compliance.
> There are six rites for the festival
> and that all should converge!

> And not to lose life for bad temper.

In Pound's context the herald's invitation refers to Wang's Declaration. "Six rites for the festival" refer to Kang's motives aimed at a constitution. The rest looks toward what is yet to come.

The rubric to *99*, echoing Confucian (*XIII*) and Parnassian (*92*) communication, fits the *Sheng Yu* into the vegetal figure which is carrying four constitutions toward maturation:

> Till the blue grass turn yellow
> and the yellow leaves float in the air

Yong's *Preface* (*99*: pp. 694–96) is then altered and extended so that Wang's
Declaration will now "incite" amendment, so that Kang's "six rites for
festival" will result in "7 instructions" (Articles), and so that all will "converge as the root *tun*[1] *pen*[3] / the root veneration" (Bill and Seal). As a
medium for "WE the People" Yong heaps up principles to be alternately
"discriminated," seen as a comprehensive "word" or common thought
("KOINE ENNOIA"), "Woven in order," broken down into a list, traced
out, and bound together. Liberty alternates with union. Uniting the Emperor's
heart and government with "our heart" and "our government," Yong speaks
for the people. His culminating principle is "Feed the people." He sums up
his heritage

> This much I, Chên, have heard. *Yo el rey.*
> Yang[3] nourish
> chih[2–5] ma[1]   set out hemp
> chung[3] mi'en[2] cotton
>   t'ung[2] all together.

Spanish signals macaronics for the Columbian as well as the Manchu heritage,
something like "Yank nourish / Gee, ma, set out hemp / chung me 'n'cotton /
tongue all together." "Yank nourish" and "chung" hint at Barlow's *Columbiad*, epic of the arts and sciences. "Gee, ma, set out hemp" remonstrates
with "ma" and "cotton tongue" Whitman's *Leaves of Grass*, epic of the
land and its people. As Barlow's "hickups" could be cured by Whitman's
"sneezing" (*XXXIII*), Pound would cure and surpass both by joining "all
together" in his epic of constitution and justice.

Wang's Declaration followed that of '76 rigorously in the form of its
argument, but deliberately amended Jefferson's urbane tone. Kang's Preamble followed the axiomatic form of '87, but the Emperor (cf. Washington)
spoke for "WE the People." The formal Declaration provided what was
missing in the form of the *Book of the Eparch*, and the formal Preamble
applied to amending the *Sheng Yu*.

Wang's Constitution (*99*: pp. 696–707), which like Judiciary interprets
Supreme Law, amends language of the law and of the state by bringing back
Wang's fiery voice. But although Yong's "7 instructions" have hinted at
Constitutional form, and although Wang will hint at the form of the Bill, those
forms await the coming American and English Constitutions. Wang's Constitution articulates "the great balance" to be achieved by "Four Tuan, and
verity," and unfolds in ten paragraphs. But the ten are not formally functional. Like an orator speaking to the people, Wang churns up his disquisition
with repetition, quotation, and other popular forms, until repletion brings a
summarizing focus.

Wang's constitution defines the functioning of a just government; reaffirms
the foundations of society in Confucian human nature, in locality, and in
the homestead; extends the argument against Buddhism; instructs against

inexact language and egoism in religion, in scholarship, and in the home; and finally urges the principle of a cooperative, not adversary, corporate state. The summary last paragraph (pp. 706–7), setting against the general principle "PANURGIA," the force of the many, "SOPHIA," by which people may determine what they will "*not* do," cites the form of the Declaration coming "Thru the ten voices of the tradition" to affirm "the right pattern" of taxation, activated "By the ten mouths of the tradition," the Bill, for maintaining peace by getting rid of criminality. The middle, to prevent "Wranglings" between "High & low, top & under," turns on the adjuration "INCORPORATE / & one body": Wang pleads "The ups are not malevolent, / you might consider their complications," and argues (of dikes for floodwater) "someone must build 'em; / must plan 'em." His final "have peace" by getting rid of criminality ends with a justicial "Catch 'em!"

Wang's constitution and Judiciary / Supreme Law shift into Yong's Bill and States/Ratification (*99*: 707–12) without transition. Yong's voice gives the popular bill a voice of urbane authority for Pound's theory of the corporate state designed for continuing revolution. "Ancestral spring making breed, a pattern" passes through pattern travestied in a book review of Pound's earlier volumes ("'12 inches, guinea an inch!'") to the basic principle "The State is corporate." The principle is elaborated in definitions, particular values, and implementations. Among the definitions the corporate state has a pulse in its body and, all through it, a root of ritual heard in the tone of all public teaching or Sagetrieb, which is making *The Cantos* (like such a state) "not a work of fiction / nor yet of one man." "The whole tribe is from one man's body, / what other way can you think of it?" The state is "order, inside a boundary"; law is "reciprocity." The plan is rooted in nature, whose emergent powers converge as they unfold from "a must at the root"; such a "must," "not one man's mere power," rules a paideumatic state. "The basis is man, / and the rectification of officers" by "the four TUAN / . . . jen, i, li, chih," which are from nature.

Particular values and implementations aim at the ideal "THE STATE SHOULD MOVE LIKE A DANCE" (the four voices of the *Sheng Yu* are also Pound's executive, advisory, perceptive, and poetic). Yong brings it all to a fourfold focus on tradition, personality, justice, and poetry:

> All I want is a generous spirit in customs
> > 1st/honest man's heart demands sane curricula
> > (no, that is not textual)
> Let him analyze the trick programs
> > and fake foundations
> The fu jen receives heaven, earth, middle
> > and grows.

Overall, detailed structure aside, Pound's presentation of revolutionary and constitutional amending processes evolves in four voices of the *Sheng Yu* while his voice interpenetrates each successively. For correction by Confucianism, the tone with which Kung was first discovered (*XIII*) and the unmediated paideumatic tone of the Chinese folk (*XLIX*) entered the voice of an American catechumen or bull in a china shop in "KUNG." Conversely an American's reverence for authority, for refinement, and for a new ethic of brotherhood defined the tone of *Pisan*. Expounding the beginning of Chinese revolution through the *Shu* (*85–87*) then balanced Chinese urbanity and American zeal in a Confucianized spirit of '76 universalized as "Sagetrieb." Expounding the culmination of Chinese revolution through the *Sheng Yu* orders all these tones into the argumentative voice, the authoritative voice, and the interpretive voice until all are focused and fused in Yong/Pound's cheerful, urbane persuasion.

Thrones 100–106

Having argued with his source in presenting the *Book of the Eparch*, and having adopted personae and their voices to amend the *Sheng Yu*, the amending statesman approaches his materials in *100–106* with the Constitution as a form in his mind and, instead of writing from a source and interpolating, gathers his own materials in his own voice. The ninth subject of *Los Cantares* realizes the ninth of *Cantos* (*1–95*), Benton, via the CHOU revolution's realization of LING^2 in I^2, city, governed by "nombreux officiers." The theme is that of the ongoing ninth draft itself: for his application of Constitutional form Pound asserts sovereign powers activated by retained rights, subsumed in (Judiciary)/Supreme Law for new world union. The form is that of Benton, Branches and Powers extended sequentially, though over seven cantos rather than two. Formal application of the Constitution advances Wang's random constituting of the *Sheng Yu* (*99*) into distinct Article-cantos. Eleusinian and Chinese constitutions are subsumed in American justicial cosmopolitanism's absorption of world law and its genius for limiting, distributing, and balancing justicial paideumas as well as governmental functions. Exercize of the American form validates the American justicial protagonist. Behind both lie the culminating constitution and "throne" of *Thrones*, the English charters and Coke to come (*107–109*).

The main purpose of *100–106* is to revaluate in the light of the world justicial mind and its ideal form European history from "Wellington's peace after Vaterloo" (*85*) to Mussolini, and American history from the period leading up to the Civil War to the world war presidents Woodrow Wilson and Franklin Roosevelt. The principal personae, defined as peacemakers, are Talleyrand, Bismarck, and Mussolini in Europe, and American presidents culminating in Buchanan; these modulate in the Powers into Pound himself, whose case is analogized to that of Ovid banished from Rome by Augustus Caesar. The function of the Constitution is not merely to serve as a model for

gathering disparate materials into viable functional relations, and not merely
to embody an inherent form of justice both stable and amendable; these
provide means for seeking external peace and a consequent peace of mind by
learning new lessons from history, so that all persons and all human faculties
may contribute to increasing the "(Paradiso) . . . 'of societies','' both of
historical states and of "states of mind." Revaluation of history and of personae, and amendment of the Constitution by its own amending process, are
inspired by interpolated epiphanies first historical and then personal, until
both converge for Ratification in a grand epiphany and a cosmic temple (*106*).

Both the Branches/Powers form and the focal materials of *100–106* appear
in the formal "palette" *100*, which is also a vestige of a possible but historically thwarted 100-canto poem. For the Branches/Powers dynamic *100* is
formally divided into "FOUR." For *100–106* a congressional mind introduces its historical subject and amendment of it. Napoleon's legal heritage
projects Talleyrand's Presidential mind (*101*). Odysseus aided by Leucothoe
to land in justicial Phaeacia projects an elaboration of divinely ordained
destiny by a Judicial mind (*102*). Amending the American Constitution and
the *Sheng Yu* project American states' rights and the homestead (*103*). Both
project Pound's elaboration of Amendment (*104*). Rationalist philosophers
include St. Anselm, whose general philosophy of mind, which lay behind the
Magna Charta, is elaborated as Supreme Law (*105*). Amor, a symbolized
temple, and peace (the end of *100*) are elaborated epiphanically for Ratification (*106*).

A rubric for the whole Constitutional mind and its activity brings Judiciary,
Presidency, and Congress together in a moment of Constitutional crisis explained by an institutional defender to a poetic defender:

> "Has packed the Supreme Court
> > so they will declare anything he does constitutional."
> > > > Senator Wheeler, 1939.

The rubric modulates through a contrasting Habsburg whose ploughing (the
source of justice) was aimed at "Eu ZoOn," the good life, into the amender's
personal instigation,

> Not that never should, but if exceeding and
> > no one protest,
> > > > will lose all of your liberties.

The constitutional mind would imitate the resourcefulnesses of Napoleon
and Lenin; Lenin's " 'Aesopian language (under censorship) / where I wrote
'Japan' you may read 'Russia' " applies to its own indirect application of its
form to eclectic materials.

A break in the text and amazement at Roosevelt's economic policy ("By
increase of debt? strengthen??") lead to the locus of Congress/States (*100*:
pp. 713–16) and of *100* itself, a money-man's remark during the Wilson ad-

ministration that they ought to " 'try to shift power to the Executive' / i.e. out of Congress.'' Trying to circumvent the Constitution calls forth the general epic cry ''PERENNE / BELLUM 'not constructif,' '' against which are mustered such positive achievements as Napoleon's law code, Cavour's unification of Italy, peace from 1870 until 1914 (credited to Bismarck), and such principles as ''representation of some sort, by trades'' and ''From ploughing . . . is justice.'' The locus for a Congressional mind is ''SUMBAINAI,'' translated earlier (of Odysseus) ''having his own mind to stand by him''(*91*) and here (from a fellow inmate in the ''bug-house'') ''Out of vast / a really sense of proportion / and instantly.' '' Congress/States culminates in President Jackson's damnation of Congress x, which in the view of states' righters has been construed to limit States' sovereignty beyond what was intended.

Dantean paradisal ''Letizia,'' a religion, brings Presidency/Amendment (*100*: pp. 716–17). ''*Virtù*'' enters, with a will good in itself (cf. Kati's ''good nature''), from the light of God's serenity. Such light brought Pound ''Out of Erebus / Where no mind moves at all.'' America sustained balance before the Civil War. To Edward VIII ''we owe three years PEACE,'' a tag which will recur in *106*. Odysseus recalls landing in Phaeacia and throwing the kredemnon back to Leucothoe ''with a fond hand.'' Napoleon's ''CODE'' functioned all over Europe. Mussolini receives credit for the economic policy of his constitution ('' 'Non della' (Verona)'') and for having done (said Santayana) '' 'More . . . for Rome than three Napoleons'' (had done for Paris).

A constitutional rubric,

Nel mezzo   the crystal

introduces Judiciary/Supreme Law (*100*: pp. 718–19), principally an extract from Wang's amendment of the *Sheng Yu* (with ideograms for light and glory) emphasizing Buddhism's lack of ''mental means for running an empire'' and sustaining peace. Included is an honor roll of pre-Civil War presidents Van Buren, Tyler, and Polk, presumably all strict Constitutionalists.

A Latin rubric for States/Ratification (*100*: pp. 720–22), ''Sky for a roof, God doesn't sell it; / Earth for a bed, but he lavishes it,'' augmented ''and that Caritas leads to serenity,'' paraphrases the temple that is not for sale. Justicial visionaries follow their ''own gods'' (states of mind), they do not ''sin by misnaming''; they move ''out of similitude into gathering'' under Fortuna (cf. the Calendar cycle, which will emerge in *106*). A list of such visionaries, all rationalist philosophers, includes Anselm and Pound. While the Norman kings of Anselm's time were playing tic-tac-toe (pictured) for cities, Anselm was writing a philosophy that led to such revolutionary poetry as Cavalcanti's ''Donna mi prega'' (''come in subjecto'') and Villon's ''La Belle Heaulmiere'' (''lisses / amoreuses / a tenir''). That Love is ''a reality sprung from a substance,'' from Plotinus's third *Ennead* (''PERI EROTAS''), precipitates the visual temple. Pound ends paraphrasing Plotinus's theory that the mind is the best self and, in its essence, remains ''aloof.'' The serenity of

Caritas is an intellectual peace. A 100-canto poem might have ended on such a note. If "Addendum to *Canto C*" were read here, it would accentuate a providential surview of the historical struggle and its aim, a "paradiso terrestre."

The Presidential mind (*101*) takes as its main subject the growth of Talleyrand's mind from the locality, landscape, and vegetation of his family estate at Perigord, one of Pound's sacred places. Analogous in nature and effect is the locality of the Himalayan Na Khi tribe of China's Yunnan Province. These are set against an American mind moving toward slavery by neglect of history and family names, by "trailer life," which is "non-productive, / non-agricultural" ("tho' avoiding the squalor of taxes / by cretins imposed"), and by "Not attempting . . . to unscrew the inscrutable." Talleyrand (and Thiers) tried to "get some sense into princes"; Talleyrand's influence led to a constitution for Italy, "Bonaparte's maximum"; to a religion "that intelligent men can believe"; and to other stabilizing policies. Such a mind is validated by Eleusinian epiphany and by Na Khi ritual. Harmony of man with nature comes to a focus in the centaur image "His horses's mane flowing / His body and soul are at peace." Such personal peace is ethical.

The Judicial mind takes as its subjects (*102*) destiny and ritual. Odysseus hears his destiny from Hermes via Kalupso, from Pallas Athena, and from Leucothoe. Senators, literate or not, must reside in the States from which they are elected. The Phaeacians devised a ritual for Leucothoe. Yeats, Eliot, and Lewis had "no ground to stand on." Black shawls were worn for Demeter in Venice in Pound's young time. Only love can make a work perfect. Anthropology ritualizes perceptions. Leucothoe's mind in the incense of her rituals opens up Eleusinian epiphanies. Na Khi ritual restrains men from wanting to "burst out of the universe," as Odysseus's godlike mind often tempted him to do. The Judicial mind rejudges Julian, labeled "Apostate" for rejecting Christianity, for refusing to be worshipped and for building graneries. It judges Domitian "infaustus" for trying to buy social or political peace with money.

The mind of the Branch/Power States (*103*) takes as its main subject American political morality leading up to the Civil War. A varied opening cites "1850: gt objection to any honesty in the White House," " '56, an M. C. from California / killed one of the waiters at the Willard," and "22nd. Brooks thrashed Sumner in Camera Senatus." Brooks's reason, " 'respectful of our own rights and of others' / for which decent view he was ousted," affirms states' rights, which are universalized in

    Homestead versus kolschoz
    Rome   versus Babylon

Of the war itself Pound adjudges slavery to have been a "red herring"; the real issue was financial speculation in land, for which the defense (too late) was the Homestead Act of 1856. States of mind are affirmed by Confucius of the LING²-theme, " 'I see its relation to one thing, / Hui sees it relation to ten.' " The crux is "Monetary literacy," without which is loss of freedom; with it people eat, the Mandate of Heaven is renewed, animals dance, the local gods come. So Pound's grandfather tried after the Civil War, in Congress, to keep some of the noninterest-bearing debt in circulation as currency. Talleyrand's, Bismarck's, and Mussolini's struggles toward peace are continued from *100.* The Branch States, marked by a break in the text, ends with the Irish revolutionary Griffith's recurring remark that you can't move people with "a cold thing" like economics; but Pound's "ut delectet" (it must delight) is turning economics into poetry as the Seal / Calendar arcanum modulated Branches into Powers from Benton *88* to *89.*

The Branch States moves into the Power States through a Mat Quay who "read greek in secret." But the Civil War preacher Henry Ward Beecher promoted the Union against states' rights by carrying into his pulpit some rusty cannon balls allegedly from Bunker Hill. In their "colossal conceit" Americans were unable to see that "Heaven made hearing and seeing" and that men, who have the rule, must prepare themselves with LING² as the HIA dynasty (overthrown by Tang, *LIII*) did not. The American constitutional struggle concludes wistfully with the public service of Buchanan as ambassador to Russia and as pre-Civil War president. His observations that men had sunk to considering the mere material value of the Union and that the Constitution was a grant from the States of limited powers augured the decline both of the Union and of states' rights. Pound's "nec Templum aedificavit / nec restituit rem / but not his fault by a damn sight" links him with Malatesta and Jackson. The personal dimension that will dominate the cantos of the amending process is introduced near the end in a comparison of Pound's exile from ideal America and Italy to Ovid's exile from Rome and from his hometown Sulmona.

For "Eight ditto, good red" in the building of a new Tempio, a précis of Paul's Lombard history frames *96–103.* That the Lombards were considered heretics links them with Hitler's heretical opposition to "Das Leihkapital" (loan-capital) and thus to Pound's. The end of *103* brings up to date a quest for world peace exemplified by "the Mensdorf letter." In 1928 Pound and Albert Mensdorf (Wormsdorf of *XIX*) proposed that the Carnegie Foundation of International Peace investigate the causes of war as well as its effects; they also suggested such specific causes as have been touched in *100–103* and requested enlightenment on what was being done to codify and implement a truly international law. By 1958 their letter has had "no publicity."

LING², the Amendment ideogram, comes back in *104* to differentiate the "great sensibility," which brings revolutionary dynasties, from sensibilities "furious from perception" like Hitler's and from an interior blindness that makes some try "to explain themselves out of nullity." LING² with all its elements—its clouds, its three voices, and its two contained figures—clarifies, harmonizes, and is the seed ("semina") of movements. Separately (i.e.,

Amendment unregulated by Supreme Law) the elements may stem from violence ("a wild-cat") or pervert (toward treasure), or destroy ("Flames withered; the wind blew confusion"). The key is Na Khi harmony with nature, which is brought back in their rituals. The bulk of the canto ritualizes Pound's acquaintances with others, mainly artists, who tried to promote harmonious change. Ovid's plight recurs. A concluding summary ritualizes sound economic policies. The aim has been to discover "What a government usefully COULD do" and to avoid "false middles," which "serve neither commerce / nor the NOOS in activity" (i.e., amending). Amendment is possible under "That fine old word . . . 'an Independence,' " which is sealed with the ideograms *pen yeh*, root patrimony (Pound's '76). *Pen*[3] *yeh*[4] has directed "Homestead versus kolschoz," "advice to farms, not control," and other beneficial amendments. Amendment ends with a Chinese version of tax as a share of local produce and with balance ("Iu's weights are still in the treasury").

The rubric of *105* —

Feb. 1956
Is this a divagation:
                Talleyrand saved Europe for a century
France betrayed Talleyrand;
                     Germany, Bismarck.
And Muss saved, rem salvavit,
                in Spain
                    il salvabile

—recalls sorrowfully the historical theme of seeking peace. The rubric for seeking Supreme Law, the ideogram *chi*[2]—the power that moves the universe or origin of that power—translated "semina motuum," seed of motions, has evolved from the "seed" LING[2] (cf. *104*). Ovid continues. Efforts to open its mysteries are solved by St. Anselm's visionary but rational philosophy of mind, a Supreme Law validating and being validated by interpolated personal perceptions.

Anselm was a philosophical revolutionary and a revolutionary against royal tyranny whose philosophy lay behind the Magna Charta. He links "ELEUSIS" and Anglo-Saxonry via Normandy. His Supreme Law is the uniting of reason with an absolute good and the ability of human nature to become godlike by using divinely endowed reason. It unites with the local laws of England, where the land itself was the source of all "*libertates*" and "*consuetudines*" (local laws) before Norman coinage, "the symbol of equity," instituted "justice . . . centralization." But by raising the interest rate from 5 to 40 percent King William Rufus, who had appointed Anselm archbishop of Canterbury, violated "Unitas Charitatis, / consuetudo diversa" and so lost "the wisdom of Kati," the basis of "something not brute force in government."[5]

---

5. Defining epic subjects in *Paris Review* 28, Pound asserted "There are epic subjects. The

Anselm withdrew to Rome and continued writing. Out of a thousand years of "savages against maniacs" Pound assembles an honor roll, mostly Anglo-Saxon, which points through Anselm toward the Magna Charta. Cavalcanti and Villon presumably read Anselm. Now Pound has. The successor will extend Anselm's reason, which somewhat slighted beauty, to his own Amor and temple.

Ratification of Cantos *100–106* takes the form of new providential inspiration received and then memorialized in an anticipation of the final temple. *Canto 106* goes all the way back to the Providences of *I*, Circe, Persephone, Anticleia, and Aphrodite, substituting Demeter for the mother Anticleia and revealing Persephone to be not only queen of the dead but also the girl of Enna who brings back the spring. All previous Eleusinian visions are extended, e.g., Odysseus's of Circe, Pound's at Pisa, and the statesman's at Castalia. The amending powers culminate in full Ovidian metamorphosis. "The rose" that has opened so slowly now opens fully as the revolutionary mind continues to "run thru his zodiac, / . . . not in memory, / in eternity / and 'as a wind's breath / that changing direction changeth its name.' " From her fruitful fields Persephone spreads a "nueva lumbre" over the great rivers of South America, suggesting Columbus's global vision. Her inspirations are "grain rite." She is like Circe but lacks the fire of Circe's eyes. Praying to her as Drake prayed to Diana (*91*) elicits a personal inspiration for perfecting the Constitutional form.

The historical theme is interpolated with diminishing magnitude. A rubric that confronts the new goddess is balanced by a pre-Confucian work on economics, the *Kuan Tzu*, founded on "The strength of men is in grain" (cf. the goddess's "grain rite"). But the opening rose reveals that while Chinese principles can guide government, Helen's breasts gave the cup of white gold at Patera. Ideal Chinese and Eleusinian government unite in "coin-skill" ("Yao and Shun ruled by jade" and Antoninus "coin'd Artemis"), but expanding vision gathers all the goddesses "in hypostasis" and elicits the prayer. The prayer, which opens the minds of the landscape, the trees, and the goddesses, is interpolated only with "Yao and Shun ruled by jade." The "three years peace" given by Edward VIII (from *100*) is only a parenthesis amid inspiration taking form as a "great acorn of light bulging outward" and as other vegetation. Good government and economic justice bring peace, but these are merely means and conditions for releasing the always abundant beauty of nature and of the mind.

The divine vision, primarily vegetal, and principles of government, art drawn from nature, come together in the building of a temple or Statue of

---

struggle for individual rights is an epic subject, consecutive from jury trial in Athens [*85, 89*] to Anselm versus William Rufus, to the murder of Becket and to Coke [*107–109*] and through John Adams. Then the struggle appears to come up against a block. The nature of sovereignty is epic matter, though it may be a bit obscured by circumstance. Some of this *can* be traced, pointed; obviously it has to be condensed to get into the form."

Liberty to "APHRODITE EUPLOIA" (of the fair voyage) by "The high admiral." Canto *106* has transformed *I* by reversing the proportions of poetic inspiration and revolutionary form. "The high admiral" is Odysseus, Columbus, Pound. The temple is a new version of Aphrodite's Mount. More locally, the whole canto has opened up a Poundian version of the Amor, the temple symbol, and the Plotinian idealism that ended Canto *100*. If we recall the Constitutional rubric to Cantos *100–106*—

> "Has packed the Supreme Court
>   so they will declare anything he does constitutional."
>   Senator Wheeler, 1939.
>   . . .
>   Not that never should, but if exceeding and
>   no one protest,
>   will lose all of your liberties

—and if we follow Pound's "Aesopian language," his relating of civic order and Amor, and the Constitution as a self-amending document guiding Cantos *100–106*, we can understand his celebrating an amendment of history under the Constitution as "the Supreme Law of the land" with

> God's eye art 'ou.
>   The columns gleam as if cloisonné,
>   The sky is leaded with elm boughs.

Beauty emergent from peace is like the Bill of Rights and a Statue of Liberty emerging from Ratification. Such a realization anticipates the last subject of *Thrones* and of *Los Cantares*.

Coke *107–109*

Pound consummates a constitutional tradition, constitutional personae, and a form of constitution in the Magna Charta and subsequent charters presented through their gatherer and commentator, Sir Edward Coke, in his *Institutes*. Beginning in 1215 and continuing into the 1600s, and extended by Pound to the Connecticut Charter saved by his ancestor Captain James Wadsworth in 1687, the English Constitution and its extensions have the form of continuing revolution by constitutional amendment. The Magna Charta, the Petition of Right, Confirmationes Chartarum "en amendement" and Articuli Super Chartas, and the Connecticut Charter, which dominate four phases of *107–109*, have the spirit and function of the Bill's Amendments and the phasal form of the Seal. They lie behind the American Constitution as an unwritten bill of Rights, "REVOLUTION . . . in the minds of the people," lay behind '76. By subject, arrangement, and arcana Pound gives his presentation of Coke the form of revolution generating Constitutional dynamic form (like *Shu 85* and *Sheng Yu 98–99*), but now the ratifying Bill and Seal impose their forms. Coke *107–109* is projected from CHIAO$^{1-4}$ . . . CHIAO$^{1-4}$ of the rock-drill—"Sagetrieb" or the speech power of the "tale of the tribe," and phasal consummation of the Bill—via the tenth subject of *Cantos (1–95)*, Amor *90–95*, to the tenth subject of *Los Cantares*, which projects a tenth draft and fourth phase. The pledge among personae and the activating reserved powers are subsumed in (States)/Ratification generating world Ratification.

Pound arranges his presentation into Coke's gathering of and comment on the Magna Charta, Coke's personal struggle against James I and Charles I, Coke's gathering of and comment on further charters, and these consummated in Captain Wadsworth's feat. Pound comments with Coke, joins Coke's struggle, joins Coke's further comments to try his own legal case, and joins his ancestor Wadsworth while revealing an antecedent of the Constitution which, as Wadsworth hid the Connecticut Charter in the Charter Oak, has been hidden in his mind throughout the poem to be saved and amended. The history of the charters and the struggles of their personae bring out the contents of the charters and irradiating epiphanies. Pound's selection and comment (like Coke's) is the method of a first phase; his analogy of Coke's and Wadsworth's struggles and his own is the method of the second. The method of a third, in which Pound's comments all but disappear, is his joining with Coke to apply the texts to his own case.[6] Selection and comment, personal analogy, and constitutional application culminate in clinching epiphanies. The four phases are both concurrent and sequential.

A general rubric, "The azalea is grown while we sleep," fits the Charters into the vegetal imagery for constitutional law which emerged in the epiphanies. "When the crocus is over and the rose is beginning" (*97*) refers to the *Book of the Eparch* and the constitutions to come. "Till the blue grass turns yellow / and the yellow leaves float in the air" (*99*) refers to the *Sheng Yu* and constitutional maturation. "So slow is the rose to open" (*106*) applies to American Constitutional form. The azalea is a rhododendron called the Greek rose. Why "we sleep" is unclear, unless a full awakening will come only with pure poetry. The azalea growing in Selinunt' and Akragas, the first of several Sicilian cities and temples, recalls the "fresca rosa" of the Sicilian poet Alcamo and Frederick II's *Book of the Falcon*, which have recurred since they appeared with Sargon's seal (*97*).

Coke on the Magna Charta and Pound's interpolations carry declaration and Congress/States (*107*: pp. 756–60). The version of the Magna Charta used in Coke's *Second Institutes* was that edited in the twentieth year of

---

6. *Impact: Essays on Ignorance and the Decline of American Civilization* (1960) had on its cover the ideogram, *jen*[2], "the full man and his contents." Its epigraph was "Bellum cano perenne, between the usurer and the man who wants to do a good job" (cf. *86–87*). Its preface was "Of Misprision of Treason" from Coke's *Institutes*, of which Pound would have been guilty had he not exposed what he took to be treason to the Constitution by the American powers that be. "Misprision" is probably also a pun on Pound's own fate, "mis-prison."

Henry III, John's successor. Charter or constitution means "certainty / mother and nurse of repose," from "CHARDE dit estre certaine" (Charter means to be certain, *109*); this tag will be elaborated in each phase. The personal theme focuses on the "clarity" of Coke's mind, "the clearest mind ever in England." Clarity appears in the original charters, but is accentuated by Coke's assemblage of legal Latin, law French, and his own English, to which Pound adds his personal and epiphanic interpolations. Pound's excerpts reflect more the historical importance of the documents than their substance, which appears in items more practical than declaratory and in words and phrases rather than in sentences and chapters—indeed the excerpts are disappointing in the light of what they mean in the history of justice, and few will feel a poetic effect more than functional. Pound seems to be emphasizing the varied languages of the law as justifications and foundations for a cosmopolitan mixture at once local and universal. Behind Coke's gathering lies Anselm's citation of liberty and local laws from Anglo-Saxonry and "justice . . . centralization" from the Norman strain (*105*); for Pound the terms are the paideumas related within American revolutionary form.

The Magna Charta "de la foresta," drawing on the Norman "Custumier" (law code) and rooted in vegetal symbol, is cited by chapters. Pound's excerpts deal with a subject's rights and duties, with ancient liberties, with the common law, and with organizations of ten-man "collegia" (an arcanum for the Declaration consummated in the Bill, see *109* below), all emphasizing exact language. Pound's interpolations declare that "the root is that charter," "our PIVOT," and that the French could not "do it" because "they had not Magna Charta." He sets the clarity of Coke's vegetally rooted mind against the mind of "that slobbering bugger Jim First," whose clerical bent "bitched our heritage" by sponsoring his version of the Bible, which by 1850 had "unfashioned" Latin and so driven truth out of school curricula. A first phase ends with application of the charters " 'as well high as low' " sealed by an ideogram for "end" and "Sapiens incipit a fine," a wise man begins from the end, which precipitates an ideogram for the "beginning" of a second phase.

"Sapiens incipit a fine" and the ideograms recall the Confucian process "things have ends (or scopes) and beginnings" (*Pisan LXXVII*, repeated *Shu 85*). Personal struggle and Presidency / Amendment (*107*: pp. 760–63, *108*: p. 764) begin with a formal garden of hedges, flowers, and herbs, containing a cardinal; Pound links his own mental setting with Coke's through a field full of larks at Allegre, above Rapallo. In a few brief extracts Coke's life begins under Elizabeth with new coin in 1560 and carries to Charles I's "Invasion of the rights of his subjects" by trying in 1628 to suspend *habeas corpus*. Against it a long epiphany is supported by other artistic personae denominated "god's antennae." A few more extracts from Coke's life center on James's execution of Sir Walter Raleigh at the insistence of Spanish Ambassador Gondomar, which Coke opposed in Parliament; they end with Coke's rebuke to James's men in Commons in 1621 that the King should seek counsel from the dead since " 'the dead will not fawn to advance themselves.' " (Coke's remark earned him a term in the Tower.) An epiphanic close to *107* reasserts "this light" to be as a river of "persistent awareness." Further personae culminate through vegetal perceptions in "The caelator's son, named Pythagora," a "heaven-reader" who provides forms for seals, coins, calendars, and revolutions.

Canto *108* continues struggle and Presidency/Amendment with a further assemblage of epiphanic personae, all leading to the end of Coke's brief biography with Charles I's granting of the Petition of Right in June 1628:

> COMMINUIT
>   there is frost on the rock's face
> nurse of industry (25 Edward III)
>   BRUM
> "alla" at Verona
>   of courage
> having none hath no care to defend it

          pen yeh

> Enrolled in the ball of fire
>   as brightness
>   clear emerald
>   for the kindness,
>   infinite,
>   of her hands
> From the Charter to the Petition   1628
>   in June and toward twilight
>   DROIT FAIT

"COMMINUIT" [broke into fragments] / there is frost on the rock's face," a delayed rubric for a second phase, alludes to Robert Frost's intervention into Pound's case, which caused the American government to commute (a punning aspect of "COMMINUIT") its sentence of indefinite confinement.[7] "Nurse of industry" amends the general rubric of the Magna Charta ("that is certainty / mother and nurse of repose").

"BRUM" (Latin "bruma," the winter solstice, and French "brumale,"

---

7. When I was visiting Pound at St. Elizabeths during the 1950s two venerable gentlemen whose names I do not recall discoursed to him that Frost's "Mending Wall" is a unique expression of American spirit of place.

wintry) makes rock-breaking winter a dismal time which challenges the courage of those who have "care to defend."[8] "BRUM" suggests "the times that try men's souls" and Tom Paine's release from the Bastille on 13 Brumaire (4 November) 1794 after fortuitously escaping execution; Mussolini's anti-usurist constitution was promulgated at Salò in November 1944. The ideograms complete the *pen*[3] of the first phase, perhaps here with a visual "T P" and a vocal "Paine, yeah!" All the defenders and "Enrolled in the ball of fire" come under the protection of the constitutional Providence Leucothoe. The return to Coke sums up English constitutional history from the Magna Charta through Coke's use of it as his declaration, to his struggle culminating in the Petition of Right. Parliament, led by Coke, refused to accept Charles I's "no" to the Petition and finally forced from him an amending "DROIT FAIT," Let right be done.

The passage has a more general application as an arcanum carried from left to right by "COMMINUIT," "BRUM," the "halves of a seal" *pen*[3] *yeh*[4], and "DROIT FAIT." Read in the light of the whole poem, "COMMINUIT" refers to the Declaration breaking the hard monolith of government tyranny, to the Preamble breaking the mind into fragments in order to reconstitute it, to amending the Constitution deformed by plutocracy and used to pervert justice, and to Pound's alleged insanity, whether of his politics or of his poetic form and style. "BRUM" refers to struggle in general while suggesting Paine, who with Mussolini exemplifies the courage of the defenders. *Pen*[3] *yeh*[4] symbolize root patrimony in general but for Pound '76 and for a third phase the Constitution symbolized by "halves of a seal"; "Brightness / clear emerald" and Leucothoe's kindness allude to the visionary, inspirational dimension opened up in *Los Cantares*. "DROIT FAIT" symbolizes a Bill of Rights—specifically the English Bill of Rights, but for Pound the American Bill of Rights derived from it.

"Nurse of industry (25 Edward III)" looks from struggle toward *Confirmations of the Charters* and *Articles in Addition to the Charters* under Edward I,[9] which dominate founding and Judiciary/Supreme Law (*108*: pp. 764–70, *109*: pp. 771–72). The keynote is the Tallage Statute, which limits the right to tax. But now, having converged with Coke's upholding and advancing of justice and liberty, Pound minimizes interpolations (argumentative or epiphanic) and makes his selections to establish a constitutional background for arguing America's case and his own against deprivation of rights and liberties by betrayal or corruption of the Constitution.

"Autarchia," a Poundian interpolation for a subject's birthright within his native land and for a policy of economic self-sufficiency, guides selections

---

8. "Saxo cere comminuit brum" illustrates from Ennius the figure of speech tmesis, in which one word ("comminuit") splits another ("cerebrum"). For details on this and on further ramifications of Pound's style, see my "Pound, Coke, or Gordon? Venus, Aeneas, or Tmesis? That's What's Wrong with *Paideuma*," *Paideuma*, Orono, Maine, Spring–Summer 1976.

9. "25 Edward III" is an error for "25 Edward I."

having a special bearing on the case of a defender-amender who has been exiled ("against his will"), disinherited ("mults des mals et disherisons"), denied the right to be "tried locally . . . according to trespass," unjustly imprisoned, and, worst of all, ignored. Edward I outlawed usury instead of exiling its practitioners. Pound is about to receive commutation only, not "our pardon" as one of the "Defenders" of the Constitution. He should have been one of the "trois prodes chevaliers / ou autres avisés" elected to protect the king's person, his laws, and his realm; also one of those specified in the provision that "the seal be in custody of four men dignioribus," as has been the case in his version of '76. Coke's English Constitution, the historical foundation of all constitutions, justifies his actions in behalf of the very Constitution that has been used to deny liberty and justice to all Americans and to their revolutionary poet.

Confirmations of Charters "en amendement," which limits the functions of government (cf. the Branches), and *Articles in Addition to the Charters*, which aim at expansion of the kingdom's economic well-being "cf. the Powers), are extended to laws from the reign of "ELIZABETH / Angliae amor" until *108* ends with provision for repairing bridges and for building new cottages under "Stat. de 31 Eliz. / Angliae amor." Such laws continue into *109* with a delayed rubric for founding and Judiciary/Supreme Law, "Pro Veritate" which brings with it a further elaboration of "certainty, mother and nurse of respose" and "Nurse of industry," "Idleness, mother of pickings"; idleness and pickings might disparage the style of *Thrones* and the handling of Coke, but for the results.

A shift to the *First Institute* generalizes Coke's achievement and Pound's inheritance while modulating toward a fourth phase. Coke on Littleton's writing, "long in the making," and his views that legal terms ought not to be changed, that no man knows everything, and that one should build "In men's heart on the rock of reason," apply to *The Cantos*; so does Bracton's "Uncivil to judge a part in ignorance of the totality." "Le Concord del fine," Coke's idea of a penalty that achieves perfect equity, is applied both to the *Institutes* and to *The Cantos* in "The *fine* cannot omit ascun chose / continuance solonques le purpot" (continuity according to the purpose, cf. "Sapiens incipit a fine"). "CHARDE dit estre certaine" and "certainty engenders repose" round back to the "certainty" and "clarity" of *107*, not for personal advantage but for the sake of one's neighbors ("ses vicines"). Time, not the king, is "mother of Manors" and of new customs. Words must be defined if one is not to lose knowledge of things. No man is born an artist.

An ancient communal organization based on separation of church and state, "Ten families in pledge and a chief pledge," assures that "Though the bishopric be dissolved / a city remaineth." A ten-part Declaration activated by the ten Amendments of a Bill of Rights runs to the Seal and Liberty (cf. the ten-man "collegium" of *107*):

Tuan et consuetudo

Tuan[1] defines the four-phase process, pictures the enduring city, and again unifies the ten Amendments in the single Bill. "Tuan" refers to Coke in "FOUR" and "consuetudo" refers to Coke in ten, or Coke as a constitution being ratified by a Bill of Rights and sealed by the Seal. This version of the Seal/Calendar arcanum applies also to the ten subjects of *Los Cantares* and its antecedents, all the way back to the prototype (*I–X*) and to the epitomes of Liberty (*I*) and of the Seal (*I–IV*), while opening up a consummating fourth phase.

"Tuan . . . et consuetudo" also introduces continuing revolution and States/Ratification (*109*: pp. 773–74) as a consummation of history and personae in a constitutional text and epiphanic Bill and Seal. Captain Wadsworth was cited earlier (*97*) as a touchstone in the constitutional struggle: "Will they get rid of the Rooseveltian dunghill / And put Capn. Wadsworth back in the school books?" Here the Connecticut Colony grants him twenty shillings "in grateful resentment" (feeling) for his feat. The entry from Hartford's records precipitates from the hidden charter an extract providing for "a Body politique" to be governed by "Seal, Governor, Deputy and 12 assistants" (cf. HORUS's Seal, ZAGREUS, PAN, and the twelve deities). Powers will be carried out under "common seal." Payment to the Crown of "Soccage," rent measured by productivity rather than "in capite," military service measured by head, is the kind of provision that should define relations between single states and some central administrative authority.

The original Charter was signed "HOWARD" by writ of the Privy Seal. Here the Charter, continuing revolution, and States/Ratification (in Coke *107–109* and in *Los Cantares*) are sealed and delivered in ten images gathered from *Los Cantares* to project a final perfection. "Wing like feldspar" (the Eagle's), and "foot-grip firm to hold balance" on a "high cliff" at Sicilian Taormina, enable the mind to move "more rapid[ly]" in sunlight where azaleas grow "by snow slope"; the image includes everything from LING[2] to Coke. Cokean clarity illuminates plutocracy's fears that Edward VIII might not sign mobilization because he had visited the hospitals. Jury trial was in Athens. Elizabethan provisions for repairing bridges and establishing homesteads are celebrated "Angliae amor." Royal power is reaffirmed over coinage. A first phase rounds the mind back to its high cliff, above "Clear deep," for "form is cut in the lute's neck, tone is from the bowl."

"Oak boughs alone over Selloi," the priests of Zeus's natural shrine at Dodona, brings back "This wing, colour of feldspar," for "phyllotaxis," the pattern by which leaves arrange themselves on a stem, previously symbolizing "affirmations of individual men."

"Over wicket gate" of an architectural shrine apppears the name of Leucothoe, which opens on the philosophers of the "Bellum perenne." Under

Helios these "thrones" are complemented by assembled churches of Rome, religious "thrones" of their visions.

Finally, crowning all, as Rome heaves over the horizon, Pound imagines that he sees from the deck of the *Cristoforo Colombo*, on which he returned to Italy, "Le chapeau melon de St Pierre." As a coda a new version of Dante's invitation to the flight through Paradiso—"You in the dinghy (piccioletta) astern there!"—challenges the reader with what the final Seal-images portend.

The tenth subject of *Los Cantares*, continuing constitution illuminated and extended by Pound's epic images, projects the tenth draft as Malatesta's post-bag, the second half of *IX*, revealed an alternative Renaissance before papal domination imposed the Renaissance of orthodox history (*X*). This last antici-pation concurs with the plan in the bill of lading, which projected from the broken Malatesta seal (*VIII*) the Renaissance idea that outlived the historical Renaissance (*XXX Cantos*). Thus the twenty-five slabs of *Section: Rock-Drill* ("First: ten. . .") and of *Thrones* ("Eight ditto. . ." and "Six of same. . .") prepare the Mount of constitutional Sections to be topped by "Eight col-umns" for a sun-temple (constitutional Articles), and by the coda "etc...with carriage, danars 151" for a roof of constitutional Branches/Powers. The closing images of *Canto 109* project from a justicial phase a consummating draft of '76, a poetic phase, and architectural culmination.

CHAPTER TWENTY

DRAFTS & FRAGMENTS

CX–CXVII & 120 CANTOS

Thru the 12 Houses of Heaven
        seeing the just and the unjust,
        tasting the sweet and the sorry,
Pater Helios turning.
   Canto CXIII

To confess wrong without losing rightness:
Charity I have had sometimes,
        I cannot make it flow thru.
   Canto CXVI

The culmination of justice in Coke's commentaries, the successfully defended Connecticut Charter, the crowning anticipatory images, and the triumphant cry near the end of a long voyage all augur a satisfying completion, if not of a 100-canto poem harmonizing twentieth-century history with a timeless conception then at least a 120-canto poem affirming a contemporary realization of the conception itself. So it looks from within the confines of the third phase and so it must have looked when the gate of St. Elizabeths opened. So it looks too as a final draft and phase opens celebrating a return to "Thy quiet house" and to paradisal landscapes.

But as *Canto CX* proceeds from the culmination of a tradition-gathering voyage to the exultance of a protagonist who finds himself at last in a new found land, and thence to an apparent affirmation of a lifelong revolutionary activity, an effort to transform the past breaks down on the ethical obstacle "That love be the cause of hate, / something is twisted." Inability to overcome evils in human nature itself throws the fourth phase back upon the ethical problem apparently resolved in *Pisan*. The cyclic vision remains in the mind, but Pound can neither complete its ideal form nor make its light and voice irradiate or "flow thru" a perfected Calendar Mount and culminating temple.

Drafts & Fragments (1968) in a deluxe, two-colored (red and black) folio recalled the two folios that began the poem and projected its end. But cantos in various stages of completion are disposed to reflect a vision but to acknowledge personal failure for historical and ethical reasons. The breakdown affects realization and tone but not form and themes. The tenth draft is not a draft, and the fourth phase is not a phase, but both are adumbrated in "Drafts of Cantos," not all completed, and in "Fragments of Cantos." The form is a chiaroscuro of the epitome and Seal-vision of a tenth draft and fourth phase, and of the prototype decad/draft.

Like its phasal antecedents Nekuomanteia *I, Pisan LXXIV*, and *Shu 85*, the epitome of the draft and phase, Liberty *CX*, is a complete model for the decad/draft evolving in "ONE, ten, eleven, *chi con me* 日̲ tan"; "to be unity" via duality, trine, and tetrad. As its phasal antecedents culminated in Seal/Calendar *IV*, in *Pisan LXXVII* and "Canto 77 Explication," and in the Seal/Calendar arcanum (Benton *88* or Amor *90–91*), Seal *CX–CXIII*, though *CXI* and *CXII* are incomplete, culminates in Seal *CXIII* with its arcanum "Thru the 12 Houses of Heaven." Canto *CXIV* is complete but *CXV* is not. Canto *CXVI* is the last complete canto, for reasons. For reasons too the rest, projected as such by Liberty *CX*, are *Fragments of Cantos* including "Addendum for C" and "Notes for *CXVII* et seq."—three fragments presumably designed to complete a broken decad with unnumbered *CXVIII* and *CXIX*—until a broken draft and the whole poem end with the seven-line, posthumous *Canto 120.*

Until *Pisan* Pound assumed that an end would occur (whether 100 or 120 cantos) and that when he got to it a pattern "ought" to be "discoverable";[1] if "the *form*" didn't "show" he would "start exegesis."[2] As reported from St. Elizabeths those who "found no plan" would be "confounded" when *The Cantos* was complete.[3] Having finished *Section: Rock-Drill* and *Thrones* he could exult "Mebbe having got in these chunks the rest of the poEM can be what is called 'POetic' and the squirmers cease to be able to say it has no subject and no FORM.'"[4] Hence the need for a formal and thematic end to consummate the repeated forms, the evolving themes (argument from tradition, personal motives, justicial form, and continuing poetry), and the accruing subjects.

By 1960, however, two years after his release and return to Italy, when asked during *The Paris Review* interview if he could say what he was going to do with the remaining cantos, he replied "It is difficult to write a paradiso when all the superficial indications are that you ought to write an apocalypse. It is obviously easier to find inhabitants for an inferno or even a purgatorio." He was, as always, trying "to collect the top flights of the mind," and the poem had carried him to the top. Asked if he was "more or less stuck" he couched the story of 1918 in a growing sense of difficulty:

1. To John Lackay Brown, April 1937, *Letters.*
2. To Hubert Creekmore, February 1939, *Letters.*
3. Daniel Pearlman, *The Barb of Time* (New York: 1969), p. 6.
4. To Ronald Duncan, 15 January 1958, Humanities Center at Texas.

> Okay, I am stuck. . . . The past epos has succeeded when all or
> a great many of the answers were assumed, at least between author
> and audience, or a great mass of audience. The attempt in an experi-
> mental age is therefore rash. Do you know the story: "What are
> you drawing, Johnny?"
> "God!"
> "But nobody knows what He looks like."
> "They will when I get through!"
> That confidence is no longer obtainable.[5]

The "top flights" of tradition and of contemporaneity having converged in the justicial minds of *Los Cantares*, however, he hoped that "the order of ascension in the Paradiso will be toward a greater limpidity" (cf. "toward limpidity, / that is exultance," *CX*). The "greater limpidity," flowing back through the mind and Mount of the whole, would illuminate or make explicit a design for a "paradiso terrestre" inherent in both. In that respect a final light would disclose an inspired pattern or form present in the revolutionary mind before the beginning.

The darker side of his remarks was reflected in his first publications, in periodicals. Published first (in 1962) was a fragment containing both the despairing *From Canto CXV* and the desolate *Canto 120*.[6] Later in 1962 *From Canto CXV* appeared in its final form along with the last complete (and also despairing) *Canto CXVI*.[7] Not until 1965 did he publish the epitome *Canto CX*, which organizes the would-be draft.[8] There he seems to have tried to fit historical, personal, philosophical, and imaginative despair into his overall historical vision: to complete the vision while registering his inability to perfect it. The personal as a medium for history is reflected in the periodical order; the personal as a medium for divinity is reflected in the final arrange-ment. Pound finished drawing God, but he could not make him speak (hence his latter-day silence?).

Formally at least, what had now become explicitly "this palimpsest" (*CXVI*), from "ply over ply" of Seal *IV*, now subsumed as a fourth phase the fourth phases of all preceding subjects. Among them were the tenth cantos or subjects of each decad and phase. Each decad/draft and each ten-part phase also would lie behind a final decad *CX–CXIX* consummated in a final draft by *CXX*. The forms of all antecedents, looking toward the final phase and decad/draft, are the Bill and the sun-vision; the theme for all is continuing revolution completing its temple.

The principal phasal antecedents are the fourth phases of the comprehensive epitome, of Seal *I–IV*, and of the prototype decad *I–X* and draft *XVI*. Cantos.

5. *Paris Review* 28.

6. *Threshold*, Belfast, Spring 1962.

7. *Paris Review* 28, Summer–Fall 1962.

8. Published for Pound's eightieth birthday, 30 October 1965, by *As Sextant Press*, New York.

As "Lie quiet Divus" would placate all those from Circe's house and the house of the dead so that Pound could invoke Aphrodite on her Cyprian "munimenta," "Thy quiet house" (the first line of *CX*) is a keynote for a return to Ithaca. A Renaissance poetic tradition consummating the Homeric tradition-discovering voyage, Ovidian rebirth, and the Dantean "bust thru" into a visionary justice in the "Gods, etc." of Seal *IV*, projected a culmination of world epic for a new era. Renaissance revolution clinched by the Malatestan Eagle (*X*) projected alternate Renaissances defined by papal excommunication and St. Peter's or by Malatestan Rimini and the Tempio. The Eagle Pound, passing through a neo-Dantean cosmos where an Elysium of founders projects continuing revolution and "the mounts of their cities" (*XIV–XVI*), envisioned from his discovery world revolution continuing through the Russian to a hoped-for revision.

The culminations of all decad/drafts also contribute: Renaissance Venice and the Renaissance constructive or destructive; '76 lost to plutocracy but Hanno's achievement and fascist possibility; "my Holy City" Siena and the exposure of Usura and Geryon; the Manchu acme; Adams's testament; "my world" affirmed against destruction; Apollonius's philosophy and Anselm's; and inheritance of Coke's mind justicially and aesthetically. Phasal culminations of declaration in Adams's testament, of struggle in affirmation of "my world," and of founding in Coke would culminate in continuing revolution, in a consummating poetry.

The spirit and themes of all initiating epitomes and of all culminations are concentrated in the epitome *CX*. All are focused into the appropriate theme and symbol as the fourth symbol of the Seal. As a consummating phasal epitome *CX* overlays its mode upon the phases epitomized by Nekuomanteia *I* (the revolutionary "course of human events"), by *Pisan LXXIV* ("my family" of personae), and by *Shu 85* ("the basic principles of government"), or subsumes previous documents in an epitome of the Bill and the previous symbols in an epitome of the sun-vision.

But as a tenth decad/draft, perfected or not, *Drafts & Fragments* is a "palimpsest," canto by canto, of all previous decad/drafts and of all previous ten-subject phases, all projected from unitary Liberty through the Eagle and Providence as "halves of a seal" and through "REVOLUTION . . . in the minds of the people" to the ten-part argument, motivation, justicial/governmental form, and activating spirit. As a tenth decad/draft *Drafts & Fragments* subsumes all previous tenths in a drafted tenth, the four-part theme of which, "moving concurrent . . . ply over ply," is the Declaration consummated in the pledge, the Preambles perfecting new union, Ratification of a world Constitution (which has modulated out of and contains a states' rights Constitution), and the Bill culminating in the reserved powers. As a tenth decad/draft and fourth phase the theme is the pledge, new union, and world Constitution subsumed in the activating reserved powers and sealed by the symbolic sun-vision.

As unitary Liberty dominated *XVI. Cantos*, as the "halves of a seal" Eagle and Providence dominated *XXX Cantos*, as "REVOLUTION . . . in the minds of the people" dominated "ELEUSIS" *LI Cantos*; and as these informed the ten-part Declaration dominating *LXXI Cantos*, the complementary Preambles dominating *Pisan*, and the expanding Constitutions dominating *Los Cantares*: so the ten Amendments of the Bill of Rights dominate the ten cantos and fragments. Cycle and phase converge toward 120 cantos of "triangular spaces" (*CXVI*) representing the symbolic Seal realized architecturally in a Calendar built of the Constitution's clauses, Sections, Articles, and Branches/Powers. Division into *Drafts CX–CXVI* and "Notes for *CXVII* et seq." reflects the aspiration that a new Renaissance founded on tradition (clauses 1–71) and personality (clauses 72–84) be built of "slabs" of justice (Sections i–xxv) until "Eight columns" should raise a temple upon the Mount and until "etc...with carriage, danars 151," by completing a whole transaction, should crown the temple with "an altar to Zagreus," "the double arch of a window / Or some great colonnade," or "a bridge over worlds" ("Notes for *CXVII* et seq.").

The plethora of subjects, themes, forms, and images present in "this palimpsest" seems to create such density that one might despair of unraveling them or might decide them to be irrelevant. Their presence, however, is precisely what enables Pound to affirm impersonal form despite personal failure and to validate a personal vision earned from tradition, struggle, and devotion to justice. In 1922 he wrote of that "epoch-making report on the state of the human mind in the Twentieth century (first of the new era)," Joyce's *Ulysses*, "And on the home stretch, when our present author is feeling more or less relieved that the weight of the book is off his shoulders, we find if not gracile accomplishments, at any rate such acrobatics, such sheer whoops and hoop-las and trapeze turns of technique that it would seem rash to dogmatize concerning his limitations."[9] *The Cantos* aims at an artistic freedom to write one's own vision earned from having wrestled with a subject given by the age. That is a meaning of "An epic is a poem containing history": history conditions the poem but the poem itself is a new achievement. If "Gods etc.," or "states of mind" have emerged from the limits of time, place, and matter, the revolutionary mind can enjoy an objective achievement "That hath the light of the doer, as it were / a form cleaving to it."

For actually composing a final illumination of his materials Pound had available as guides any or all of the foregoing palimpsest. From the end of *Thrones*, "You in the dinghy (piccioletta) astern there," he could look back through the concluding images and through the mind of Coke and see nine drafts projecting a tenth; looking ahead through Coke's mind and through those same images he could foresee the cantos of a tenth draft. The aim all along, however, had been to carry "ten head" along with "Live man goes

9. "Ulysses," *Dial*, New York, June 1922.

down into the world of Dead'' through ''The 'repeat in history,' '' and through the ''magic moment'' of justice revealed, to a transformation of ''world of Dead'' into the undying ''states of mind'' of ''Gods, etc.'' inherent in ''ten head.'' The most pertinent guide, therefore, was the Seal-vision and Calendar form received as Circean inspiration (''ONE'' and ''ten head''), the entry of this revolutionary vision and mind into history until it revealed the Renaissance heritage of Malatesta (*I–X*), and finally the Malatestan heritage reaffirmed despite apparent defeat through the omen of the Eagle and through the irrepressible cheerfulness of Malatesta's last will and testament (*XI*). The intervening subjects having extended that spirit to the world, given it new life, and augmented it with new justice, a new version of the Tempio might crown a later effort.

Narratively, then, a voyage ends with an exultant arrival at ''Thy quiet house'' and Pound settles into his place of colonization. ''I am all for Verkehr without tyranny'' posits a destiny and pledges with fellow declarers a new world. He is about to focus originally motivated union from achieved liberty toward new union for a new era, of which *The Cantos* will be a universal plan of an illuminated ''WE the People.'' Having ratified a states' rights Constitution in unpromising circumstances, he will try to ratify a world Constitution evolved from it. All will be activated by the freedoms of expression (''Verkehr without tyranny'') extended to the reserved powers, of which he has enough left to pray for divine power but of which he will not have enough left to do more than outline the intended ''paradiso terrestre.'' He has built the Mount to 109 cantos but cannot complete either the circle of light or ''the shrine'' and eye within it. There will be only the echo of a celebratory ANNUIT COEPTIS.

The main working form canto by canto is the dominant Bill perfecting the Declaration; the Preambles and the Constitution are subordinated. Overall the Bill's private rights (*CX–CXIII*) sustain a troubled vision coming through the Declaration's premises. The legal rights applied to the cases (*CXIV–From CXV*) try human nature in general and Pound in person. The common law rights try a declaration of independence (*CXVI*), which fails between the vision and the ethical cases. With common law rights circumscribed, so are political rights and reserved powers. *Fragments of Cantos* register a failure of political rights and reserved powers to realize independence, sovereign powers, and a pledge. But ''the great ball of crystal'' or ''great acorn of light . . . coheres all right / even if my notes do not cohere.''

Drafts of Cantos

Canto *CX*, since it projects a decad/draft, and Canto *CXIII*, since it projects from a Seal-vision a Calendar form for the decad/draft, are two of the four completed cantos (leaving aside the coda Canto *120*).[10] Canto *CX* has the ten-part form of the "old" and "new" epitomes Nekuomanteia *I* and Canto *XXXI*, the one '76 prophesied and the other '76 being realized, and of the phasal epitomes *Pisan LXXIV* and *Shu 85*. A hemicycle and phase in six subjects without ideograms, followed by a hemicycle divided into four subjects and three phases by ideograms grouped two by two, anticipate the Seal/Calendar arcanum to be revealed in Canto *CXIII*.

"Thy quiet house" from before the beginning and after the end of a sea voyage fuses in tranquility Circe's house, Kimmeria, Erebus, Elpenor's tomb, Divus's grave, and Aphrodite's "munimenta." "I am all for Verkehr without tyranny" states the revolutionary ideal. The dismal discoveries of Nekuomanteia *I* are transformed into perception of a boat's wake cresting on a Venetian sea-wall in a crozier's curve, in a snail's spiral ("caracole"), or in feathery white "as a dolphin on sea-brink." "Wake exultant" seen in "panache," and "paw-flap, wave-tap" heard, elicit "gaiety."

Landing at "the place / Aforesaid by Circe" and performing the general rites of colonization become "exultance" in a Na Khi mountain landscape and in its ritual atmosphere. The "wind sway" suggests the motions of a suicide ritual. The land draws one to "see with eyes of coral or turquoise," to "walk with the oak's root." Yellow iris roots itself into a river bed with transliterations of ideograms disposed on a vertical axis.

The axis points to transformation of Odysseus's rites to the dead, here the Na Khi *muan bpo* ritual or sacrifice to heaven performed at a textually arranged shrine on Mount Sumeru. On left and right are oaks for heaven and earth; "in the center / is / juniper" for the emperor. The ritual results in "The purifications."

The evoked mind of the dead becomes "And in thy mind beauty, O Artemis," which beauty is elaborated by a setting at Lago di Garda where "rock-layers arc'd as with a compass" were used by astute designers to build a mountain road.[11] The exultant arrival in Venice, the ritualized Na Khi perceptions, the formal Na Khi rituals, and Garda's divine beauty perceived and followed by constructive road-builders, epitomize the themes of the respective cantos of Seal *CX–CXIII*.

The discord between Odysseus and the dead becomes memories of Italian acquaintances killed in war (cases "triste e denho di memoria") and a recollection of "one hell of a row / in the Senate" when President Wilson presented the Treaty of Versailles for ratification; violence is checked here by "cypress versus rock-slide." Recognition of and pity for "our friend Elpenor"

10. *Drafts & Fragments* recurred to roman numeration with "Canto" title until the regularization to roman numeration only after the 1970 collected *Cantos*. I retain the "Canto" title and the arabic "Canto 120" given in *Anonym 4*, Buffalo, N.Y., April 1969.

11. This and other "Mindscapes" appeared in the *National Review*, Orange, Conn., 10 September 1963.

become a married spouse's happy ending and love for Kati though he has been dead for 5000 years. These cases project the trials of human nature in Canto *CXIV* and in "From *CXV.*"

Elpenor's gloomy voyage to Erebus becomes a beautiful voyage to a place (a "Mindscape") where he may be an Orpheus to "all Eurydices," an Apollo to Daphne (or the reverse), an Endymion buried beneath an altar to Phoebe (Artemis). His guide, like Odysseus's, has been Leucothoe of the beautiful shoulders ("KALLIASTRAGALOS"). Placated, he advises Odysseus with the doubled ideogram *hsin*[1] translated "to go forth by day," or Chinese revolution given its aim and its sun in a phrase from the Egyptian *Book of the Dead* (cf. Elpenor as Tom Paine and OSIRIS). But solicitude and rebirth run into the ethical block "That love be the cause of hate, / something is twisted," which projects the verdict of the trial of human nature (*CXVI*). A restless, jealous spirit (Awoi) sets "bare trees walk on the sky-line" against a hope "that one valley reach the four seas." But sunset limns the mountain and is disturbingly inverted.

Tiresias's recognition of the "man of ill star" and his dire prophecy, intended to be amended through a stirring Divus and an invoked Aphrodite, bring instead destruction projecting *Fragments of Cantos*. Despite the peace and beauty of Byzantine tombs and of "thy quiet house at Torcello,"[12] war destroys restaurants where friends plan revolutions; with the courage of such "resisters" "blacked out," "the mind jumps without building . . . and there is no *chih* and no root." Tiresias's recognition and prophecy are accented by the doubled ideogram *chih*[3], the revolutionary and his scope. That there is "no *chih* and no root" leaves only "these fragments" "From time's wreckage" "shored against ruin." Pound cannot reconstitute and build them as Malatesta did his Renaissance or as Pound did Malatesta.

Continuation of "these fragments shored against ruin" into "and the sun 日 jih[4-5] / new with the day" turns from wreckage by completing "*hsin*[1] . . . *hsin*[1]" ideogramically and rendering "go forth by day." This transformation of Divus's rebirth elicits for Pound's example the anthropologist Joseph Rock, who still hopes to climb Mount Kinabalu in Borneo even though his "fragments," collected over twenty years, were sunk by a Japanese submarine during World War II. But violence, supervening, elicits a cry for light at a shrine "seen and not seen" in chiaroscuro (cf. Aphrodite's

---

12. Torcello, the first Venetian island settled when the peoples of the Veneto were seeking refuge from invading Goths, has an air of recurrence to prehistory. Its basilica, the oldest in Venice, is unique in having in the apse, behind the altar, tiered thrones for the bishop and the clergy. Except for the basilica and a few buildings that housed the old government, the ancient city has wholly disappeared. The return of nature and the atmosphere of the lagoon give Torcello qualities which must be experienced to be appreciated. There history and nature, man's struggles and his spirit, beauty and peace tinged with the melancholy and lustre of tragedy, all come together in such a way as to place one somewhere between the bustle and grandeur of San Marco and a premonition of what Pound meant by "oblivion" and "arcanum."

"munimenta"). A projected second *jih*[4-5] retreats to *ching*[4], pray. "There is power" "From the roots of sequoias," but luminous Aphrodite is blurred to jealous Awoi and muted to "the oval moon" of Fortuna.

The title "Notes for *CXI*" suggests a special unfinish. But a dual theme of war and peace, violence and serenity, marks the main subjects. An intermediate publication added emphatic framing.[13] Then, when he put the "Notes" into the sketched draft, Pound added for the right to bear arms of the imagination, from the Na Phi sensibility of *CX*, the rubric

> I, one thing, as relation to one thing;
> Hui sees relation to ten.

All men have natural rights, but all are not created equal. The opening frame recalls Wadsworth's ingenuity, regrets a political martyr stoned to death, and reminds that the power to issue is basically the power to tax. The concluding frame recalls that the Lombard Rothar, though he issued a prologue of laws, "Coin'd gold" and "bumped off 8000 Byzantines." The equivocal theme recalls epiphanies emerging from violence in Seal *II* and in the second draft, which end respectively with the chiding of Proteus "in the half-light" and with a Renaissance chiaroscuro.

Between the frame a first subject regrets Napoleon's lost opportunities to effect a Malatestan renaissance ("post-bag") and his fatal letch for conquest. He ignored the "Whole lesson" of Talleyrand, "Wu / Hsieh (heart's field) / Szu," Have no twisty thoughts, for Pound the essence of the Confucian *Odes*.[14] The meaning of words themselves was changed from one conference to another. He was "a blessing" as long as he ruled with constitutional guarantees and cared about civilization, but finally "a nuisance." By the time of writing the drift to violence has become "600 more dead at Quemoy— / they call it political."

A second subject tries to counter with "A nice quiet paradise" by opening up pity, for Pound's guild socialist mentor A. R. Orage the basis of a cooperative, humane politics. A "Gold mermaid" ("Cold" in the latest text) is lured up from the sea like Tyro or Ileuthyeria (*II*), but she becomes mixed with Geryon (cf. the second draft). Splendor, as in Venice, hints at "Veritas, by anthesis" (the opening of a flower); but in Geryon's undertow the eyes hold trouble and there is no light "ex profundis" (from the eyes' depth, from the sea's depth, from the soul). "Feigning" imaginative metamorphosis will

13. These "Notes" consisted first only of a Napoleonic passage balanced with a mermaid passage (*Agenda*, London, March/April 1963). The frame of mixed evidence and mixed motives was added later (*Cantos 110–116* published without authorization by the FUCK YOU press, New York, 1967, hereafter cited FY). The comprehensive rubric was added for *Drafts & Fragments*. Such stages of composition reflect persistence of the constitutional vision despite recalcitrant times and the consequent inability of their poet.

14. Pound used the three ideograms to end his translation of the *Shih, Classic Anthology Defined by Confucius*, 1954.

avail nothing. "Serenitas" comes only when "Soul melts into air." Rothar returns imaginative equivocality to politics.

"From *CXII*," elaborating the Na Khi paradisal landscape and ritual of *CX*, is integral but partial. A "Mindscape" of mountains, fertile land, clear air, temples, "The firm voice amid pine wood," and "the clear discourse / as Jade stream," where "we have been . . . from the beginning," echoes the aboriginal godscape of Seal *III* which inspired Pound's climb up Confucian temple steps and My Cid's ride up to Burgos seeking justice. Justice inheres in the Na Khi rituals to earth, without which "nothing is solid," and to heaven, without which is "no reality"; it carries government by consent sought by soldier-lawmakers who are allowed into houses of government. Pound has been such a justicer. The setting and the rituals bring "The purifications," but his destiny has been

> Winnowed in fate's tray

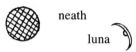 neath

luna

The winnowing tray *mun*, a fate or a fated life, is applied to his own life under Fortuna, whose new moon might allow the sun to emerge.[15] The Fortune wheel at the end of *The Seventh Canto* contains such an encircled grid of diamonds and triangles as a pattern for building a Mount of Constitutional constituents.[16] We can see in the axial symbol and in the temporal measures on the right a version of the Seal/Calendar arcanum.

Canto *CXIII* consummates the phasal Seal/Calendar cantos of tradition (Seal *IV*), of personality (*Pisan LXXVII*), and of justice (Benton *88*) with a revelation of the revolutionary mind:

> Thru the 12 Houses of Heaven
>> seeing the just and the unjust,
>> tasting the sweet and the sorry,
> Pater Helios turning.

It consummates an unfulfilled Seal *CX–CXIII* by opening up "And in thy mind beauty, O Artemis" from *CX*. It transforms Seal *CX–CXIII* in phases intellectual, ethical, justicial, and poetic. Its theme is continuing revolution activated by the right to privacy except by proper warrant (here Pater Helios).

---

15. FY accentuated the positive with the ending "Until Di Marzio quotes Guicciardini," a World War II version of "Nec Spe Nec Metu" preferred during that dark night of the soul by the editor of *Il Meridiano di Roma*. Cf. "Nothing impossible to him who holds honor in sufficient esteem," the concluding note to the translation of the *Chung Yung* done at Pisa, cited *Rock-Drill 92*.

16. See "The Mathematical Symbolism of Ezra Pound's Revolutionary Mind," *Paideuma*, Orono, Maine, Spring–Summer 1978.

It tries to affirm the creativity of the revolutionary mind, but the mind remains in Hell on an Ixion wheel, ''unstill, ever turning.''

Canto *CXIII* formalizes the revolutionary dichotomy, which has been emerging as conflict, in conflict between Pater Helios and Fortuna. As ''Mortal blame'' had no sound in Fortuna's ears (*100*), neither does ''Mortal praise''; remaining subject to her without making ''gods out of beauty'' is ''$\Theta\rho\tilde{\eta}\nu o\varsigma$,'' ''a dying.'' ''Yet,'' the rhetoric reverses, the aim remains ''to walk'' and ''take thy mind's space'' in an intellectual paradise with the great dead, ''the Men against Death,'' ''out of dark,'' '' 'neath overhanging air under sunbeat.'' Curses (Malatesta's) break the glory, but something as spontaneous as '' 'now bigod I have done it' '' brings on a certain day ''why not spirits?,'' which, two days later, brings the reversal ''But for the sun and serenitas'' and a re-experiencing of the original inspiration from *Cantos* ''pre-history.'' Oscillation between dichotomies settles finally into

> The long flank, the firm breast
> > and to know beauty and death and despair
> and to think that what has been shall be,
> > flowing, ever unstill.

A first phase ends with a destiny accepted.[17]

A ''partridge-shaped cloud over dust storm'' brings the dichotomy ''The hells move in cycles, / No man can see his own end.'' In ethical debate one voice says the gods have not returned. A second rejoins they have never left us. The first insists they have not returned. The second counters ''Cloud's processional and the air moves with their living.'' The first cites the ethical crux ''Pride, jealousy and possessiveness / 3 pains of hell.'' The second sees ''3 lights in triangulation'' in the heavens over Portofino and adduces apples of the Hesperides falling into laps from phantom trees. Elegiac memories cover the apple orchard with sorrow, ''but,'' turning to sensibility, ''there is something intelligent in the cherry-stone'' and Venice's beauty is self-evident. ''But to hitch sensibility to efficiency?'' The problem is ''grass versus granite,'' ''For the little light and more harmony.'' The plea ''Oh God of all men, none excluded'' modulates into ''howls'' for cheap money by the popular faction during the Constitutional debates of 1787. Alas, nothing is new but human ignorance, ''ever perennial,'' of everything from proper sacrifices to proper interest rates.[18]

If the foregoing appears to be ''Error of chaos,'' those who ''demand belief rather than justice'' might consider that ''Justification is from kindness of heart'' (one's motives) and that ''from her hands'' (one's Providence) ''flow-

---

17. The first phase was published in *Poetry*, Chicago, October 1962.

18. FY added this second phase, designated ''Canto 113/2.'' The rest of Canto *CXIII* appeared in the 1968 edition.

eth mercy.'' Waiting for an American ''pyramid builder'' to be born and
finding the justicial ''body'' not ''boxed for economy'' but ''inside the soul''
shatters the darkness and reveals ''the fragment'' in or as a ''lifting and
folding brightness.'' Yeats saw the symbol over a portico in Paris (Pound
reverses the spoof of *Pisan LXXXIII*). A bull is mastered by ''the force that is
in him.'' One can know ''interest from usura'' and the ''prezzo giusto.'' ''In
this sphere''—a Na Khi landscape as in ''From *CXII*''—is ''Giustizia.''
''But'' (again) ignorance spreads: ''Article X for example''—actually Congress Section x, which limits the powers of the States—was ''put over,'' and
it has taken a hundred years to get back to the ''awareness'' of ''what's his
name in that Convention.'' To end a third phase ''all men's'' Constitutional
debates have passed to the lawyers' instituted document.

''And in thy mind beauty, / O Artemis'' (fourth) raises the emerging ethical
question of human nature. ''As to sin, they invented it—eh? / to implement
domination / eh?'' ''Largely,'' Pound agrees (with himself). There remains
''grumpiness,'' even malice (''malvagità''), but it can be absorbed into all-
inclusive nature. Further, somewhere in ''the snarl'' of every woman is ''a
tenderness, / A blue light under stars.'' But what about ruined orchards, trees
rotting, tools unused? All cry out for ''a little magnanimity somewhere'' and
''to know the share from the charge.'' Lack of both has forced Pound (like
Dante) to climb another's stair (''scala altrui'') and eat another's bread. He
can only beseech Artemis and himself ''God's eye art 'ou, do not surrender
perception.''

The revolutionary mind has run a cycle in Seal form. It finishes building a
canto with a coda. The beauty of Artemis's mind moves like Daphne fleeing
Apollo, but ''in vain speed.'' An echo of ''Homage to Sextus Propertius'' VI
anticipates the poet's own death with a broken seal (''the Syrian onyx'').
''Out of dark, thou, Father Helios, leadest,'' but the mind remains ''as Ixion,
unstill, ever turning.'' The mind has found itself unable either to build a
complete Mount or to irradiate it.

The unfinished Seal/Calendar *CX–CXIII* prepares an ethical case tried by
due process, Canto *CXIV*, and a passage of a justicial case given fair trial,
''From *CXV*.'' As the creative value of Seal *CX–CXIII* was beauty (for the
premises and the personal rights), the destructive power of the cases (from
''That love be the cause of hate, something is twisted,'' *CX*) is hate. Canto
CXIV sets ''the vision'' against individual motivation in the manner of *V*,
where Pound celebrated ''the vision'' but Varchi subjected it to due process in
the assassination of Duke Alessandro by his cousin Lorenzaccio. ''From
CXV'' faces a failure to clarify individual and collective motivation as fair
trial clarified Odysseus's by adducing Eleanor of Aquitaine's and Cunizza's
influences on kings and troubadors (*VI*).

Voltaire insists that he hates no one, not even Fréron; his apologia puns
on brother and echoes Odysseus (*85*). Nor did John Adams hate Timothy
Pickering, whom he discharged from office for disloyalty in one of his latter

acts as president (*LXX*). Hate is ramified into France's ingratitude toward John Law, who was ruined by debt. Contradicting a good book (like *The Cantos*?) is not hate, but respect. The historical rubric introduces (like *V*) an interior view of "the vision,"

> Amid corridors and ambassadors
> > glow worms and lanterns, and this moving is
> > > from the inward

But as the cyclic mind moves within the "Great bulk, huge mass, thesaurus" of history and draws its materials into its own "triangular spaces," are it and its materials of the same substance or different? The Renaissance Platonist Giordano Bruno, burned as a heretic, thought "di diversa natura."[19]

Bruno's natural philosophy joins that of the Neo-Platonists of *V* and of "serious characters" like Aristotle against the transcendental "belly-aches" of Plotinus and St. John of the Cross. The vision "falls white" upon the senses as in Cavalcanti's love canzone (*XXXVI*) but may be unseen because of "Their dichotomies (feminine) present in heaven and hell": the female dark may obscure the gods wherever the mind may be. Nevertheless "triangular spaces" have been made into "Gems sunned as mirrors, alternate"— into cantos laid in tiers, alternately on base and on apex—to build a single triangular Mount.

Affirmed vision is turned against the "3 pains of hell," pride, jealousy, and possessiveness. Simple men have fought against jealousy and "To mitigate ownership." Claiming that his own family contained "good guys," or "feminine gaiety—quick on the uptake," or reputed conversation, or public spirit, is not vanity; he denies the snobism of coats of arms for "the *tribù*." The antidote to "pains of hell" and to "Fear, father of cruelty," a "Mindscape," is "the delicacy," "the kindness"; must he write "a genealogy of the demons," or is it better to illustrate "ubi amor, ibi oculus" by noticing that a lizard's feet are "like snow flakes"?

"But these had thrones" passes from what has been to what is now. Once the thrones in his mind were "still, uncontending," not moving to "possession" but firm in "hypostasis." Resolving possession into hypostasis seemed to make the mind "Some hall of mirrors" and its creation a tapestry in the Louvre; such a mind seemed able "to reign, to dance in a maze, / To live a thousand years in a wink," whether in "York State or Paris." Now, however, the crushing "Nor began nor ends anything" has supervened. He can only take a cue from a boy in a fruit shop who would also have liked to write something but knows that one must be "portato" (carried) by "The kindness,

---

19. In *Text Und Kritik*, Aachen, October/November 1965, Canto *CXIV* consisted of four passages separated by dotted spacings (indicated here by my paragraphing); to give apparent continuity the final version simply replaced the dotted spacings with four binding passages (a few lines each), the last an ending of the fourth. So Pound's composition reflects his archetypal form.

infinite, of her hands." Yeats knew it when "the mist came." The ethical case ends "that the truth is in kindness."

"From *CXV*," the first printed and original source of Canto *120*, seems to be the end of a canto, a hemicycle, and a phase.[20] It begins "The scientists" ("color che sanno" of Pound's "paradiso terrestre") "are in terror / and the European mind stops." A fellow revolutionary, Wyndham Lewis, chose blindness rather than have his mind stop, as Pound has suffered to continue his mental activity. The key to the case against "our . . . British brethren," by the brethren themselves, is "When one's friends hate each other / how can there be peace in the world?" Pound confesses "Their asperities diverted me in my green time." Now he is "A blown husk that is finished," "But" (the turn) "the light sings eternal" over the marshes at Torcello (a "Mindscape"). Revolving "Thru the 12 Houses of Heaven" has revealed the philosophical "Time, space, / neither life nor death is the answer." It has led to the ethical and justicial verdict "And of man seeking good, / doing evil." The mind as "meiner Heimat / where the dead walked / and the living were made of cardboard," complementing and framing the visionary "Thy quiet house," completes a hemicycle and affirms a phase of tradition.

Canto *CXVI*, like *VII* in the prototype and *Pisan* in the drafts, sums up and transforms the foregoing tradition in a mode of personal struggle. Despite the verdict delivered upon human nature Pound tries to declare the independence and integrity of the poetic imagination by drawing on the common law of nature and human nature. Canto *CXVI* is projected from the epitome Canto *CX* by the placated, many-personaed Elpenor's advice "*hsin* . . . go forth by day . . . *hsin*" lapsing into "That love be the cause of hate, / something is twisted," which has conditioned all the foregoing cantos. The last finished canto affixes that condition definitively for what remains.

Transforming the introduction to a mind of history, foam cresting "feather-white, as a dolphin on sea-brink" (*CX*), "Came Neptunus / his mind leaping / like dolphins" (plural) introduces a mind of nature. Neptunus reactivates "the European mind," gives new life to the dead "In meiner Heimat," and affirms the mental achievements of the "*tribù*," of which *The Cantos* is "the record." So European epic emerged out of the sea via Homer's "ear for the sea-surge" (*II, VII*), and so Gemisto Plethon's Platonism, which "stemmed all from Neptune," the concrete universal, inspired the Tempio. From such a mind "the human mind has attained . . . these concepts," all *The Cantos* before and after this line. As motives, the concepts have been "To make

---

20. "From *CXV*" appeared in at least four versions. The *Threshold* (Belfast, Spring 1962) version contained the present text and Canto *120*. The present text appeared in *Paris Review* 28 (Spring–Summer 1962). The present text adding meliorative lines (some from a "Mindscape") appeared in Eva Hesse, ed., *Ezra Pound: Cantos 1916–1962 Ein Auswahl* (Munich: 1964). The darker *Paris Review* version finally prevailed and lines from the first version became Canto *120*.

Cosmos— / To achieve the possible—"[21] "Muss." applied them to the corporate ideal but was "wrecked for an error." "But," the argument reverses, "the record / the palimpsest" affirms the value of a tradition irradiated at least partially by "a little light / in great darkness"—even though an "old 'crank'" like Pound, probably John Brown, lies dead in Virginia;[22] even though "Unprepared young" are "burdened with records"; and even though "The vision of the Madonna" shows only "above the cigar butts / and over the portal." "Muss."'s error was to have made (unlike Justinian) "a mass of laws" but no sane letters, or like Pound "a tangle of works unfinished."

Canto *CXVI* formalizes the oscillative "But," as in "But the record, the palimpsest," in four phases. Personally, "I have brought the great ball of crystal; / who can lift it? / Can you enter the great acorn of light?" Pound has been adjudged insane, "But the beauty is not the madness / Tho' my errors and wrecks lie about me." He is not a "demigod" and he cannot "make it cohere." Ethical failure is both personal and general: "If love be not in the house there is nothing. / The voice of famine unheard." All the more baffling, therefore, is how "beauty" came against "this blackness," "Twice beauty under the elms" on the lawn at St. Elizabeths, where he was "saved by squirrels and bluejays?" Aids have been "Disney against the metaphysicals" and unexpected "deeps" in Jules Laforgue and Linnaeus, instances of comrades "chi crescerà i nostri"—who will increase our loves.[23]

The possibility of increased loves precipitates a justicial "but about that third heaven," Venus's, where "again is all 'paradiso' / a nice quiet paradise / over the shambles." The regained vantage point recalls "some climbing" (of the Mount) before an anticipated "take-off." The mode would be "to 'see again,'" not to "'walk on,'" as in the land-periplum of *VII* and *Pisan*. Seen again "it" ("The palimpsest," "the great ball of crystal," "the great acorn of light") "coheres all right," "even if my notes" (*The Cantos*) "do not cohere." "Many errors" have overwhelmed the "little rightness" that might

21. FY edition reads, interestingly, "To make cosmos— / To achieve human order, / To precede the possible."

22. In "Interview with Mrs. Unterguggenburger" (*Globe*, Milwaukee, Wis., October 1937) Pound clinched the Mayor of Worgl's experiment with Gesellite currency (*Pisan LXXIV*) "Johnnie Brown wasn't all killed when they killed him."

23. Asked in the *Paris Review* 28 interview "Do you think that the modern world has changed the ways in which poetry can be written?" Pound cited as new "competition" "the serious side . . . , the Confucian side of Disney," in a squirrel film, *Perri*, where Disney took an ethic and asserted "the values of courage and tenderness" in a way that "everybody can understand." That is "absolute genius," "a greater correlation of nature" than achieved since Alexander the Great ordered fishermen that if they found out any specific thing about fish that was interesting they were to tell Aristotle; that correlation brought ichthyology to "the scientific point where it stayed for two thousand years." The camera permits "an *enormous* correlation of particulars"; its "capacity for making contact" challenges literature as to "what needs to be done and what is superfluous."

"excuse" Dante's Hell and Pound's paradise. "That love be the cause of hate, / something is twisted" (*CX*) and "men seeking good, / doing evil" (*CXV*) surge back: why do men "go wrong, / thinking of rightness"? "Who will copy this palimpsest?"

With but little daylight left amid a great circle of shadow, the soul responds "But to affirm the gold thread in the pattern" at Torcello, "Thy quiet house," and at Rapallo, as in a narrow street of Gold ("Vicolo d'oro"). He must "confess wrong without losing rightness," but he has had "Charity" only "sometimes," and cannot make it "flow thru." All he has managed is "A little light, like a rushlight / to lead back to splendour." Formally he has achieved a tradition and a persona, but he will not achieve even formally justice and poetry. If the foregoing cantos had been completed, Canto *CXVI* would have ratified states' rights through a declaration of independence, motives for a new union, and common law; it does so only formally. As to new world union, vision persists but the sequels will be fragments.

Fragments of Cantos and Canto *120*

Drafting a tradition having remained unperfected (*CX–CXV*), and a protagonist's struggle having been found the chief cause (*CXVI*), the modes of justice and poetry had to remain *Fragments of Cantos* and a providential coda had to be reserved as a posthumous gesture. *Fragments of Cantos* are the immediate consequence of the consolatory "From time's wreckage shored, / these fragments shored against ruin" (*CX*); of the affirmative "That the body is inside the soul— / the lifting and folding brightness / the darkness shattered / the fragment" (*CXIII*); and of the resigned "my errors and wrecks lie about me" (*CXVI*). In a longer view "Addendum for *C*," written about 1941 and already expounded for the transition from *LXXI Cantos* to *Pisan* (see Chapter Ten), memorializes the shift after 1941 from a 100-canto poem to a 120-canto poem while presenting a vestige of the 100-canto poem (cf. *Thrones 100*, see Chapter Eleven). "Notes for *CXVII* et seq." and Canto *120* evidence an inability to complete the 120-canto alternative. Moreover, *Drafts & Fragments of Cantos CX–CXVII* refers to "Eight columns" in the bill of lading, while "Notes for *CXVII* et seq." and Canto *120* refer to an edifice and a transaction to be completed, signed, sealed, and delivered "etc...with carriage, danars 151." Constitutionally, however, since neither the drafting nor the memorializing, signing, sealing, and delivering of Articles I–VII/VIII can be completed, Branches/Powers—"Notes for *CXVII* et seq."—remain *Fragments of Cantos* while Canto *120* is completed formally but tenuously and dismally.

With reference to transformation of the prototype *Fragments of Cantos* reflect the transition from *I–VII* to *VIII*, "These fragments you have shelved (shored)," which precipitated through the dispute between Truth and Calliope the instance of Malatesta and his broken seal, a fragment then reassembled, interpreted, and expanded into *VIII–XI*. *Fragments of Cantos* and Canto *120* have been projected from the Malatesta cantos, through the repeated, trans- forming drafts and phases, and through the fragments into which Canto *CX* devolves, to a final re-expression of Malatesta's effort. It can be inferred that three "Notes" followed finally by Canto *120*, Pound's last will and testa- ment, are Poundian versions of the history of Malatesta's life (*VIII*), of his effort to build a temple inspired by Isotta (*IX*), and of an apparent failure at least momentarily averted by appearance of the inspiring Eagle (*X*). Canto *120* then becomes Pound's version of a Malatestan effort continued to the last moment and handed to posterity as a spirit, a model, and an inspiration, if not an achieved end (*XI*). By sustaining the vision and the prototype form, the end of Pound's poem repeats Malatesta's effort even if it fails to culminate in Malatesta's irrepressible good cheer.

The first "Note" (an eighth unit of a projected draft and a "Mindscape") transforms the Malatestan-American seal by its phases into a pattern for a temple. "The blue flash and the moments / benedetta" appear like the con- stellation in a mind of history (the shield); but a tradition subjecting the young to the old is tragedy. When one beautiful day brings peace, Brancusi's sculpted bird (the Eagle) seems to take new life in nature under a twilit sky (not "gleaming," as in *106*) "leaded with elm boughs" (a cosmic shrine). Under the Rupe Tarpeia, from which Roman criminals were thrown to their deaths (a justicial Mount), Pound adjures himself "weep out your jealousies" so that "without jealousy" he can "make a church / or an altar to Zagreus" (god of the fourth phase) "like the double arch of a window / Or some great colonnade" (sun-vision and temple of Providence). He is asserting the inde- pendence of his vision despite cruel and unusual punishments (tragedy, ad- judged criminality, jealousy). Memorializing, signing, sealing, and delivering the Constitutional dimension of *Drafts & Fragments of Cantos CX–CXVII*, and perfecting "Eight columns," are alluded to but unachieved. The compre- hensiveness of the vision symbolizes Congress/States.

The second "Note" (a ninth unit) is little more than a personal cry of inspiration lost during struggle:

> M'amour, m'amour
> > what do I love and
> > > where are you?
> That I lost my center
> > fighting the world.

Recalled is Malatesta's effort inspired by Isotta and evidenced by the post- bag, which Malatesta carried out under declared sovereignty and retained rights. For Pound, however, the effort "to make a paradiso / terrestre" is reduced to "The dreams clash / and are shattered." The personal focus manifests Presidency/Amendment.

The third "Note" (a tenth unit) makes a wistful pledge activated by failing reserved powers. Pound associates himself with a Parisian bankrupt ("fail-lite"); with a lark flying high toward the sun and then "falling"; with the "farfalla" (moth) gasping "as toward a bridge over worlds"; and with kings who would "meet in their island . . . after flight from the pole."[24] "Two mice and a moth my guides" and "Milkweed the sustenance / as to enter arcanum" seem deliberately opaque, and all but the "falls" remain hypotheses or motives. The culminating "To be men not destroyers" hypothecates a pledge and reserved powers. It recalls Malatesta's response to the Eagle, "All I want you to do is to follow the orders, / They've got a bigger army, / but there are more men in this camp" (*X*). Pound redirects his inspiration away from "fighting the world." Justice manifests Judiciary/Supreme Law.

When Pound looked back upon his overall achievement he did not celebrate it ANNUIT COEPTIS or even see it as he saw Malatesta's, "In the gloom, the gold gathers the light against it" (*XI*). Nor did he end a grand failure with Malatestan jocularity and cheer. Though he "ratified" the "states of mind" of "the tribe" formally—one can see in the four sentences an historical effort, a recourse to nature, and appeals first for impersonal and then for intimate justice and mercy—he had never adjudged himself and his work so directly:

> I have tried to write Paradise
>
> Do not move
>   Let the wind speak
>   that is paradise.
>
> Let the Gods forgive what I
>   have made.
> Let those I love try to forgive
>   what I have made.

After seven decades, out of the silence deliberately chosen as a destiny, or a discipline, or a penance, or a sounding board of his last years, there was nothing more to say. The rest is silence.

24. "Larks at Allegre" merge with Provençal phrases about Bernart de Ventadour's lark "letting himself fall" after having moved "his wings for joy" against the sunlight. Ventadour's lark arrives from each previous phase: from *VI*, from *Pisan LXXIV*, from *Rock-Drill 91* (the musical epigraph). A composite of its appearances touches the italicized phrases in a translation included in *The Spirit of Romance*, 1910:

> When I see the lark *a-moving*
> *For joy his wings against the sun-light*
> *Who forgets himself and lets himself fall*
> *For the sweetness which goes into his heart;*
> Ai! what great envy cometh unto me for him whom I see so rejoicing!
> It marvelleth me that my heart melts not of desiring.

By simply giving itself to its nature the lark can "make it flow thru." For men, it depends.

AFTERWORD

"Some one said I was the last American living the
tragedy of Europe."
    Interview, 1960.

Pound has been vilified, charged with treason, and declared mentally in-
competent by medical authorities who held him for thirteen years until he was
released as incurably insane. In certain undeniable perspectives "the case of
Ezra Pound" has been proved and closed, to many fair-minded persons justly.
Conversely, friends, literary critics, poetry lovers, cultists, and disciples,
some of whom espoused the least attractive ideas which Pound at one time or
another expressed, have written testimonies, apologies, rebuttals. Adversary,
judicious, and apologetic have left out, short-circuited, or muted too many
questions of which even Pound, on his more sensitive side and in his poetry
(if not in his polemics), was aware.
    Extra-poetic judgments ignore the motives and the poetry. Ignoring extra-
poetic judgments and trying to concentrate on the poetry alone leads to irrele-
vancy, since it denies Pound a subject, an aesthetic, a motive, and a method
all of which deliberately and necessarily involved him in events and their
consequences. No writer has ever committed himself more absolutely to
"ends (or scopes) and beginnings" that contain and enforce a chosen destiny.
No writer has ever asked more directly to be judged intellectually, ethically,
morally, and legally as well as aesthetically. Only by taking all these things
into account, therefore, can one confront "the case of Ezra Pound" whole.
We can judge the whole only in the light of the poem, as one day posterity will
judge. Insofar as posterity adjudges success, it will have arrived at and in part
been shaped by Pound's scope and end, a "new *forma mentis*." Since the
"new *forma mentis*" will be the poem, the light of "a poem containing
history" is the only "proper lighting" in which to consider all cases at once.
    The comprehensive view expounded in this book substantiates a conversa-
tion on Lago di Garda between Pound and Serafino Mazzolini, minister of
foreign affairs of the Republica di Salò, some time after Pound had walked
from Rome to the Tyrol following the fall of Mussolini and the fascist regime.
Reported by the journalist Damaso Riccioni in 1955, the conversation dwelt
on Imagism and on the poetical patrimony of Greece and Italy, but it turned
particularly to the medial crisis of Pound's career and of his poem, World
War II. In discussing Italy, Hitler, and Stalin, Pound defended himself against
accusations about his "Anglo-Saxon radio transmissions." When asked about

the duties of a citizen to put aside his own feelings when his country was at war, Pound recurred to his lifelong poetic motive and vision:

> Socrates was accused of impiety and the subversion of the laws of his country; still he was not impious or subversive, and subsequent history has shown this. I am accused of betraying my country, which I love as much as you love yours. But one, who like me, acts in the light of a truth interiorly felt, and foreseen, anticipates in the present a most certain future reality.
>
> Over the radio I tried to make my countrymen understand that my ideas are above warring factions, because they are inspired by a vision far above the relations among peoples. As a citizen I do not speak nor stand against my country; as a thoughtful man I stand for points of view which I consider closest to the aspirations of my free spirit, under the spell of a vision of a ''sacred union'' of all peoples called by destiny to lead humanity by virtue of their advanced evolutionary state, intellectual and social. Besides, my very own countrymen at a time not far hence will have to admit the correctness of my convictions, even if before that time they will have sent me to the electric chair.
>
> Poets are somewhat like seers. The value and character of an action are judged from the point of view of repercussions in boundless dimensions of time; that is to say, in the foreshadowing of what sooner or later becomes history. And history—and Schopenauer also says this—often changes tomorrow the titles of chapters which today have a contrary sense. Today my countrymen (I wish they could read my pamphlet of two years ago, *Visiting Card*, for the explanation of some absurd aspects of this war) give to the present tragic chapter a title that they themselves will change tomorrow by compulsion of events resulting from the fatal game of ideas and interests in evolution.

At the end of the interview, Riccioni reports, they got into Pound's hired boat. As they rowed to Salò in the light of a splendid sunset, the poet seated himself next to the boatman, took one oar, and in rhythm with his strokes recited sotto voce some English verses. Pound said they were Milton's.[1]

Because a view ''above warring factions'' was conditioned by economic relations and mechanisms, by cultural idealism, by the ideal pattern of '76, and by motives toward ideal beauty, Pound misunderstood the crisis and struggle of 1939–45. Since he believed in the possibility of enlightenment based on an essential human goodness that would prevail if minds and hearts were informed, he misunderstood or did not even see either the Italian regime's brutality and bad faith or barbarism made policy by Germany and Japan. In effect the poet who was trying to save mankind from blind and

---

1. The account is reported by Harry Meachem in *The Caged Panther: Ezra Pound at St. Elizabeths* (New York: 1967), pp. 26–27.

perverse forces neglected the fact that the roots of the nightmare of history disappear below the observable and teachable human heart.

Pound always put his faith in the expert, in the man with "the lowdown," in "the opportunist who is RIGHT," in "the light of the doer." For politics men of civic responsibility, whom he thought had been virtually snuffed out in England and America (hence his own exile), ought to bring these to bear for the executive, advisory, perceptive, and inventive (or poetic) functions. The man with intellectual interests would be motivated by the good and by justice because he had a positive vision of them. He had learned this Platonic ideal not only through his "Plymouth Rock conscience landed on predilection for the arts" but also from his first social and political mentor, A. R. Orage, who had demanded "an ideograph of the good" from writers to whom he would open *The New Age*.

Inspired by visions of the good, Blake and others (*XVI*) shout against "the evil" of a Hell (*XIV–XV*) "without dignity, without tragedy." (Eliot found it to be a Hell "for other people.") Evil is principally a deprivation of enlightenment and therefore a cause of "human error." For Elpenor, Alessandro dei Medici, the Lotophagoi, and the voices from the stone pits (*XXV*) the cause of error is "abuleia" or will-lessness, the absence of "direction of one's will" and "Worthy will to the chosen end." The decline of the Renaissance makes it appear that "Time is the evil" (*XXX*), though the underlying cause is the failure of "aesthetes" to understand and to resist the forces of decay, a failure rebuked by Artemis's "Compleynt" that pity has softened merciless beauty into a Circean opiate. Such a failure of "the tops," coupled with the aimlessness of Tovarisch, both allows decay and prevents constructivity. Ignorance and will-lessness join with deliberate perversion in "criminals have no intellectual interests," applied to the prisoners at Pisa sympathetically but therefore all the more severely to usurers who have sent helpless slaves "to the slaughter . . . to the sound of the bumm drum." Only under impacts from without does evil strike deeper than a secular interpretation of Dante's "l'hanno perduto il ben dell'intelletto."

Pound's myopia and error can probably be explained by the demands of his subject and method, both of which had to be open-ended and had to allow for contingencies. The motive stated in *Paris Review 28*—"I am writing to resist the view that Europe and civilization is going to Hell. If I am being 'crucified for an idea'—that is, the coherent idea around which my muddles accumulated—it is probably the idea that European culture ought to survive, that the best qualities of it ought to survive along with whatever other cultures, in whatever universality"—may even explain his attribution of European paideumatic motives to the collaborators Vidkun Quisling, Maréchal Petain, Pierre Laval, and Phillipe Henriot. Even the scurrility and scatology of the broadcasts, however repellent, might be rationalized by theories and models of satire, though the radio medium could hardly accommodate American bluntness and folksiness remembered, laced with verbal violence and vulgarity, and directed toward an American audience known only from a distance for more than thirty years. What is hardest to explain away, what can only be mitigated by personal remorse and absorbed into the larger dimensions of *The Cantos*, is the strident insistence on race and the obsession with Jewry at a time when race had become a justification for public policies of genocide.

Pound's emphasis on action was not the Fascists' substitution of the clenched fist for reason, but American enthusiasm coupled with the American imperative to get things done. "The curse of me and my nation is that we always think things can be bettered by immediate action of some sort, *any* sort rather than no sort."[2] This confession, made to Joyce when Pound was trying to persuade Joyce to meet him at Sirmione in 1920 (Joyce did), strikes a chord with the native Americanism defined at the end of the 1960 *Paris Review* interview. Asked "You said the other day that as you grew older you felt more American all the time. How does this work?" Pound replied:

> It works. Exotics were necessary as an attempt at a foundation. One is transplanted and grows, and one is pulled up and taken back to what one has been transplanted from and it is no longer there. The contacts aren't there and I suppose one reverts to one's organic nature and finds it merciful. Have you ever read Andy White's memoirs? He's the fellow who founded Cornell University. That was the period of euphoria, when everybody thought that all the good things in America were going to function, before the decline, about 1900. White covers a period of history that goes back to Buchanan on one side. He alternated between being Ambassador to Russia and head of Cornell.

As he wrote in "Antifascisti" (1941), "No American from 1900 to 1910 *imagined the possibility* of a world *not* dominated by a fat and dirty usurocracy, by commercial vulgarity and by the swinish power of gold." To combat it, "No laboratory existed. It was necessary to build one."[3]

It can never be overstressed that for Pound "my spiritual father" was Whitman, who "is America." "In America there is much for the healing of nations." " 'His message is my message. We will see that men hear it.' "[4] "I find in him what I should be ready to call our American keynote"—"a certain generosity; a certain carelessness, or looseness, if you will; a hatred of the sordid, an ability to forget the parts for the sake of the whole, a desire for largeness; a willingness to stand exposed."

> "Camerado, this is no book;
> Who touches this touches a man.

"The artist is ready to endure personally a strain which his craftsmanship

2. To Joyce, 7–8 June 1920, Forrest Read, ed., *Pound/Joyce: Letters & Essays* (New York: 1967).
3. Chapter Sixteen, p. 291.
4. "What I Feel About Walt Whitman," 1909.

would scarcely endure.'' Whitman embodies the strength of a people, that it "will undertake nothing in its art for which it will not be in person responsible."[5]

Pound never ceased being the young man of 1907, one of whom Whitman prophesied "Poems and the materials of poems shall come from their lives, they shall be makers and finders":

> Thirty years ago in the last and after midnight train from Philadelphia a tough bloke reproved me for hoarding knowledge. I was dead tired, I had with me a pile of books appertaining to graduate study, and suddenly two minutes before my station it emerged that the tough customer envied me to the point of dislike. He thought it just as unlikely that fellows that "had learning" would unbuckle and hand it out to someone that hadn't, as that J. Wanamaker, whose country place lay alongside the railway, would hand out a slice of money.
>
> Such shocks come once in a lifetime. It was a thick and heavy voice: "Huh! 'n 'yuh fellers! Wot got a lot of learnin' wouldn't *give* any of that!'' That call to order has stayed with me thirty years.[6]

From such experiences and from his own near paupery in London came his indignation against all kinds of injustice and a perception of relations between intellectual and economic sharing, between currency of knowledge and of money. A sympathy for the underdog (and cat) and a revolutionary attitude joined his aristocratic tastes with the plight of the deprived on different grounds than those held by opportunists and by ideologues of various stripes, liberal, fascist, or Marxist. He took as his model "the normal man wishing to live mentally active," and his "Plymouth Rock conscience landed on a predilection for the arts," struggled for "all men." His poetic ideals, stated in "Propertius" and "Mauberley," were complementary: to write "something to read in normal circumstances" and "to resuscitate the dead art / Of poetry; to maintain 'the sublime' / In the old sense." Both were perhaps impossible in an age of experiment and revolution, but both had nonetheless to be the aim of a man who would "voice the general heart."

In eschewing "originality, i.e., unless it happens,"[7] he was seeking to tap the paideuma shared by all men, not only "the taught" but also "the not taught" found in the bones, in the mother's milk, in the locale, in "the oral tradition." In the sense that paideuma is "thinking in poetry," from roots in Homer and in the Confucian *Odes*, Pound tried throughout his life to get back

---

5. "Patria Mia" XI, 1912.

6. "When Will School Books . . . ? An Author's Idea on 'What's Wrong with Modern Education.' " *Delphian Quarterly*, Chicago, April 1937.

7. He wrote to Wyndham Lewis about the alleged attack in *Time and Western Man* (1927): "You [are] almost only who has writ any real criticism of [*crossout*: me] (fools called it attack - - - - got the point esp. re no originality - - precisely the not-to-be-desired/i.e./unless it happens" (about 1951, Cornell University Library).

to Homer and to the simplicity of the *Odes*. He tried to turn the new modes of experience embodied in '76, which had been only imperfectly realized in the literary tradition, into something inherent in its origins, the Manifest Destiny of One World. In this respect all his work is written and voiced in an American language aspiring hysteron proteron toward its consummation. Its destiny is rooted in Columbus Day, in Thanksgiving, in the Fourth of July, in the national birthdays, in Old Glory, in the pledge of allegiance. Its hymns are "My Country 'Tis of Thee," "America the Beautiful," "The Star-Spangled Banner," "Columbia the Gem of the Ocean," "The Battle Hymn of the Republic," most of them sung to traditional melodies with new lyrics—like most American culture, palimpsests. Pound was simply reversing the process to "make it new" again.

The Cantos may be incomplete, may contain errors, may be a rash attempt at epic in an age of experiment. It may be too bulky, too obscure, too idiosyncratic. Despite Pound's remark about Buckminster Fuller's similar geometric (or geodesic) vision—" 'Buckie' has gone in for structure (quite rightly) / but consumption is still done by animals" (*Thrones 97*)—it may be too schematic. Such details as building the Constitution and measuring out the form of a civilization in one sense constitute an infernal machine that could have sunk Pound's effort in *l'ésprit de géometrie*. Certainly it made him a servant to his conception and to whatever his historical destiny might bring. He could alter his poem no further than by shifting to the 120-canto alternative and selecting the proper subject that might come to hand. As he said in the *Paris Review* interview, "There has been a great deal of work thrown away because one is attracted to an historic character and then finds that he doesn't function within the form, doesn't embody a value needed. . . . The material one wants to fit in doesn't always work. If the stone isn't hard enough to maintain the form, it has to go out." Doubtless rejected matter will eventually come to light and will be related to the poem as Pound left it. But such can be used only to clarify the formal publication that defines the canon. In the face of principles sustained over a lifetime even the notorious palinode made to an Italian journalist in 1963[8] is but a momentary crack in the silence that defined the public man of the last years while the poet was preparing his last will and testament. Even a posthumous testament could be only a gesture by a different Pound than the Pound who lived *The Cantos*.

The Cantos takes its place in the line of American inheritances of structural visions from China, Egypt, Sumeria, Greece, Rome, the Gothic Middle Ages, Freemasonry, and the Enlightenment. Benjamin Franklin, an adept with magic squares and magic circles, mapped ethical time and space by laying out on a grid the days of the week and thirteen moral instructions. Jefferson, by

8. Grazia Livi, "Interview with Ezra Pound," *Epoca*, Milan, 24 March 1963, translated by Jean McClean in *City Lights Journal*, Number Two, San Francisco 1964.

cutting up the Gospels and laying out parallel columns of Greek, Latin, French, and English, schematized a religious tradition in a fresh notebook. Washington surveyed the West. Such minds and Adams's legal mind made a revolution and devised a "system of government / AS of a demonstration of Euclid." Paine's vision, derived from the orrery and "The Spacious Firmament on High," resulted not only in intellectual, ethical, legal, and religious structures, but also in his iron bridge. Someday the similar structures of Whitman and other verbal architects will be charted. Pound tried to set the whole tradition to his own kind of music.

If not too schematic, *The Cantos* may fall too far into Pound's suggestion about William Carlos Williams's work (applicable also to Malatesta's and Whitman's), "Art very possibly *ought* to be the supreme achievement, the 'accomplished'; but there is another satisfactory effect, that of a man hurling himself at an indomitable chaos, and yanking and hauling as much of it as possible into some sort of order (or beauty), aware of it both as chaos and as potential."[9] When he received E. E. Cummings's *Collected Poems* (1938) he wondered if Cummings might be "le Whitman de nos jours? the message of looseness?"[10] In the speeches gathered in *If This Be Treason......* Pound is at particular pains to differentiate an American style from "the end" of a style and of the capitalist system rendered in *Ulysses*. He cites Jeffersonian neologism, Jamesian "parenthesis," "that just unfinish" of Whitman, and Cummings's style, particularly in *Eimi*, where Cummings had "defined" the new subject Russia, "carryin on from old Hen. James (measurin one race by another) carryin on from Thoreau natr. wild natr. all that Silver Lake background."

More specifically Pound explained:

> Now in part mr cummings teaches a doctrine which is very ably
> condensed (dichten: condensare; to write poetry is to CONDENSE),
> Mr C. teaches a truth which a contemporary German author has stated
> quite clearly, as follows: "what we used to call public opinion is based
> only in very small part on personal experience of particular persons or
> indeed on the knowledge of individual voters, but for the most part
> on a collective representation (collective picture) which brings about
> in a very obstinate and persistant way a so called process strangely
> clarificator of the problems."
>
> Now the use of a great writer to his race is due to his having precisely
> PERSONAL direct perception, and putting it down on paper/ dont matter
> what he thinks is doin, his USE to his race or nation consists in seeing
> the OBJECT and writin down what he sees/ and not falsifyin record/
> mebbe by and by afterwards that word photo, that diagram; that TRUE

9. "Dr. Williams' Position," *Dial*, New York, November 1928.
10. To Mary Barnard, 21 March 1938, Collection at Yale.

diagram can serve to enlighten his people. dont' forget they are HIS people as they will never be the people of any member of congress.[11]

Pound's eschewal of traditional forms and methods of scholarship and thought were probably necessary to avoid narrowing specialization and to uphold the tradition of the Renaissance man. He espoused the challenge and response faced by the Odyssean opportunist, and modified it by the ethic of the Confucian self-directed and self-disciplined man who listens to "the heart's tone," in order to perfect the American jack-of-all-trades, bull in a China shop, autodidact, self-made man, "simple separate person," inventor, and "genius." Eliot labeled Pound's Yankee ingenuity "isolated superiority." The narrator of Ralph Ellison's *Invisible Man* calls such a Ford, Edison, or Franklin a "thinker-tinker."

Such weaknesses may be unavoidable corollaries of Pound's strengths: of the scope of his subject, of the necessary submission to its claims, and of such ethical qualities as energy, purpose, endurance, and faithfulness to an epic vocation that could hardly have been a more exacting mistress. Error, from simple errors of fact to the cataclysmic error of allying himself with historical fascism, may have been part of the cost of trying to realize the motive "To build the city of Dioce whose terraces are the colour of the stars" in a poem that might become "reading matter, singing matter, shouting matter, the tale of the tribe" precisely *because* he had made his life the vehicle for trying not only to perfect the vision but also to make it fact. He made himself not only the poet of many voices seeking to constitute the mind and life of the normal man wishing to live mentally active in a complacent era, but also the champion of "these simple men who have fought against jealousy," of "the sensitive" (as he perceived Joyce when he first met him in 1920), of the artist-saint like Constantin Brancusi—both of what the simple heart feels and of what the intense mind does and might do. If he presumed to voice "The enormous tragedy of the dream in the peasant's bent shoulders," he did it by becoming "the last American living the tragedy of Europe."[12]

The passage quoted earlier becomes by Pound's having lived it extraordinary enough to be quoted again:

> To act on one's definition? What concretely do I myself mean to do?
> I mean to say that one measure of a civilization, either of an age or of a single individual, is what that age or person really wishes to *do*. A man's hope measures his civilization. The attainability of the hope measures, or may measure, the civilization of his nation and time.

In *Confucius To Cummings* his translation of Metastasio's lyric "L'età d'oro" reaffirmed a declaration made in "Prolegomena" and "Credo" (1912), "the age of gold pertains":

11. Olga Rudge, ed., *If This Be Treason......*, (Siena: 1948).
12. *Paris Review* 28.

Age of Gold, I bid thee come
To this earth, was erst thy home!
Age of Gold, if e'er thou wast
And art not mere dream laid waste!

Thou art not fled; ne'er wast mere dreaming;
Art not now mere feigned seeming.
Every simple heart knows this:
Candour still thy substance is.

An epilogue to *A Lume Spento* is ''Make strong old dreams lest this our world lose heart.'' ''A man's paradise is his good nature.'' ''What whiteness will you add to this whiteness, / what candour?'' ''Out of all this beauty something must come.''

APPENDIX A

THE SEAL OF THE

UNITED STATES

Proceedings that led to the design of the Seal and official interpretations of its heraldry may be found in Gaillard Hunt, *The History of the Seal of the United States*, Washington 1909; (first edition 1892). To design a seal a committee of the Continental Congress including Jefferson, Franklin, and John Adams was appointed on 4 July 1776. The Seal was first used by Washington on a document for an exchange of prisoners in 1781. It was officially adopted by Congress on 20 June 1782:

> On report of the secretary, to whom were referred the several reports on the device for a great seal, to take order:
> The device for an armorial achievement and reverse of the great seal for the United States in Congress assembled, is as follows:
> ARMS, Paleways of thirteen pieces, argent and gules; a chief, azure; the escutcheon on the breast of the American eagle displayed proper, holding in his dexter talon an olive branch, and in his sinister a bundle of thirteen arrows, all proper, and in his beak a scroll, inscribed with this motto, *"E pluribus Unum."*
> For the CREST. Over the head of the eagle, which appears above the escutcheon, a glory, or, breaking through a cloud, proper, and surrounding thirteen stars, forming a constellation, argent, on an azure field.
> REVERSE. A pyramid unfinished. In the zenith, an eye in a triangle, surrounded with a glory proper. Over the eye these words, *"Annuit Coeptis."* On the base of the pyramid the numerical letters MDCCLXXVI. And underneath the following motto, *"Novus Ordo Seclorum."*
> The Escutcheon is composed of the chief & pale, the two most honorable ordinaries. The pieces, paly, represent the Several States all joined in one solid compact entire, supporting a Chief, which unites the whole & represents Congress. The Motto alludes to this union. The pales in the arms are kept closely united by the chief and the chief depends on that Union & the strength resulting from it for its support, to denote the

Confederacy of the United States of America & the preservation of
their Union through Congress. The colours of the pales are those used
in the flag of the United States of America; White signifies purity and
innocence, Red, hardiness & valour, and Blue, the colour of the Chief
signifies vigilance perseverance & justice. The Olive branch and arrows
denote the power of peace & war which is exclusively vested in Congress. The Constellation denotes a new State taking its place and rank
among other sovereign powers. The Escutcheon is born on the breast
of an American Eagle without any other supporters, to denote that
the United States of America ought to rely on their own Virtue.

Reverse. The pyramid signifies Strength and Duration. The Eye over
it & the Motto allude to the many signal interpositions of providence
in favour of the American cause. The date underneath is that of the
Declaration of Independence and the words under it signify the beginning of the new American Era, which commences from that date.

APPENDIX B

SIGISMUNDO'S POSTBAG

The bill of lading is not in the 1454 postbag, but has been extracted by Pound (with considerable alterations) from a lengthy contract, covering many more items, made in 1455 by representatives of Sigismundo with a sculptor and a supplier from Verona. After a descriptive title, notarization, and a general statement of responsibility, the contract proceeds thus (I translate the Latin only of those portions from which Pound draws, italicize his phrases, and mark his alterations with a preceding "n.b."; note that the repeated Arabic "15" is entirely his own interpolation):

> *First.* fine *red slabs* of [n.b.] good member without flaw, in number *ten*, *seven* feet long *by* [n.b.] five feet wide *by one third* of a foot high, slabs six and two thirds feet long and three and one third feet wide and one third high.

> Item. *Eight good red* slabs without flaw [n.b.] five feet long *by three and one third* feet wide by one third foot high.

> Item. *Six pieces* of good [n.b.] red slab as above, five feet long *by one* [n.b.] *and one* fourth feet wide of aforesaid height.

After three more items:

> *Eight* [n.b.] red *columns* [n.b.] five feet long by two thirds high

After seven more items that contain none of the measures Pound uses:

> *All these stones* are to be *transported* from the mountains and are to be sufficiently good and clean without flaw.

For these items and services Malatesta's representatives agreed to pay

> . . . *one hundred fifty one danars* in gold

The means of payment is specified, after which the parties date the document and sign it.

The Italian *La Prima Decade* (in *L'Alleluja: Poesie di Ennio Contini e La Prima Decade dei Cantos di Ezra Pound*, Mazara 1952) returned to the original Latin and condensed further while almost wholly suppressing the design (again I translate):

442

First: fine red slabs (ten)
      seven long by five wide,
Eight good slabs without flaw...
                  five by three feet,
Six pieces of good slabs as above
      etc...transported from the mountains,
              151 danars of gold.

La Prima Decade, *I–IX* and *X* lines 1–55, was translated by Pound's daughter "in collaborazione personale con l'autore." Why he should have countenanced suppression of his design or himself ordered such suppression must remain a speculation.

APPENDIX C

TOM PAINE'S PRISON POEM

FROM THE CASTLE IN THE AIR,
TO THE LITTLE CORNER OF THE WORLD.

In the region of clouds, where the whirlwinds arise,
   My Castle of Fancy was built;
The turrets reflected the blue from the skies,
   And the windows with sunbeams were gilt.

The rainbow sometimes, in its beautiful state,
   Enamell'd the mansion around;
And the figures that fancy in clouds can create,
   Supplied me with gardens and ground.

I had grottoes, and fountains, and orange tree groves,
   I had all that enchantment has told;
I had sweet shady walks, for the Gods and their Loves,
   I had mountains of coral and gold.

But a storm that I felt not, had risen and roll'd,
   While wrapp'd in a slumber I lay;
And when I look'd out in the morning, behold
   My Castle was carried away.

It pass'd over rivers, and vallies, and groves,
   The world it was all in my view;
I thought of my friends, of their fates, of their loves,
   And often, full often of YOU.

At length it came over a beautiful scene,
   That nature in silence had made;
The place was but small, but 't was sweetly serene,
   And chequer'd with sunshine and shade.

From Moncure Daniel Conway, ed., *The Writings of Thomas Paine*. 4 vols. Vol. 4,
Appendix VII. New York 1894–96.

I gazed and I envied with painful goodwill,
   And grew tired of my seat in the air;
When all of a sudden my Castle stood still,
   As if some attraction was there.

Like a lark from the sky it came fluttering down,
   And placed me exactly in view,
When whom should I meet in this charming retreat,
   This corner of calmness, but YOU.

Delighted to find you in honour and ease,
   I felt no more sorrow, nor pain;
But the wind coming fair, I ascended the breeze,
   And went back with my Castle again.

APPENDIX D

RICHARD OF ST. VICTOR

Pound described Richard's process most elaborately in a note to Guillaume De Lorris, Belated: A Vision of Italy, *Personae* 1909 (see pp. 67–68). Richard's process lay behind Dante's four senses and three realms. It doubtless is related in Pound's mind to the process of "European nature," "to act, observe and believe" consummated in Amor, which is related to "The Confucian Four TUAN," Love, Duty, Propriety, Wisdom, and to the American nature reflected by the Declaration, the Preamble, the Constitution, and the Bill of Rights, and symbolized by the Seal.

In "And Therefore Tending," a final testing of his own Neo-Confucian ethical system against Aristotle's *Nichomathean Ethics* (Chapter 54, *Guide To Kulchur*, 1938) Pound acknowledged in an otherwise severe critique of the source of Western ethics that their father's

> dissociation of the "five" kinds of knowing is not to be sneezed at. BEGINNING with (1) teXne, skill in an art, in making things (2) knowledge of rules and invariables, such as multiplication table, acquirable by the young, (3) phronesis or good sense in conduct due to perception of variables, (4) wisdom or the knowledge with a head and proportions, (5) what Rackham calls intuitive in a special way, the faculty that permits one to "see" that two straight lines can't enclose a surface, and that the triangle is the simplest possible polygon.
>
> It will be seen that NO. 1 can exist without the others; 2 and 5 have a certain relation to permanents, that 5 is in a sense above 4 (the sophia) and is in another sense part of it.

He then set against Aristotle's epistemology:

> R. of St. Victor's gradation of processes (1) the aimless flitting of the mind, (2) the systematic circling of the attention around the object, (3) contemplation, the identification of the consciousness WITH the object.
>
> 600 page parenthesis here required to discuss the implications of this confrontation (supplementary rather, I trust, than contradictory) with remarks on arabic ideas about *atasal*, union with the divine.

(For *atasal*, see *Pisan LXXVI*.)

He tested Aristotle further against "Mang Tsze (The Ethics of Mencius),"

446

Criterion, London, July 1938. A summary explanation of Confucianism at the end of *Confucio: Ta S'eu Dai Gaku Studio Integrale* (1942) offered anyone who wanted to confront the doctrine and method of Confucius with Western thought three points of reference:

Dante, De Vulgari Eloquio. II 2.75/85 (directio voluntatis)
Omero. Odissea I–34 ὑπεζ θοζόν
Aristotle, Etica Nichomachia Lib. VI.iii Τέχνε, επιστημη, φρενήσιζ, σοφία, νους; e forse Metafisics, Lib. X.

A letter to Santayana (about 1951) sets an ideogramic-graphic layout of "Confucian Four TUAN" against "Aristotl / division of faculties (teXne in Nicomac/ omitted in Mag. Moralia. greek splitting." The "Four TUAN" are called "Places you start to build from, principles, or, if analyzing, clues" (see p. 73).

The locus for St. Victor is *Rock-Drill 90. Canto 90*, Versione di Mary De Rachewiltz, English and Italian, Milan 1956, was augmented by "Richardi Excerpta Accurante Ezra Pound (1956)," twenty Latin excerpts culminating in the Latin epigraph to *90*.

APPENDIX E

"TO R. B."

___

Having worked through all Pound's published poetry in interpretive detail, I still had a blank for some persuasive hint of the Calendar from Pound's earliest years. I found it in an unpublished poem of 1907. Here is the text, lightly edited, from a letter to Viola Baxter dated 1907, at Yale.

To R. B.[1]

___

    Begin with a different or a new idea and as we grow, following that idea in all its byways and branches, so we grow to comprehend it but a part of some greater thought tree, seen before in some other part and not known of us to be the same. So my Cavalcanti growing, joins Sordello. Sordello whom my faint understanding failed to comprehend till Guido stood ready for the acting.
    Then looking on the fruits of both these men
    For fruit is the tree's token,
    Lo thou one branch,   and I
    A smaller stem have broken,
Both of one tree and in quality the same,
Thou show'st th' incomprehensions   self
Being greater and poet.
I being,   or striving to be what [I] would be,
Show the outward act of this same lack of grasp.
Thy script stands sealed
To them   who may not read,
Mine plainer writ is yet unto the blind a secret,
May hap we work to one same end
Thou greater and I less.

The lyric maid Balustion   mad to great deeds
Might filled   of that old poet

___

1. "To R. B." is the eighth in a packet of twelve poems ending with a note, actually part of the letter to Miss Baxter, "One of a series more nearly connected with what I had to say about ecstasy at the beginning. The others I think need more introduction and explanation than I have time for now." Apparently Pound was writing groups and series in 1907.

Of the wind and sea   — thy words I borrow
Being best man's words I know   —   She led men,
A remnant of the whole,   on to great deeds
And thought greater mayhap.   Thought go'th fore deed alway.
Well thou and I'd do likewise
And haply might we.   And all three
Understood at best by some few Kameiros,
Or what other island village, town,   earth
star   we be best known and loved in.
"She with others music?" sayst one.
Nay we all sing others music,
Would we,   would we not.
Thoughts circle reach'd long syne
And shot beyond,   ours the blending
Of old mad thought to truth;
To show the folly truth's self mis-seen;
To show — not all truth
Were we mad enough to dream we saw,
But just so much of truth we see,
As best may help our stumbler on the road to All ends.

Not give all our wealth t' th' inn-keep'r,
But "a penny for his lodg'ment"
And "If there be more expense —   to my account"
If all our store way giv'n,
We must stop and labour
Eer we reach the friend-waited goal.
No hardship p'rhaps.   But
He that could not bear his own small store
'Thout robbery, how shall he in safety bear our treasure?
Or if by sudden wealth giv'n pow'r,
Who knows he'll not spend for folly
—Aye and worse,   he'll feed   of our good earned store?
Or,   the inn-keep's half rascal.
Trust him with no more!
He'll leave his half dead
Foundling to the dogs
And to Araby, quick bought camel quick-sped
Houris and amber,   myrrh-soaked bed
And sybarite at weeks end
While our road friend, the Samaritan*
Works out his bruises as best he may.

* Pound's note: "Cowper slips here. It was not the Samaritan that fell among thieves."
Pound's correction accentuates dramatic verisimilitude.

Therefor,   for his lodgement night and day
Two pense;   rest to my chargè
When this way,   I pass next time.

So haply give we our truth to the worlds needs
Or to friends;   foes well and welcome
Be they fair foes;   unto each as days need is,
Not enough to weary with new burden,
But such as may give nights lodgment,
Day's food,   and chance for next day — labor
Or new finding.   He'll beg or steal perhaps,
At least I give him not the power
To raise an army and take myriad life,
Or play the riotous fool
And curse me later for an enemy.

Be he wise man,   a tool beside the tuppence,
An he wish it he may ply trade
Be he true,   well tried of old
P'rhaps even coin press—
The crafty'd use it for false coin—
Therefor to few true only—
Better left at mint,   temptation's strong
And brass passes easily where all cheat.
But I ramble as ever,
Thought half-cut from next thought—
Two radii ill seen are blurred to one.
And in o'er great confusion
The priest and levite passing,
See no radii,   as such,   at all;
Nor even guess the circle and its laws
Or know a centre and that lives lead thither.
Or living mid mixed lines,
Have no chance to hear
The harmonies of thought God-leading.

Thou swing'st the texts great line,
For the full synagogue,   too high,
—we use not millions for the children's sum—
Thou singst the text.   I in my lesser place,
Make plain the meaning to some dozen nearest me,
that caught of thy words but rumbling echo
sans form,   sans sense;
Or to some deaf ones who haply
misunderstood thy words,

Or well ear'd that lacked the wit
to know their essence;
Traveler from far land that but part knew our language:
To these odd dozen
May I help make plain thy meaning—
As I see it;   So hap
I stand more nearly to thy reading desk than they.

New exposition of old truths misunderstood,
Distinguishing twixt th' evil and the good,
By such means as may best serve
Our next neighbors turn—.   One fellow broke the path.
I blaze the trees—So piecemeal make we road.
Th' roads been traveled once to end,
And track left.   Can we follow: so aid we,
Here a tree,   there   a branch out of next fellows way,
Seek path 'round this swamp—track lost—bridge down?
"One swam this meer"   Well my neighbor's no water-bird.
I must needs plan way 'cross water for him,
Where there is of surety no track.
Or,   beacon far-lit aids not Myop,
Wherefor must I set smaller lights mid-distance
In the same old-traveled way.
The far beacon tells me there's no novelty
In my direction.
Or as I have said lang syne
"That others following in the way
"I went may say,
"There passed a man this way,   as Lo
"The foot-prints here do show,
"Leaving things fashioned and men made,
"In stronger,   fairer semblance than before.
"Riches be cob-webs and fames flame is naught
"Let this sentence to my praise be brought."[2]

2. *Paris Review* 28. Pound often complained that his "designs" had been missed. He claimed that "Collected Prose Works" designed as a "work in progress" accompanying *Personae* and *The Cantos* would show "some proof" that he had "started with a definite intention," and that what had appeared to be "an aimless picking up of tidbits" had been "governed by a plan which became clearer and more definite as I proceeded" ("Postscript (1929)" to "Praefatio Ad Lectorem Electum" to *The Spirit of Romance*, in *Prolegomena 2*, 1932). Of many claims that *The Cantos* has a form, two of the last were that those who "found no plan" would be "confounded" when *The Cantos* was completed (reported from St. Elizabeths by Daniel Pearlman in *The Barb of Time*, page 6), and that "Mebbe having got in these chunks" (*Section: Rock-Drill*

Browning wrote "Balaustion's Adventure" at the request of, and dedicated it to, "The Countess Cowper." It sets Euripides's *Alcestis* within an imaginary semi-dramatic narrative spoken by a girl exiled from her home because she declined to forego her allegiance to Athens in favor of ascendant Sparta. Similarly Pound has invented a pseudo-historical occasion within Browning's life in order to try to "explain," through an interpreter who tries to "explain" his own motive for writing. (Browning)Balaustion : Euripides :: (Pound) Cowper : Browning. In an "Apology" more than an "Adventure," Cowper apologizes not only for himself as interpreter but also for Pound as one poet who would interpret another in order to adapt, continue, and perfect once more the struggle toward Truth. Cowper has already hit on the relation between lyric persona and narrative persona, and between poet and successor poet, with which Pound will prepare *The Cantos*. Cavalcanti will become his first "Etude" ("study in form") and then a locus for intellectual renaissance and revolution (*XXXVI*). The Ur *Cantos* of 1917 will open "Hang it all, there can be but the one 'Sordello' " (cf. the present *II*) and will in effect "interpret" Browning's poem by seeking a form and a figure for Pound's own "meditative, semi-dramatic, semi-epic story." "Th' incomprehension's self" and "this same lack of grasp" are terms for arcanum and for ultimately infinite and so inscrutable Truth.[3]

---

and *Thrones*) "the rest of the poEM can be what is called 'POetic' and the squirmers cease to be able to say that it has no subject and no FORM" (to Ronald Duncan, 15 January 1958, at Texas).

3. Browning wrote "Balaustion's Adventure, including A Transcript from Euripides," and "Aristophanes' Apology, including A Transcript from Euripides, Being The Last Adventure of Balaustion." Pound has fused ("con-fused") the two.

INDEX TO SUBJECTS

I–IV and IV–VII, 19; states' rights,
19, 51, 97, 102, 311, 339, 343, 355, 372,
402, 416, 418; and government, 20,
199; use of in *Cantos*, 77, 91, 94, 100,
119, 128, 131–34, 156, 159, 172,
177, 192, 198, 206, 228, 250, 252, 262,
265, 281, 309, 329, 335, 344, 349,
350, 354, 362, 365, 387, 398, 405, 409,
410, 417, 436; as religion, 347. *See
also* Preamble
Constitutional Convention of 1787, 6,
103, 198, 200, 202, 232
Constitutional debates of 1787, 423
Constitution of 1787, 27, 30, 279
Constitutions, 71, 115, 117, 140, 171,
174, 255, 310, 396; Confucian, 7;
American, 7, 351, 352, 353;
Eleusinian, 7, 398; British, 271, 275;
Massachusetts, 276; French, 279;
English, 280, 350, 351, 396, 410;
Chinese, 351, 392, 398; Manchu,
353; world, 376, 416, 418
Continental Congress, 275
Convention of Messina, 146
Conybeare, F. C., 381
Cremona, Italy, 156
Crusade: Third, 146; Second, 148
Crusades, 146, 361; Albigensian, 185
Cuba, 167
Culture, 4, 58, 59, 60, 63, 106, 233;
European, 4, 58; world, 303;
American, 436
Cultures, 73, 299, 355; world, 385
Cummings, E. E., 437
Cunizza da Romano, 145, 148, 192,
197, 214, 312, 317, 424
Cythera, 338

DTC. *See* Disciplinary Training Center
Danae, 138, 139
Daniel, Arnaut, 54, 148, 149, 193
Dante, Alighieri, 5, 28n, 46, 93, 94, 121,
144, 151, 153, 157, 169, 171, 184,
213, 378, 380, 383; as Pound's model,
53–55, 65, 67–69, 76, 132, 301,
304, 412, 424, 433
Daphne, 420, 424
De Born, Bertran, 146, 147, 148, 334
Declaration of Independence, the, 6,
12, 27, 159, 169, 206, 249; use of in
Cantos, 13, 17–19, 31–32, 44, 49,
112, 114–17, 131, 140, 142, 144,

147–48, 150, 153, 156, 174, 175,
177, 179, 196, 203–4, 214, 229, 238–39,
250, 252, 260, 267–68, 281, 283,
309–10, 314, 350–51, 397, 409, 416,
418; quoted, 15–16; and revolution,
29, 99, 108, 141, 194, 219–20, 225, 266,
270–74, 276, 289, 292, 335; as
symbol, 78, 94, 97, 102–3, 133, 170,
171, 407
De Gourmont, Remy, 383
Delaware River, 159
Del Mar, Alexander, 389
Delphos, 156
DEMETER: in Calendar cycle, 42, 138
Demeter, 401, 404
Democracy, 47, 286; economic, 217
Destiny, 199, 227; revolutionary, 208
Diana, 81, 82, 94, 136, 137, 149, 404
Dído, 152
Dionysius of Syracuse, 157
Dionysus, 127, 133, 136n, 143, 177,
316; rites of, 181, 374
Disciplinary Training Center (DTC),
296, 314, 315, 333, 341
Divus, Andreas, 48, 110, 111, 114–19,
121, 129, 246, 260, 419, 420; as Pound,
133, 142, 245, 285, 313, 317, 319
Dos Santos, José Maria, 167, 168, 330
Douglas, Major C. H., 217, 221, 224,
225, 233, 237, 369
Drake, Sir Francis, 374, 375, 376,
381, 390, 404
Dumas, Alexandre, 333

Eagle: and Malatesta, 18, 49, 141–42,
149, 156, 162–65, 175, 188, 196, 206,
219, 223, 224, 340, 416, 418,
429–30; and Calendar, 42–43, 108, 135,
244; as symbol, 45, 66, 110–11,
119, 126, 133, 137, 152, 161, 167, 170,
171, 214, 216, 239, 269, 307, 310,
322; and Seal, 50, 58, 75, 79, 135, 154,
239, 320, 417; ideograms and, 73,
100, 258, 264, 360; illustrations and, 80,
84, 88, 91, 97; revolutionary, 107;
and Confucius, 168; as Geryon, 227, 236;
Odyssean, 306, 308–9. *See also*
Pound, Ezra: as Eagle
Eagles, 66
East, the, 91, 174
Eaton, Peggy, 215
Eblis, lady of, 149

INDEX TO TITLES

INDEX TO CANTOS

474

PS3531 O82 C296
+'76, one world a+Read, Forrest.

0 00 02 0205916 8
MIDDLEBURY COLLEGE